METART.COM™
WHERE FLAWLESS BEAUTY MEETS ART

VivThomas.com

Collected and edited by Rose Eden

EDITION Skylight

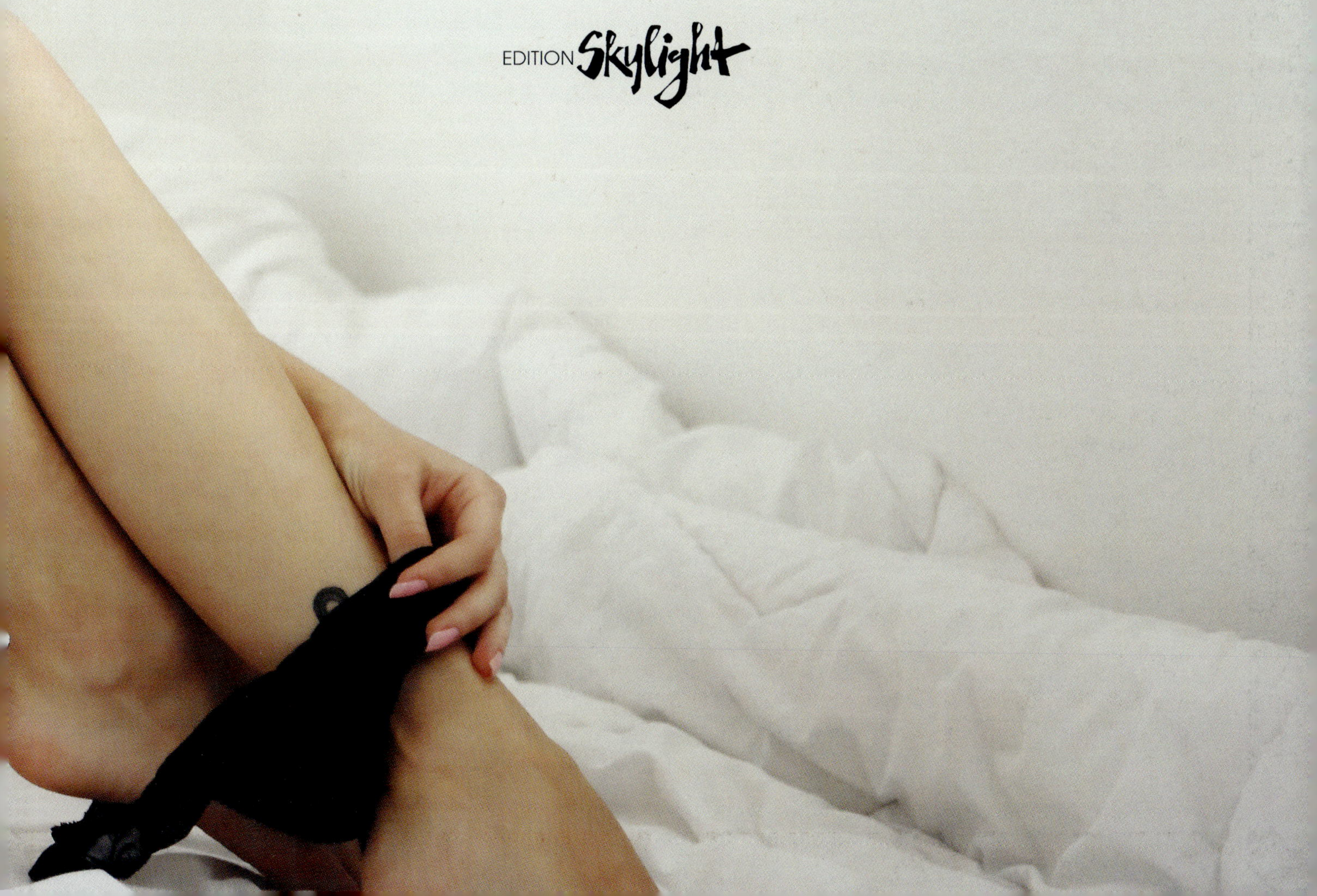

First edition 2026

EDITION SKYLIGHT
Rosengartenstr. 13B
CH-8608 Bubikon/Zürich
Switzerland
info@edition-skylight.com
www.edition-skylight.com

ISBN 978-3-03766-719-4

Bibliographic information published by Die Deutsche Bibliothek
Die Deutsche Bibliothek lists this publication in the Deutsche Nationalbibliografie; detailed bibliographic data are available in the Internet at http://dnb.ddb.de.

Printed in Bosnia and Herzegovina

"I believe women deserve admiration and respect, and I think we portray that in our films." – Vivian Thomas

VivThomas.com is part of the Metart Network, the world leader in high-class adult entertainment, presenting stunning girls who are confident, sexy and desirable; in short, modern women for a modern world.

Vivian Thomas started out as a photographer for men's magazines in South Africa, which led him to set up Rolling Images, a video production company he established in Wandsworth, South London. The firm then moved to North Acton in the west of the city and was renamed Vivthomas.com. Eventually, Thomas moved his entire business to the Algarve in Portugal. Known for producing artistic erotic films with an emphasis on high production values, Vivian Thomas has, over the years, been nominated for numerous awards, and also won prizes at the AVN Awards. Vivian Thomas is a master of photography, and this site exhibits his best work, which for years he directed pretty much by himself. These days, directors such as Andrej Lupin, Sandra Shine and Pierre Collant continue to carry the torch, keeping his signature style alive. The soft lighting, emotional depth and a unique artistic touch set it apart from the ordinary.

The site features over 1,200 models and over 3,000 erotic photosets. Thomas' work has starred almost exclusively Hungarian, Czech, and other central European models, although he does feature some British performers. His scenes are the perfect mix of erotic and artistic elements: beautiful to watch and still as hot as hell! Since the site joined MetArt in 2013, the quality of the models has improved.

Connoisseurs of high-class lesbian action will love the luxurious locations, sexy lingerie, complex stories and, most of all, the emphasis on tastefully explicit, genuine girl-on-girl pleasure.

Stunning pussy-hungry girlfriends bring authentic passion and intense sexual chemistry to the screen in each sizzling erotic encounter, pleasuring each other with fingers, tongues and toys. Real lesbians only! See explicit, uninhibited girl-on-girl sex at its best. Visually speaking, things have got a little more erotic over the years. Earlier, scenes tended to focus on wide, full-body shots whereas now, you'll see more close-ups, including tasteful pussy shots that turn up the heat without killing the vibe. This book presents a one-of-a-kind collection which really has enduring value. Enjoy the hottest girls selected from the best portfolios!

Of course, with a name like Rose Eden any connoisseur thinks it must be a pseudonym. And they would be right, because it is. There is an actual Rose Eden, of course, but she's not known under that name. So, her fictional biography we present as follows: born yes, location unknown, age unknown. What is her task? Rose Eden lives and works in Europe and Los Angeles and she loves to explore erotic photography, especially around everything concerning the Metart universe. So, if you want to have more detailed information on this secret star, I'm afraid we're sworn to secrecy! Just enjoy these hot selections of our «under cover» top editor!
— Rose Eden

„Ich glaube, Frauen verdienen Bewunderung und Respekt, und ich denke, dass wir das in unseren Filmen auch darstellen."
– Vivian Thomas

VivThomas.com ist Teil des Metart-Netzwerks, dem weltweit führenden Anbieter von hochwertiger Erwachsenenunterhaltung, der atemberaubende Mädchen präsentiert, die selbstbewusst, sexy und begehrenswert sind – moderne Frauen für eine moderne Welt.

Vivian Thomas begann in Südafrika als Fotograf für Männermagazine, was ihn dazu veranlasste, eine Videoproduktionsfirma namens Rolling Images zu gründen. Er ließ sich in Wandsworth im Süden Londons nieder, zog dann nach North Acton in London und benannte seine Produktionsfirma in Vivthomas.com um. Schließlich verlegte er das gesamte Unternehmen an die Algarve in Portugal. Thomas ist bekannt für die Produktion künstlerischer Erotikfilme mit dem Fokus auf hohe Qualität. Er wurde für zahlreiche Preise nominiert und hat in der Vergangenheit bereits bei den AVN Awards gewonnen. Viv Thomas ist ein Meister hinter der Kamera, und für diese Website hat er seine besten Arbeiten geschaffen und jahrelang so ziemlich alles selbst inszeniert. Heute führen Regisseure wie Andrej Lupin, Sandra Shine und Pierre Collant sein Erbe fort und bewahren seinen unverkennbaren Stil – sanfte Beleuchtung, emotionale Tiefe und künstlerische Akzente, eben alles, was seine Arbeiten auszeichnen.

Die Website bietet über 1.200 Models und mehr als 3.000 erotische Fotoserien. In Thomas' Portfolios sind fast ausschließlich ungarische, tschechische und andere mitteleuropäische Models zu sehen, obwohl er auch einige britische Darstellerinnen zeigt. Seine Szenen sind die perfekte Mischung aus Erotik und Kunst – appetitlich anzusehen und trotzdem verdammt heiß. Seit die Website 2013 dem MetArt-Netzwerk beigetreten ist, ist die Qualität der Models nur noch besser geworden.

Kenner hochwertiger Lesben-Spiele werden die luxuriösen Drehorte, die sexy Dessous, die komplexen Geschichten lieben – und vor allem die Betonung auf geschmackvoll explizitem, echtem Girl-on-Girl-Vergnügen. Atemberaubende, muschihungrige Freundinnen bringen in jeder heißen erotischen Begegnung authentische Leidenschaft ihre intensive sexuelle Chemie auf den Bildschirm und verwöhnen sich gegenseitig mit Fingern, Zungen und Spielzeugen. Nur echte Lesben! Sehen Sie expliziten, hemmungslosen Sex zwischen Frauen vom Feinsten. Optisch ist es im Laufe der Jahre etwas erotischer geworden. Frühere Szenen konzentrierten sich eher auf Ganzkörperaufnahmen. Jetzt gibt es mehr Nahaufnahmen, darunter geschmackvolle Muschi-Aufnahmen, die für zusätzliche feuchte Hitze sorgen, ohne die Stimmung zu zerstören. Dieses Buch präsentiert eine einzigartige Sammlung von bleibendem Wert – die heißesten Mädchen, ausgewählt aus den besten Portfolios, VivThomas zum Genießen!

Na klar, denkt der Connaisseur, ein Name wie Rose Eden, der kann doch nicht wirklich stimmen? Und da liegen Sie richtig, denn es handelt sich um ein Pseudonym, die Rose Eden gibt es in der Realität schon, aber eben nicht unter diesem Namen. Also, die fiktive Biographie präsentieren wir wie folgt: Geboren ja, Ort unbekannt, Alter unbekannt, immer auf der Suche nach aussergewöhnlicher erotischer Fotografie, speziell Metart betreffend. Rose Eden ist eine Agentin «under cover» und lebt und arbeitet in Europa und Los Angeles.
— Rose Eden

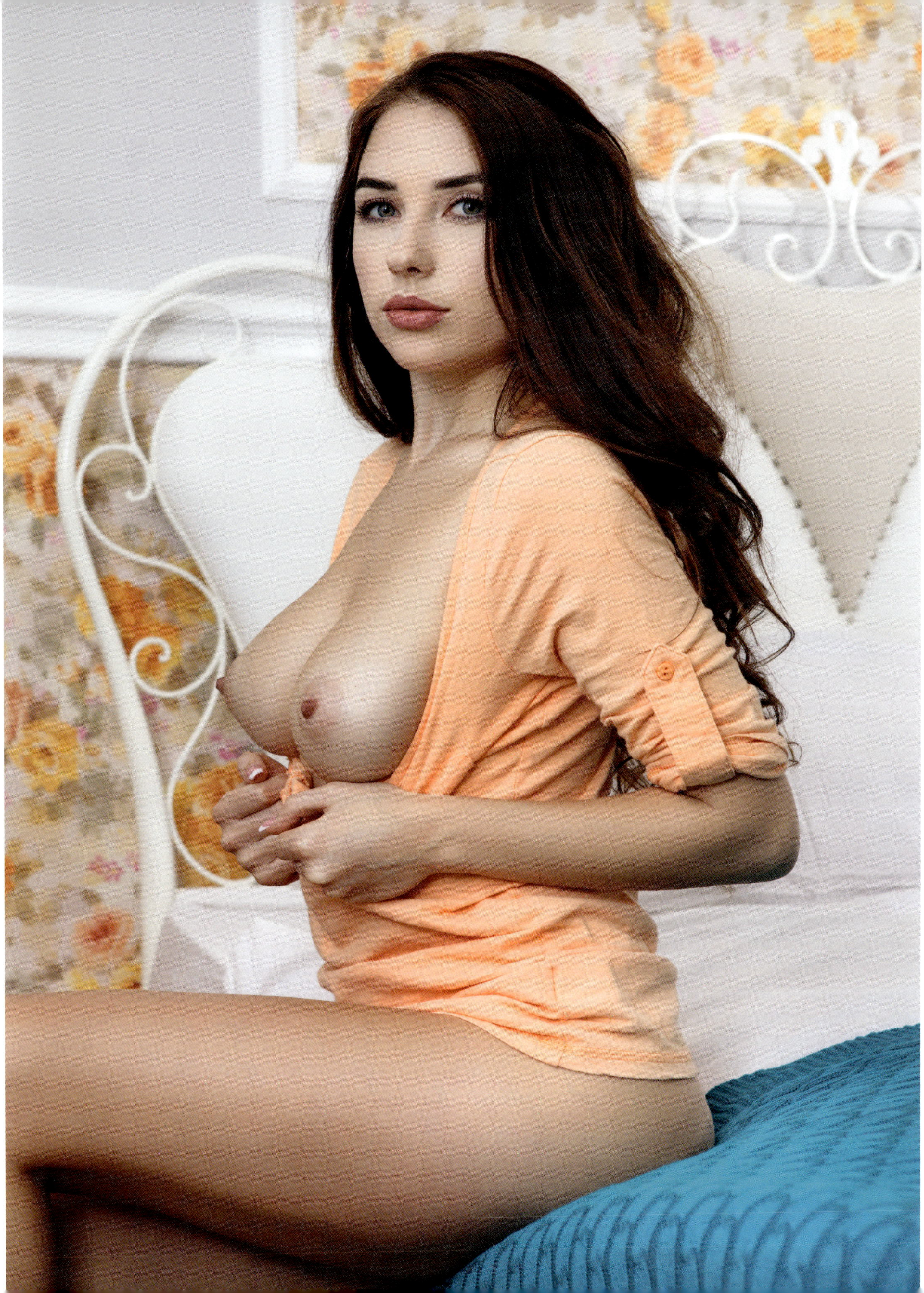

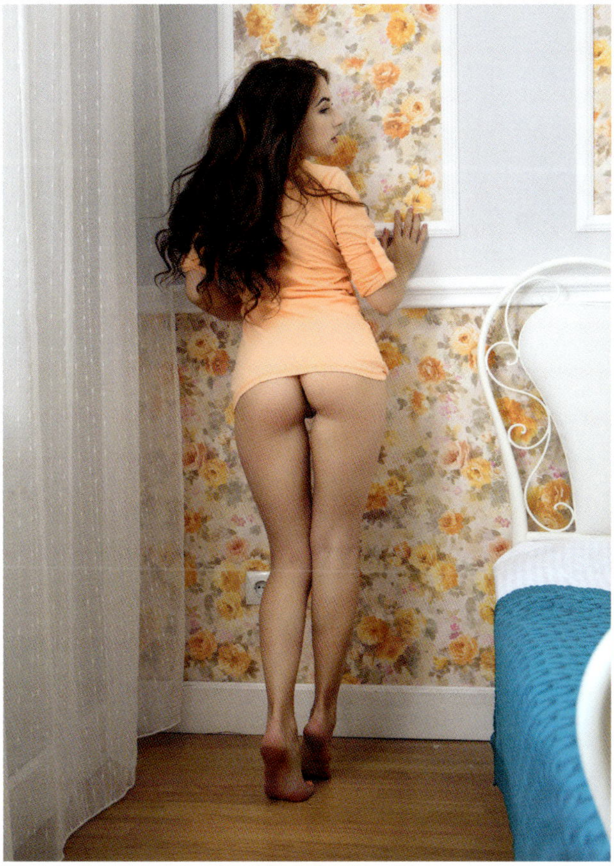

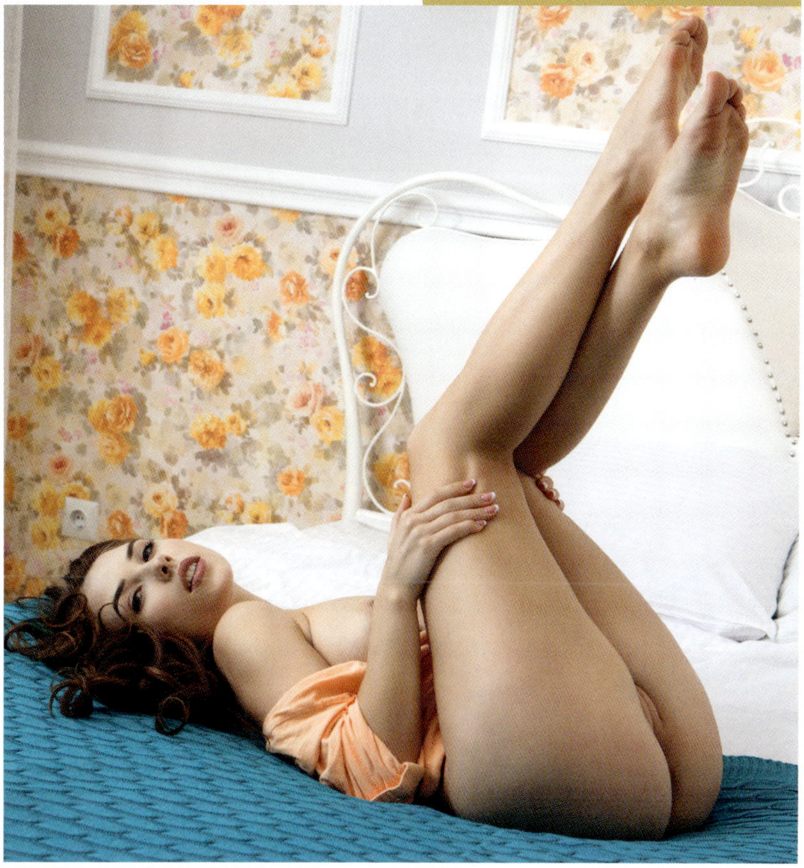

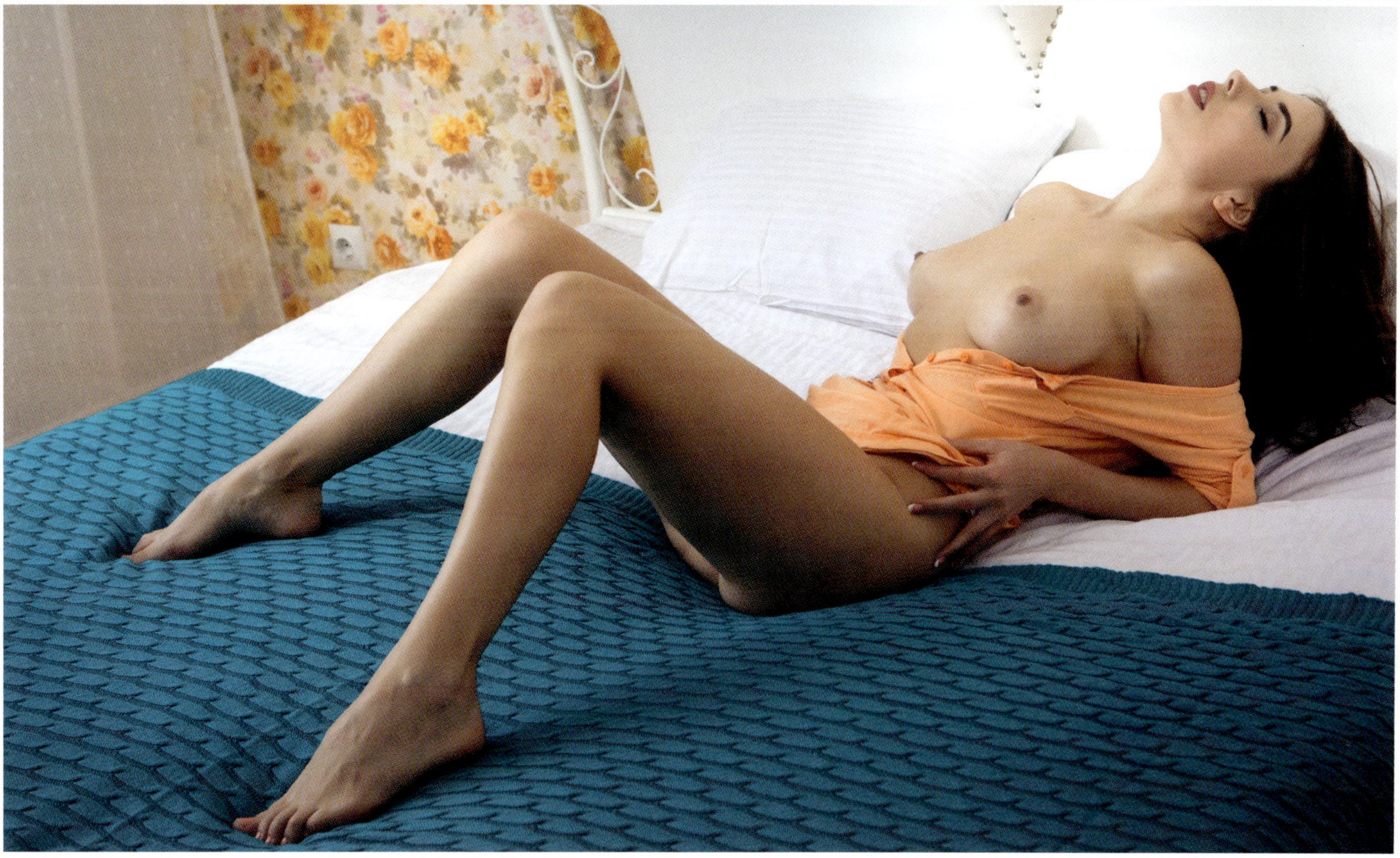

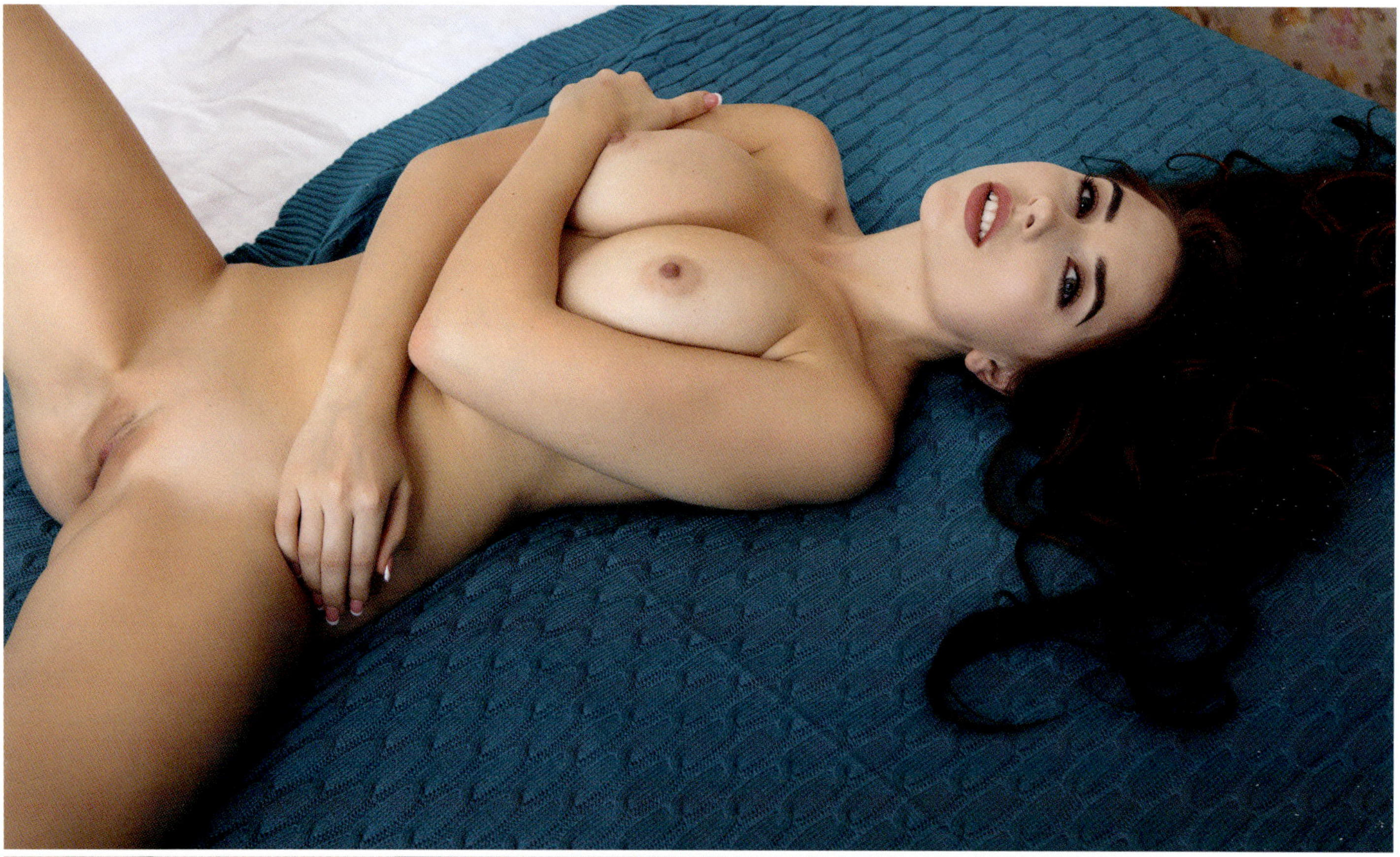

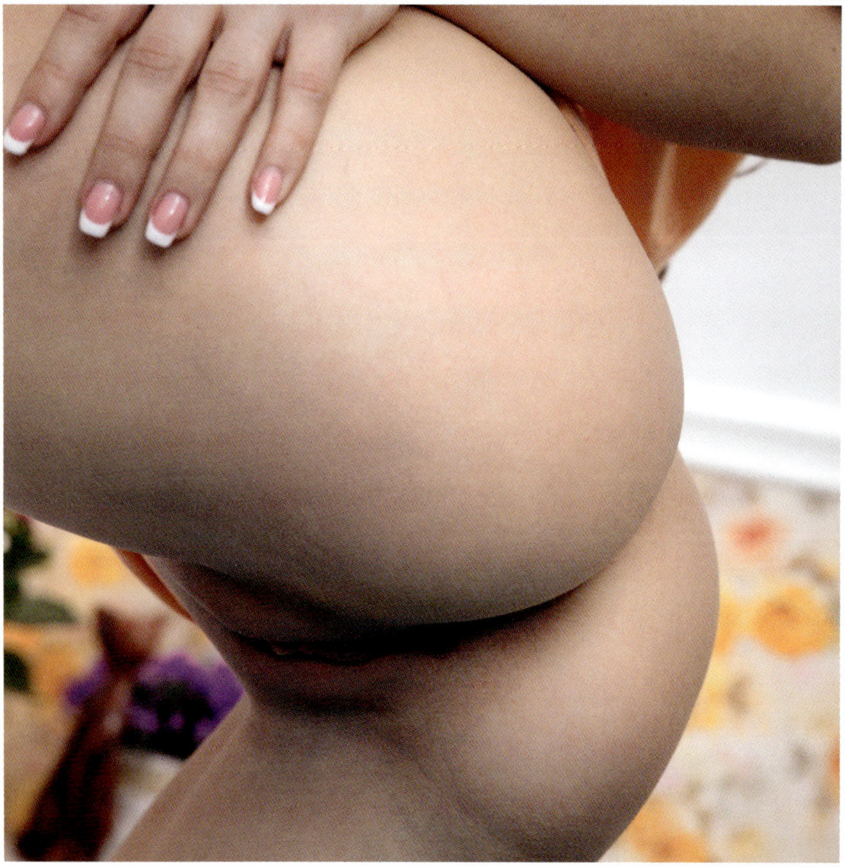

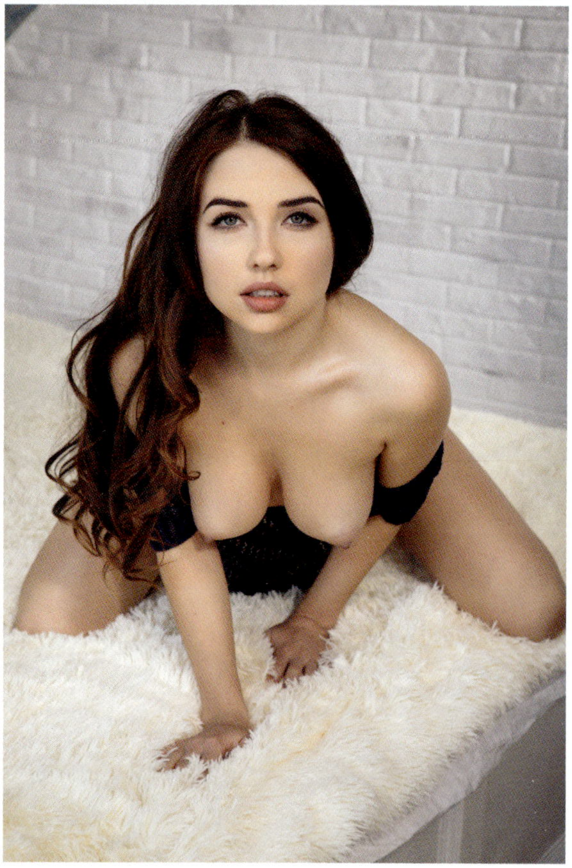

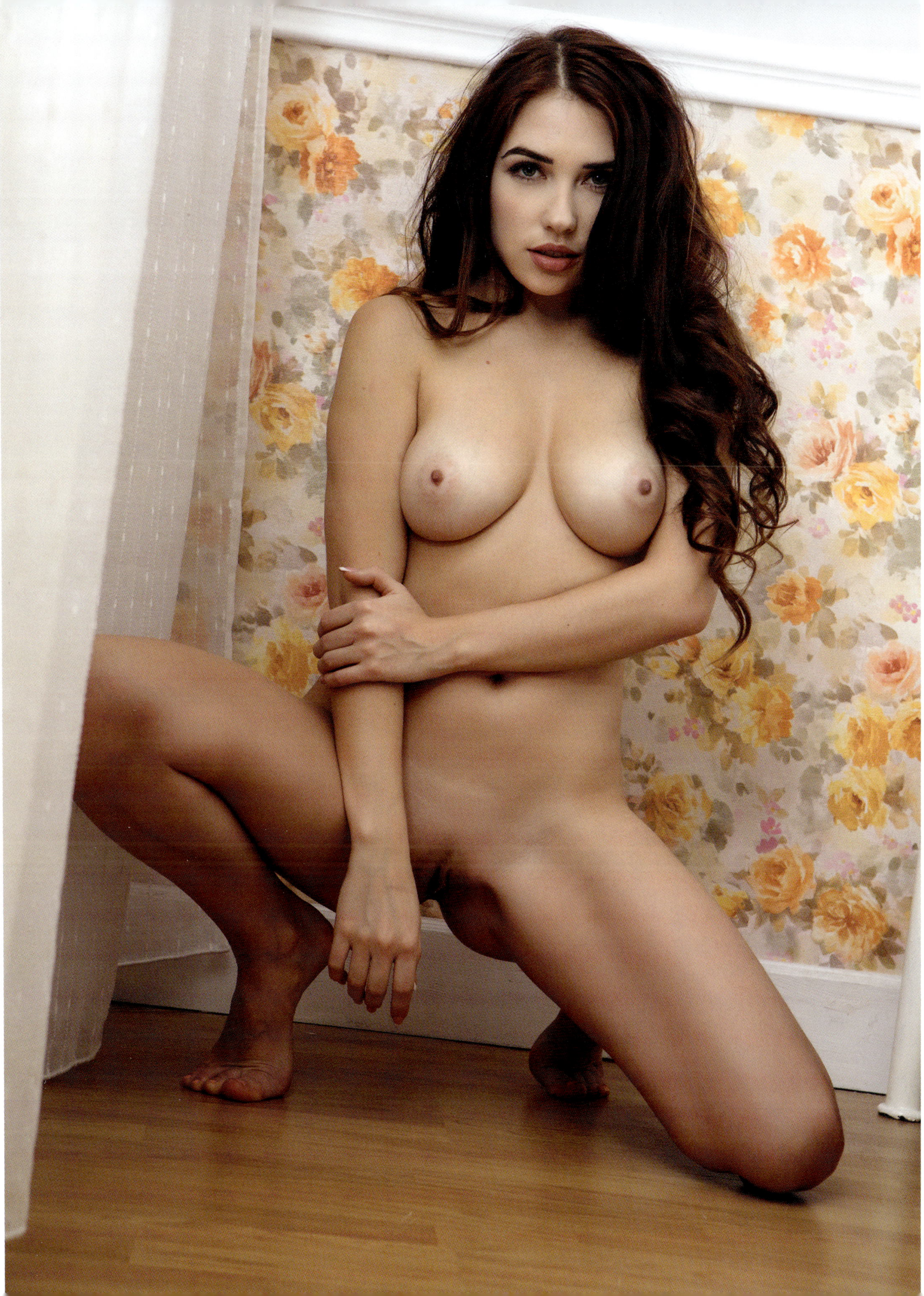

Angel E

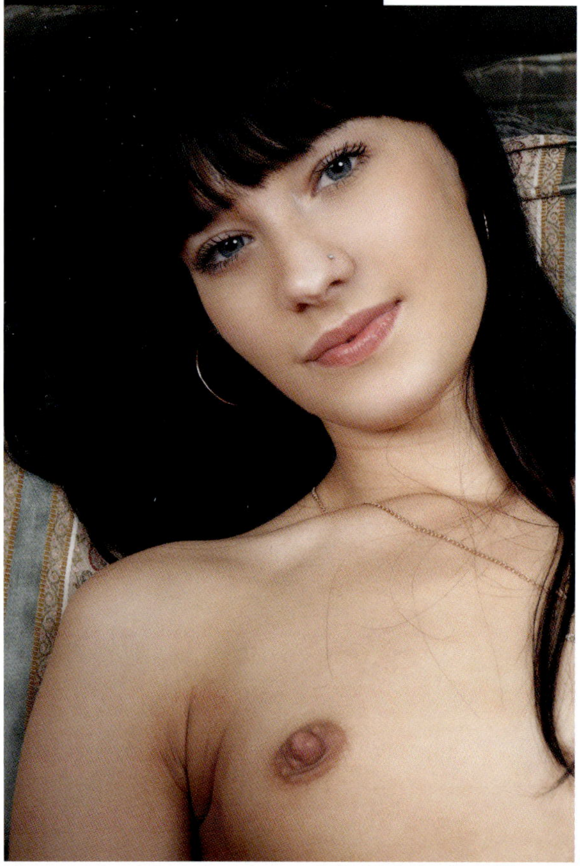

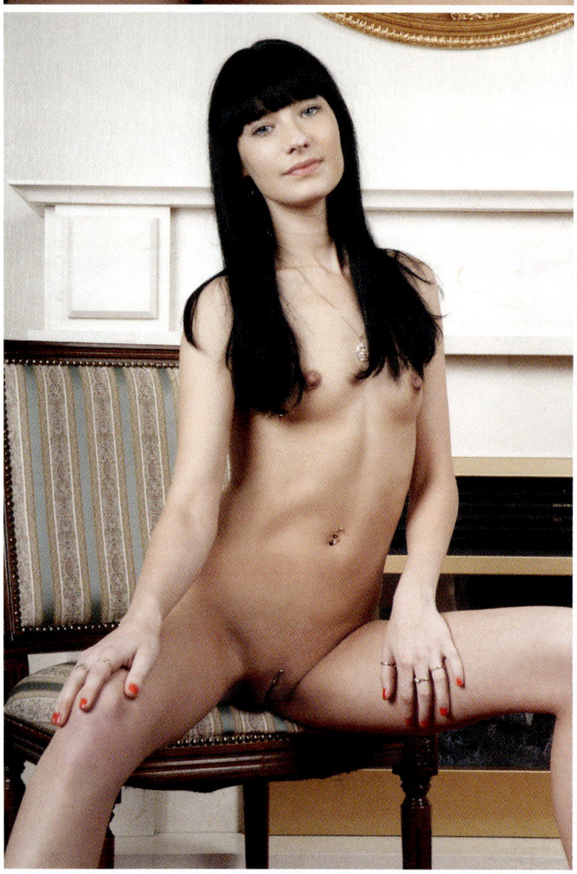

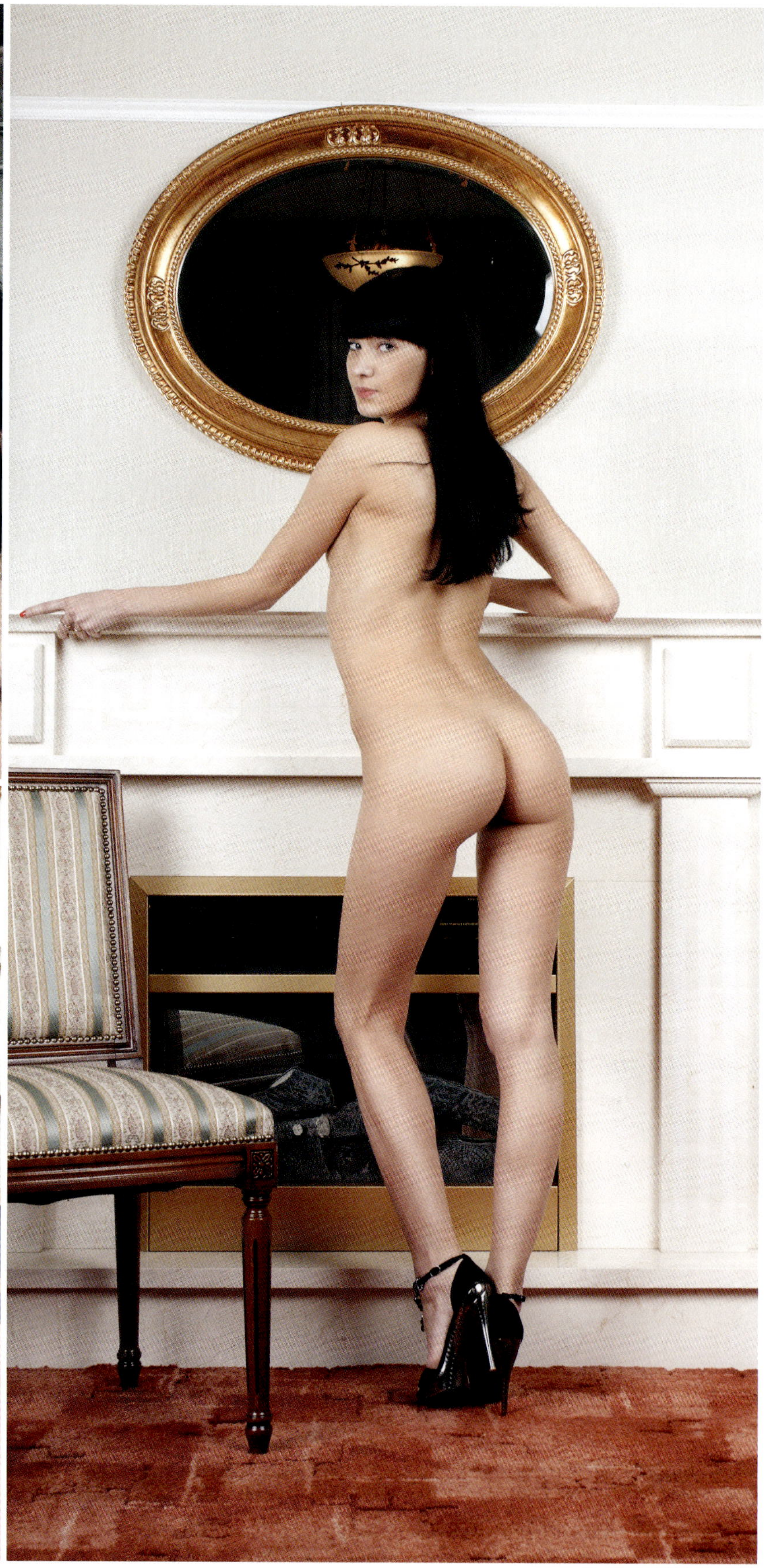

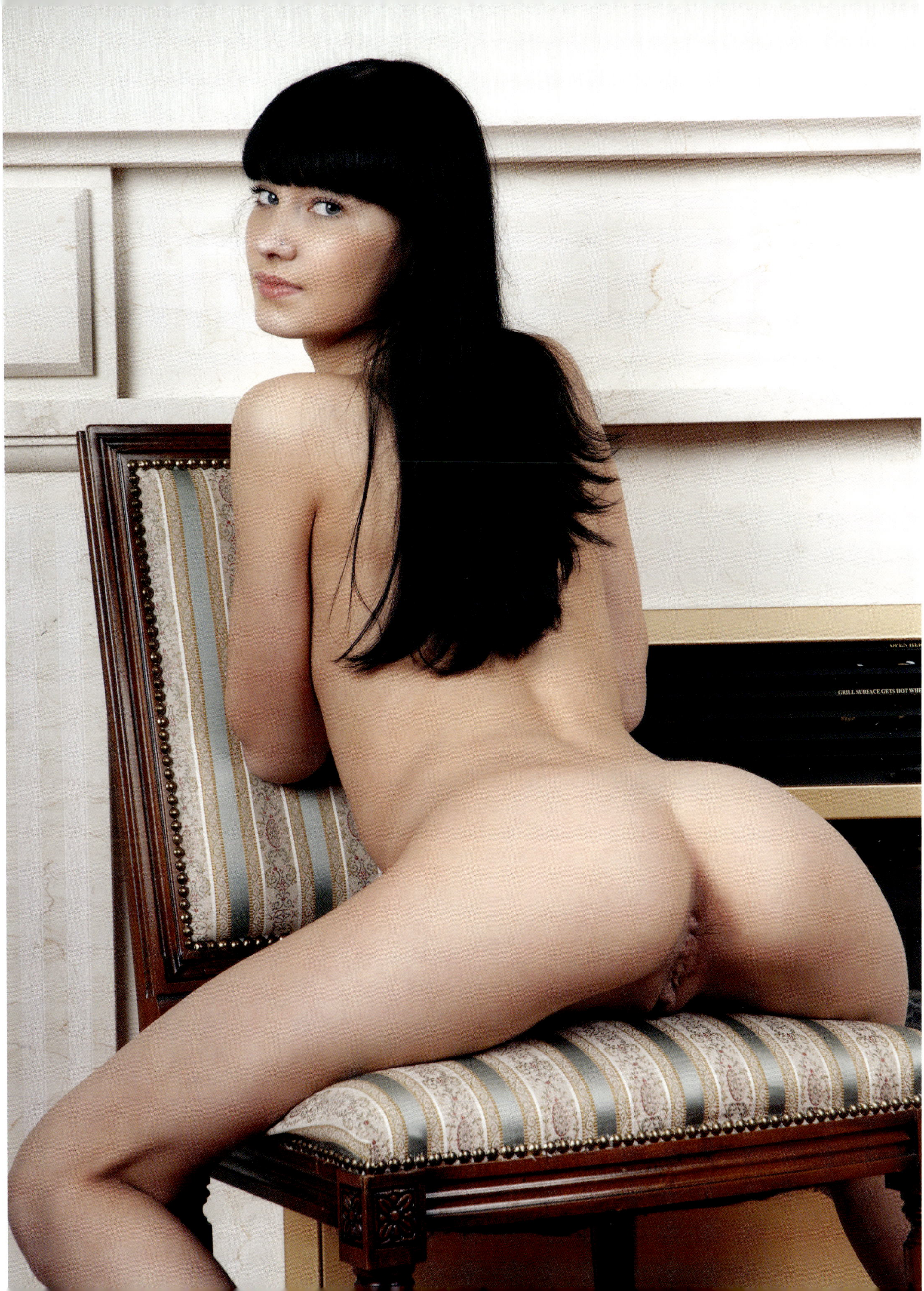
GRILL SURFACE GETS HOT

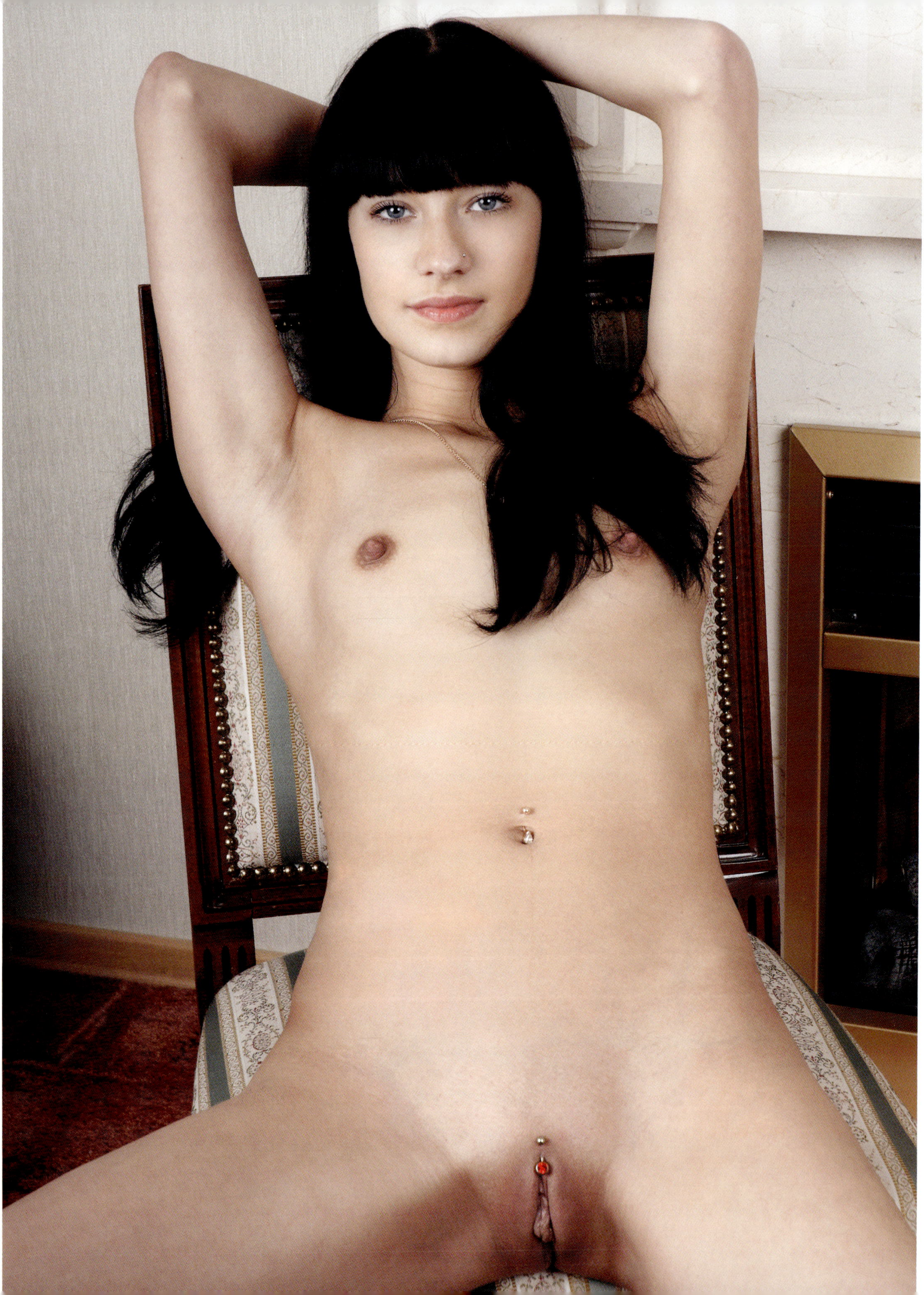

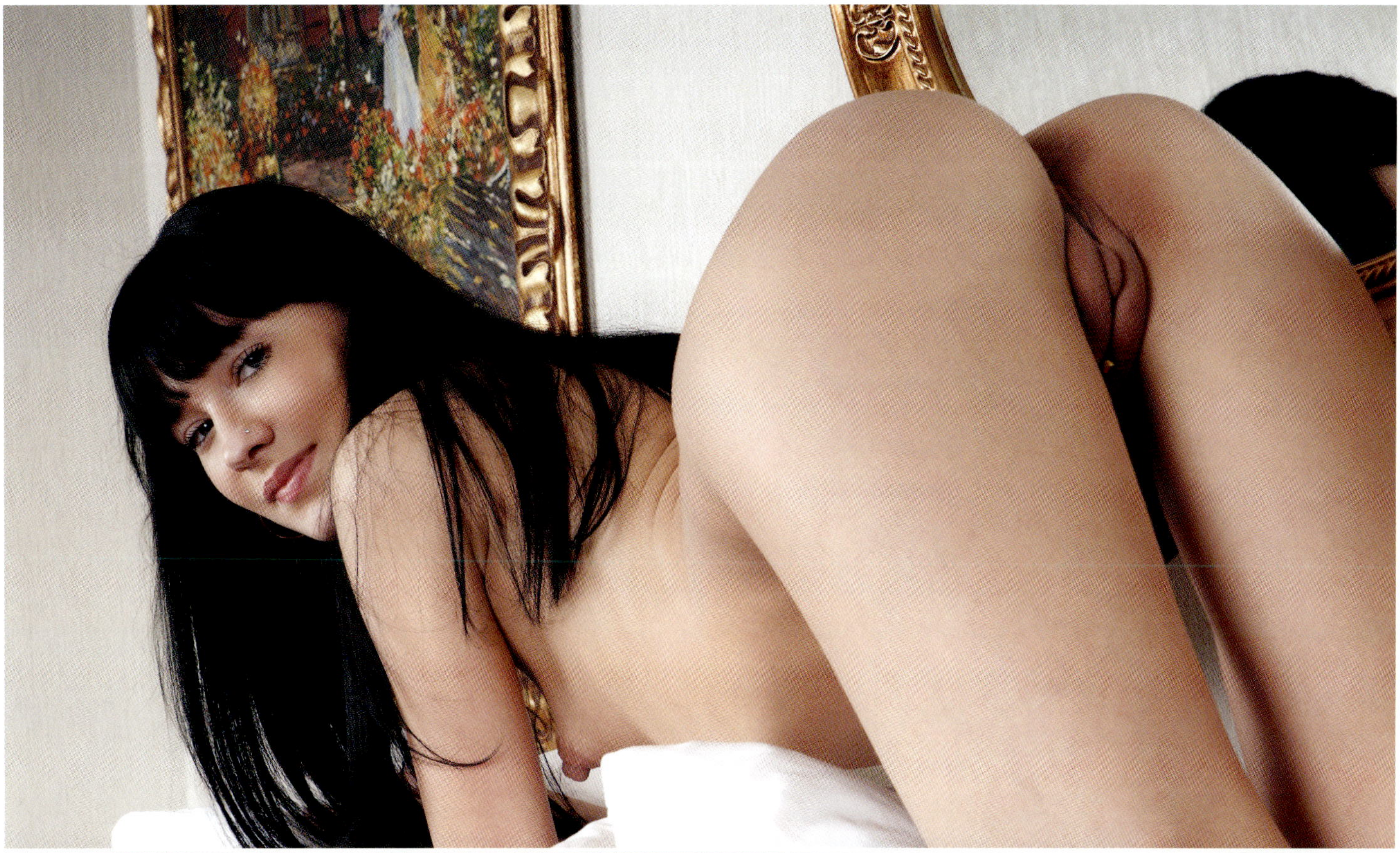

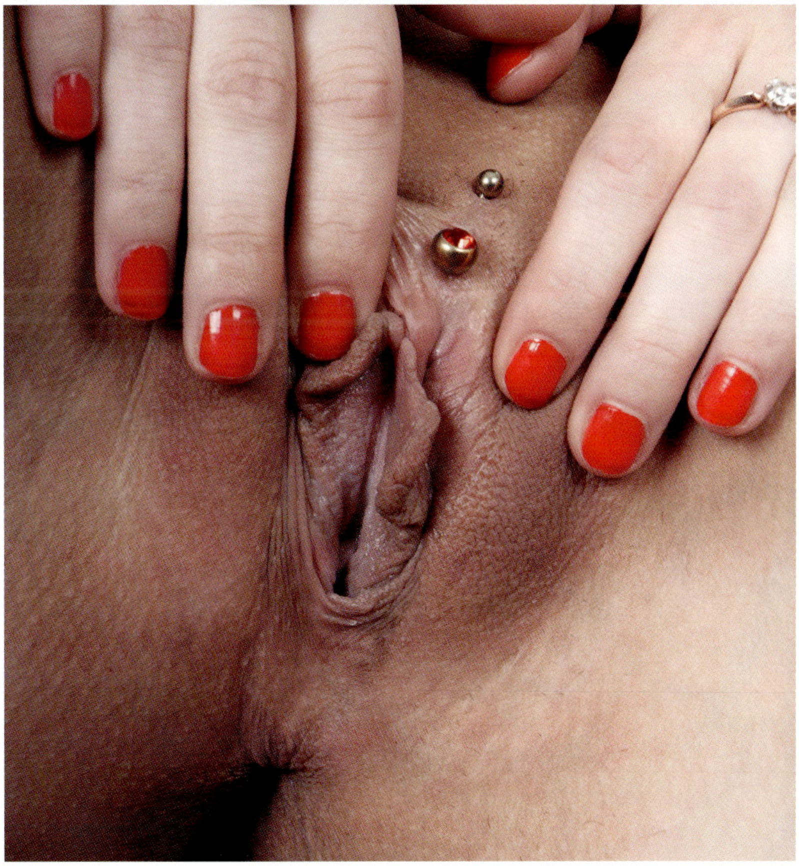

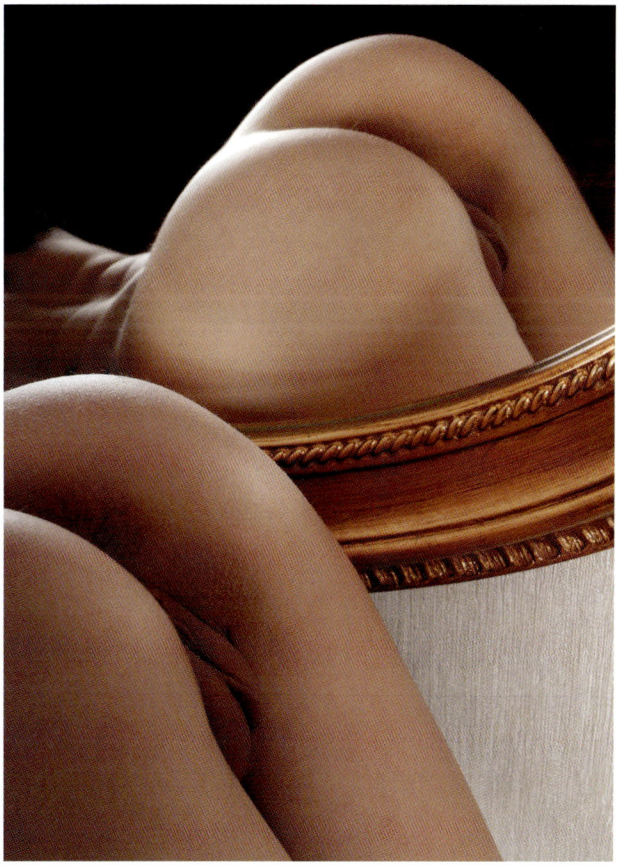

Alexis Crystal
Lilu Moon

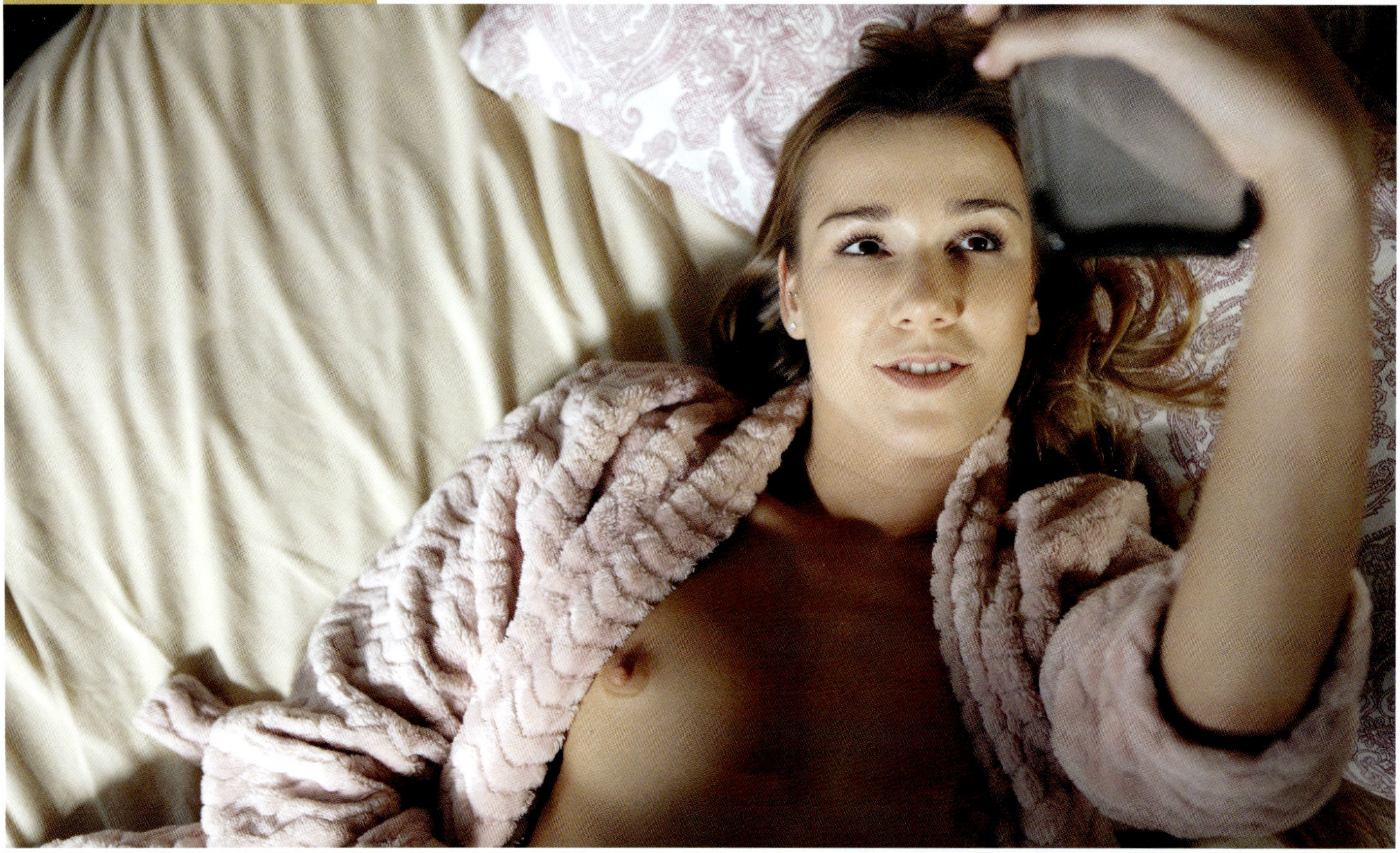

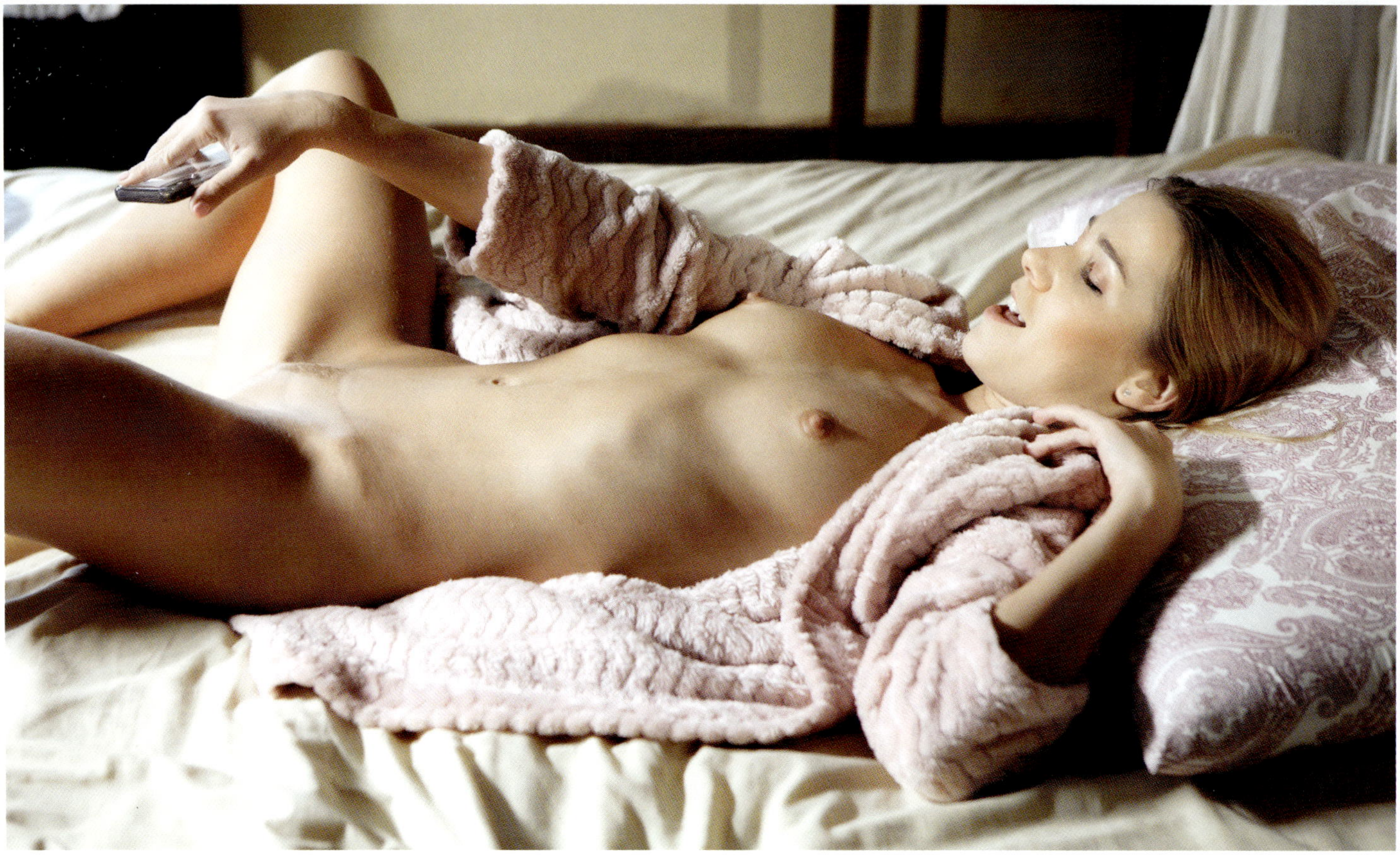

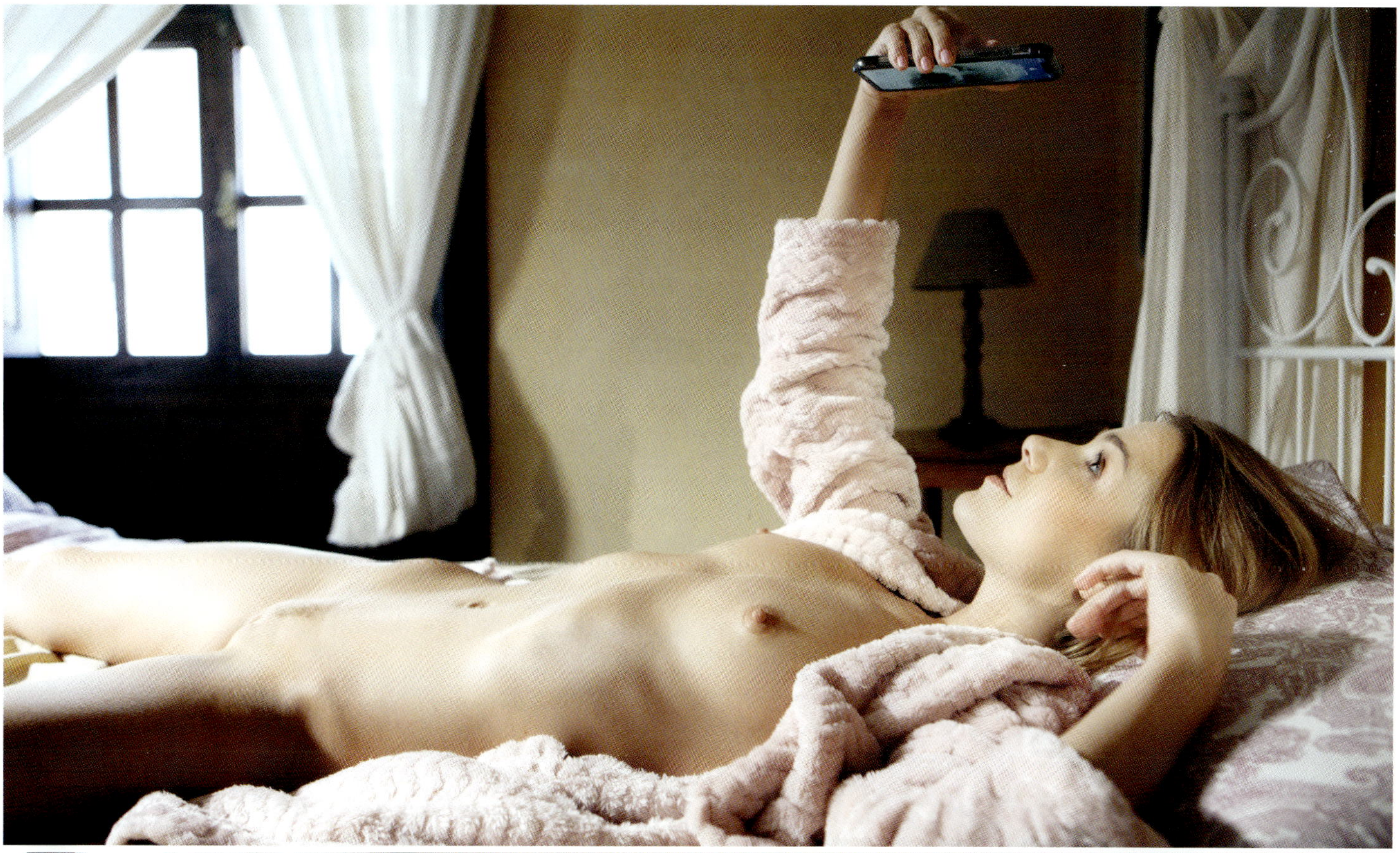

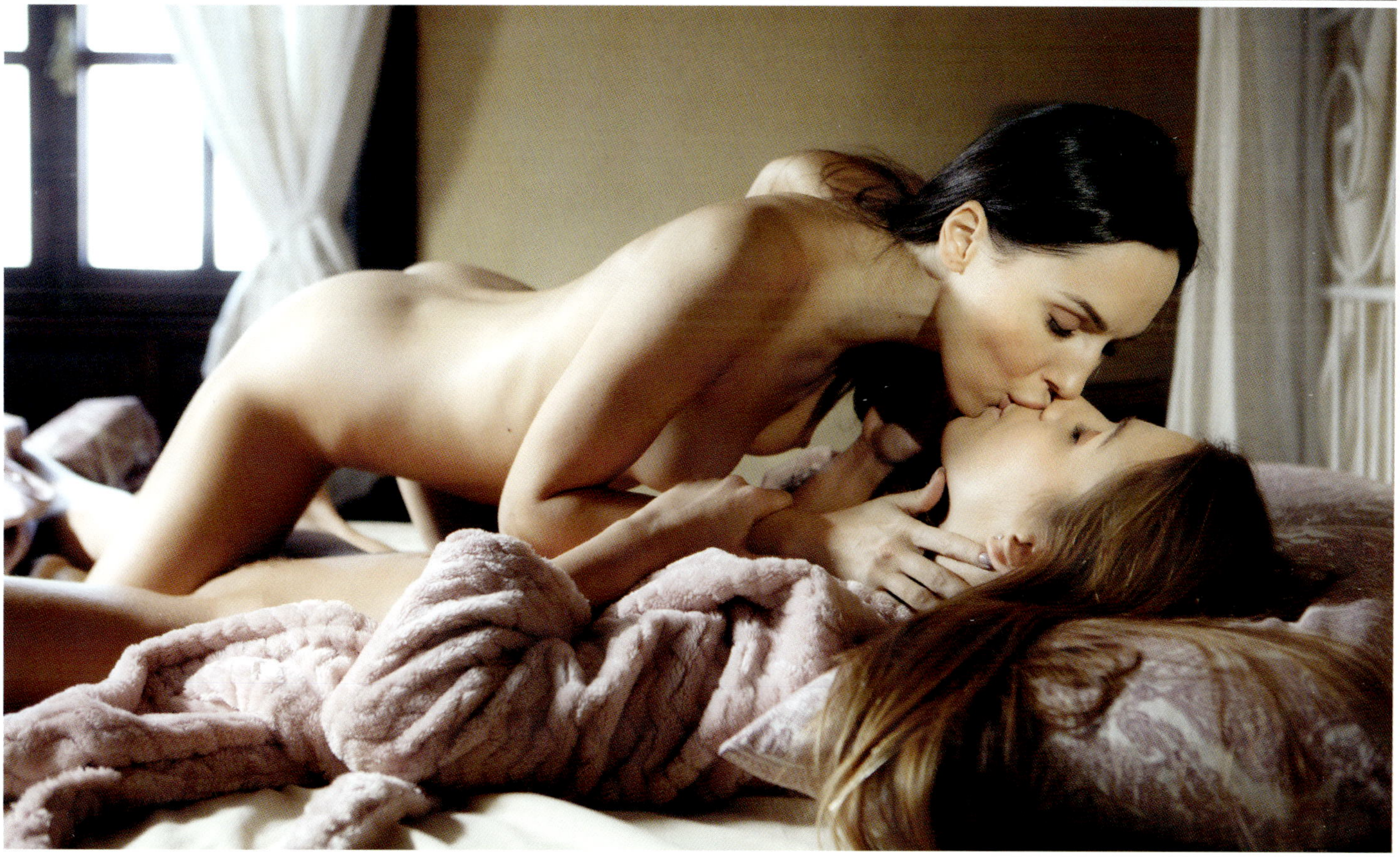

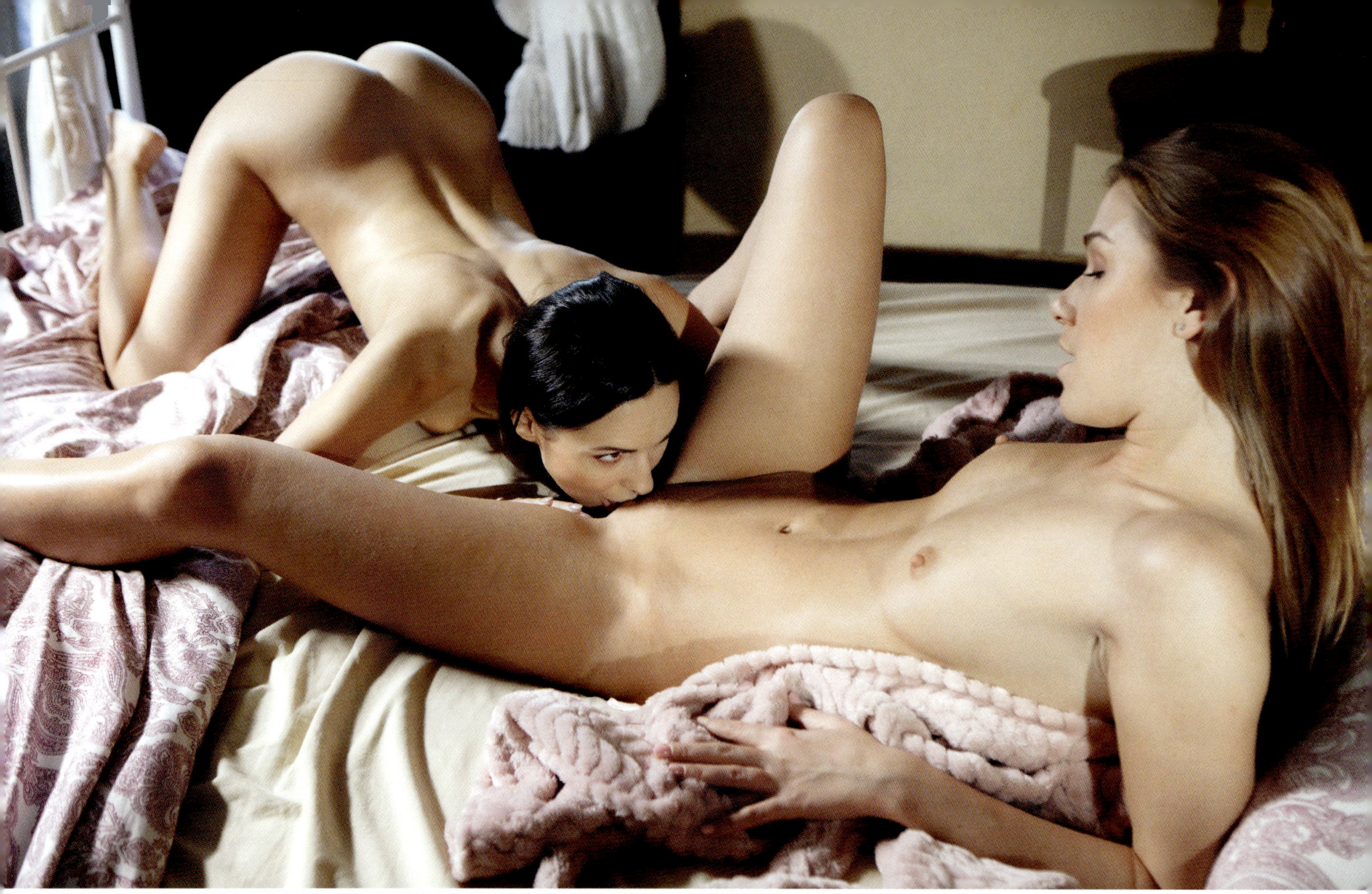

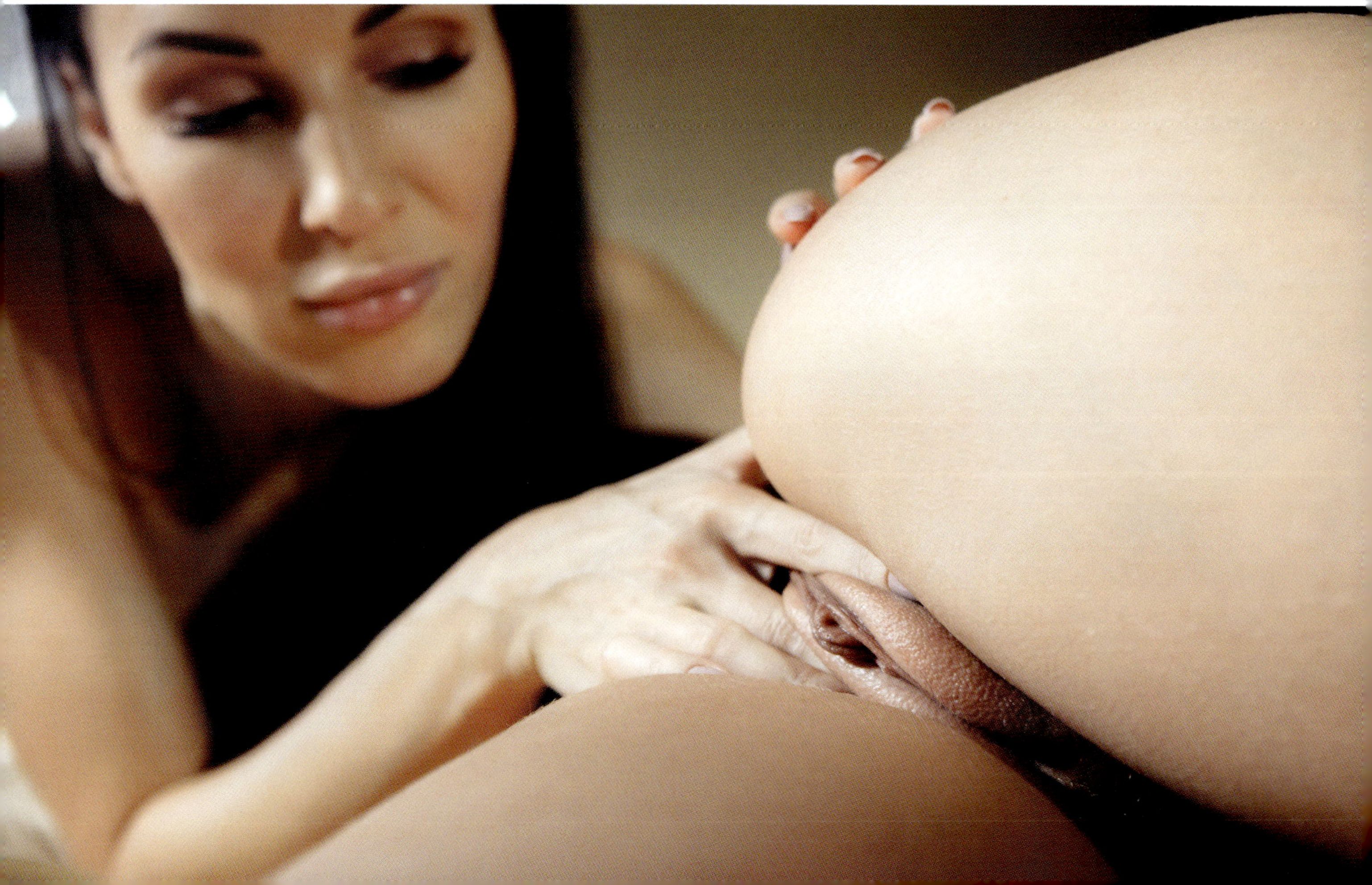

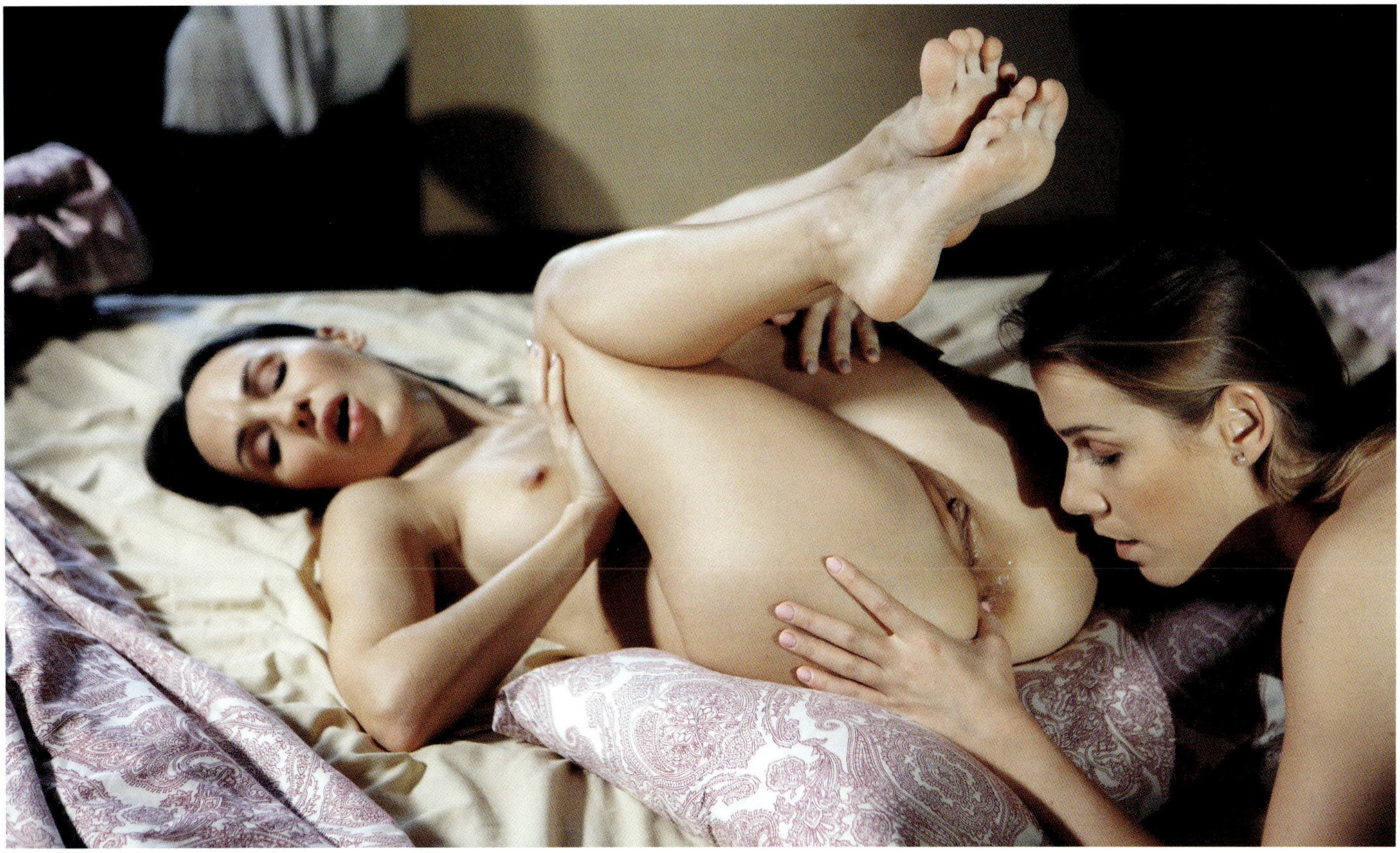

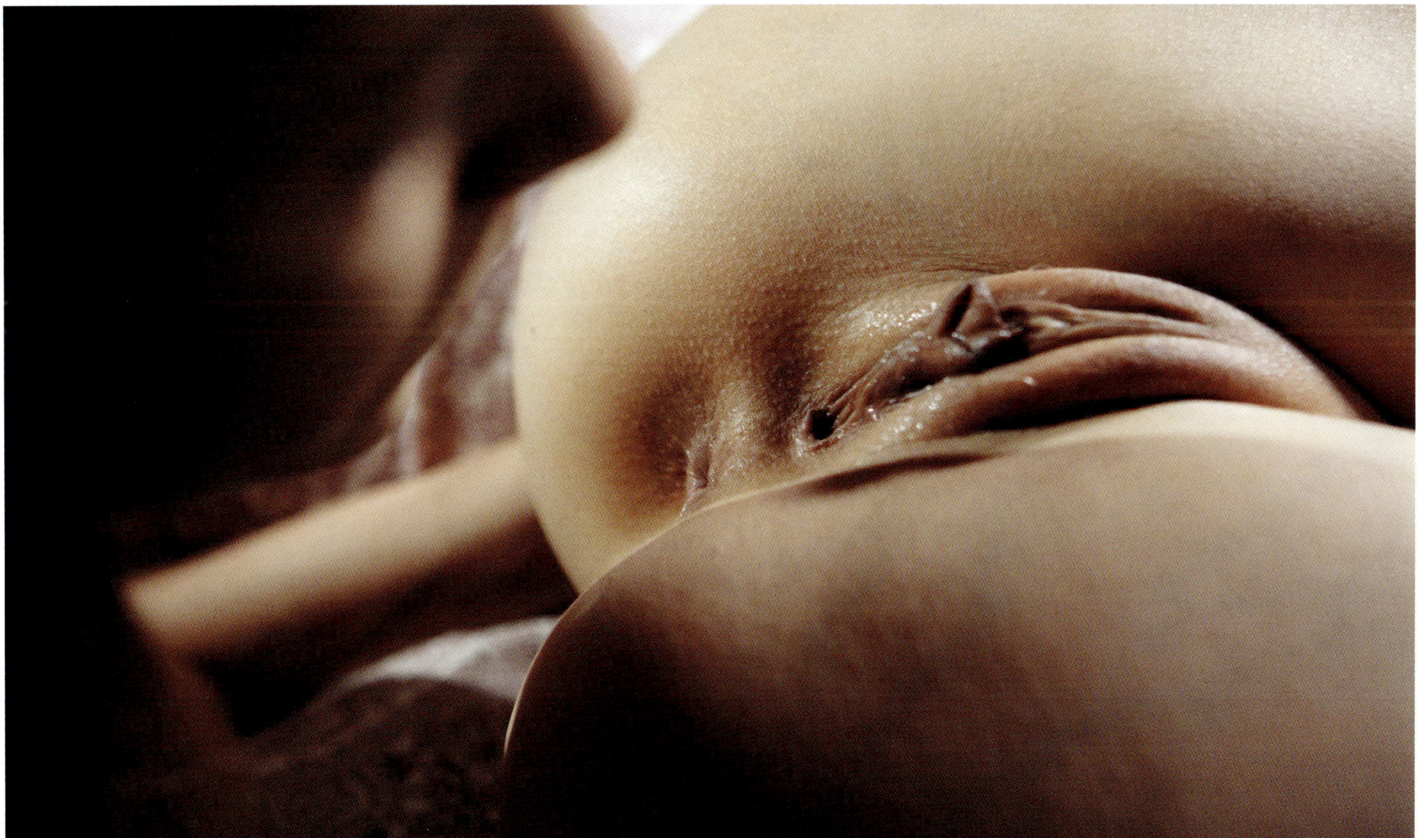

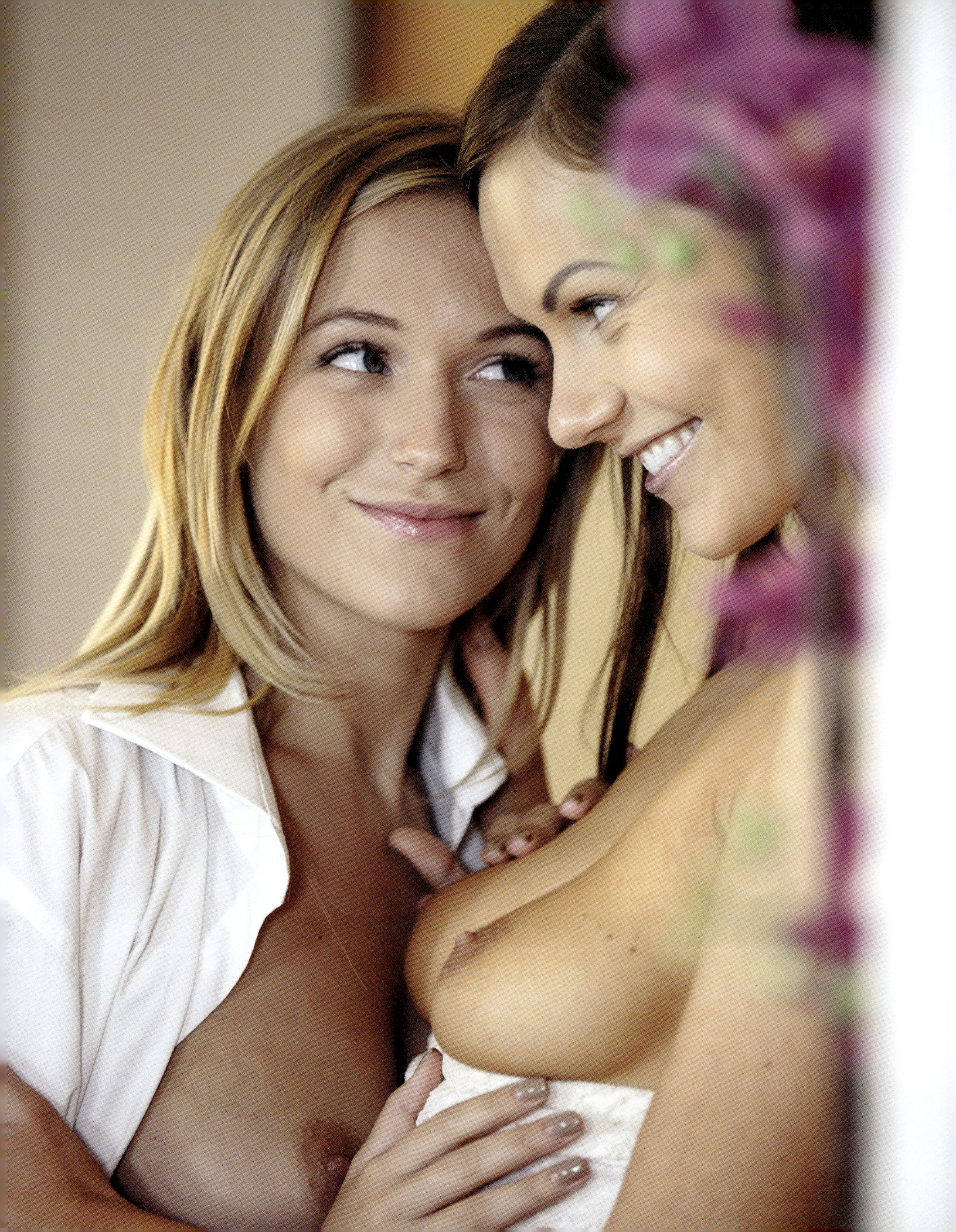

Aislin
Tina Kay

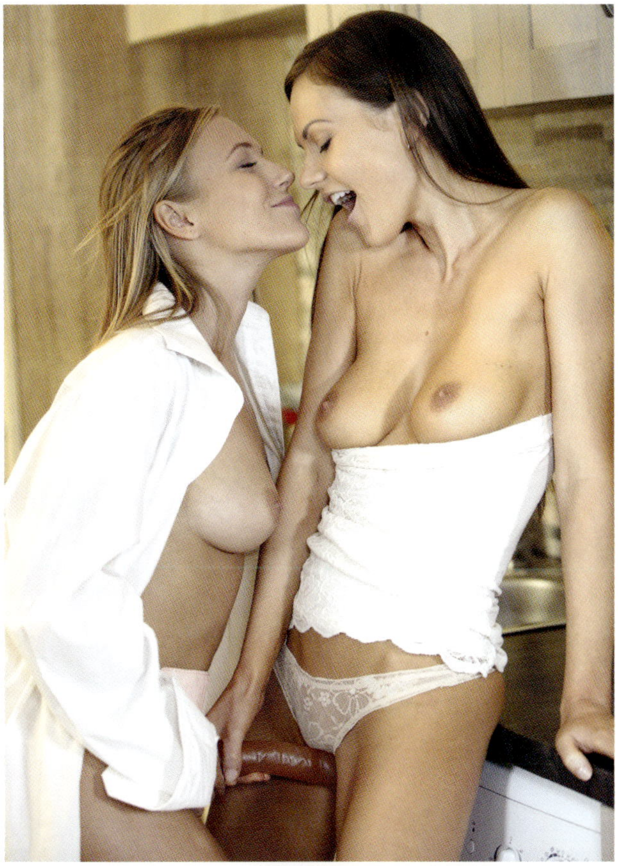

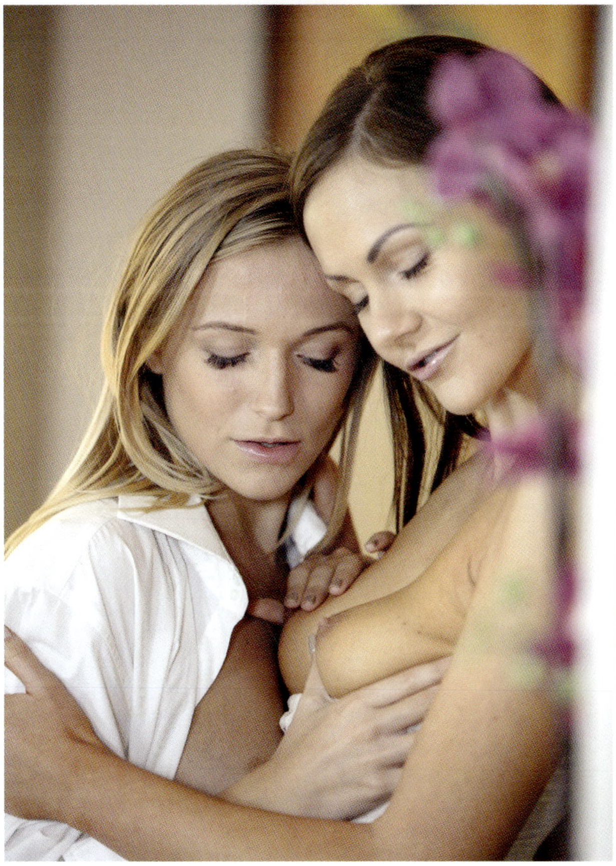

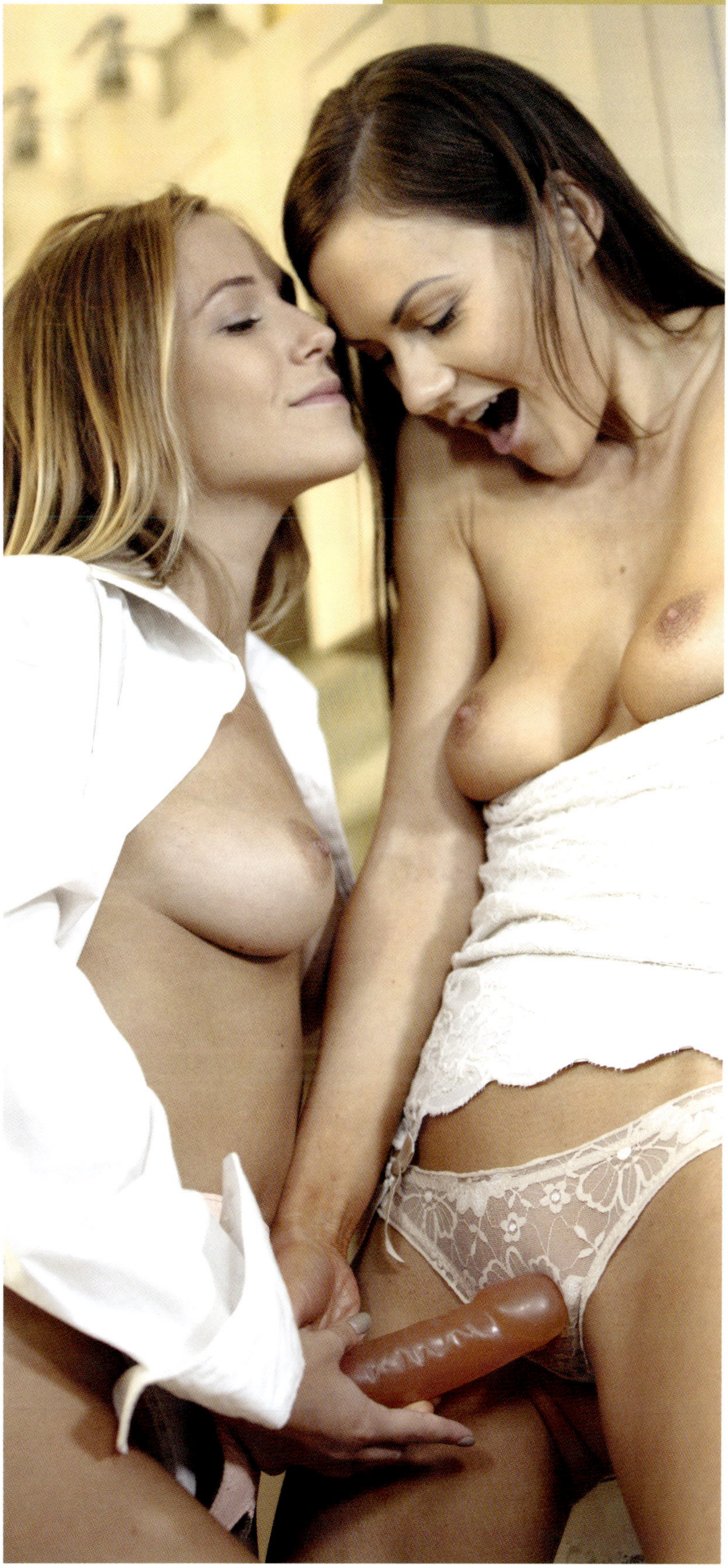

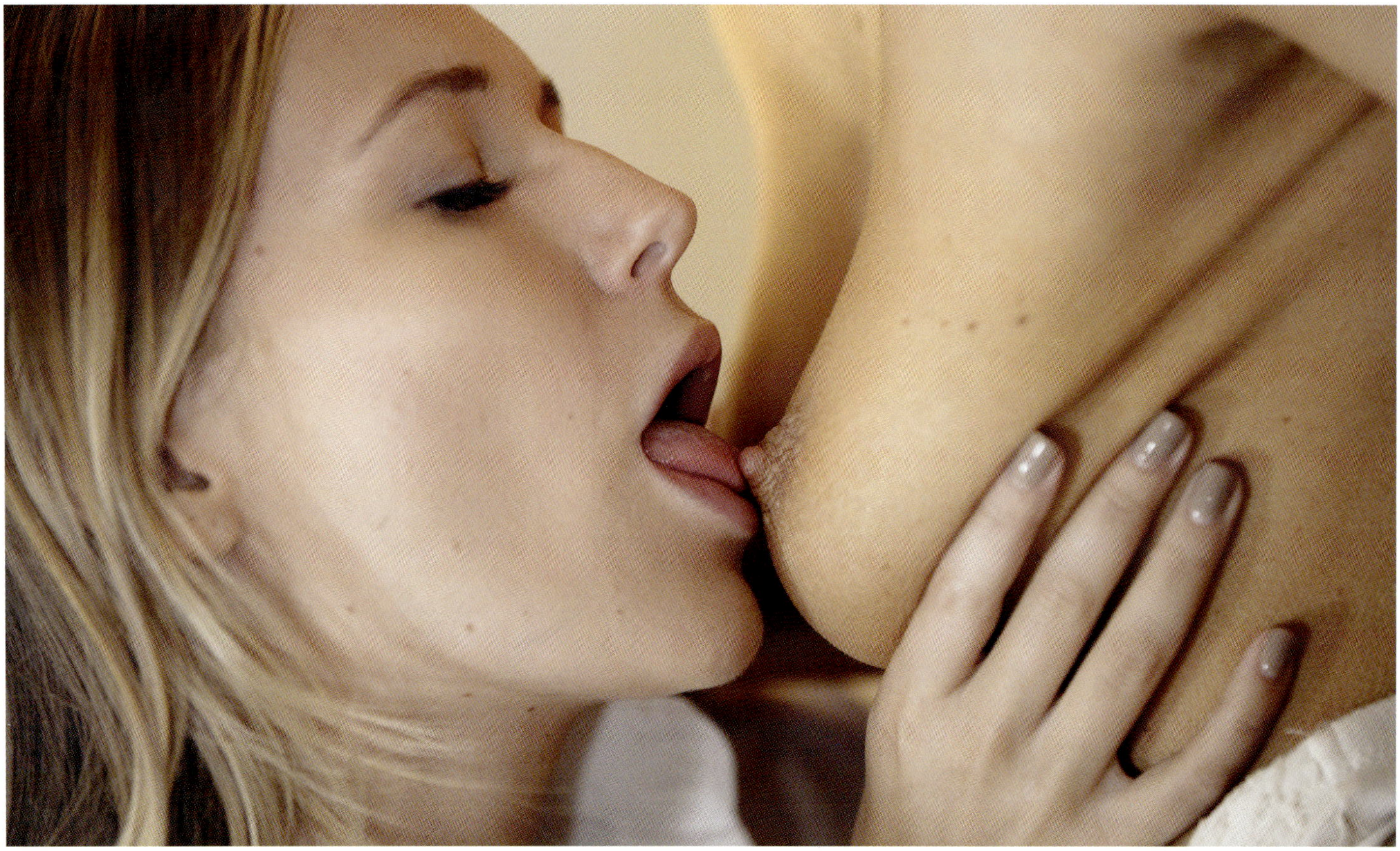

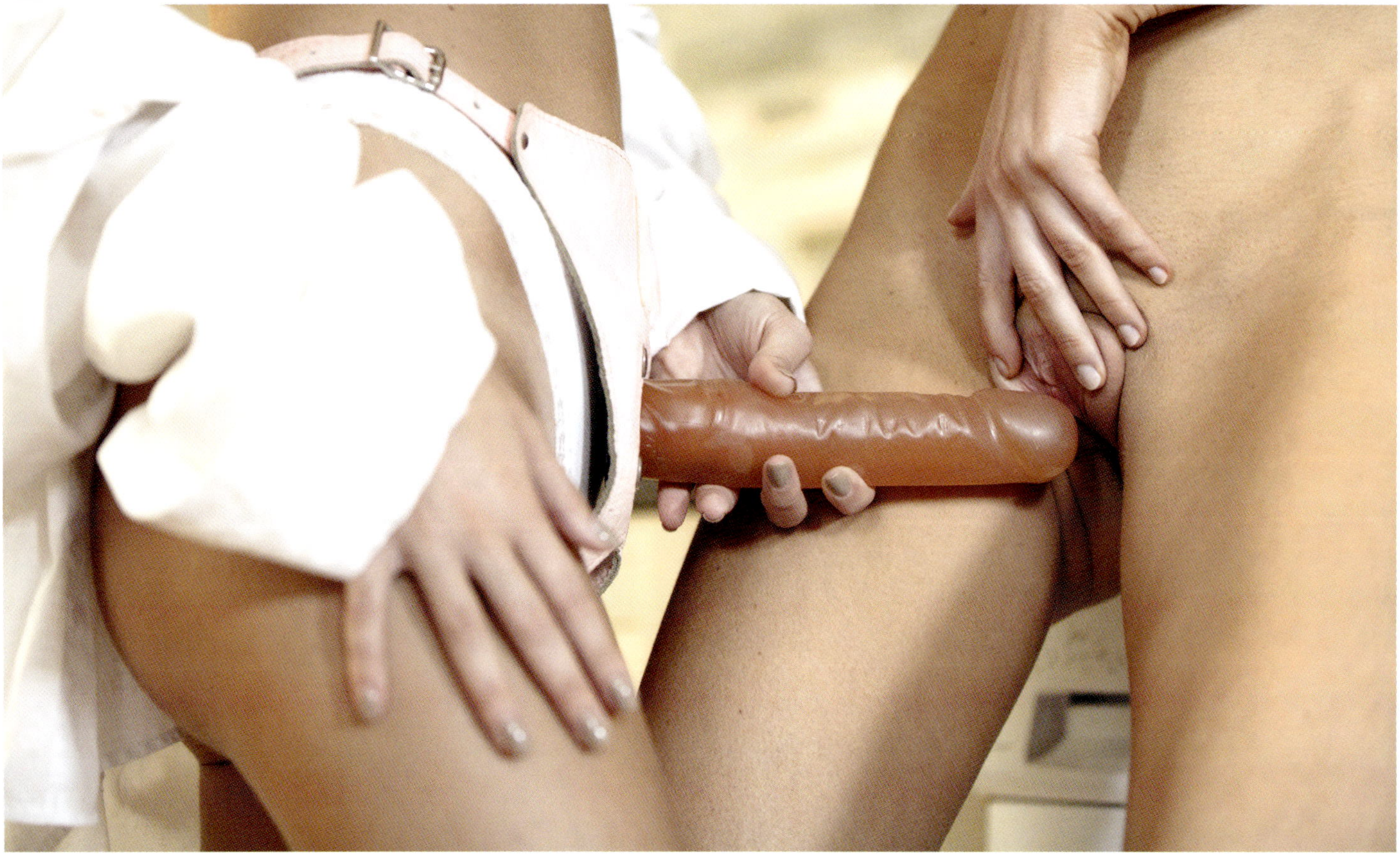

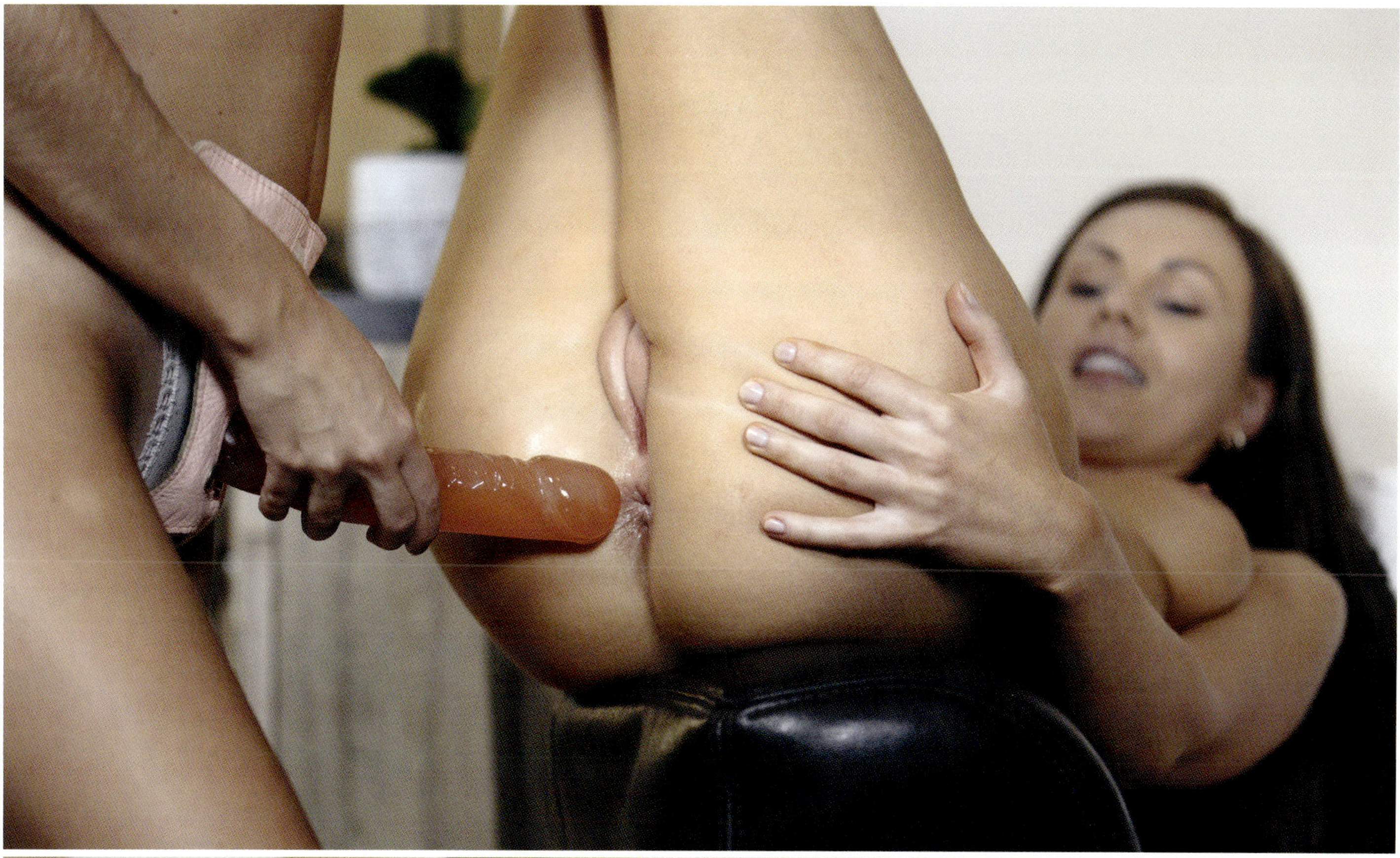

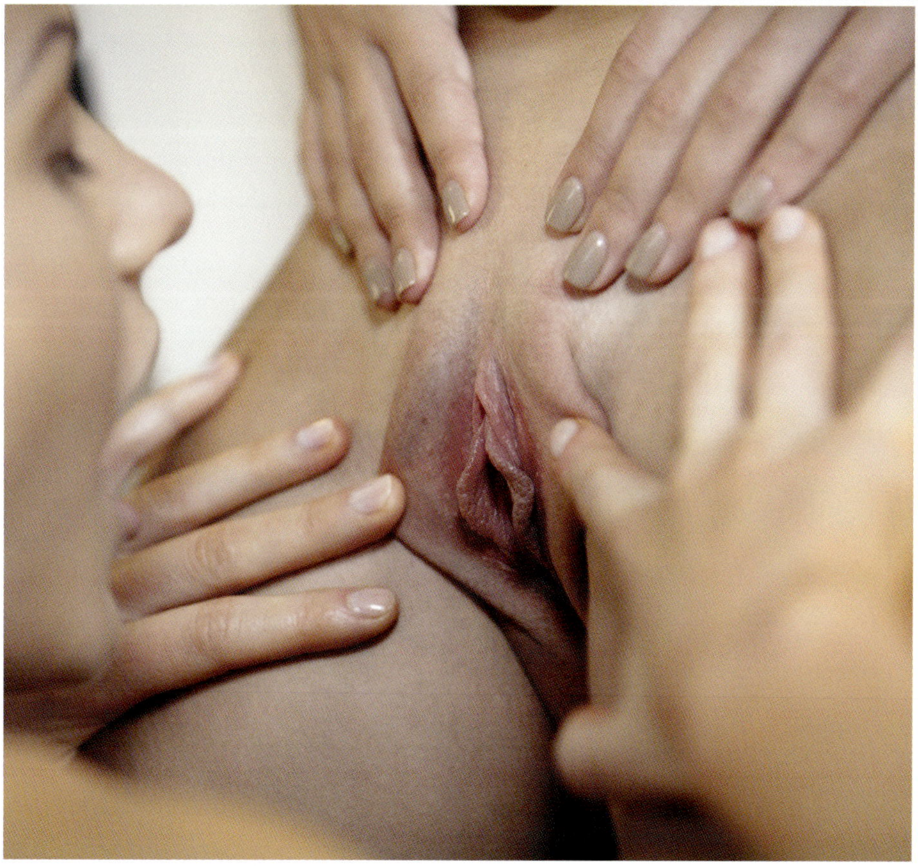

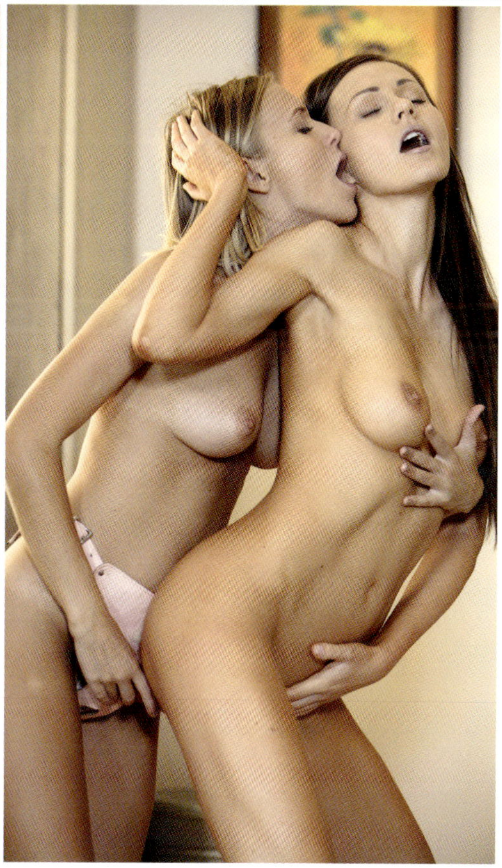

Amelie B

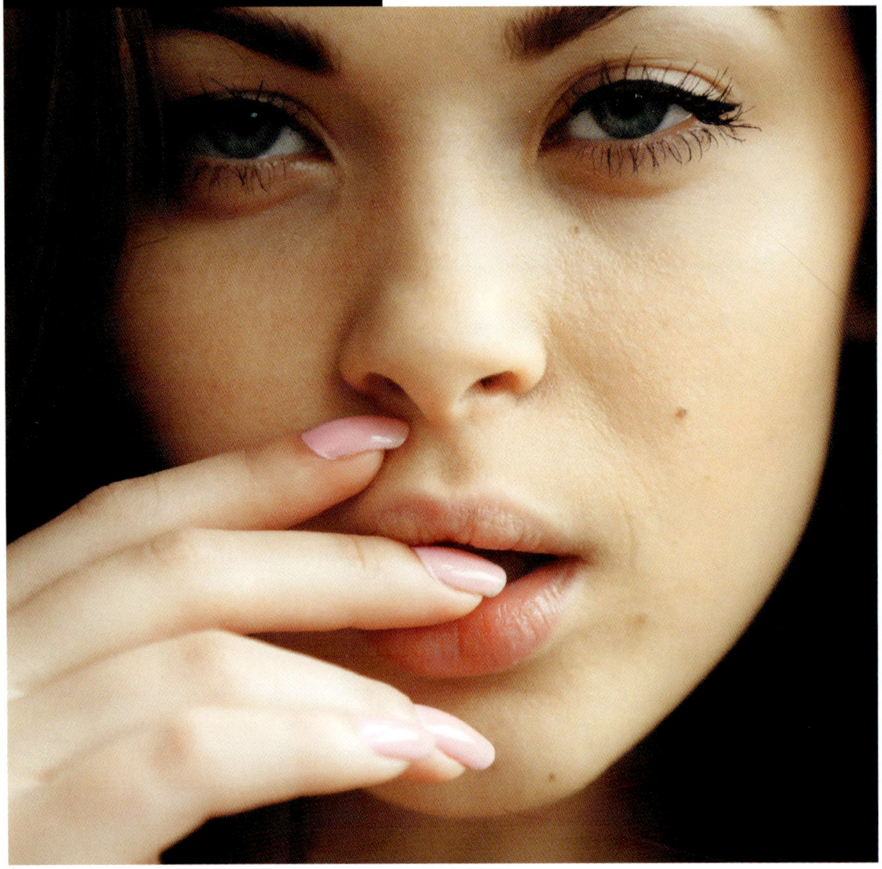

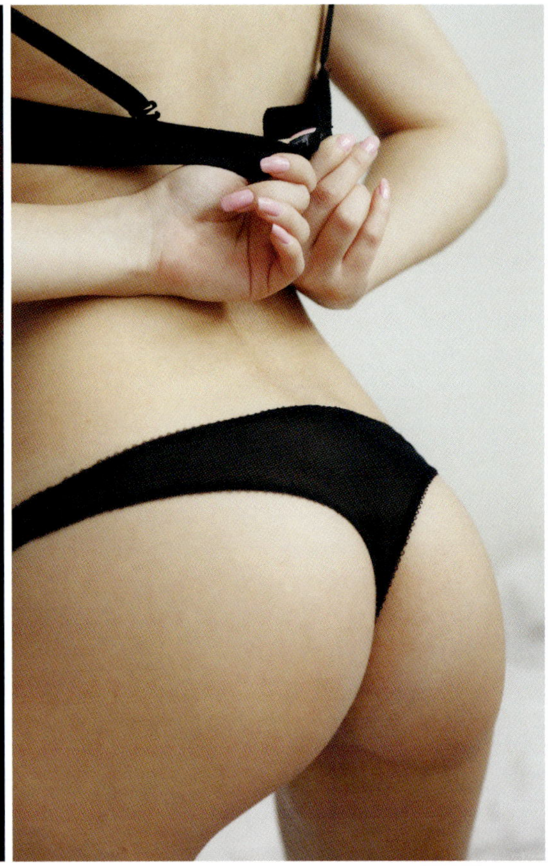

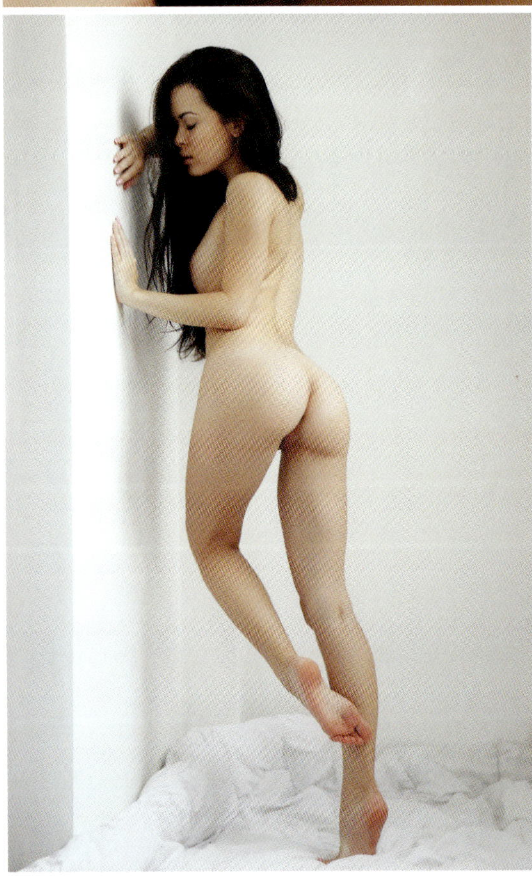

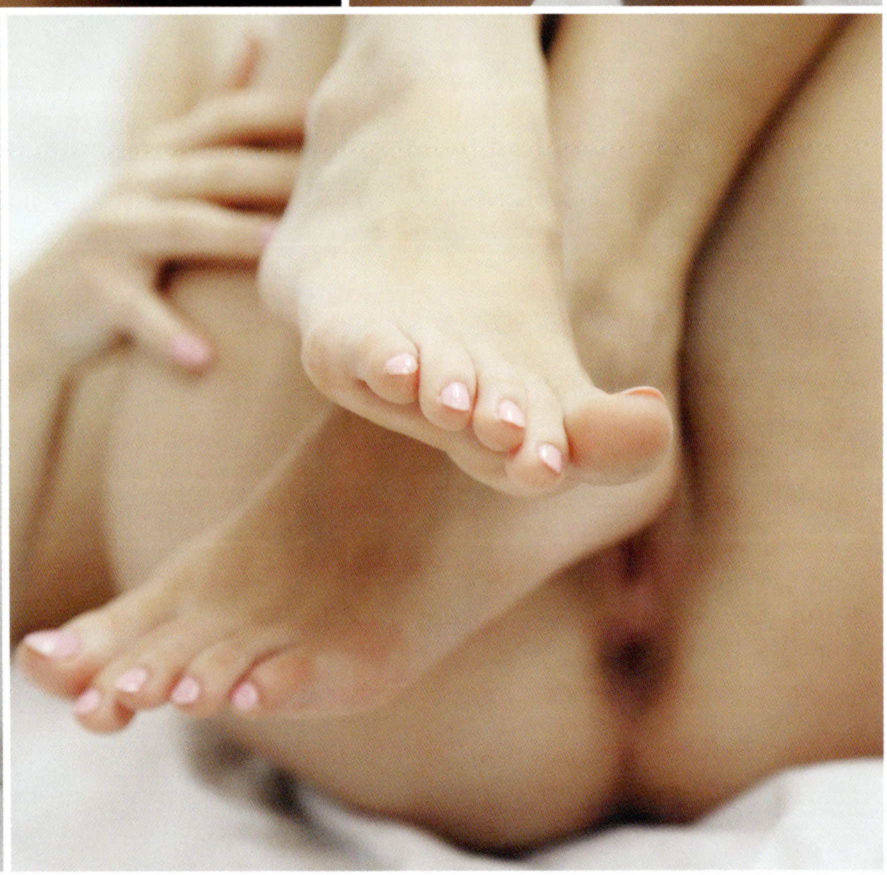

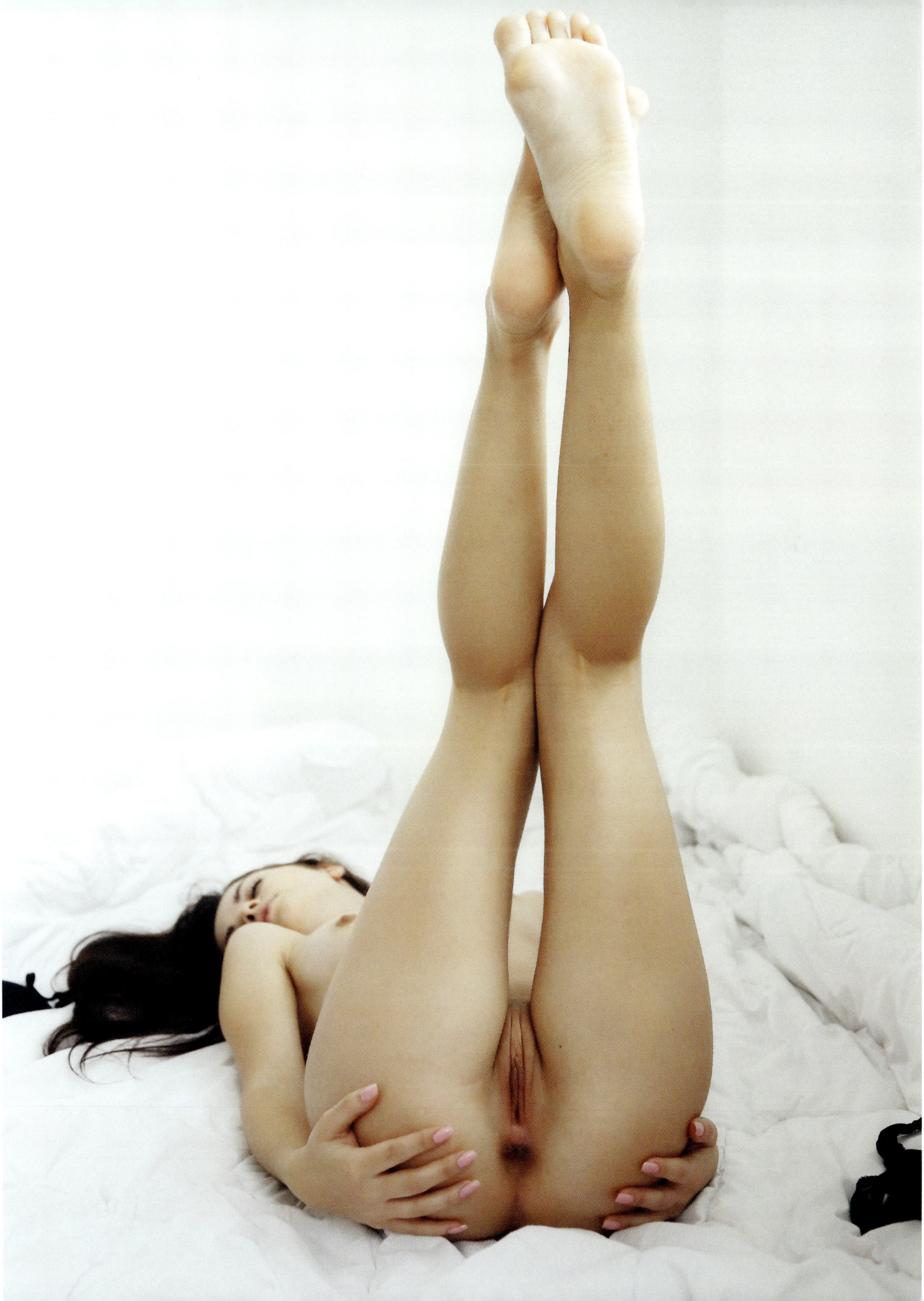

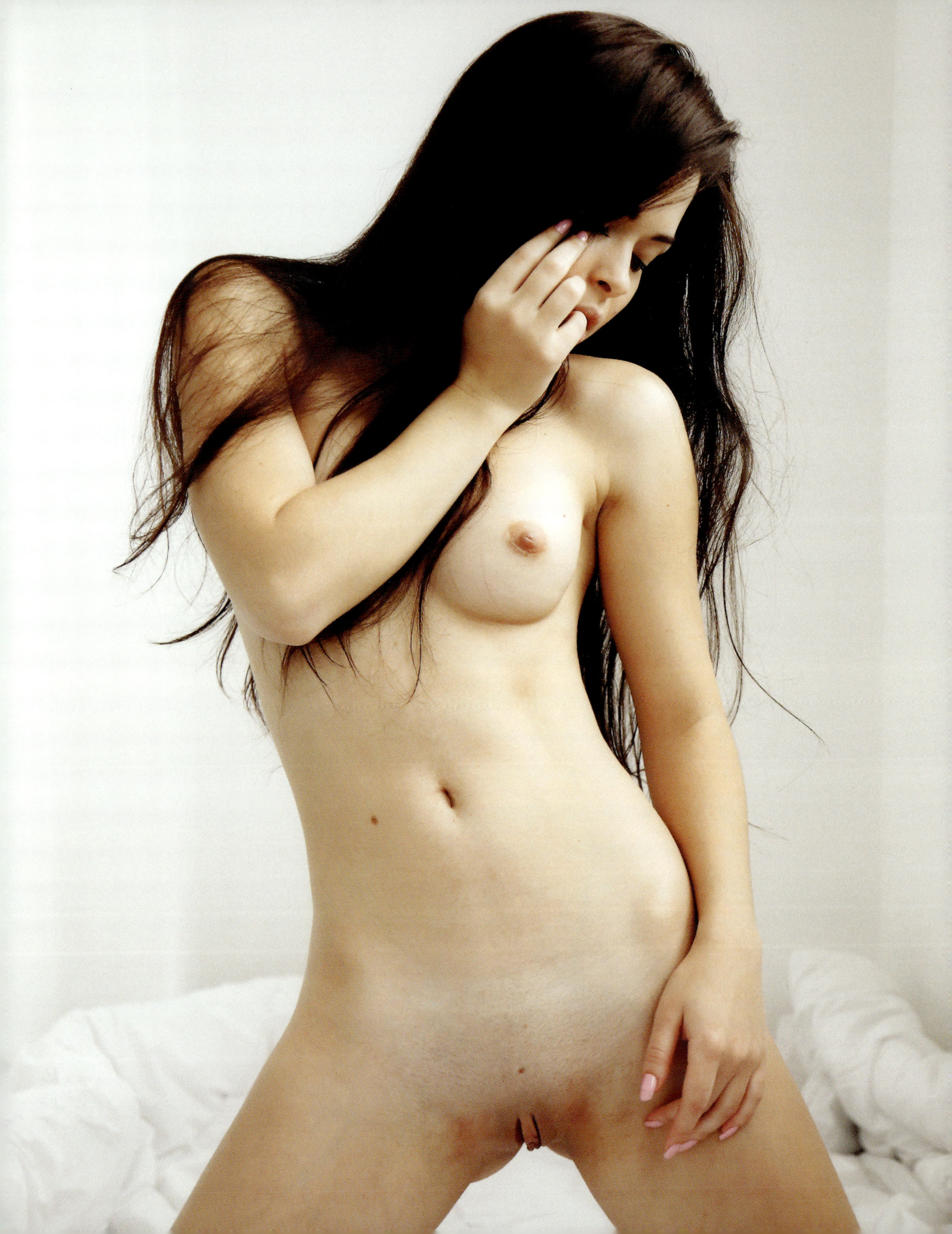

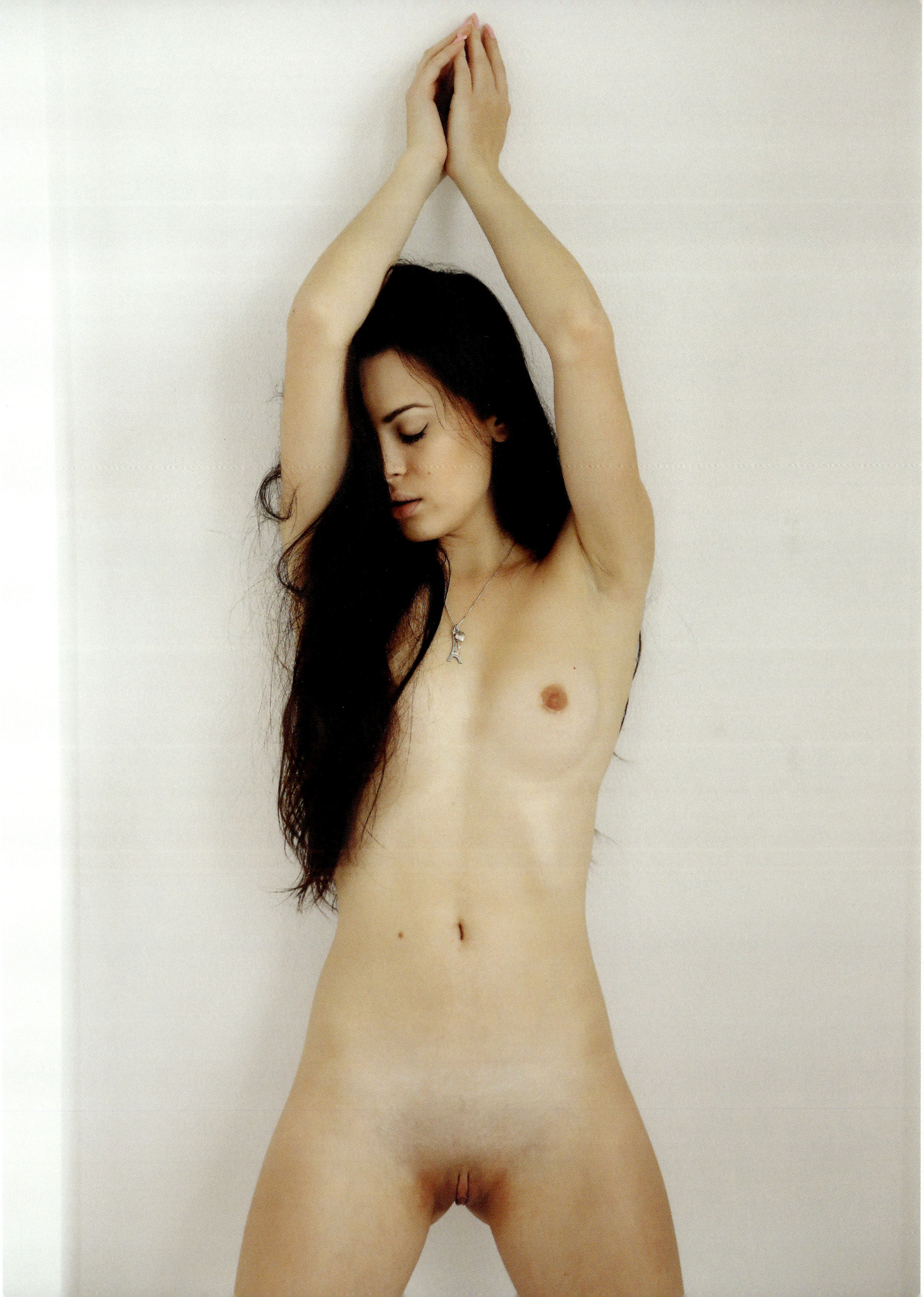

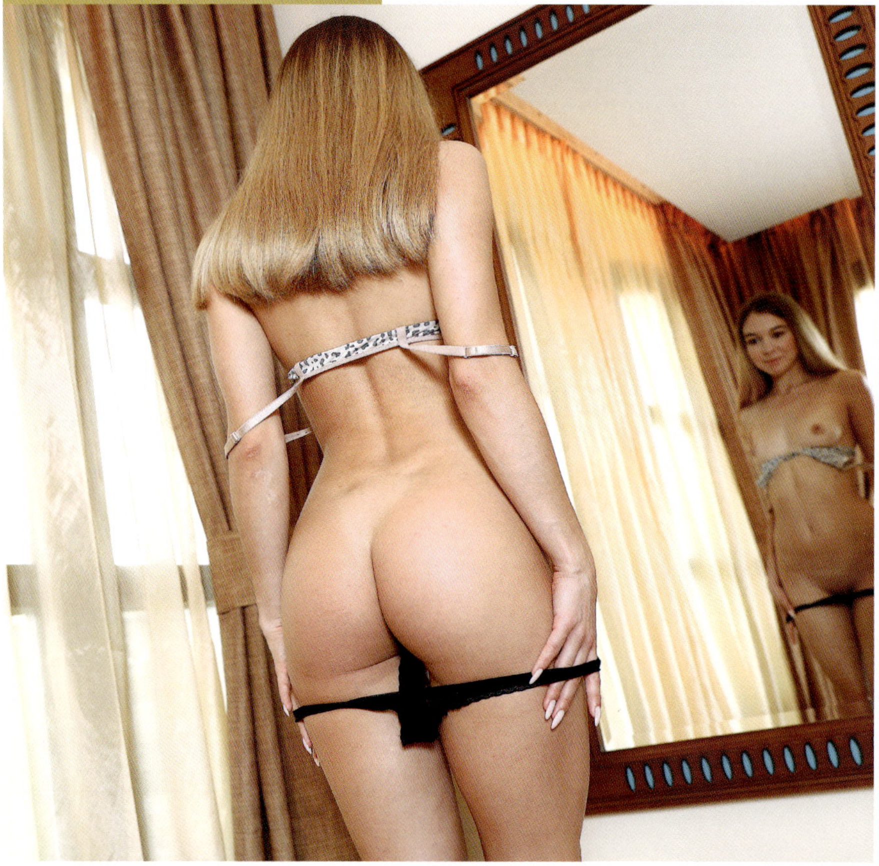

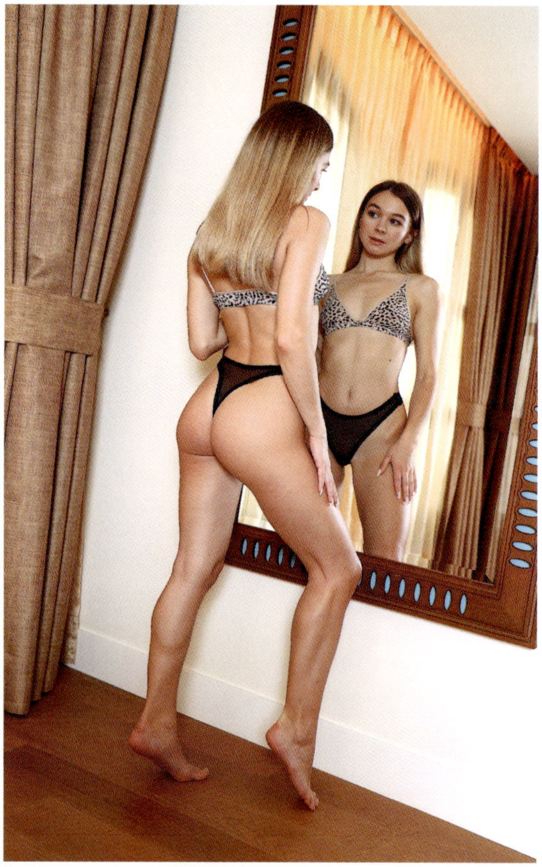

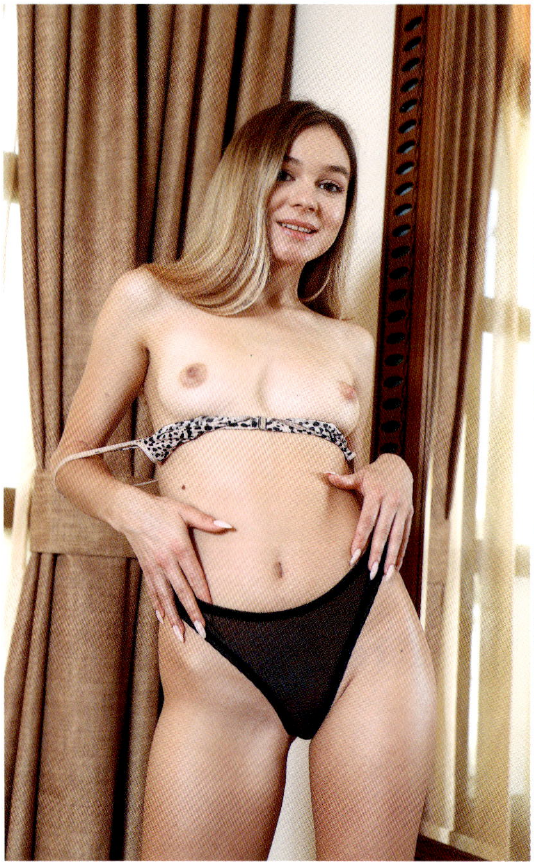

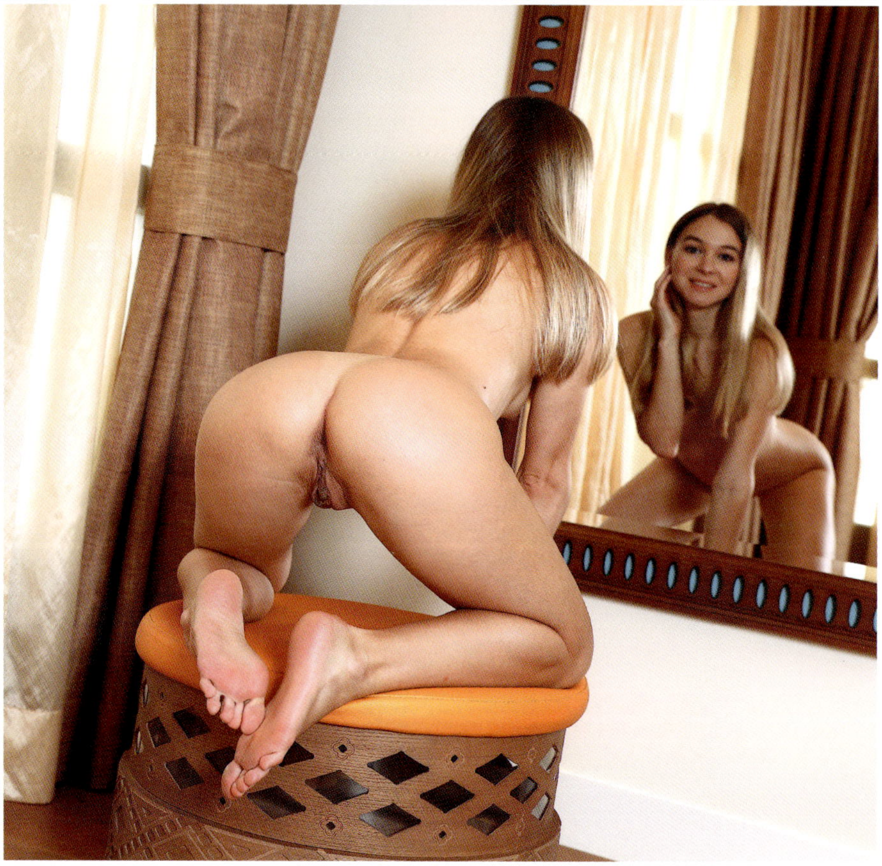

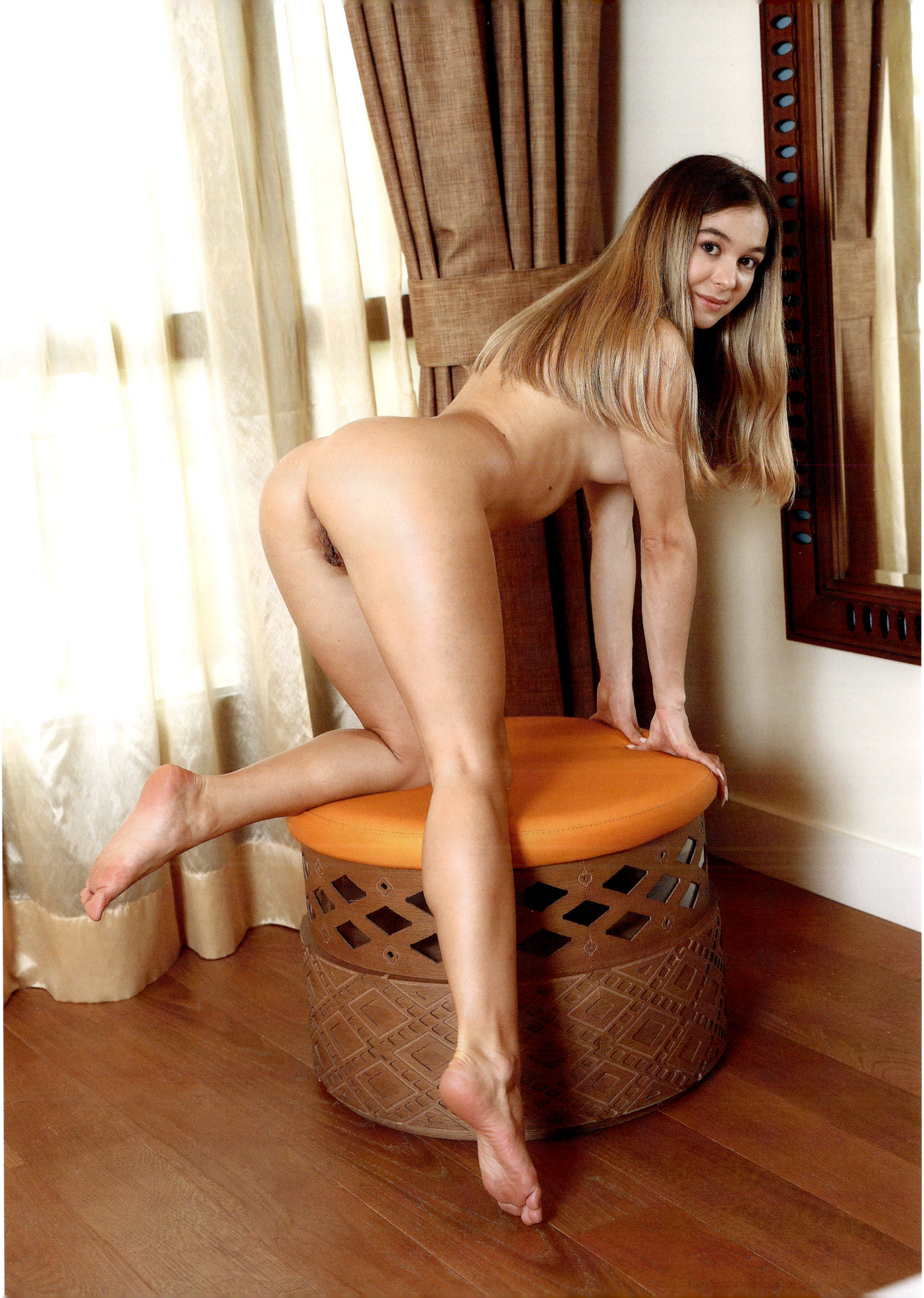

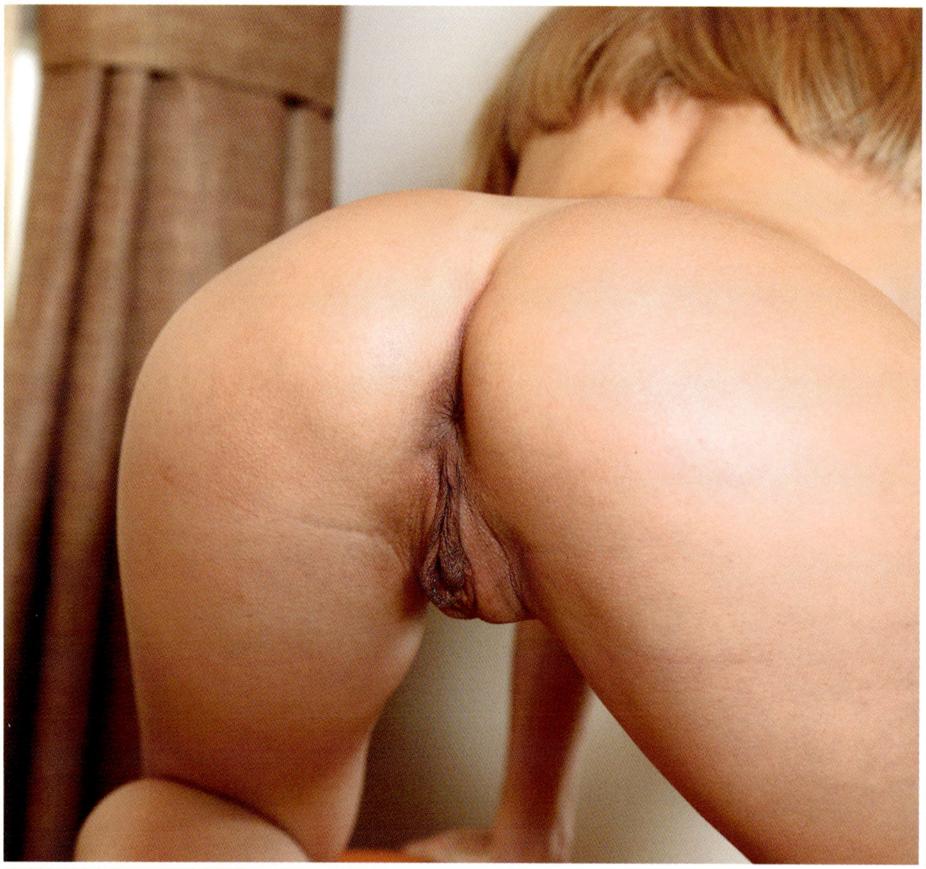

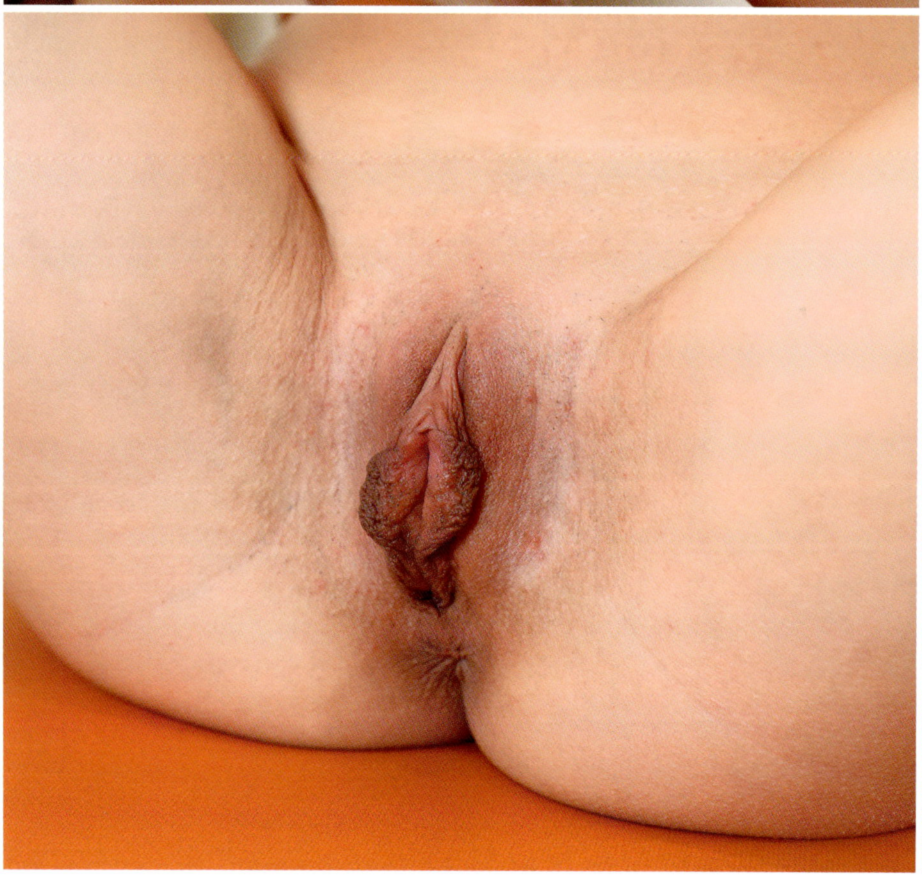

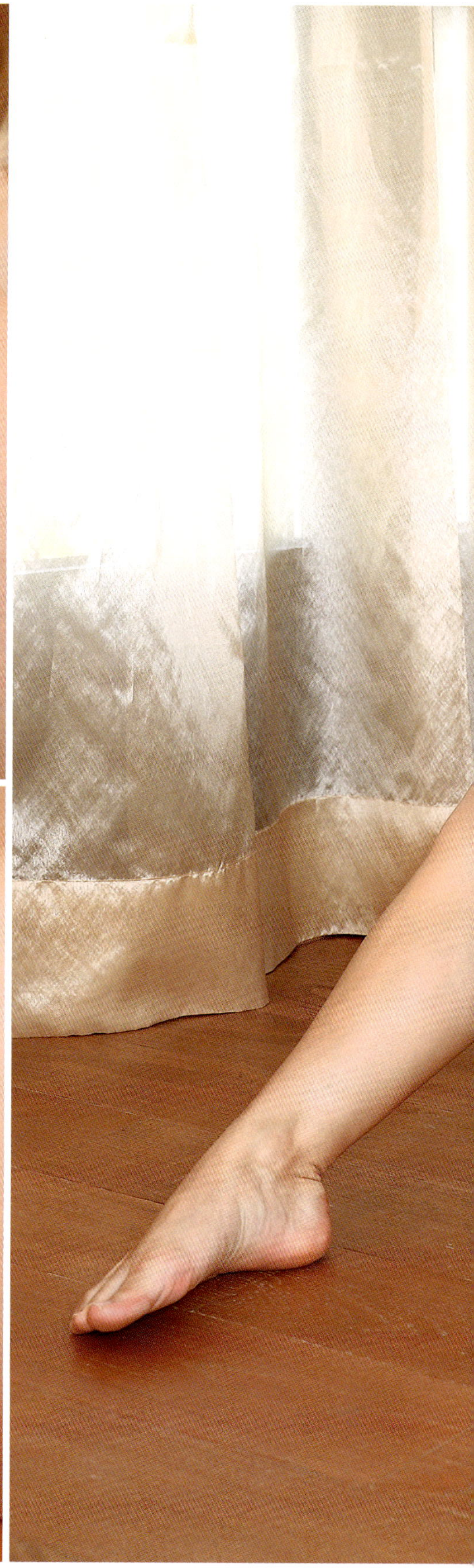

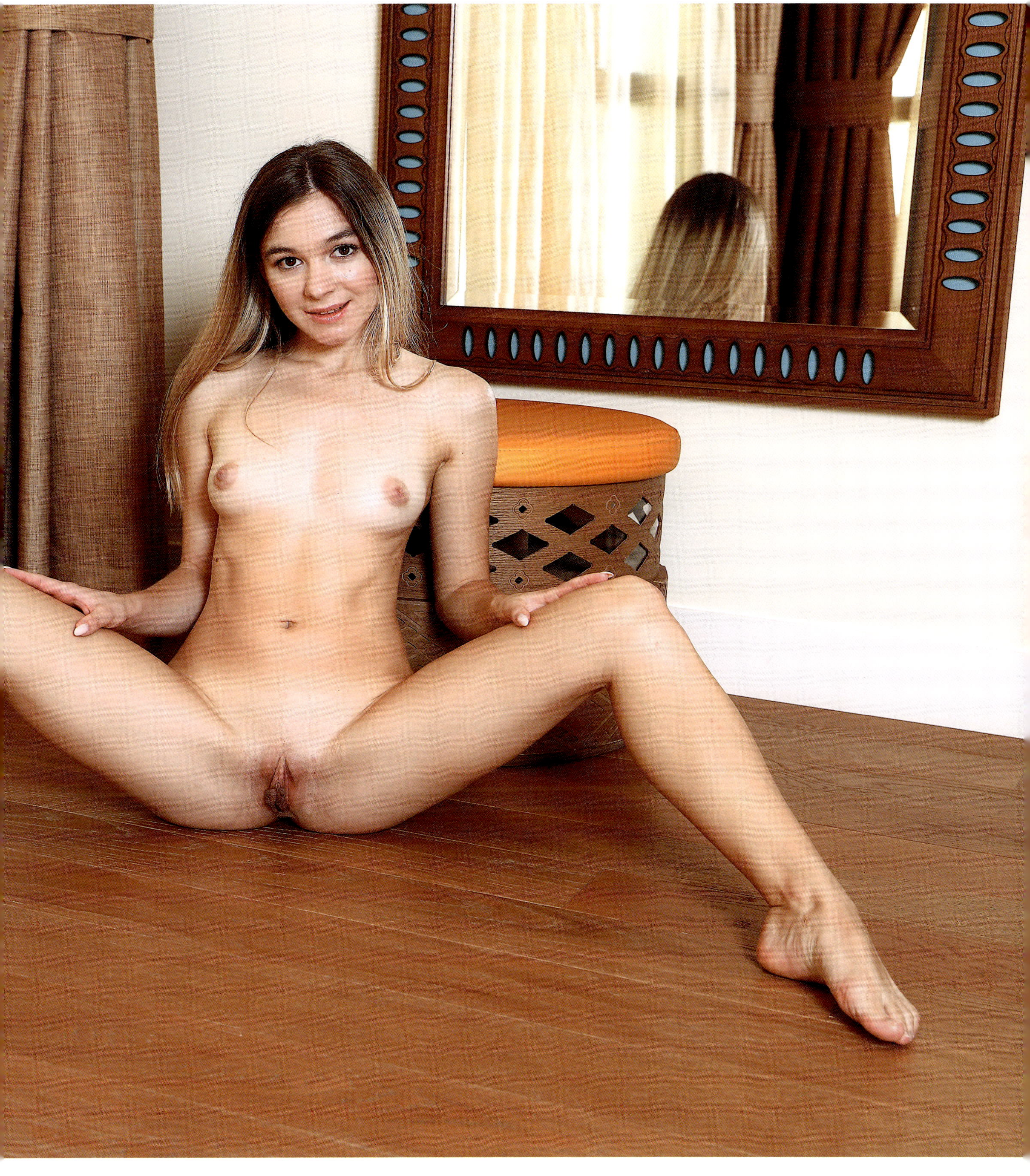

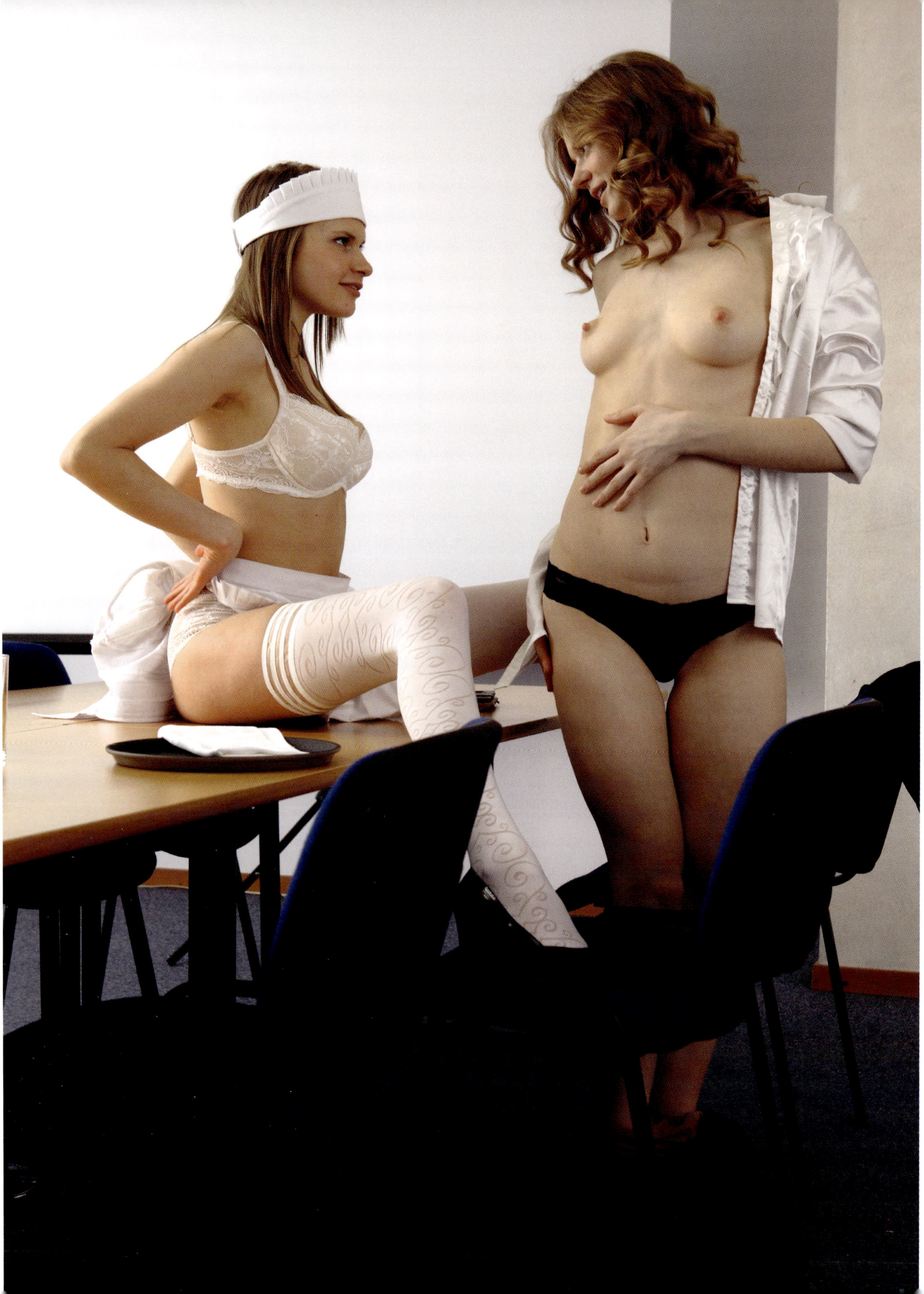

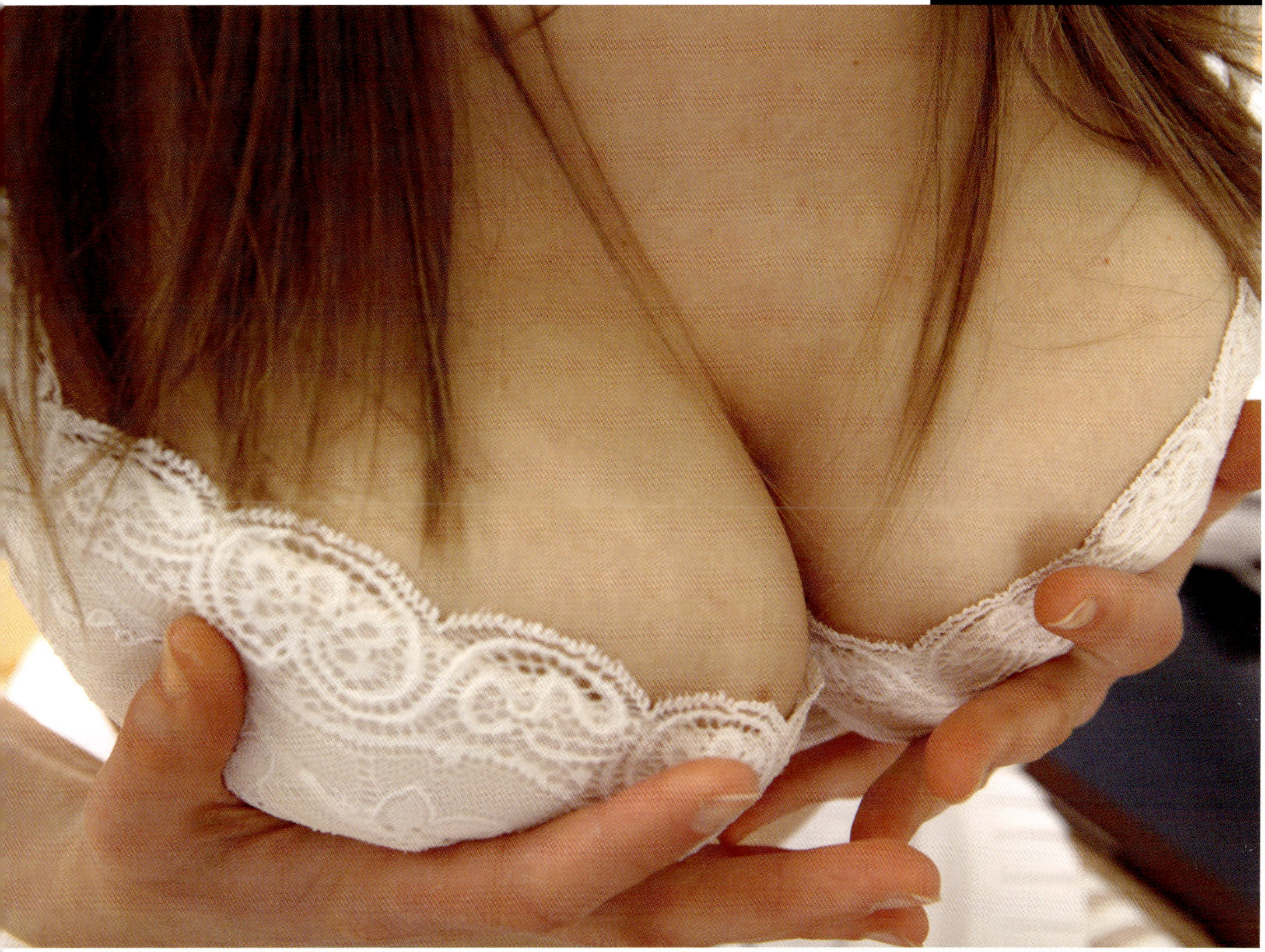

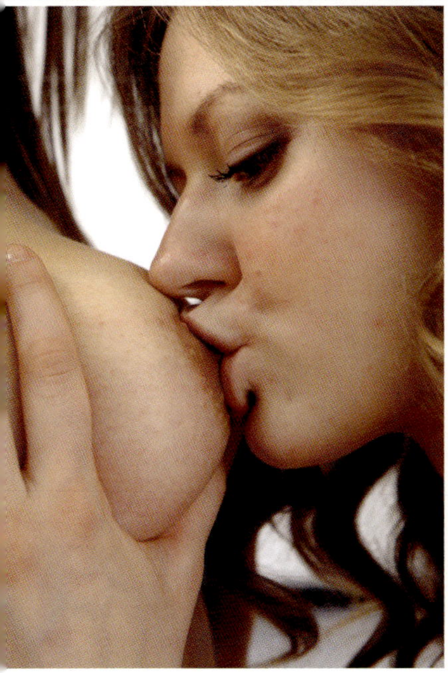

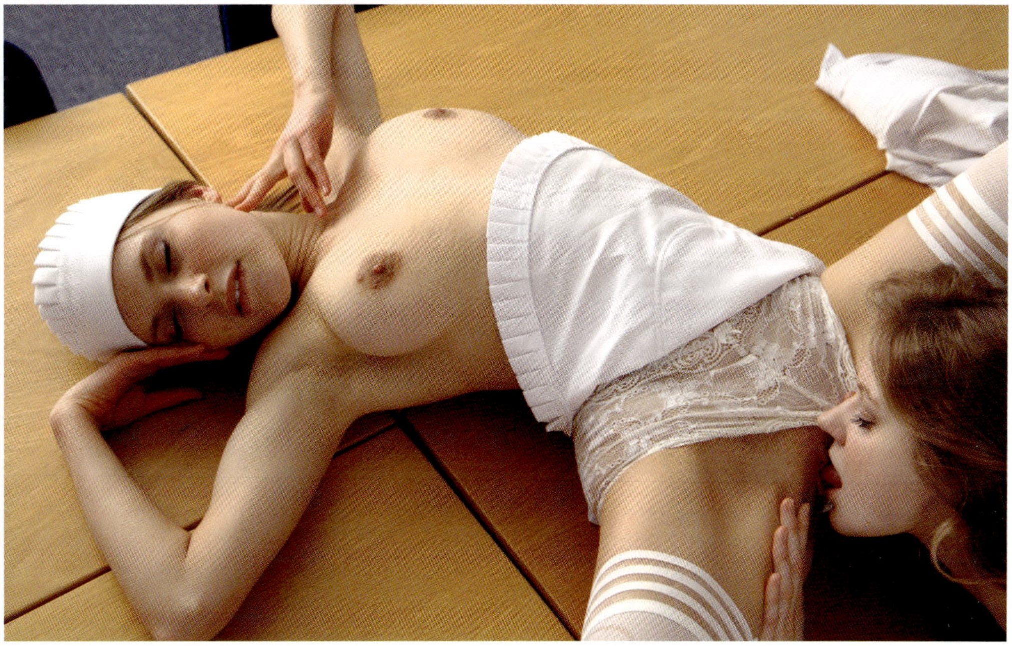

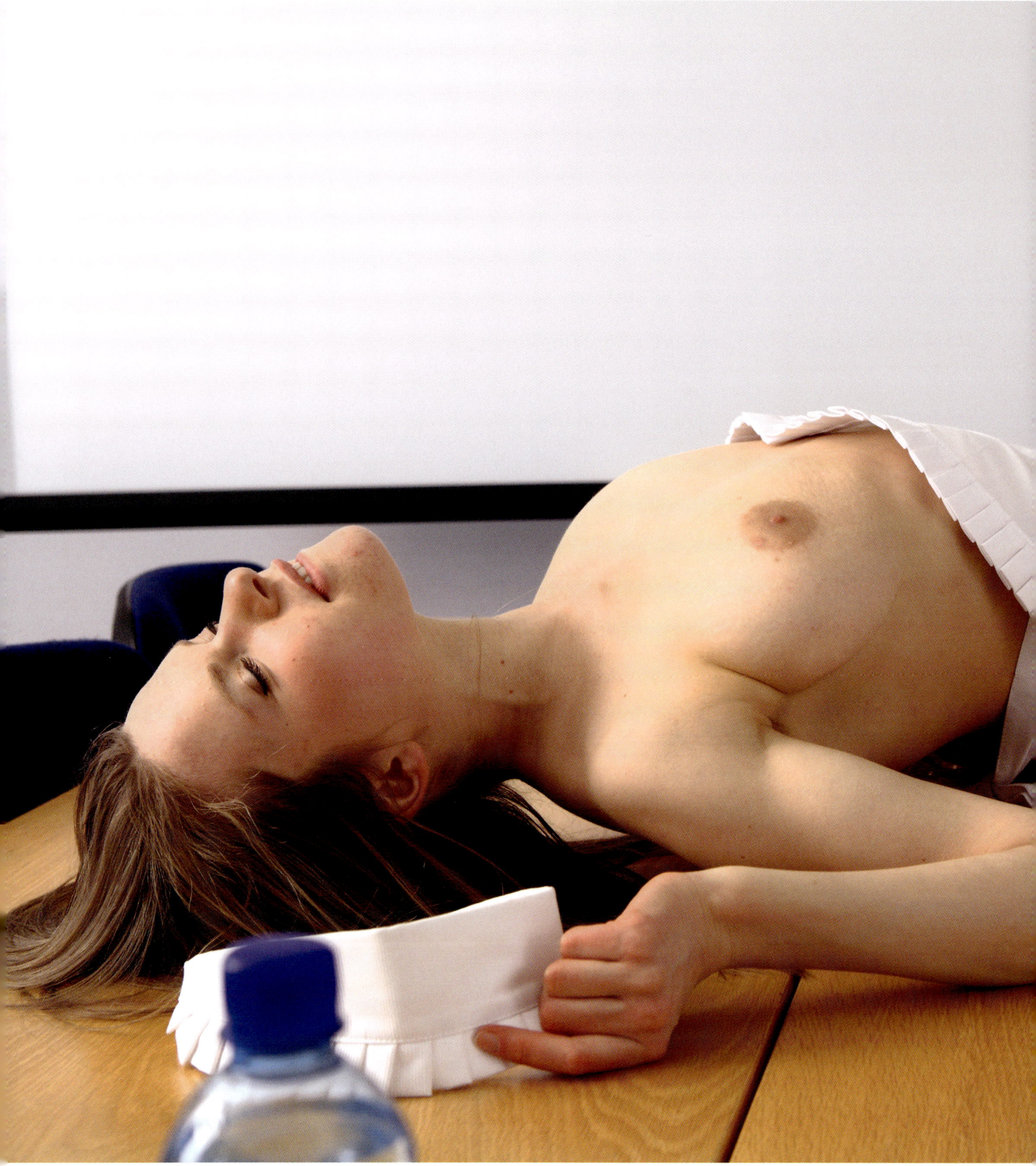

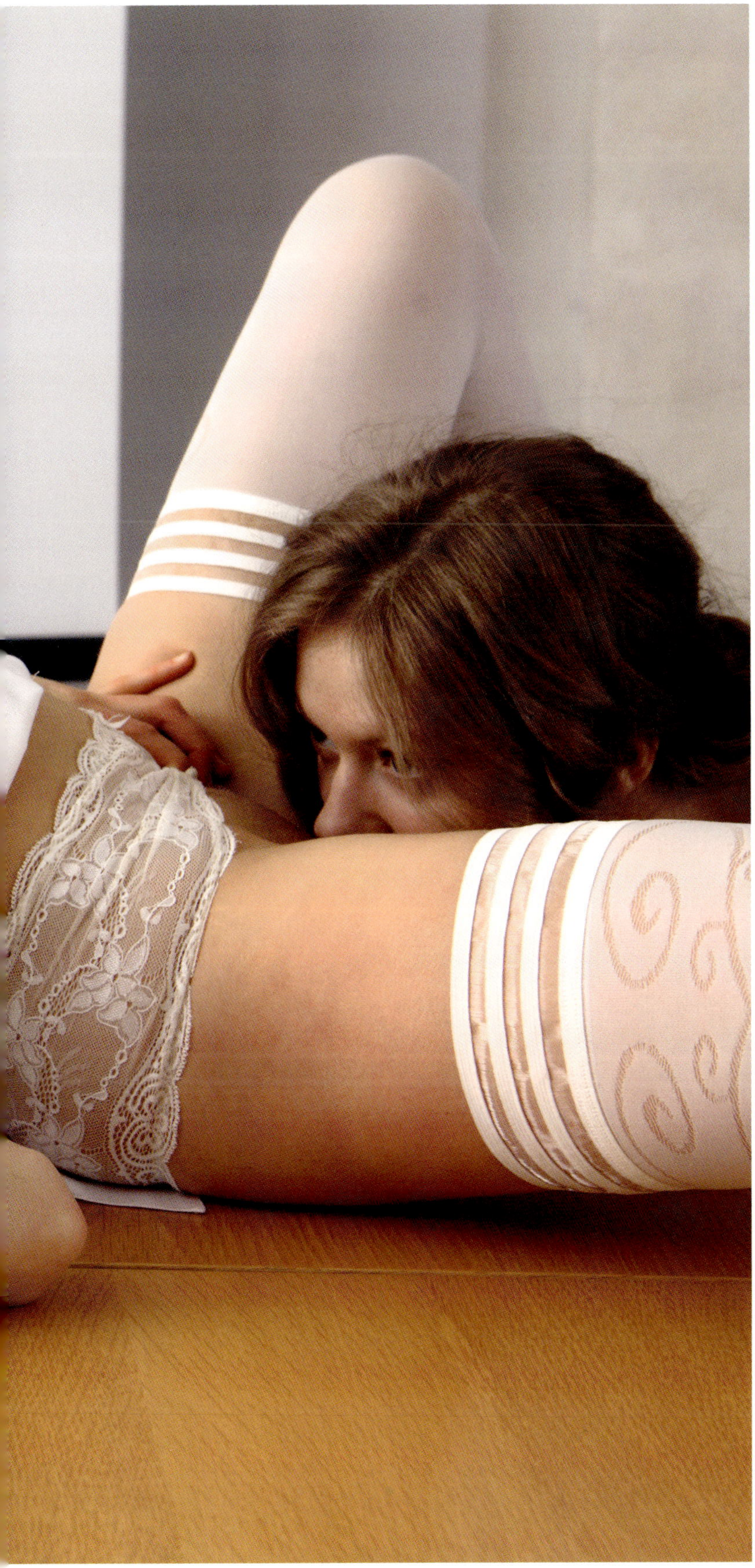

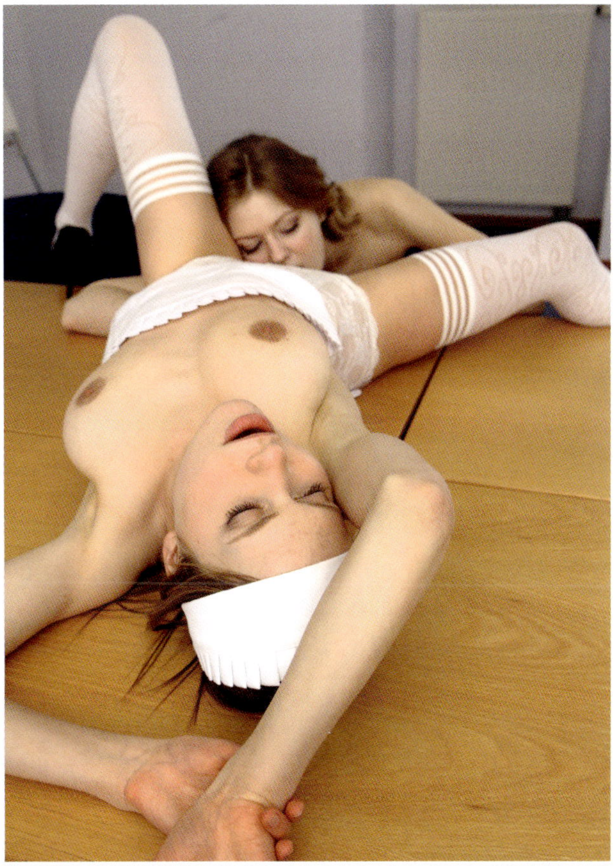

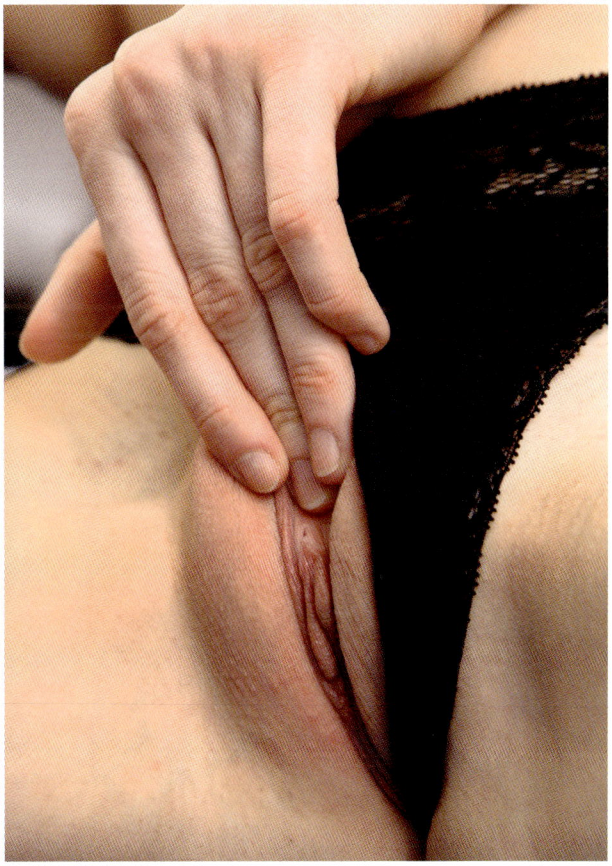

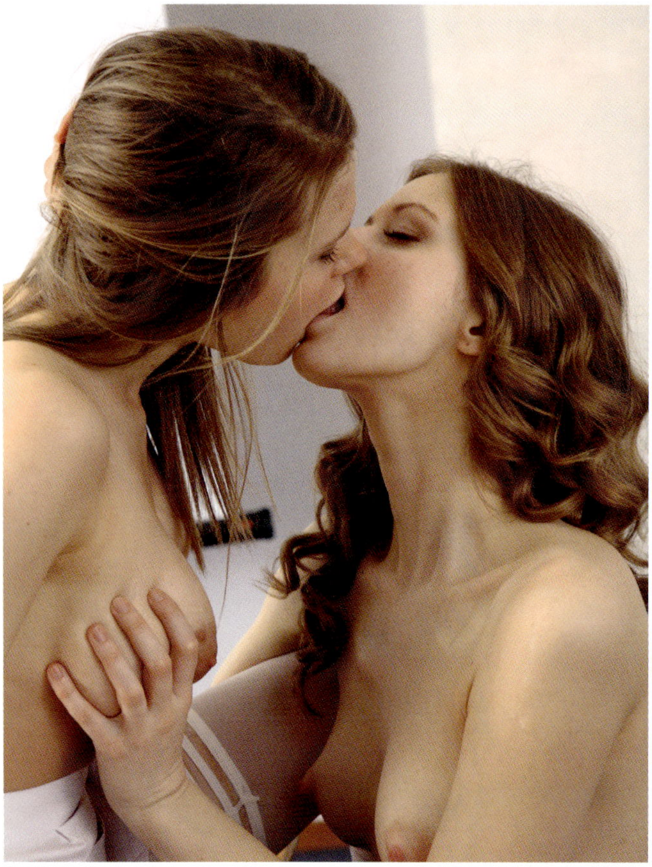

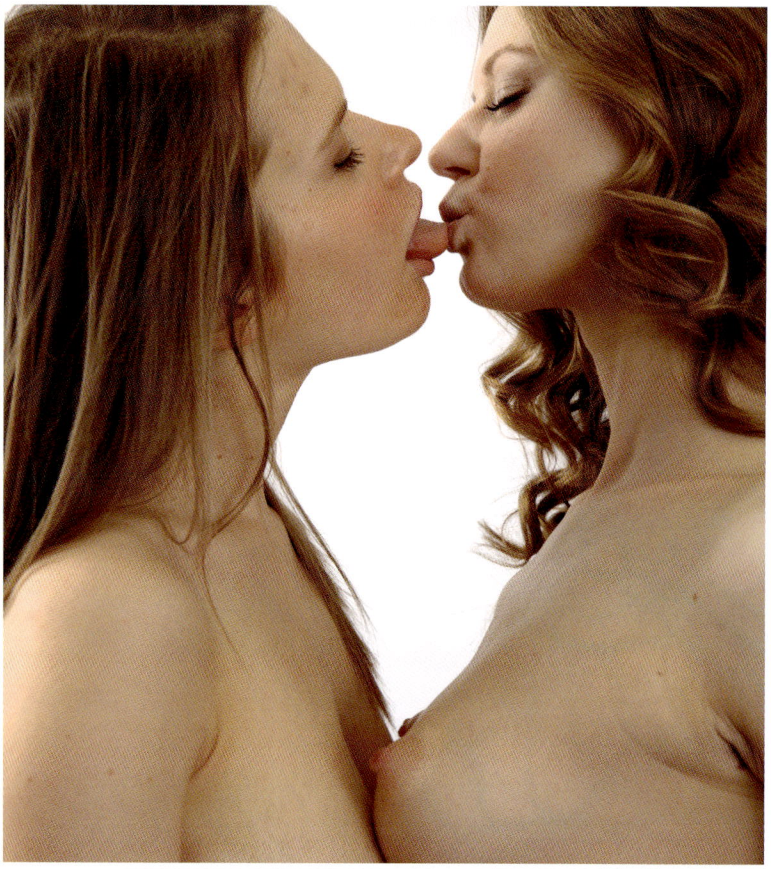

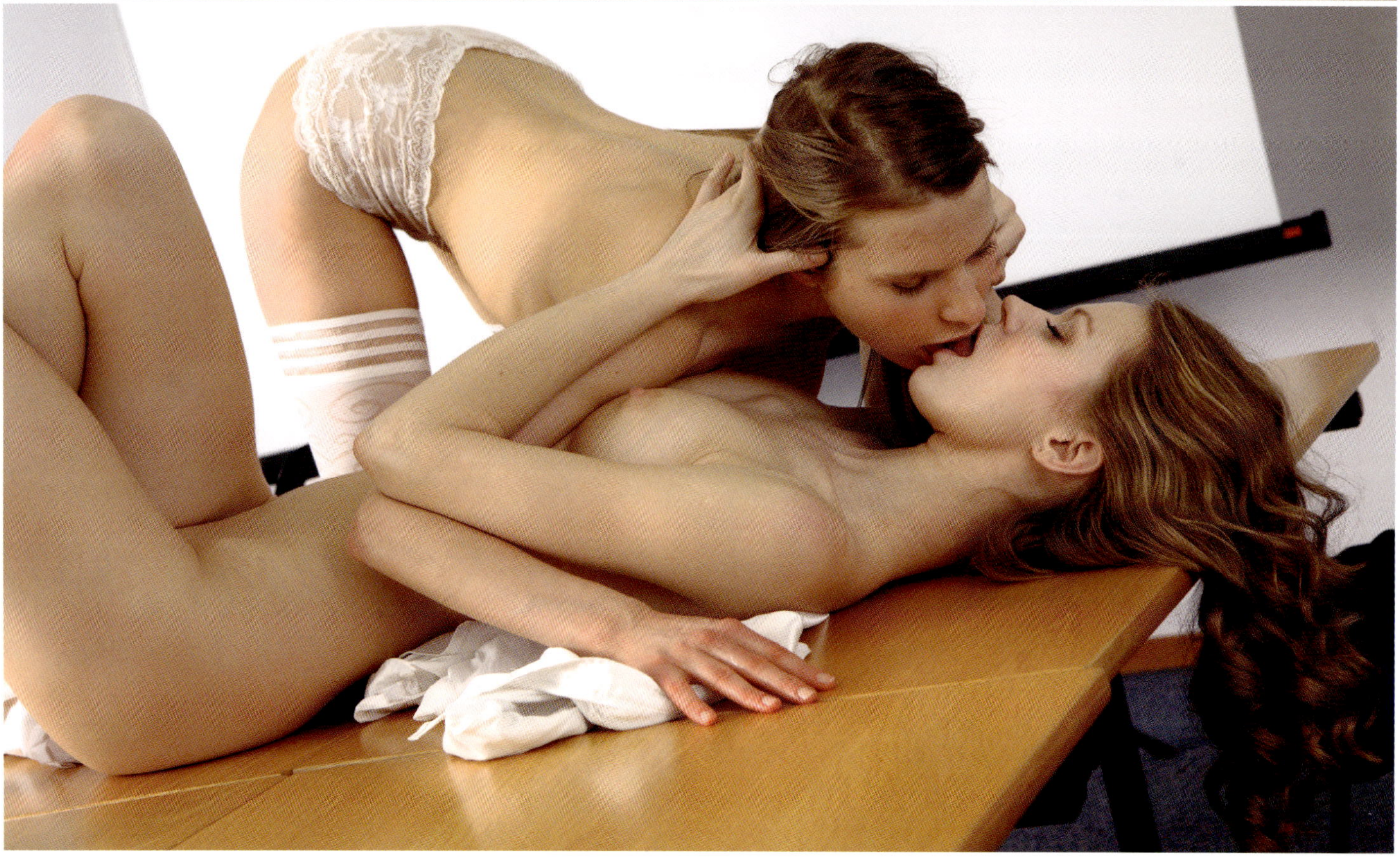

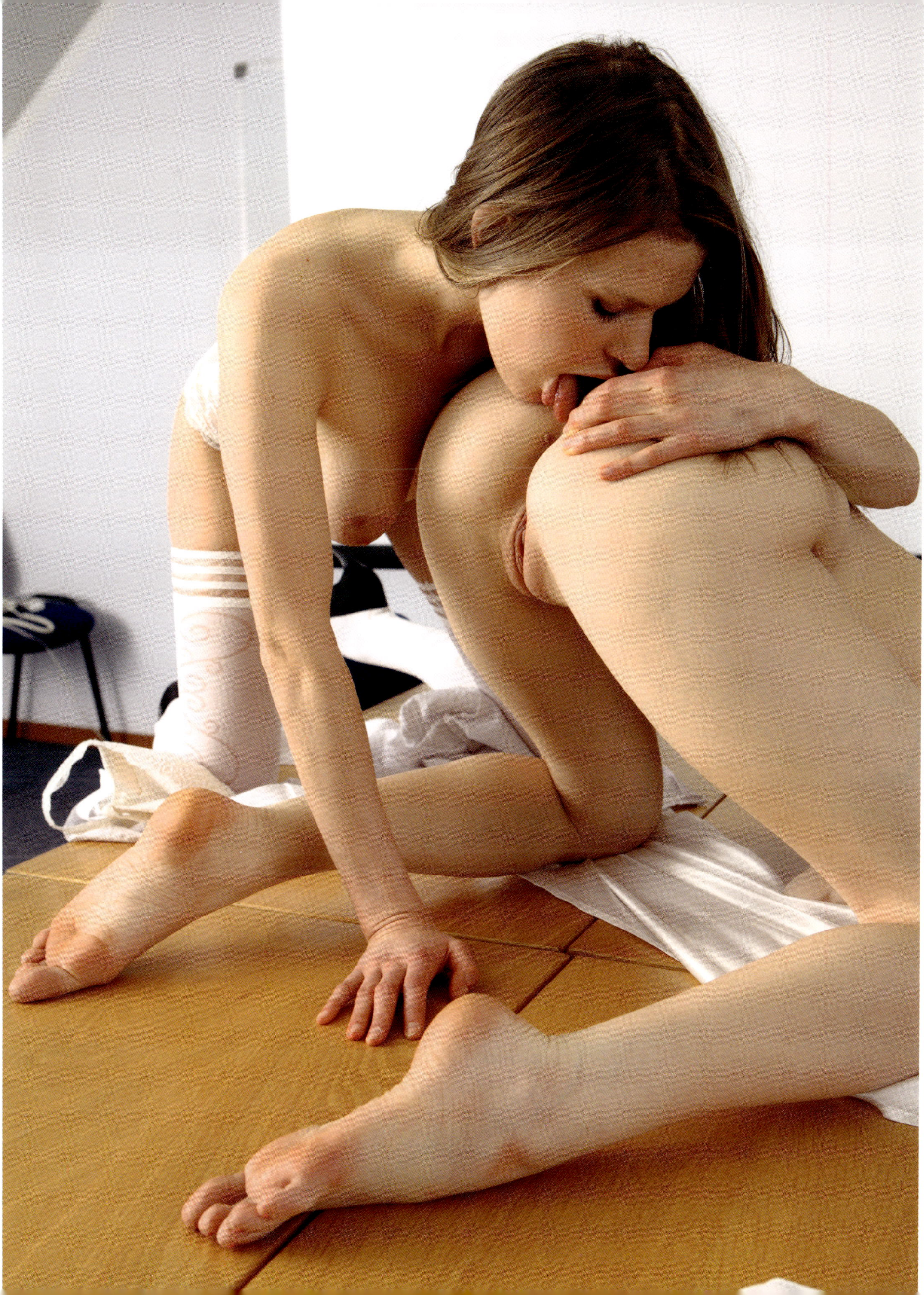

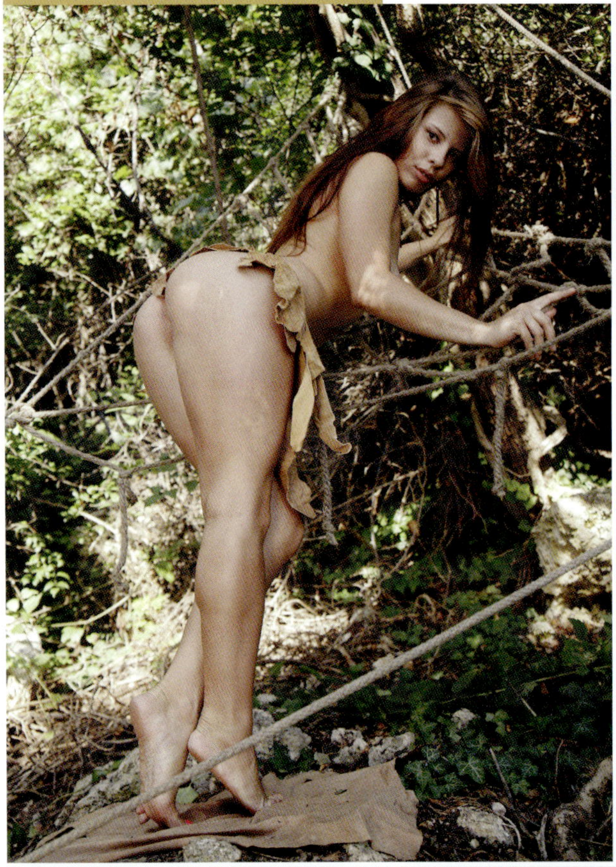

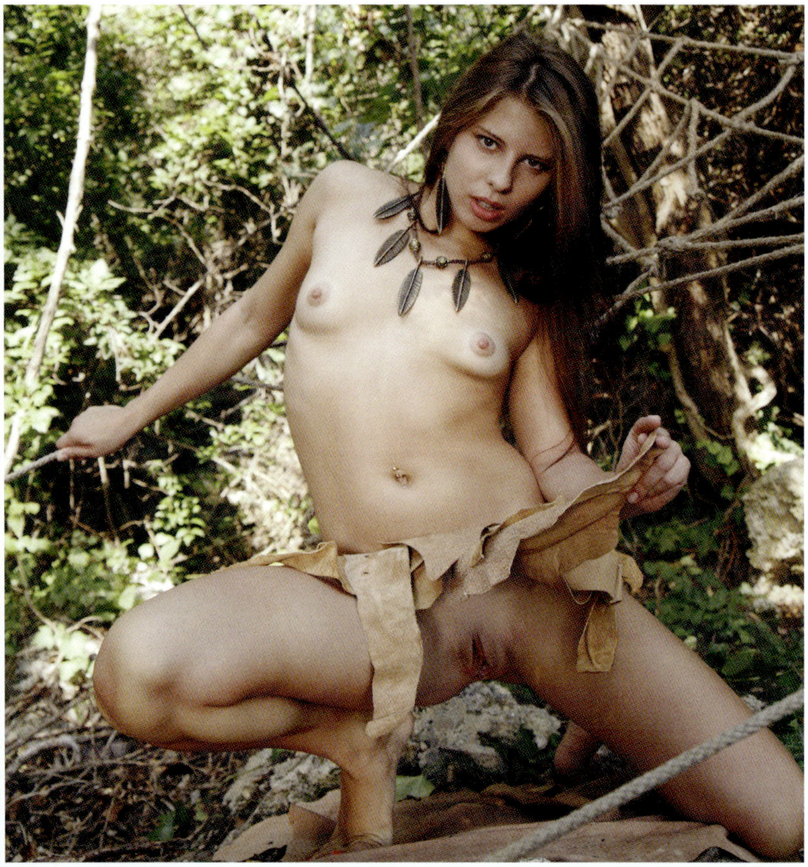

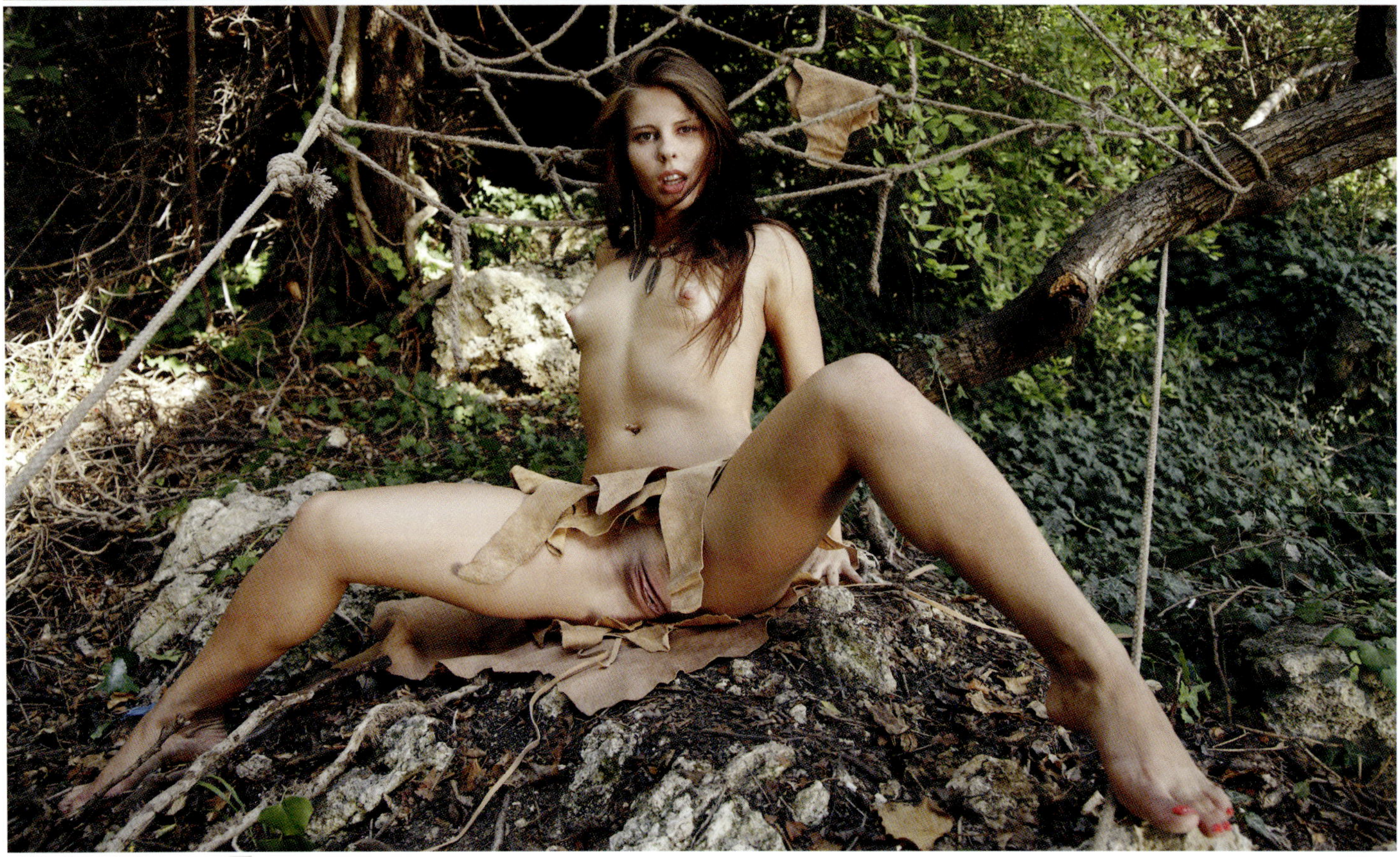

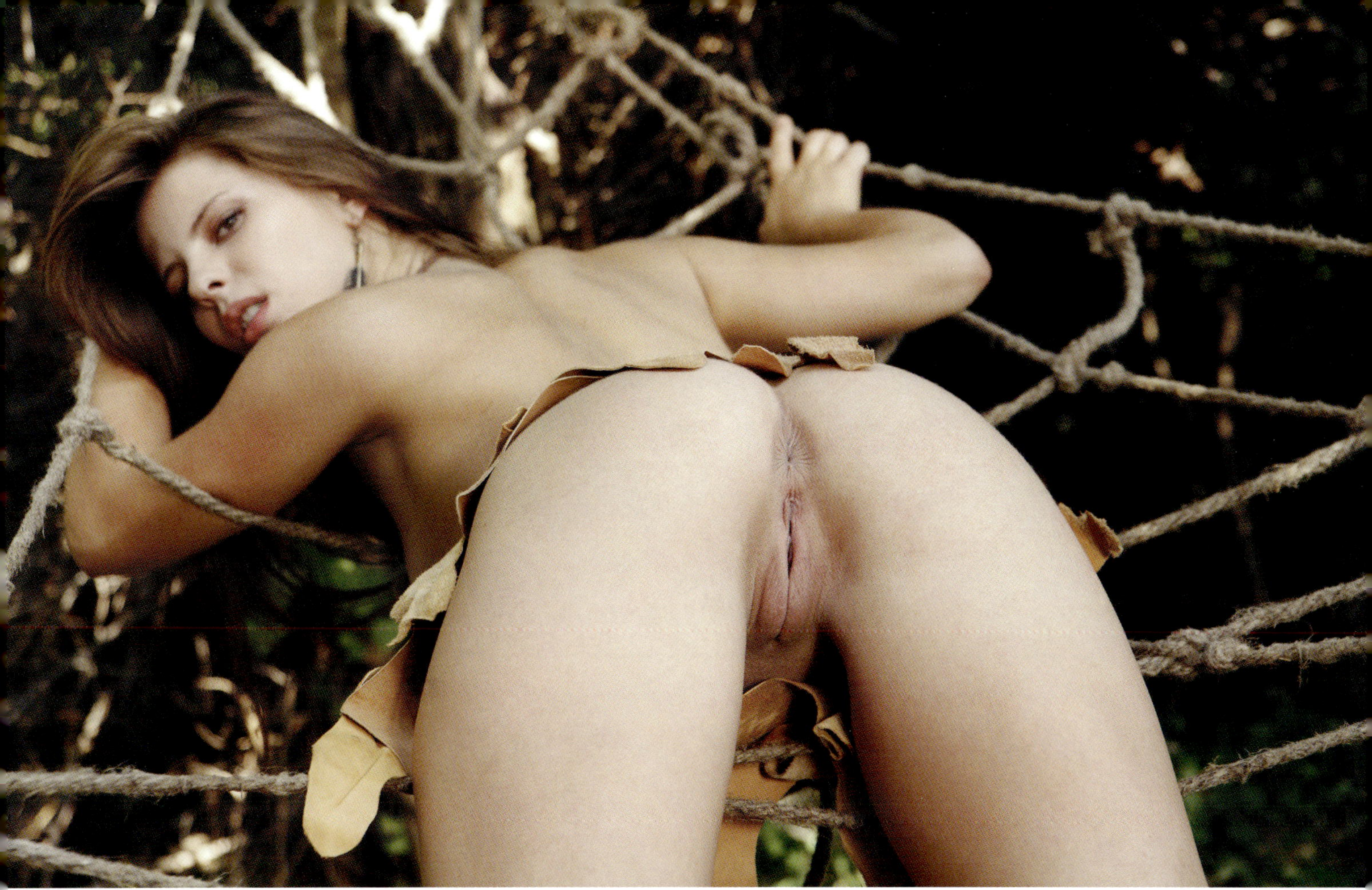
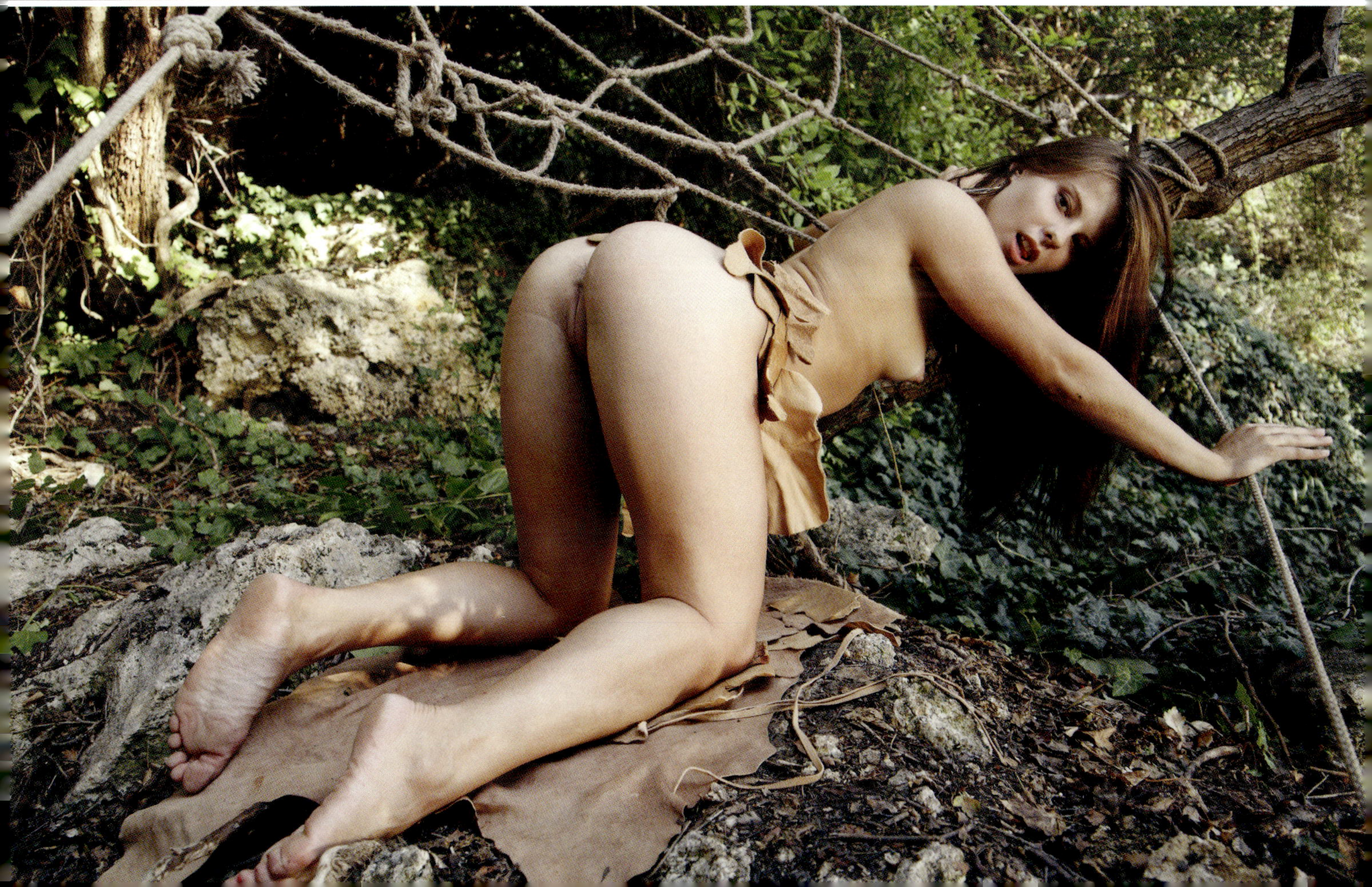

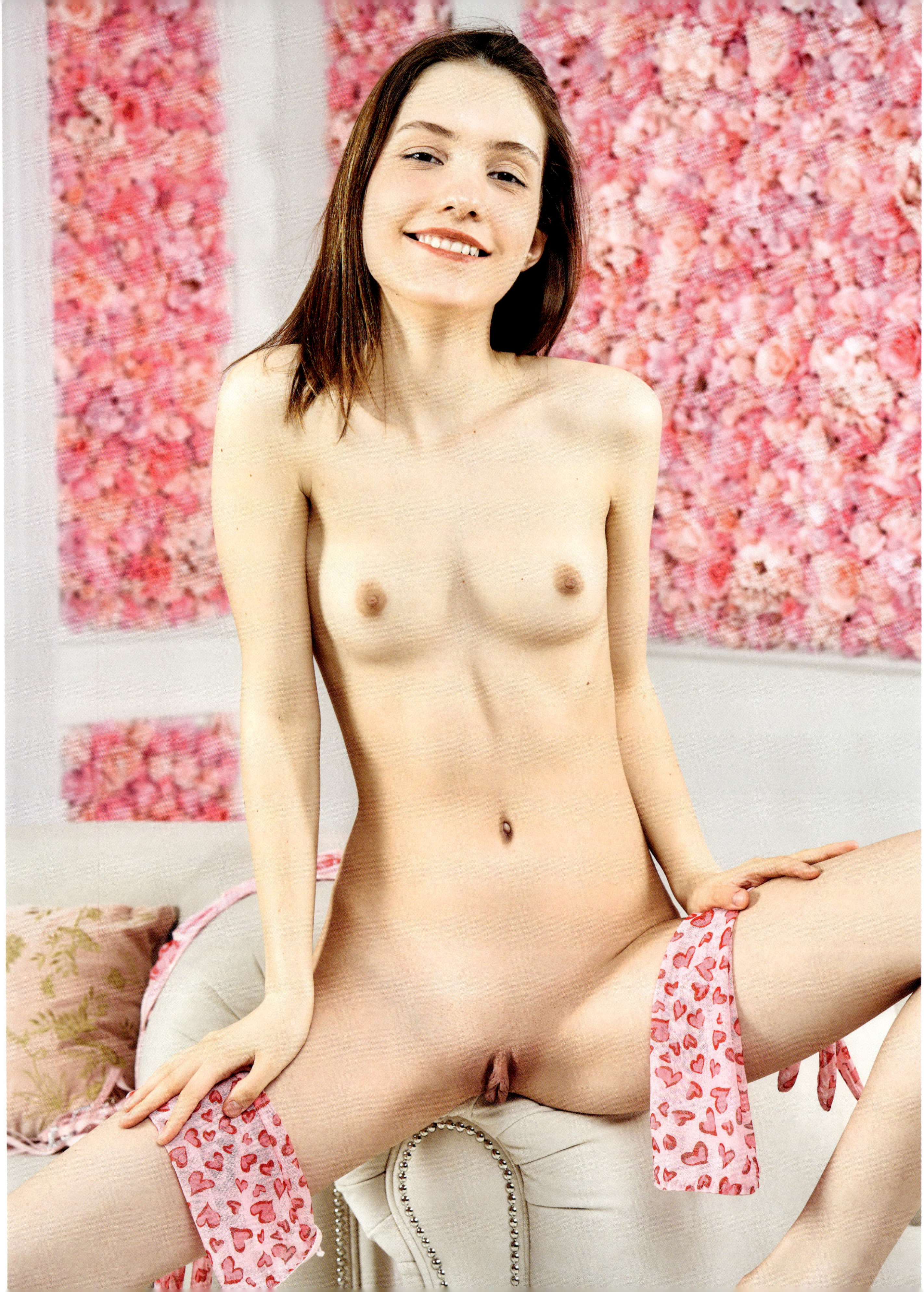

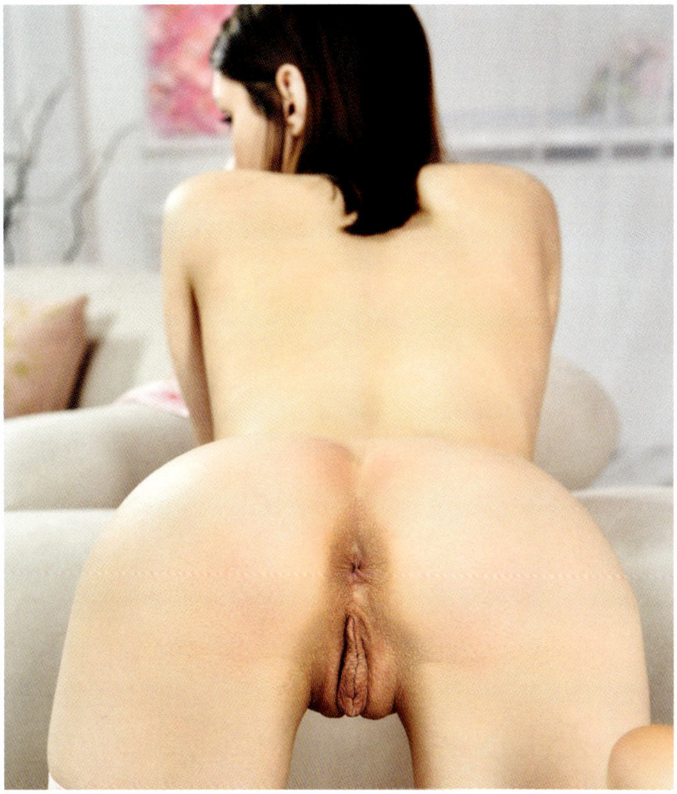

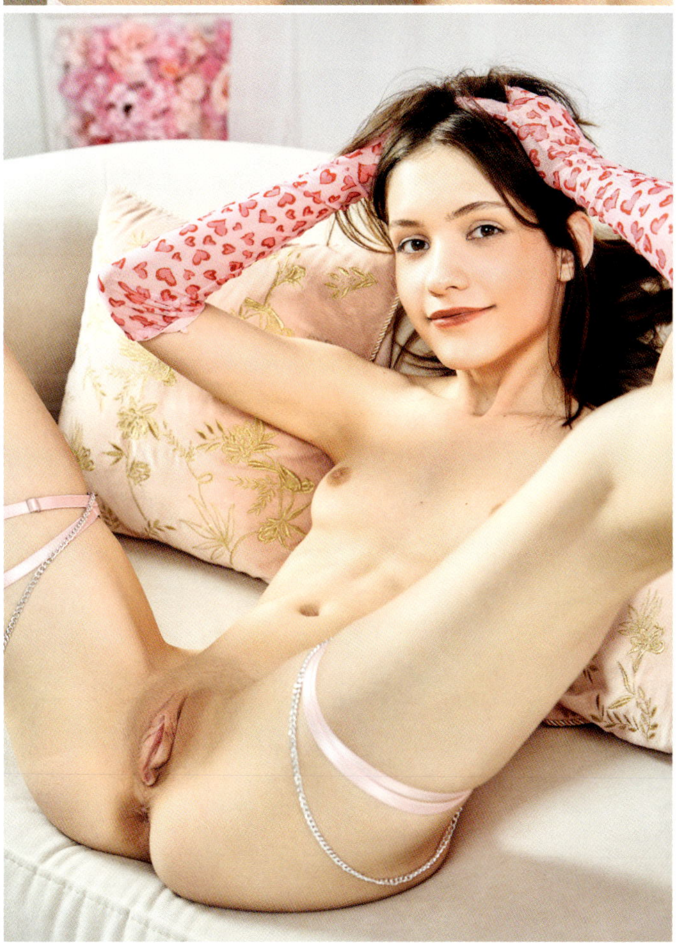

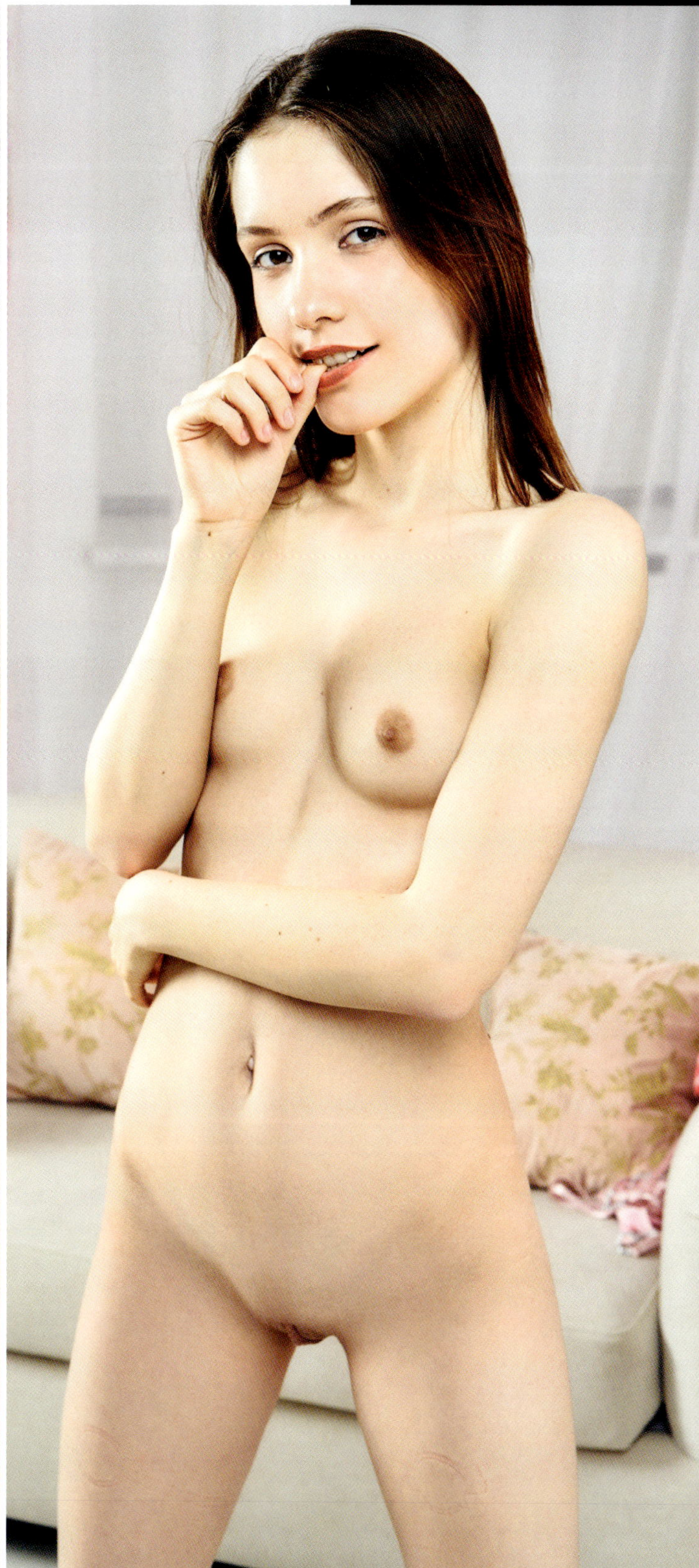

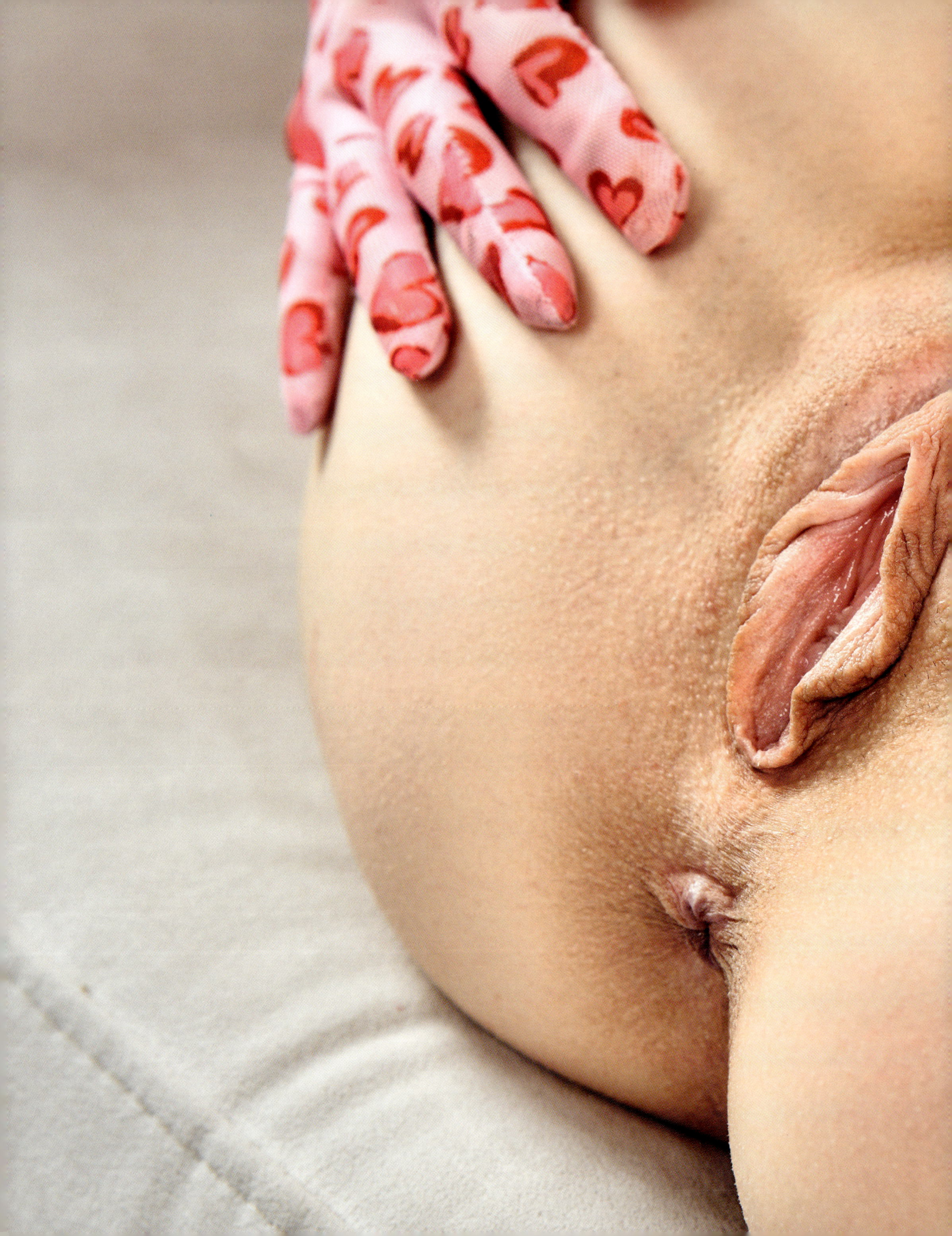

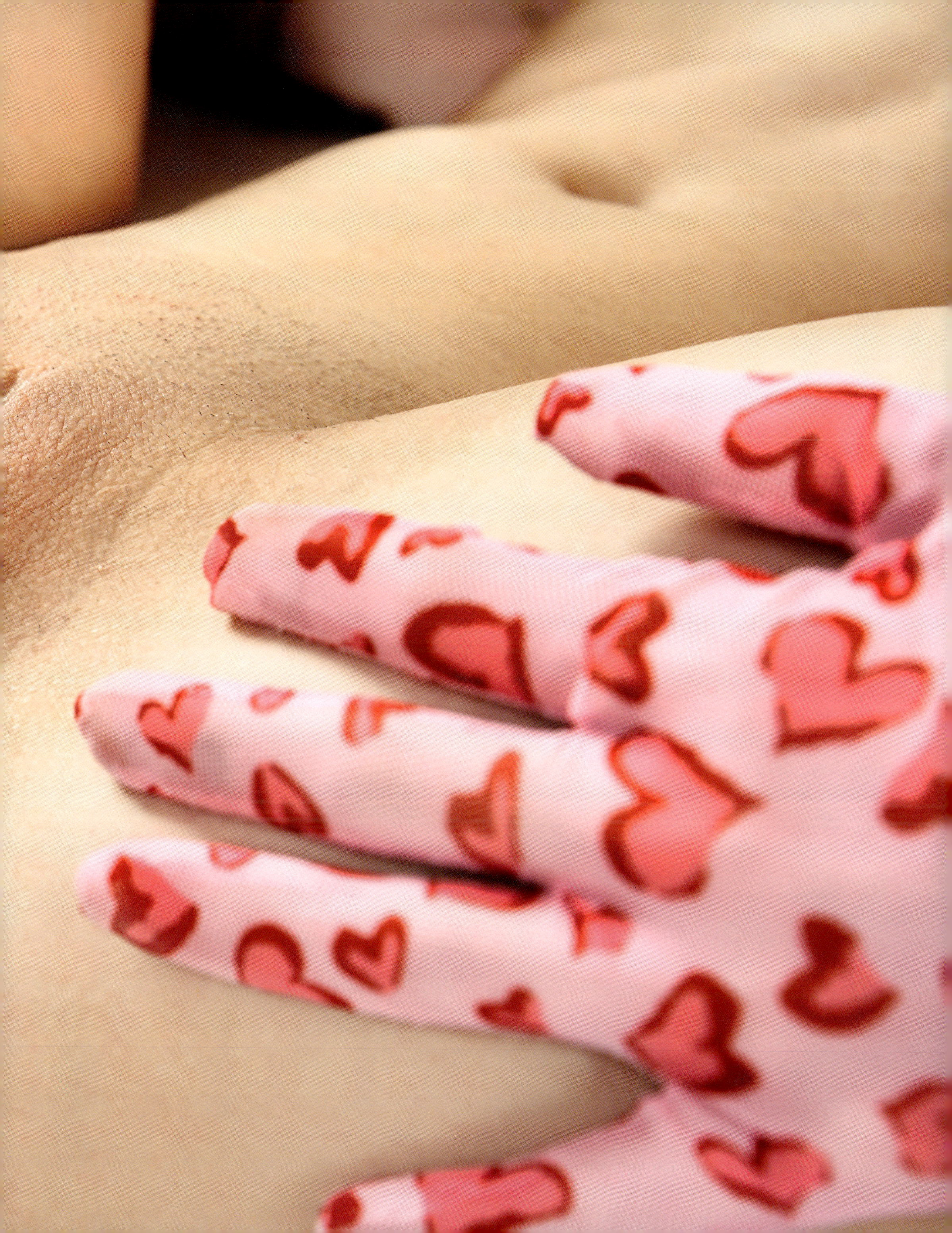

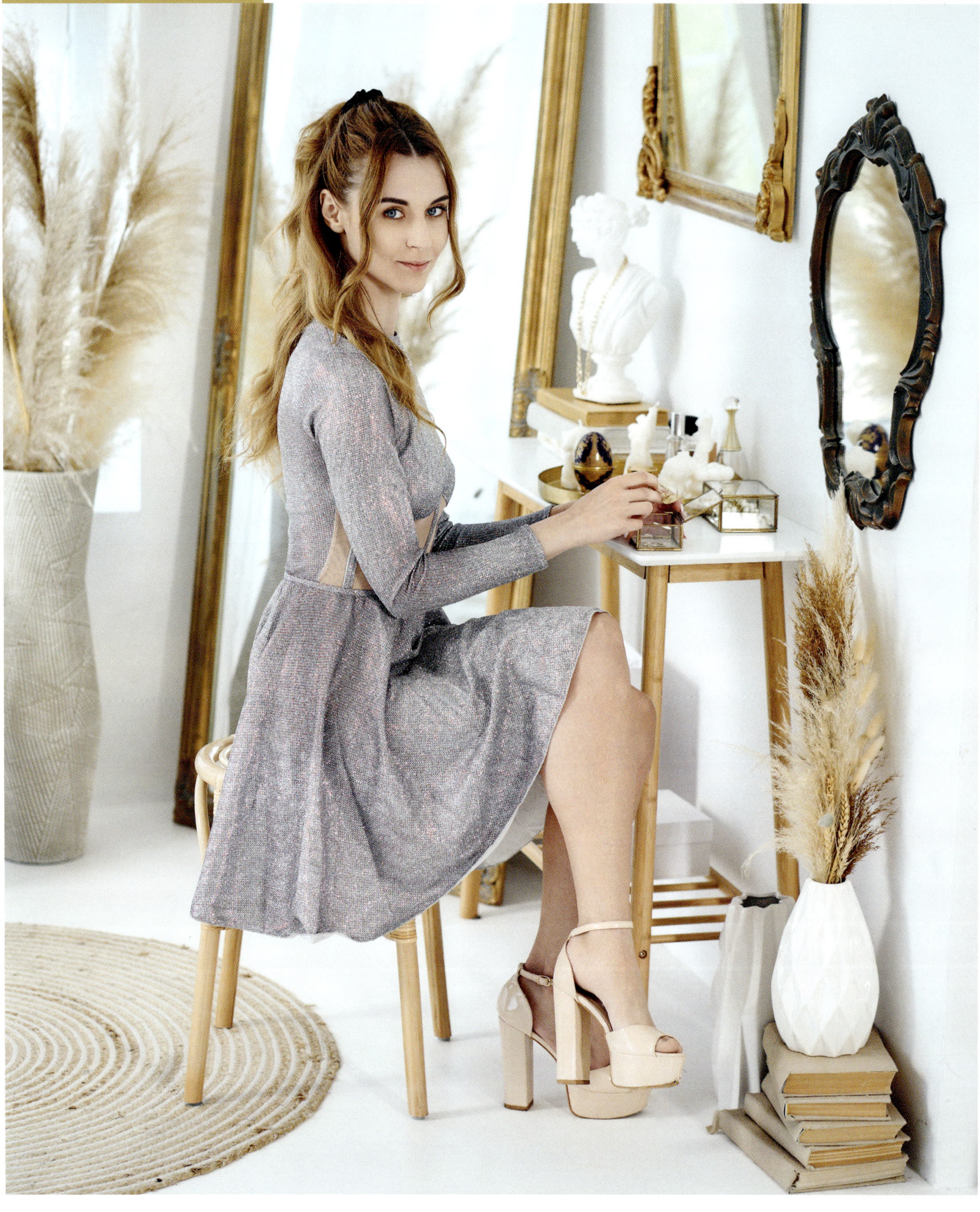

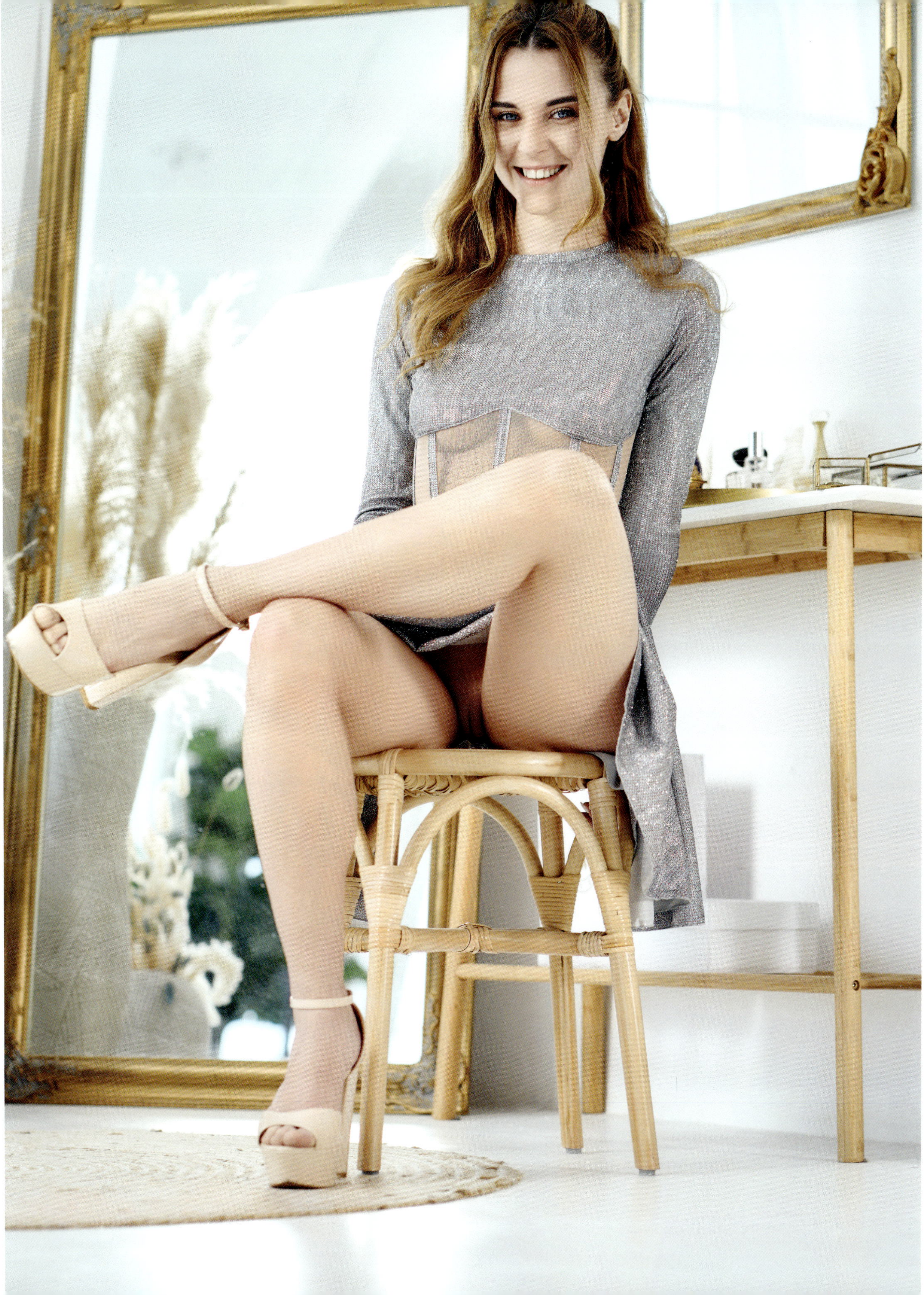

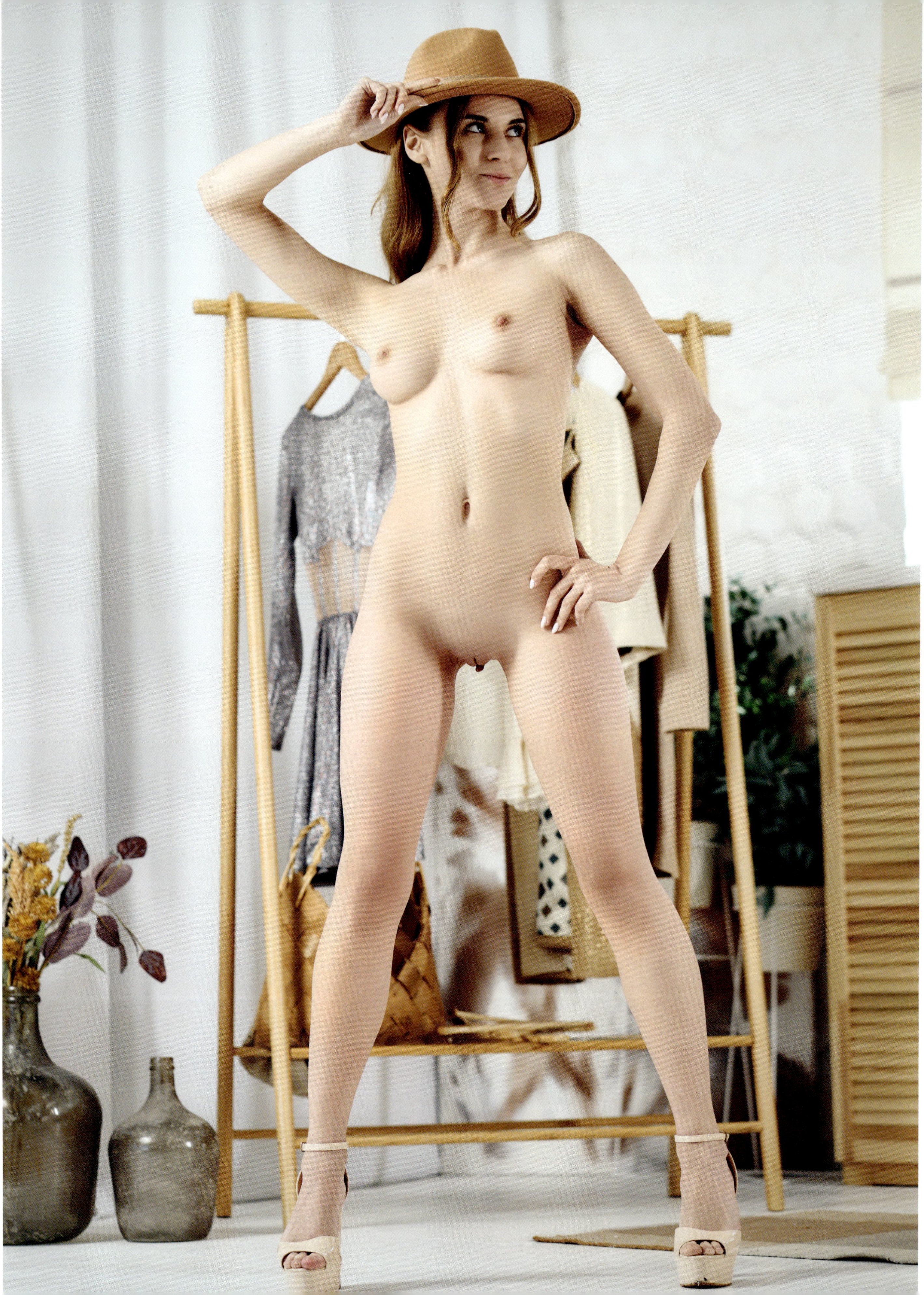

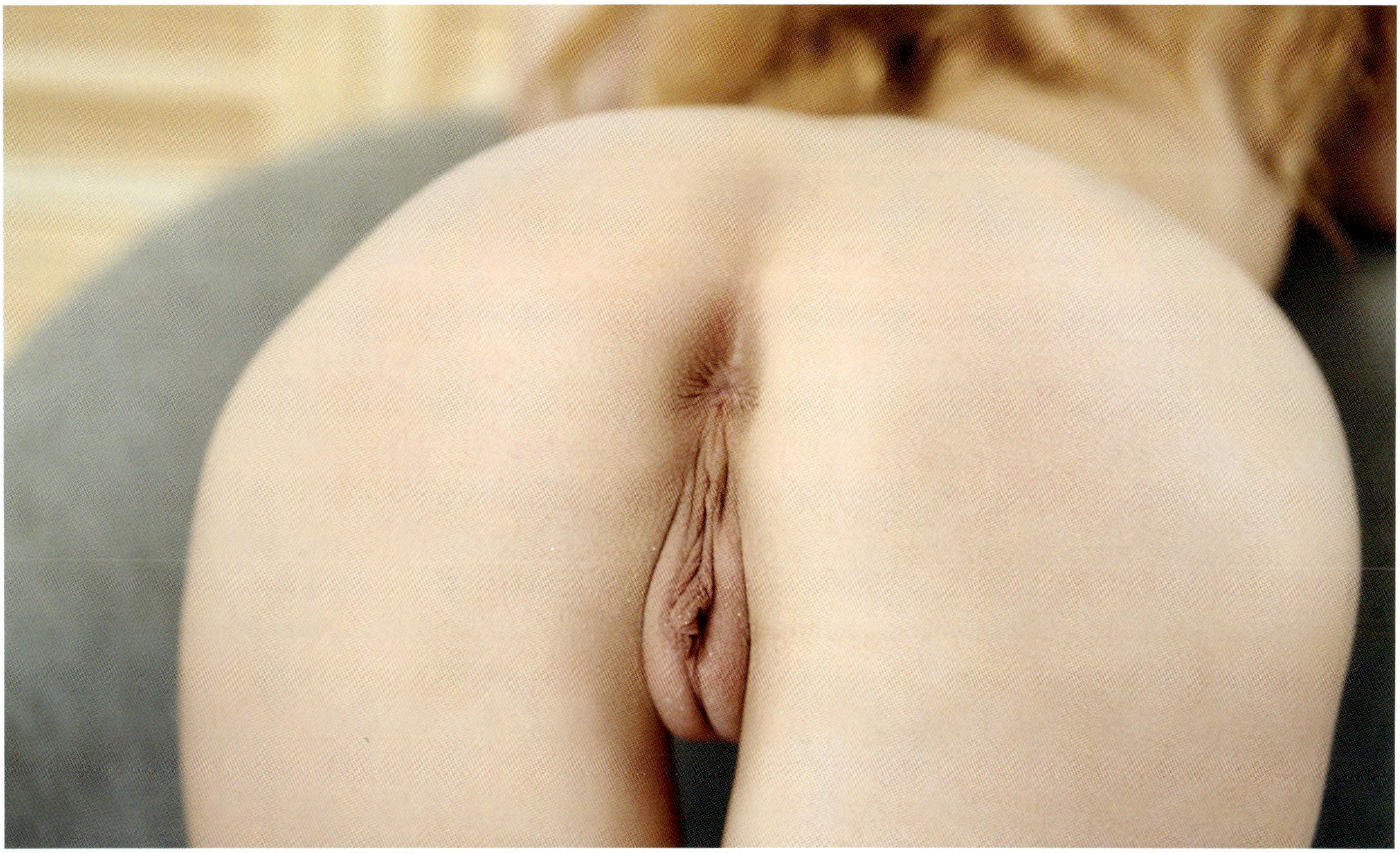

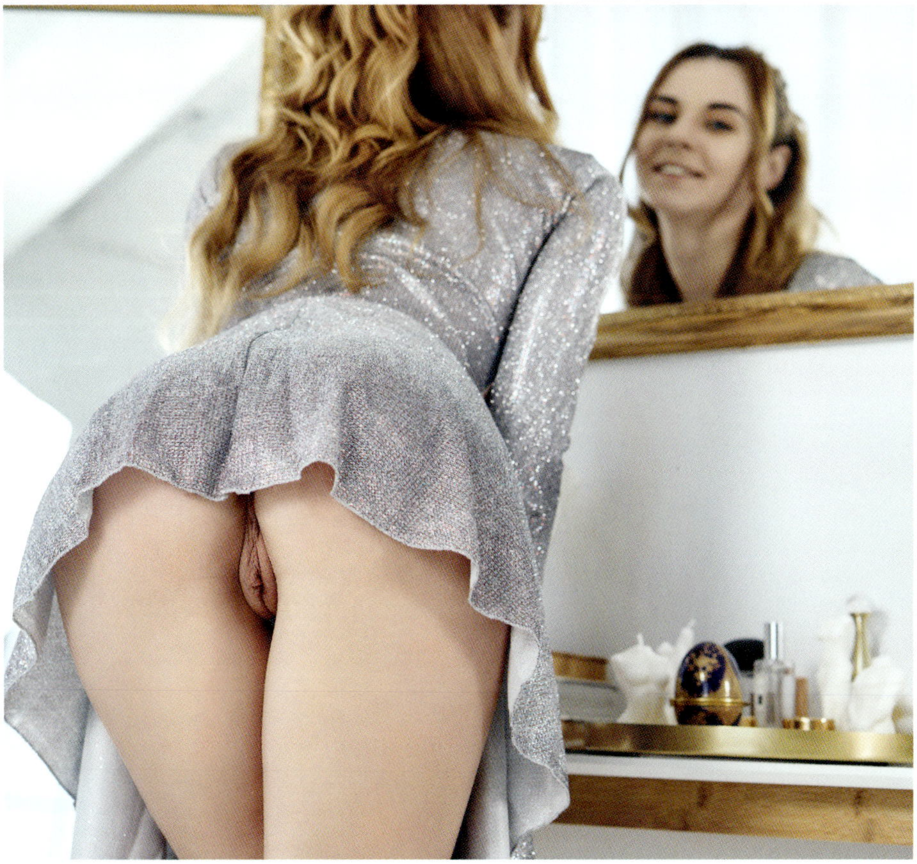

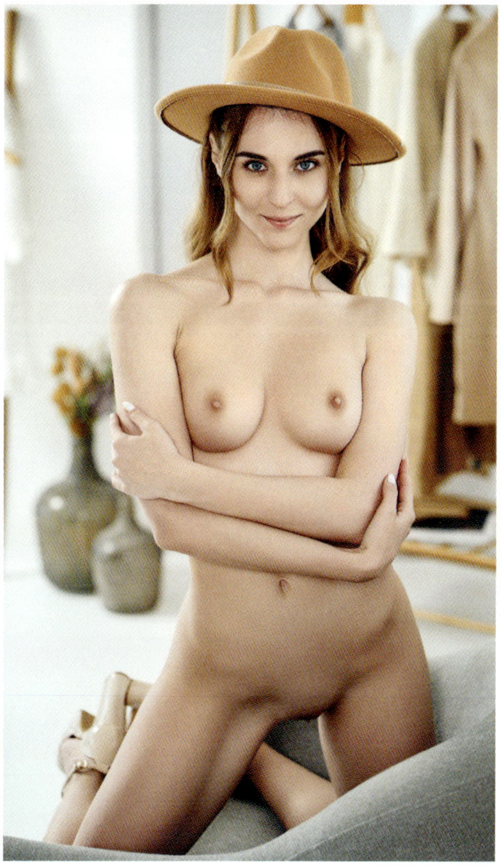

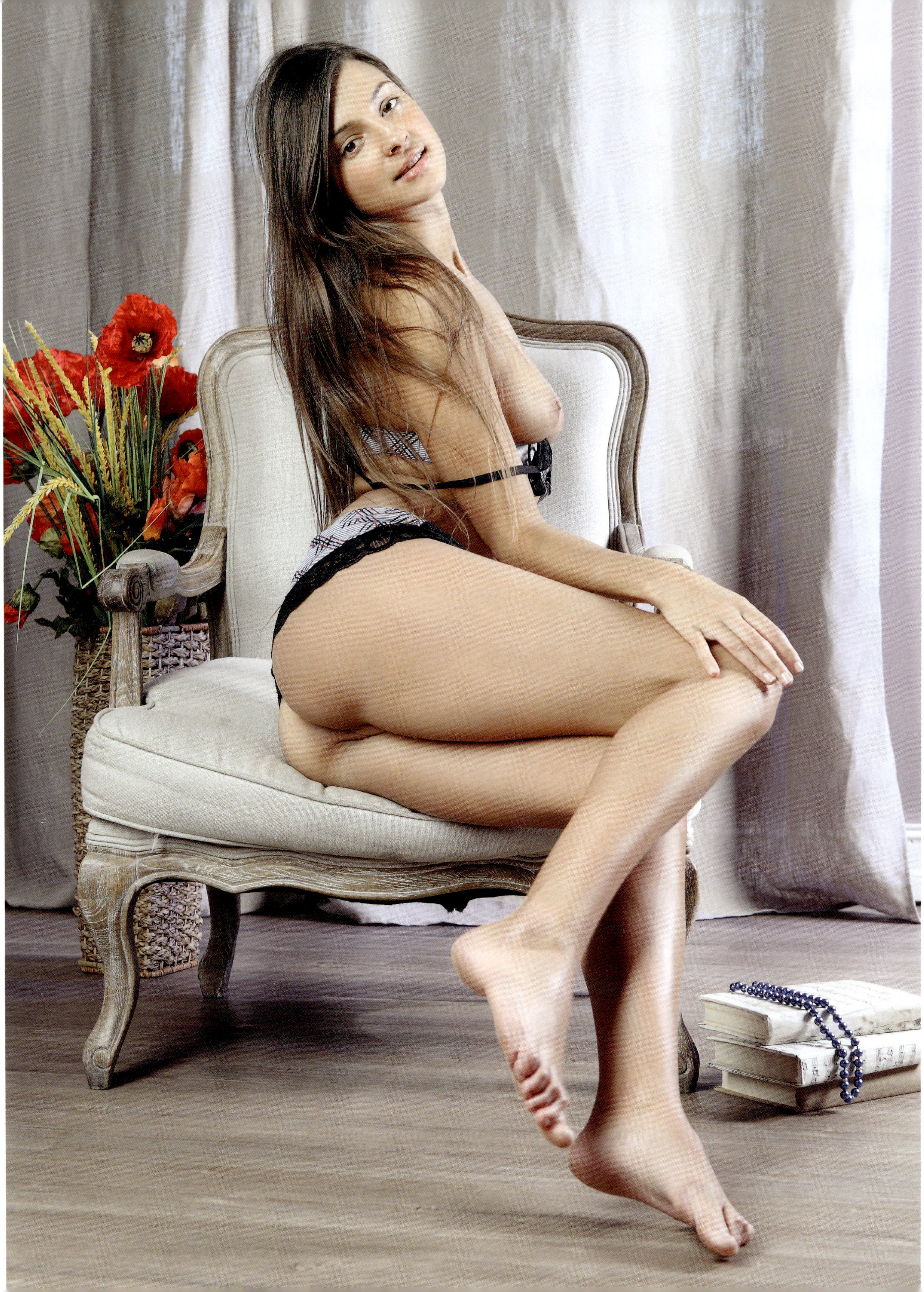

Melena A

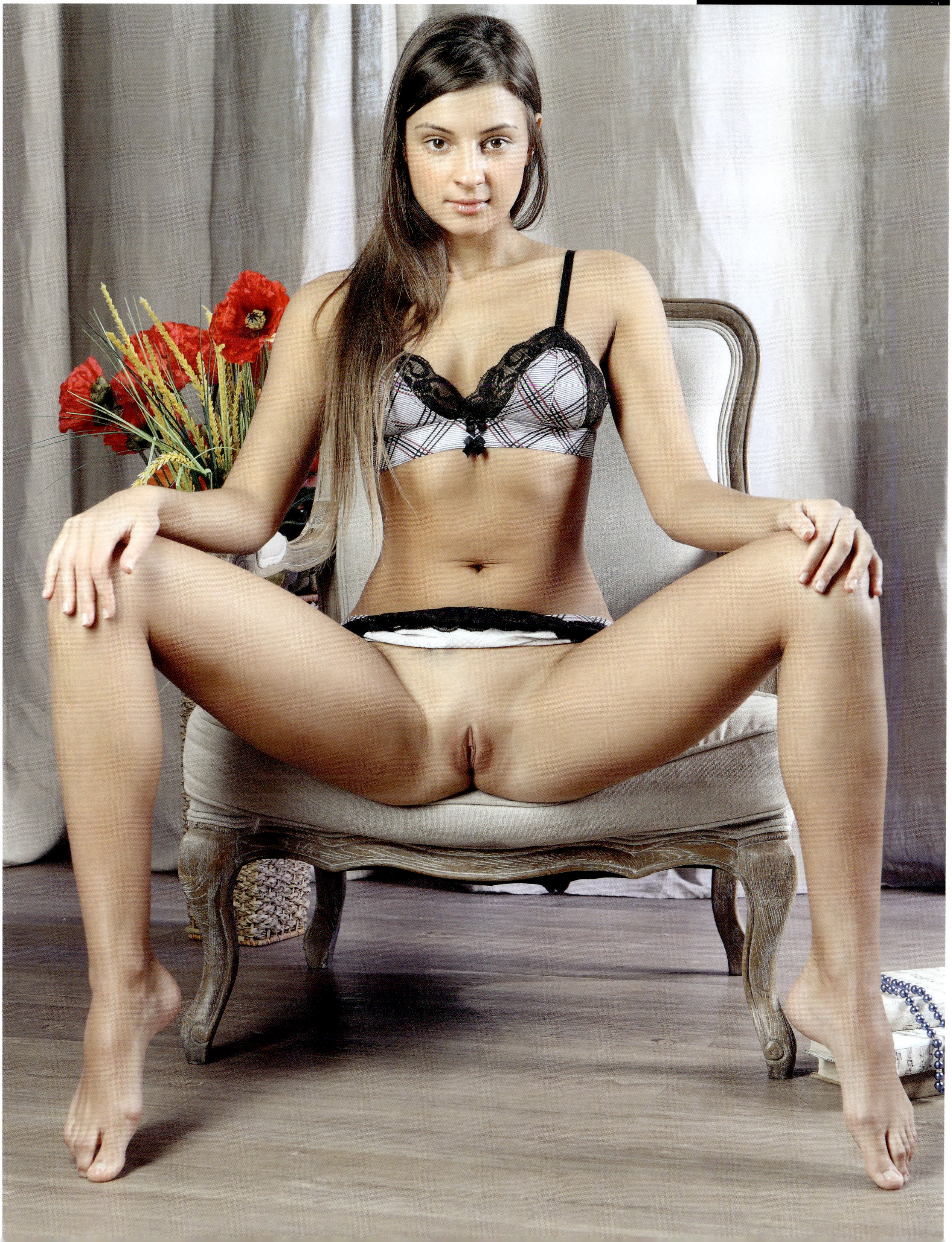

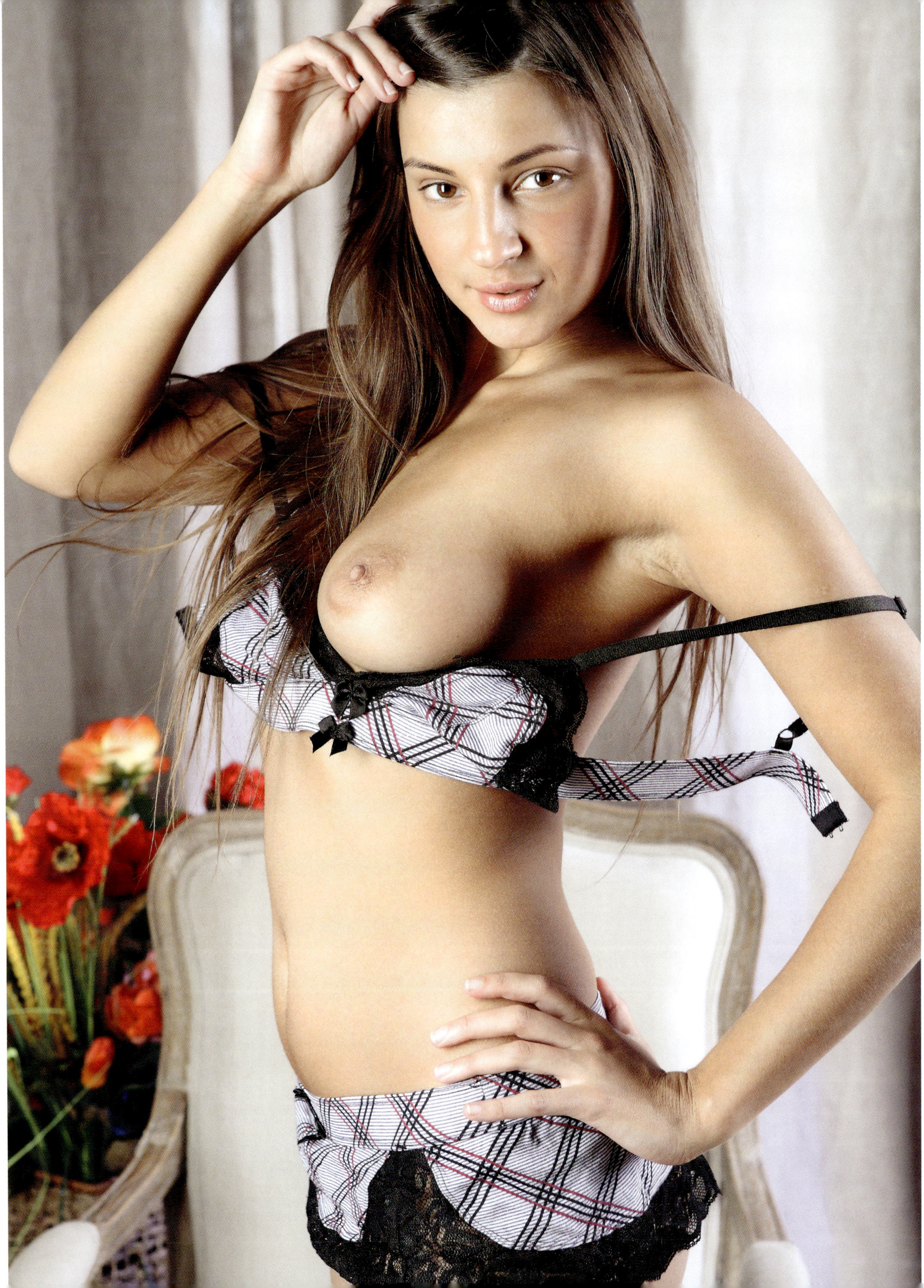

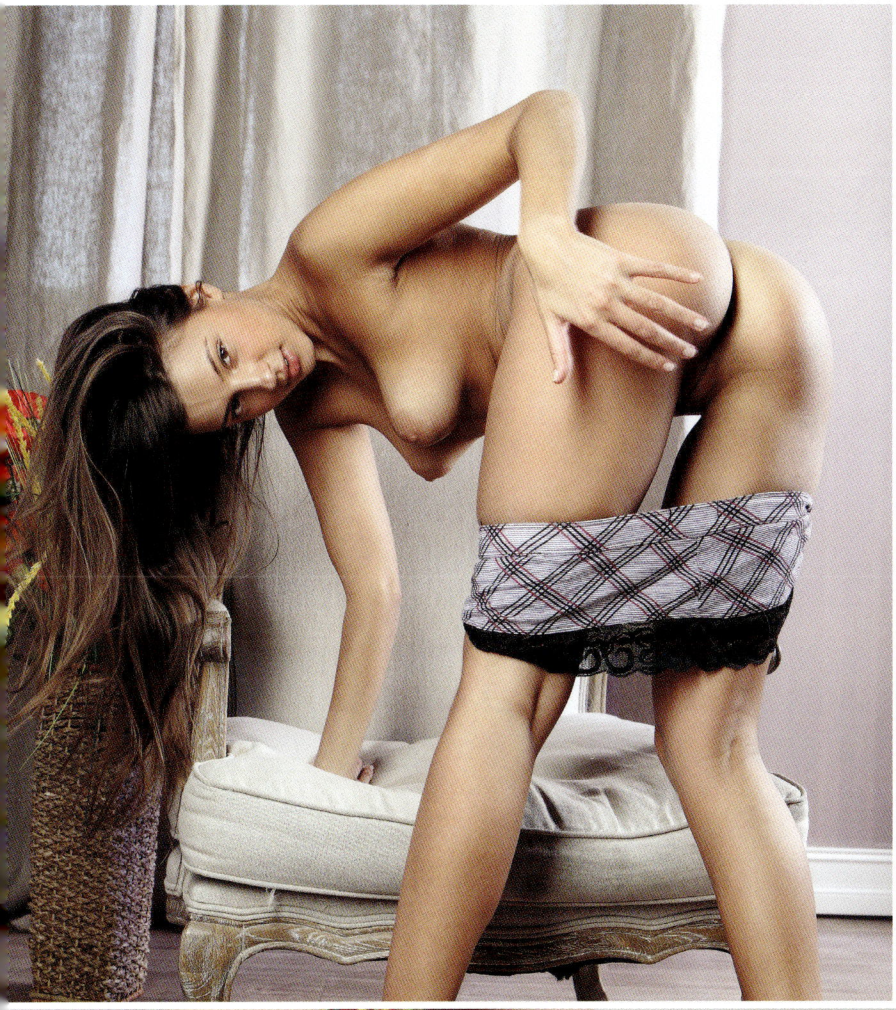
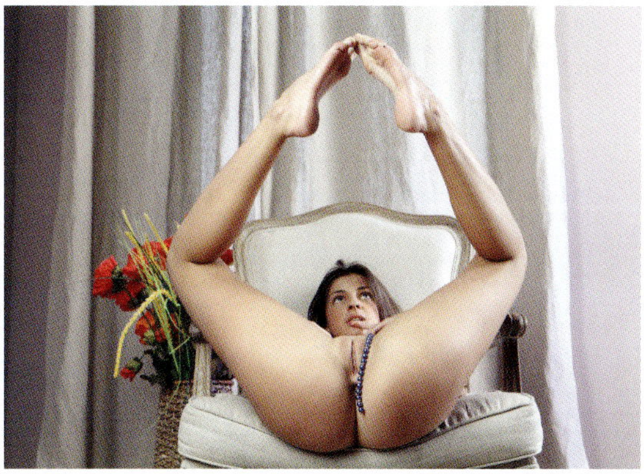
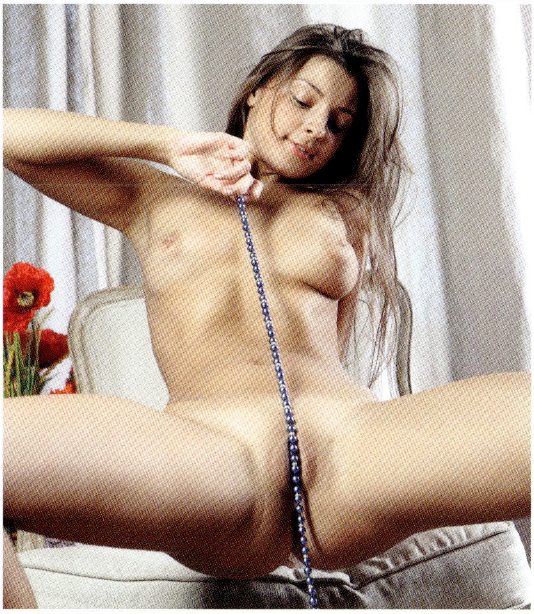
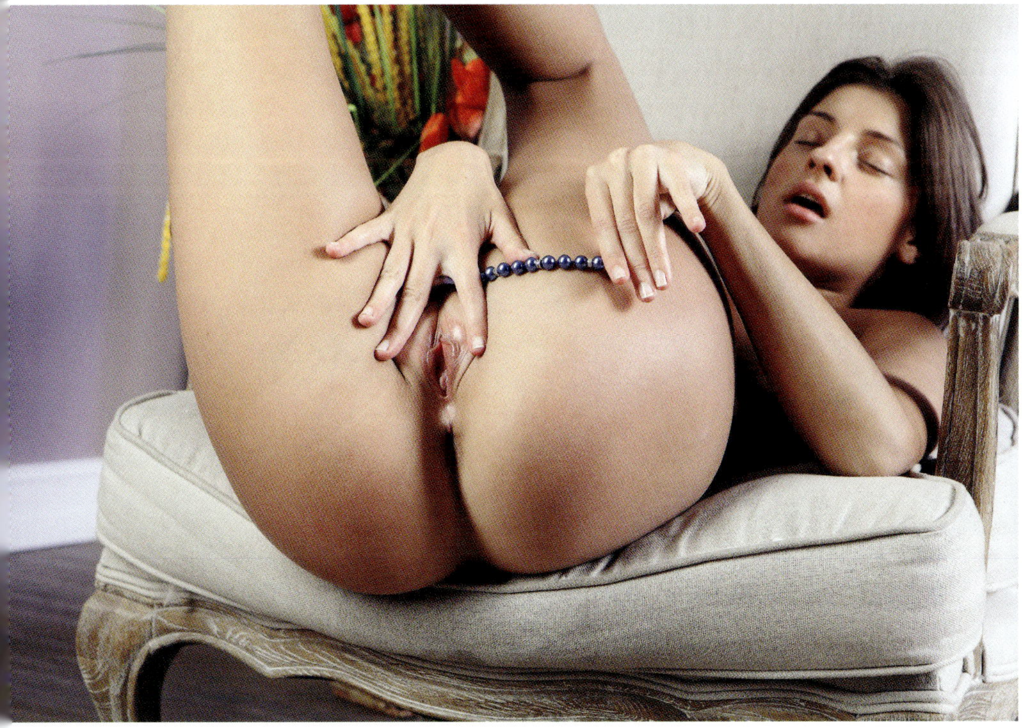
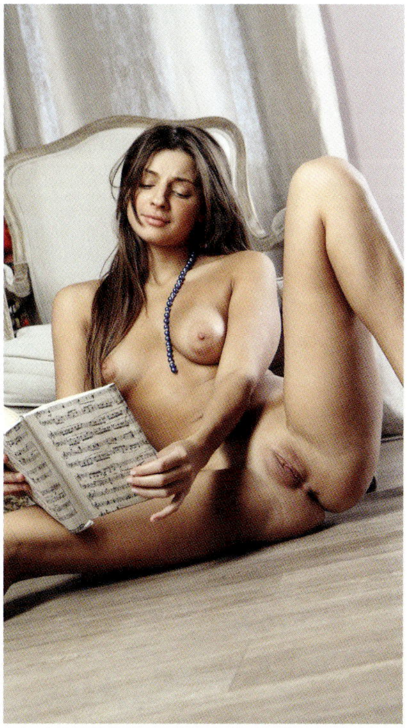

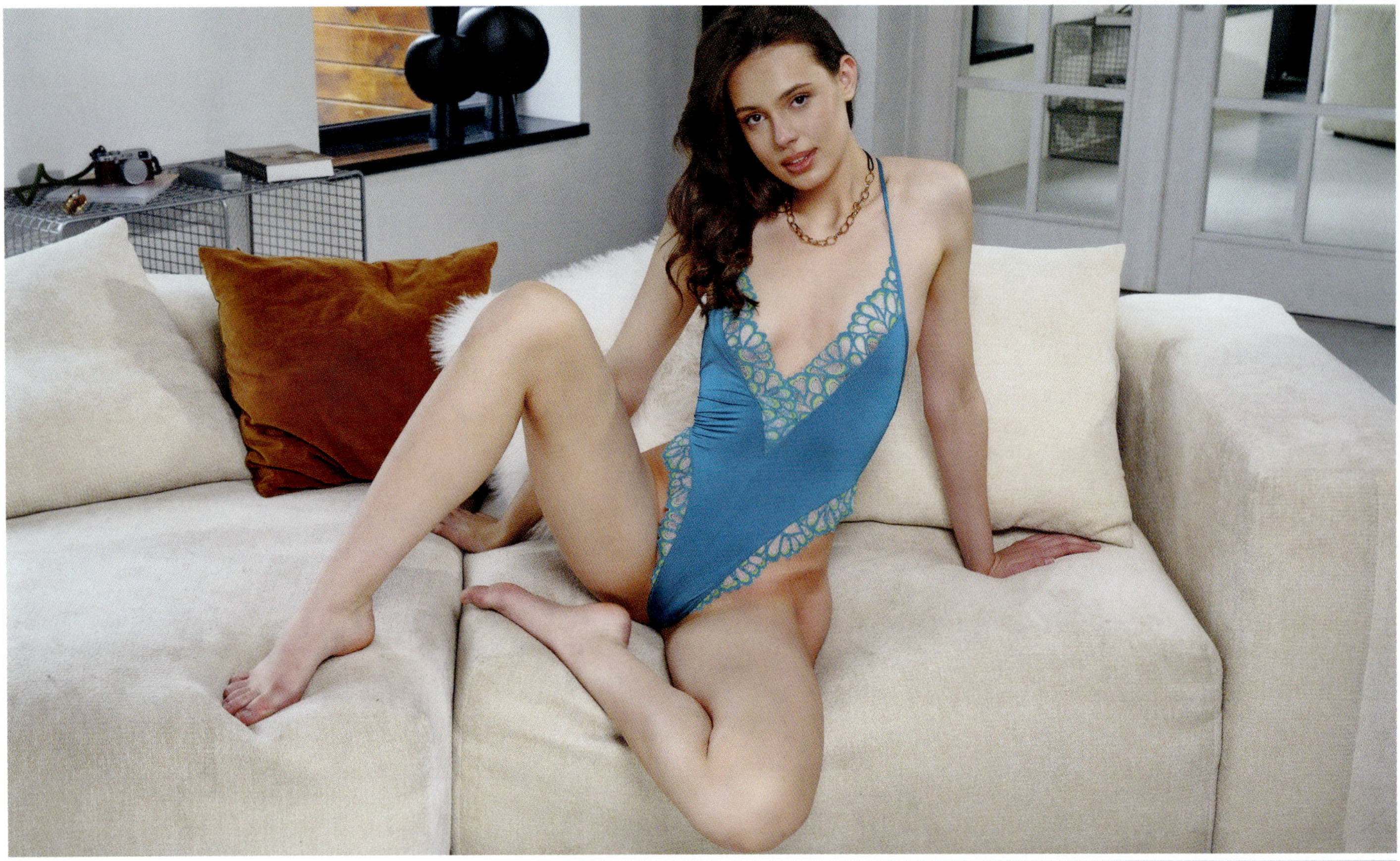

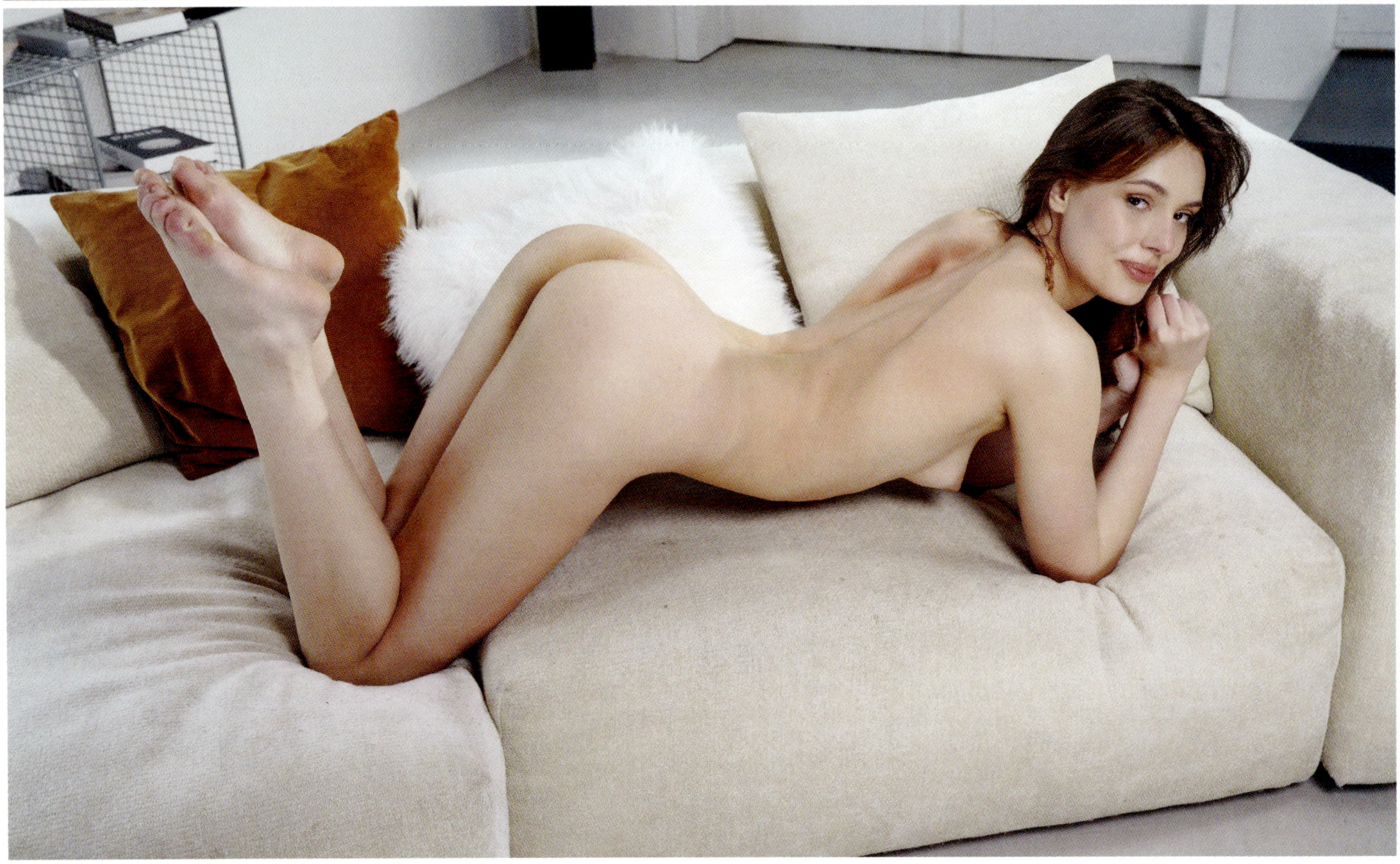

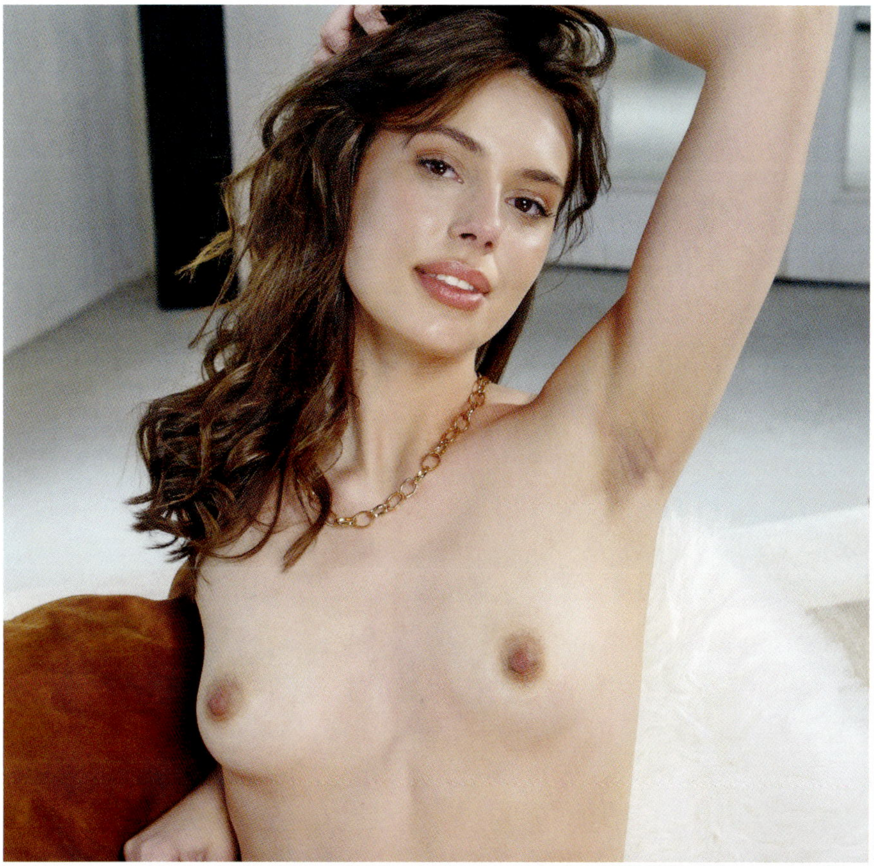

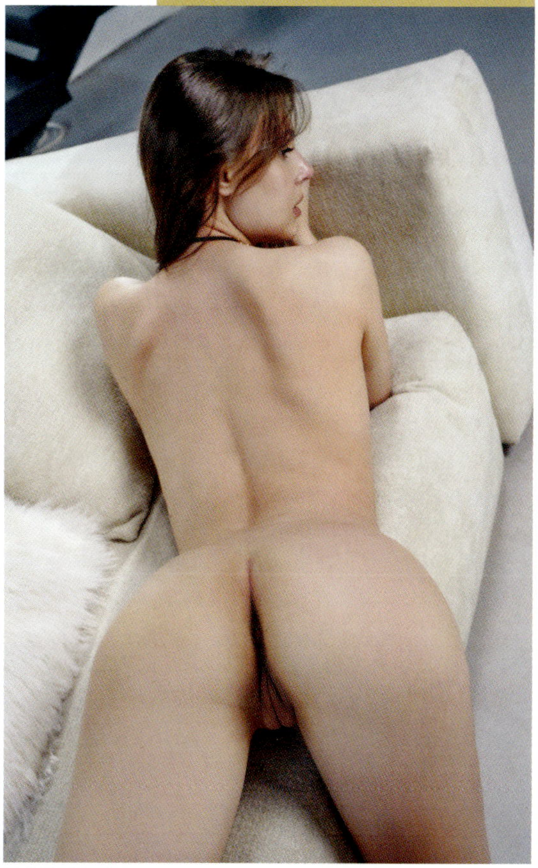

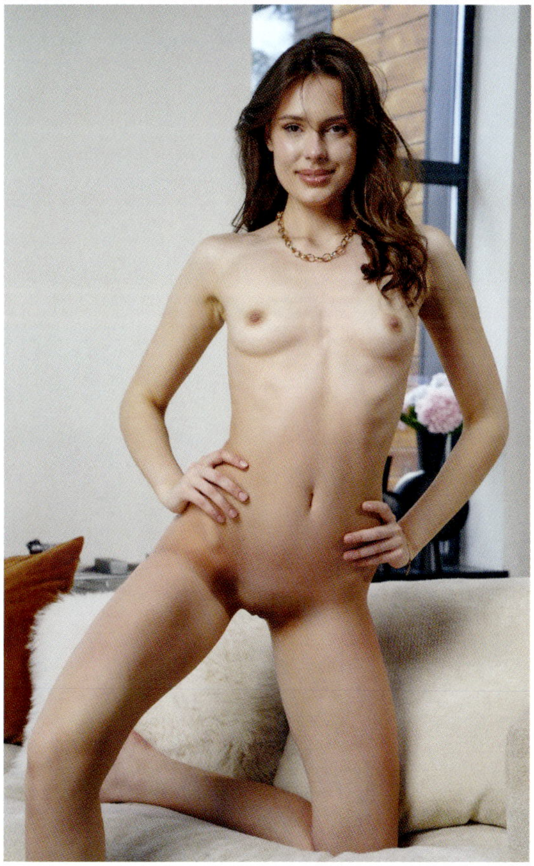

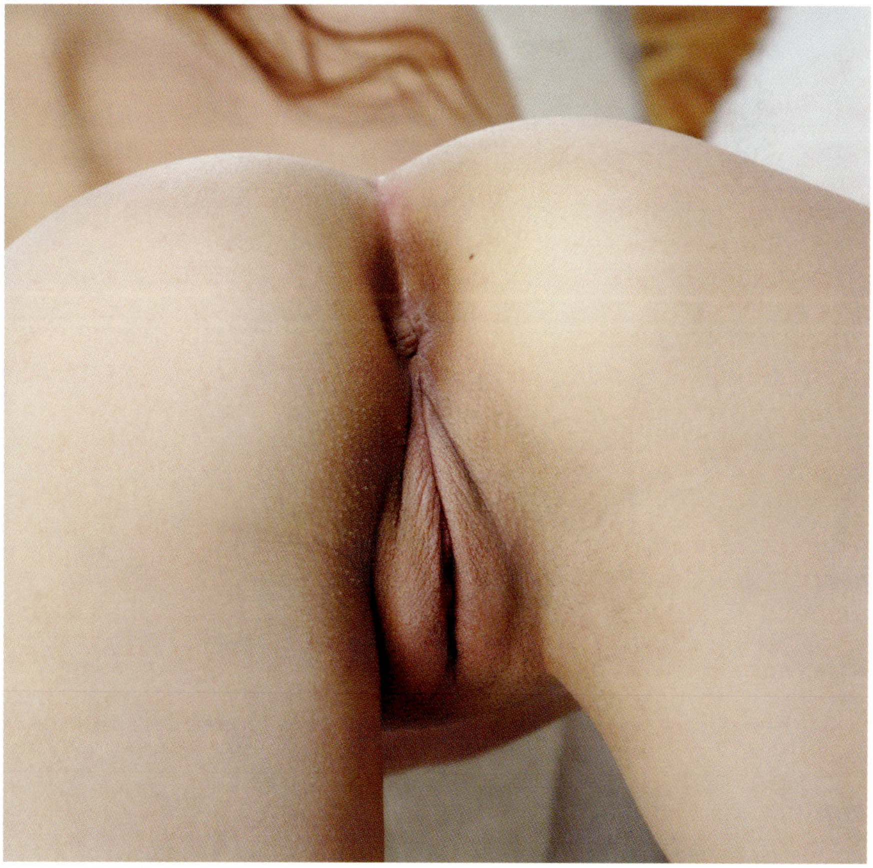

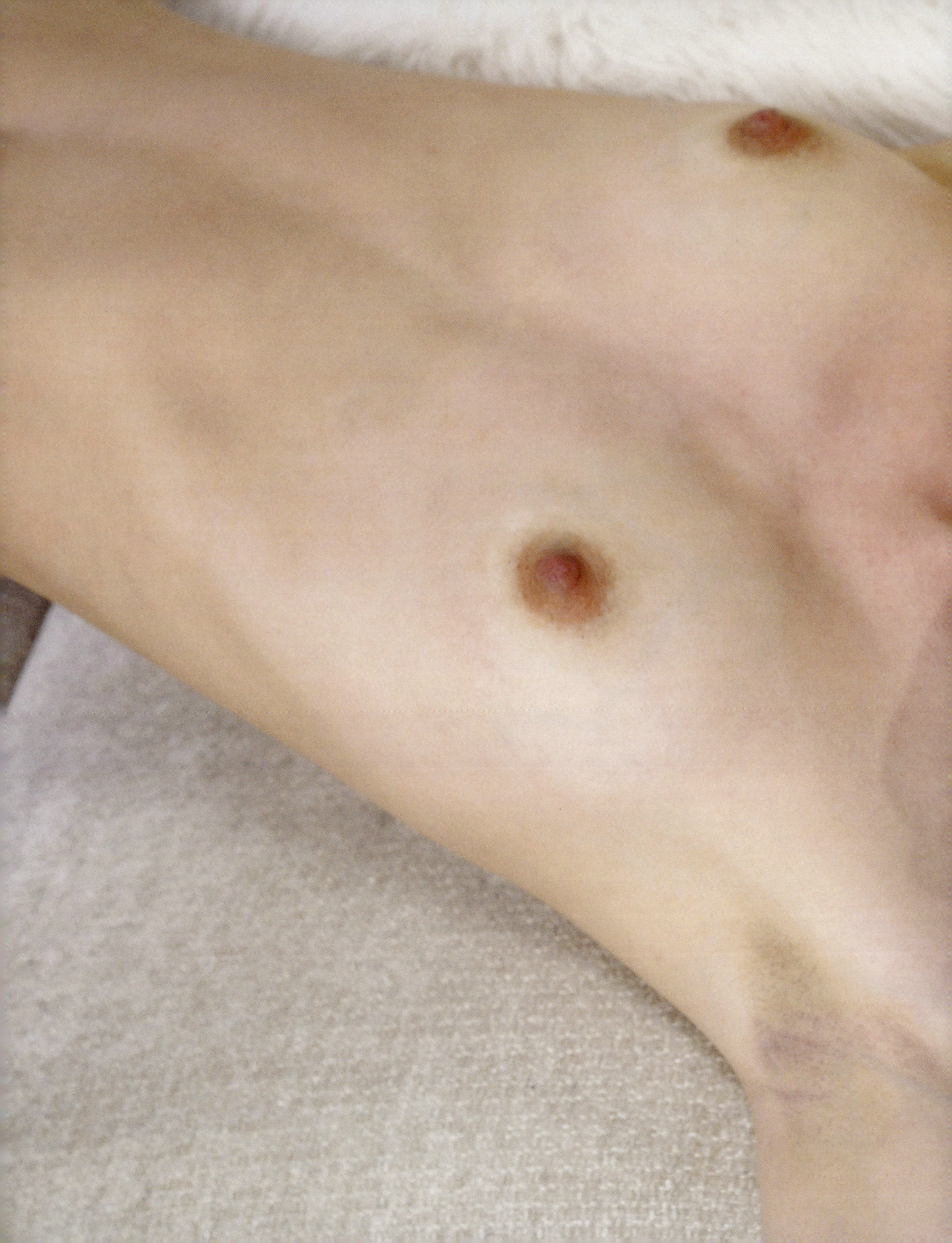

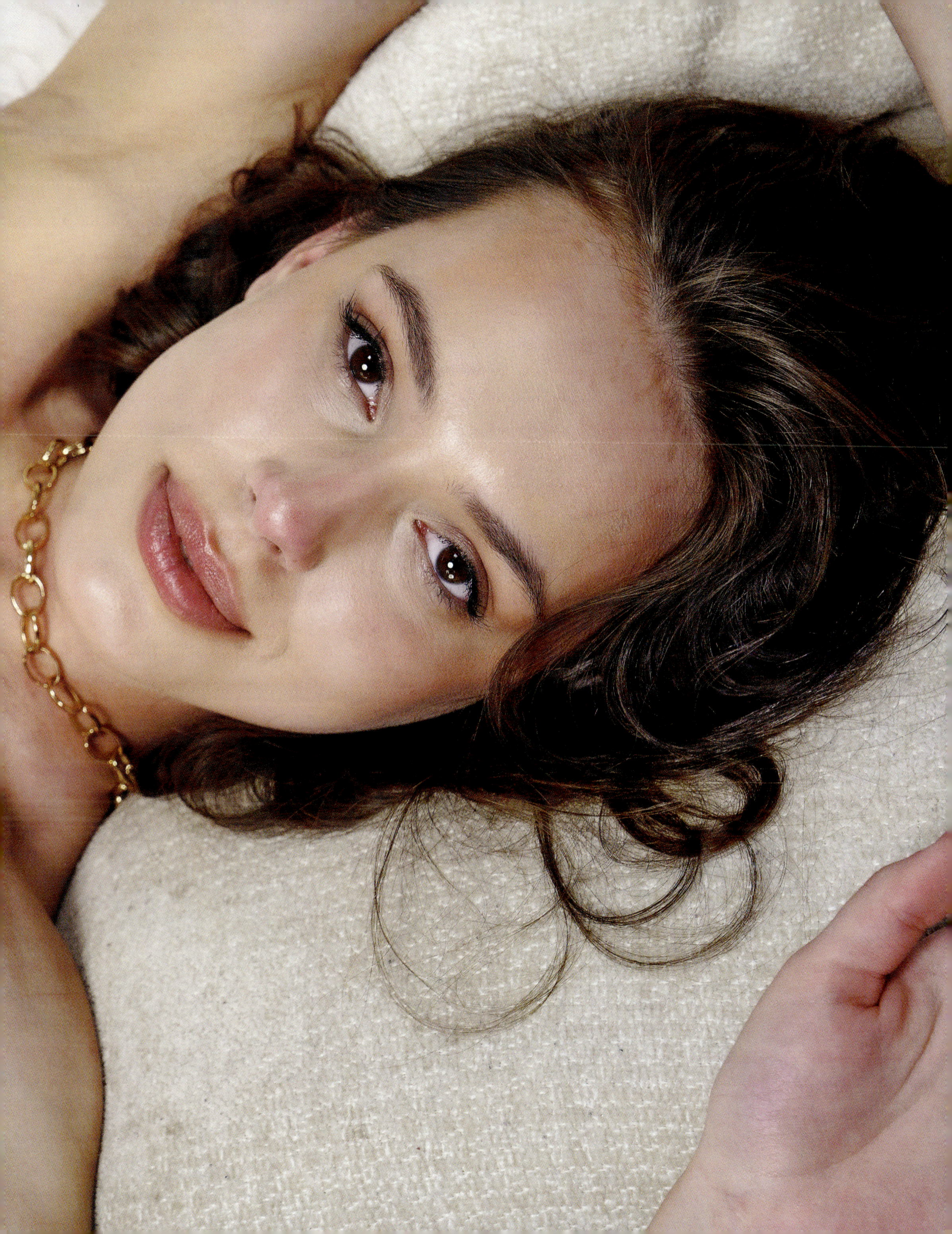

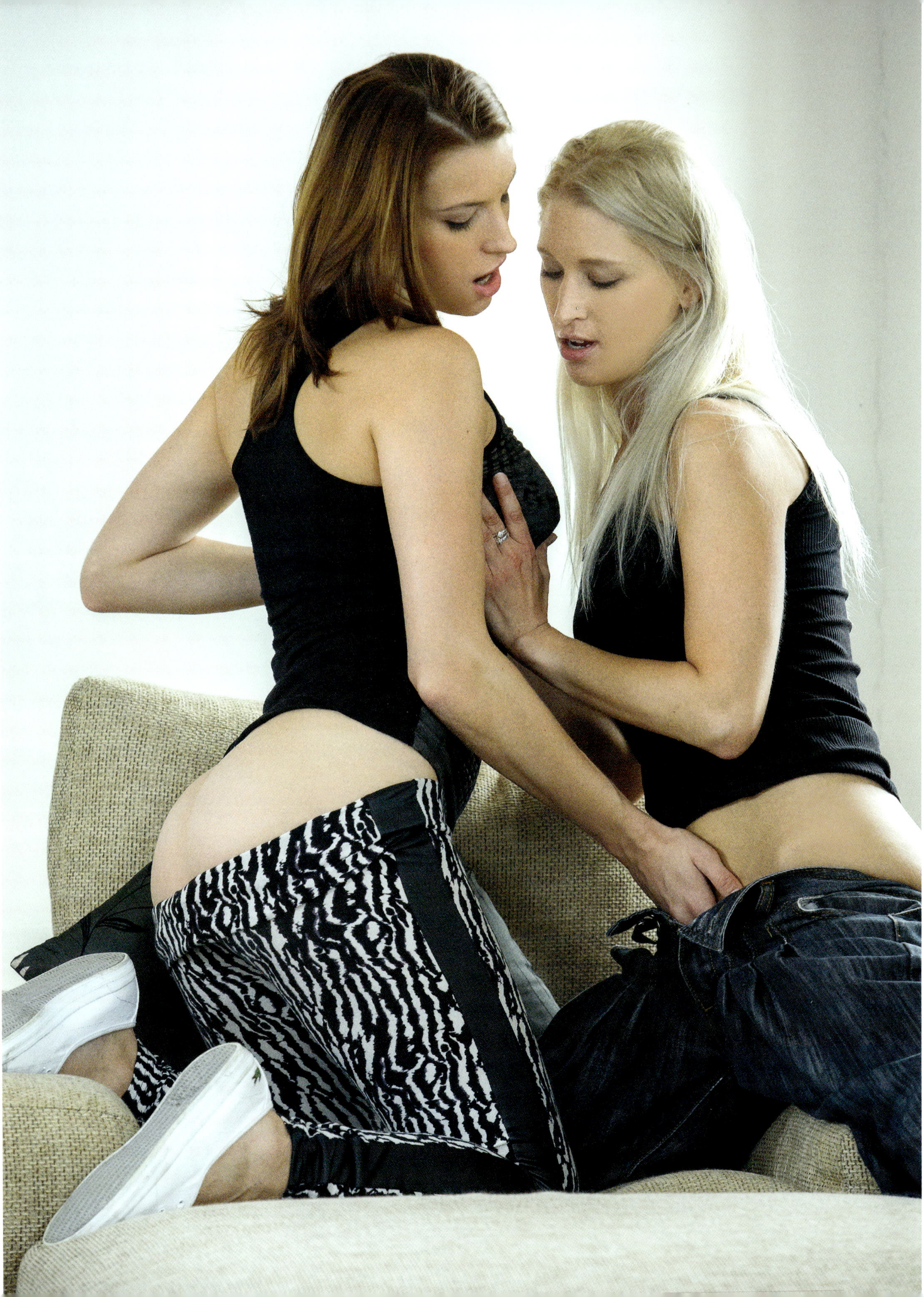

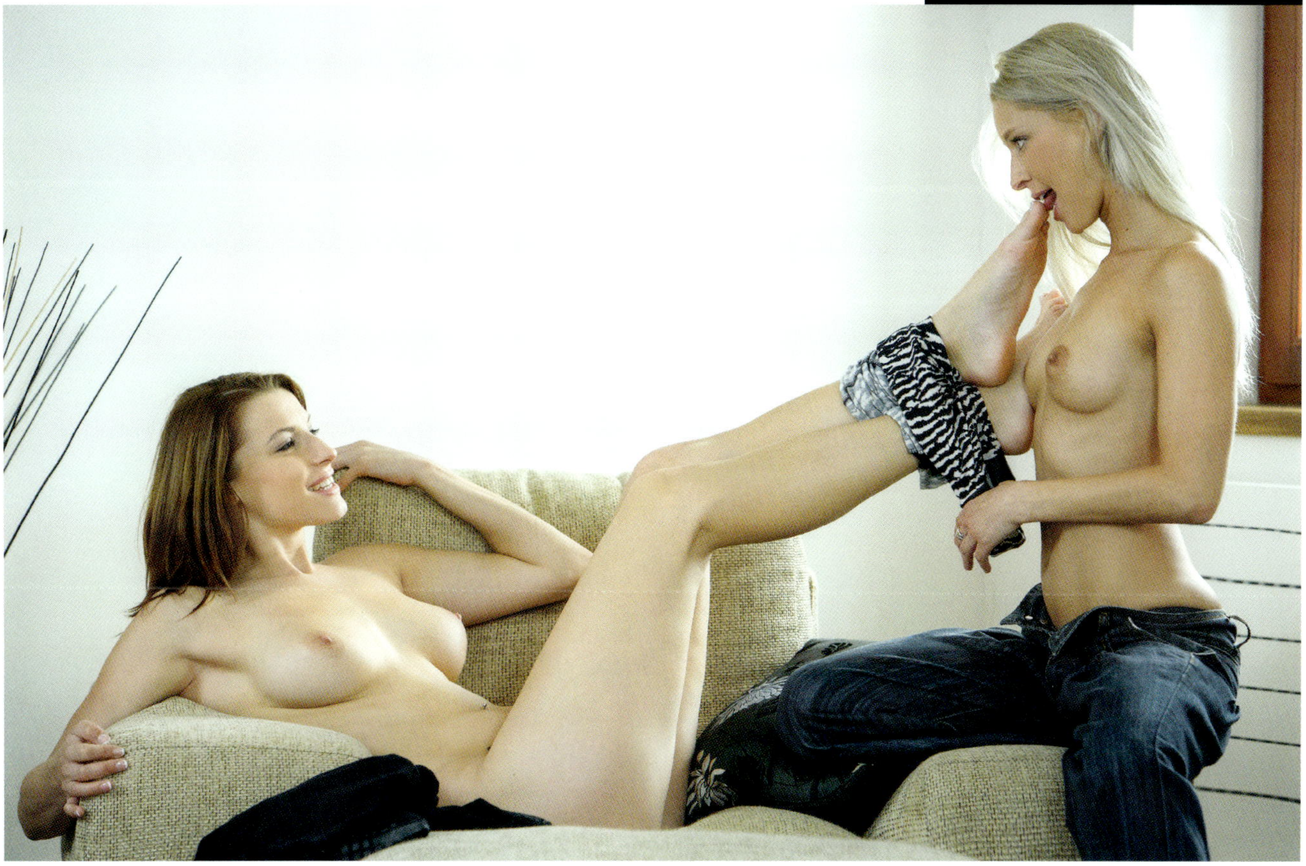

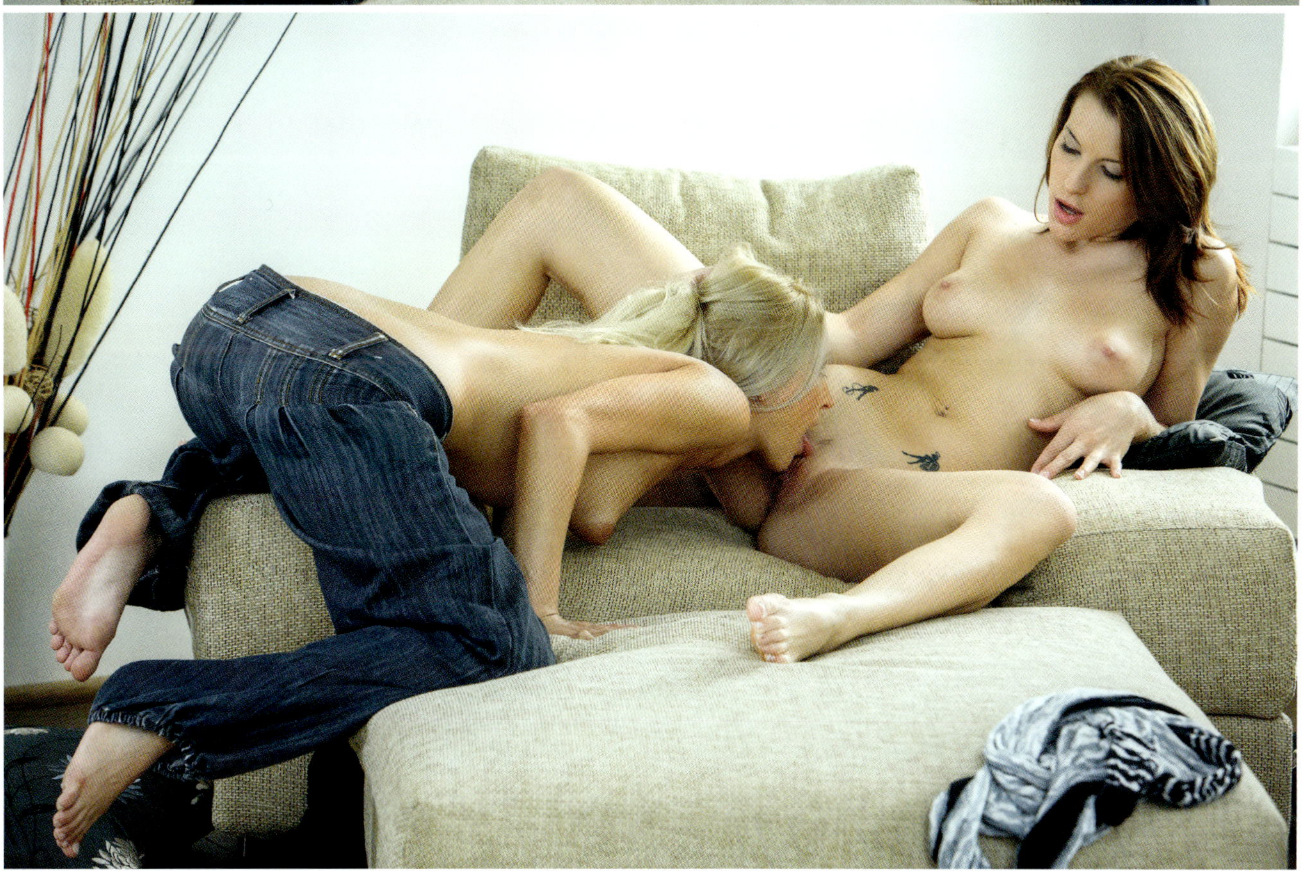

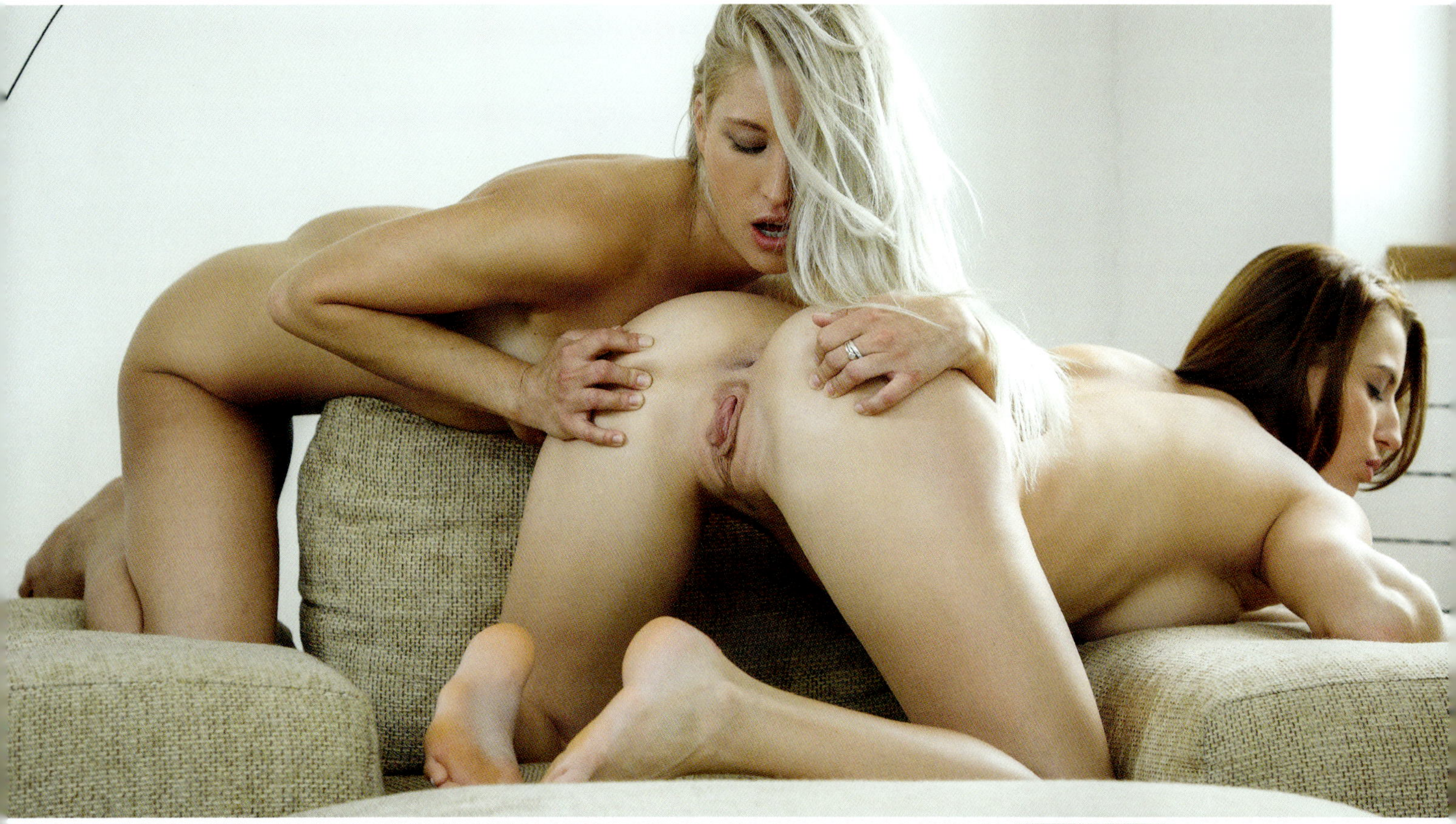

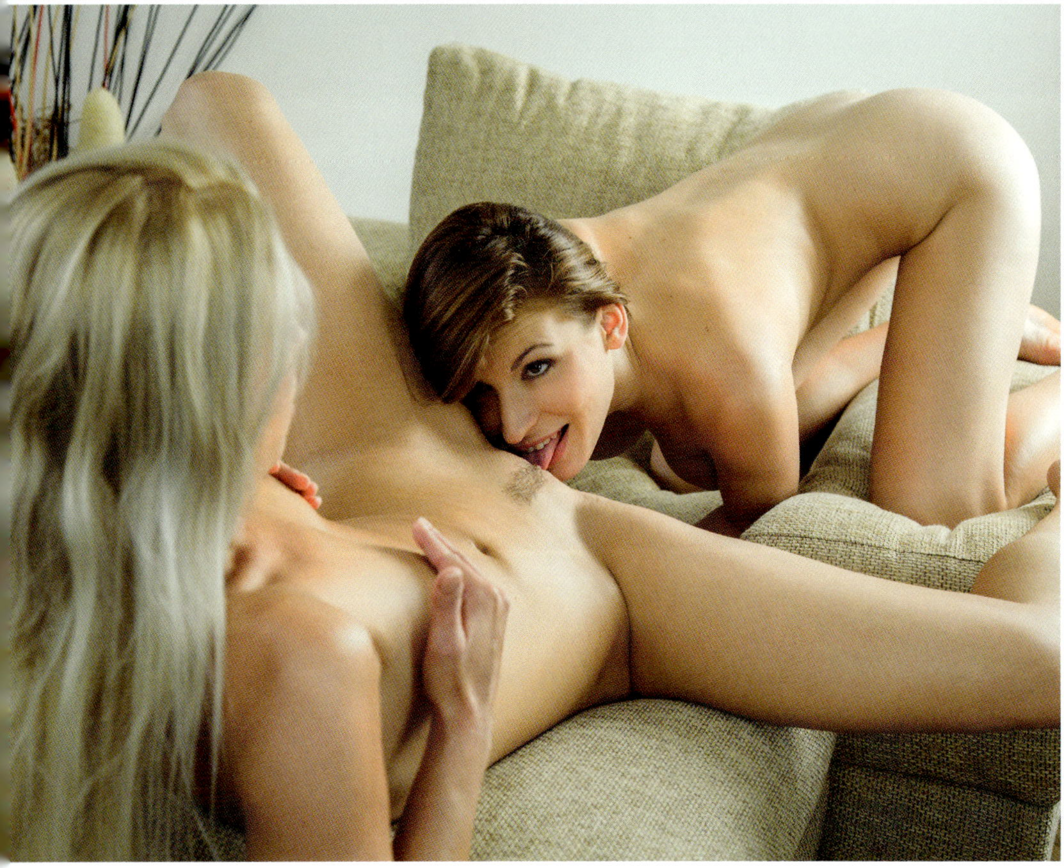

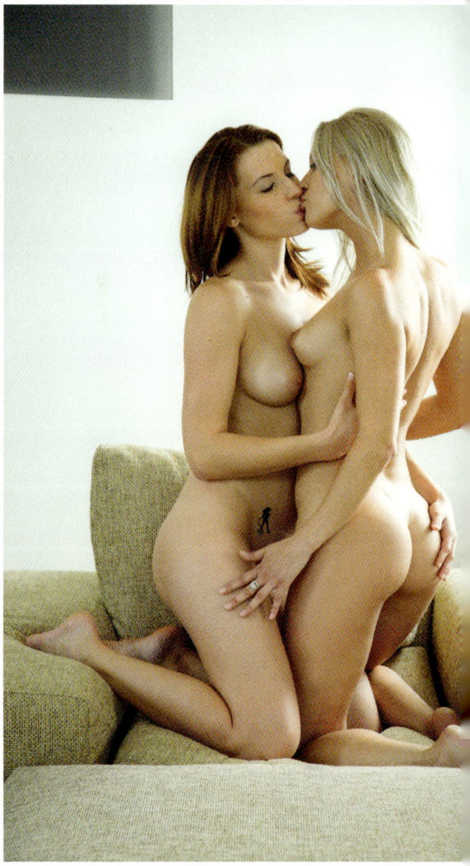

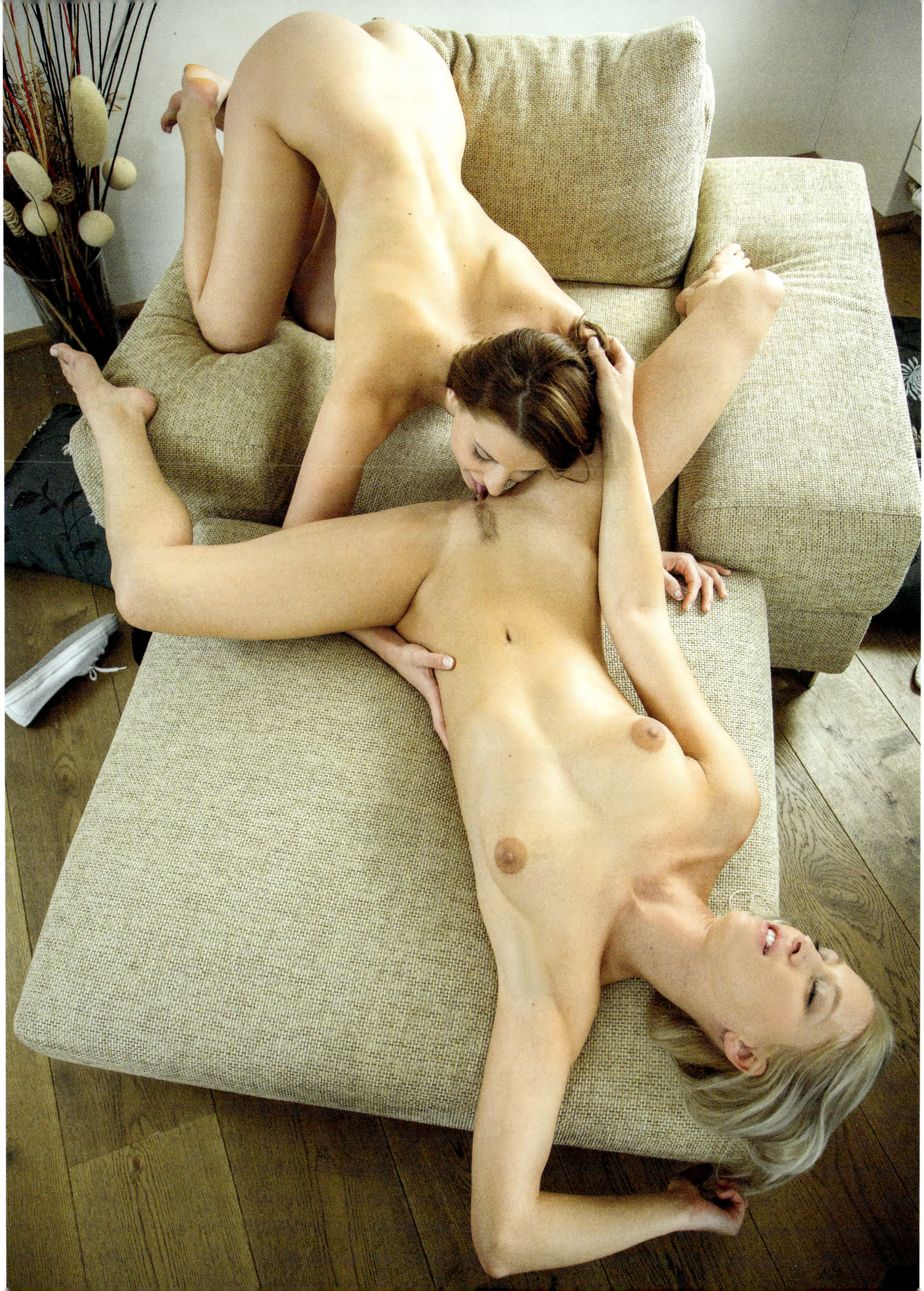

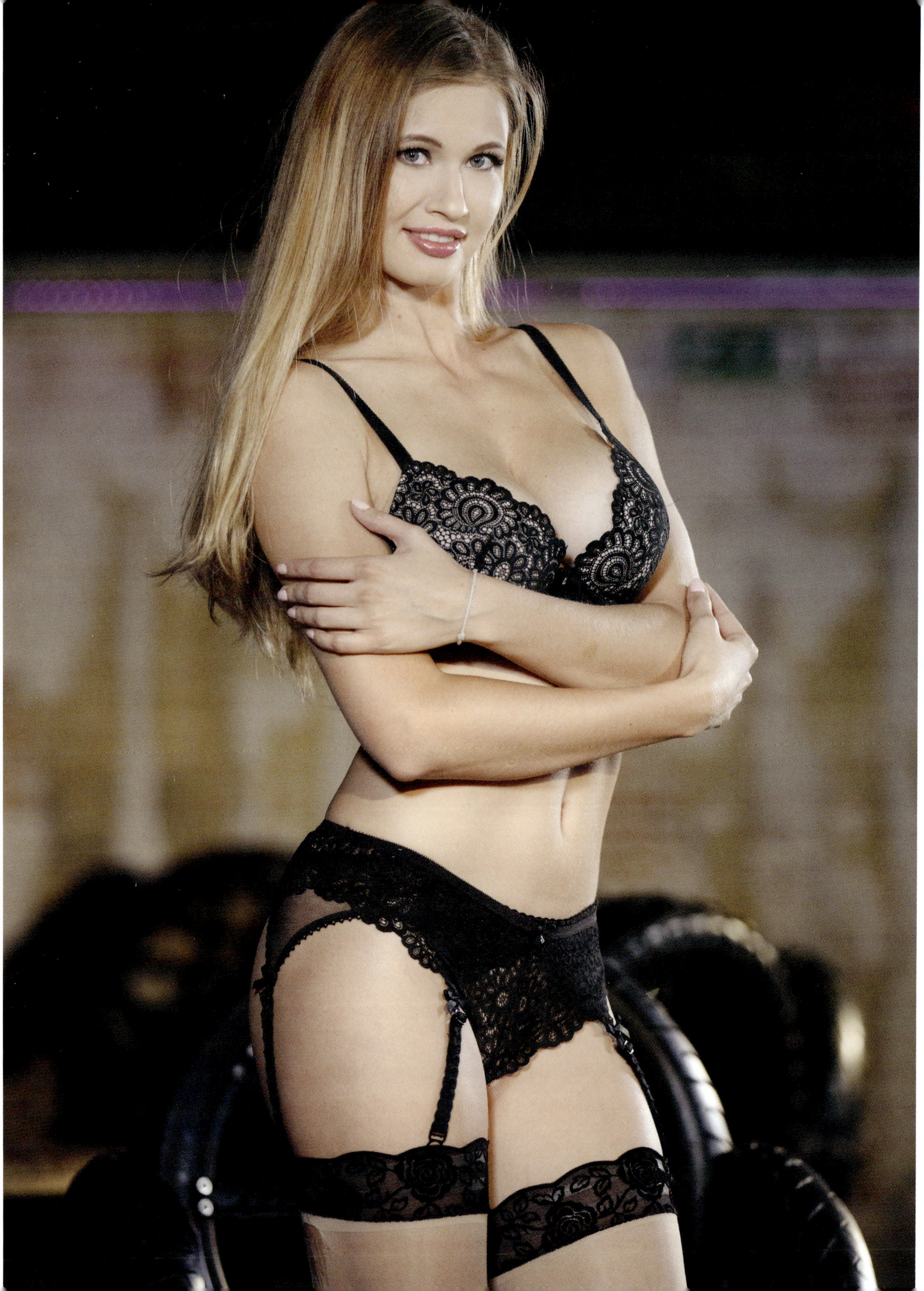

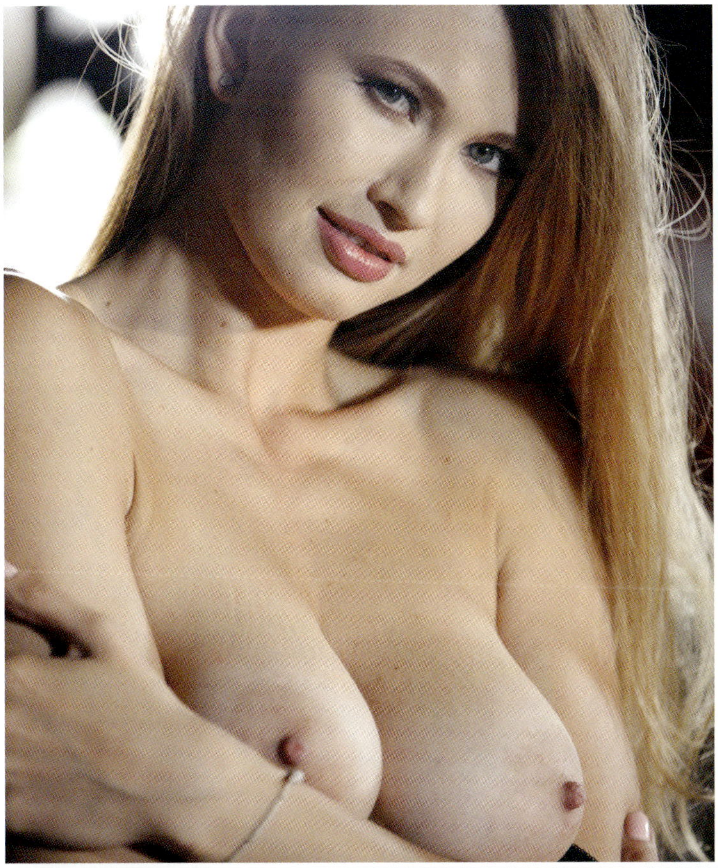

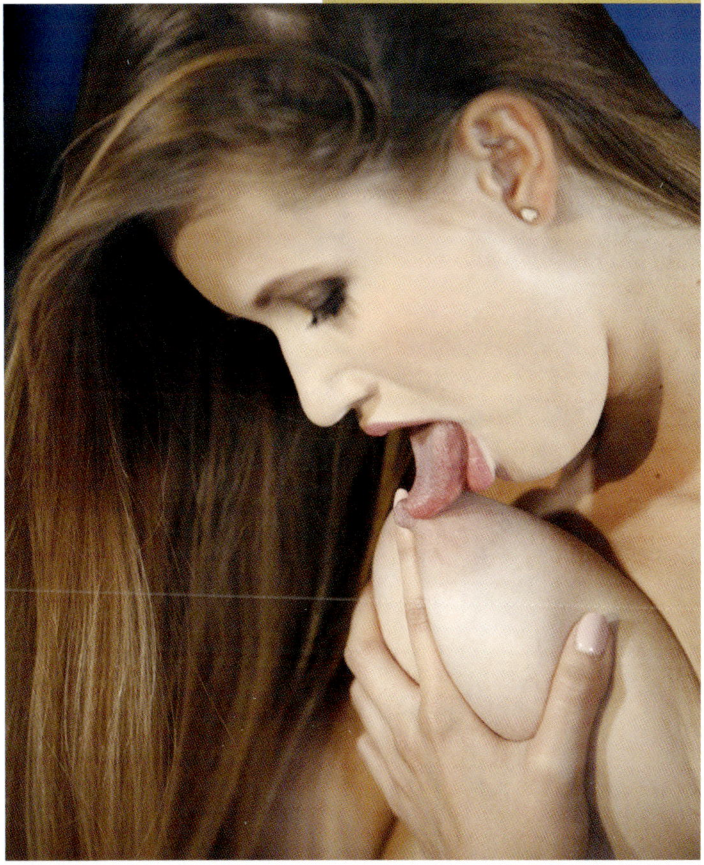

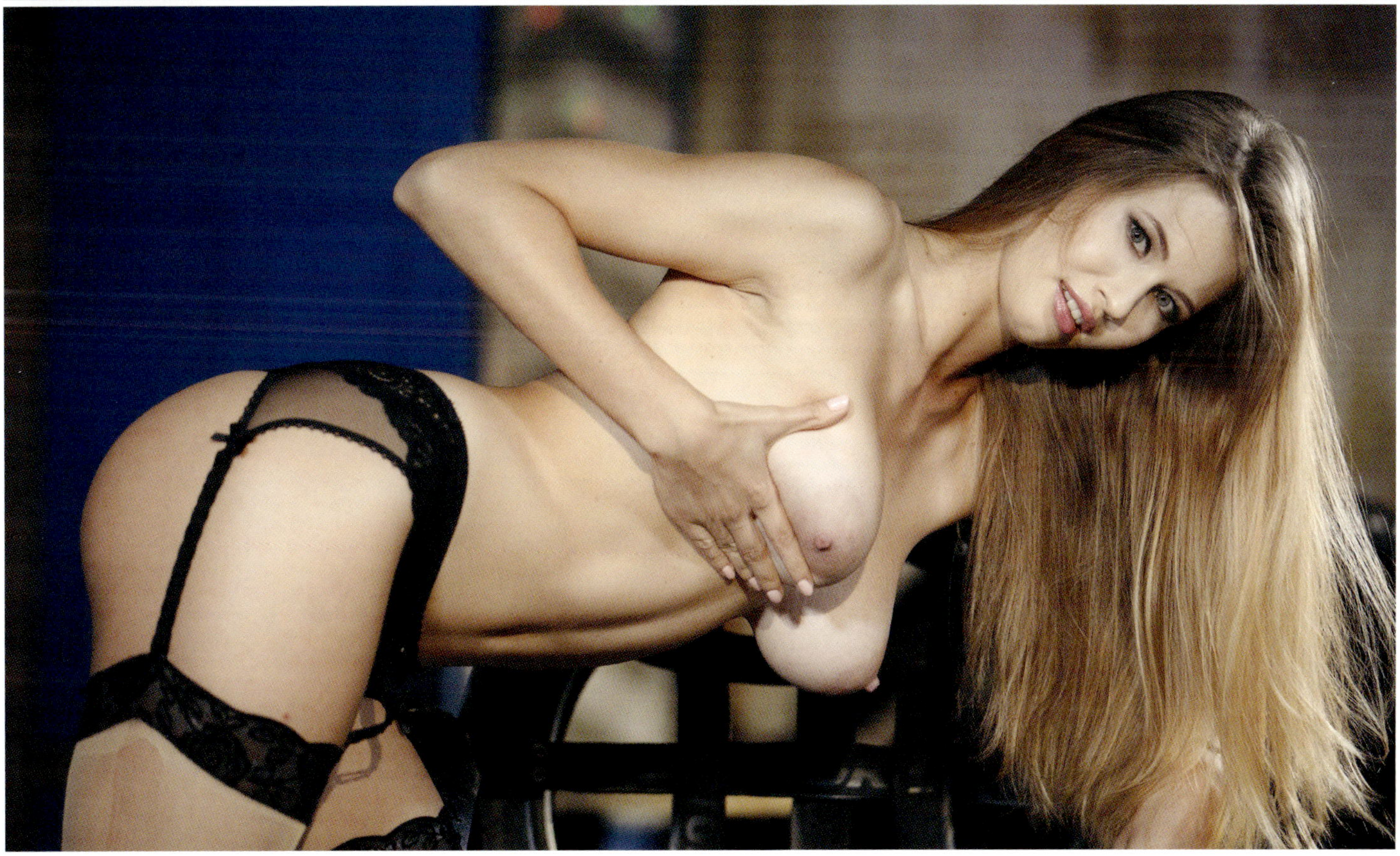

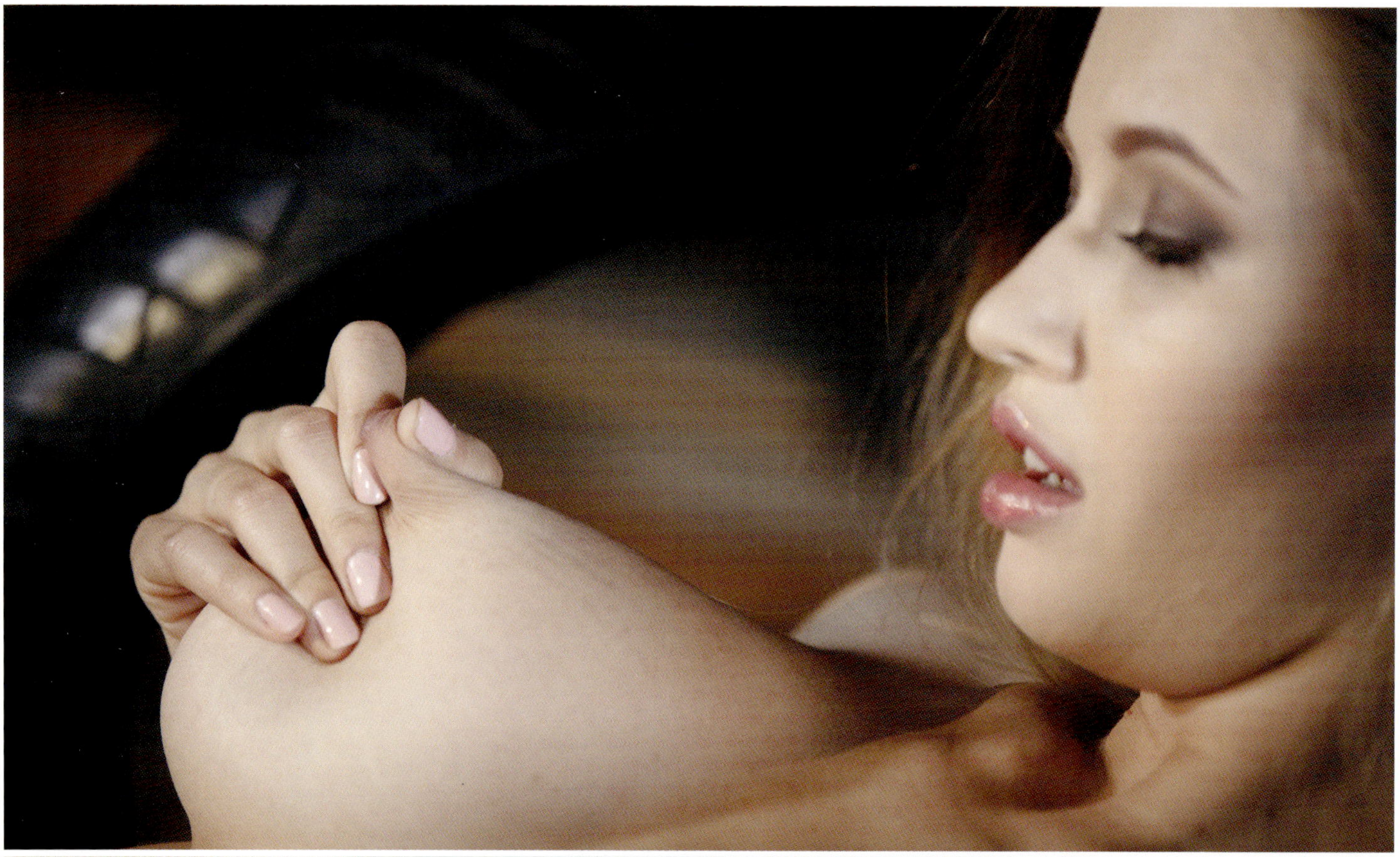
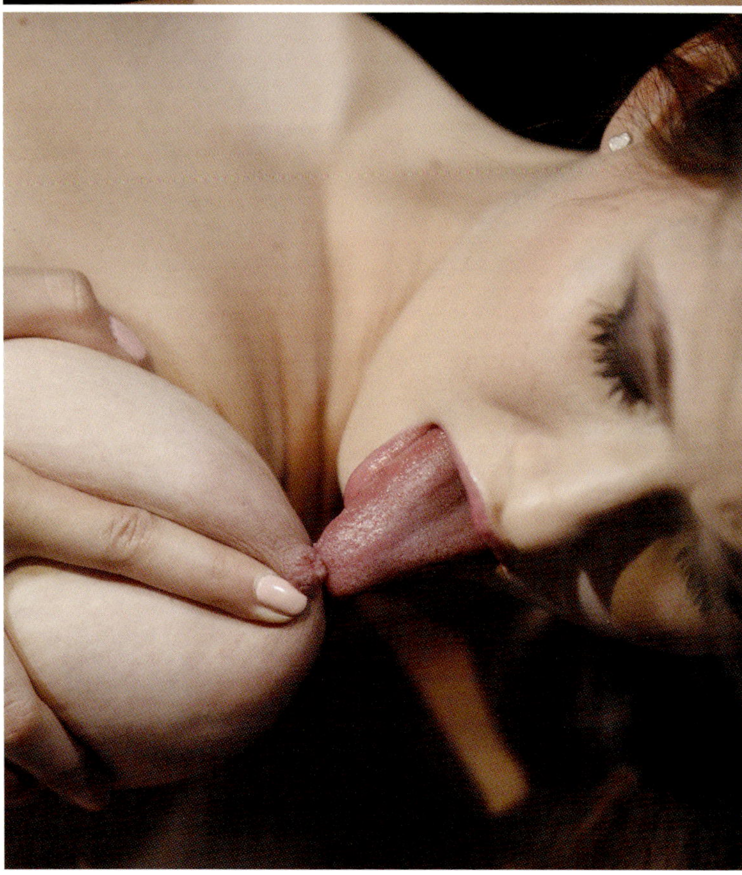
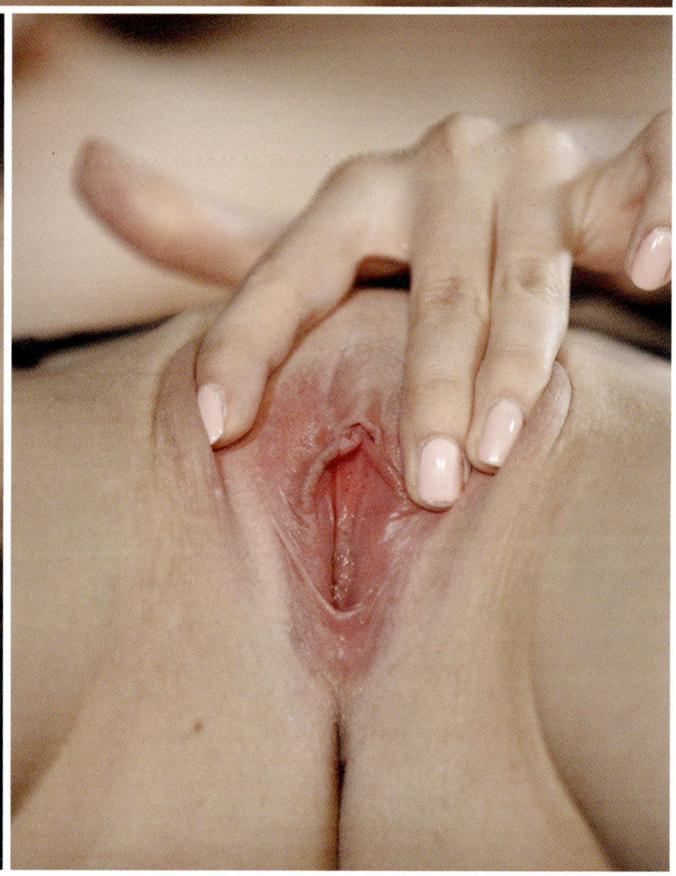

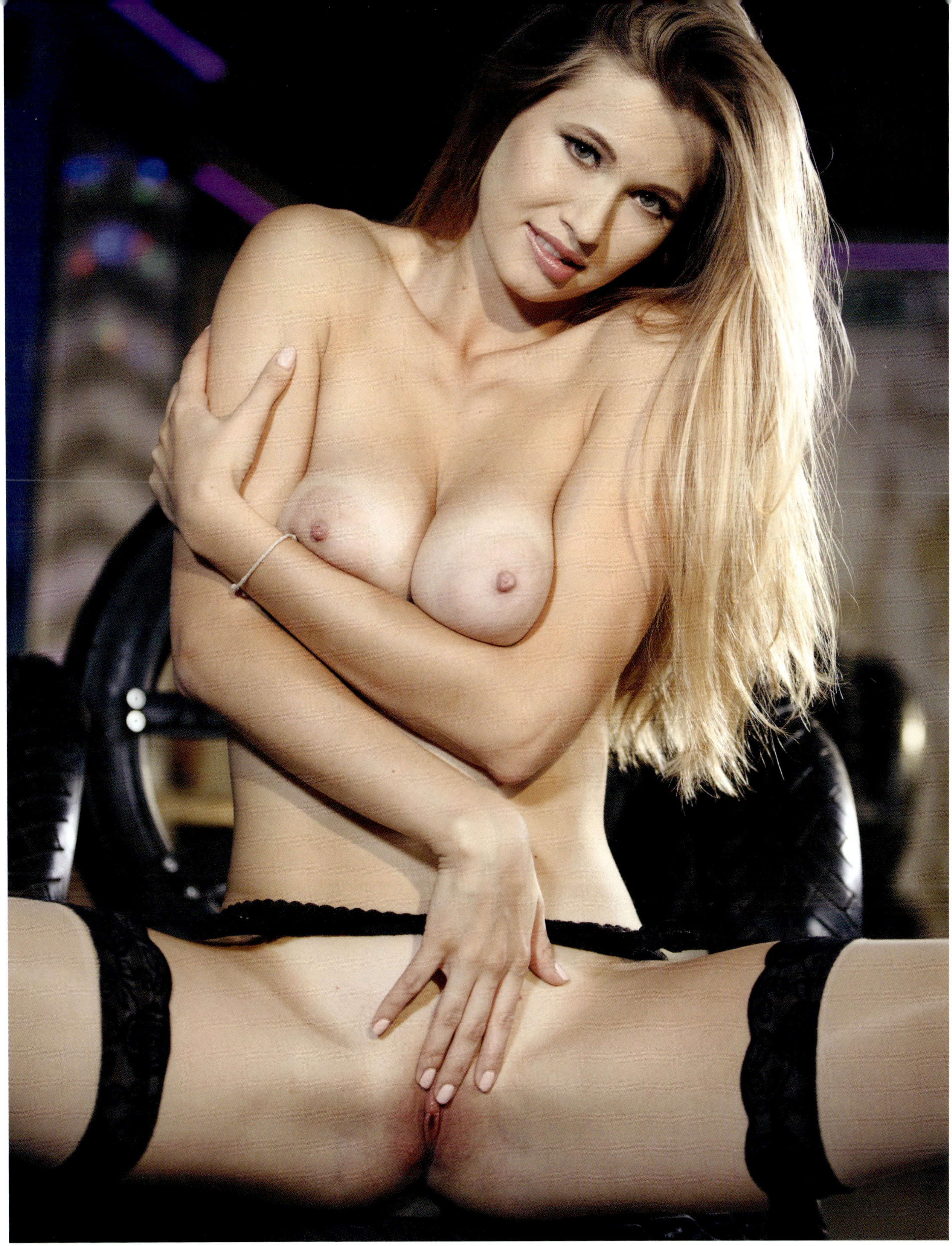

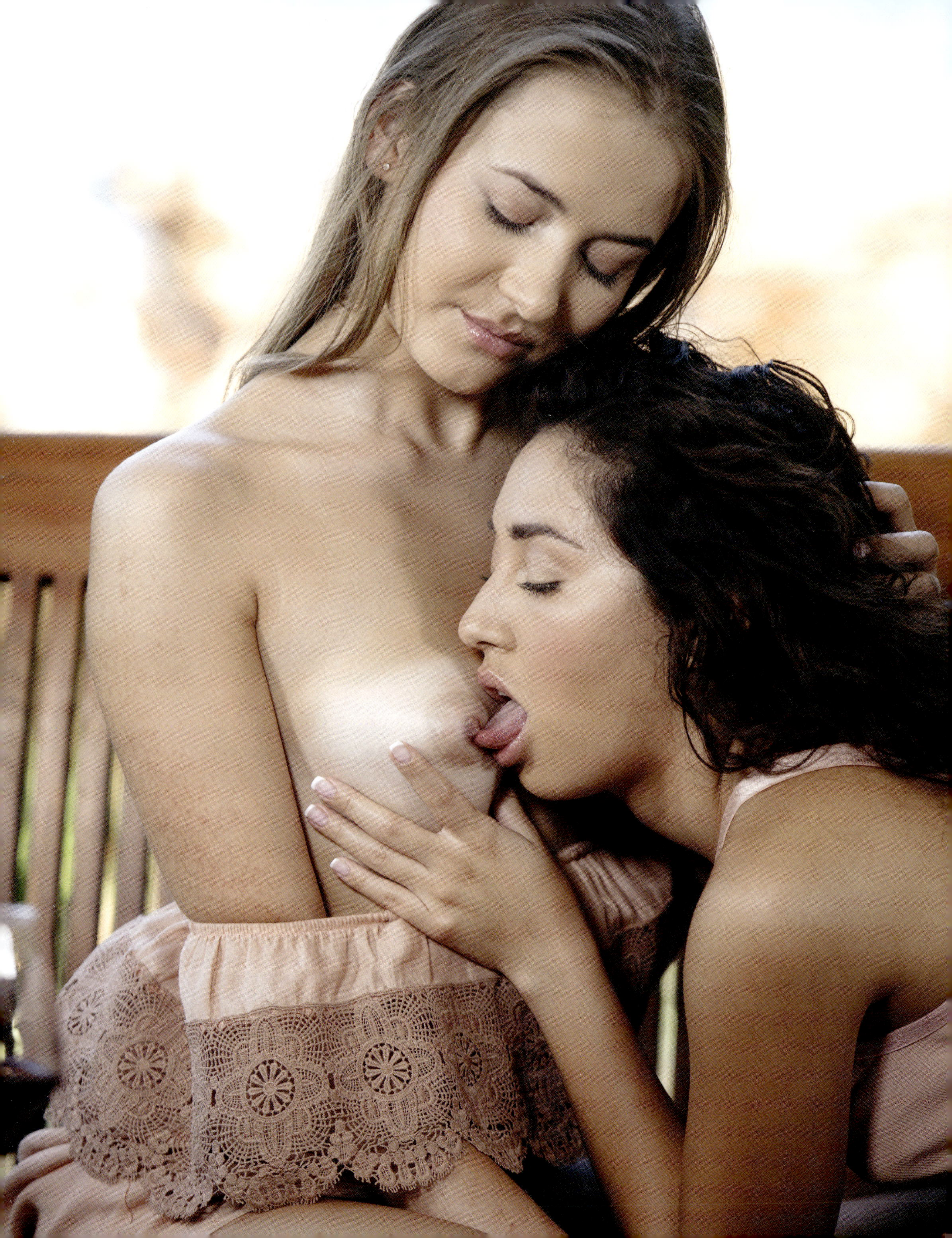

Melody Petite
Swabery Baby

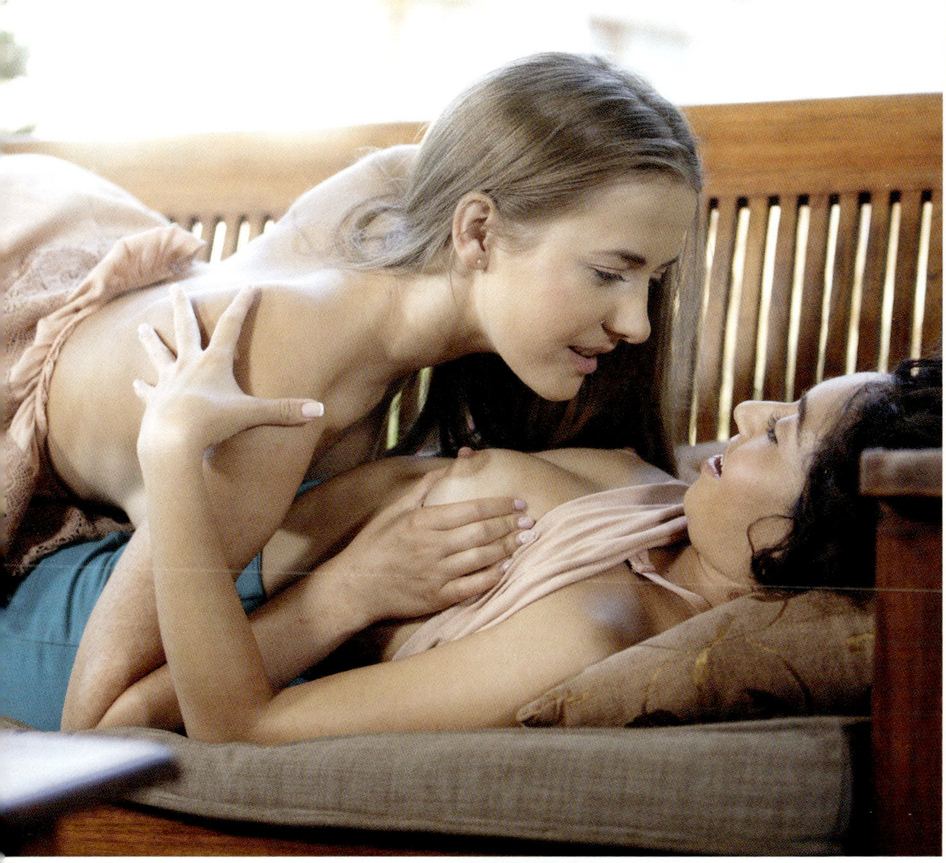

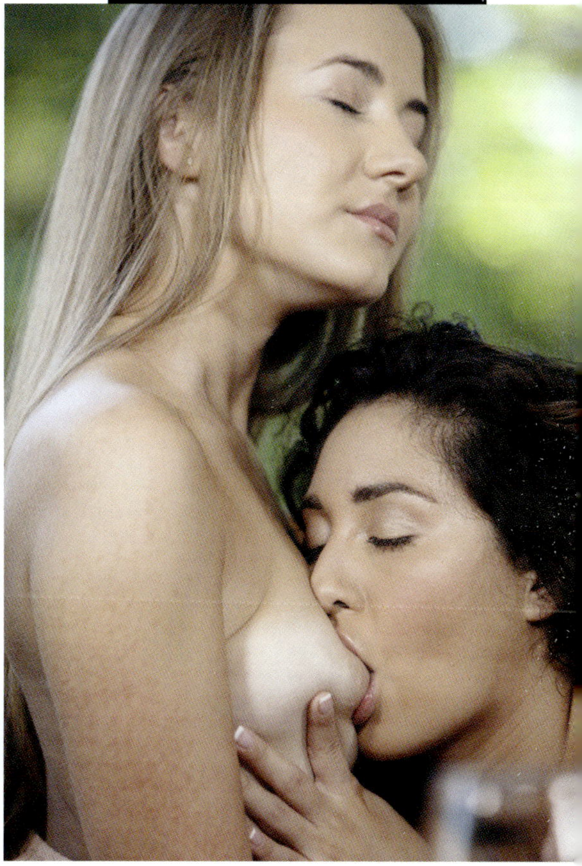

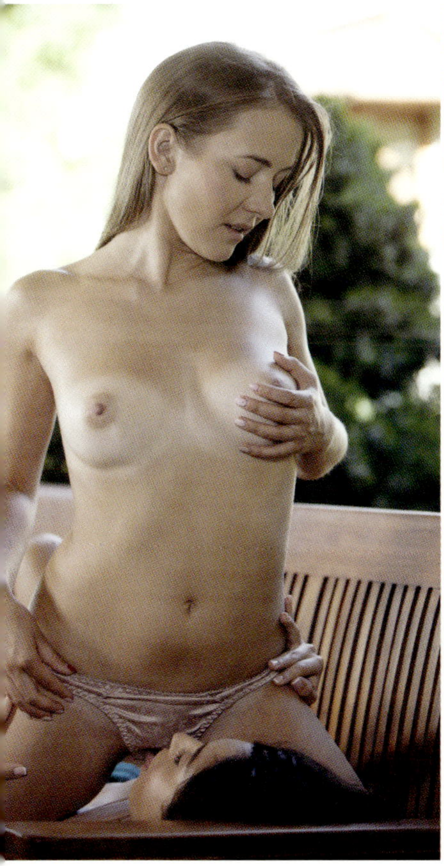

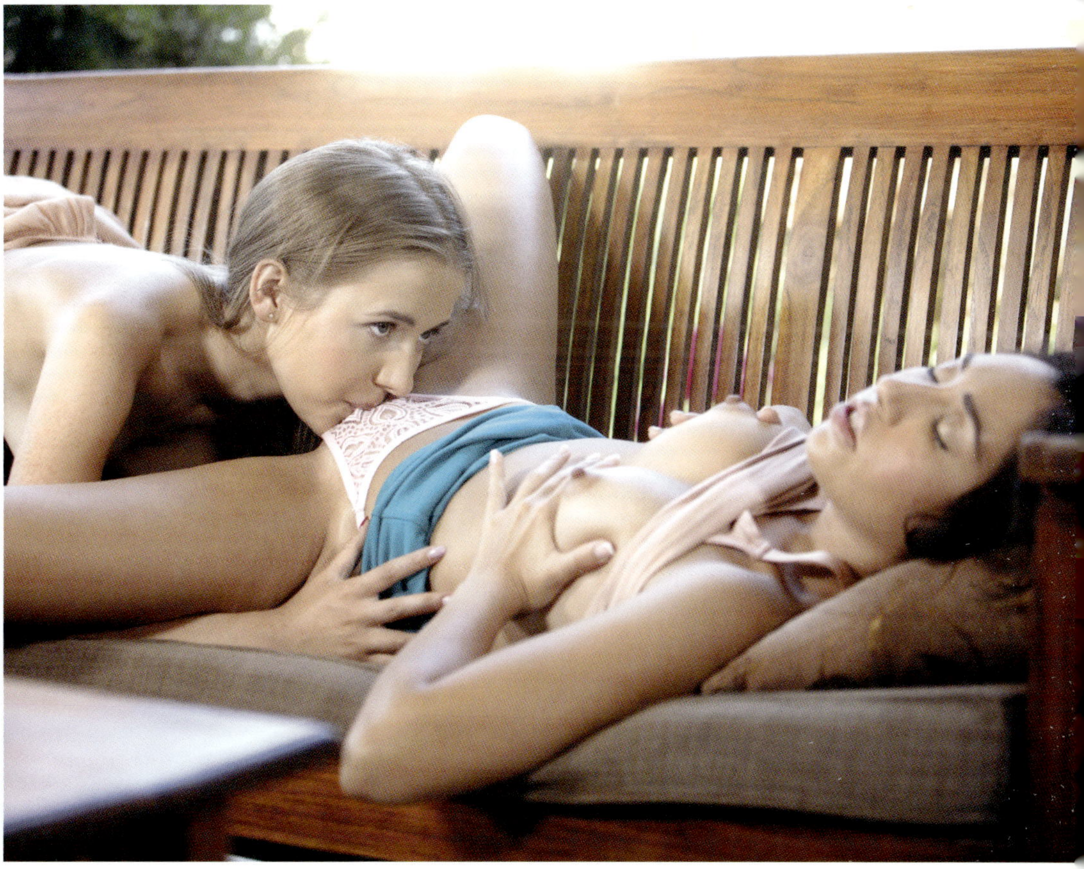

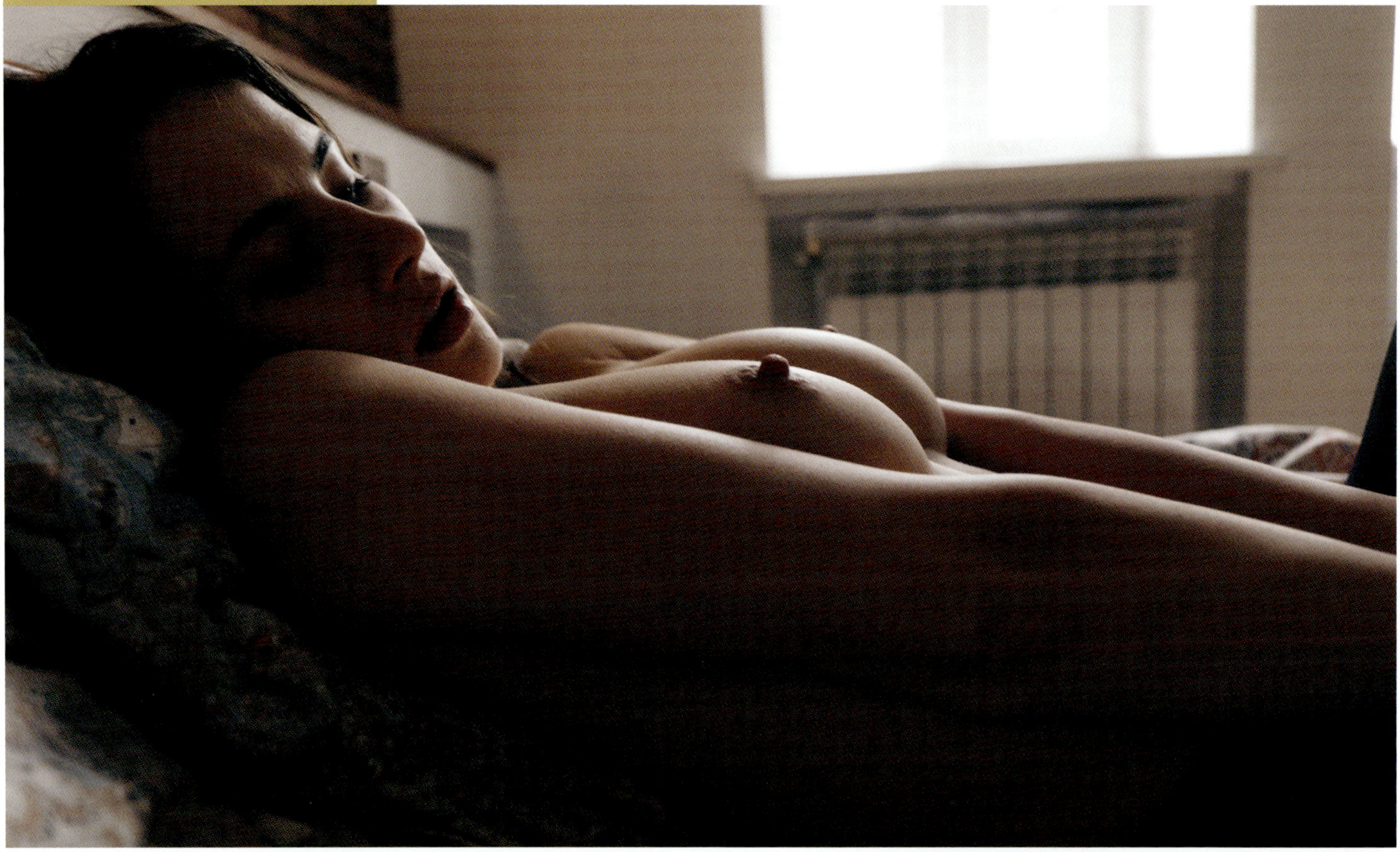

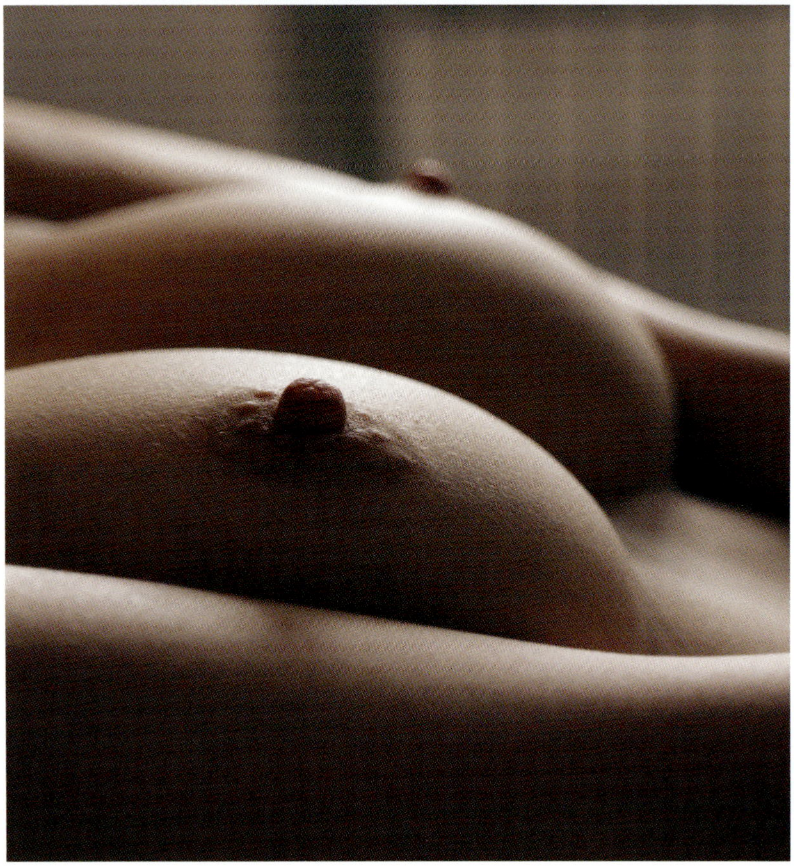

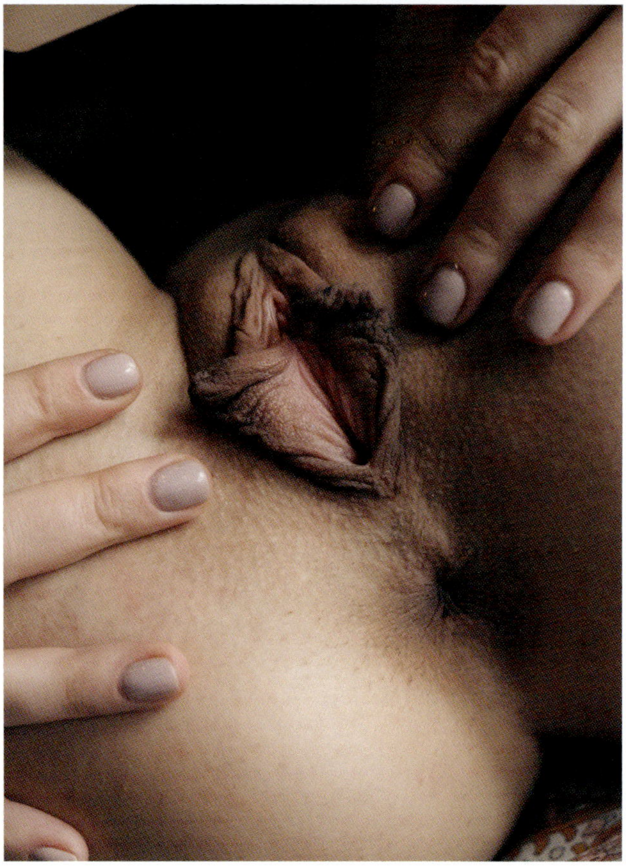

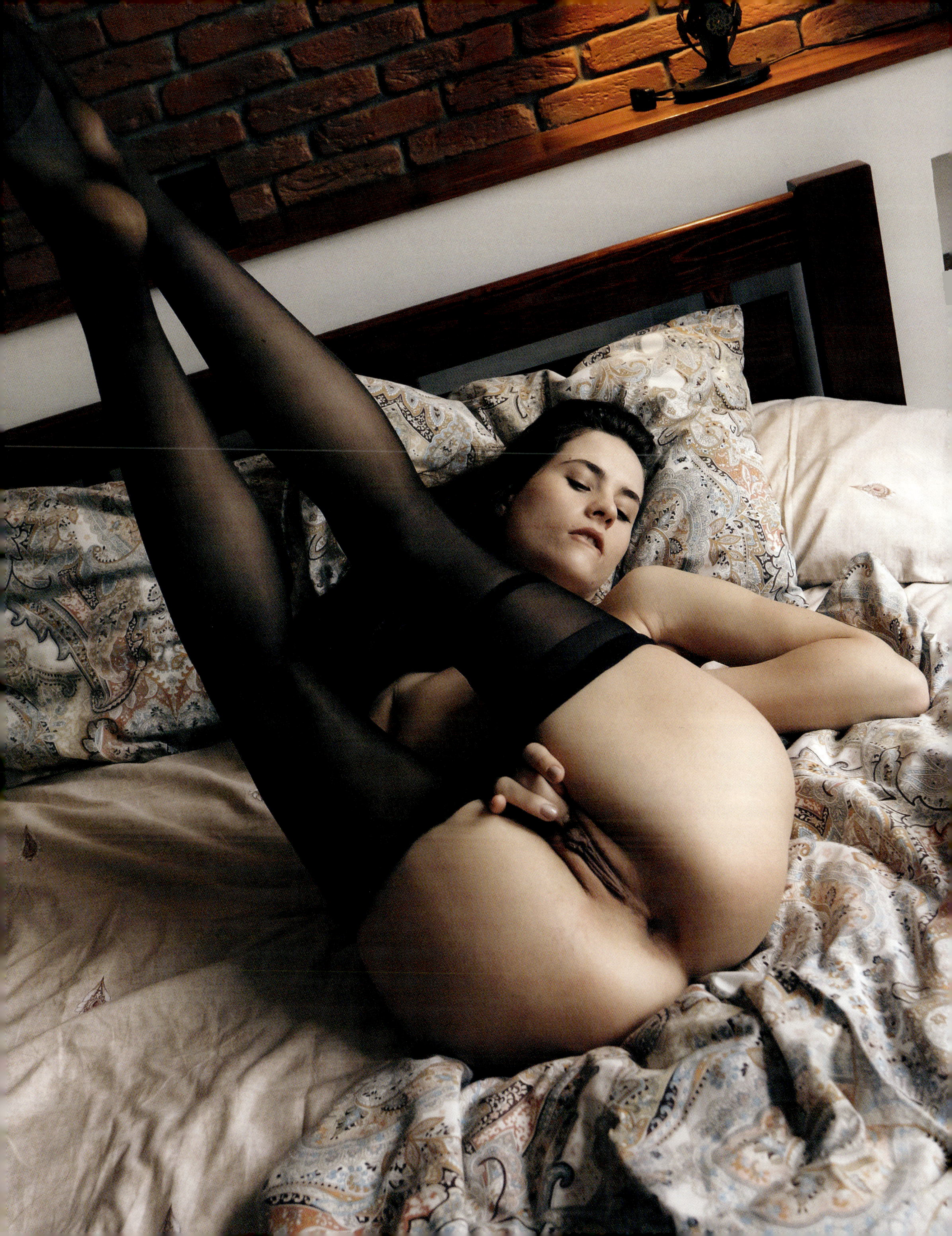

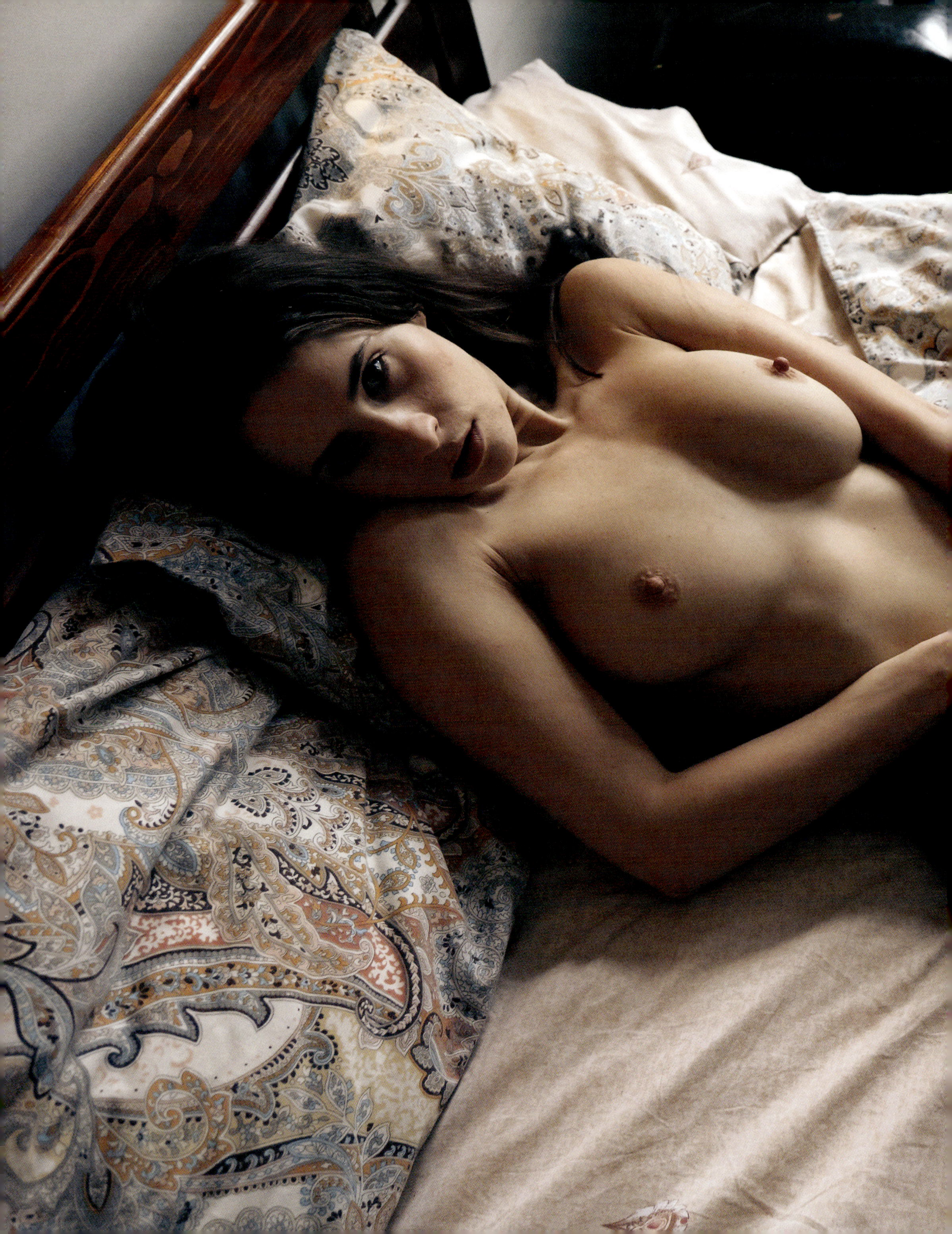

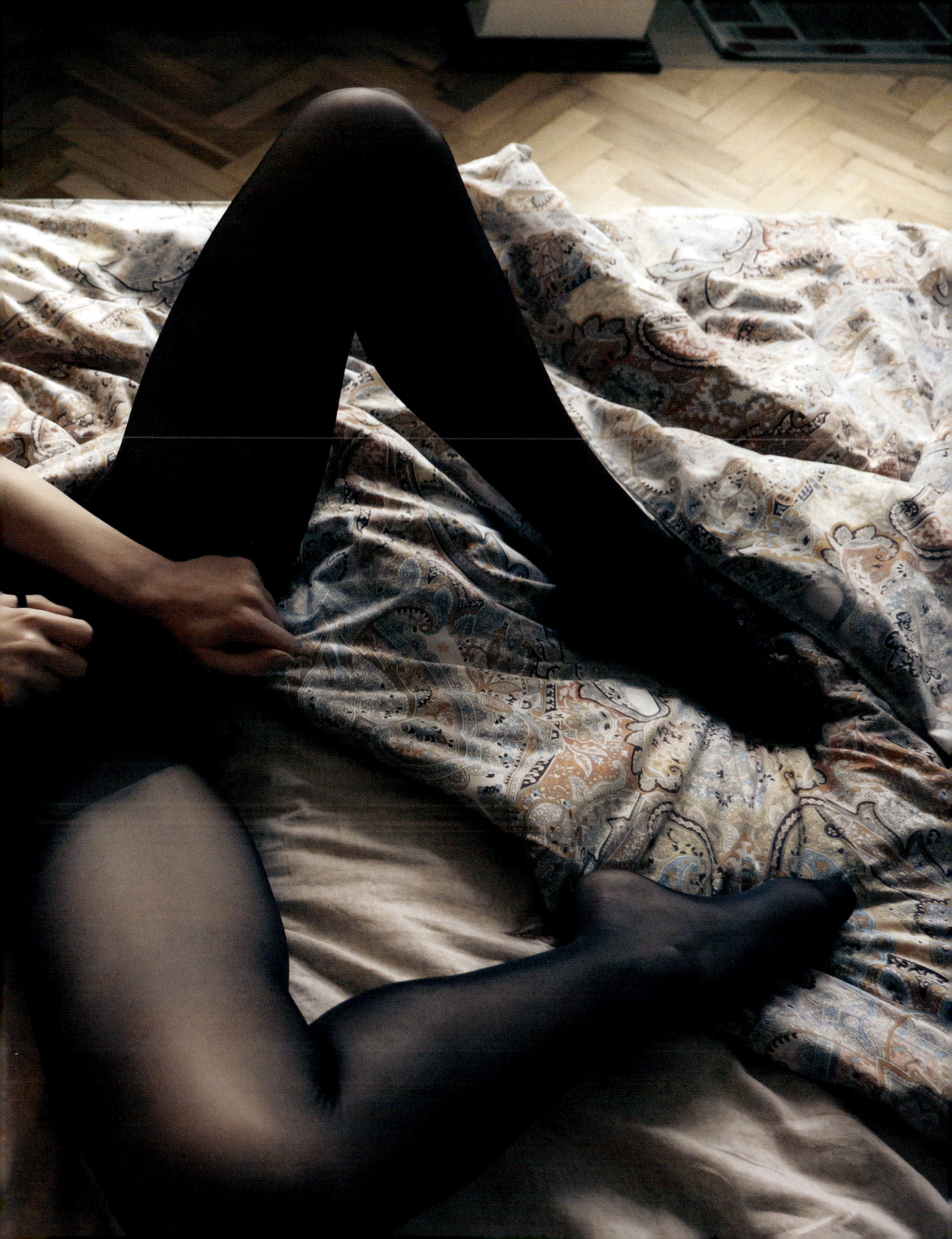

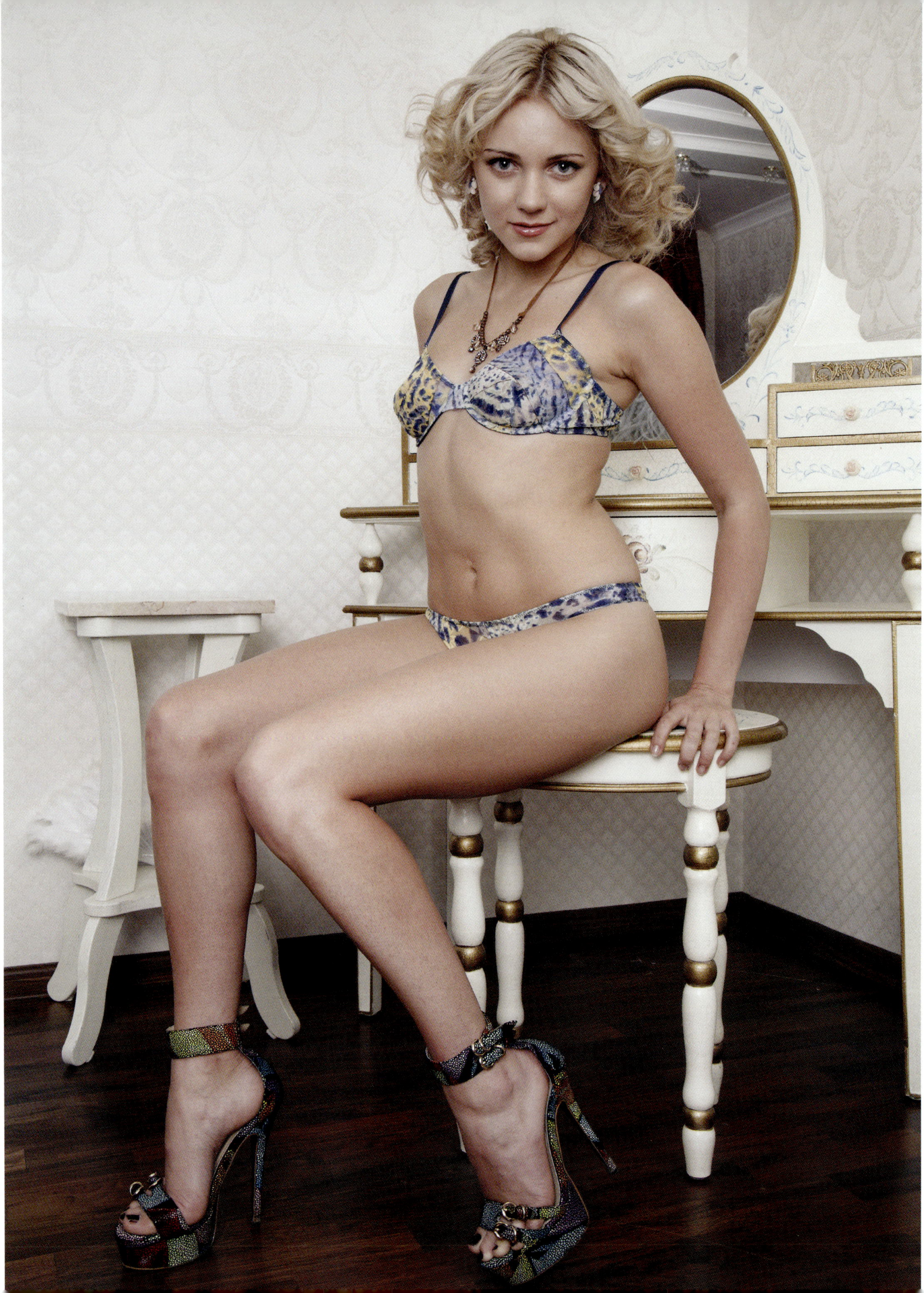

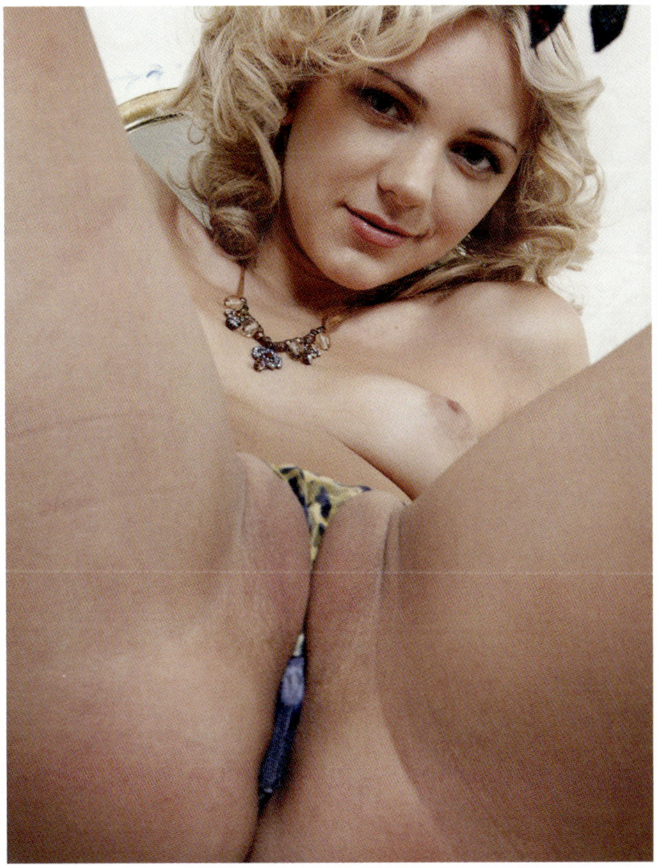

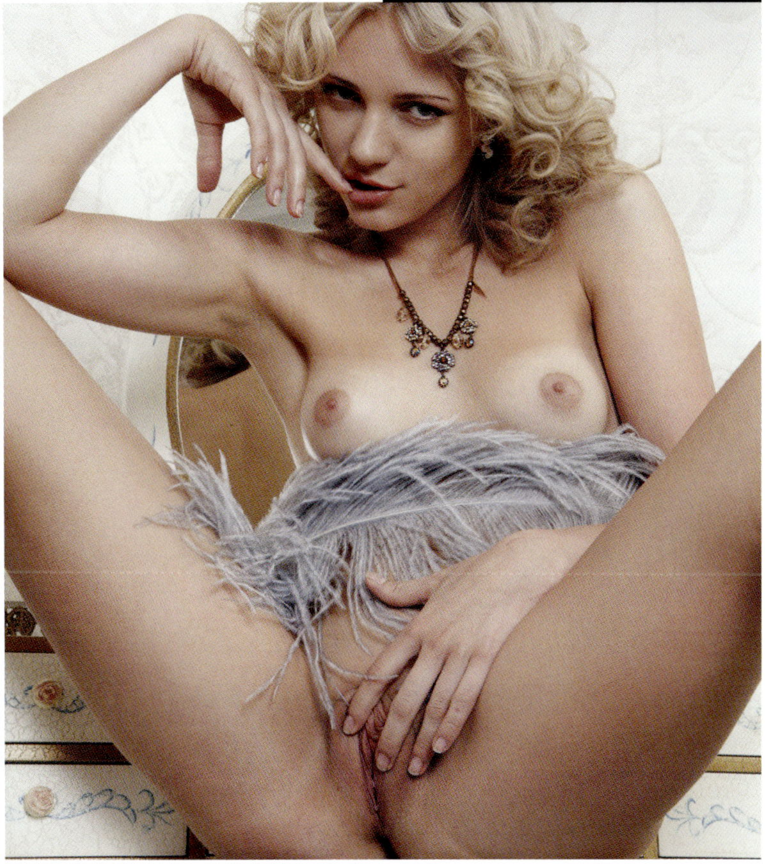

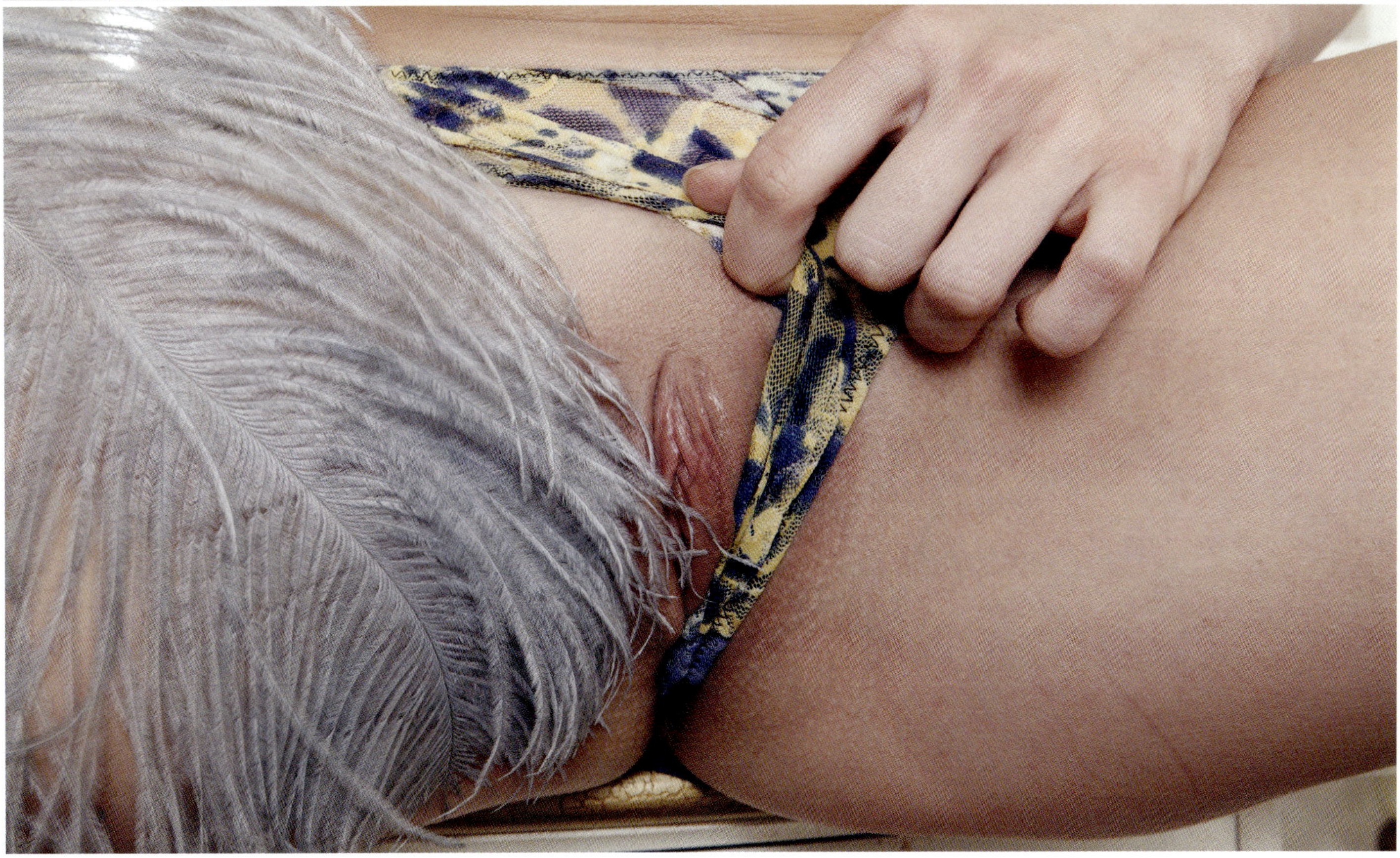

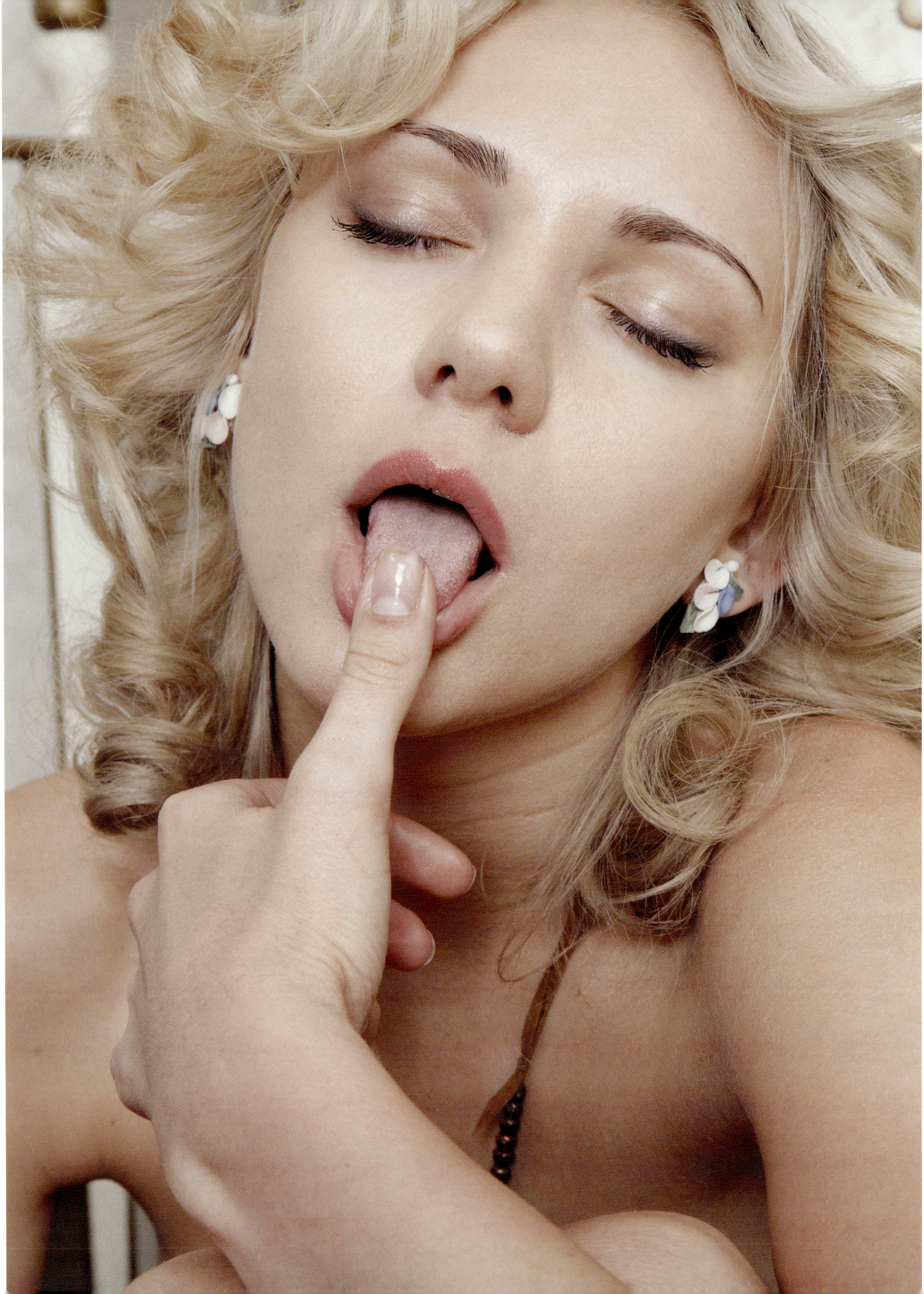

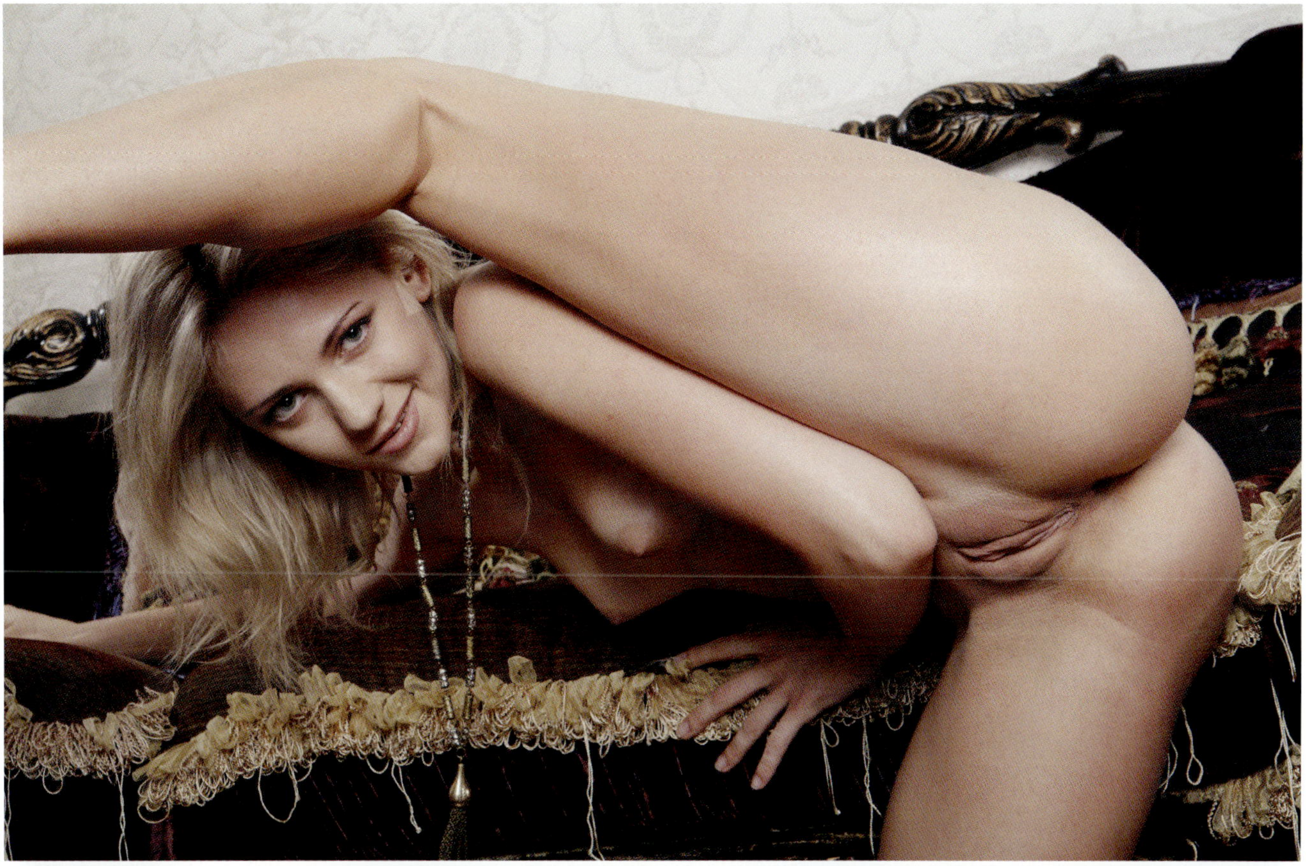

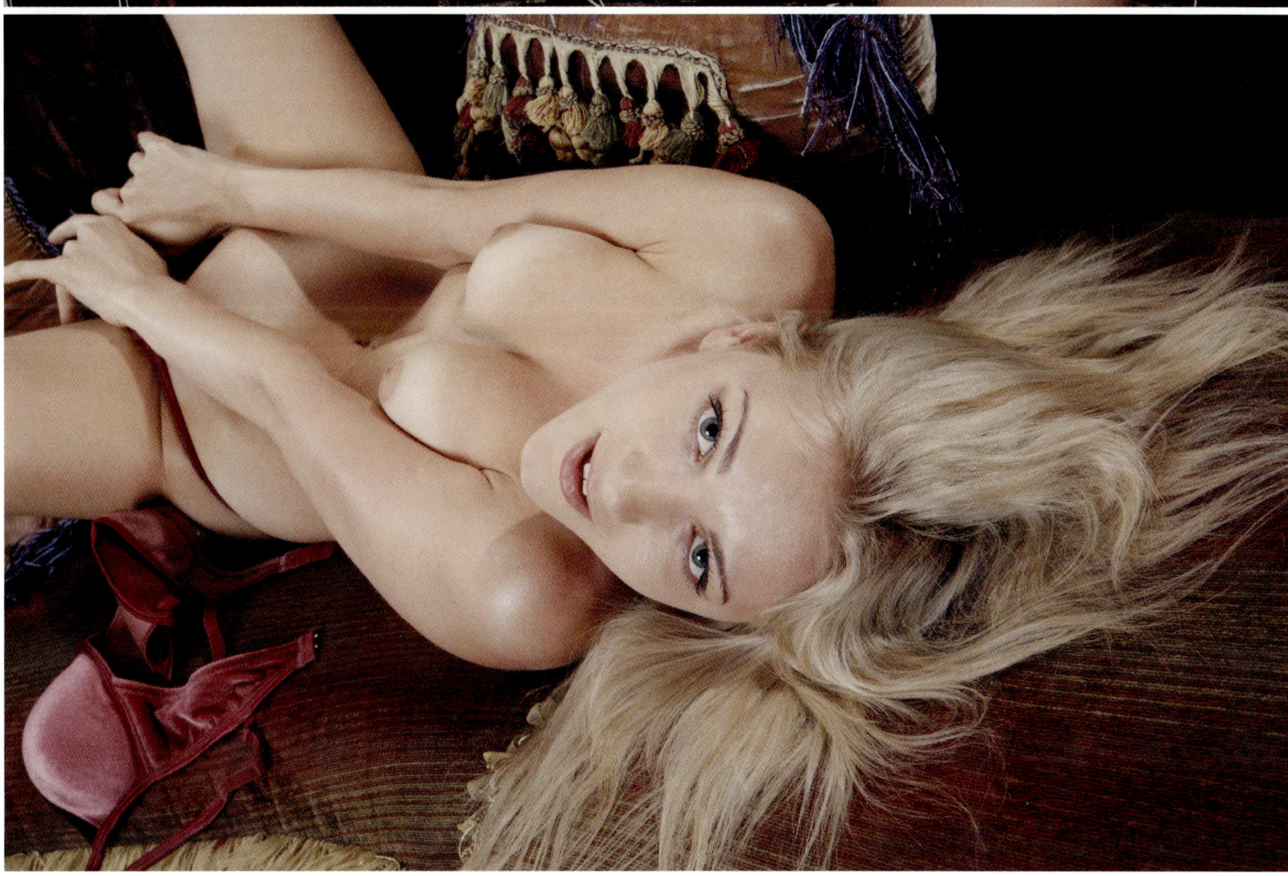

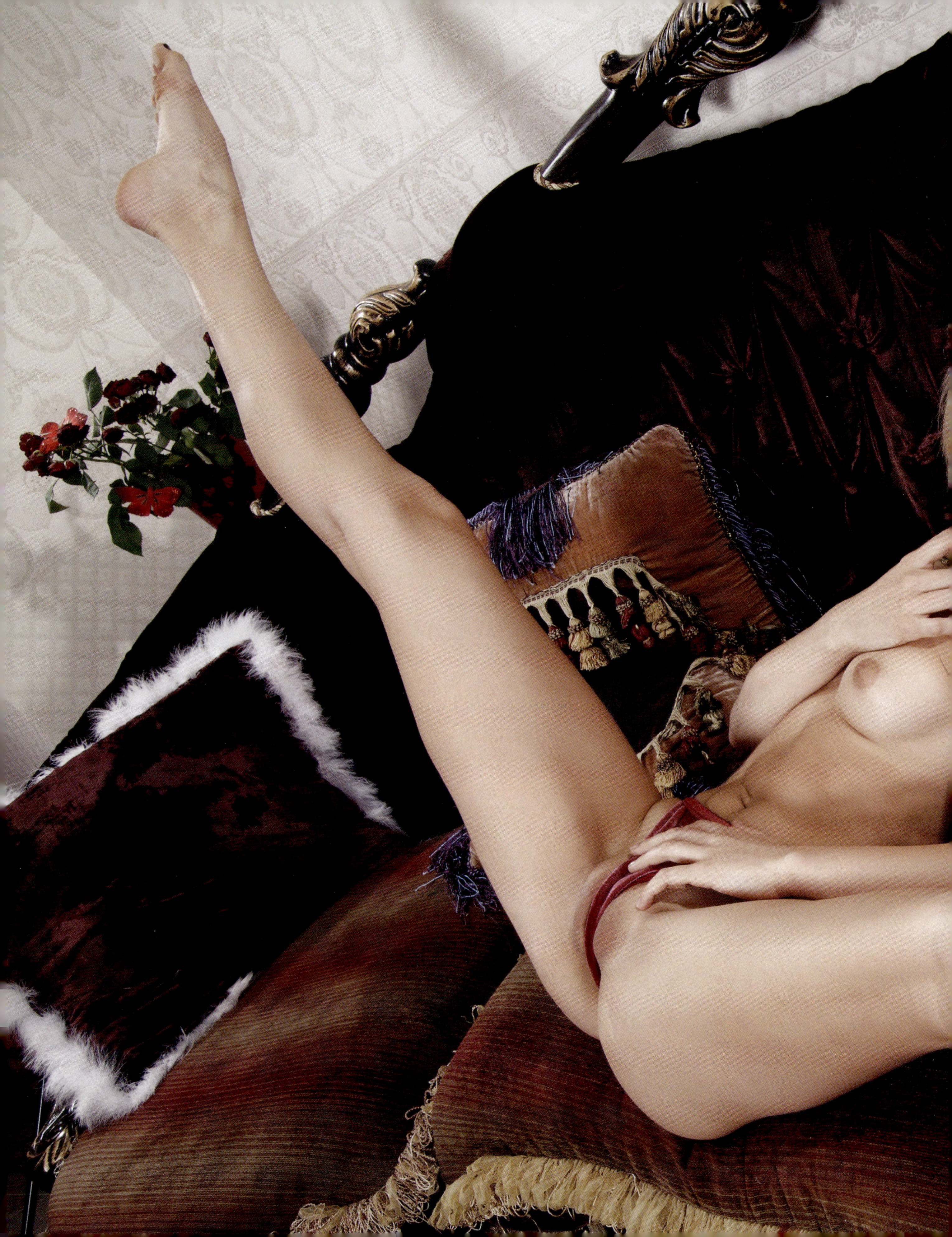

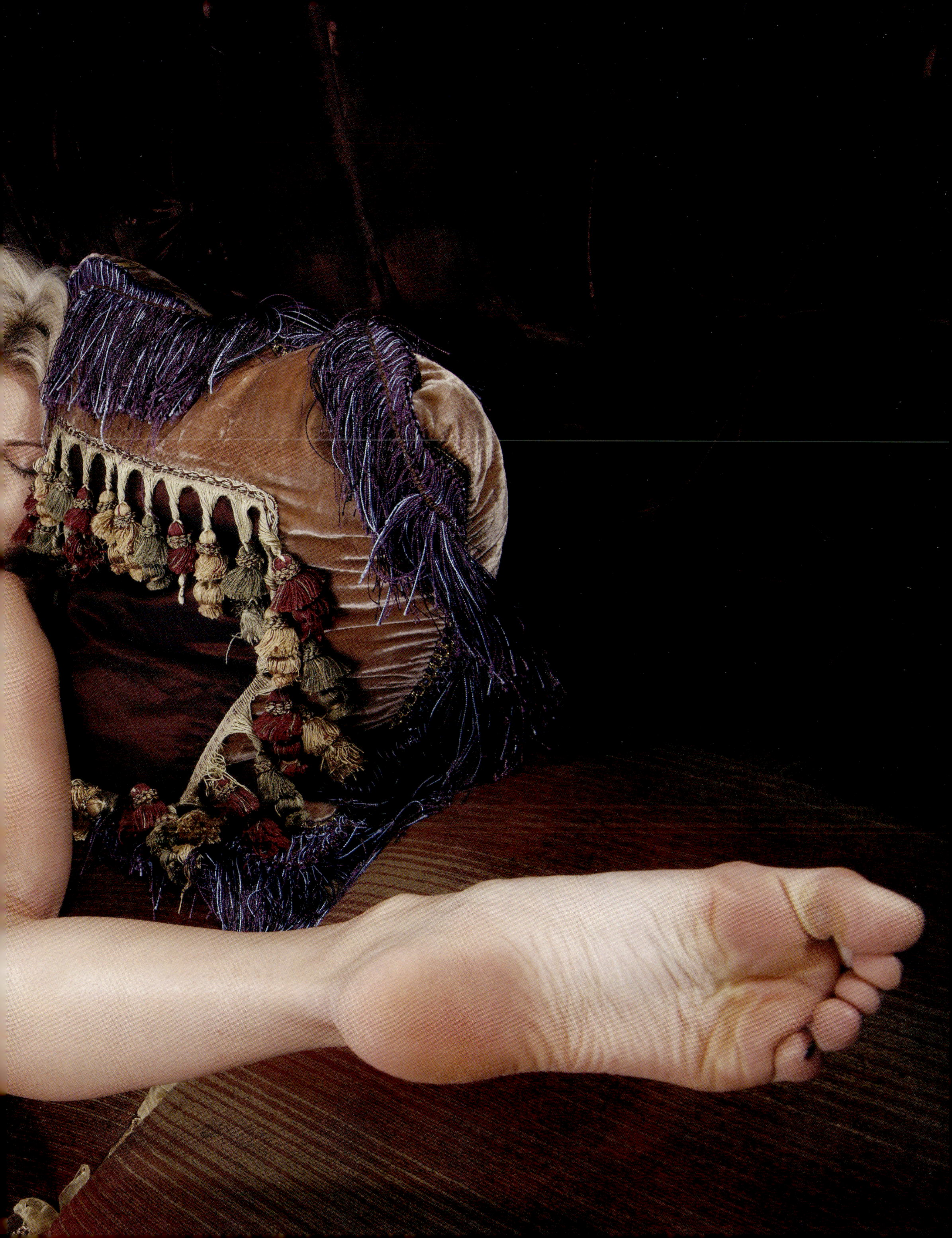

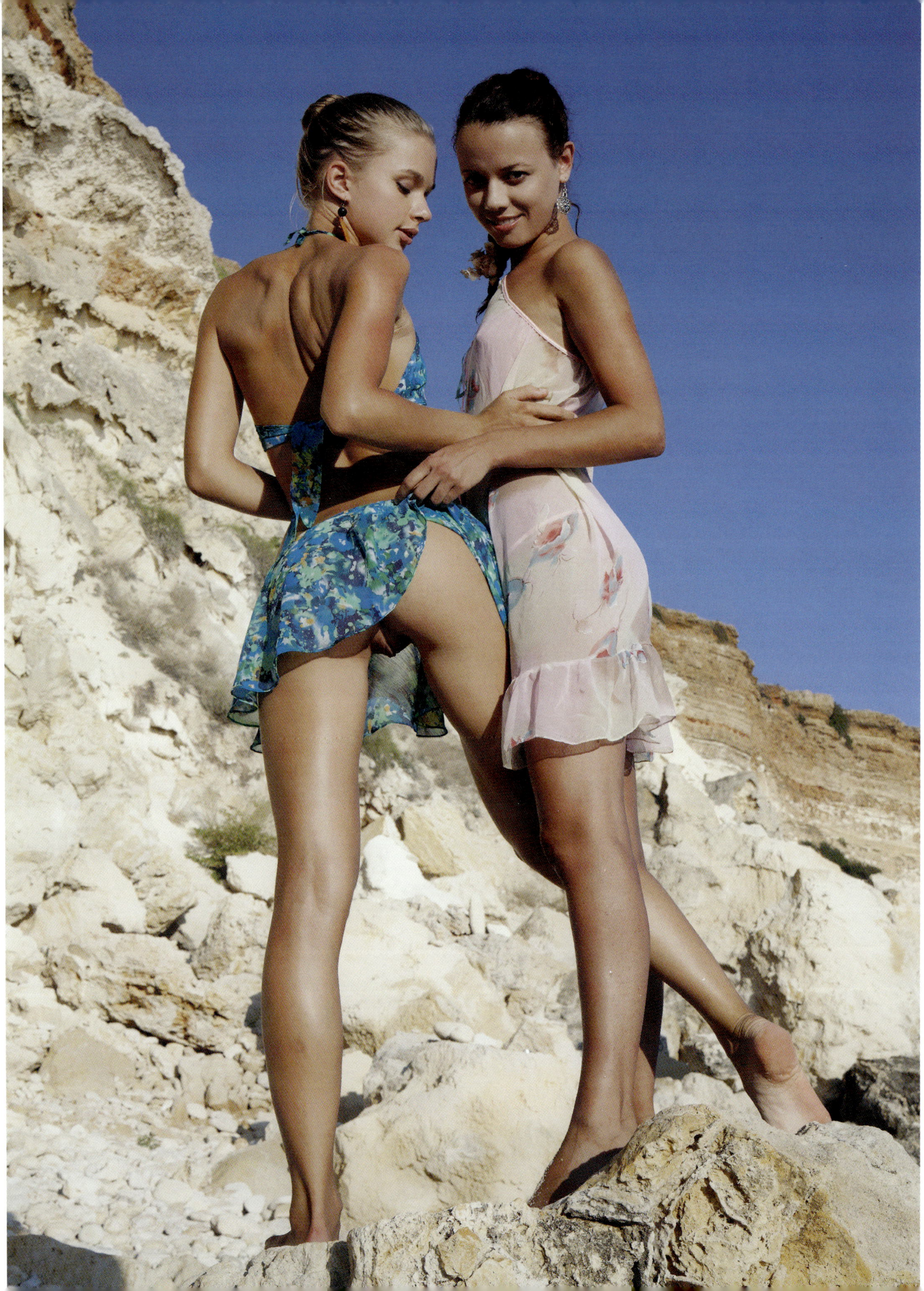

Korica A
Milena D

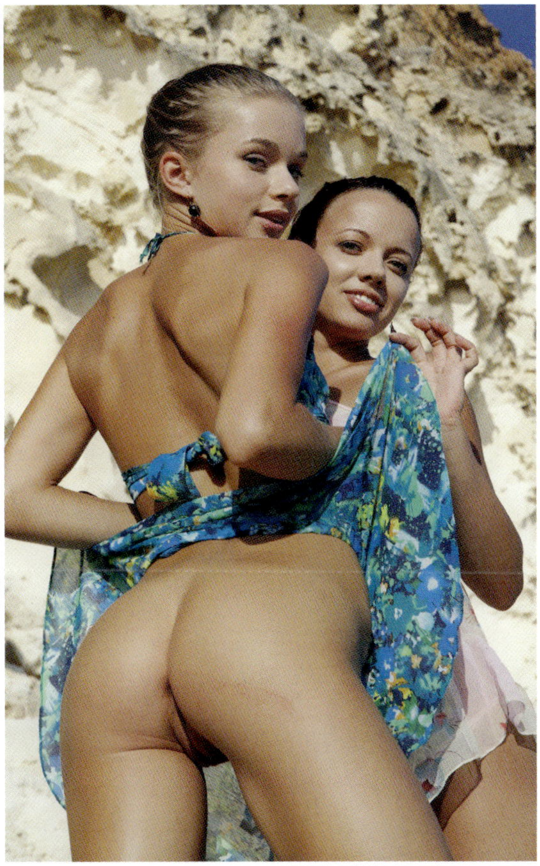

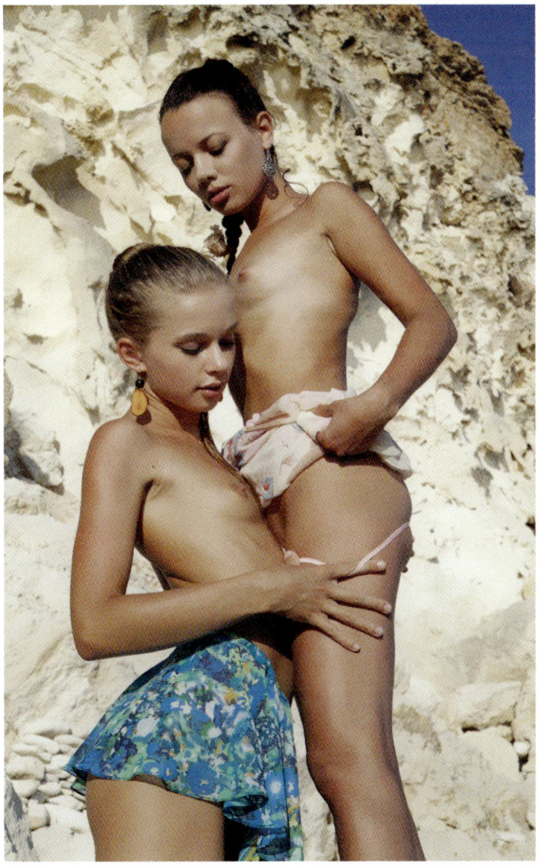

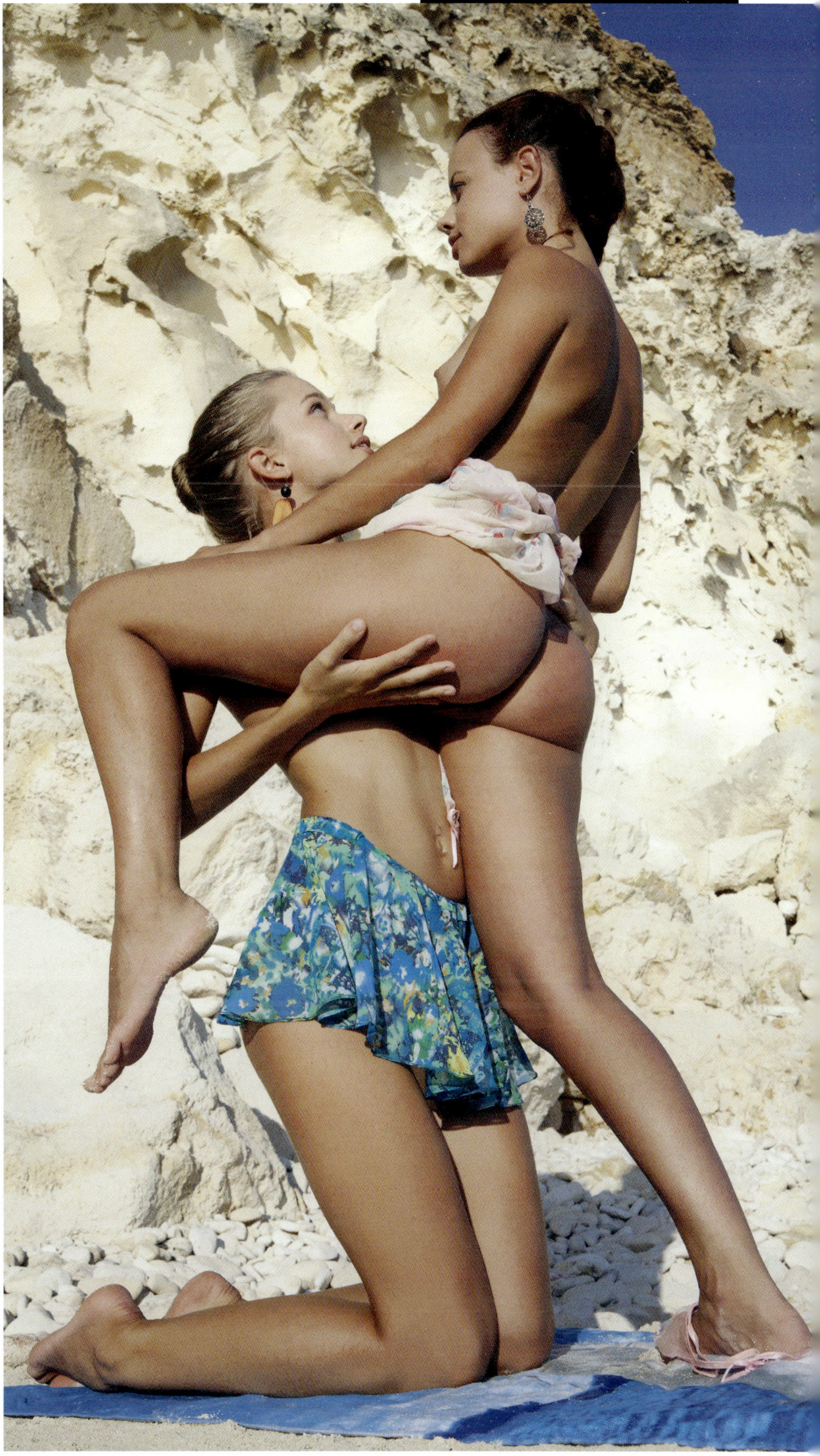

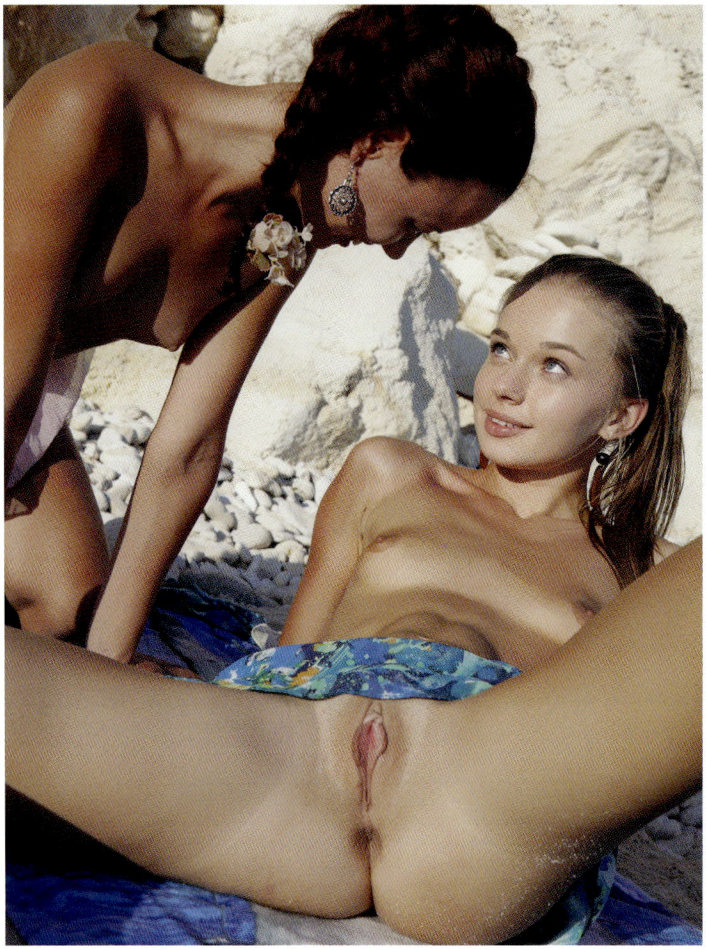
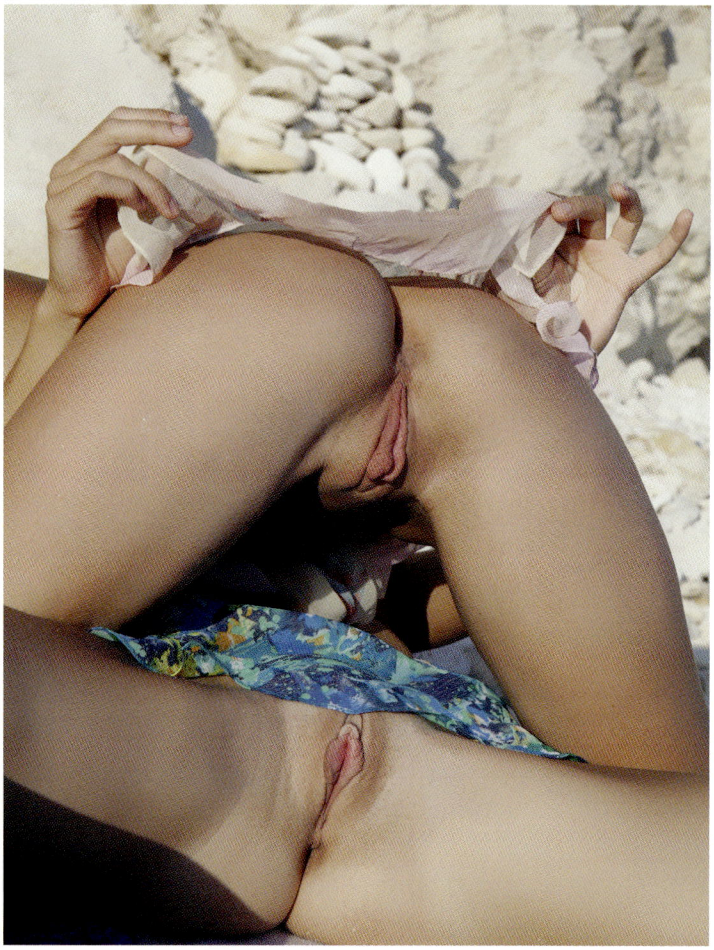
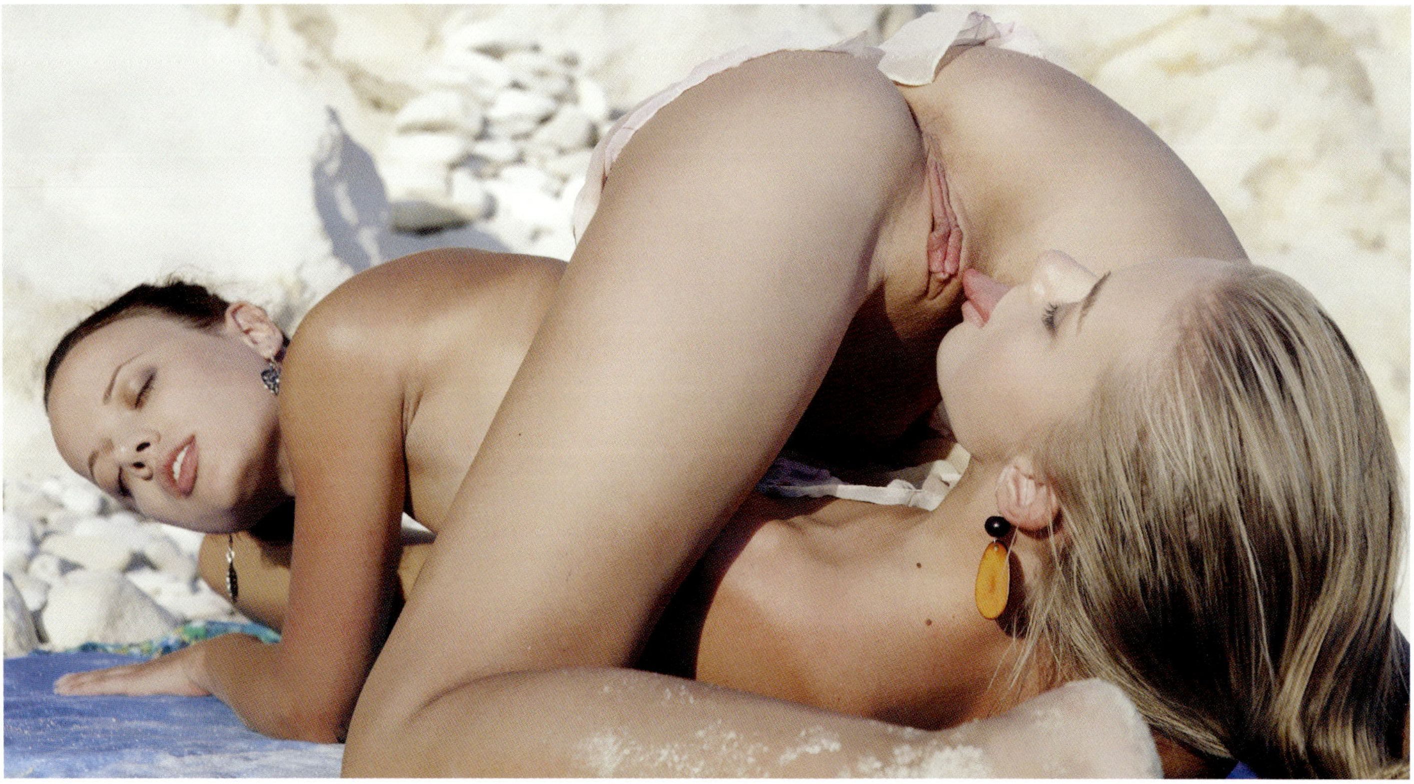

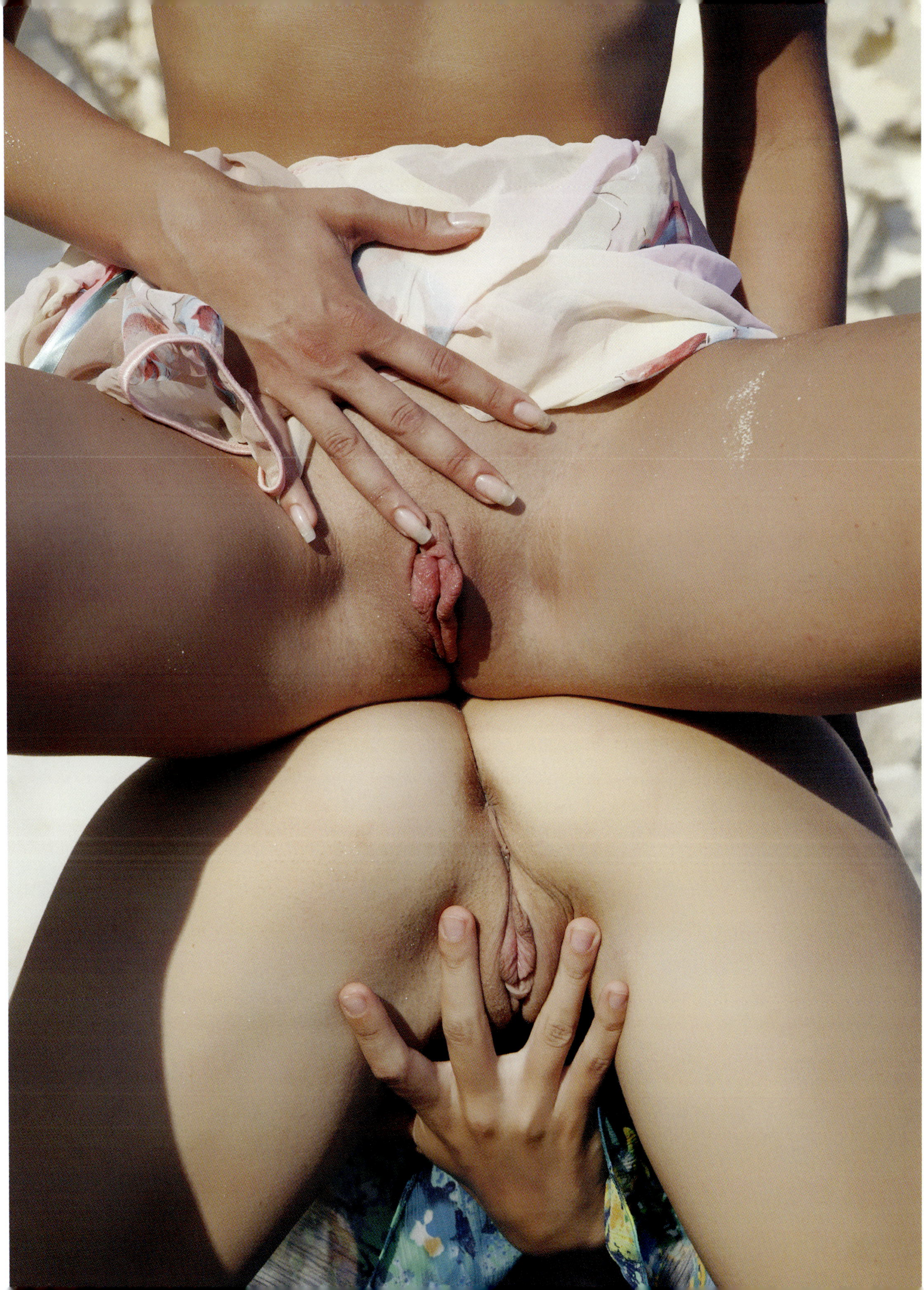

Kelly Collins
Sirena Milano

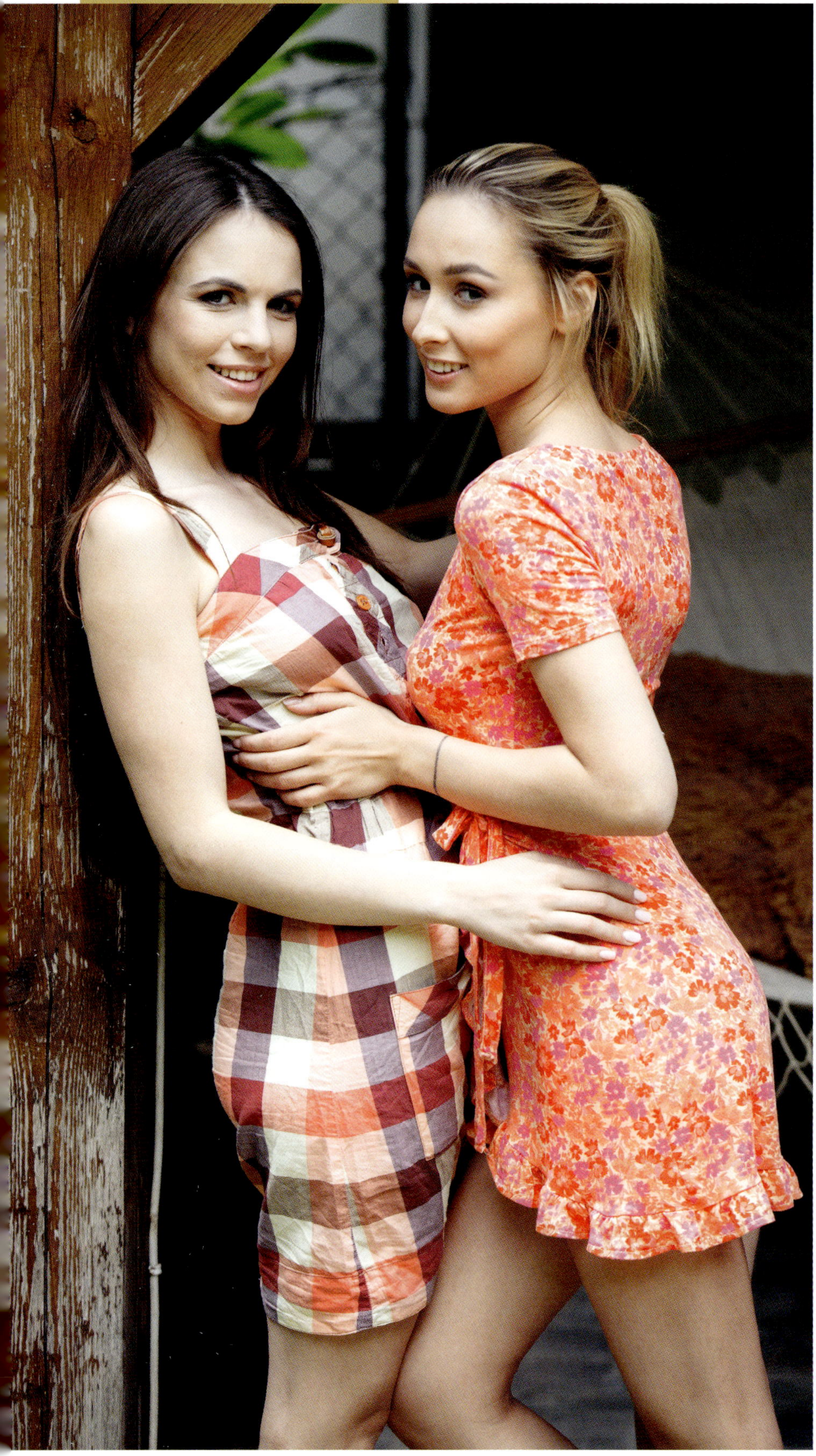

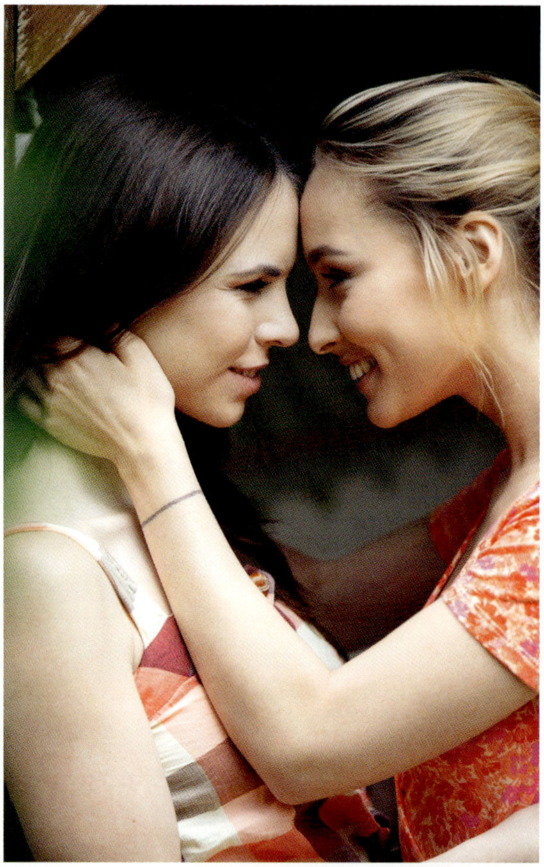

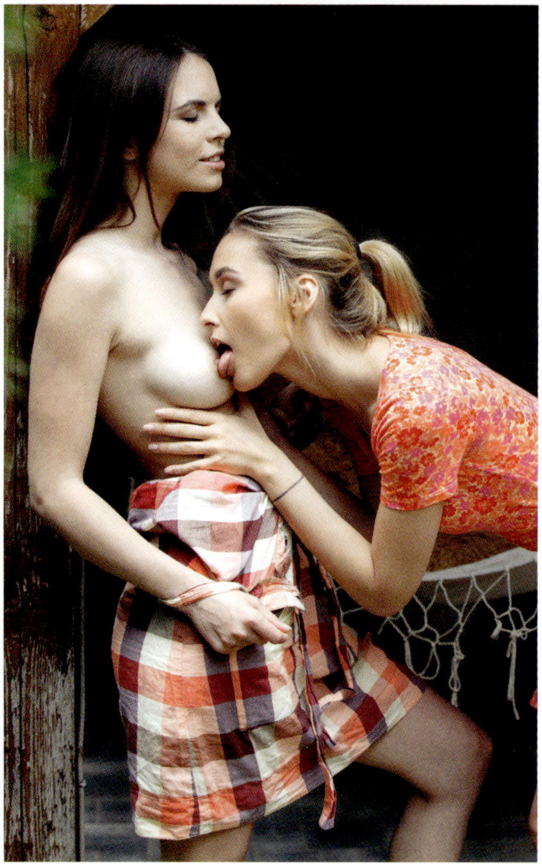

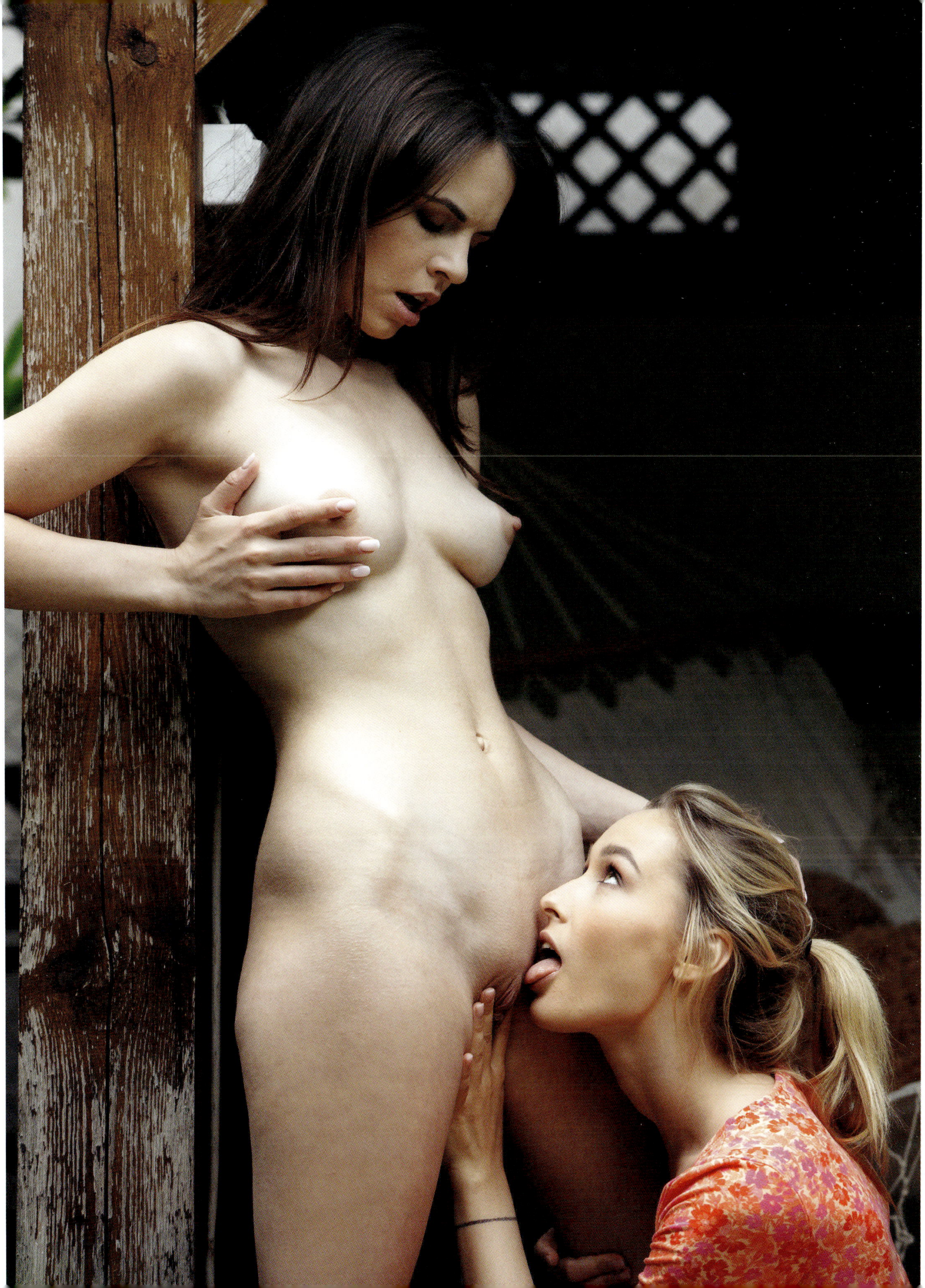

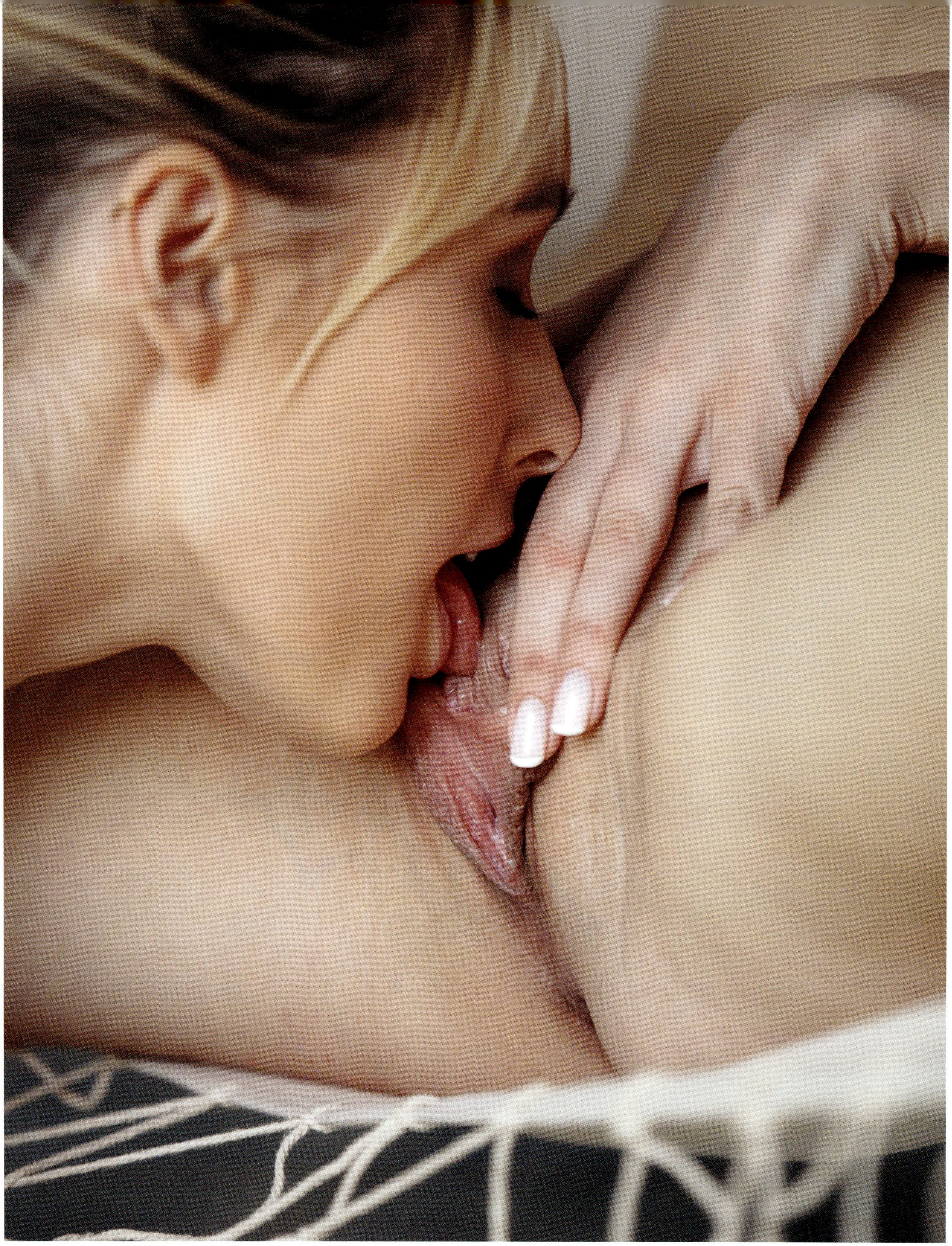

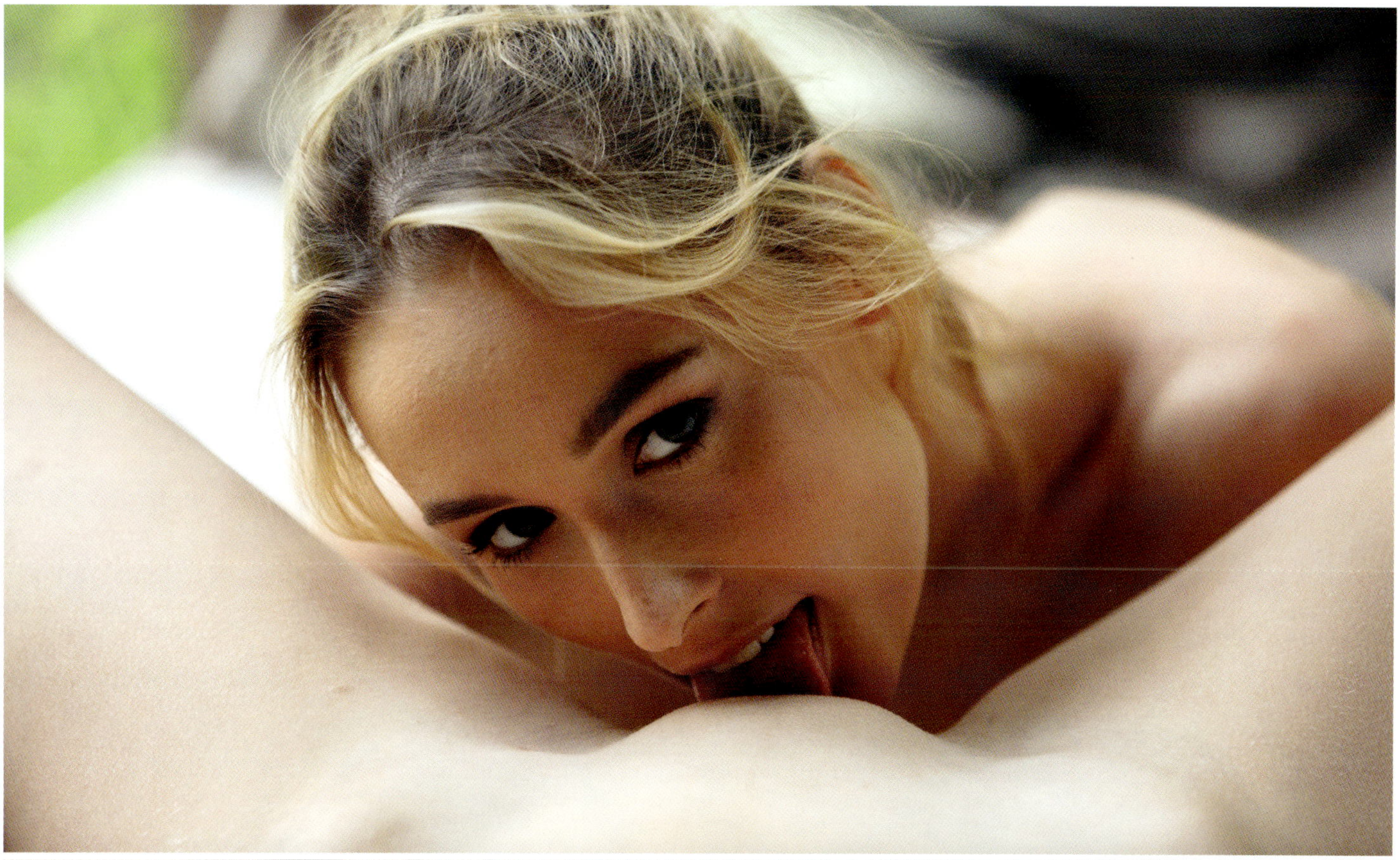

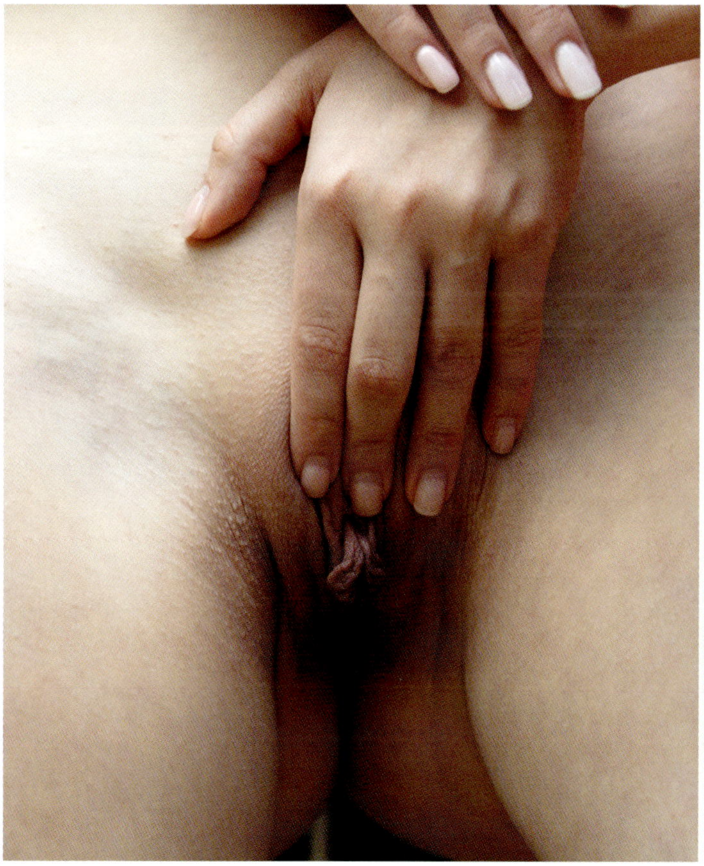

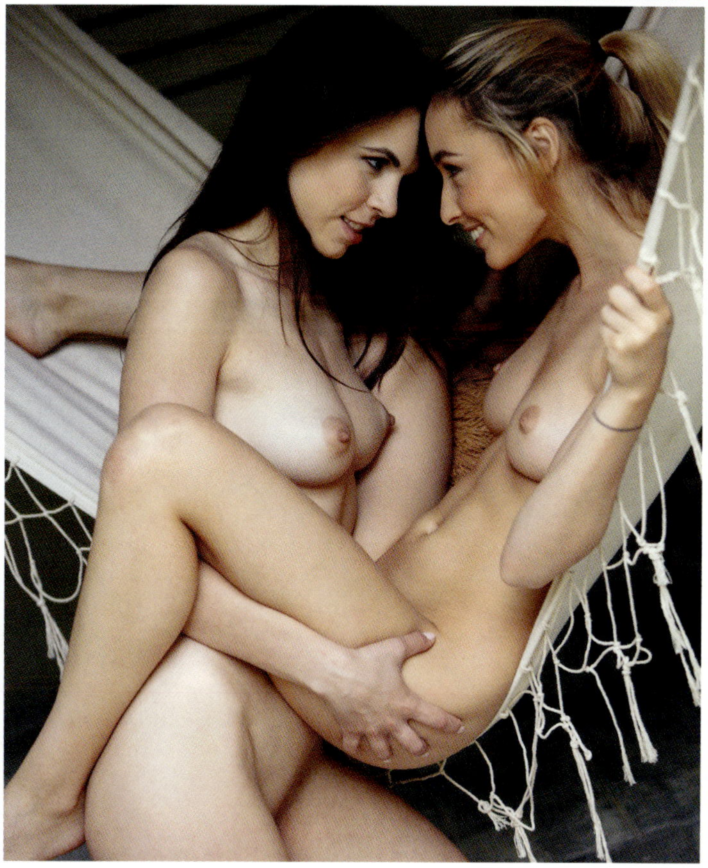

Kari A
Rosaline Rose

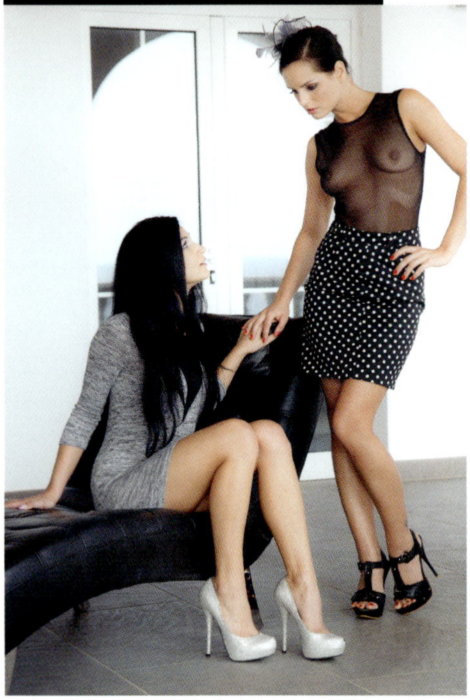

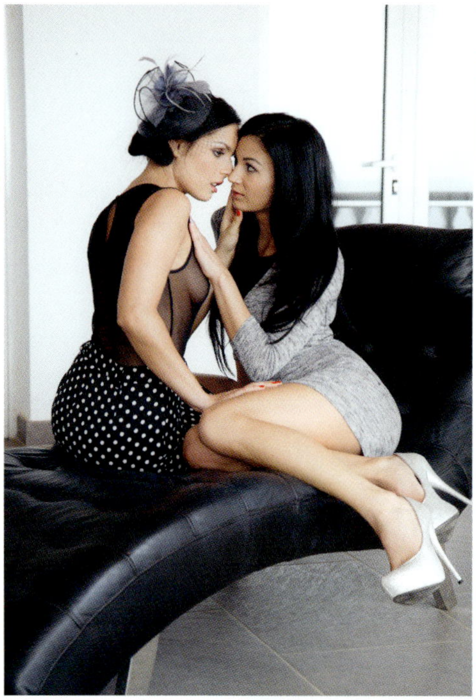

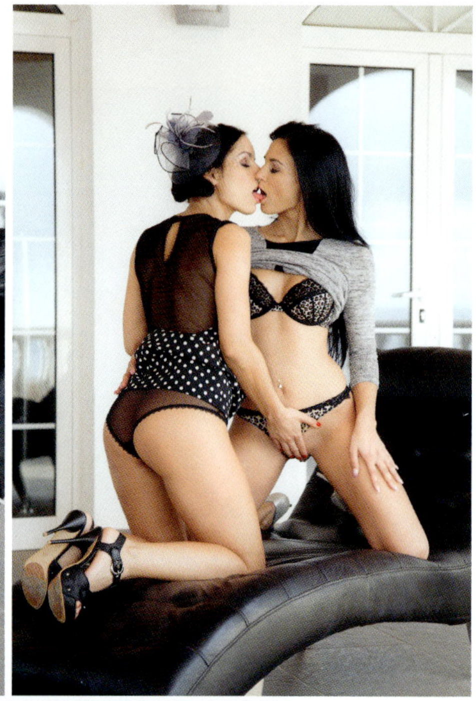

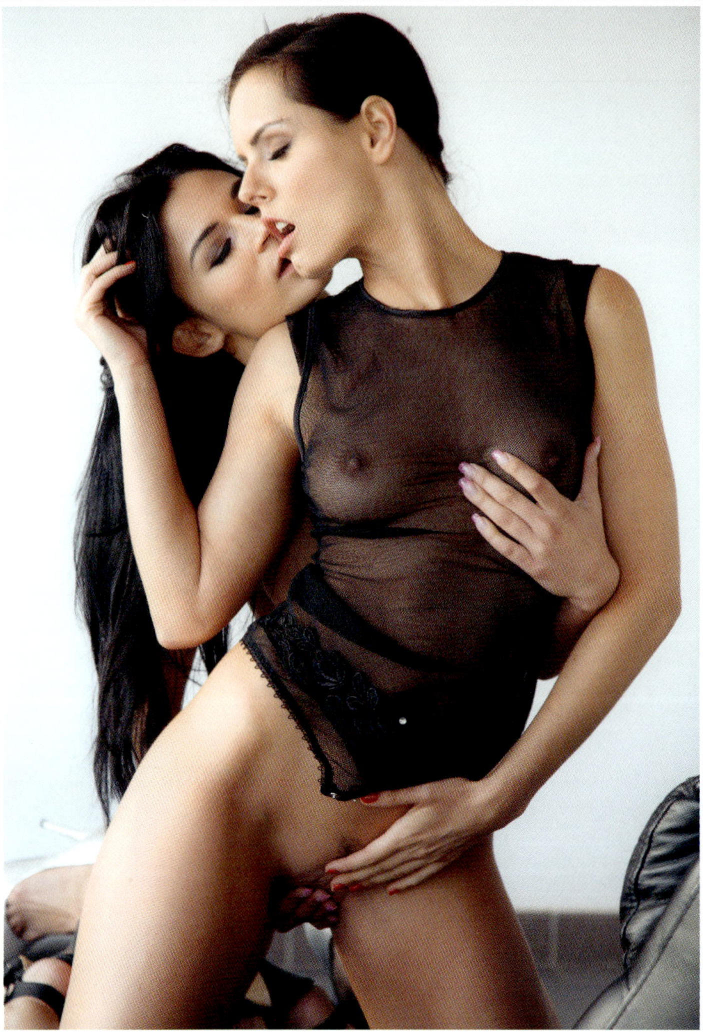

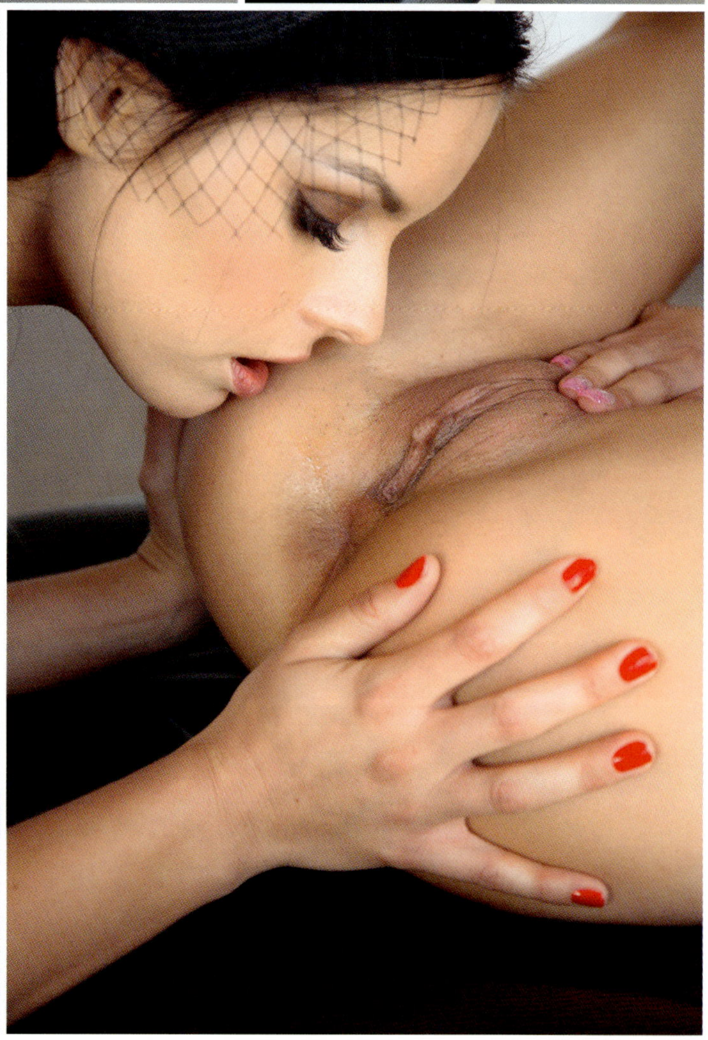

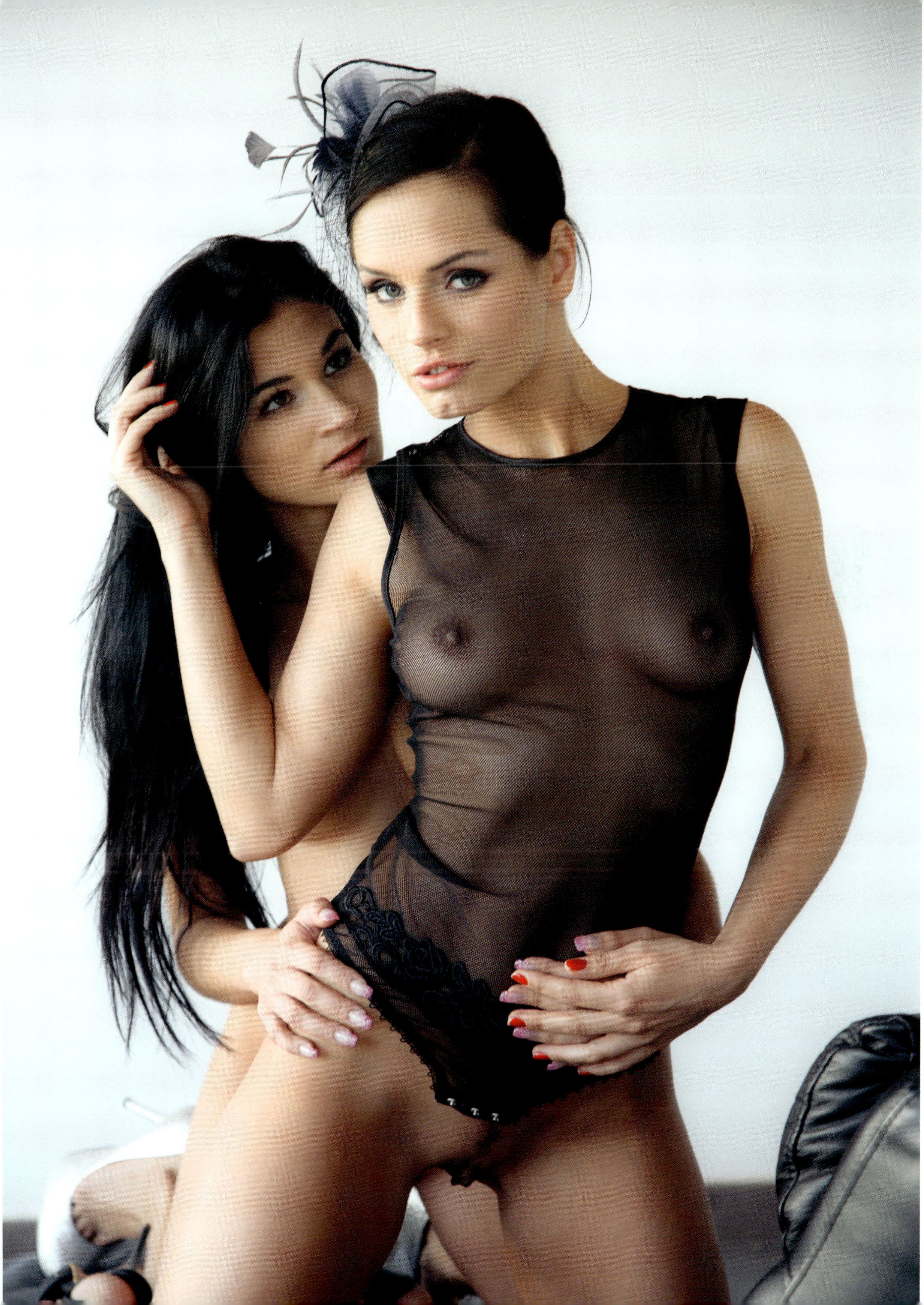

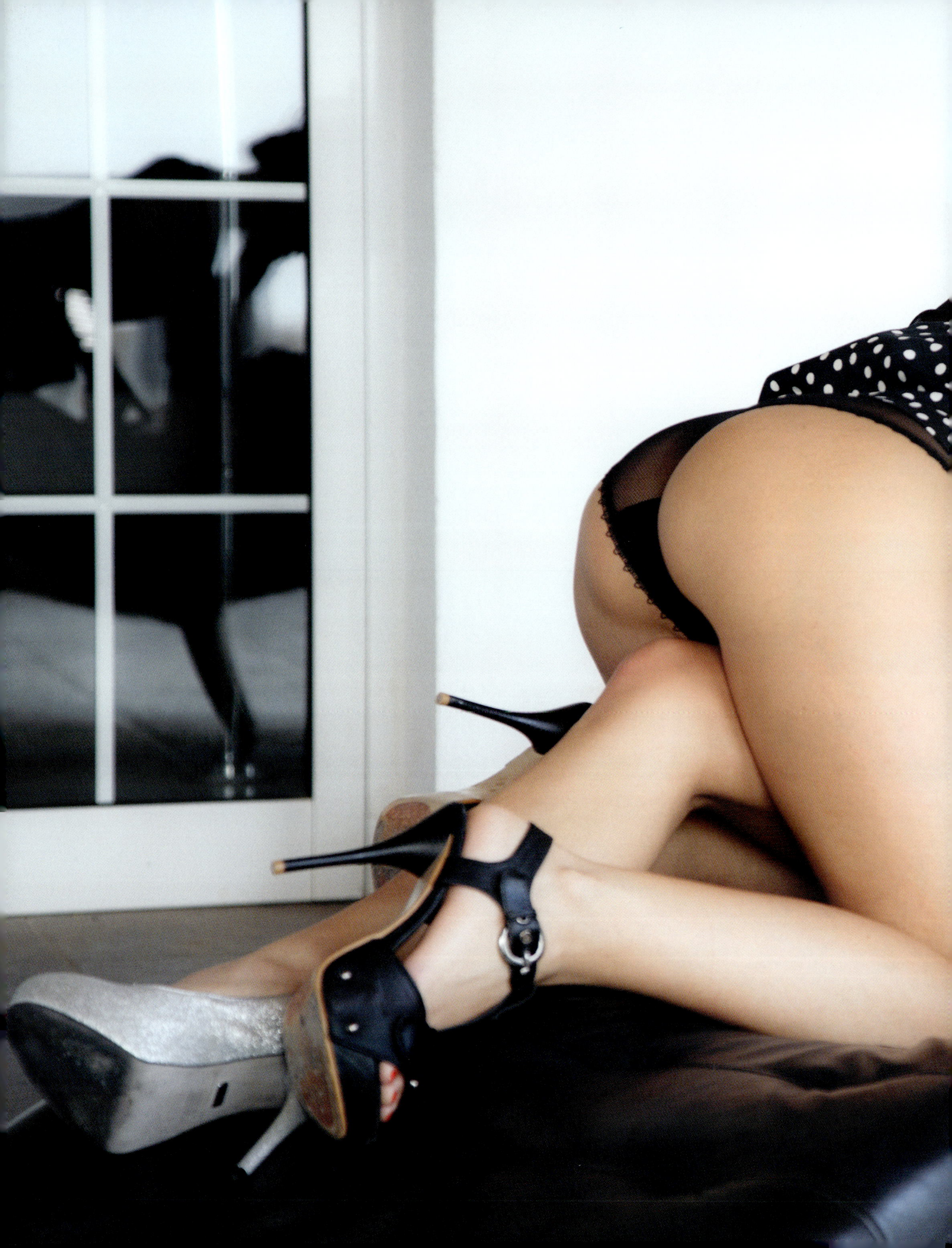

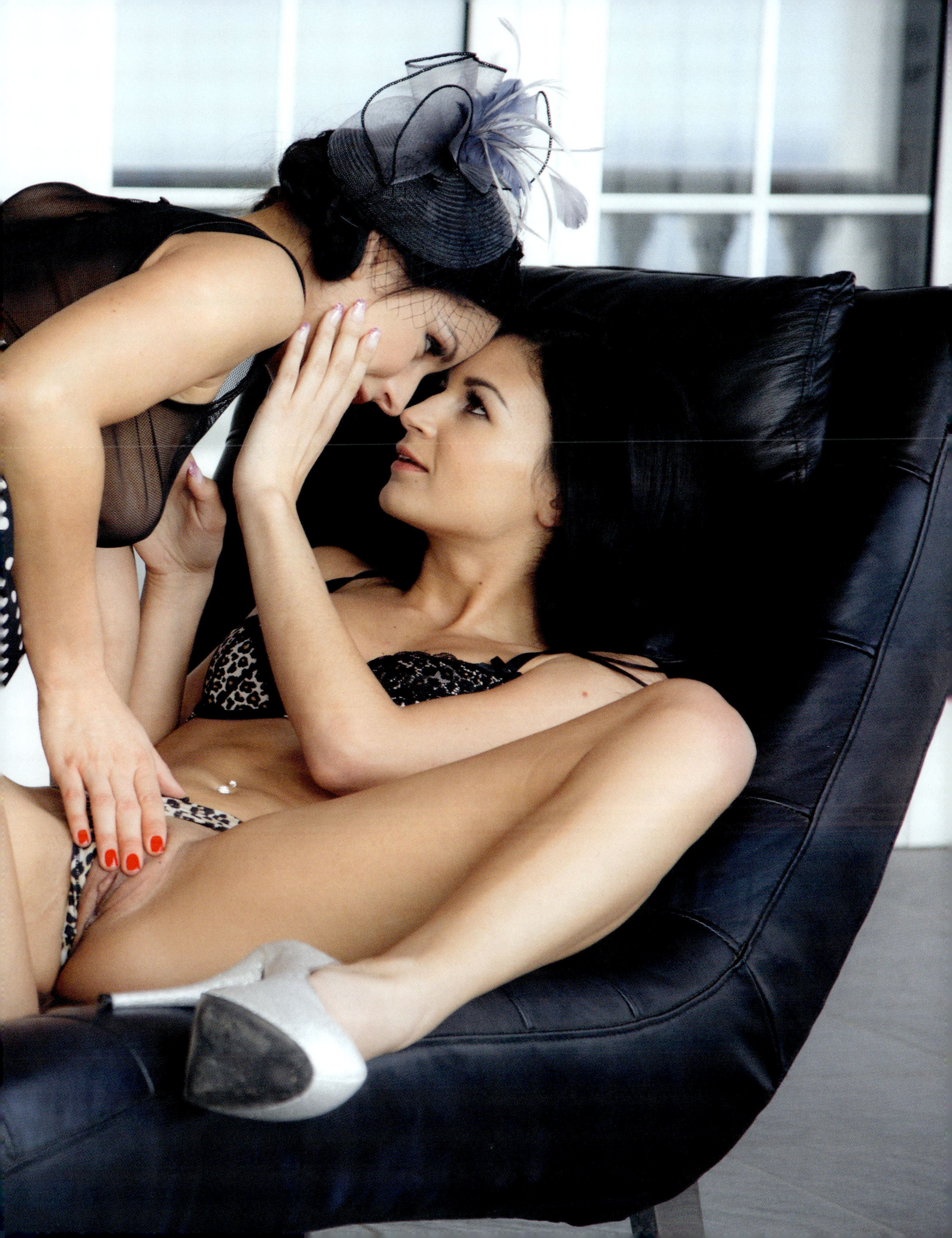

Jia Lissa

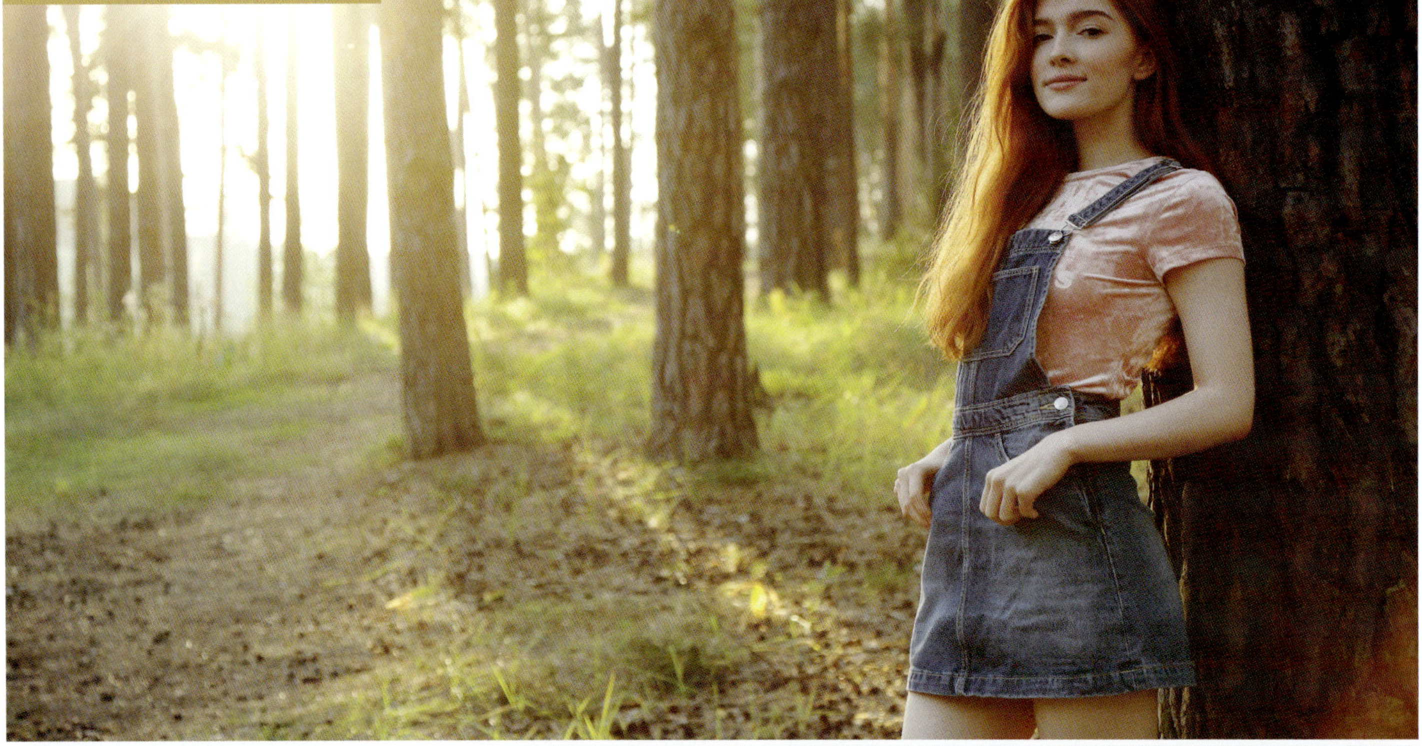

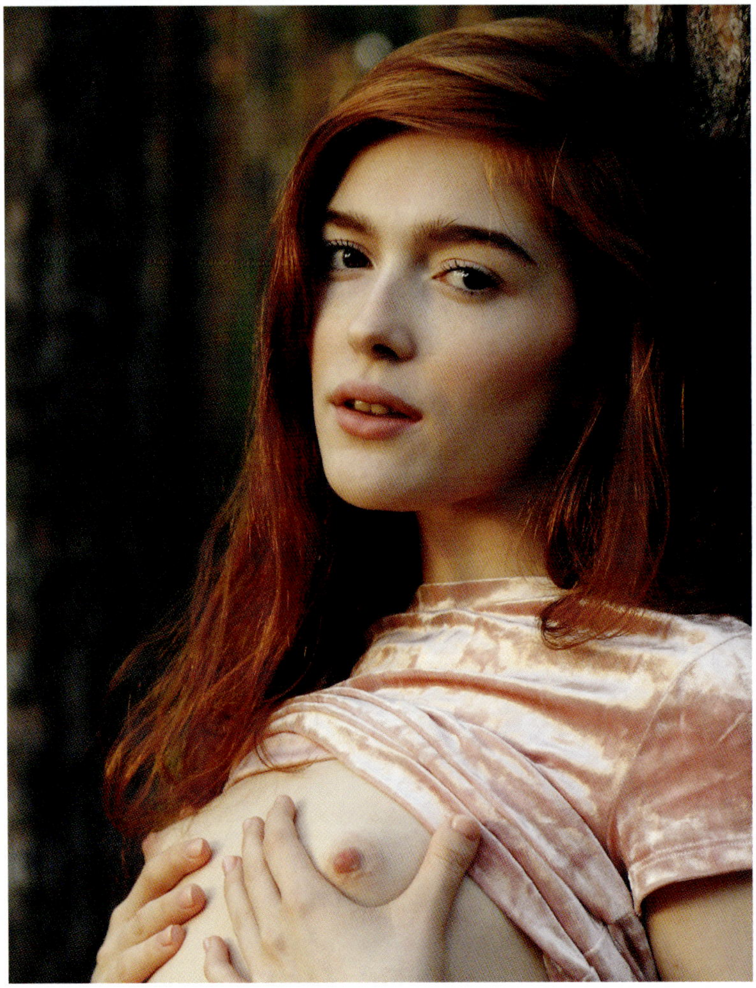

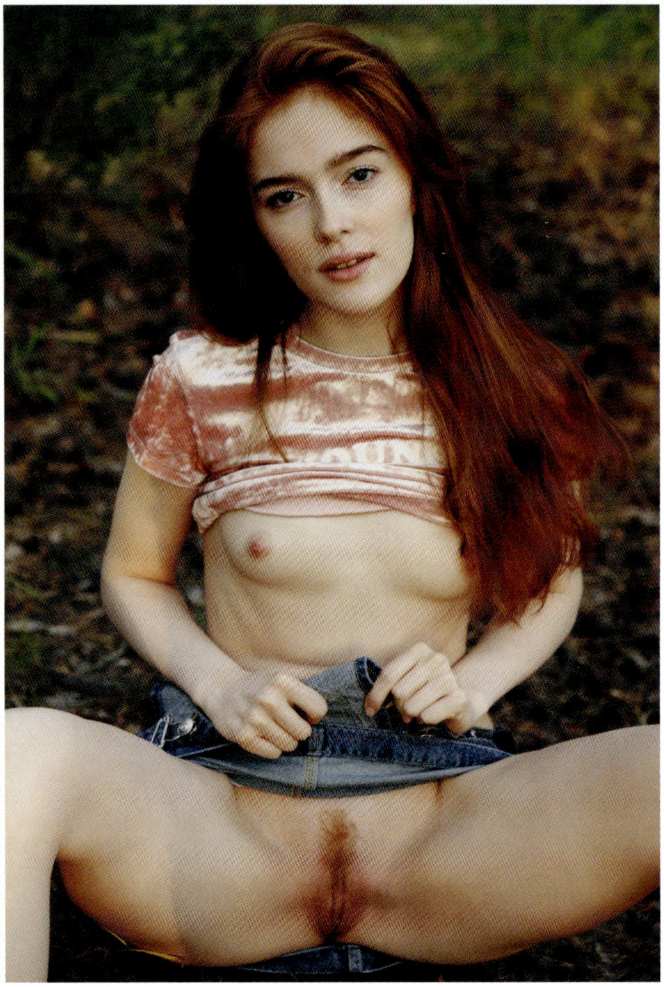

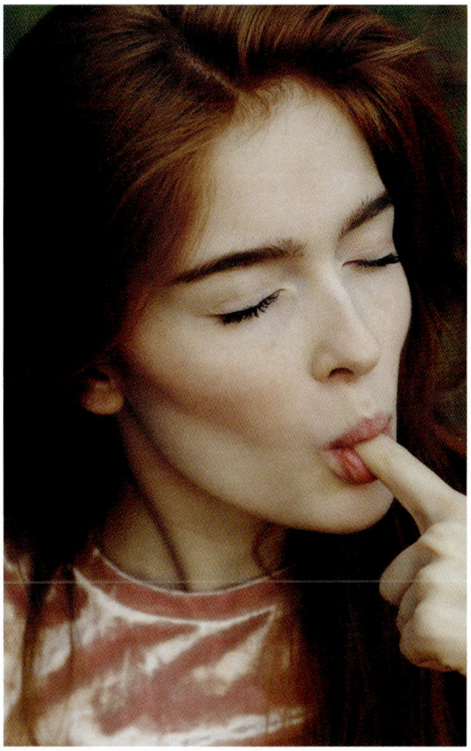

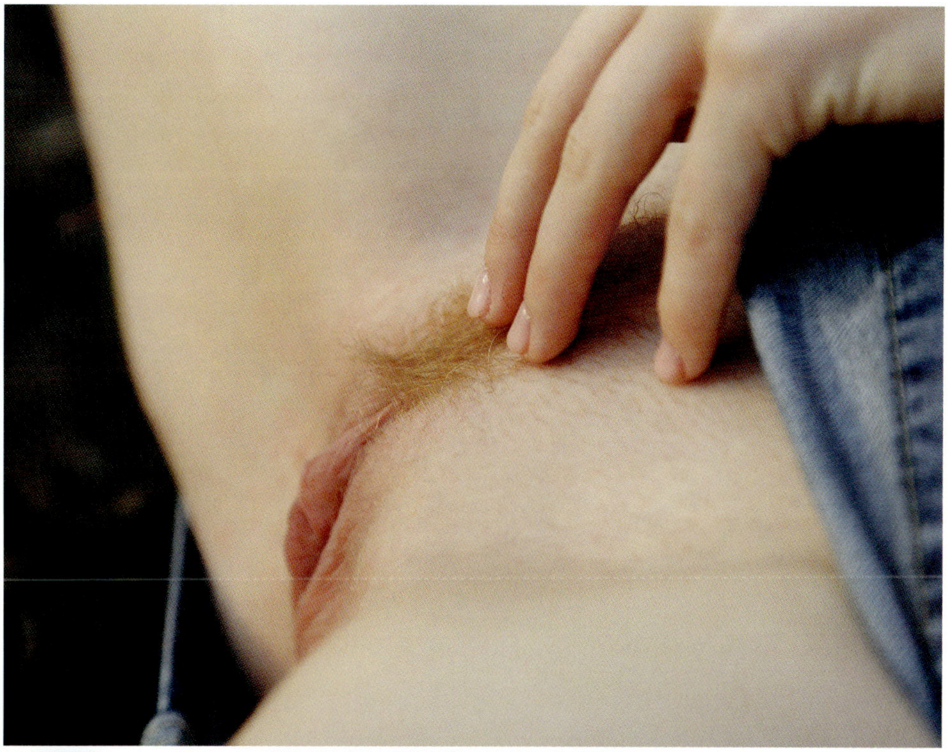

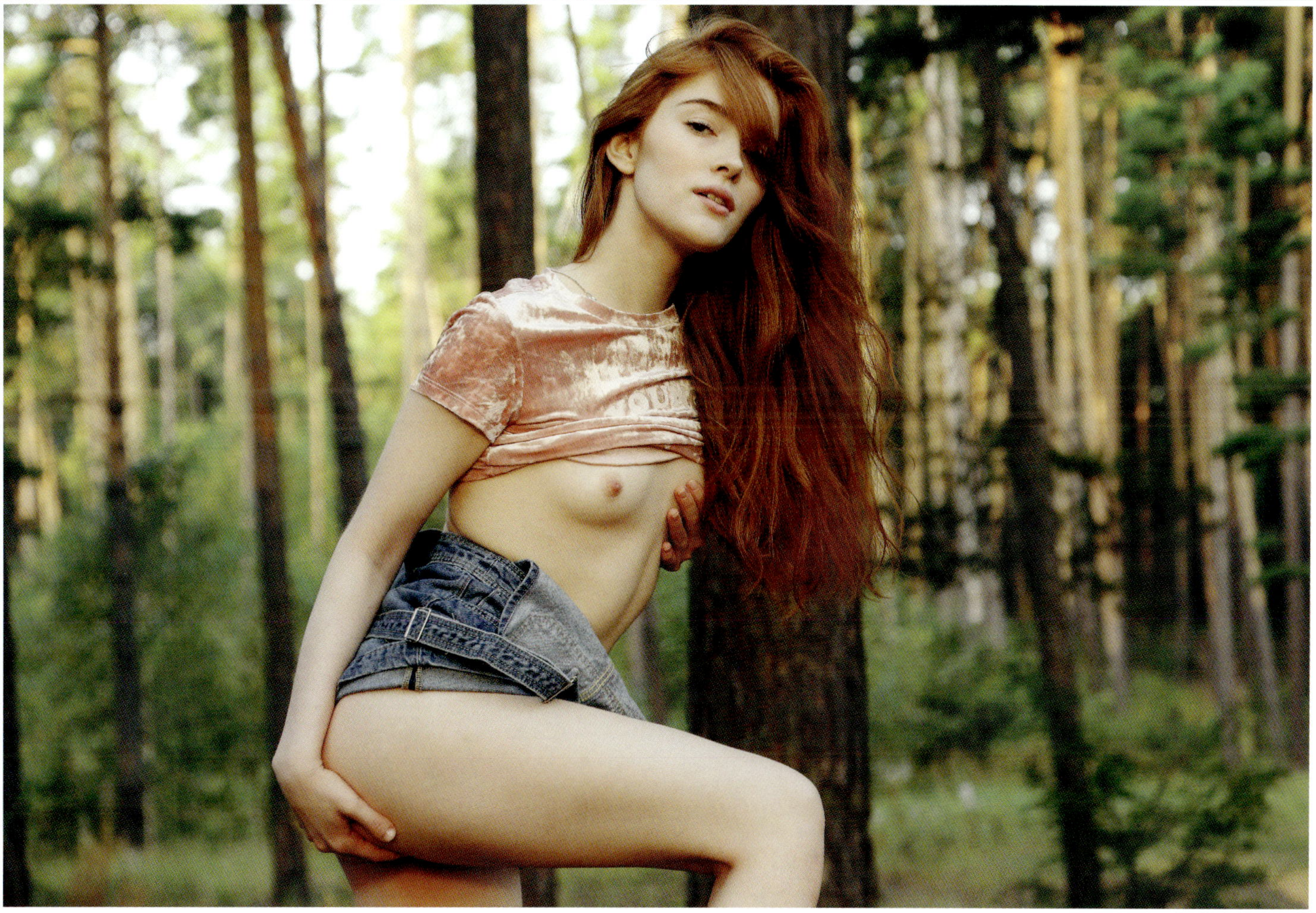

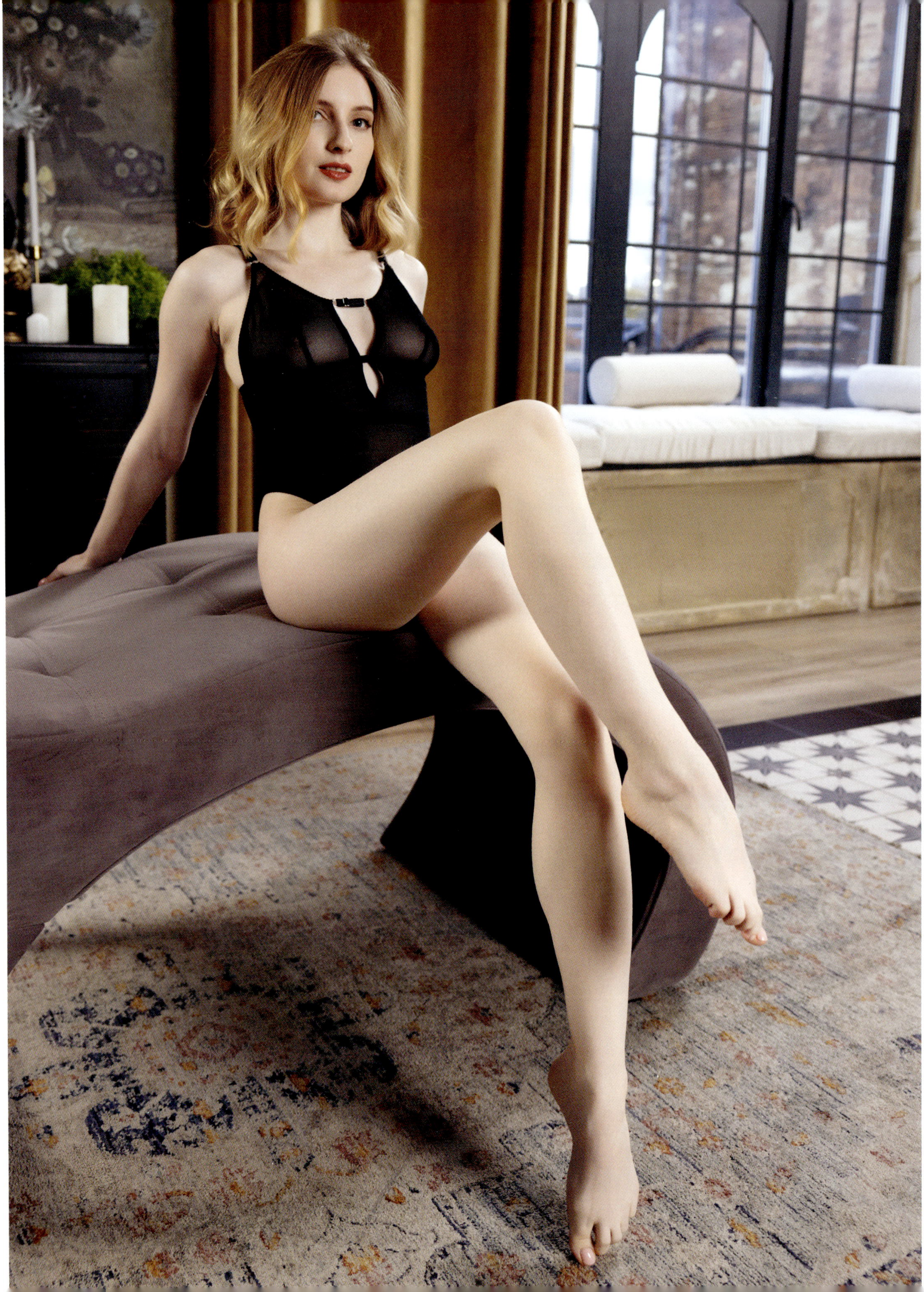

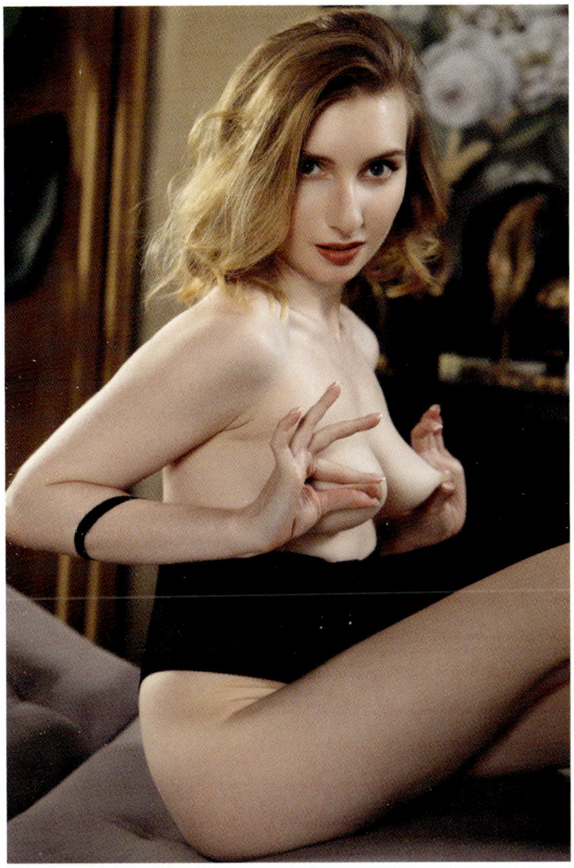

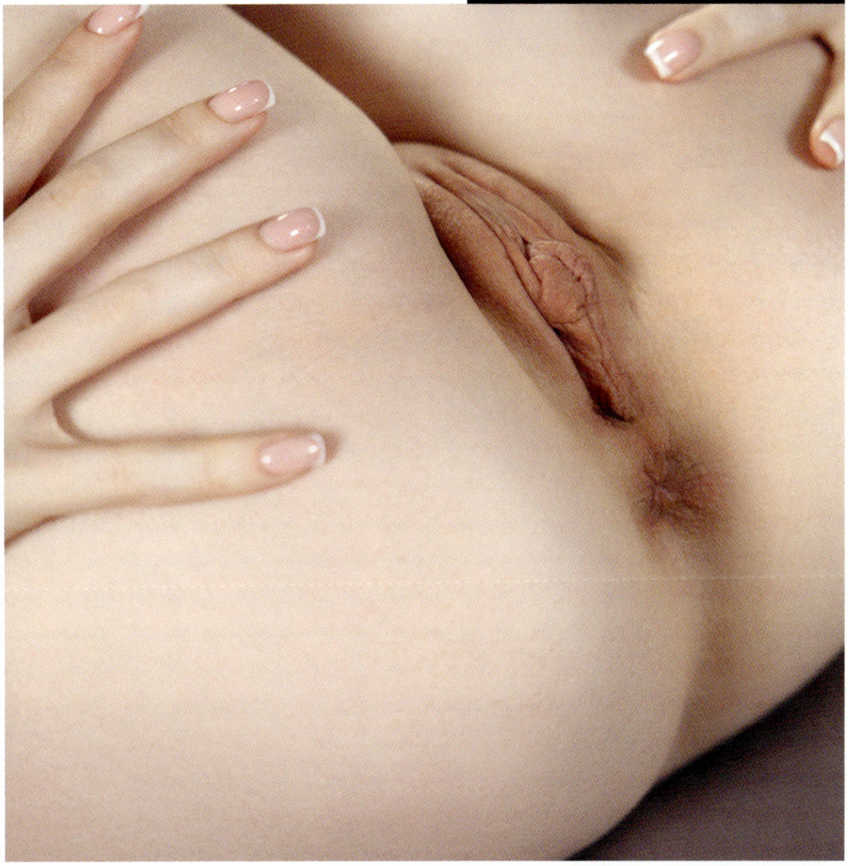

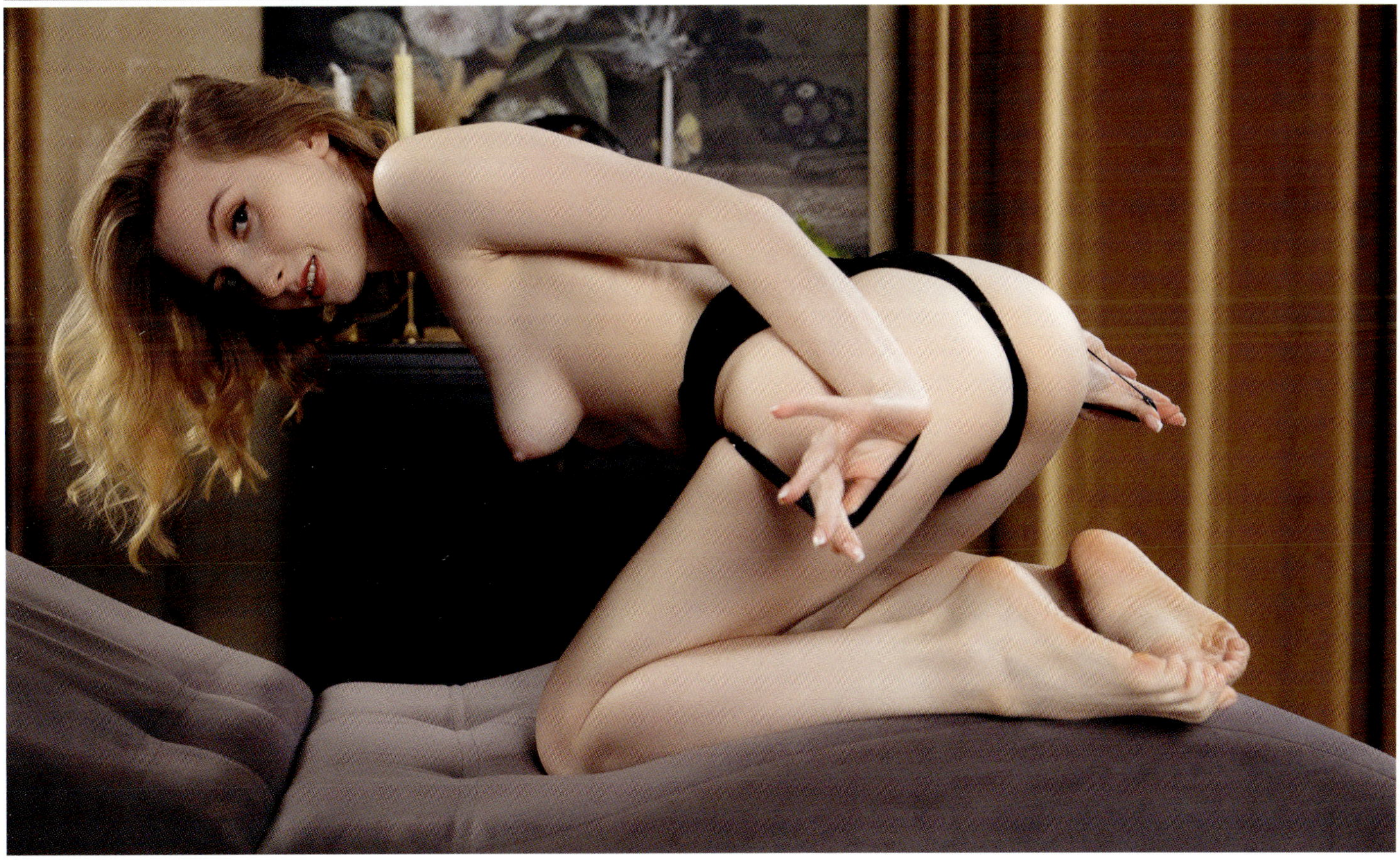

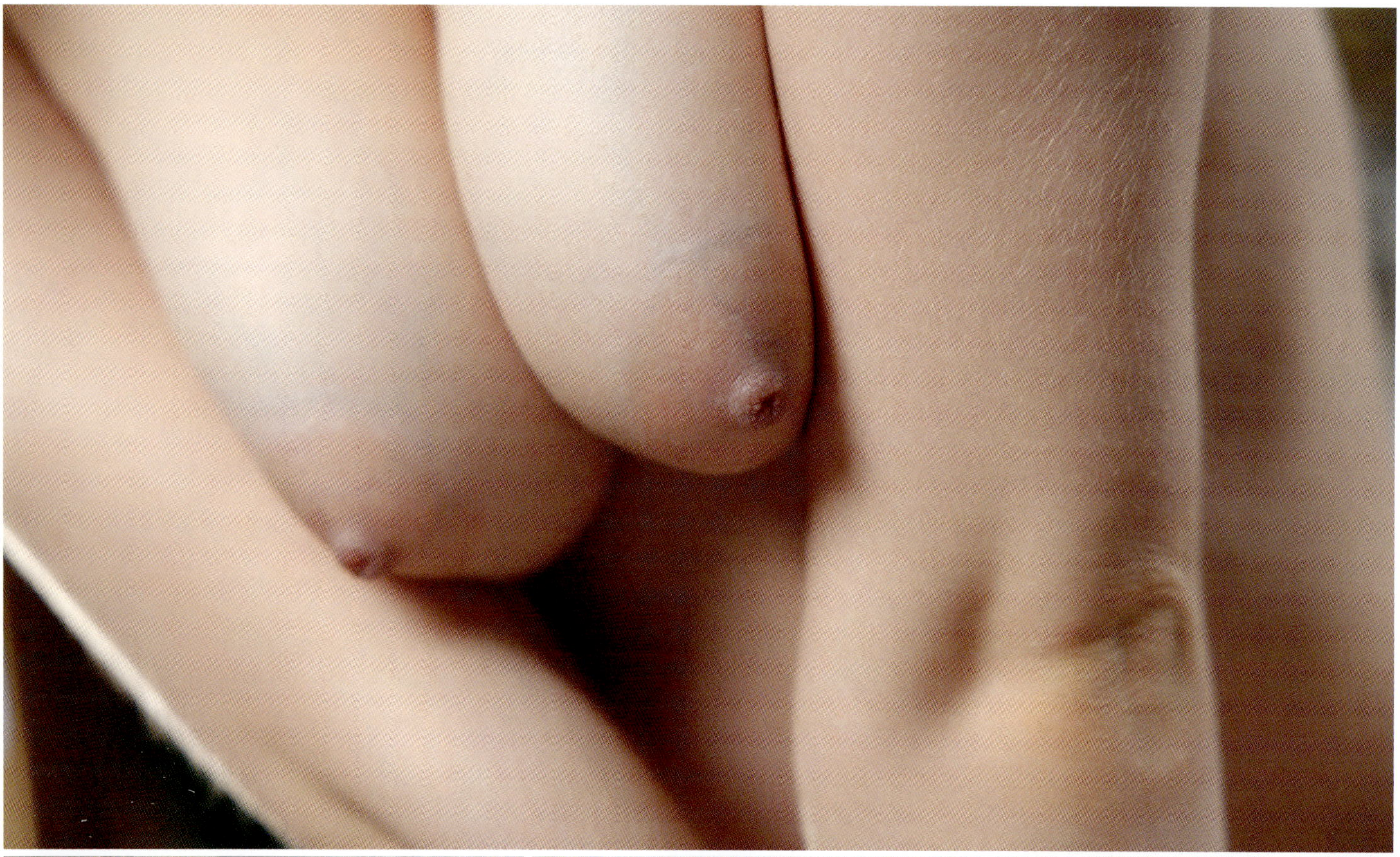

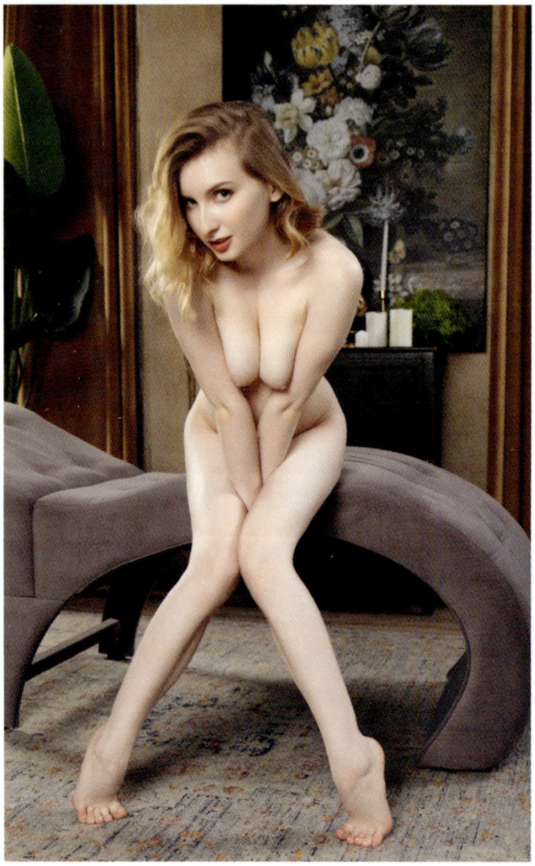

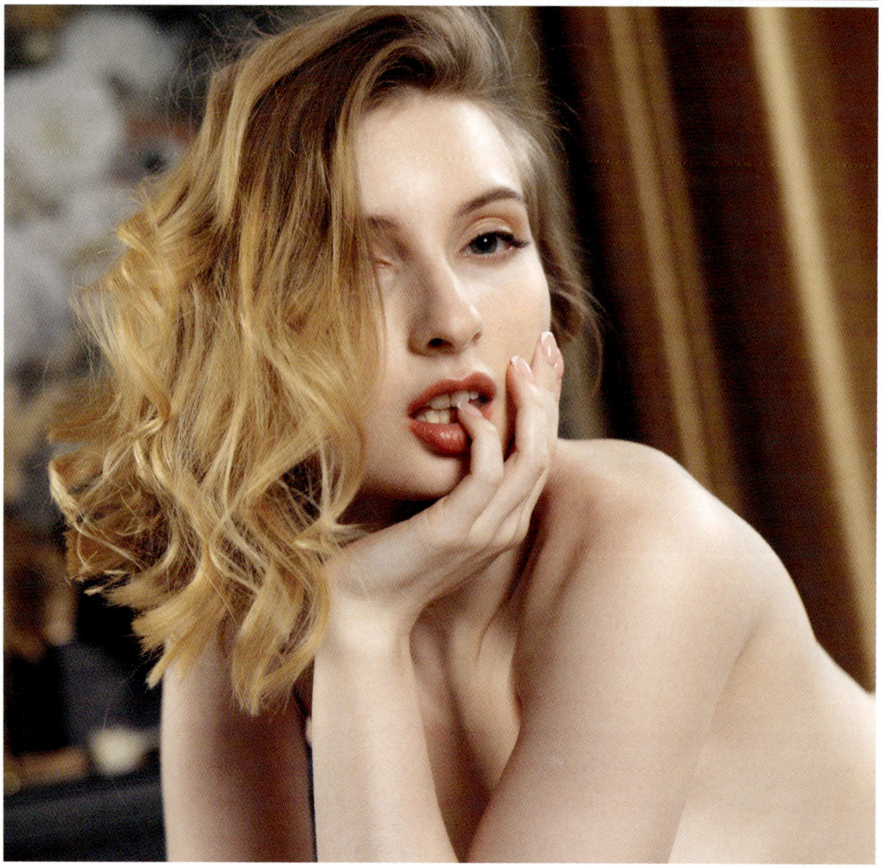

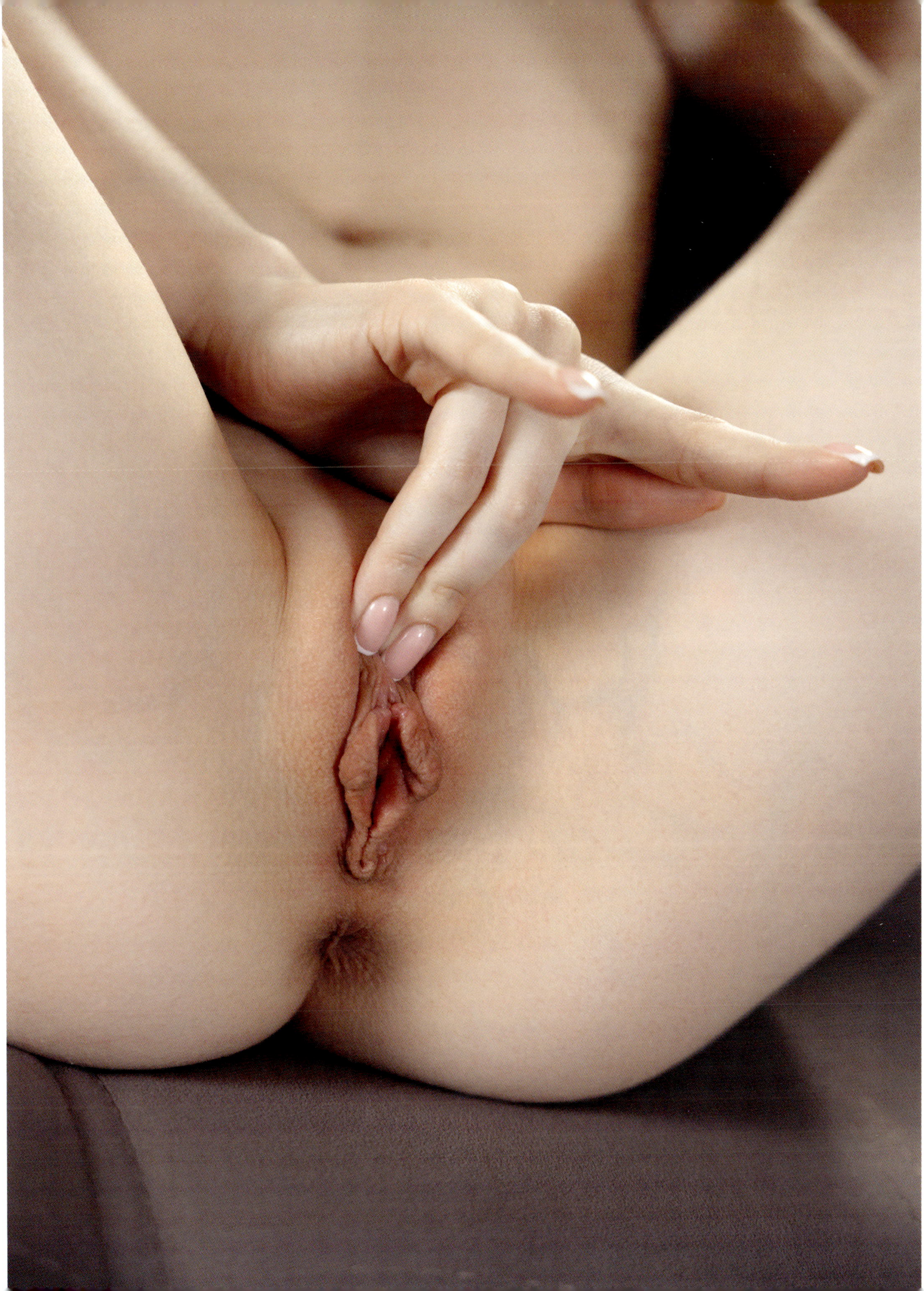

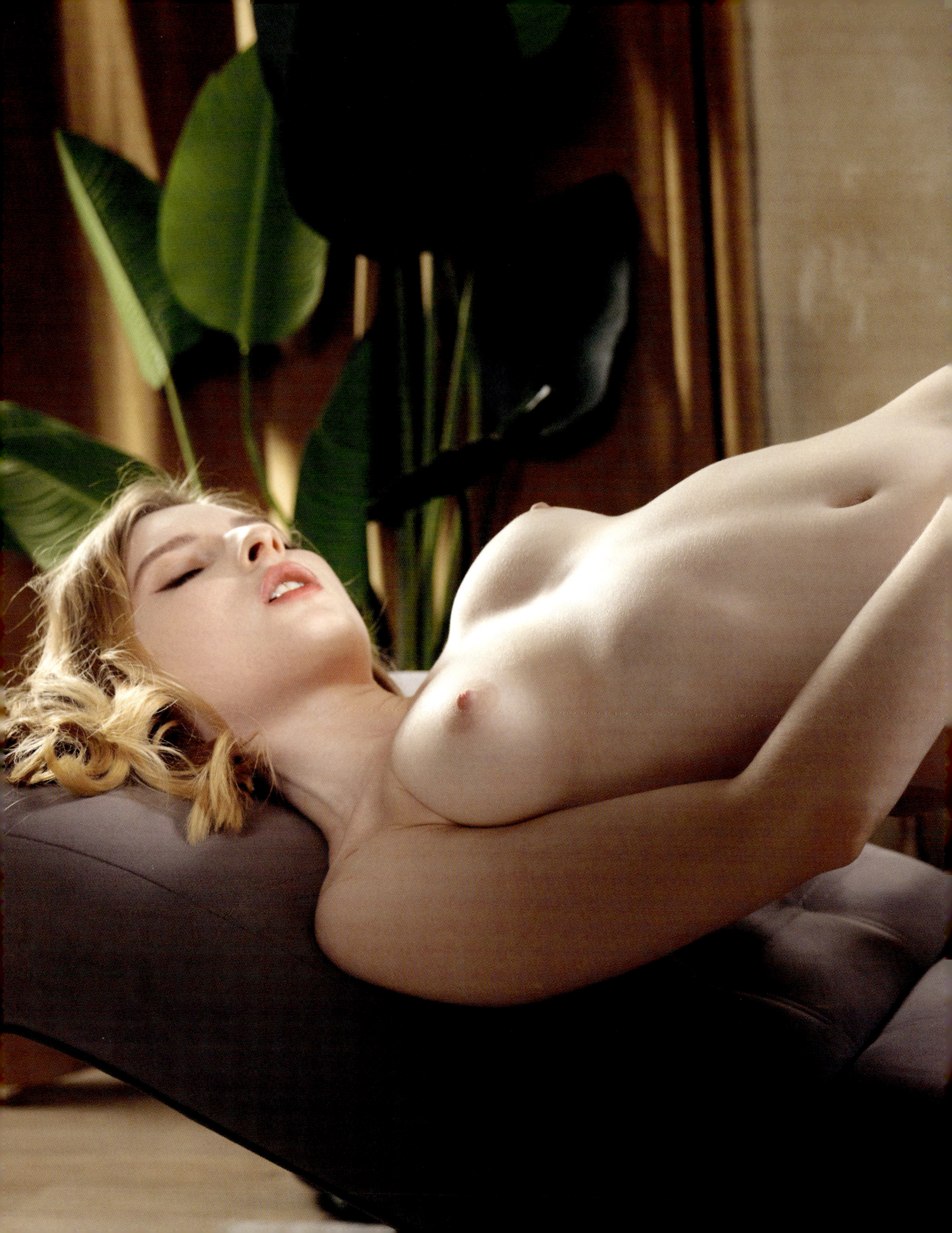

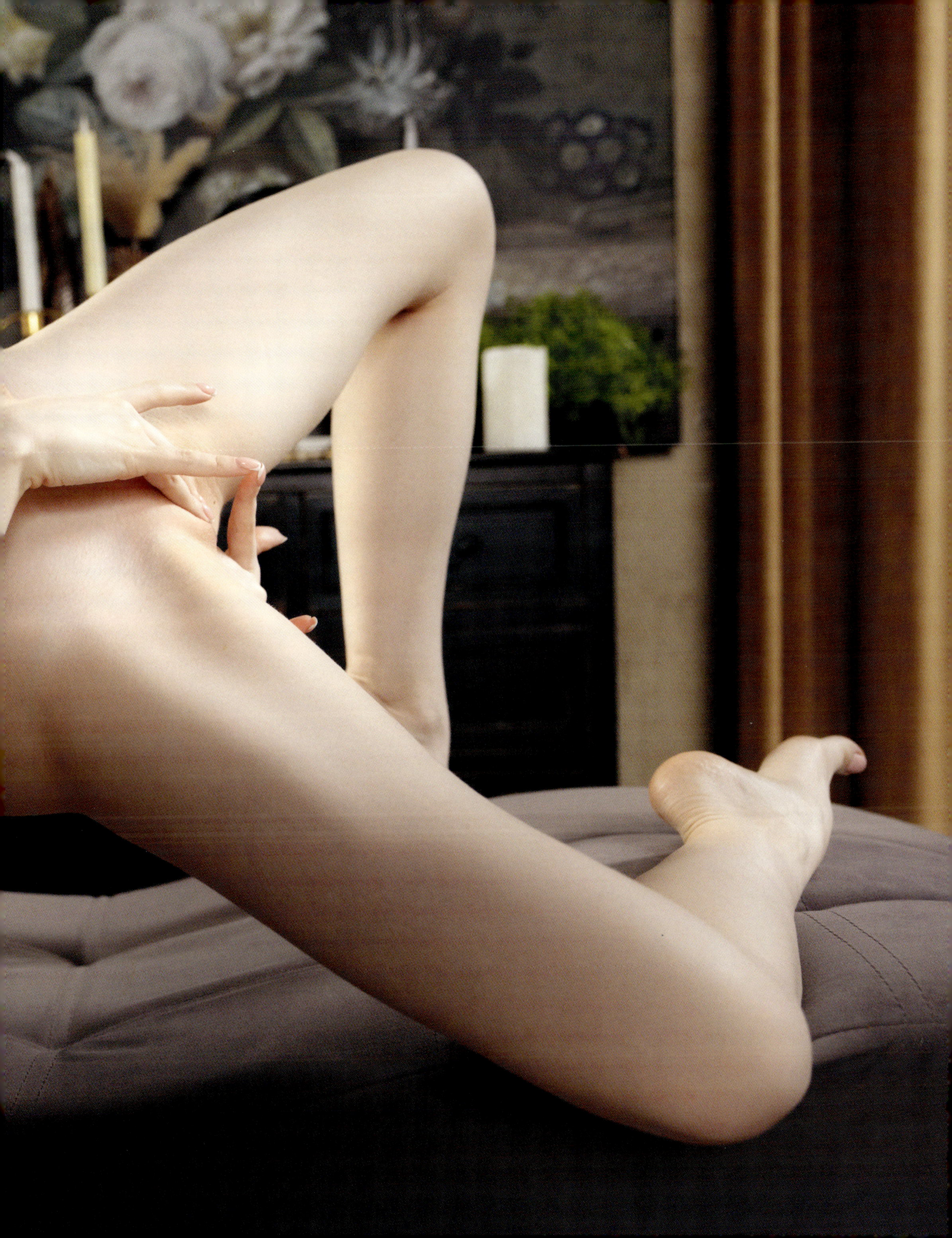

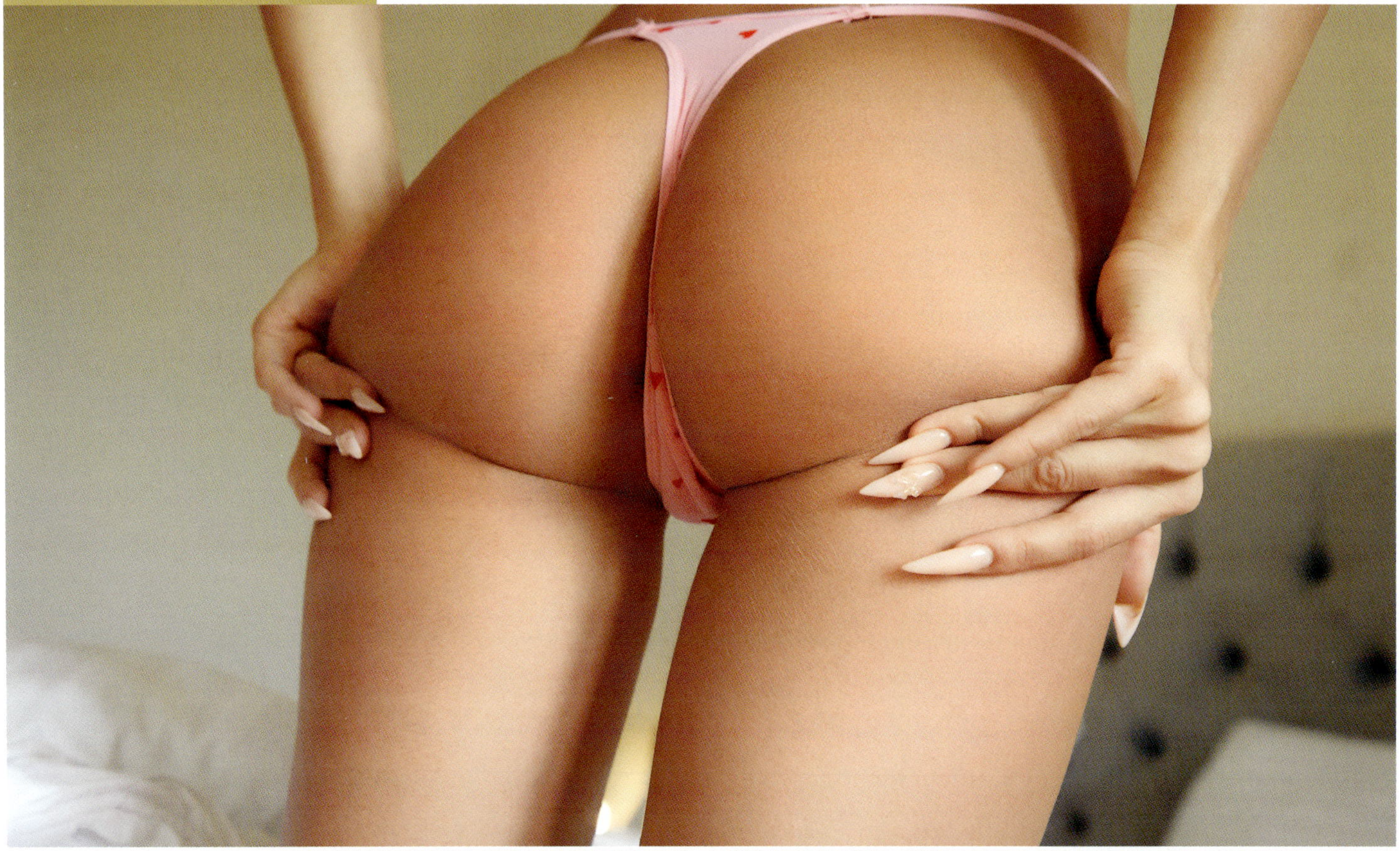

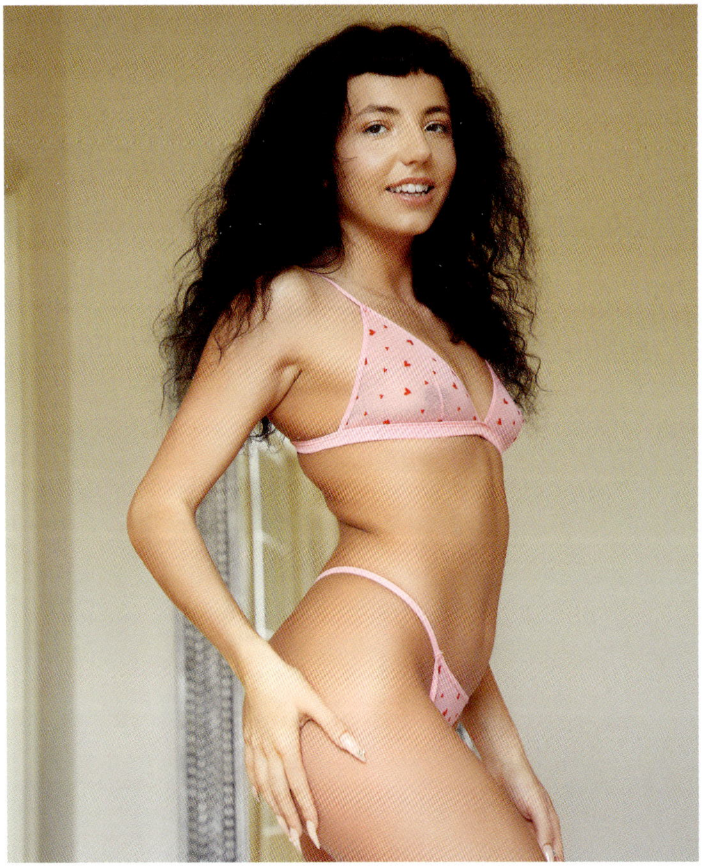

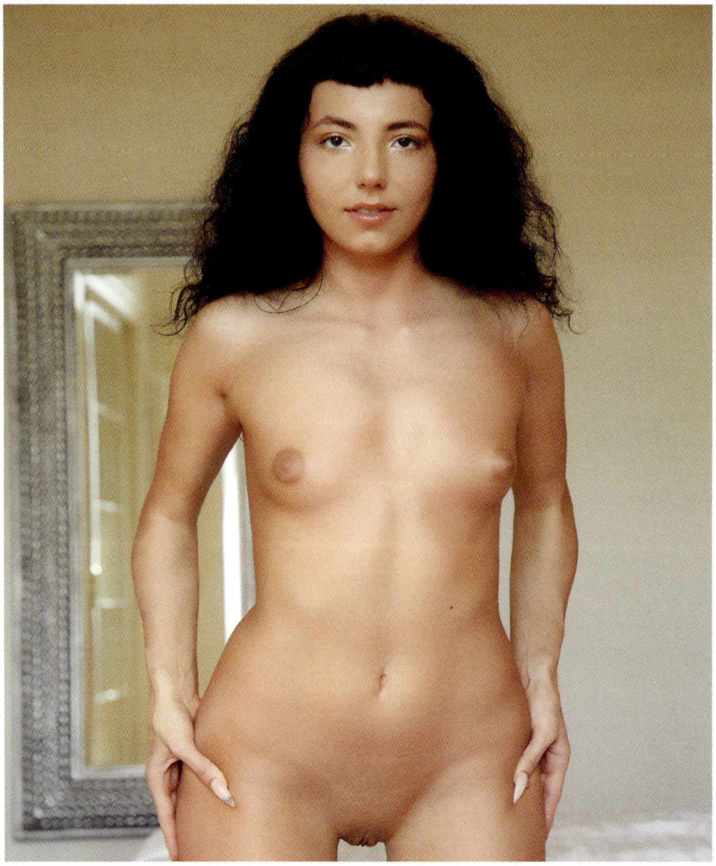

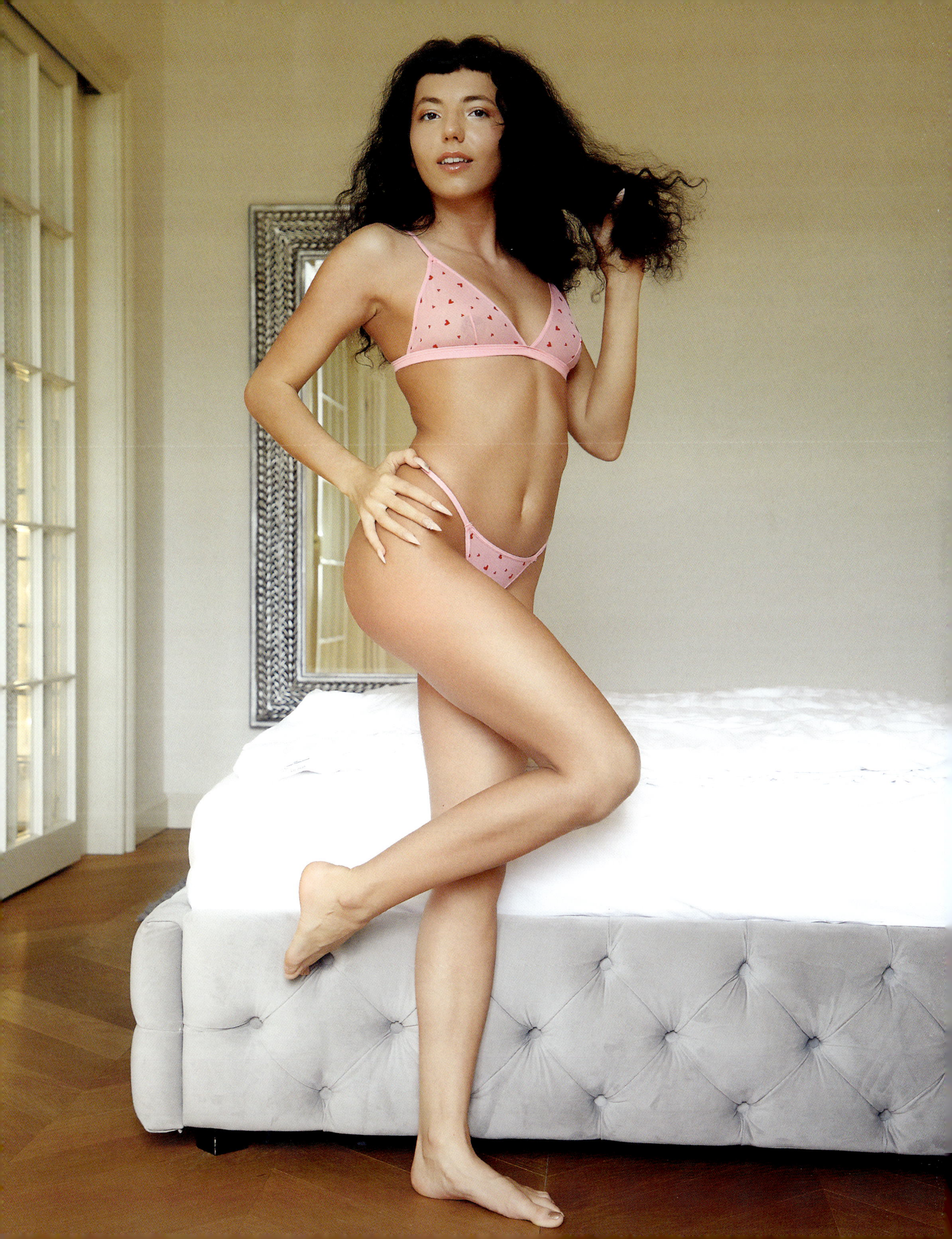

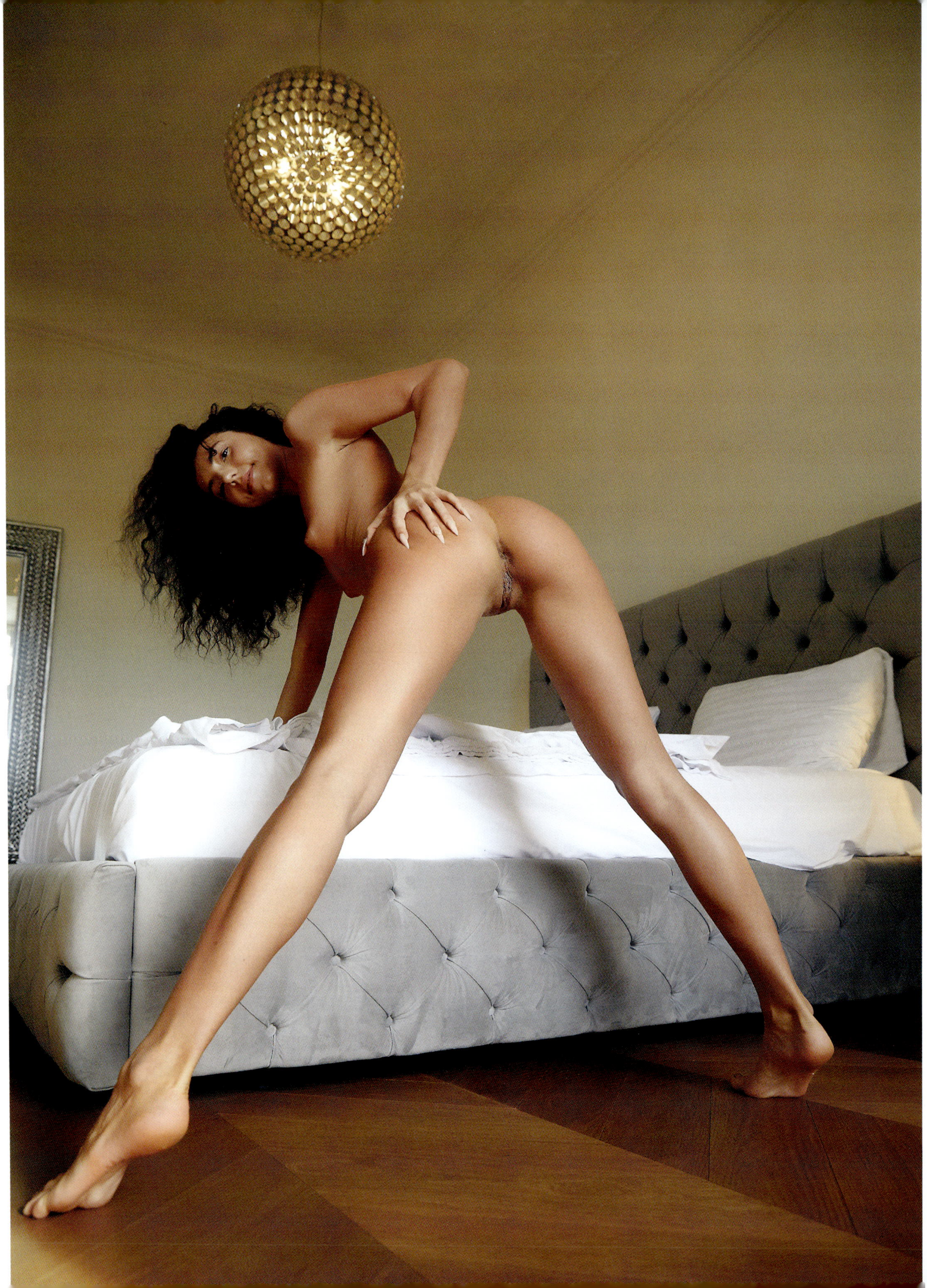

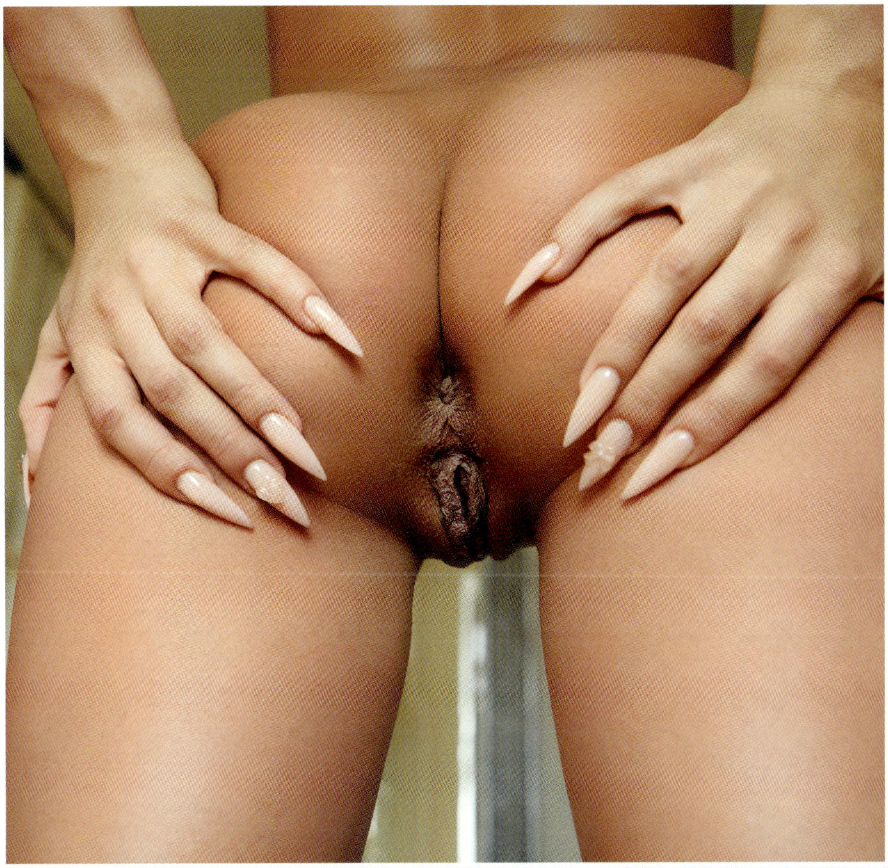
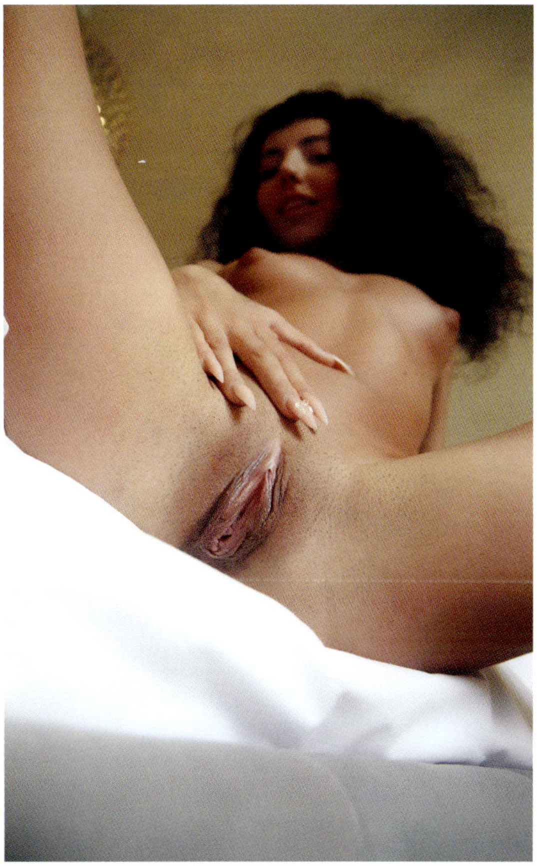
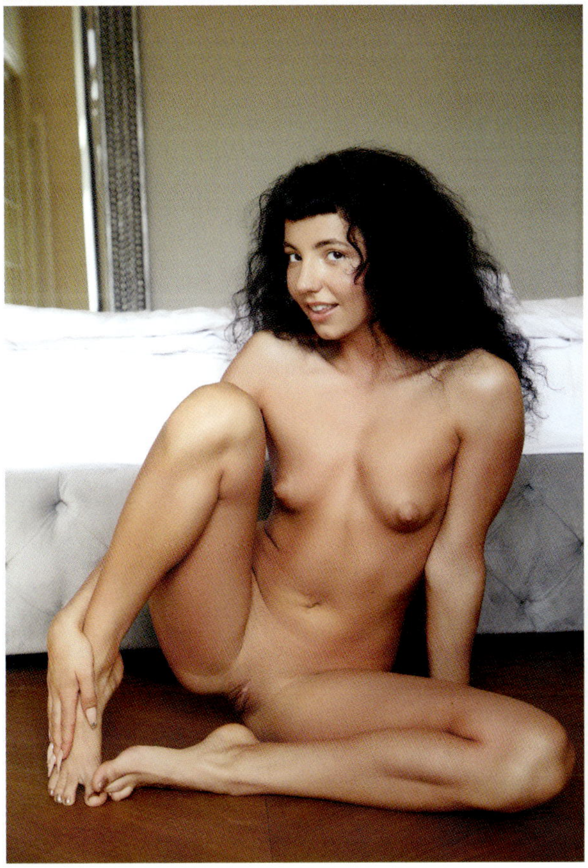
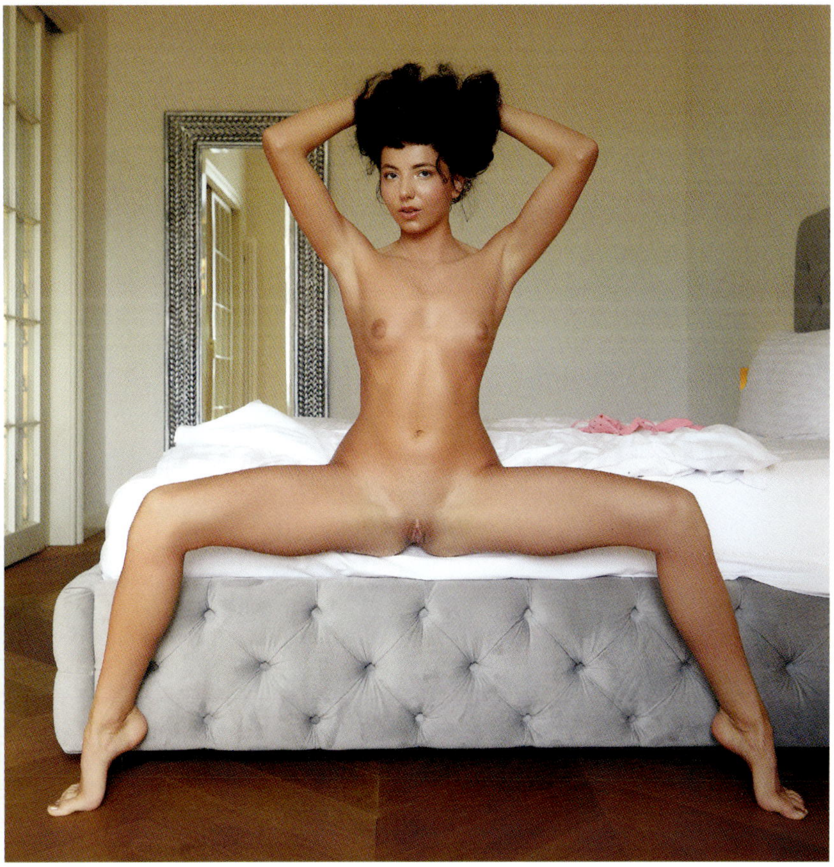

Nikita Bellucci
Sweet Cat

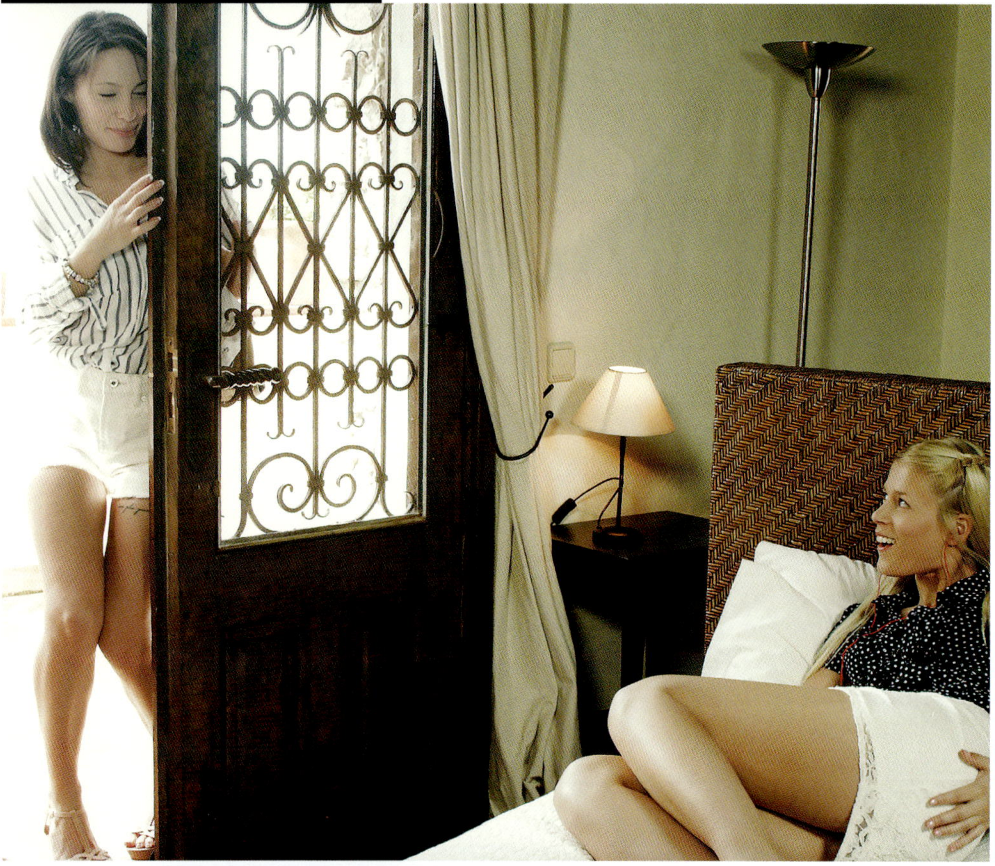

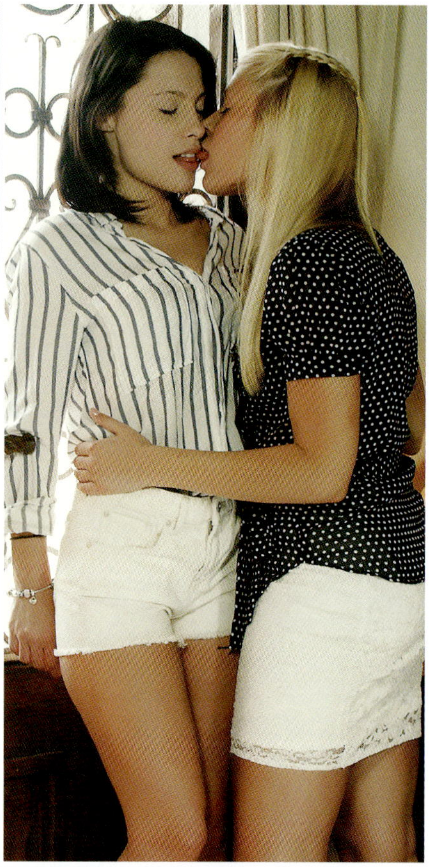

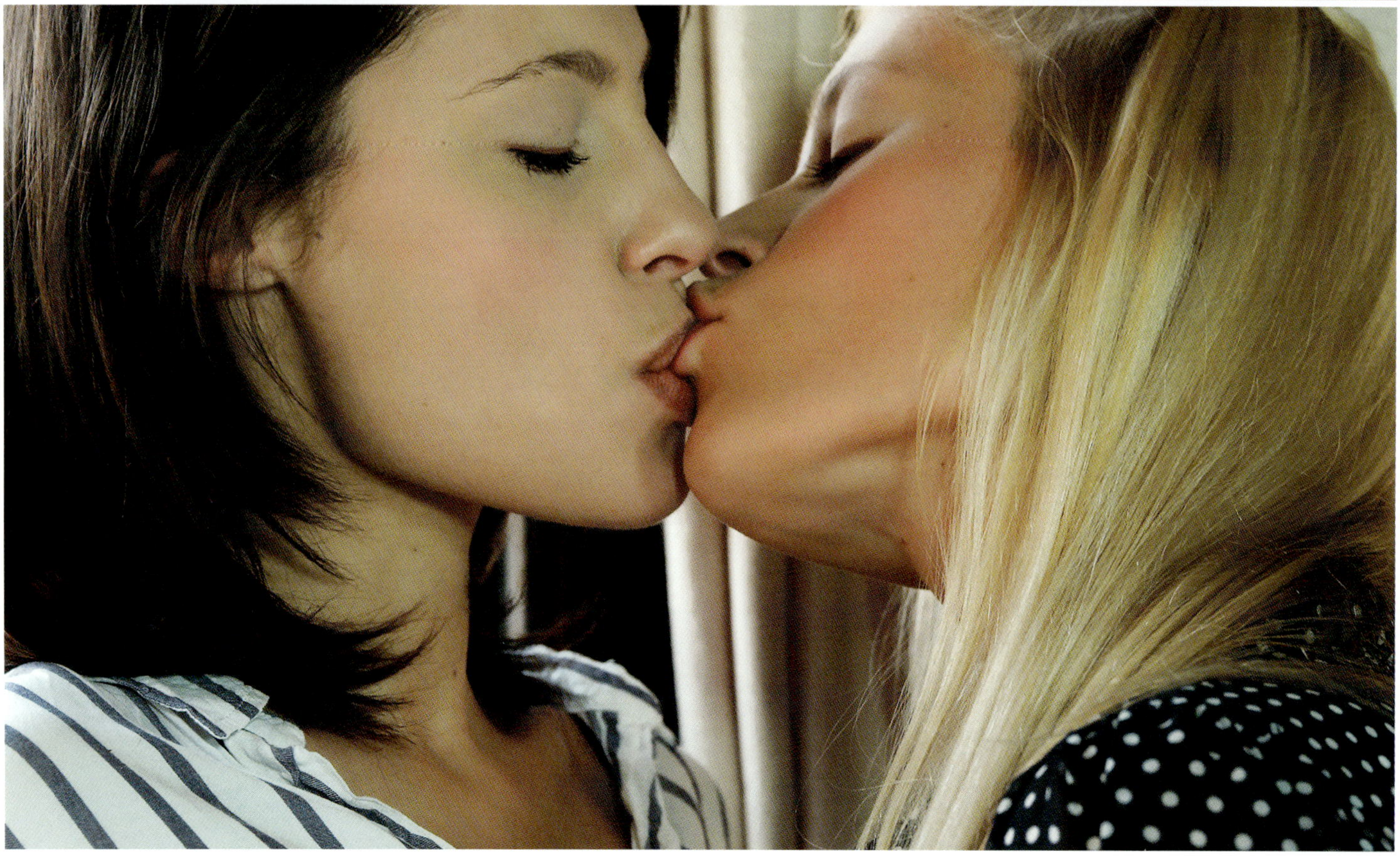

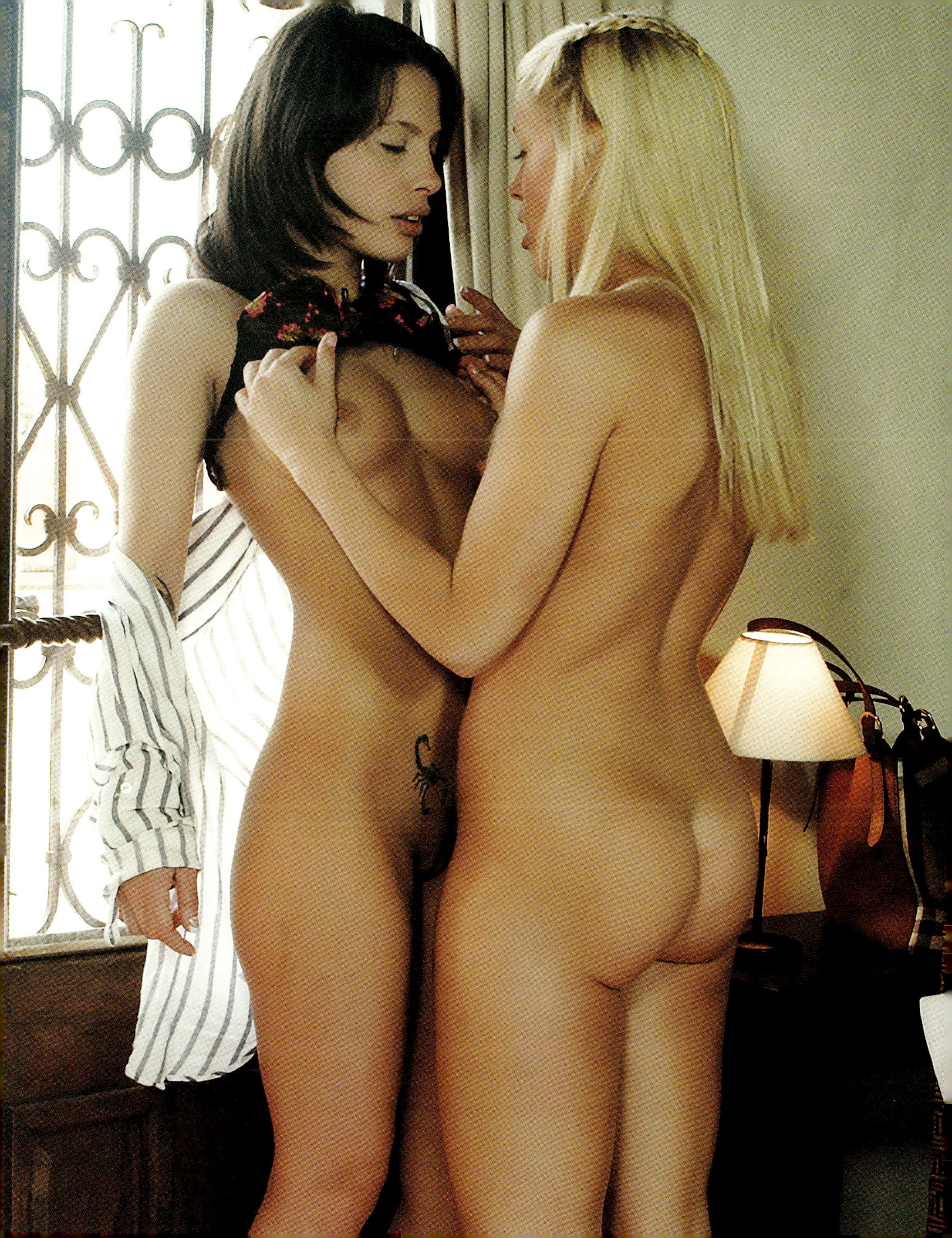

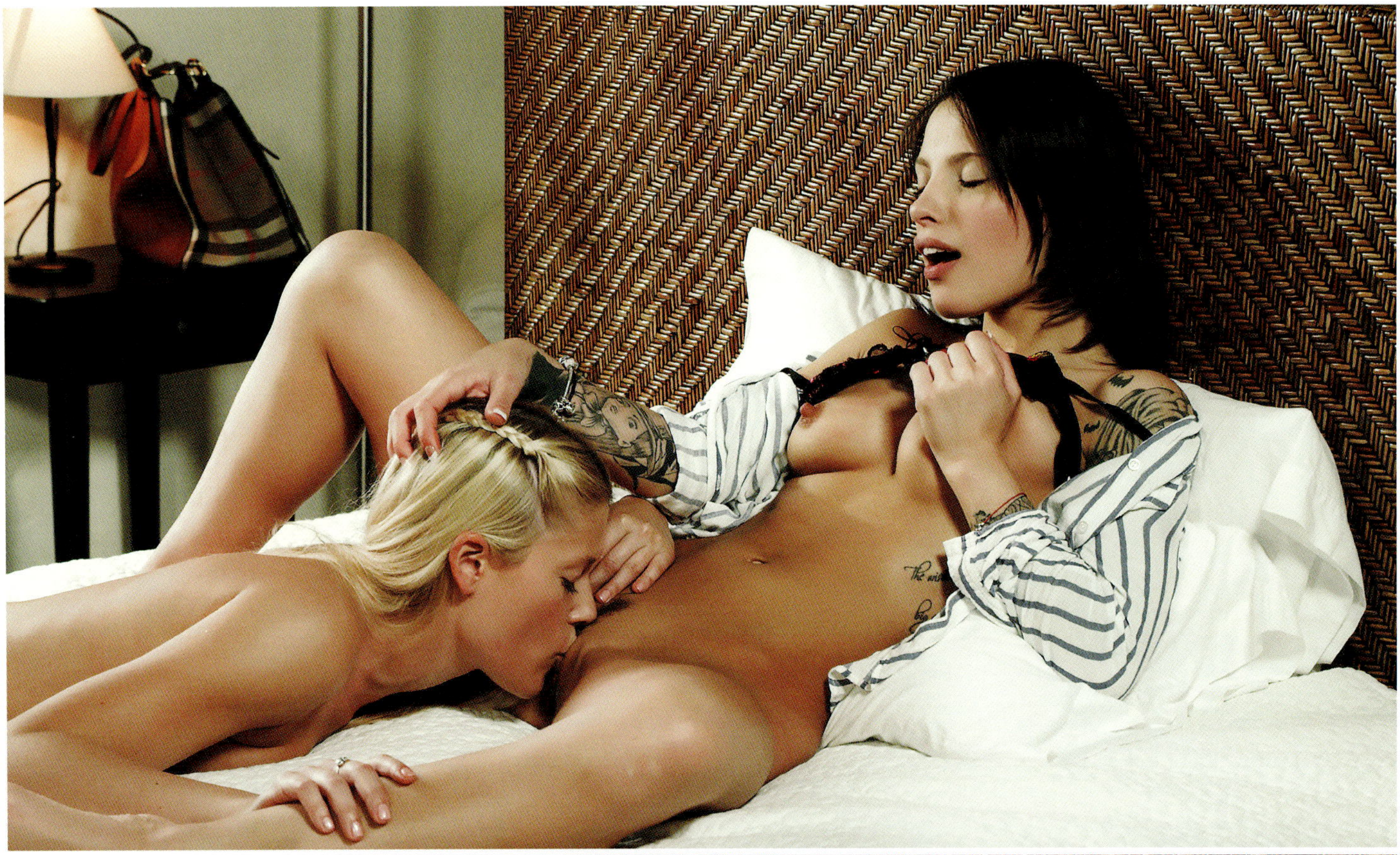

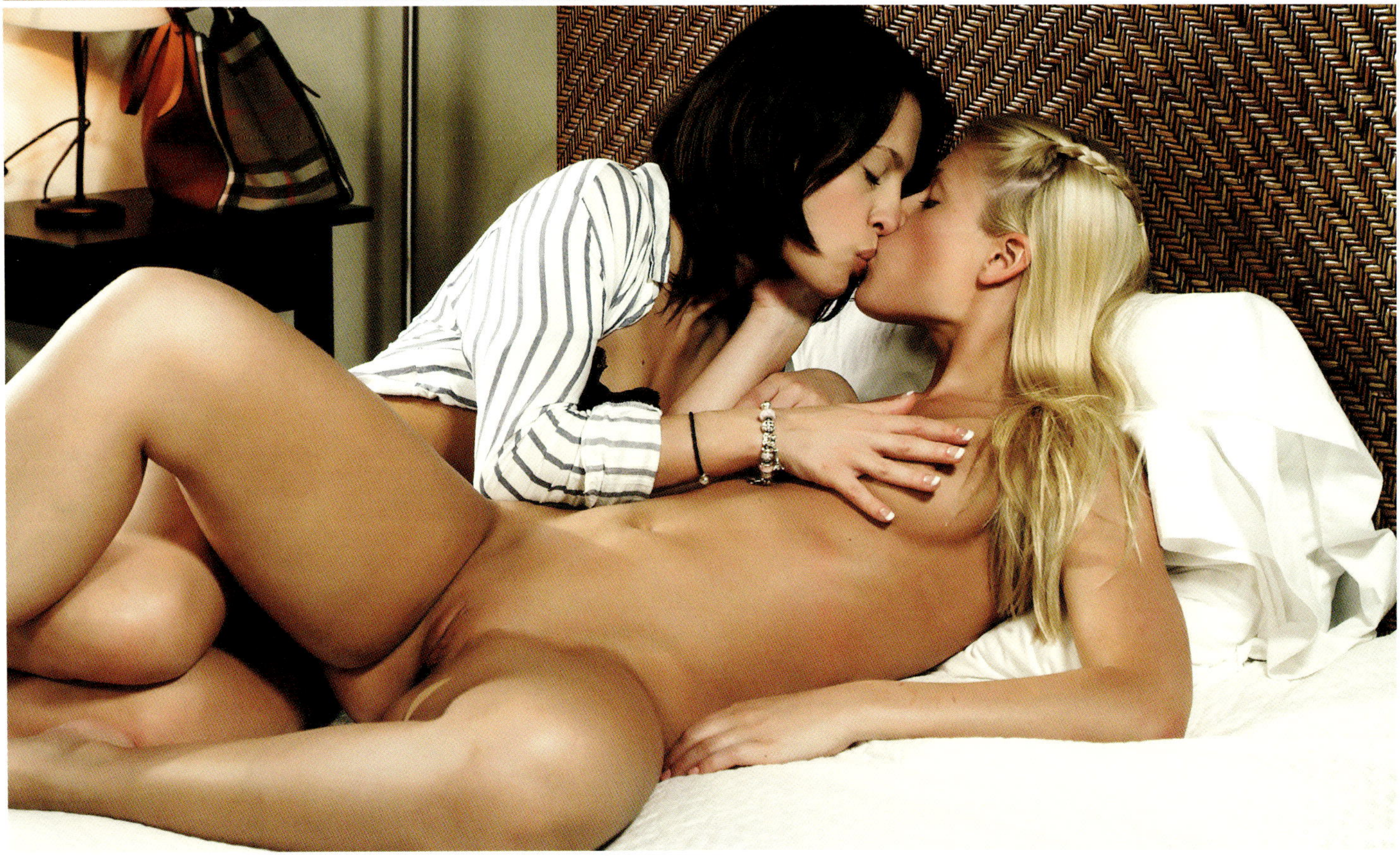

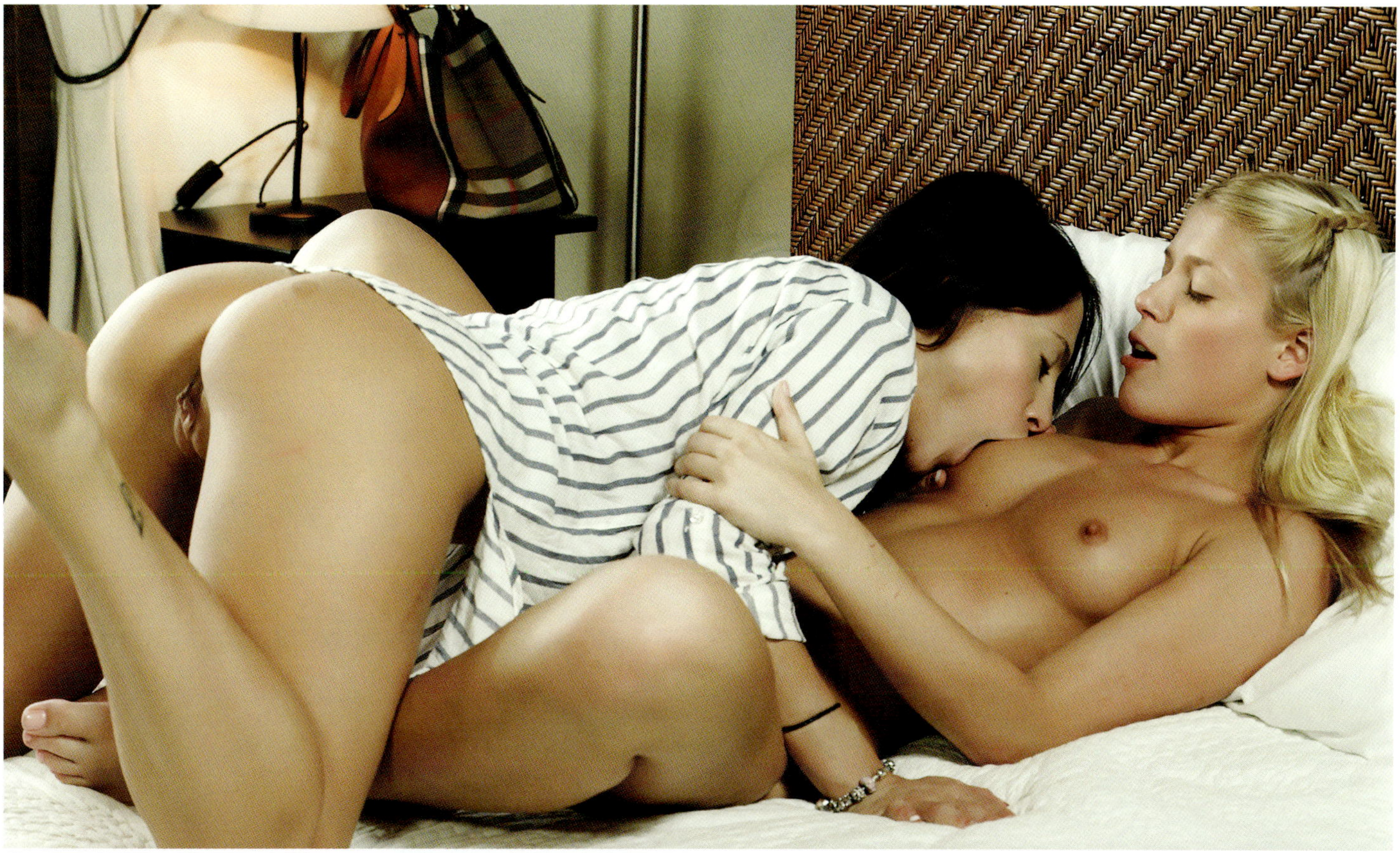

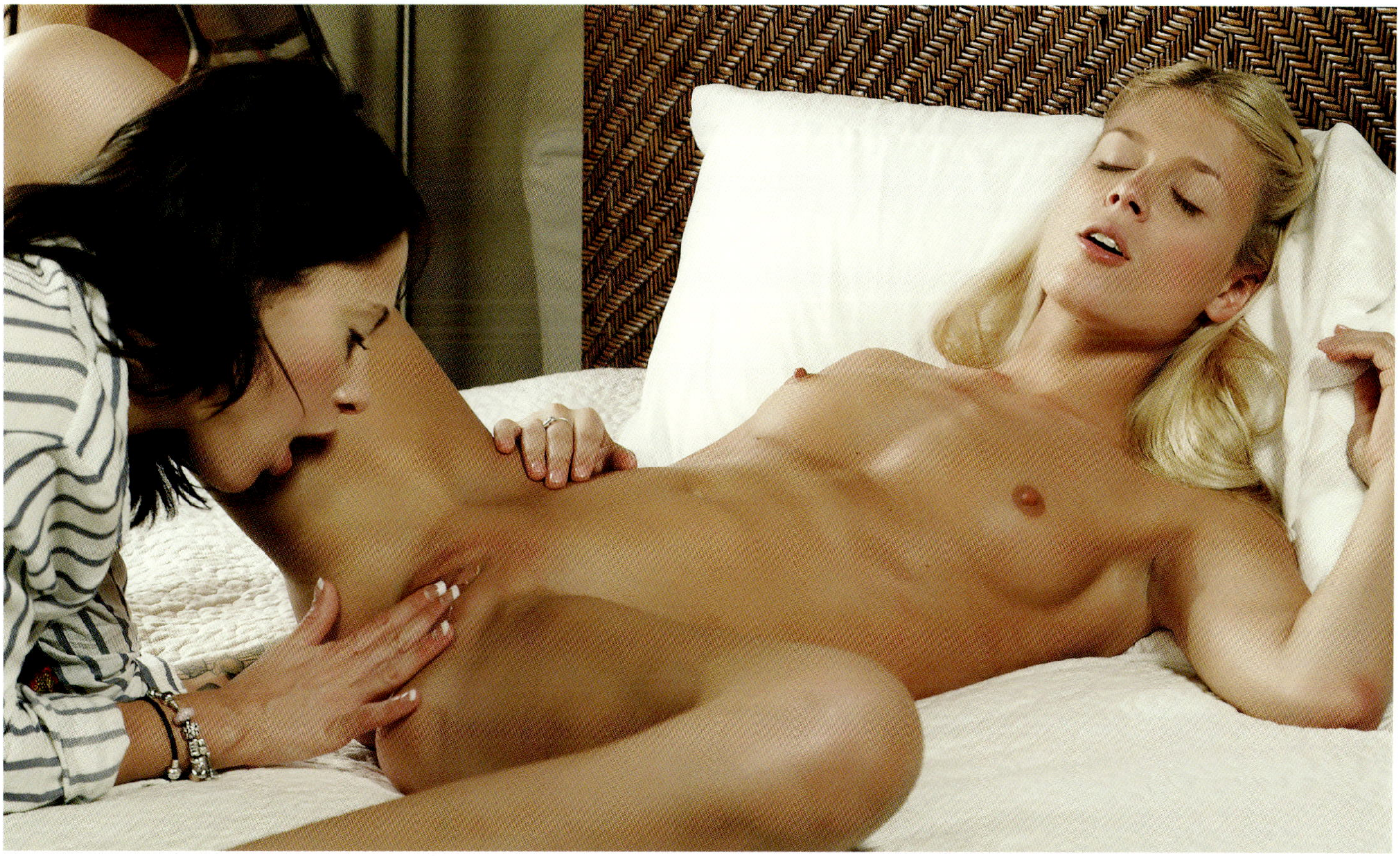

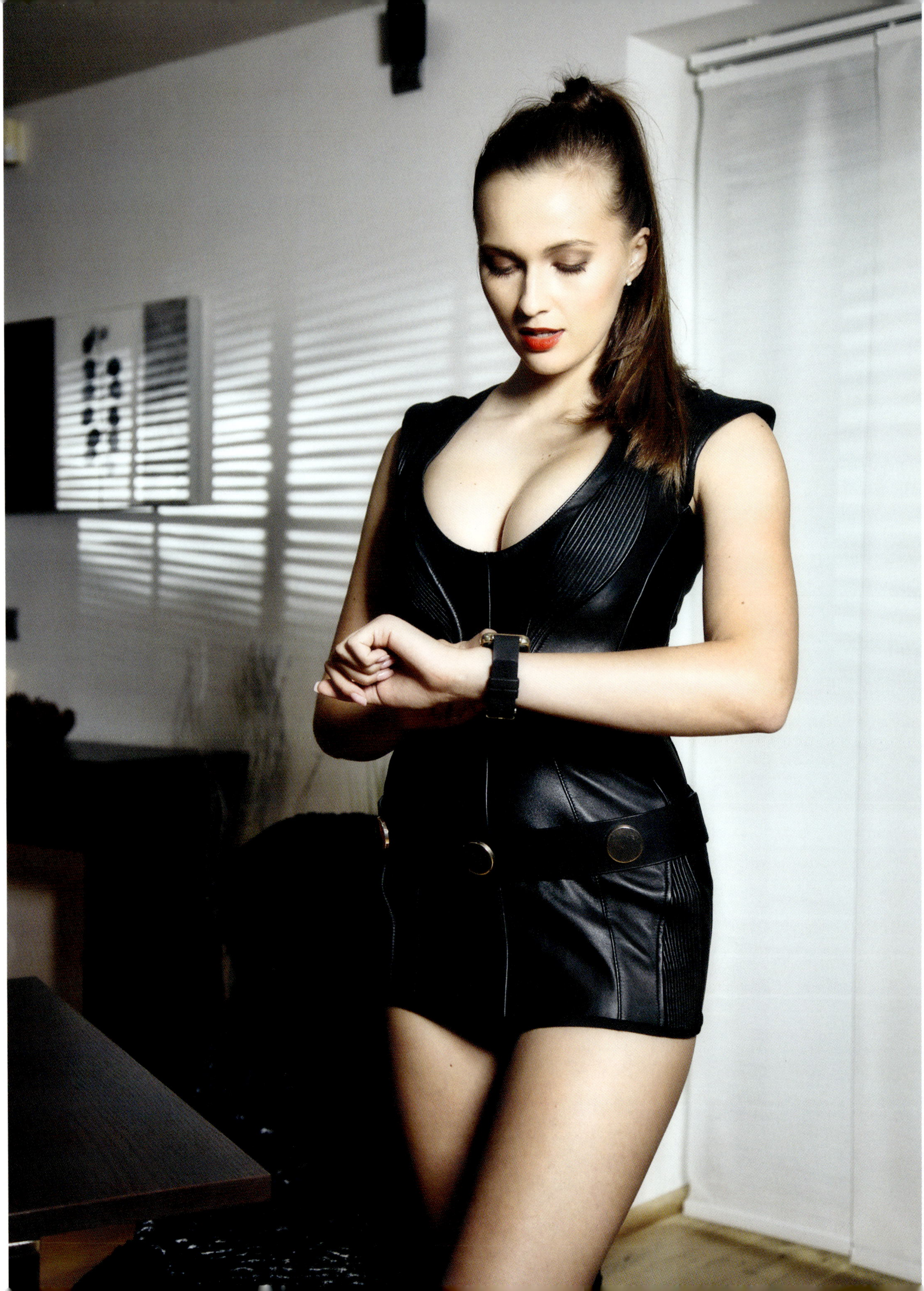

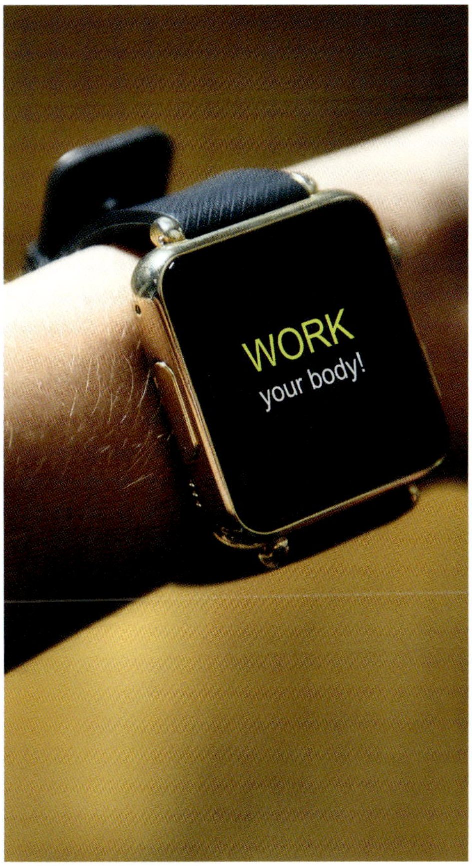
WORK
your body!

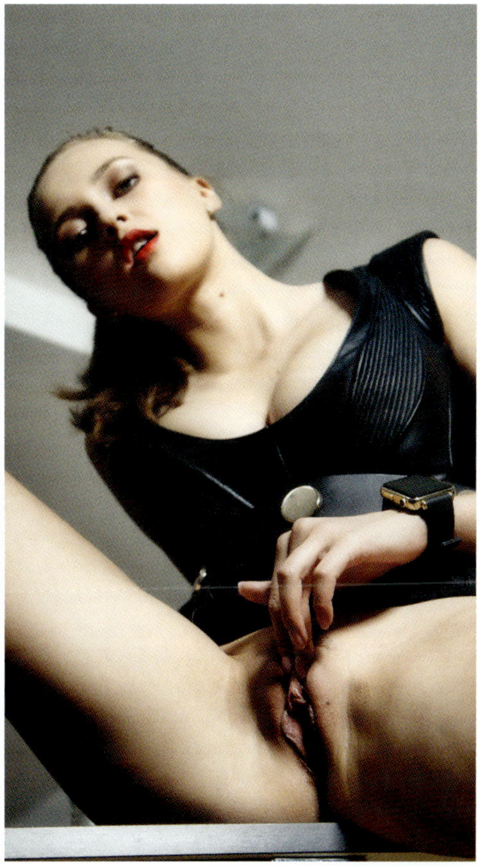

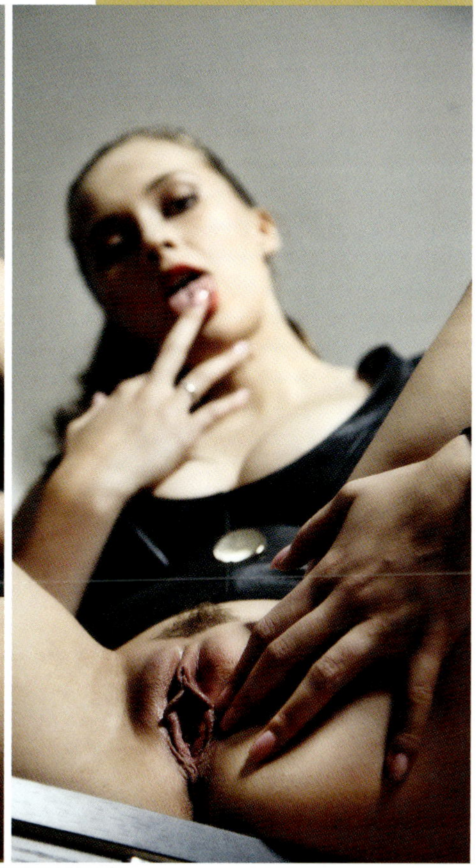

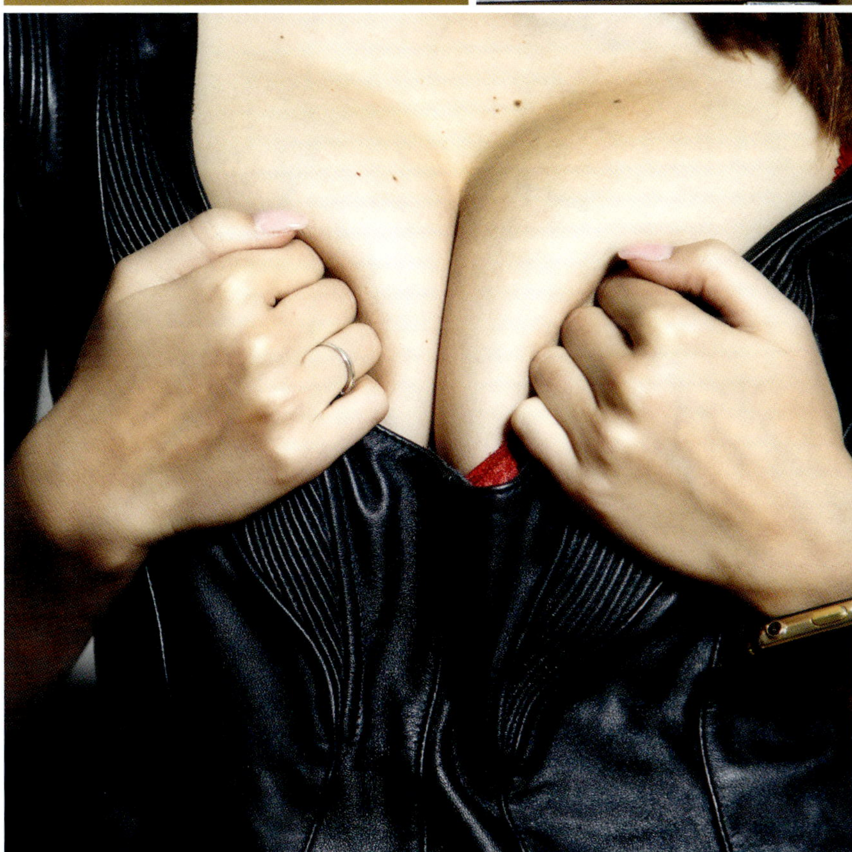

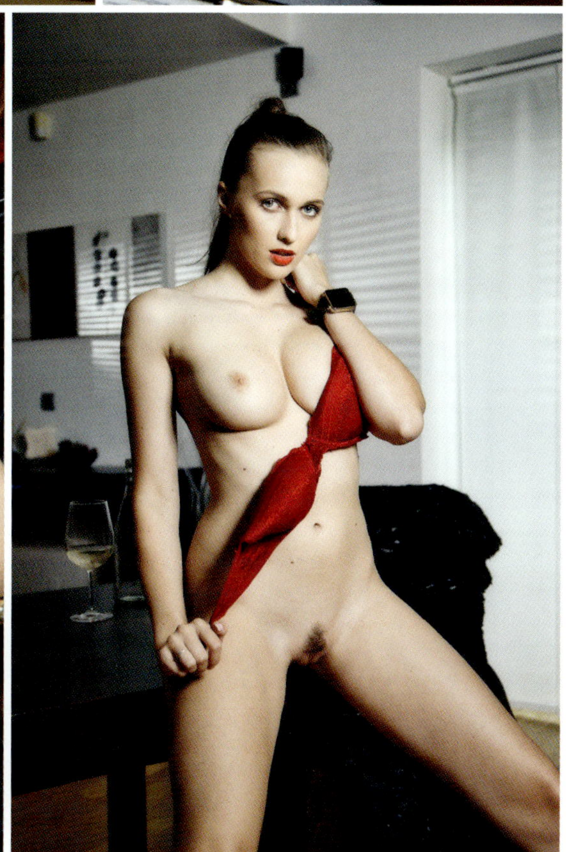

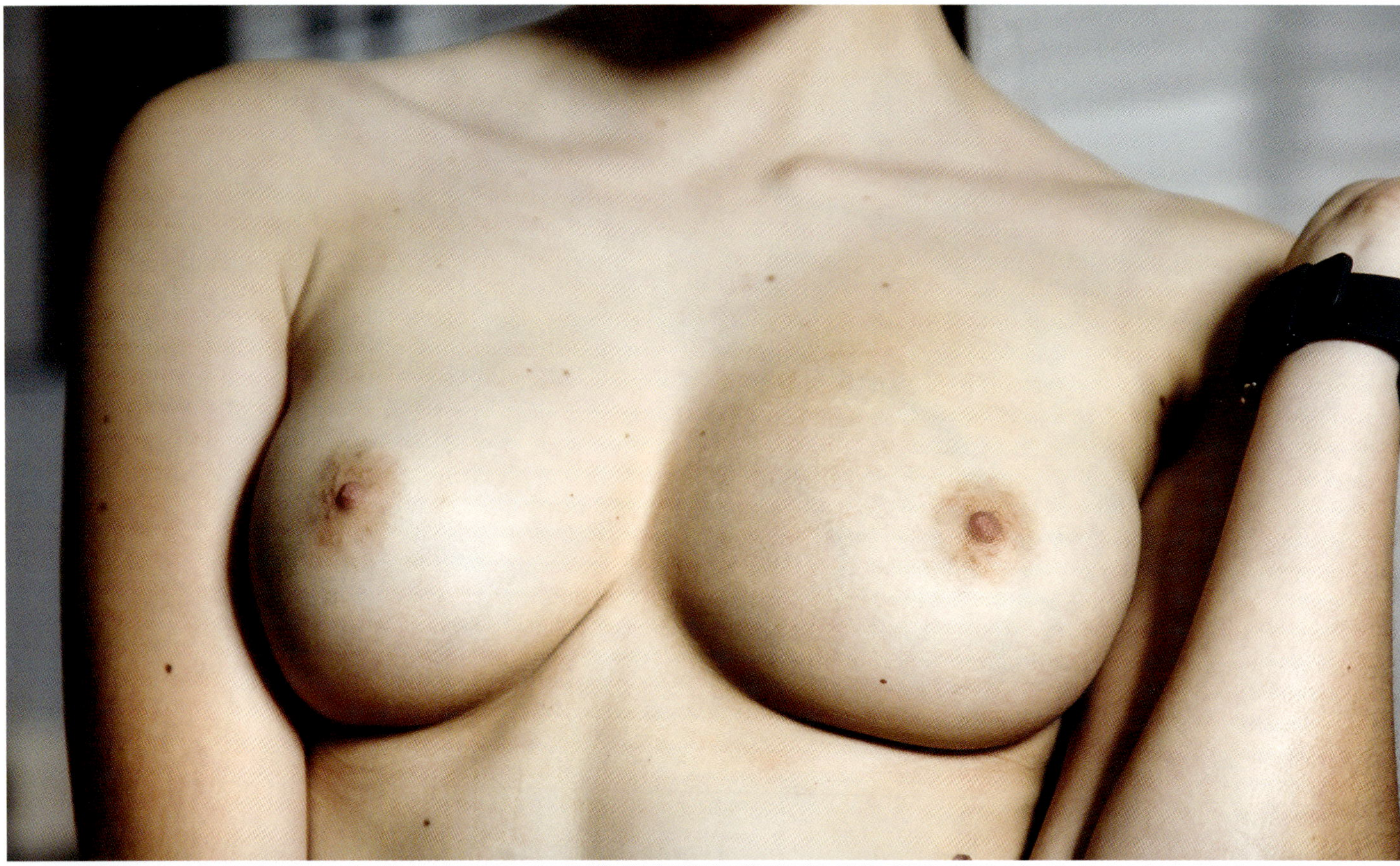

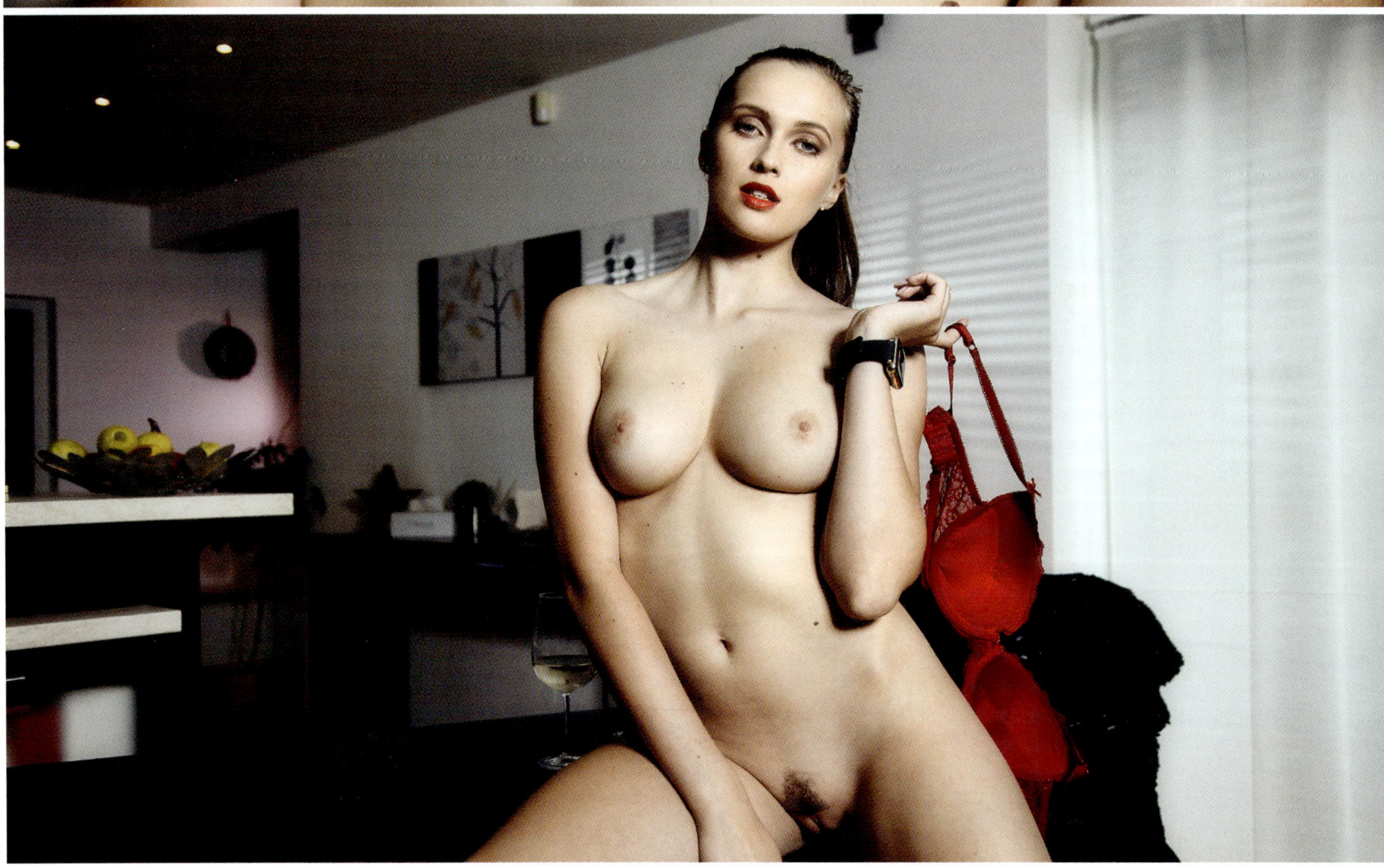

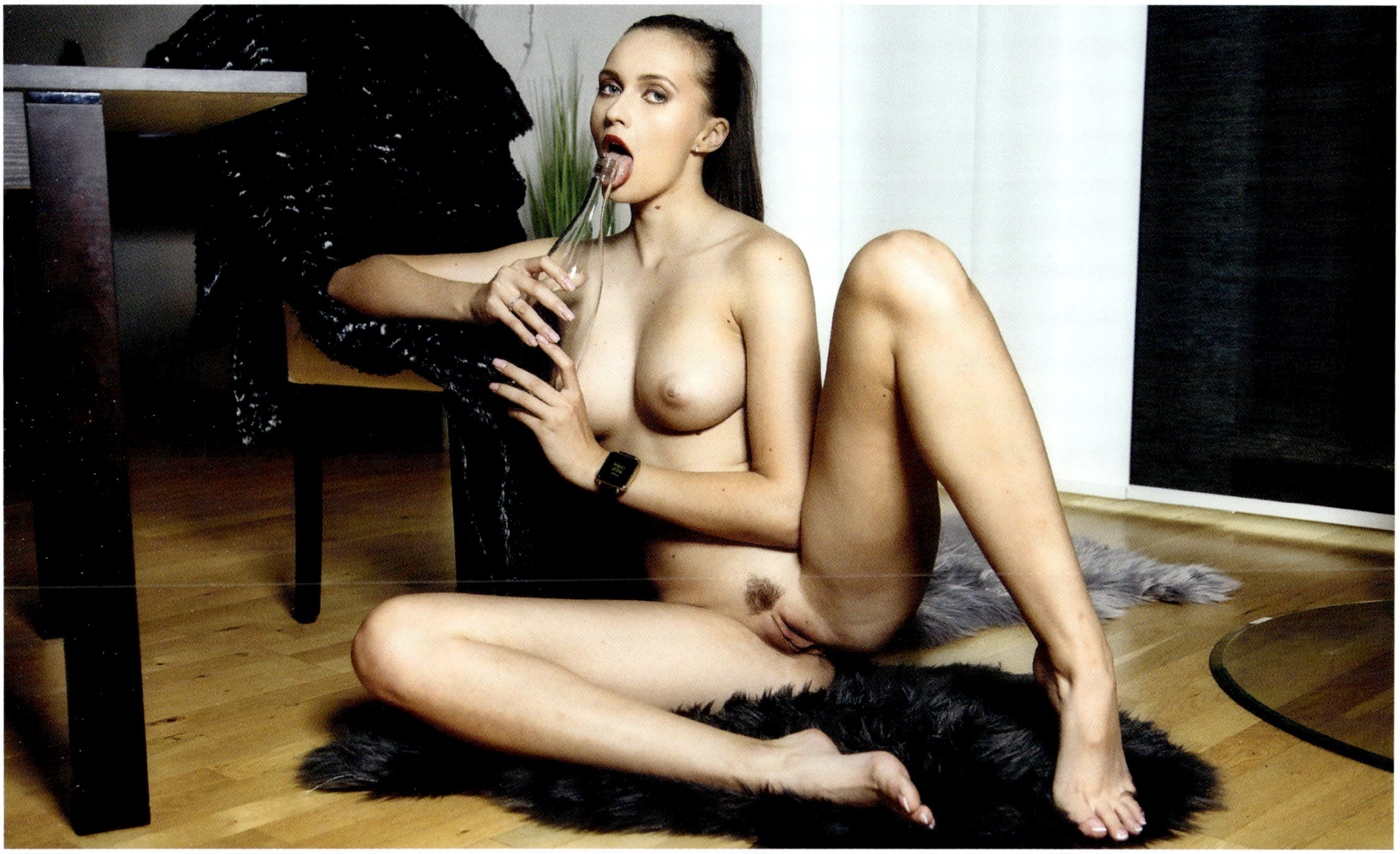

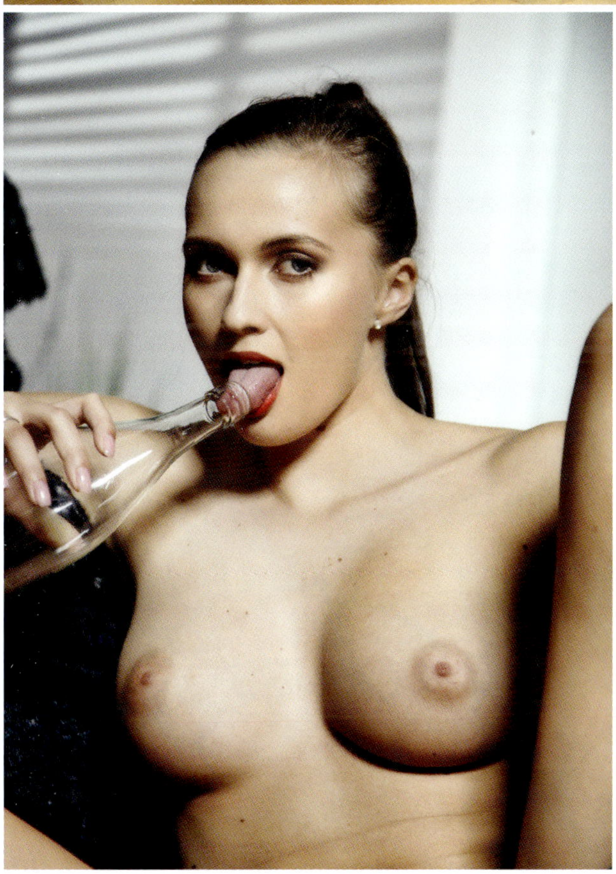

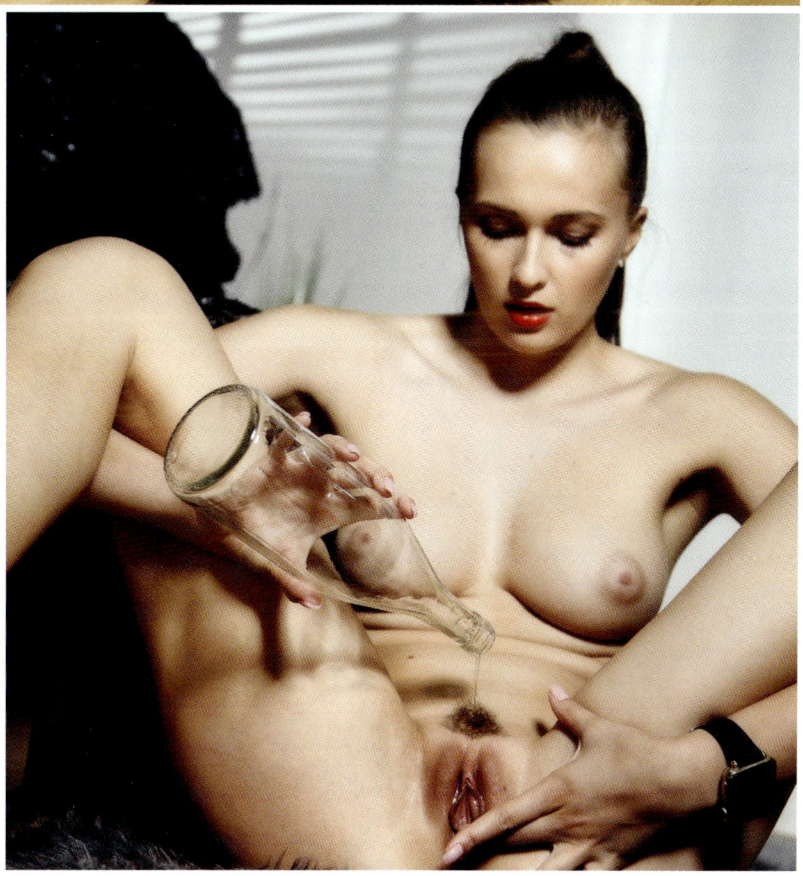

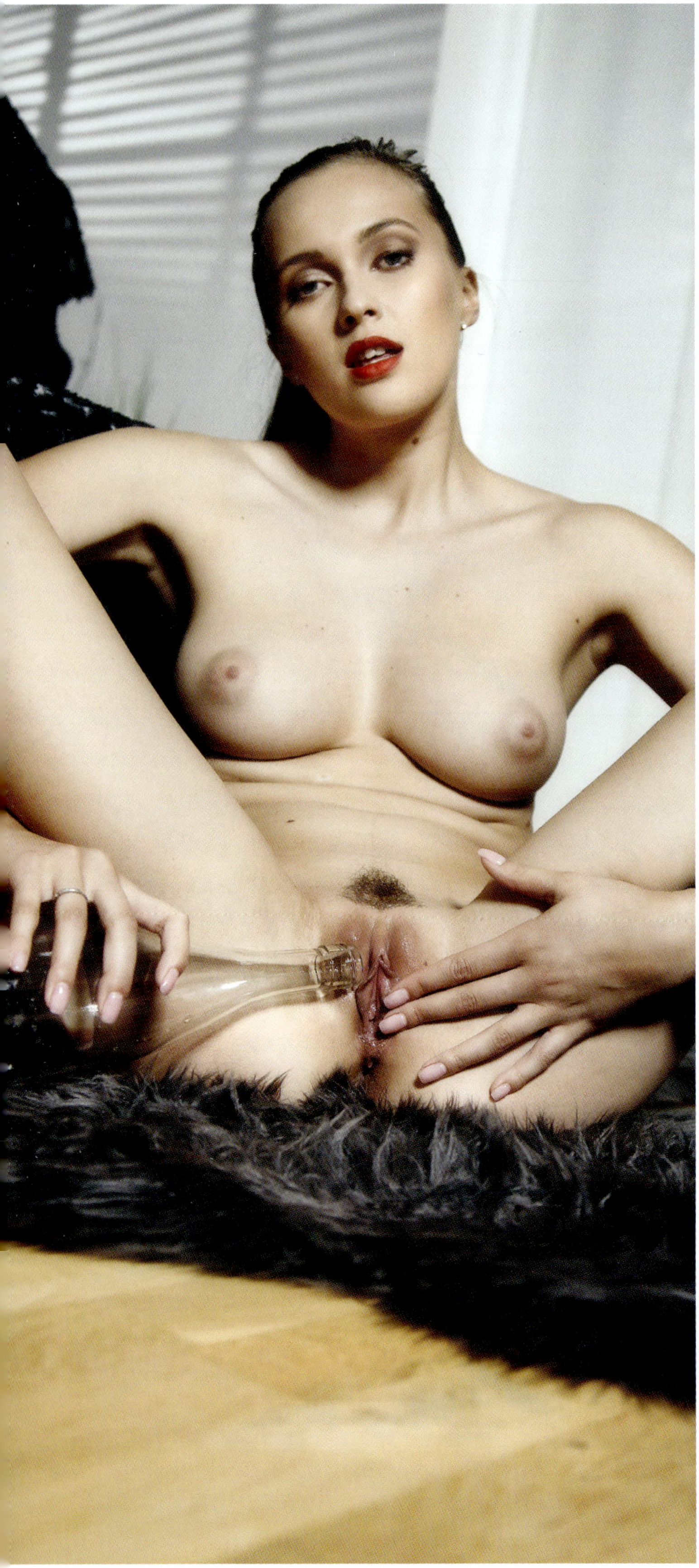

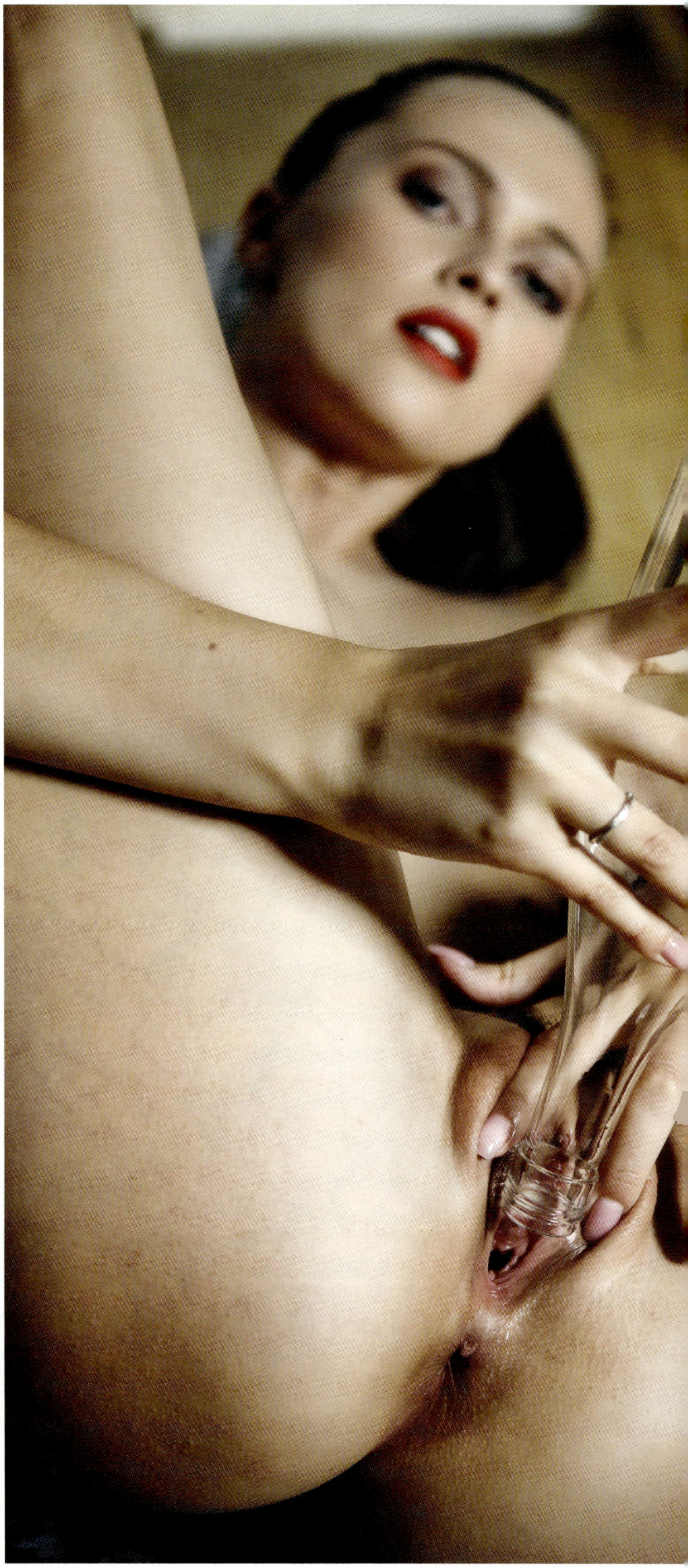

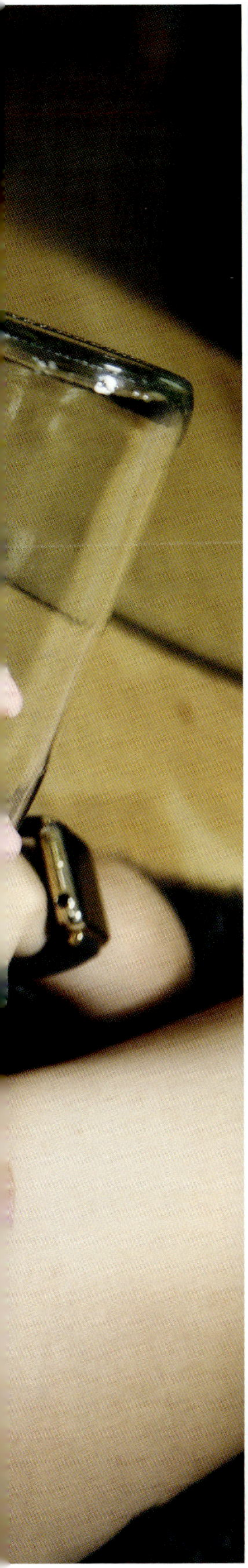

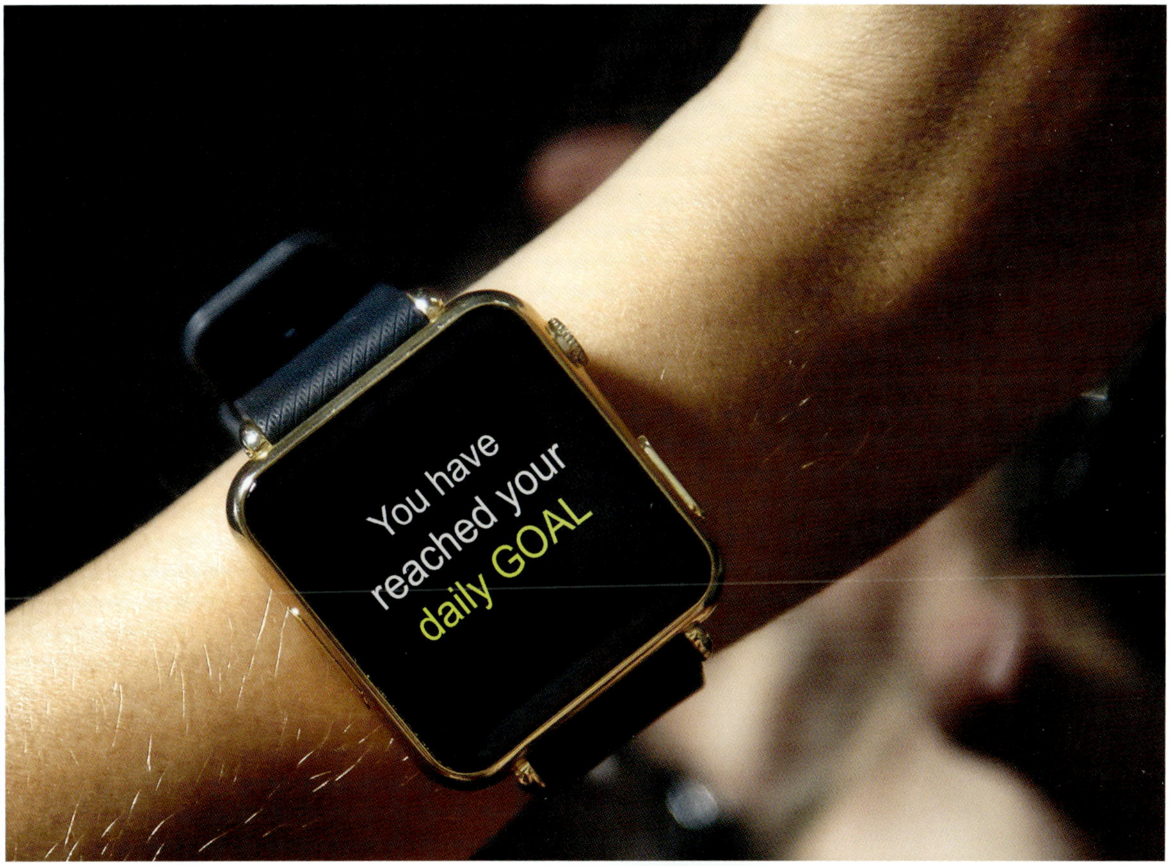
You have
reached your
daily GOAL

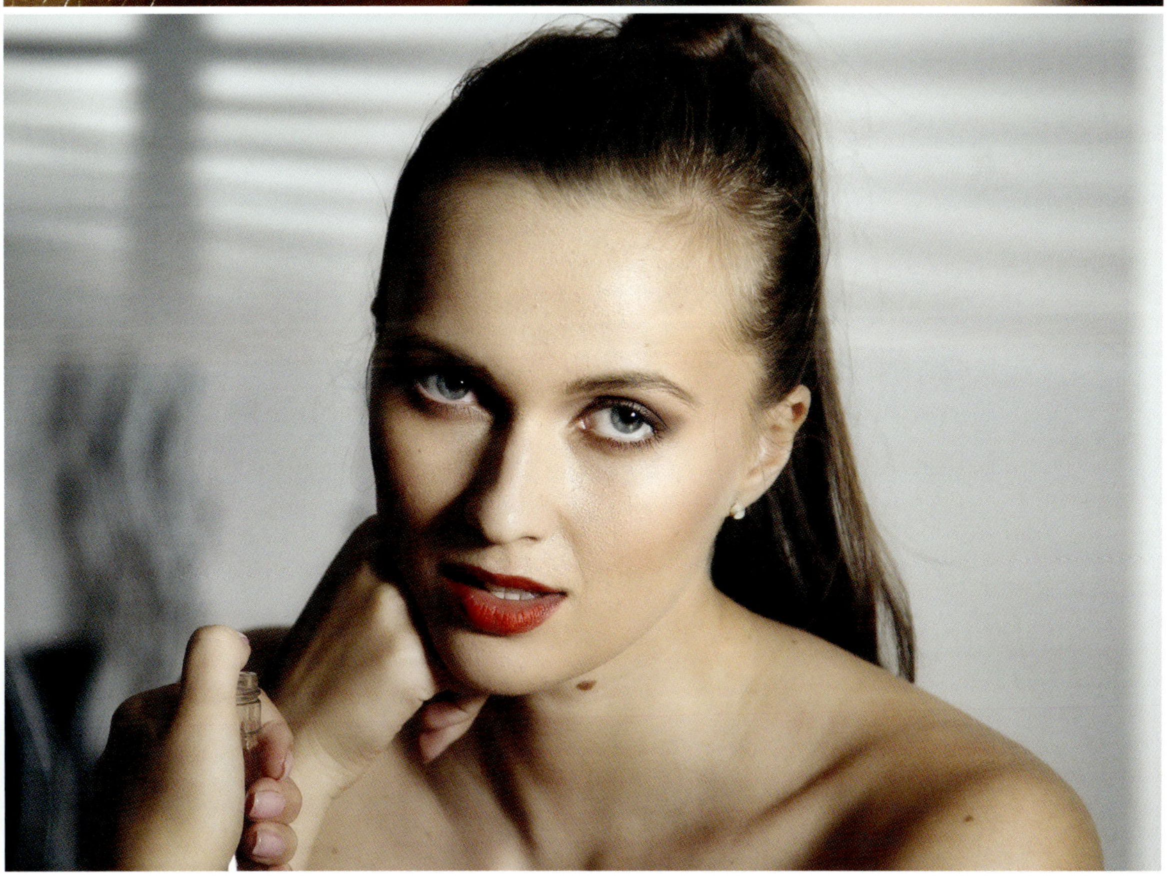

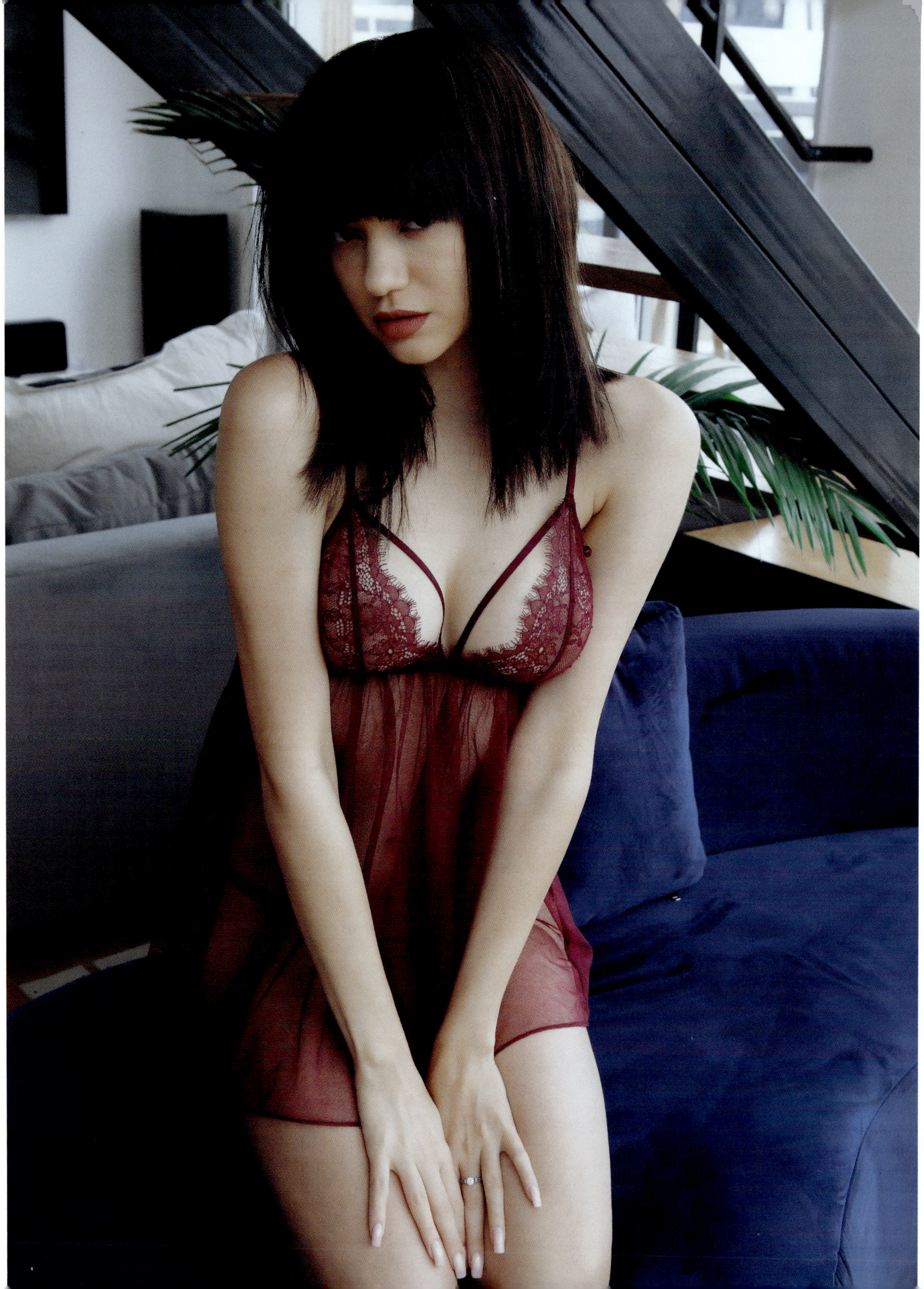

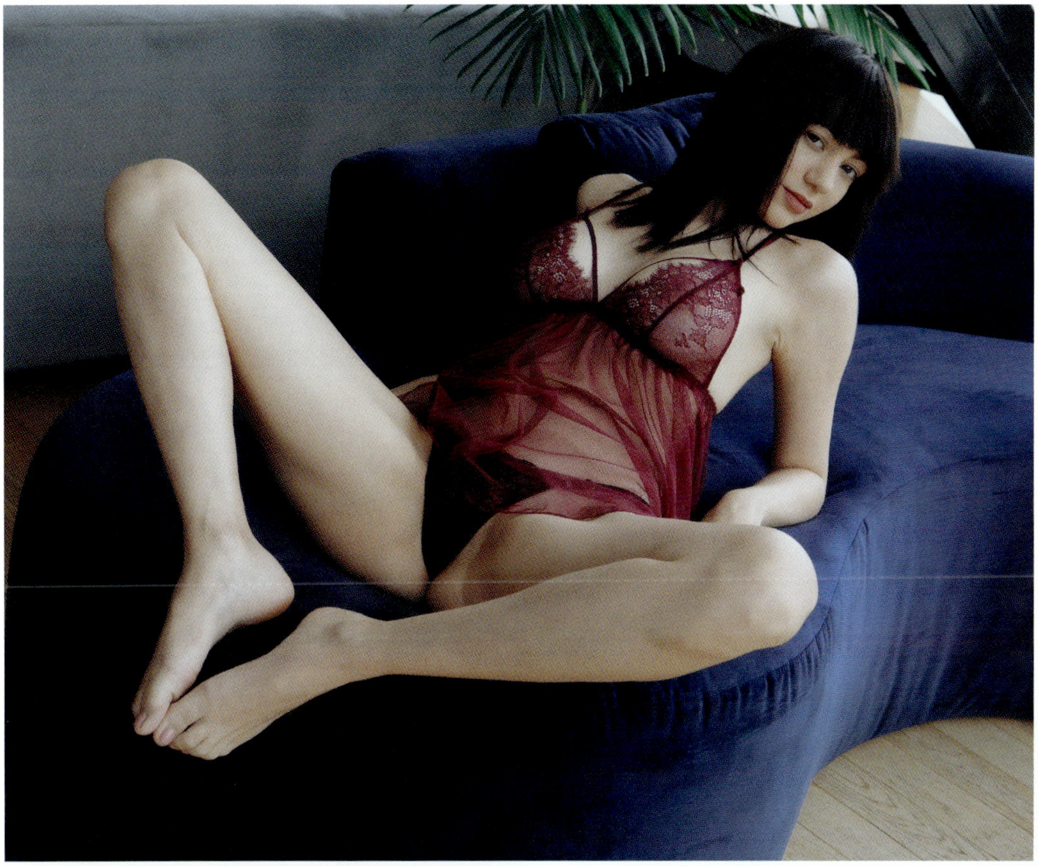

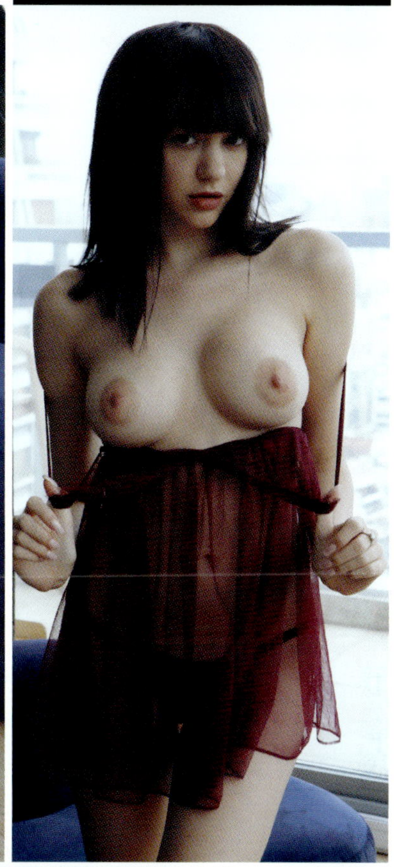

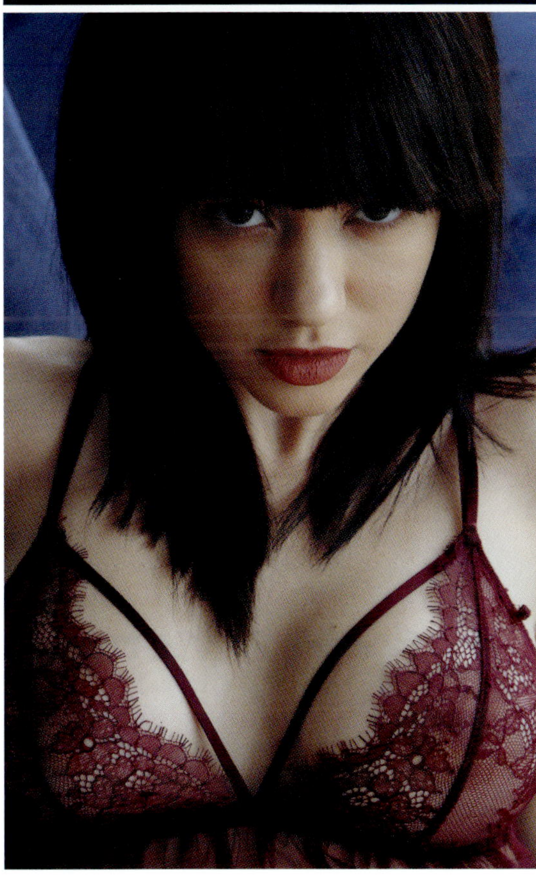

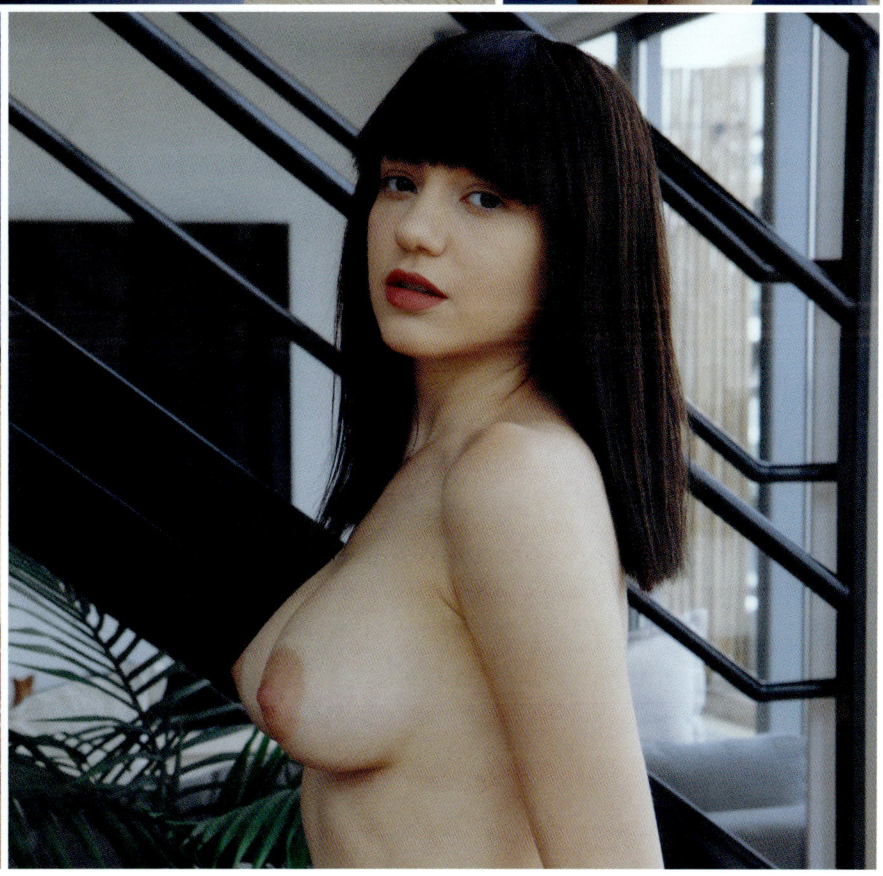

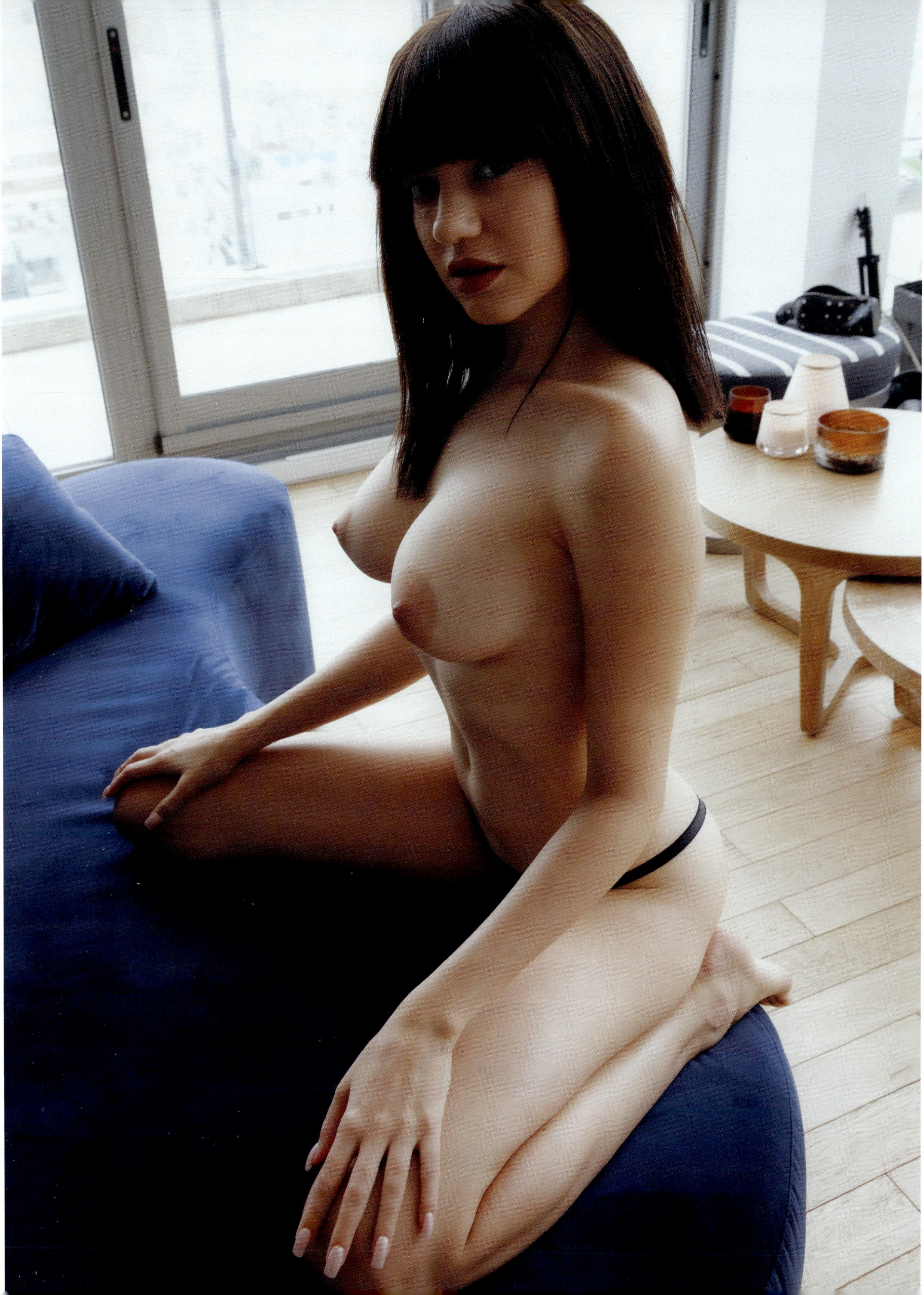

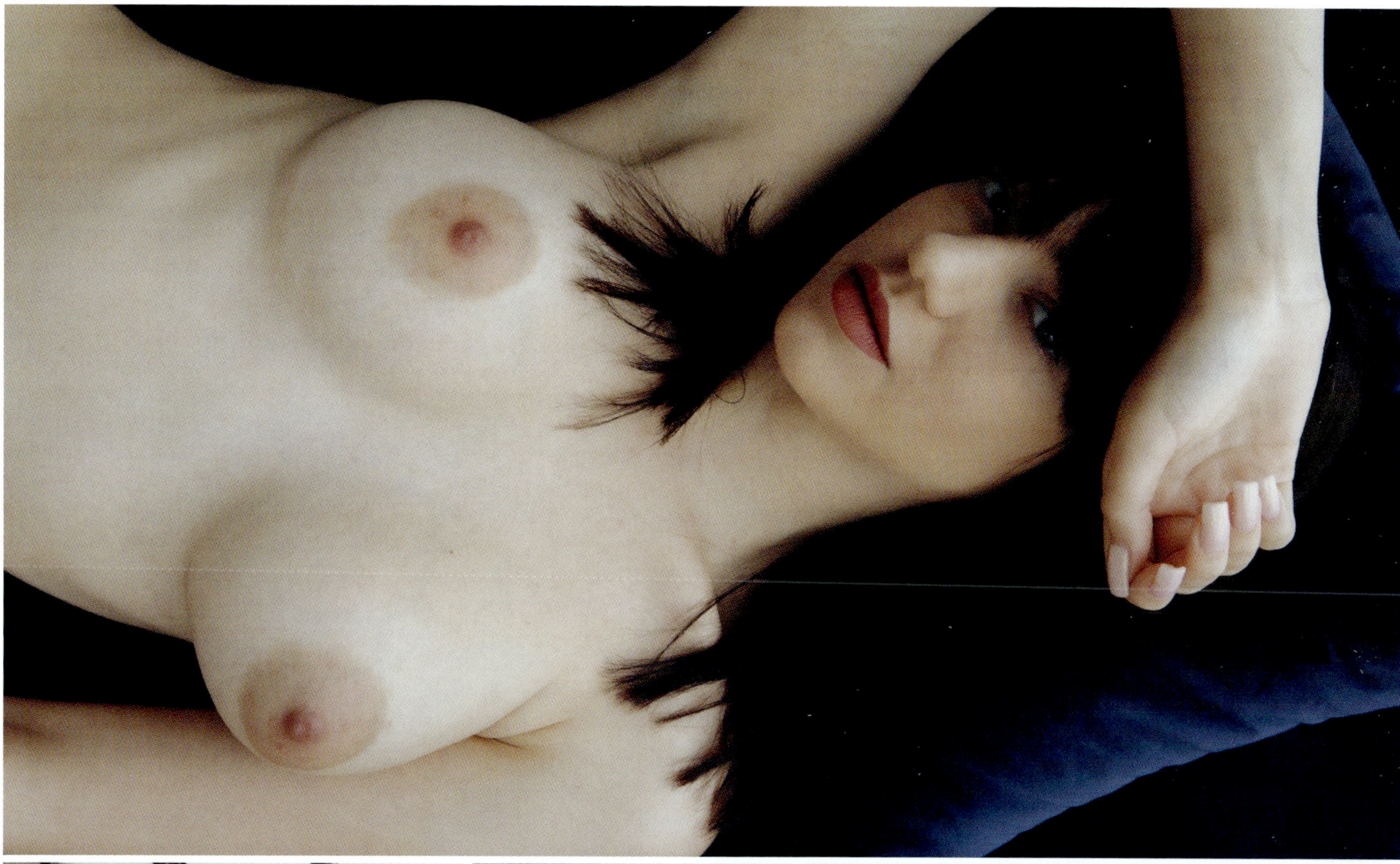

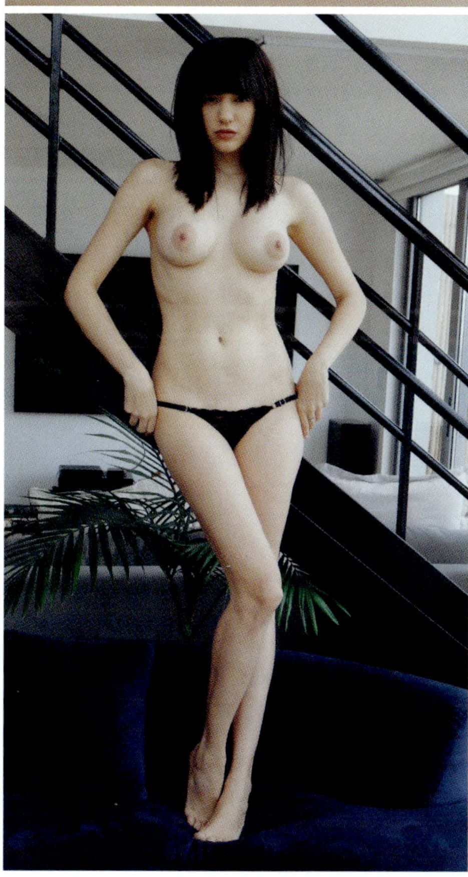

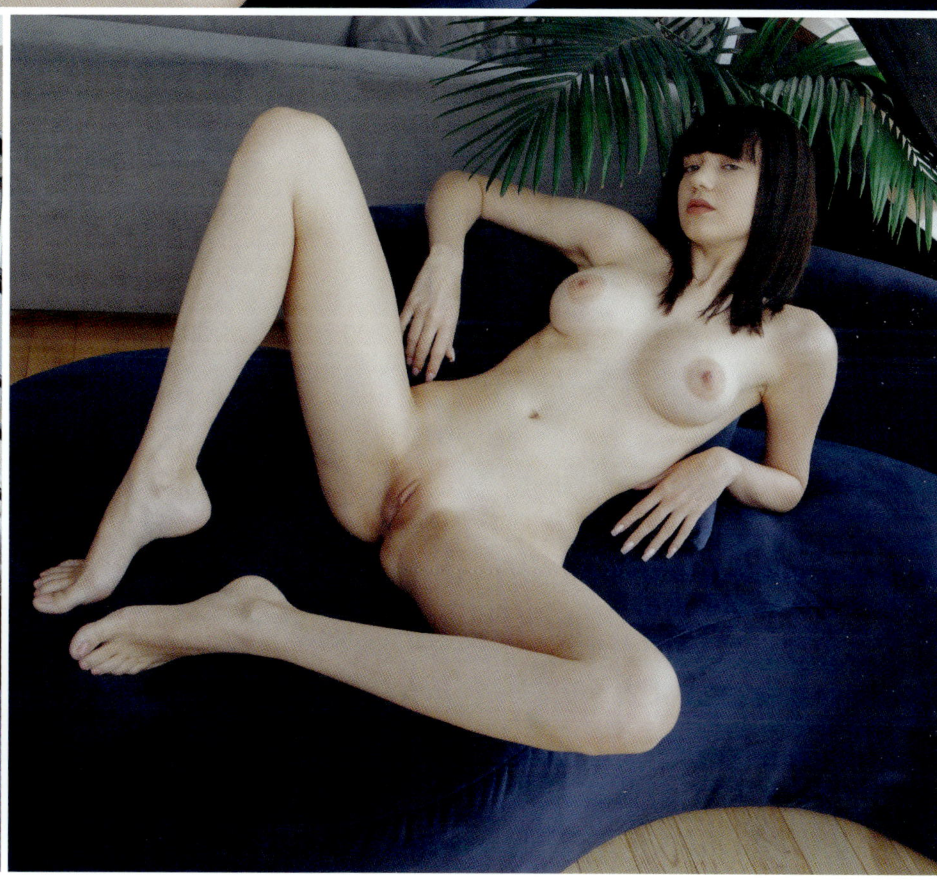

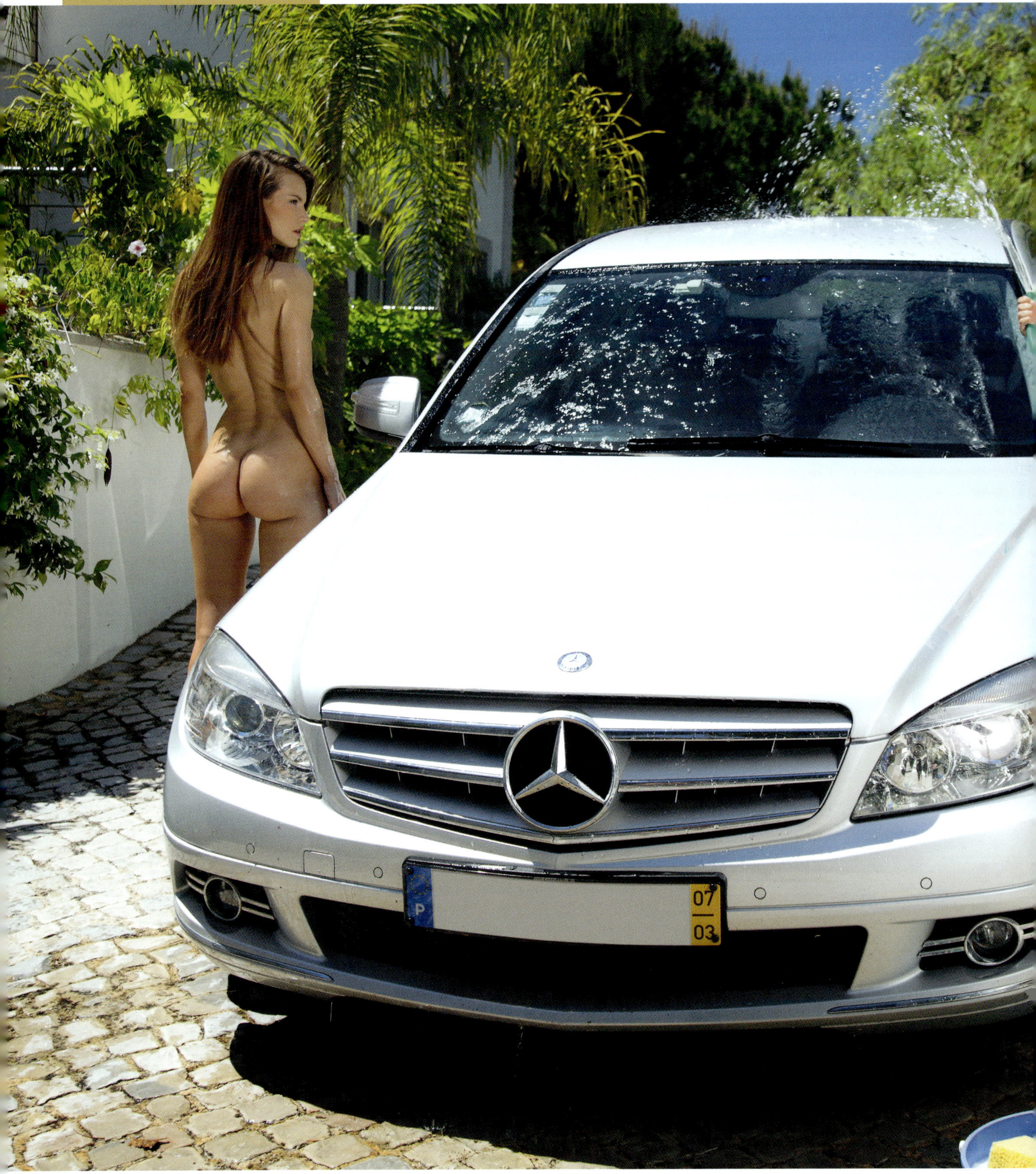
P
07
03

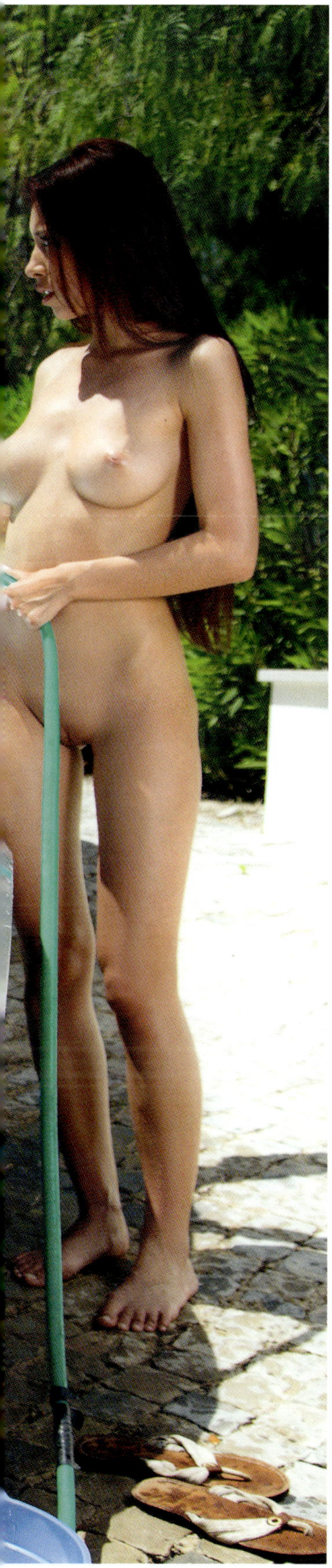

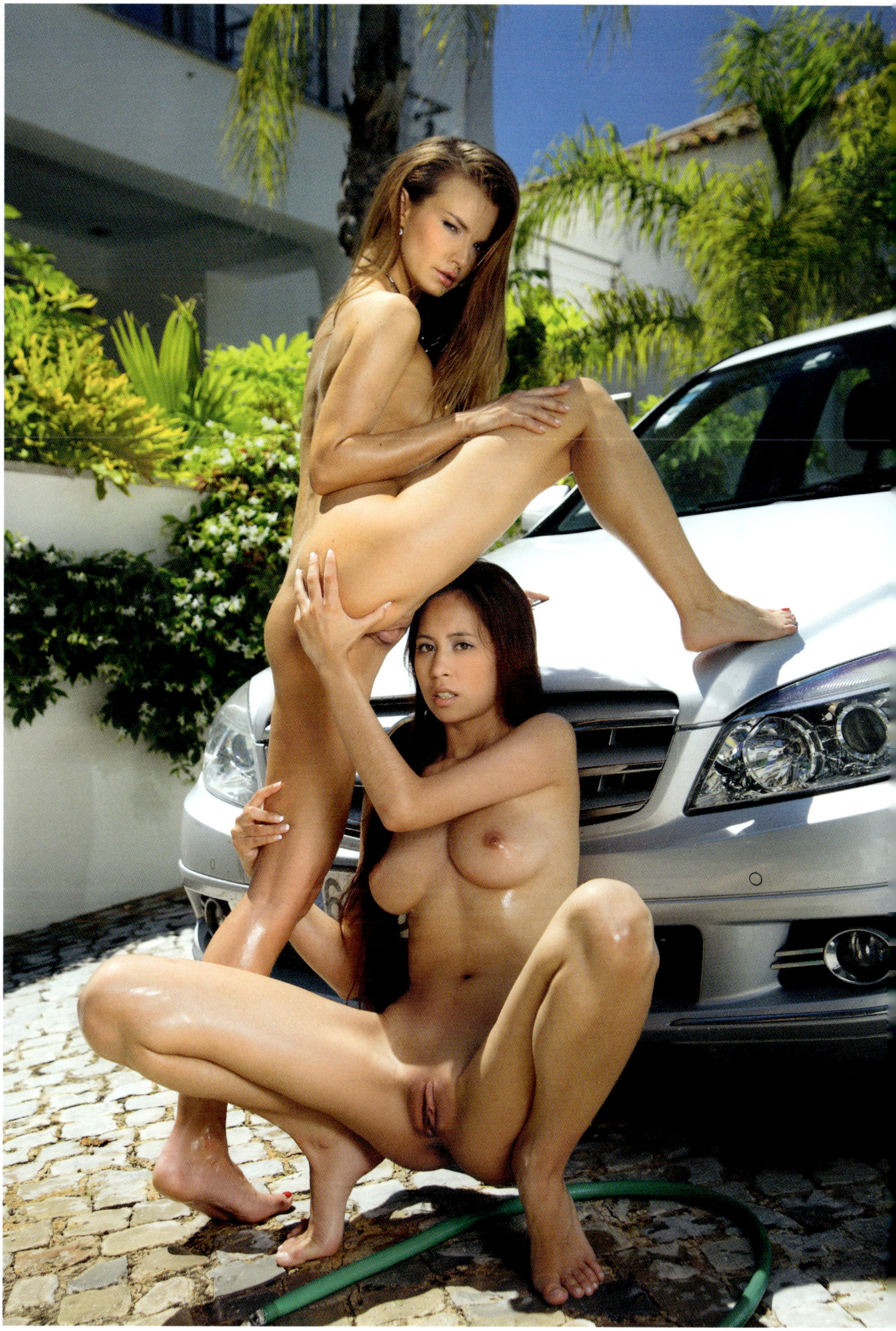

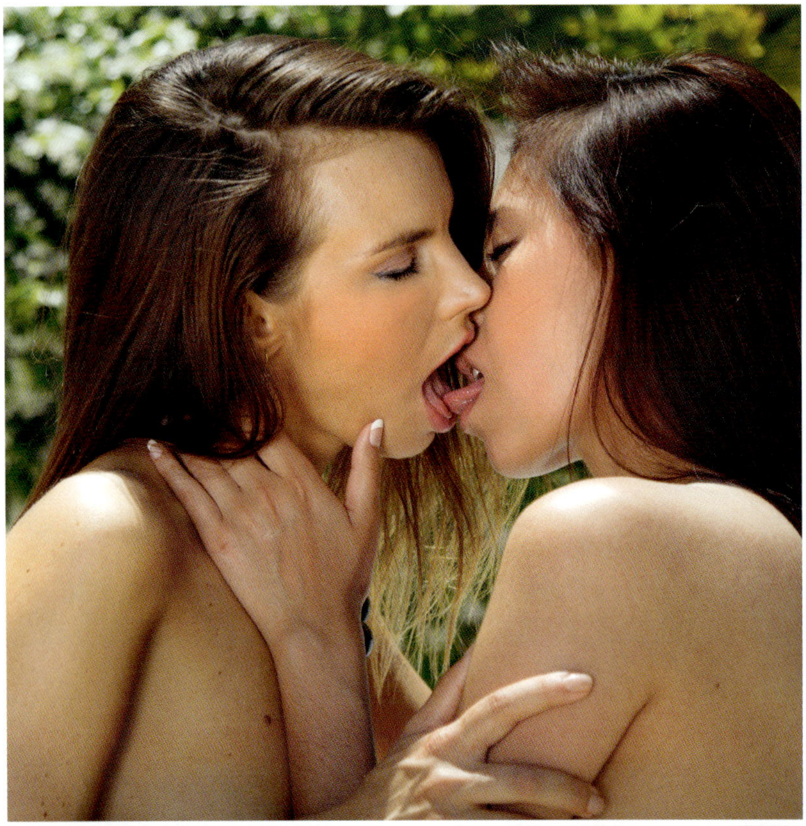
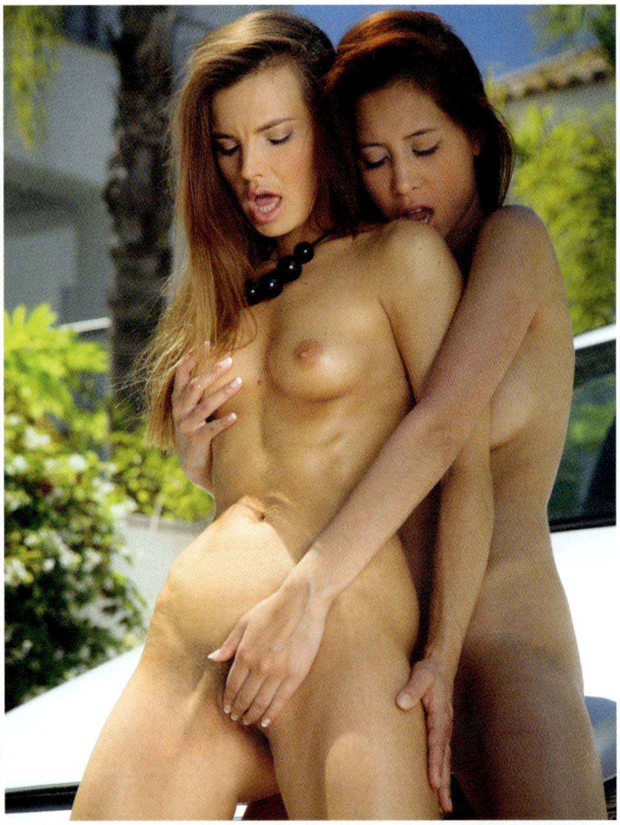
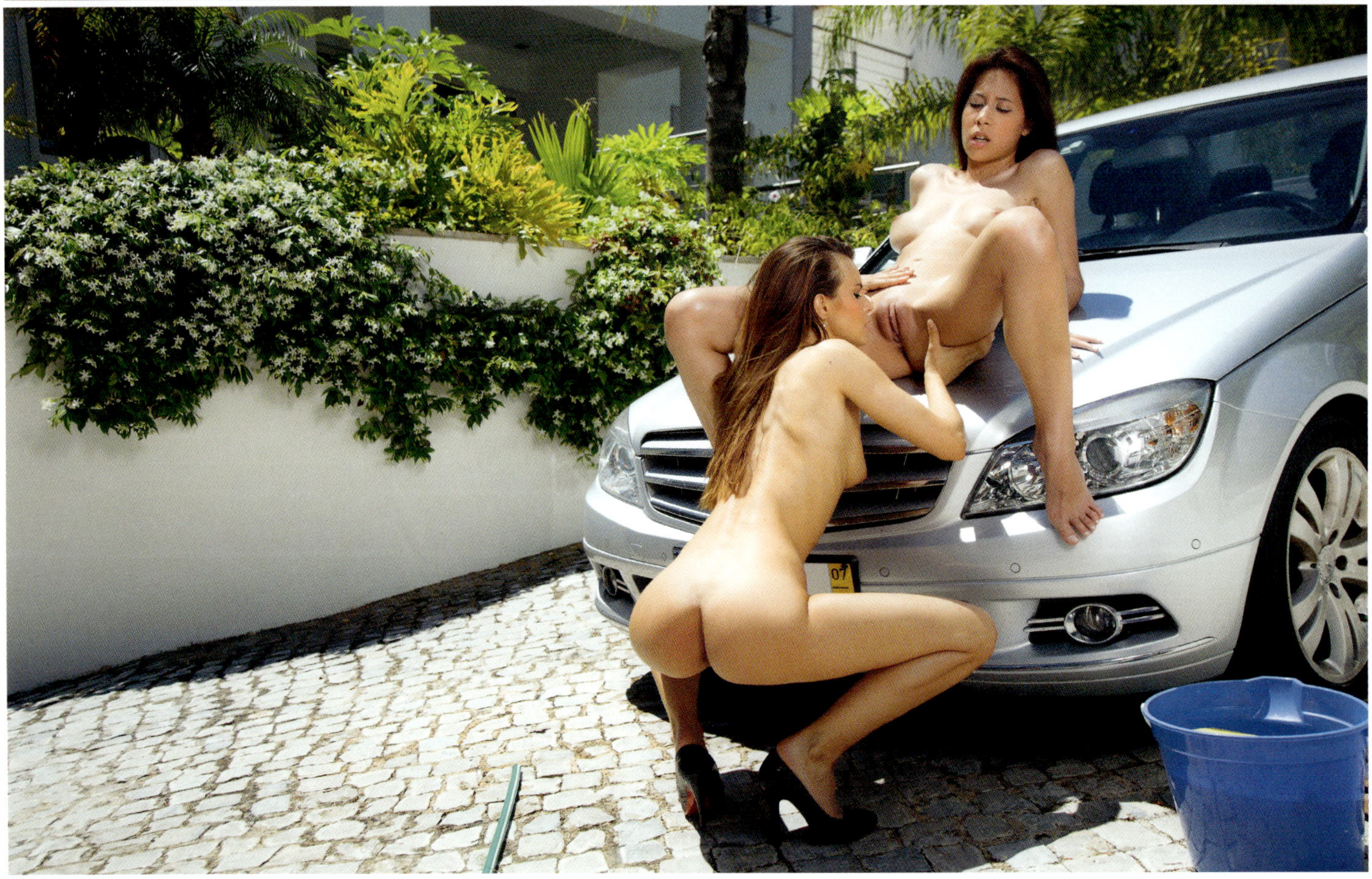

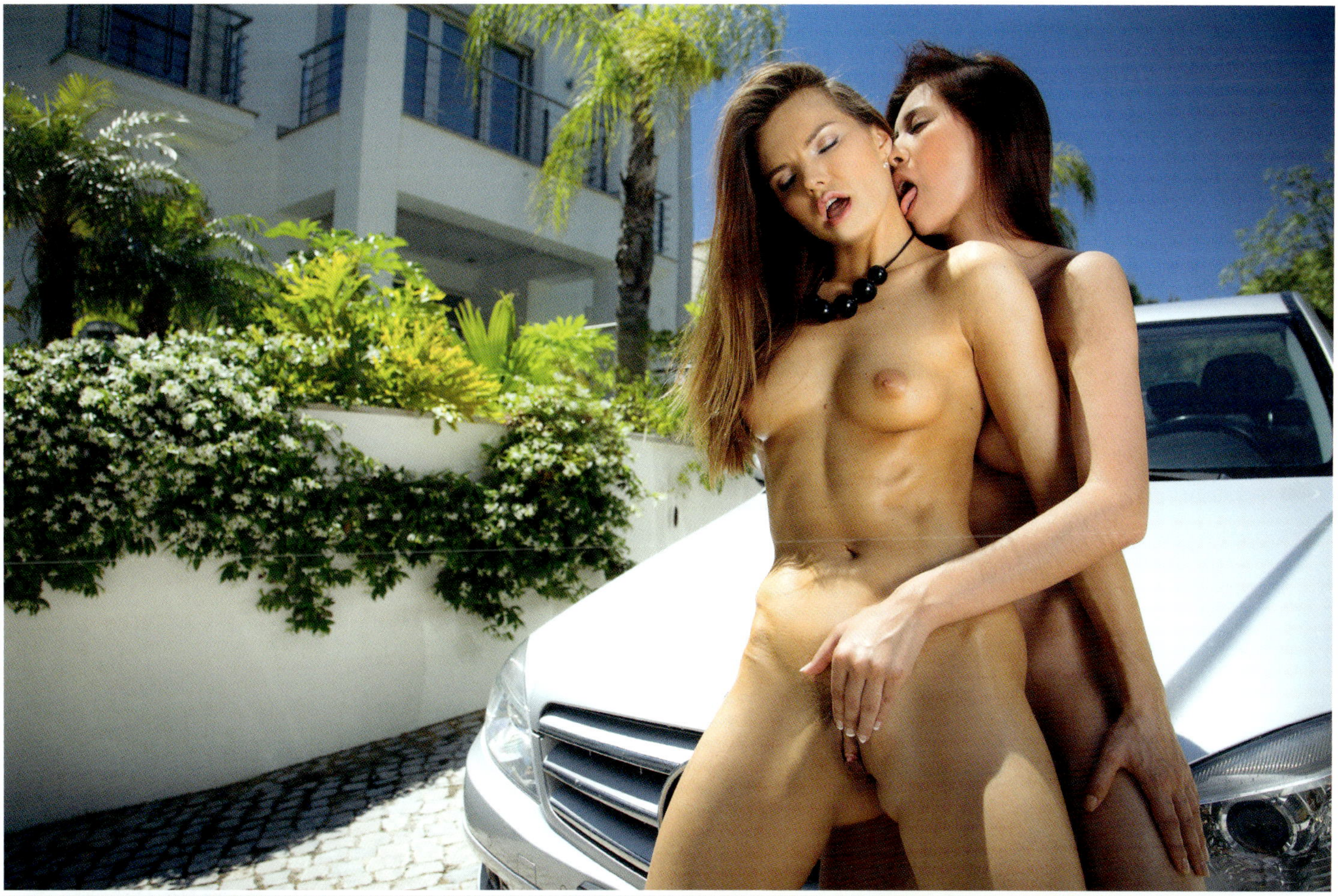

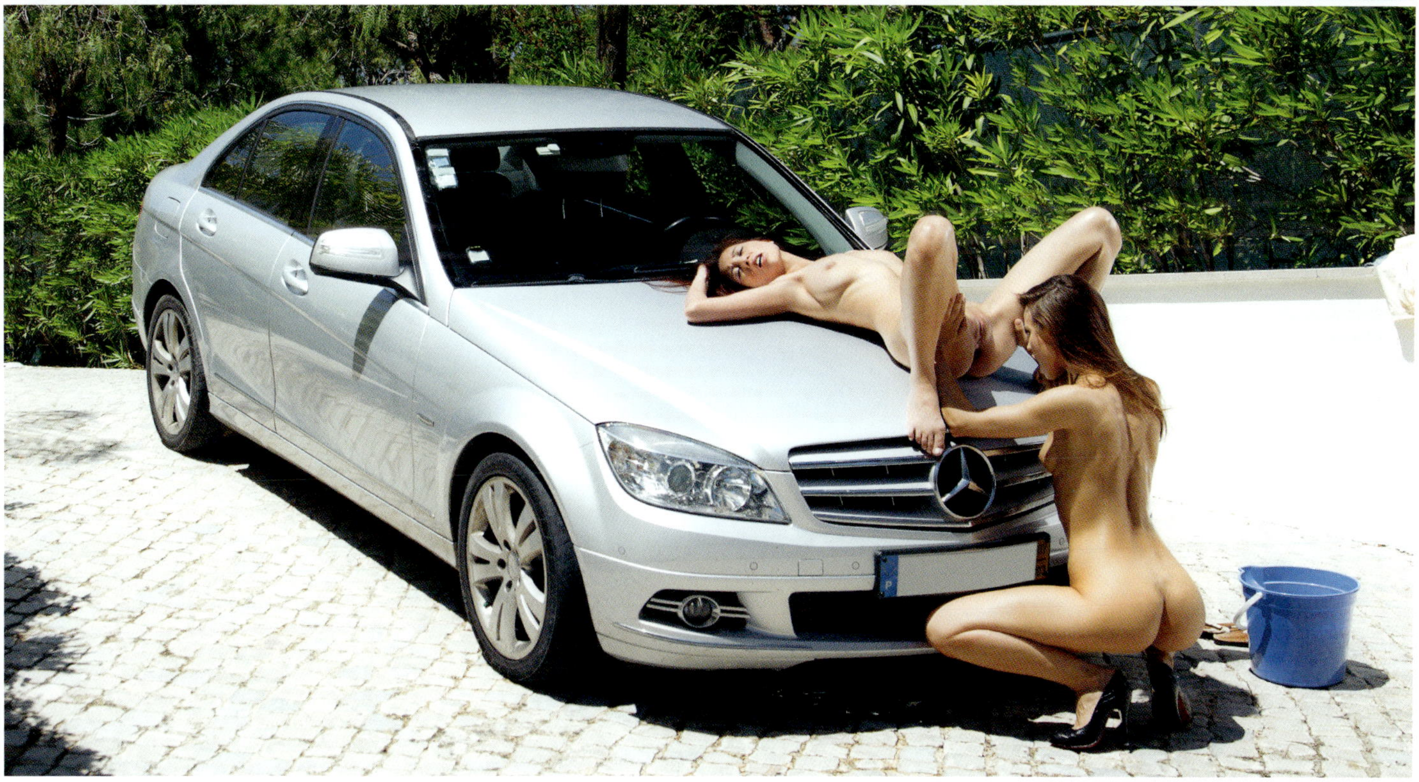

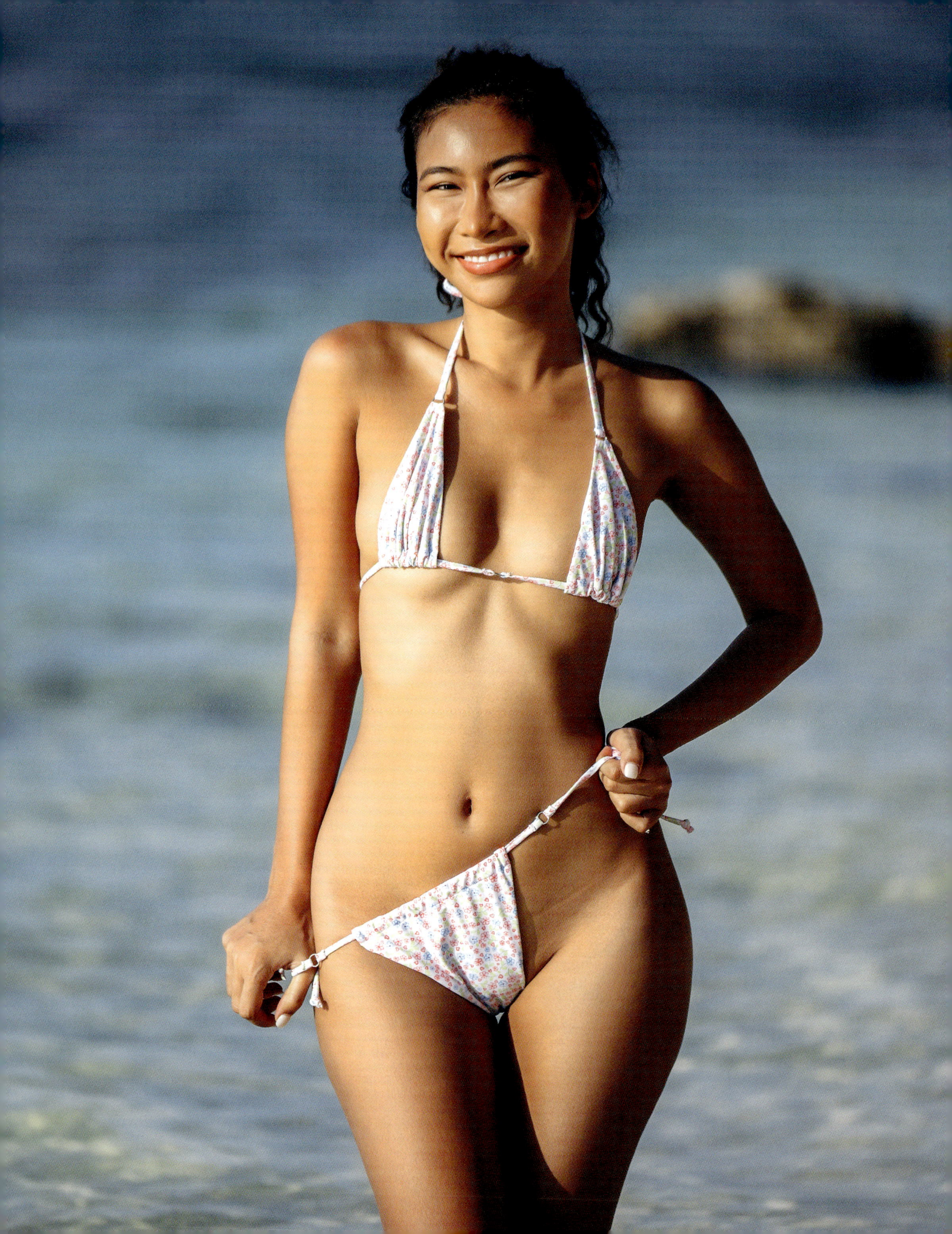

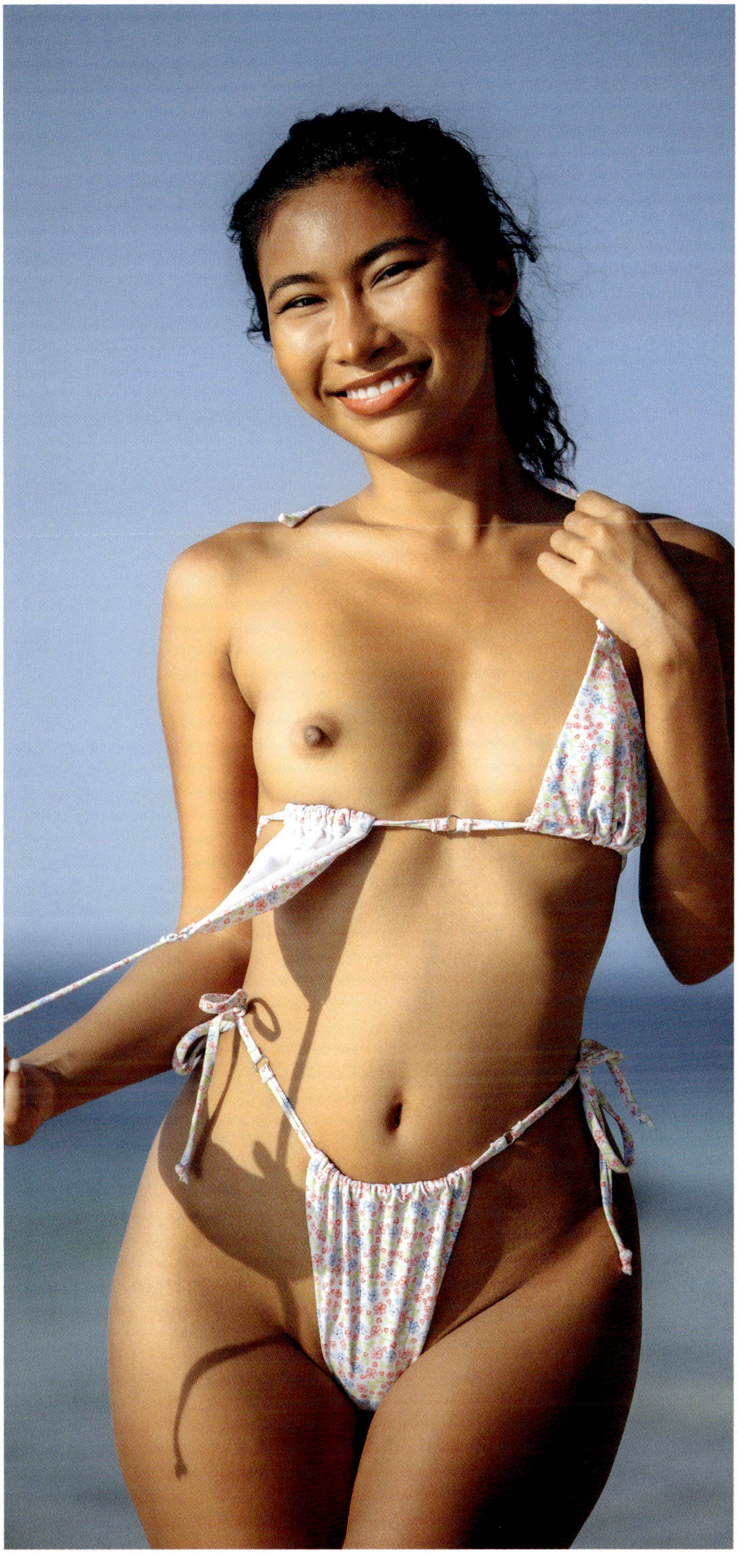

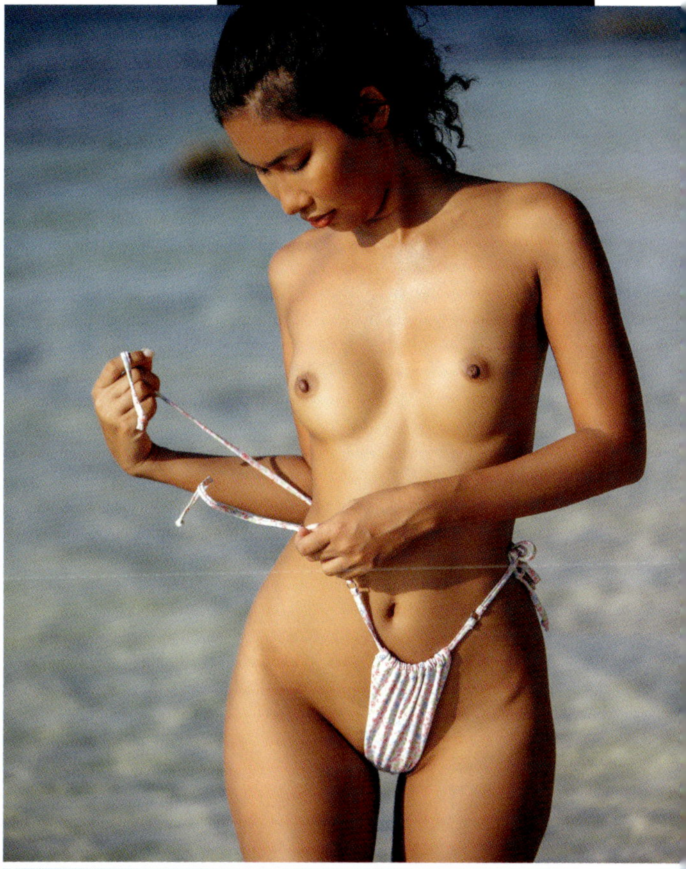

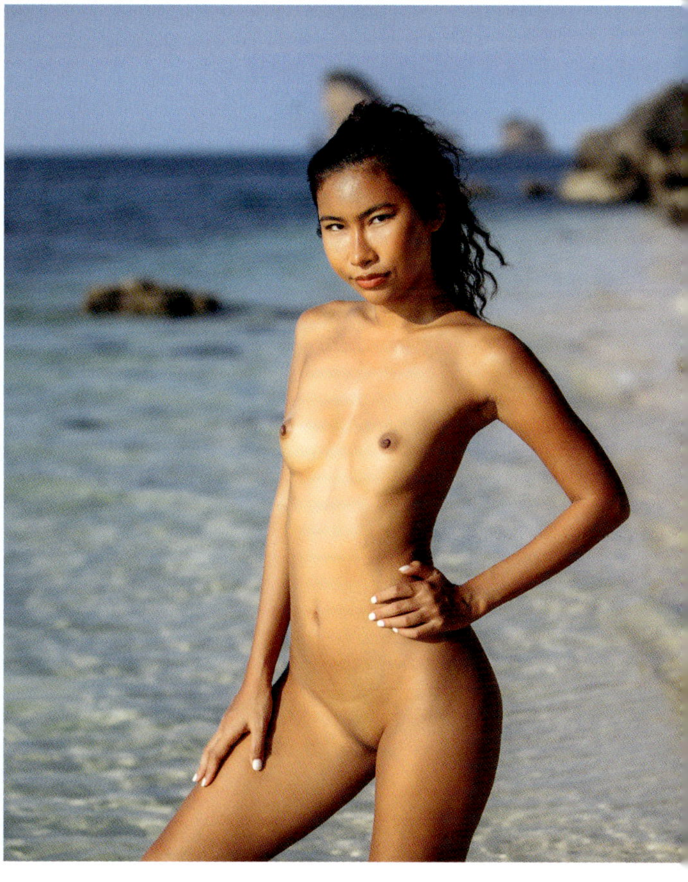

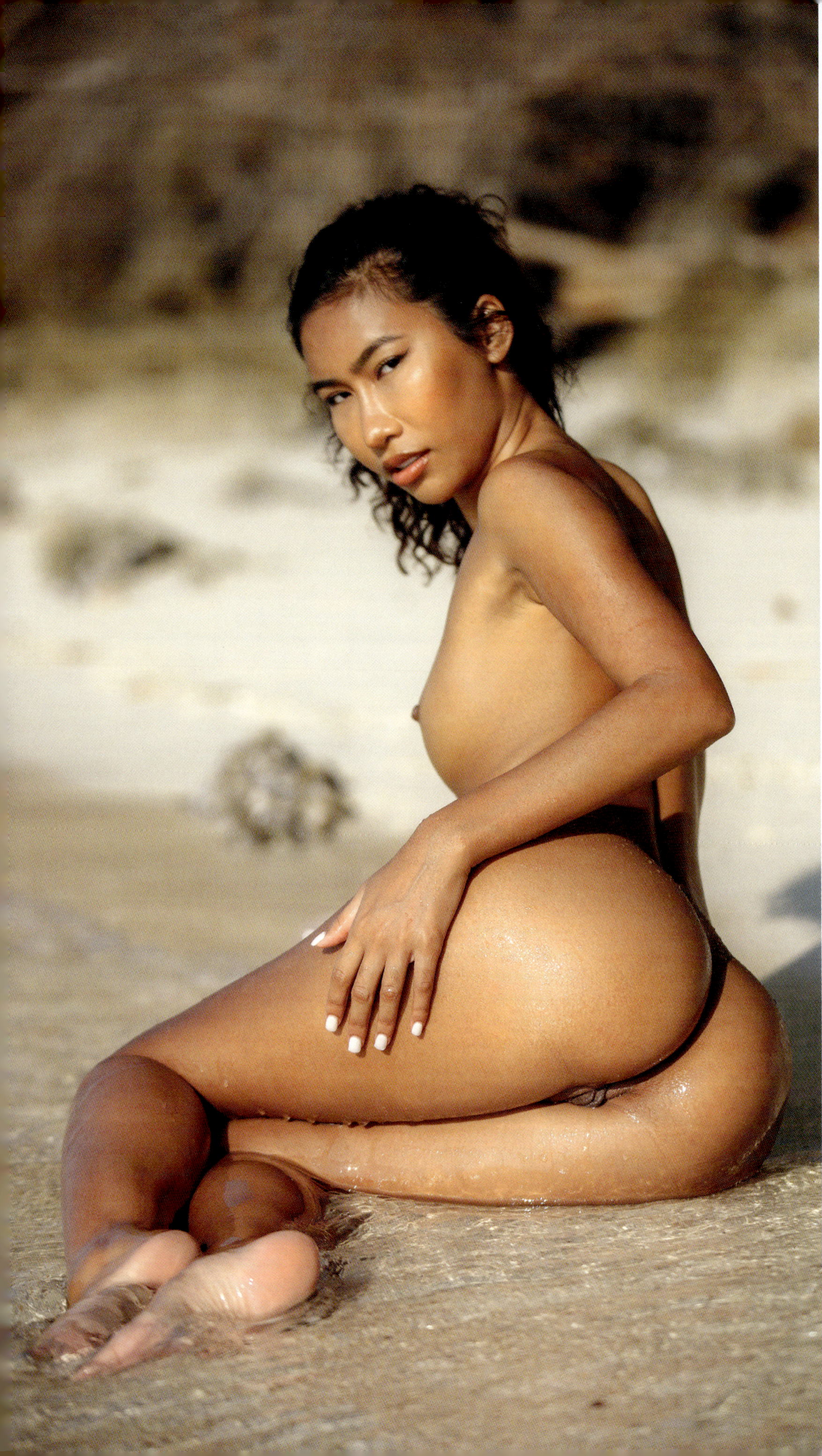

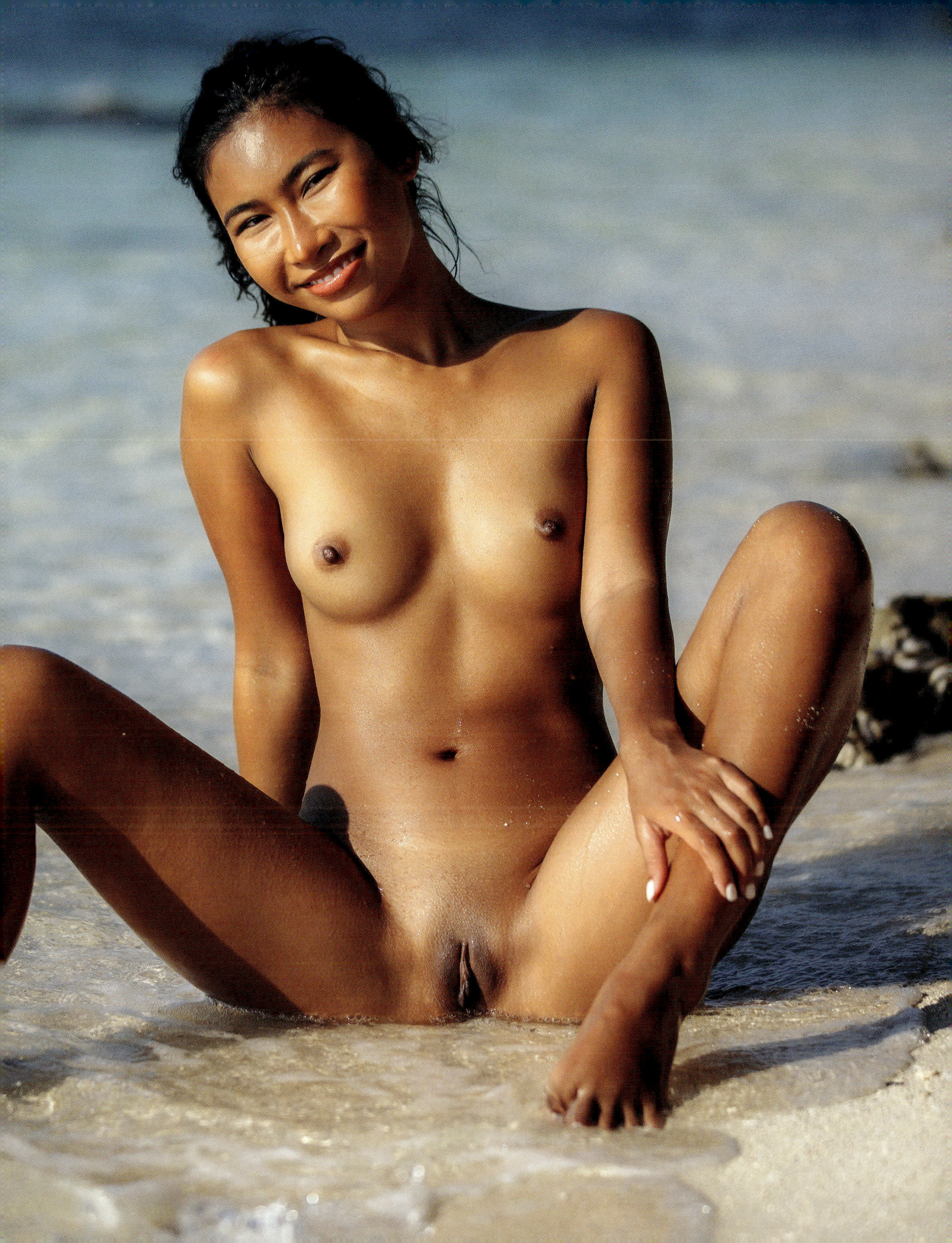

Ellie Luna
Kelly Collins

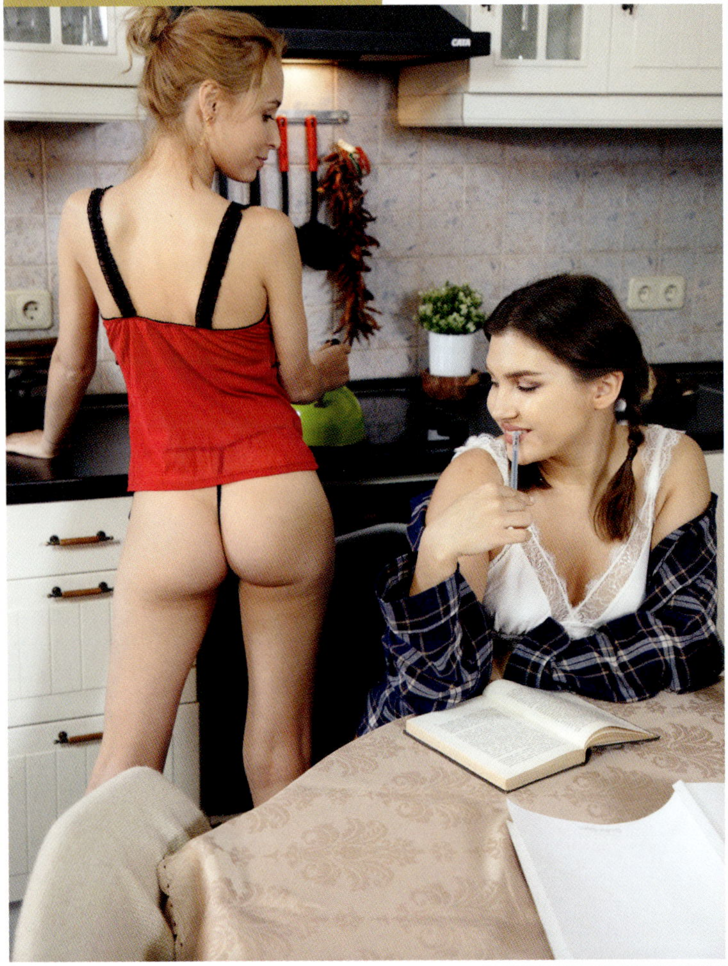

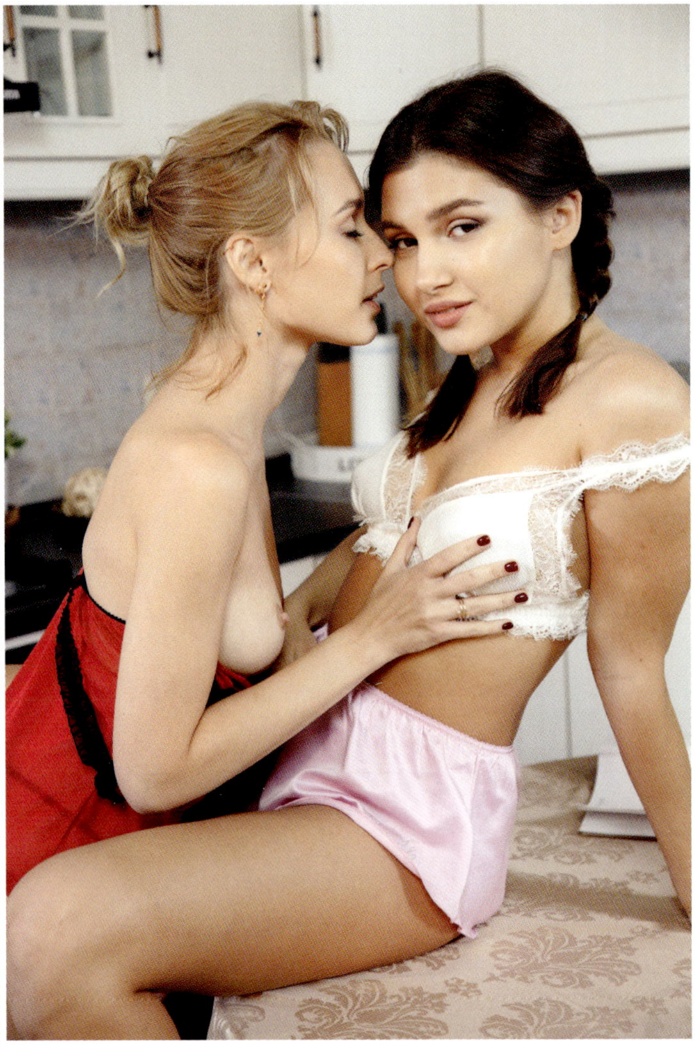

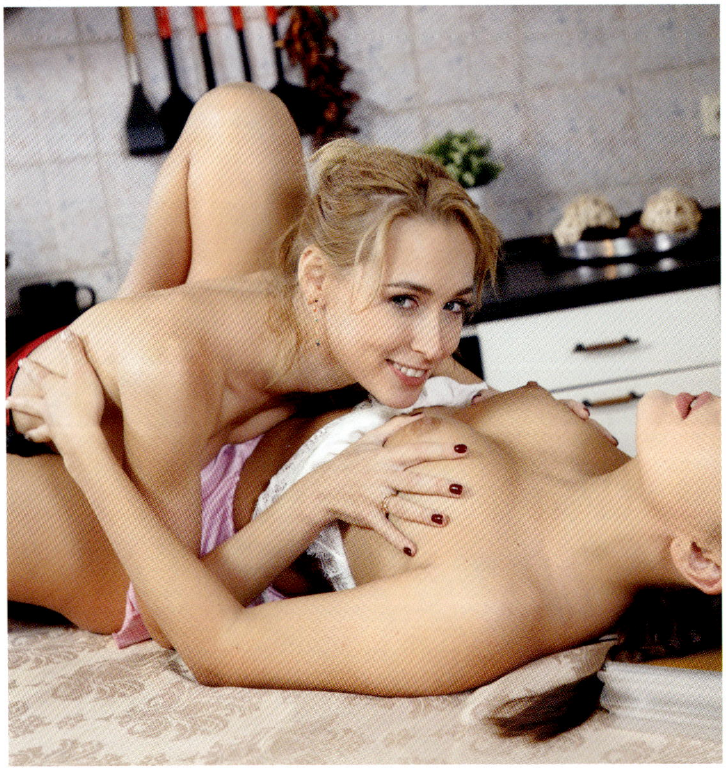

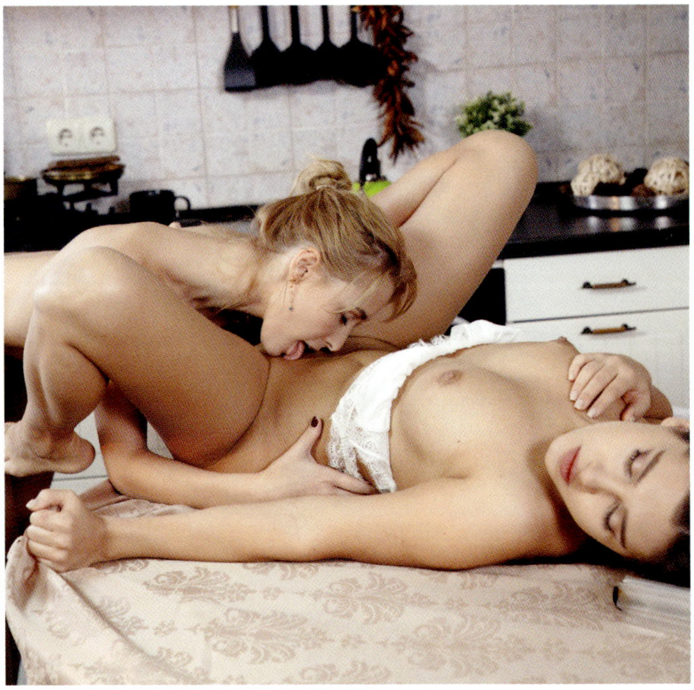

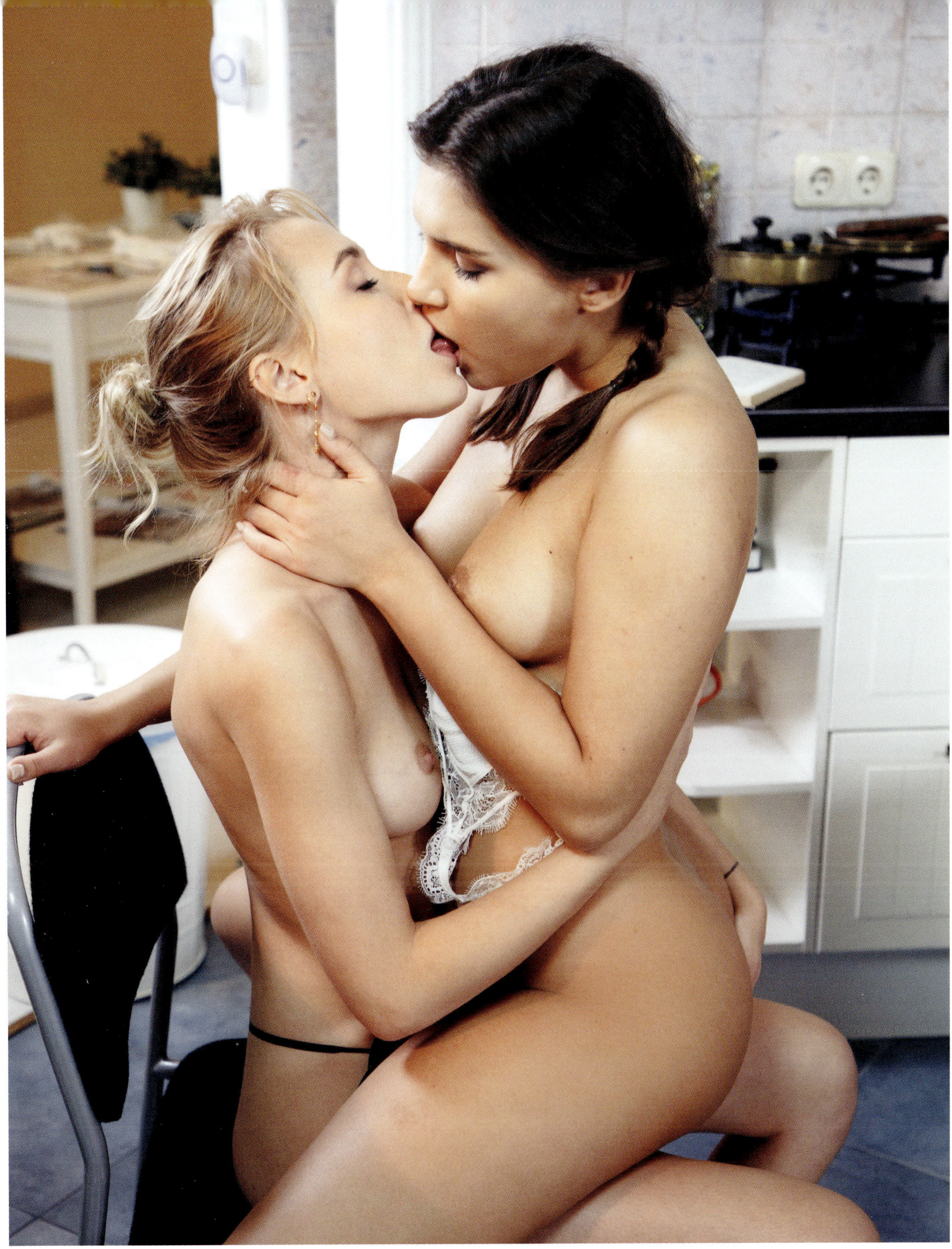

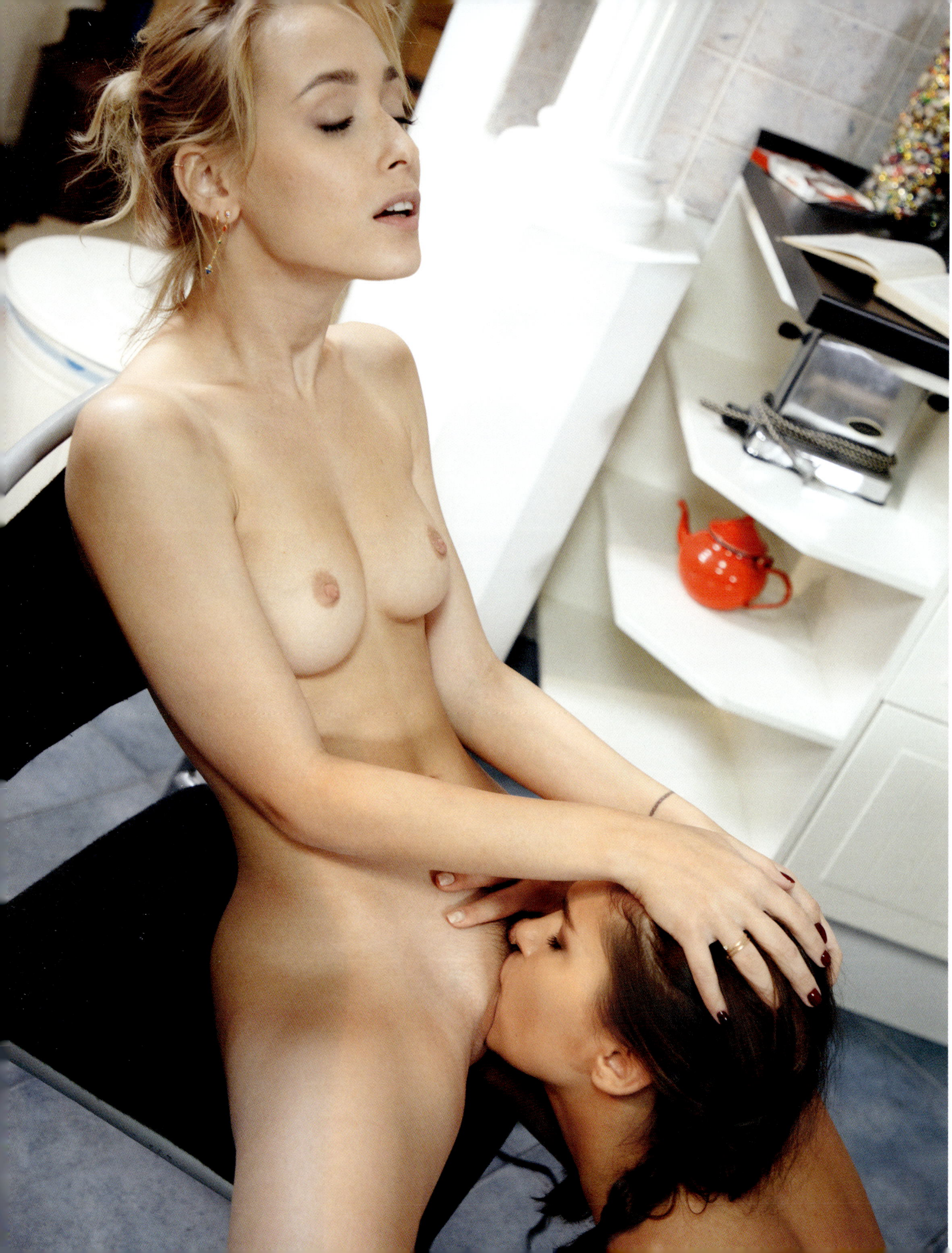

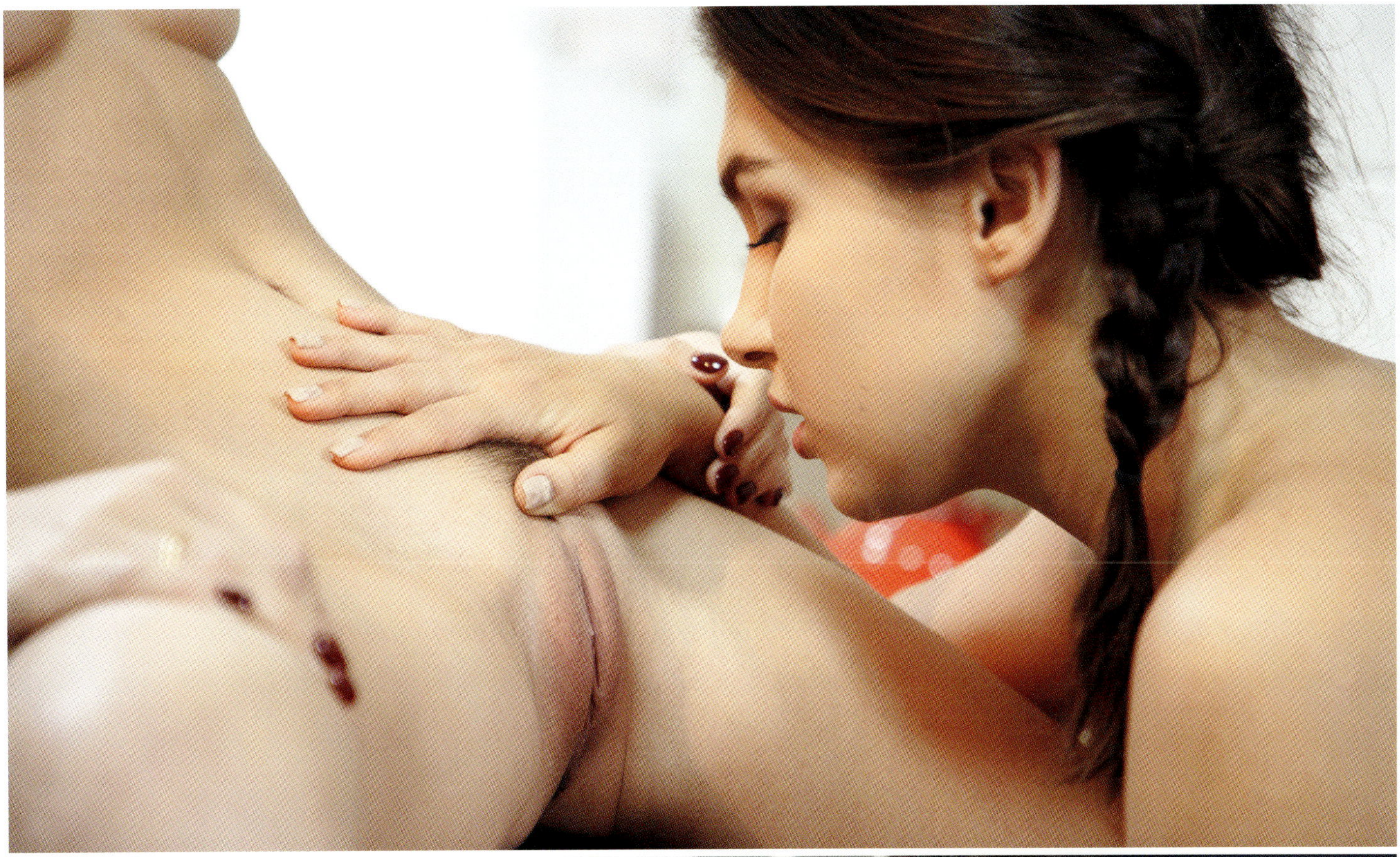

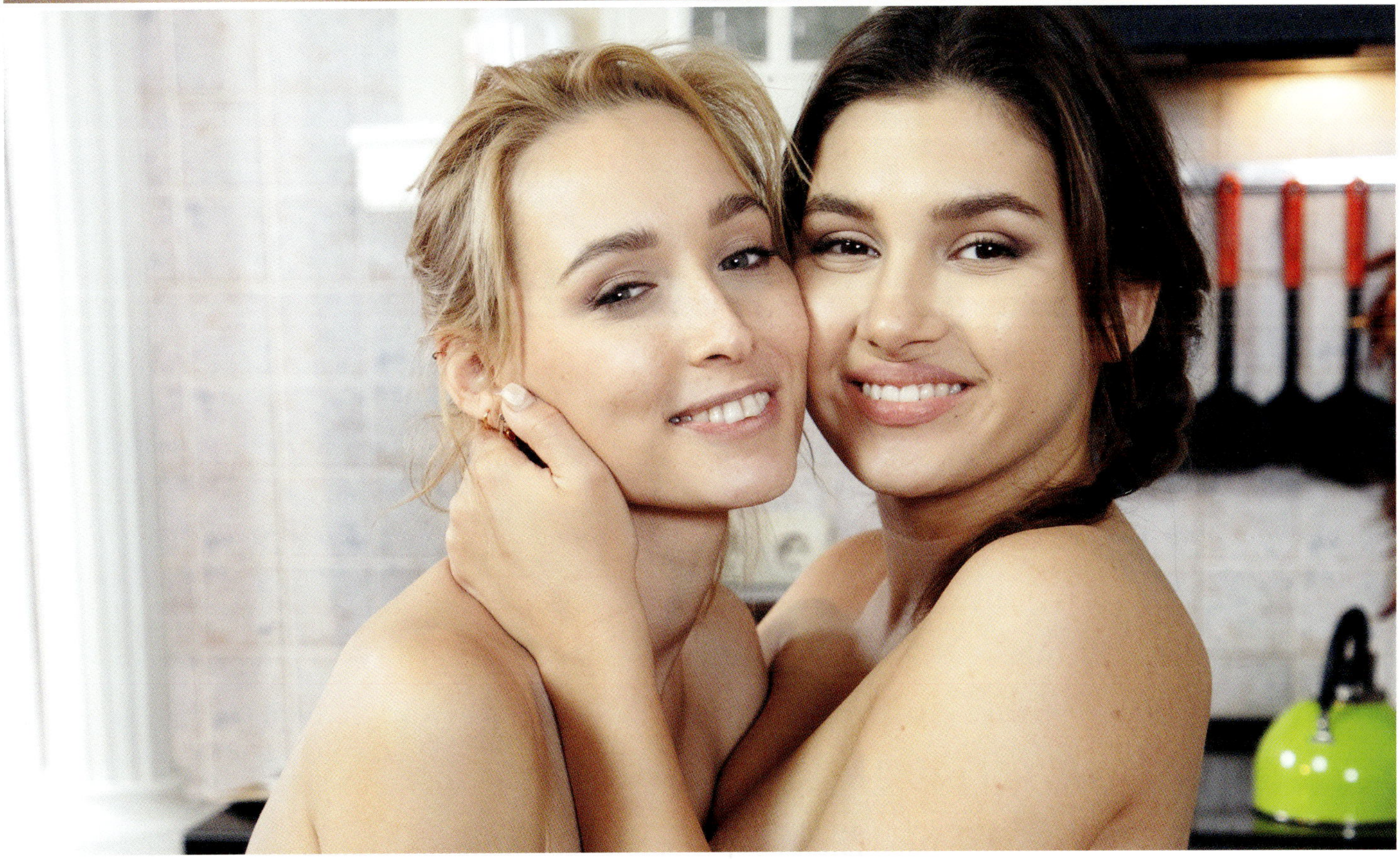

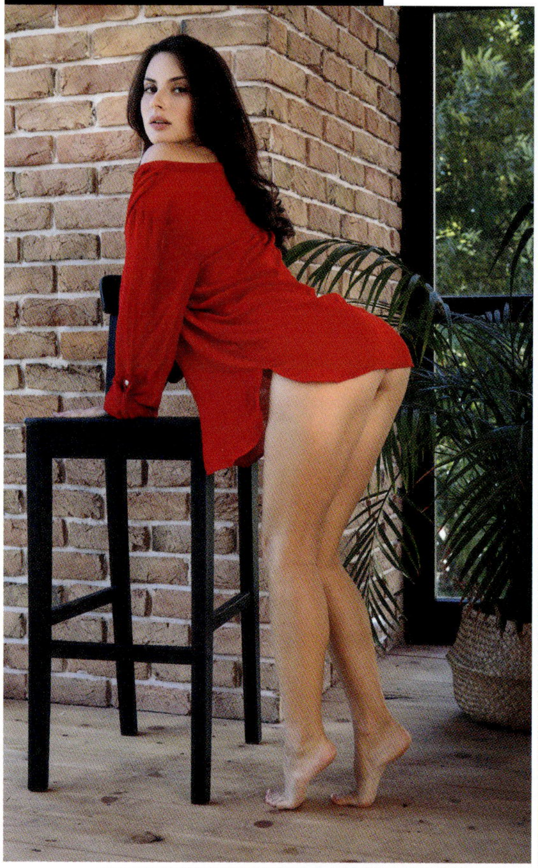

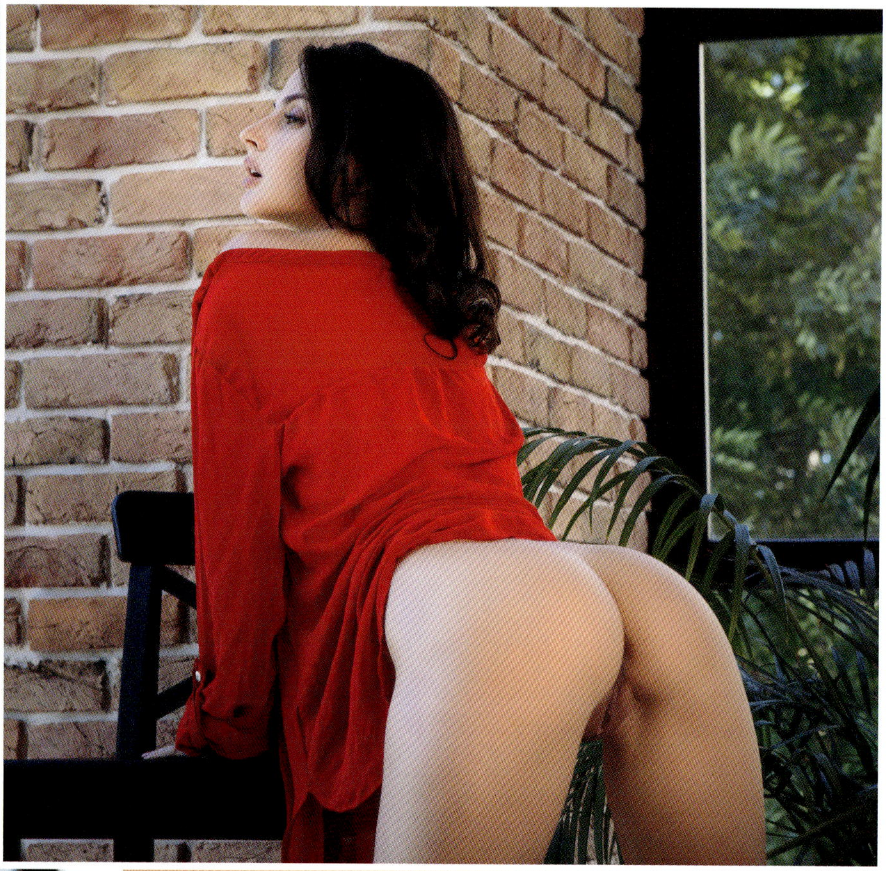

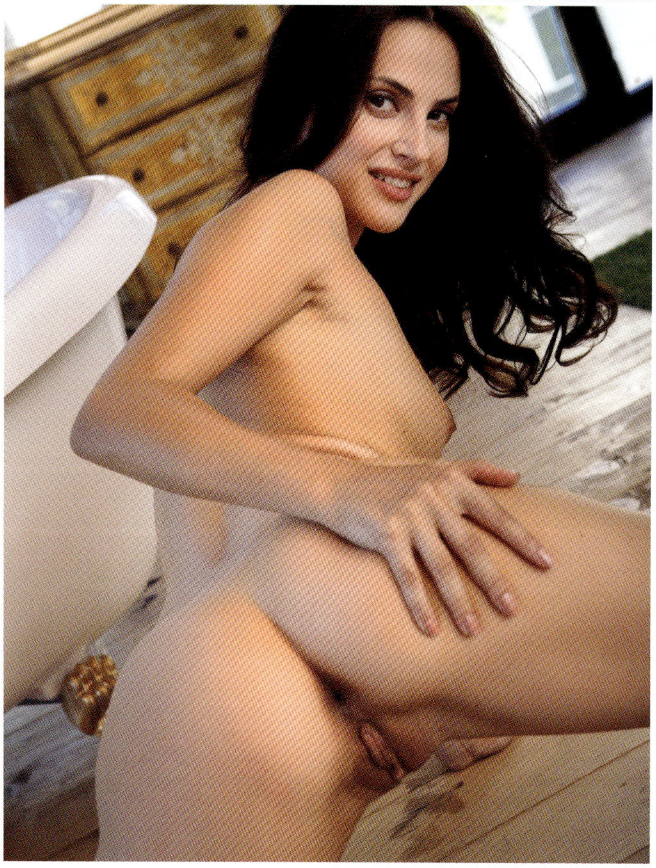

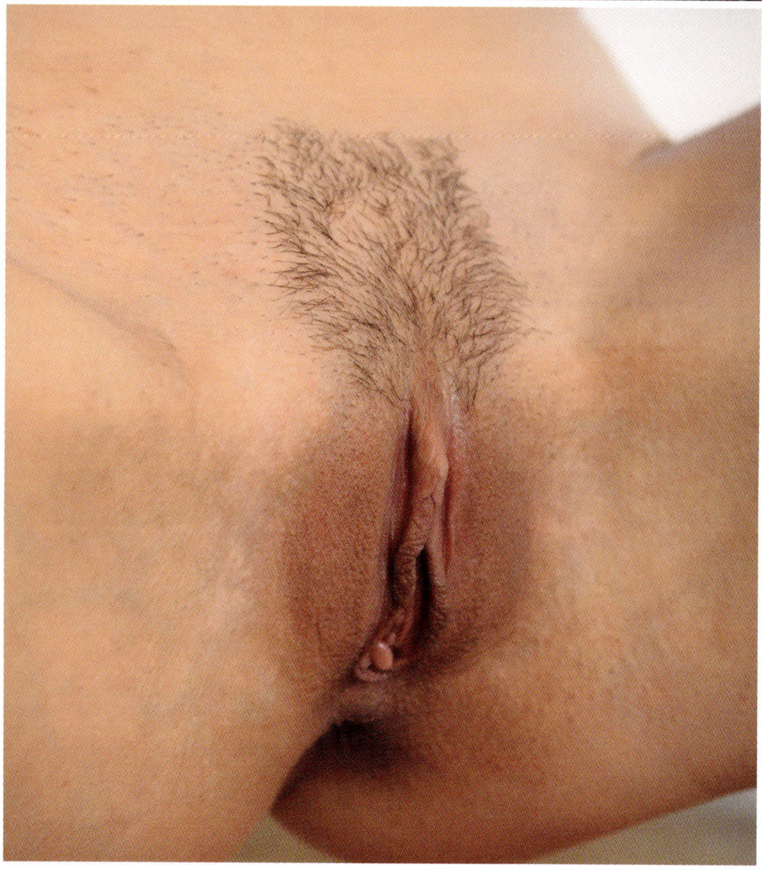

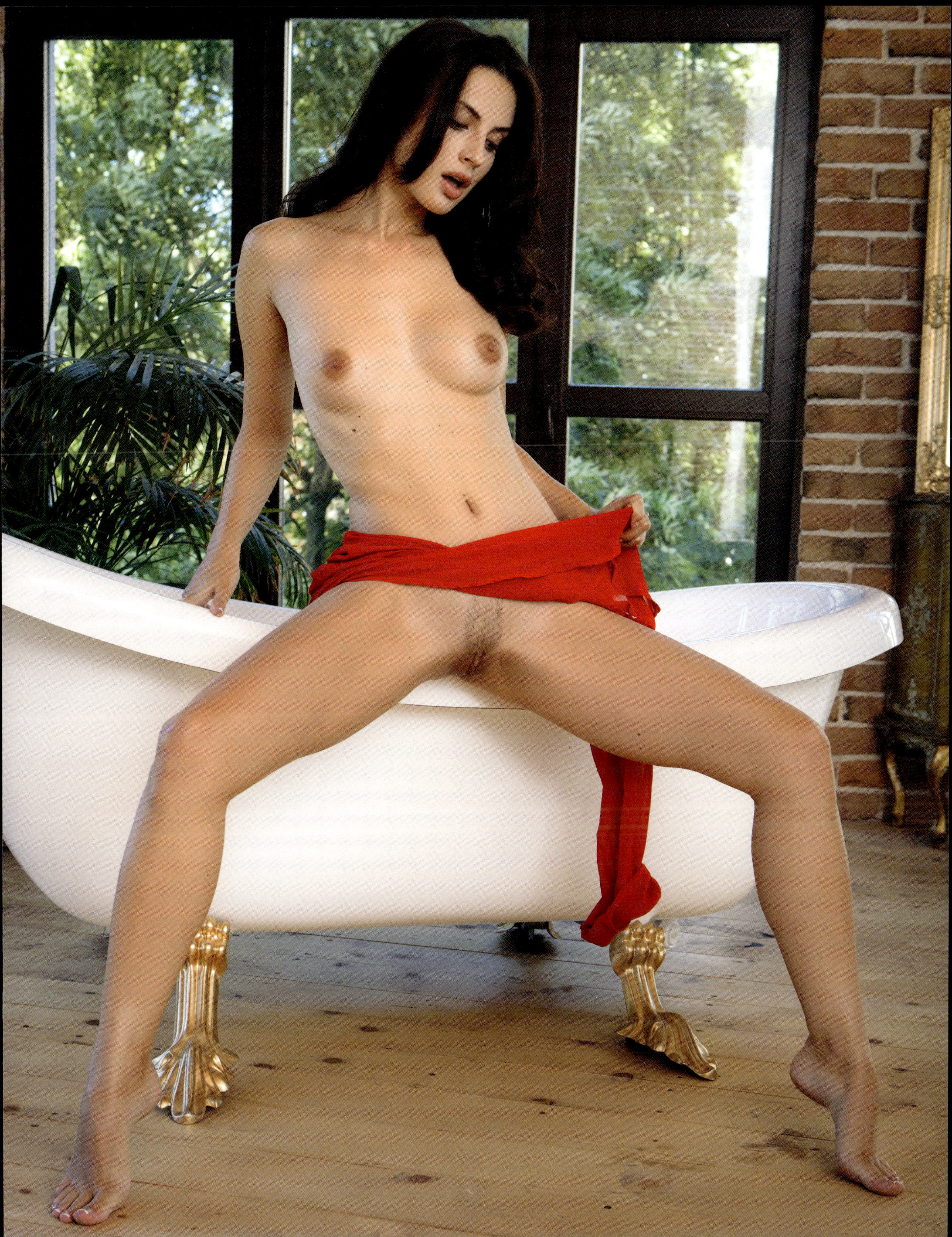

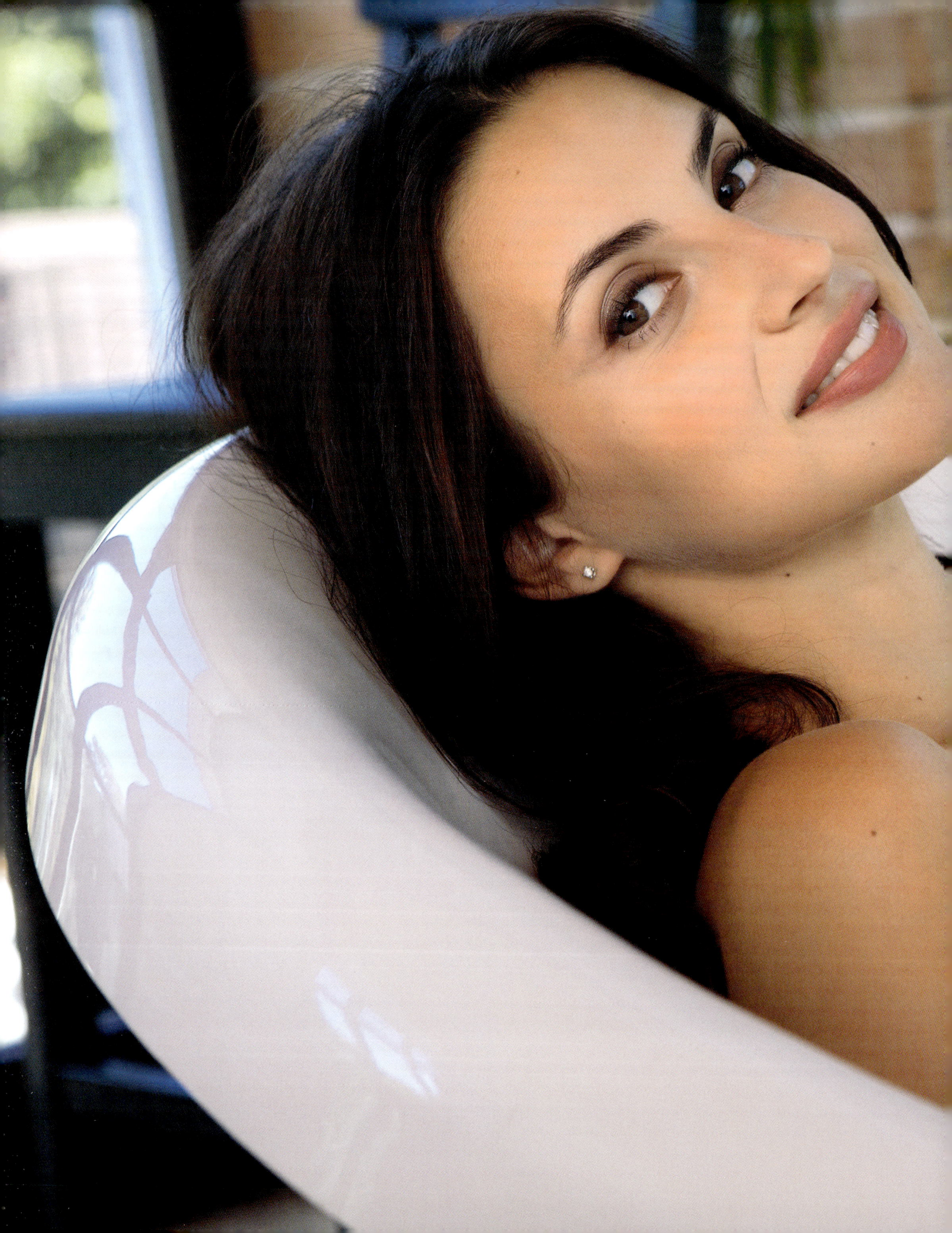

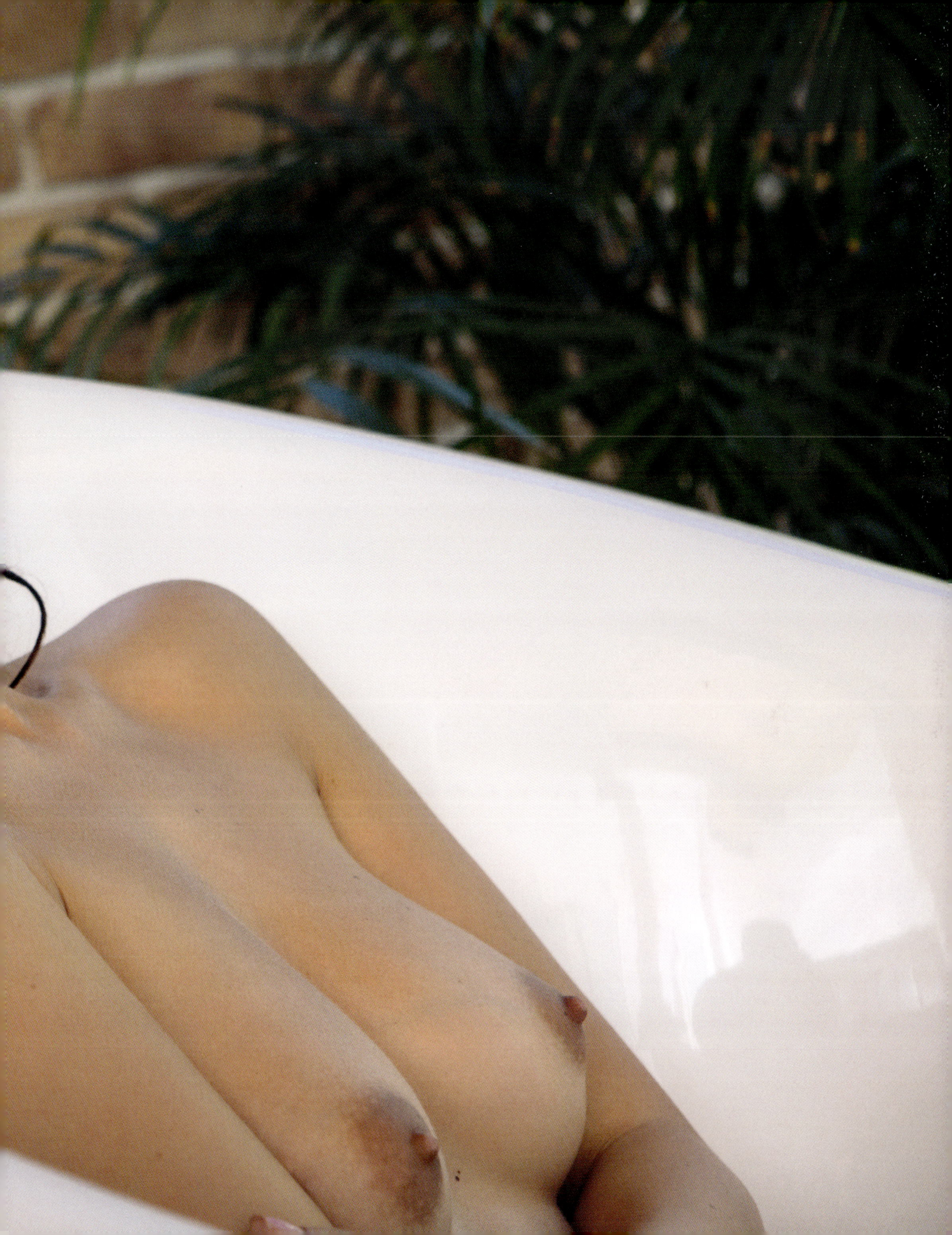

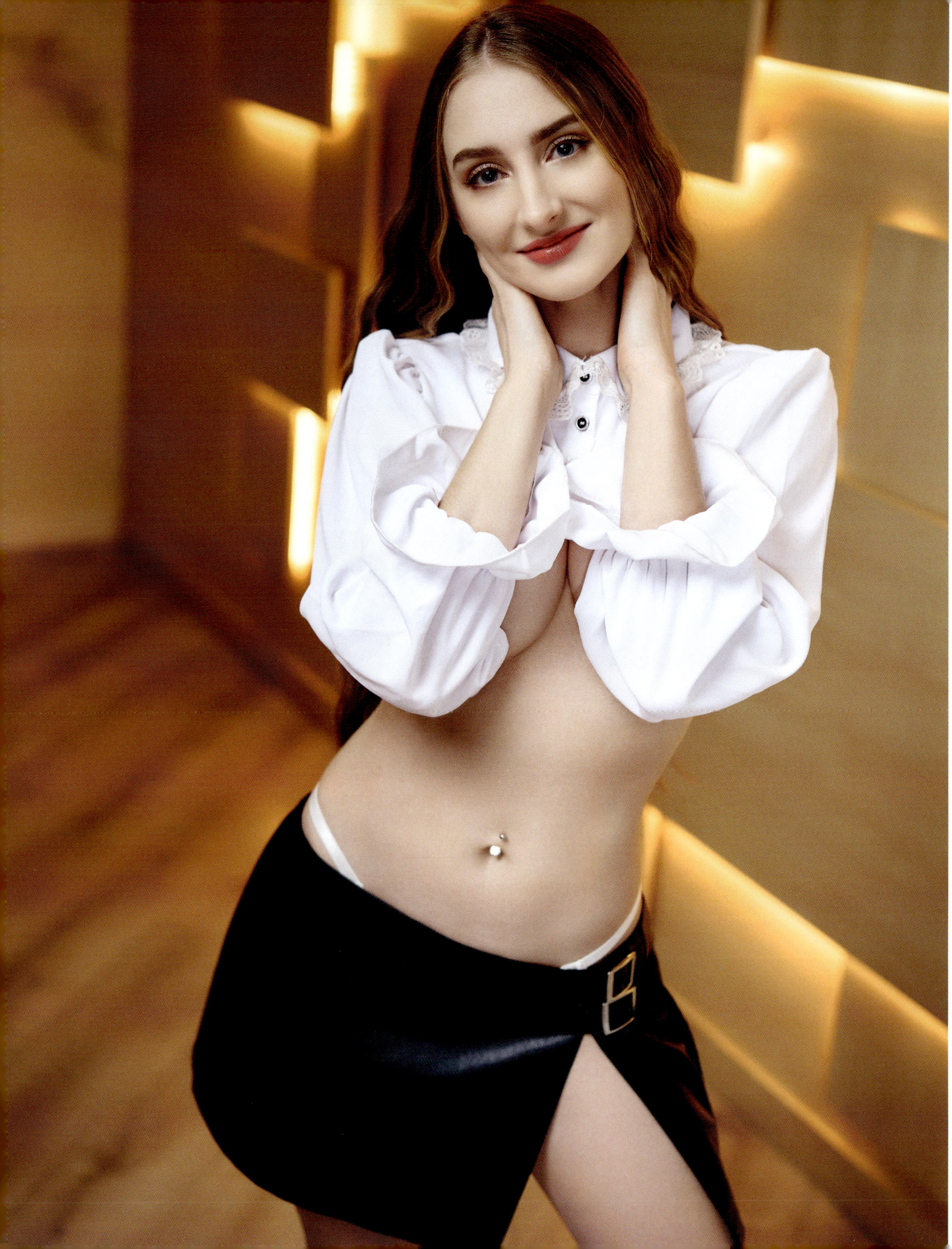

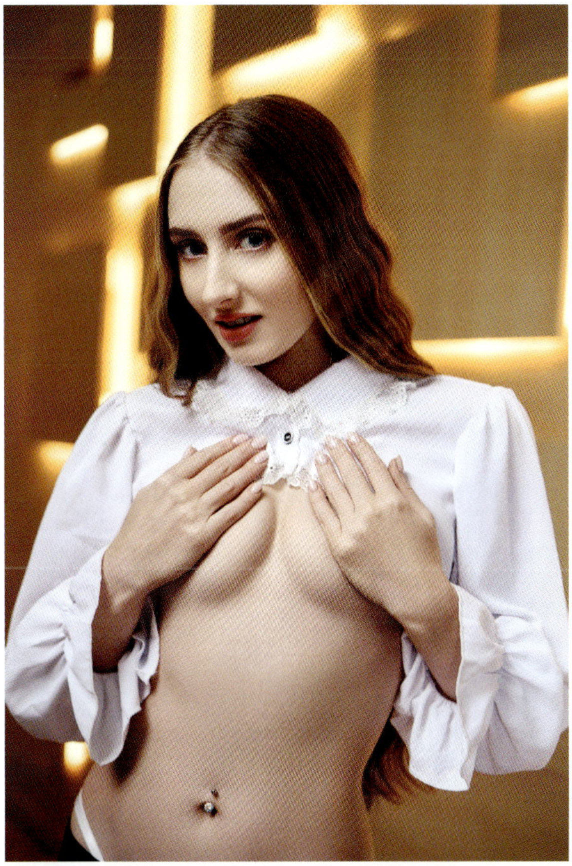

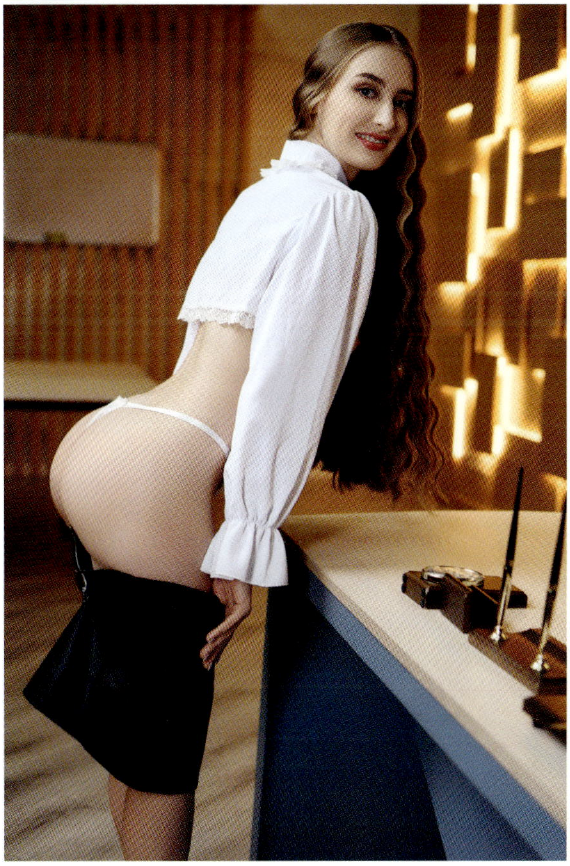

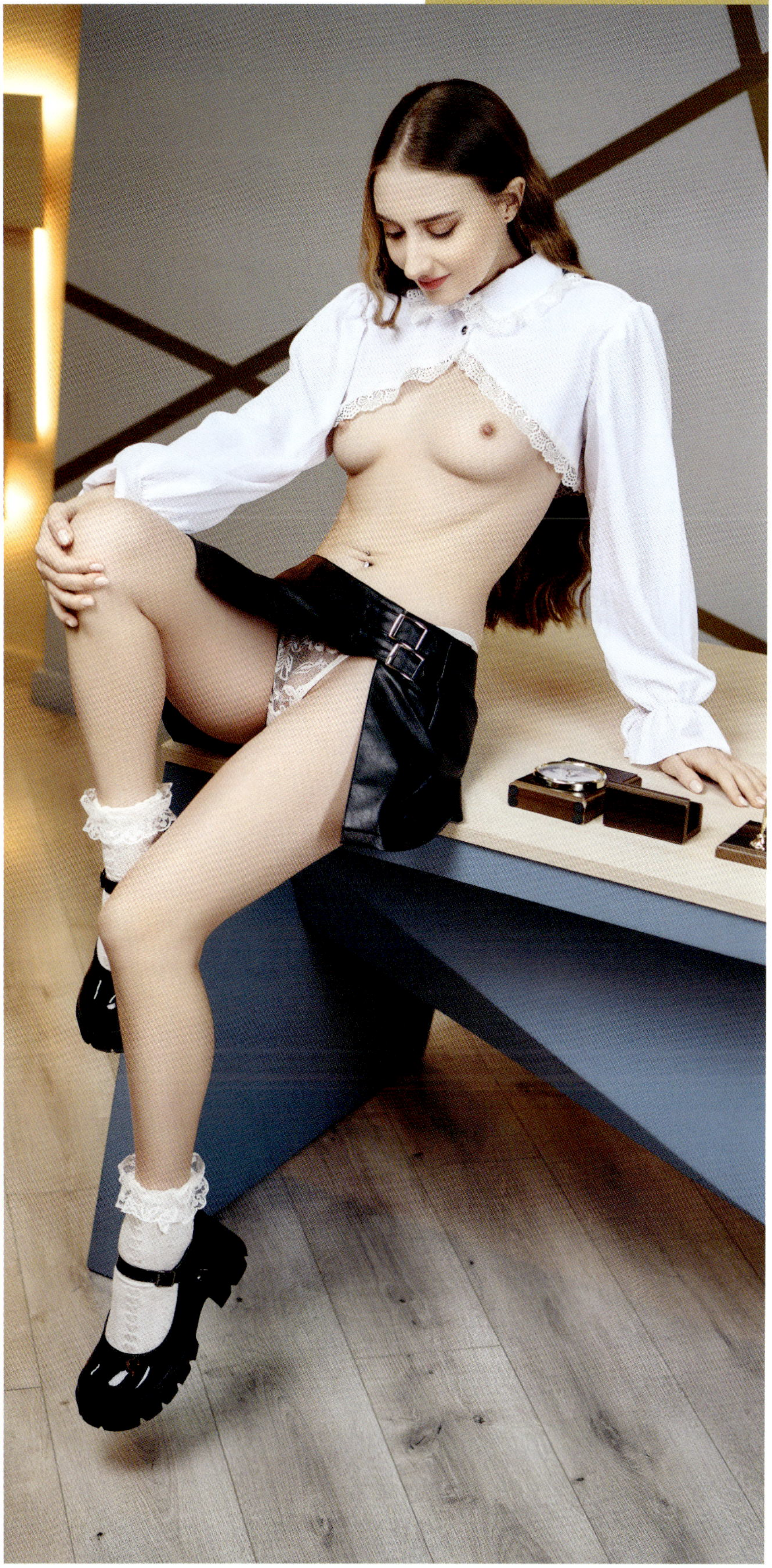

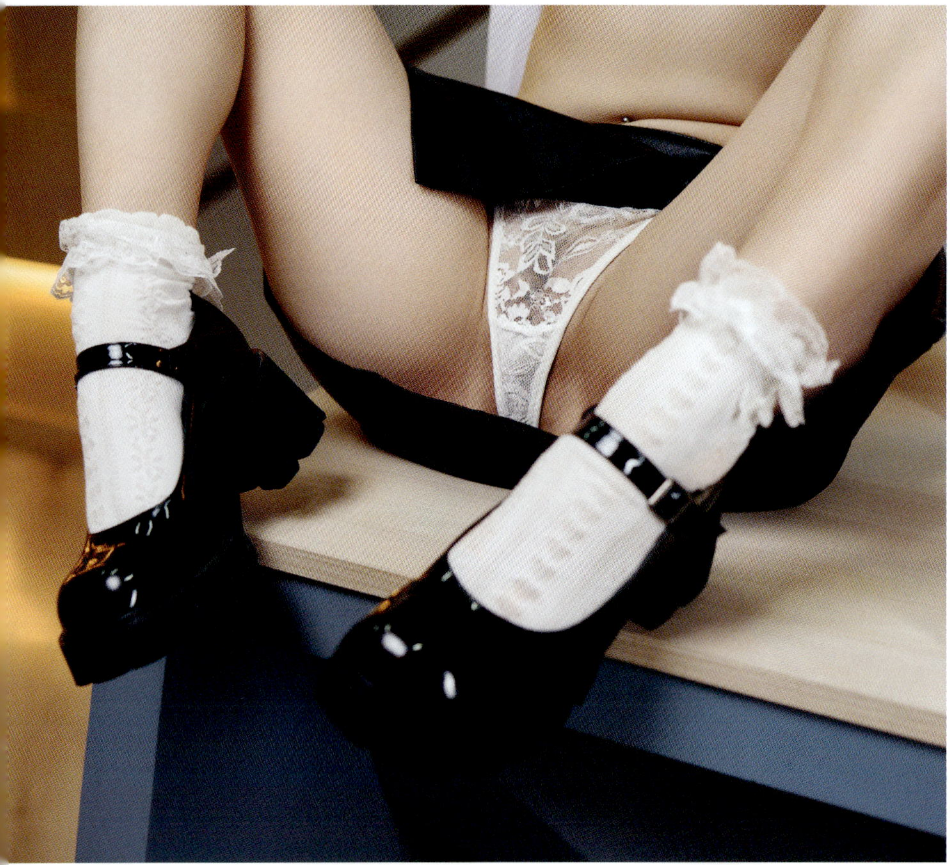
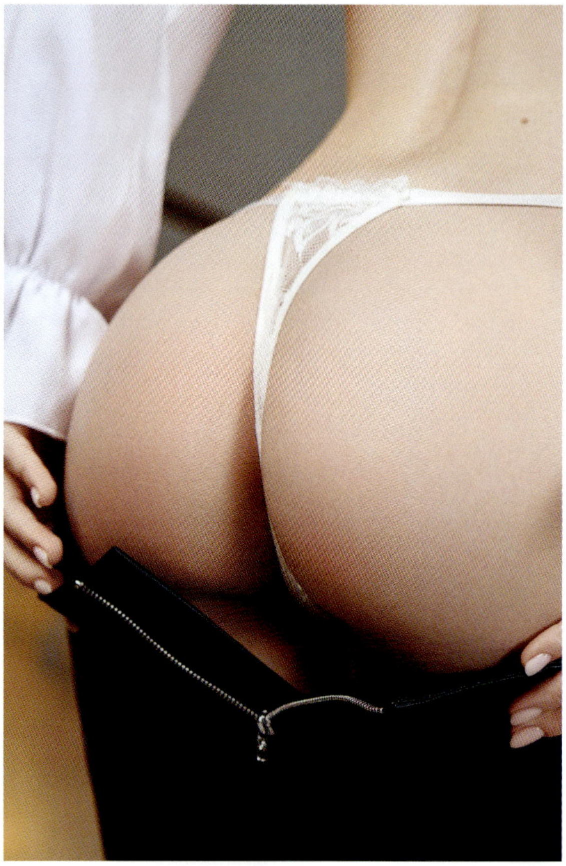
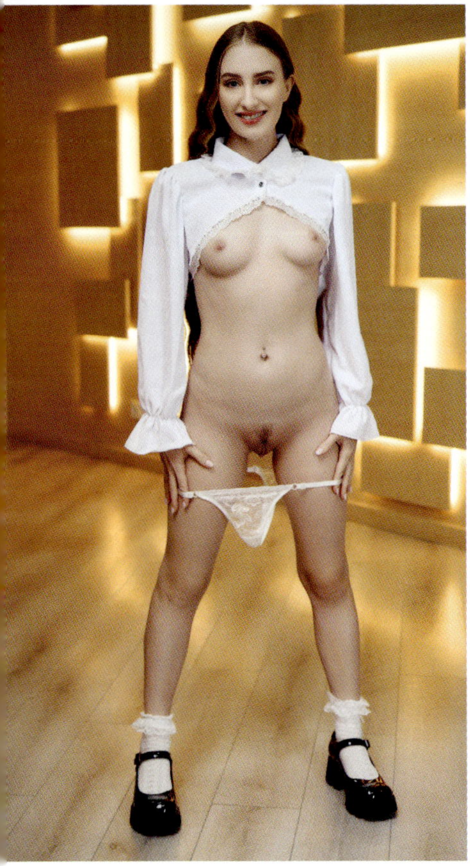
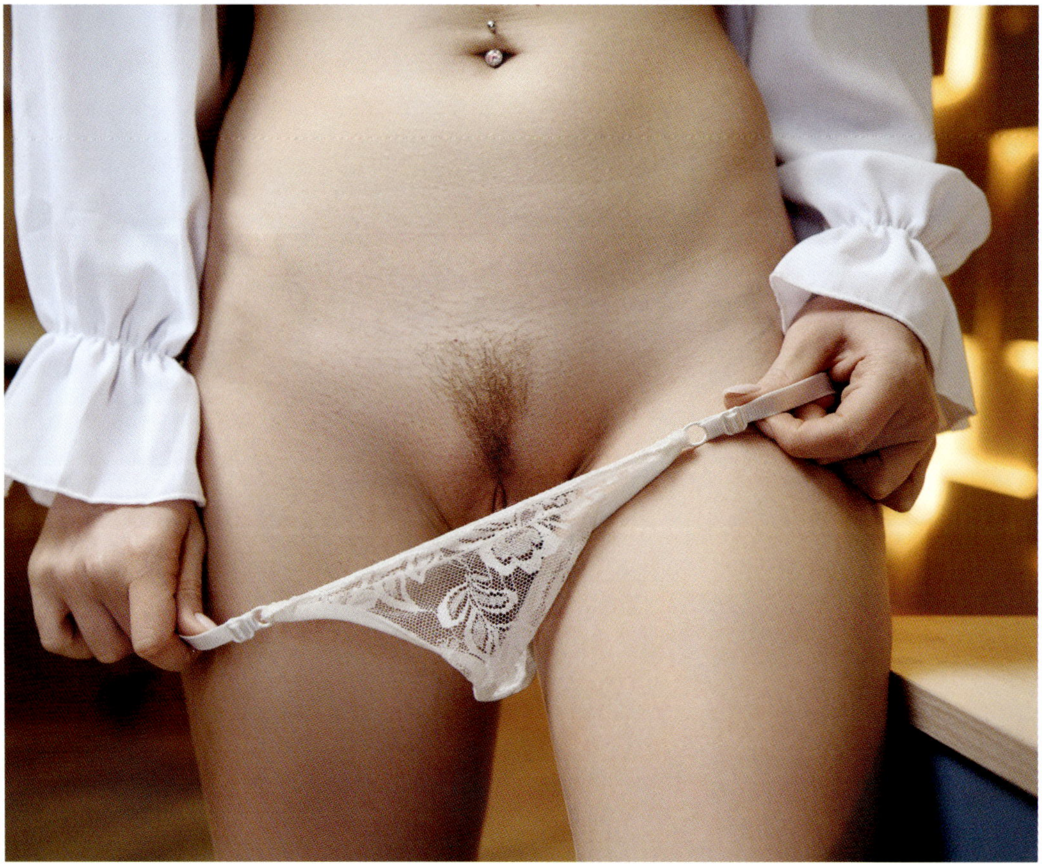

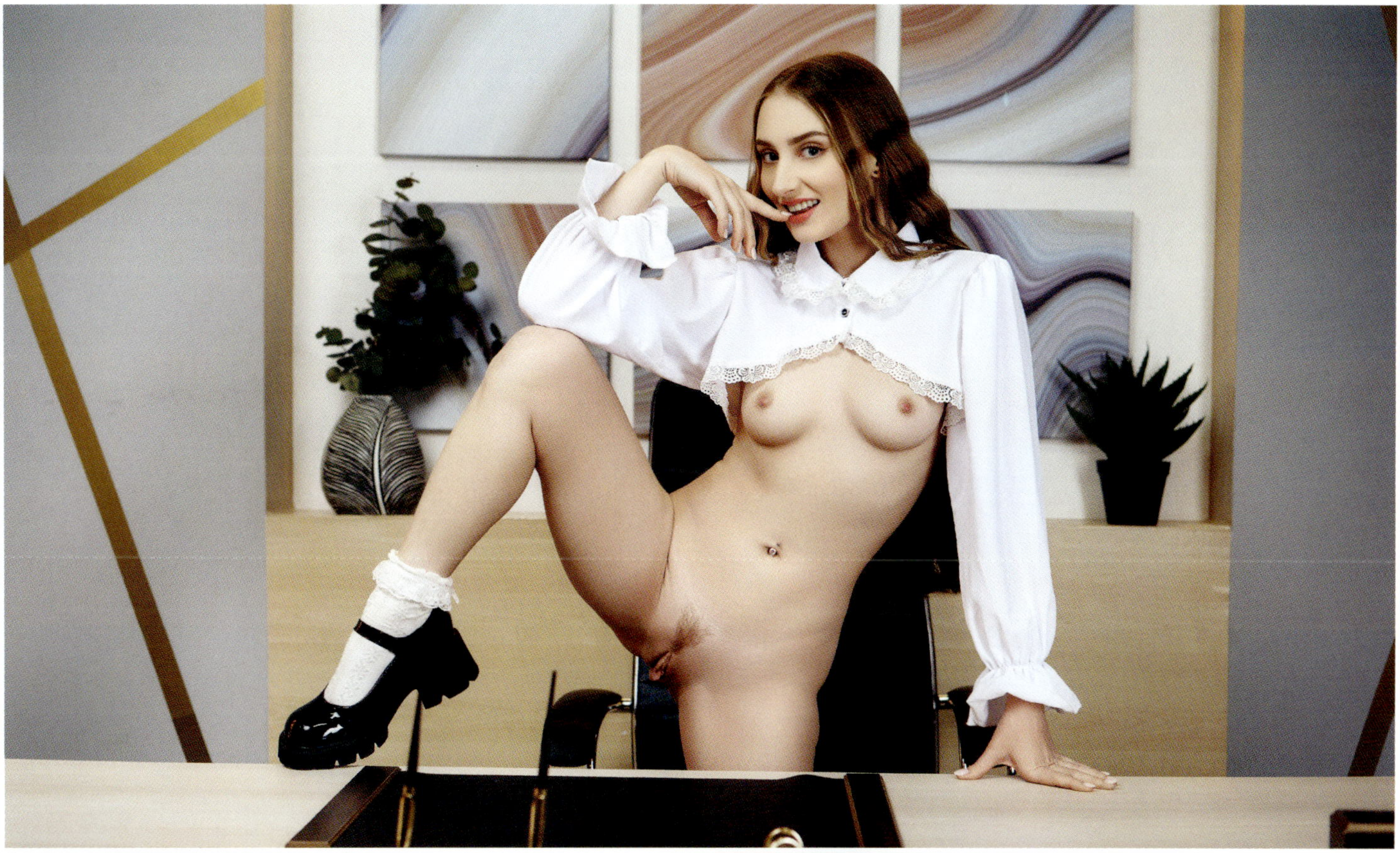

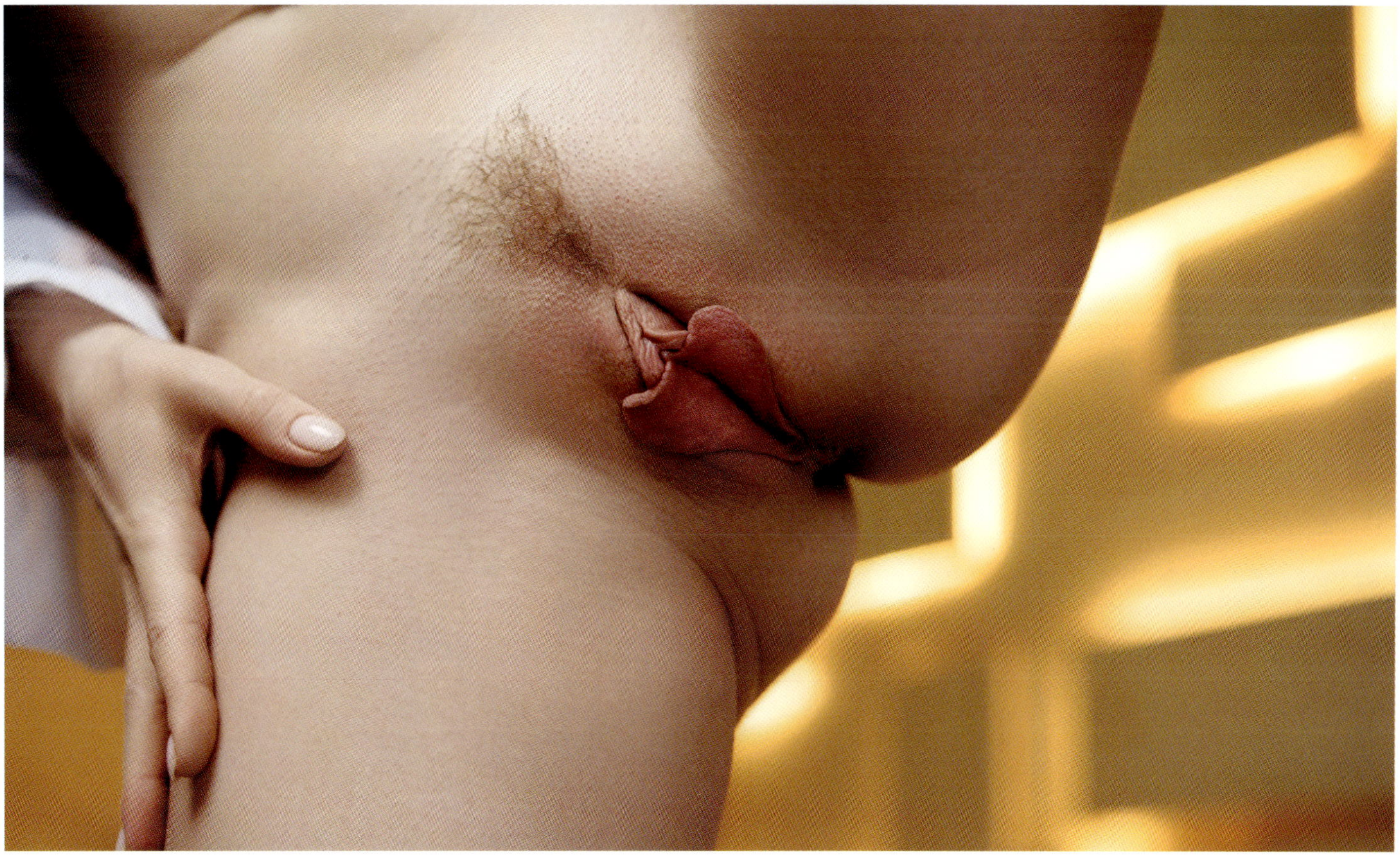

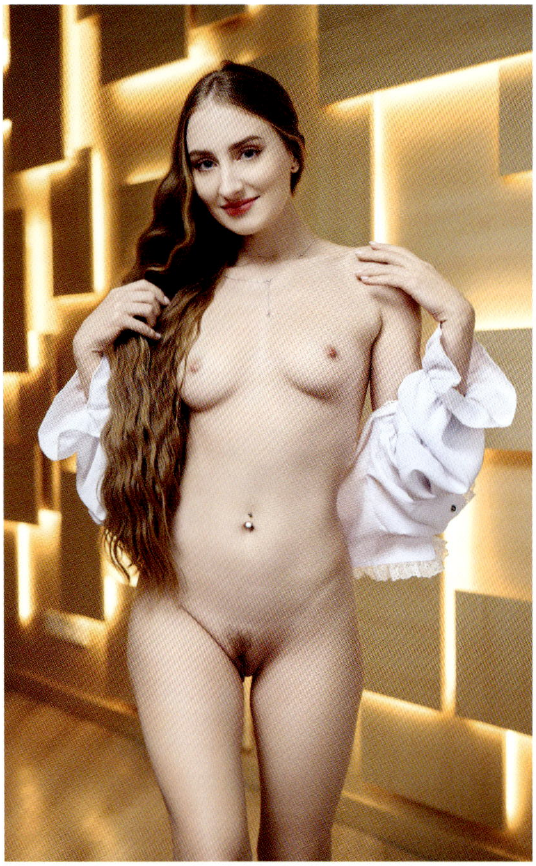

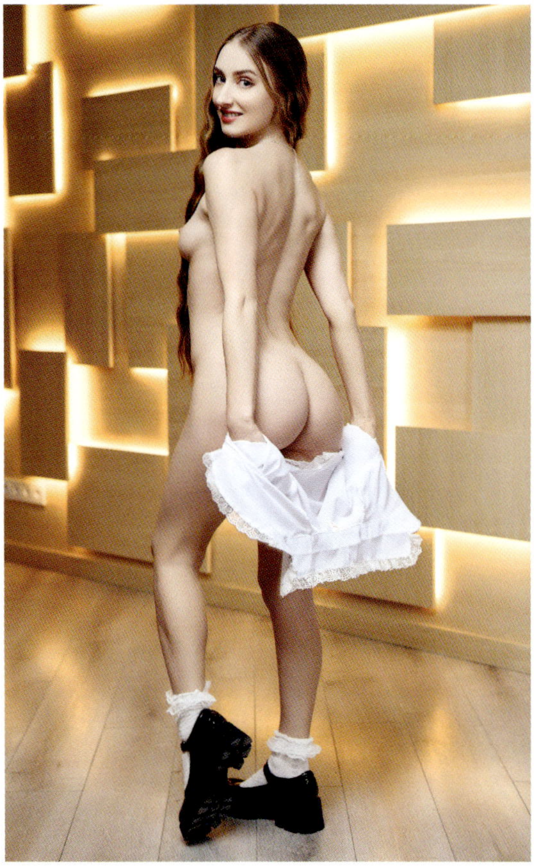

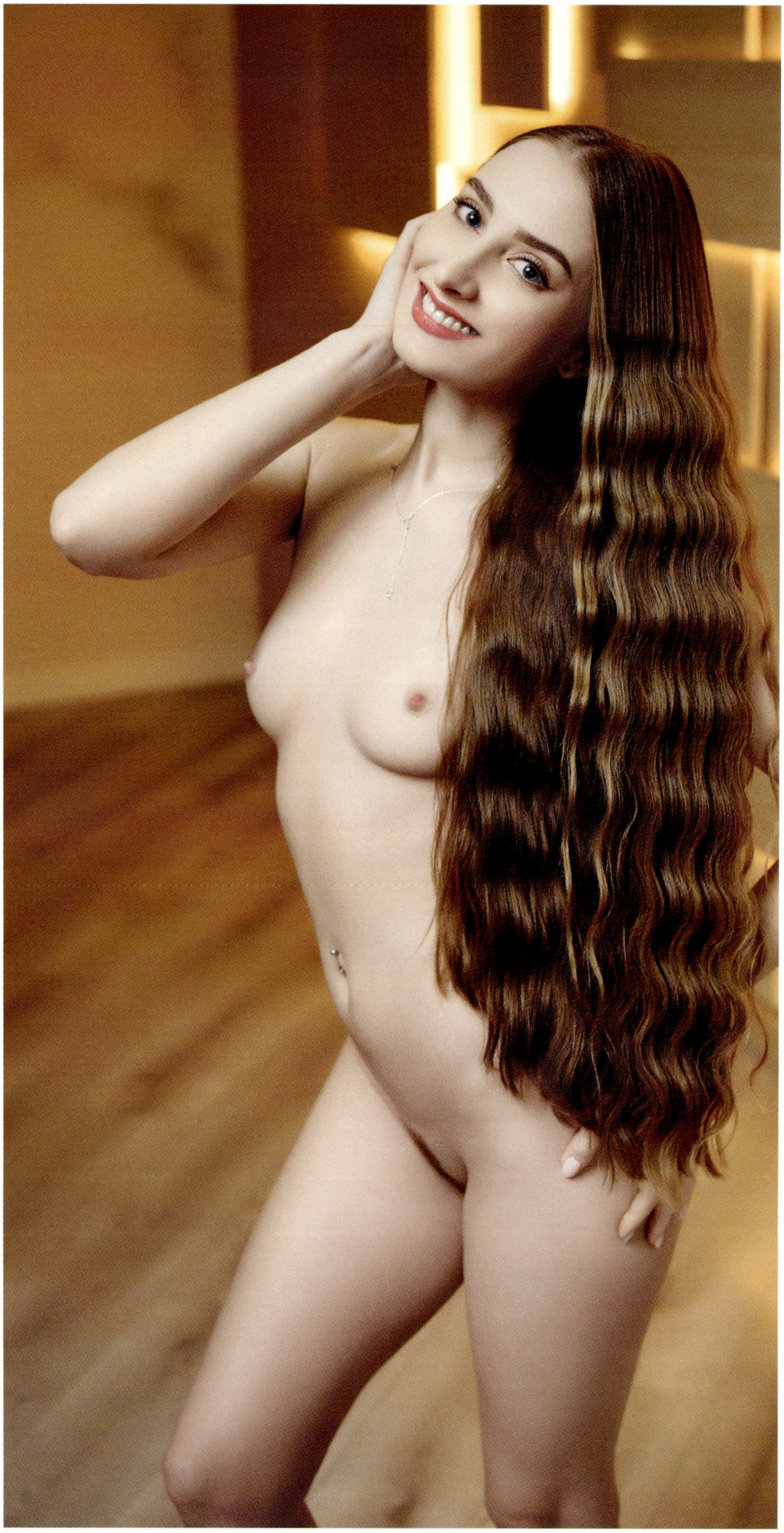

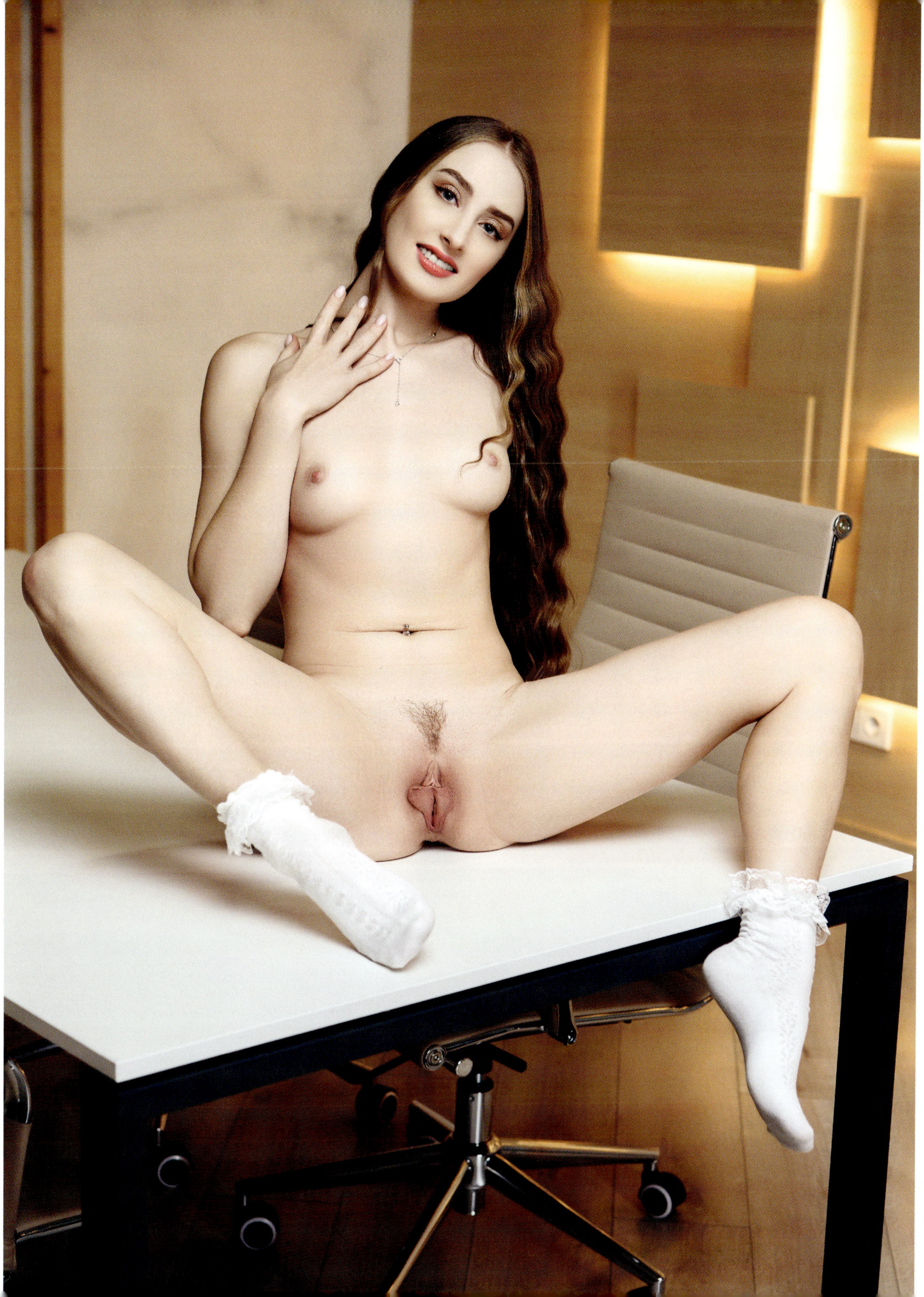

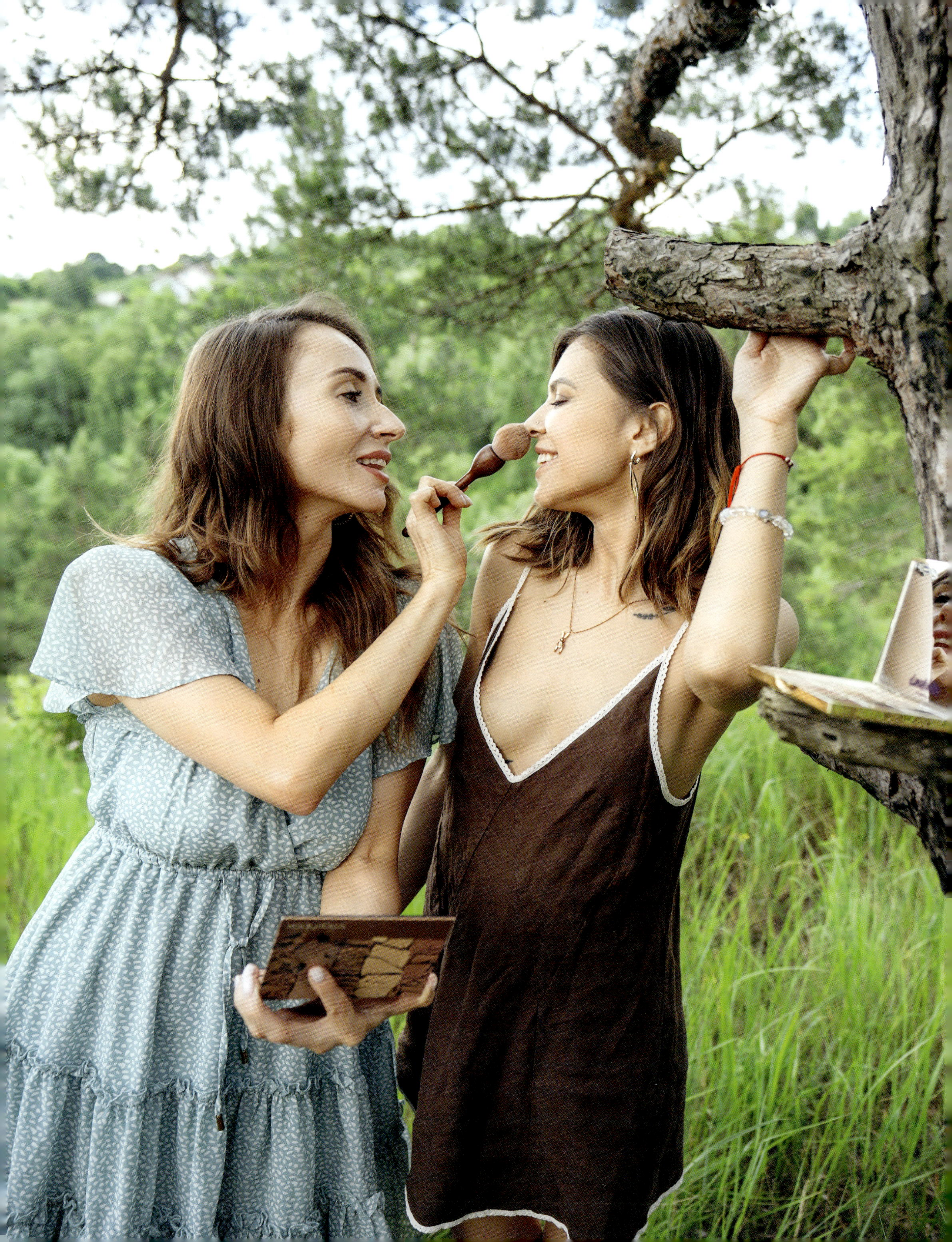

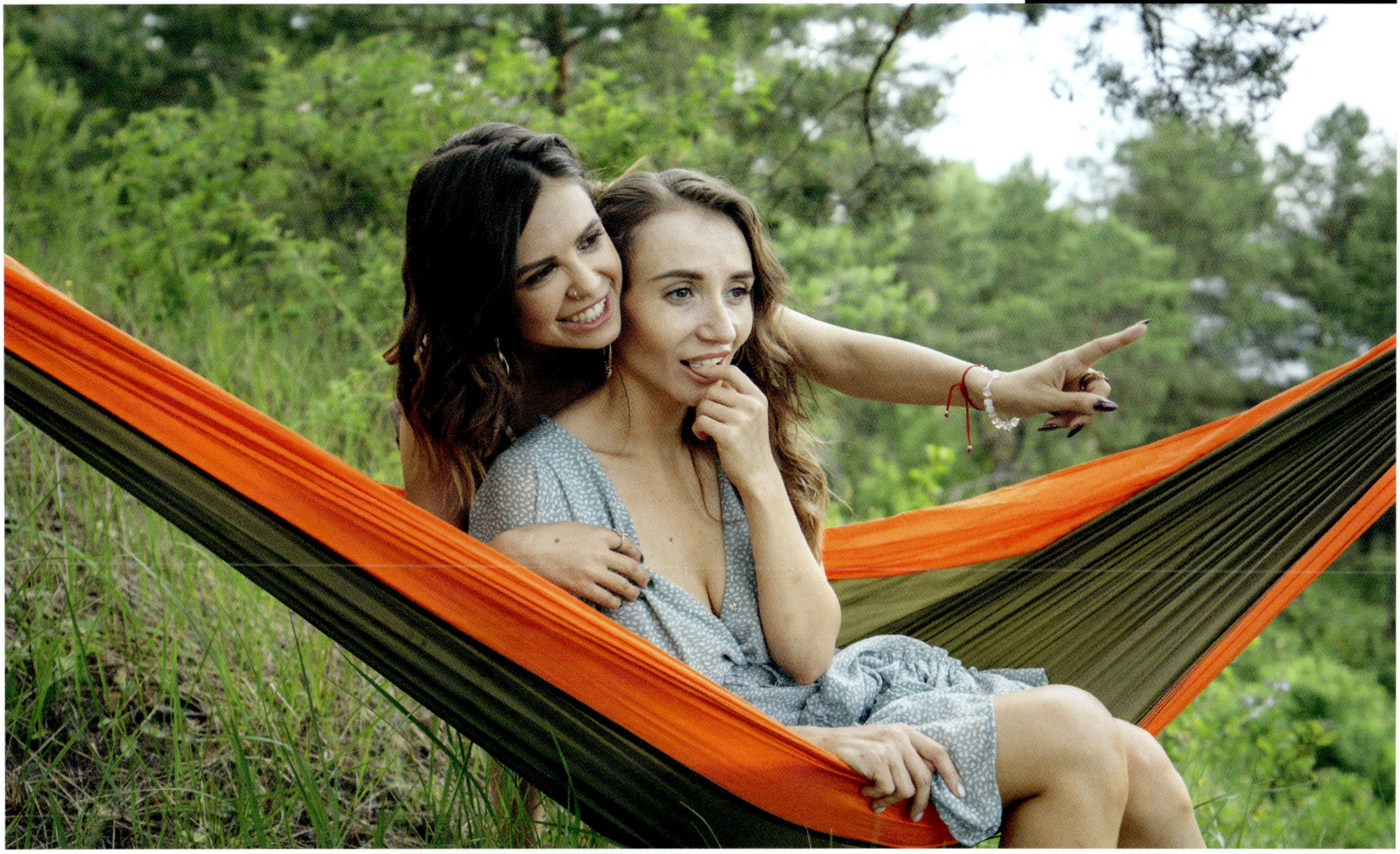

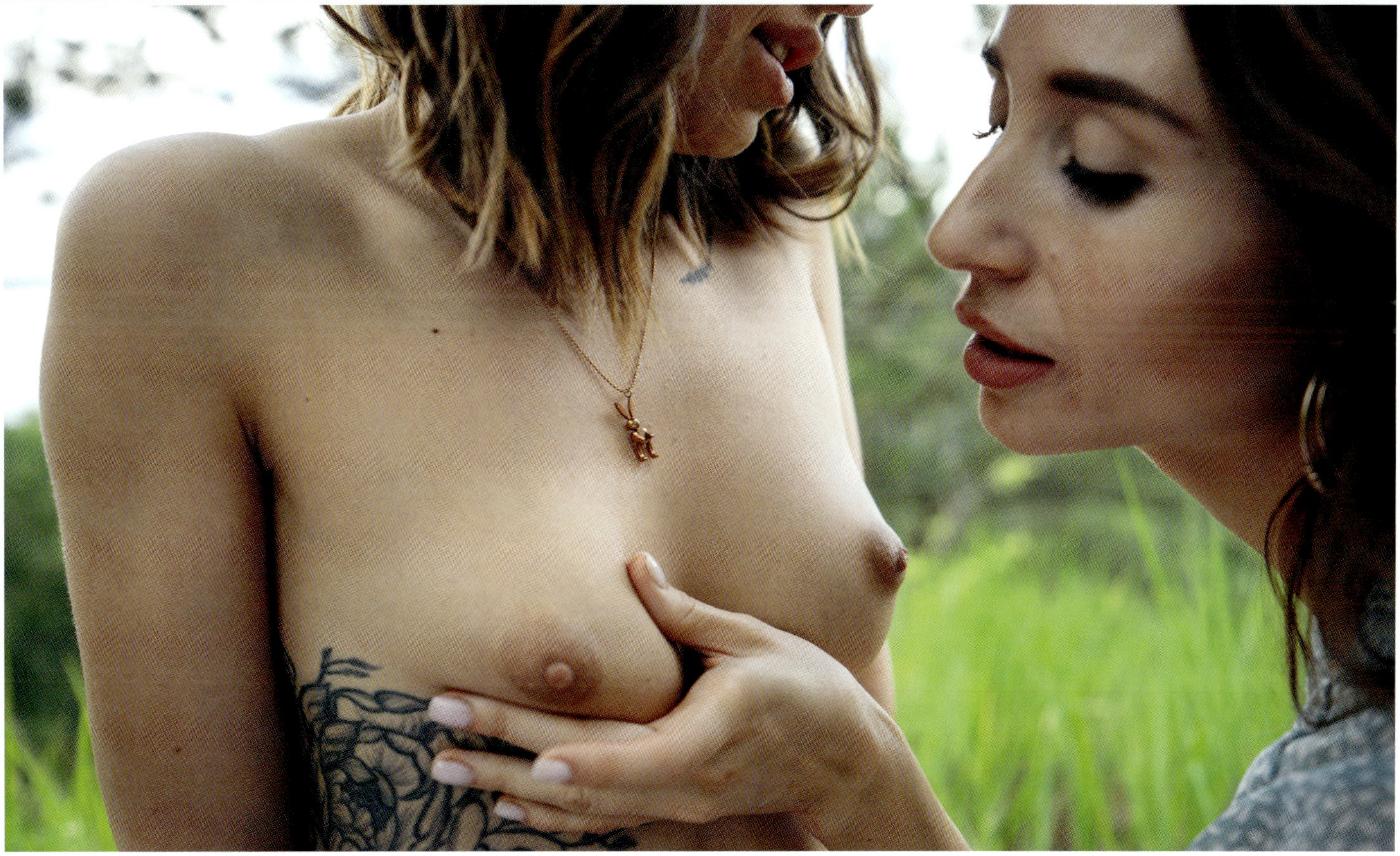

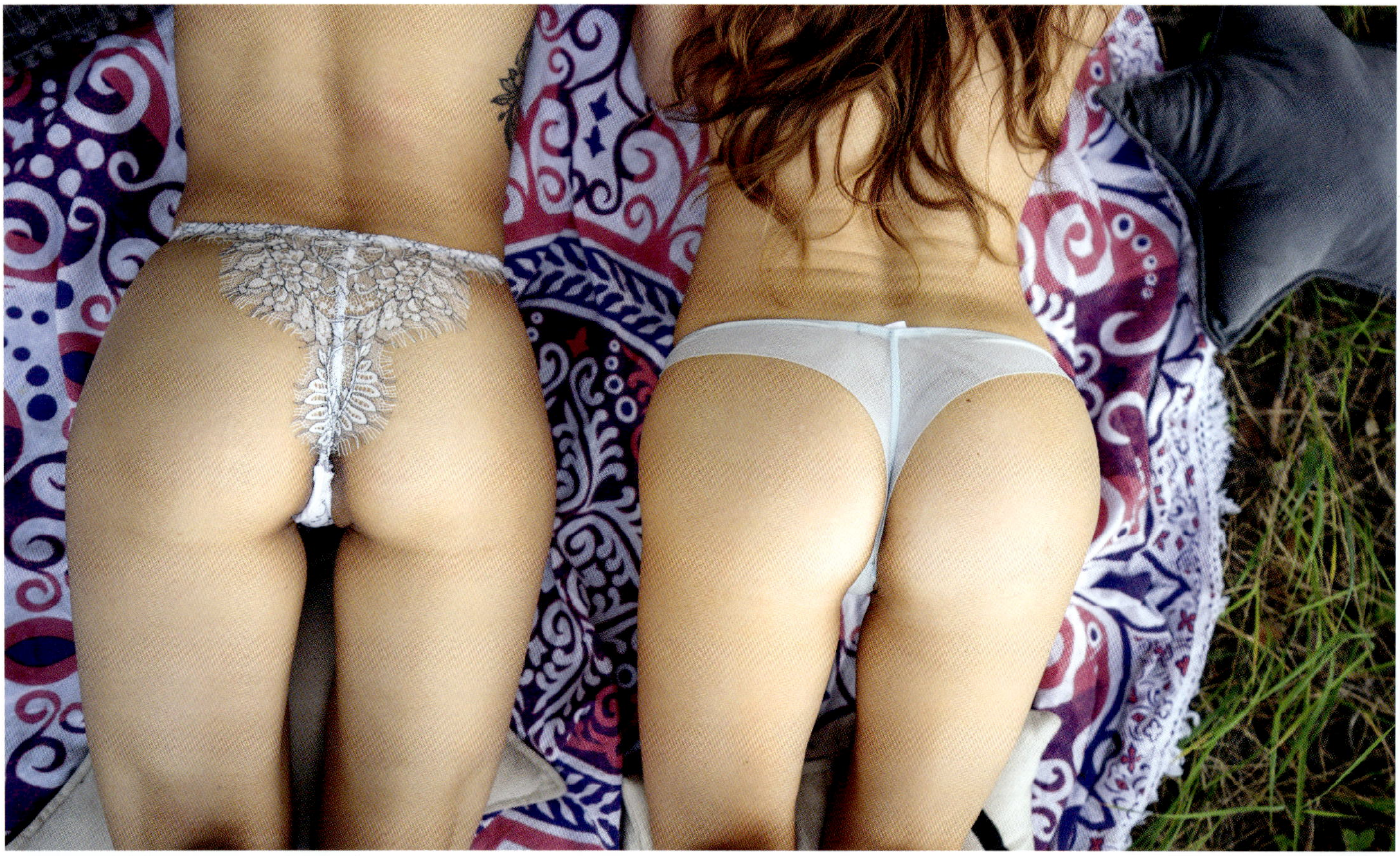

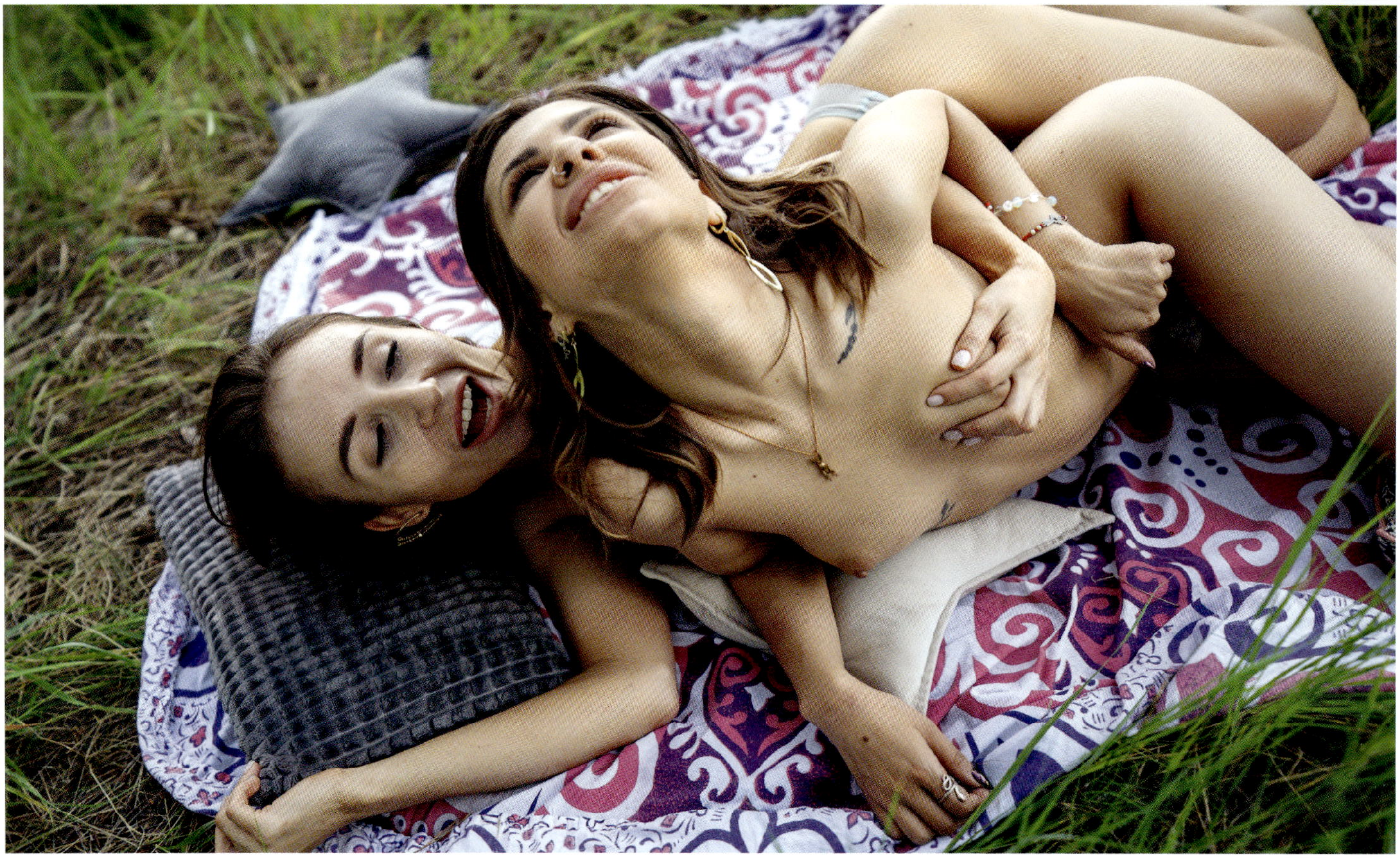

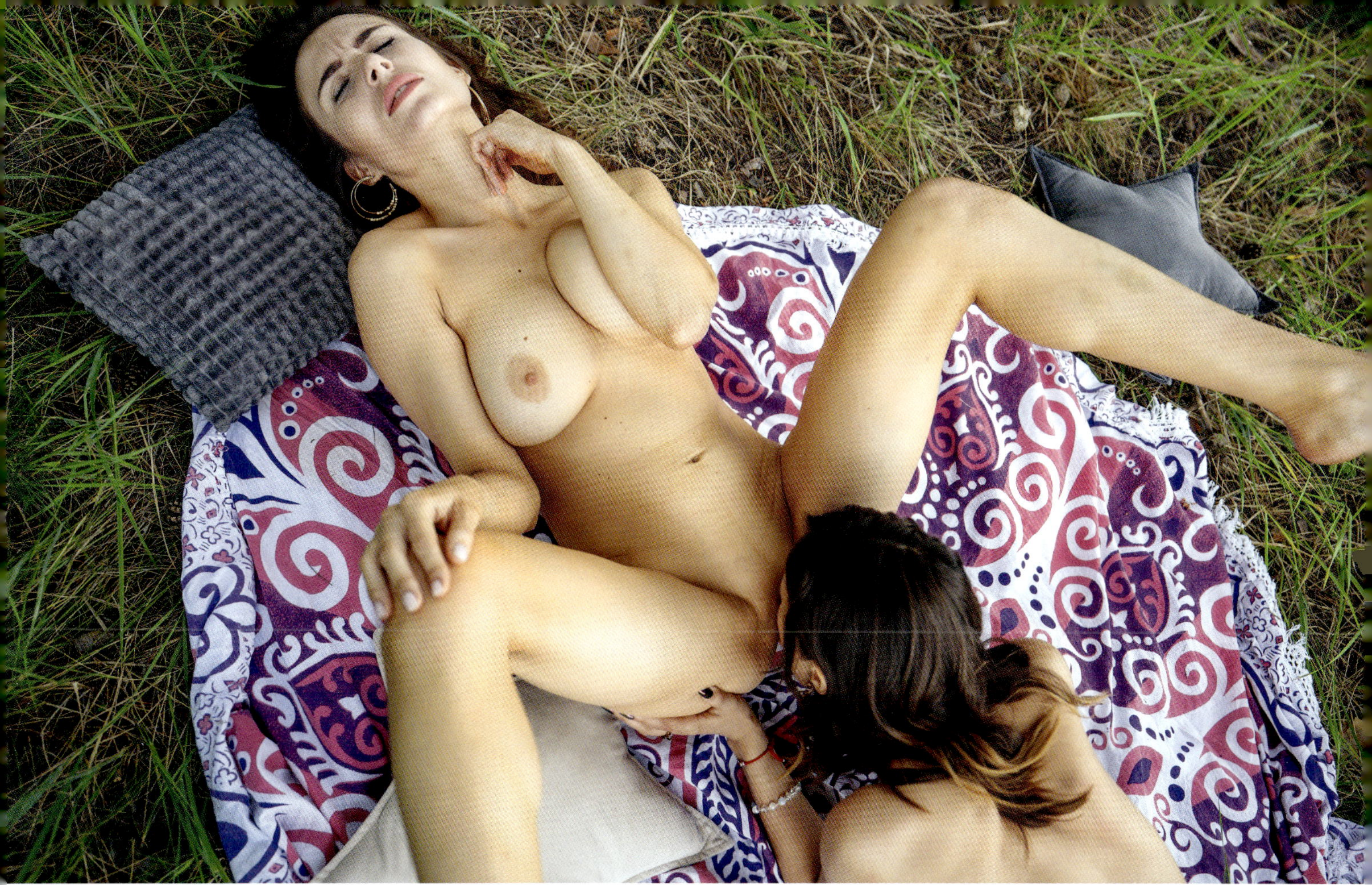
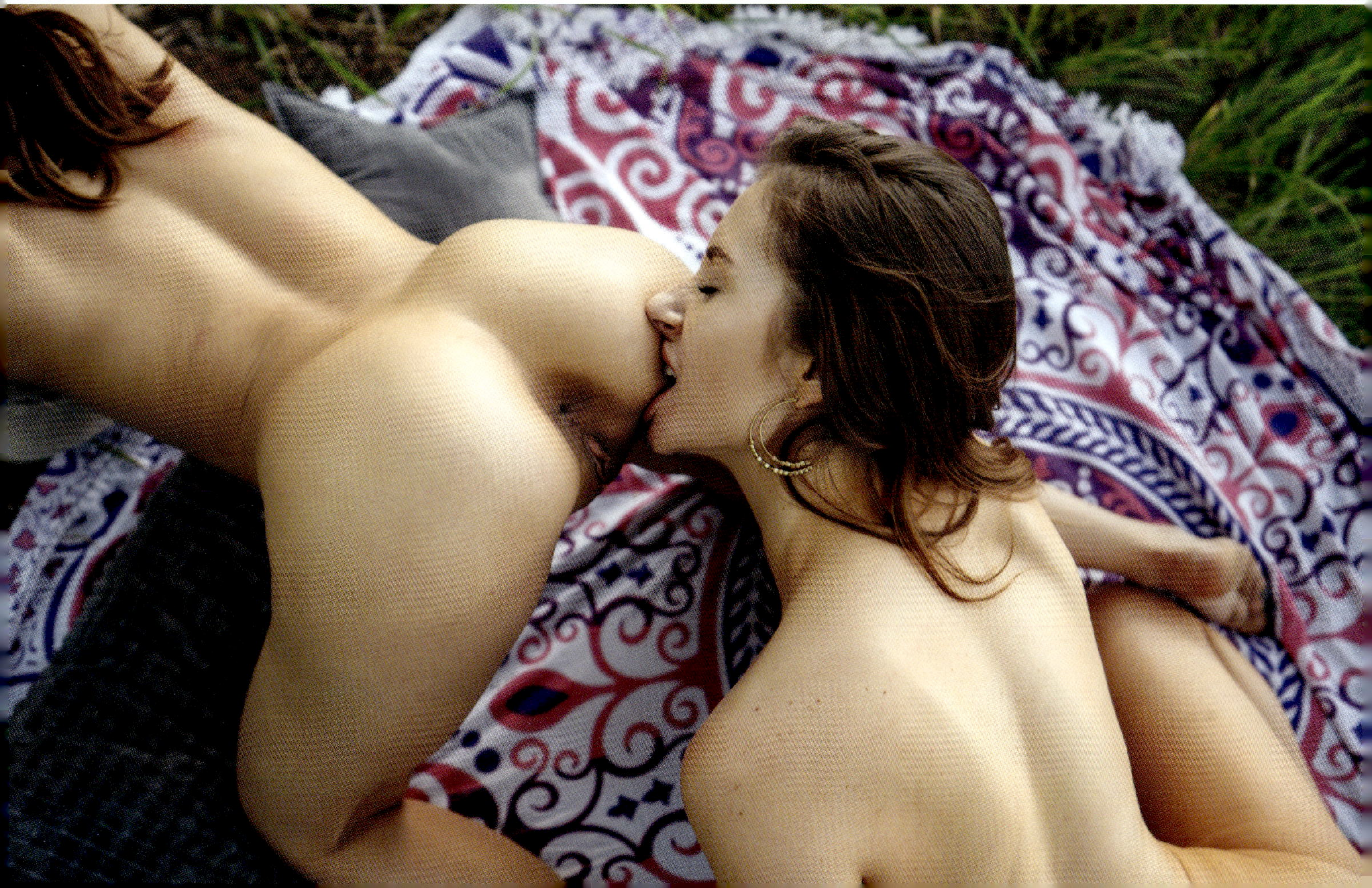

Anie Darling
Cristal Caitlin

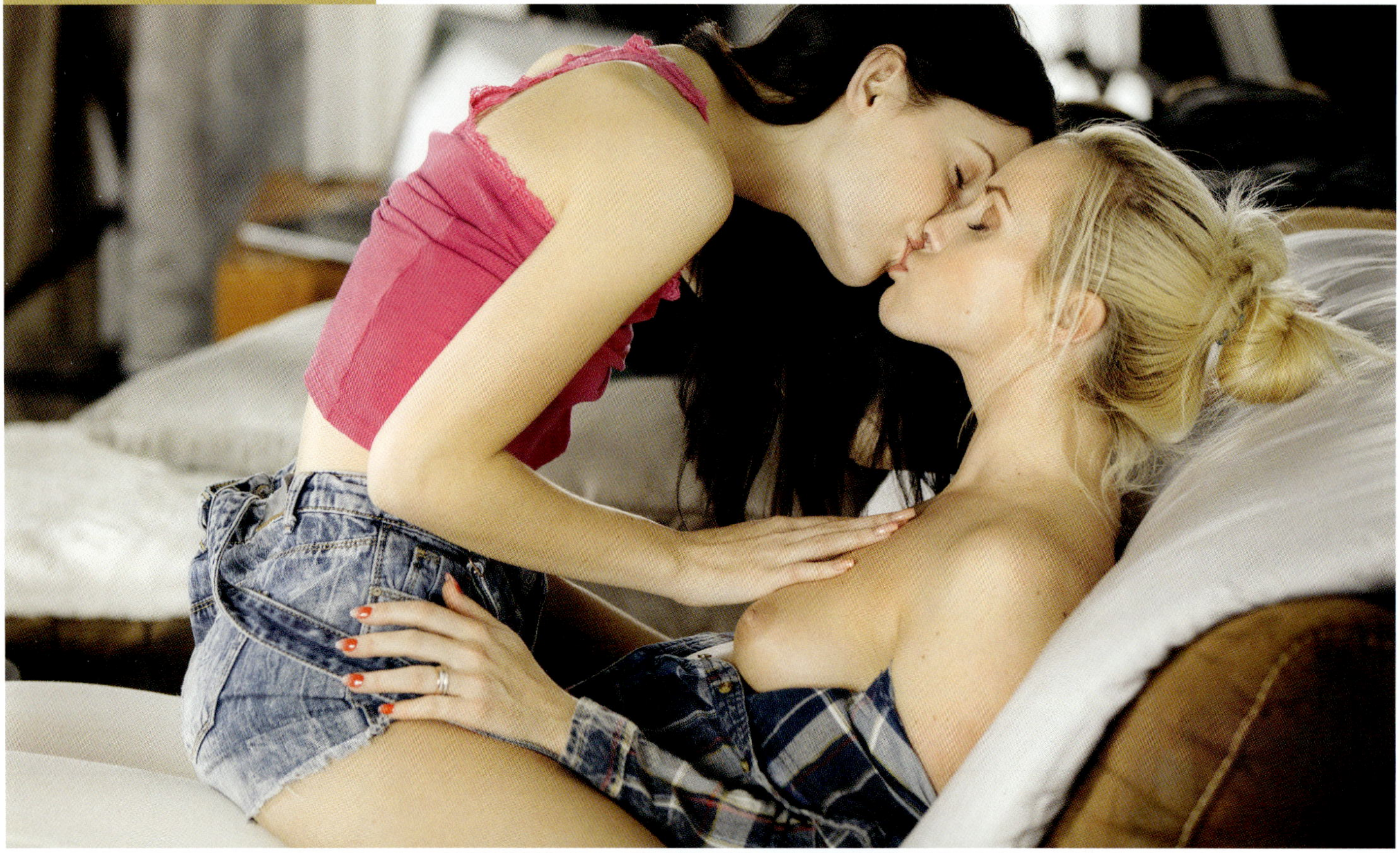

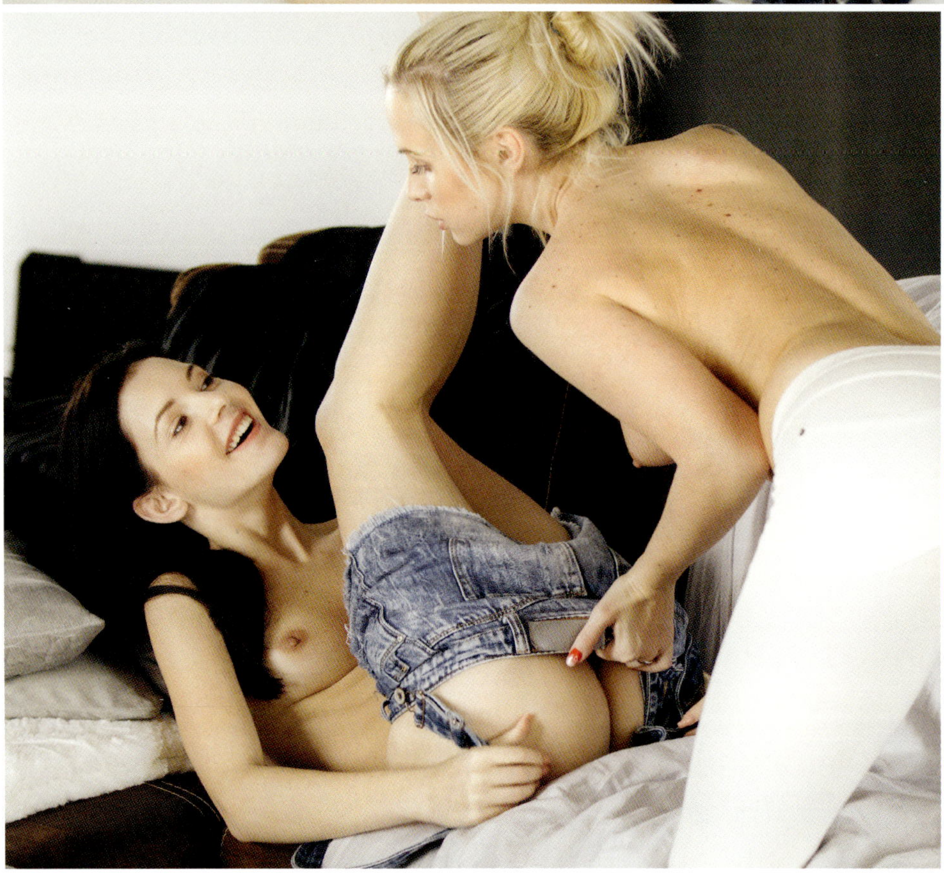

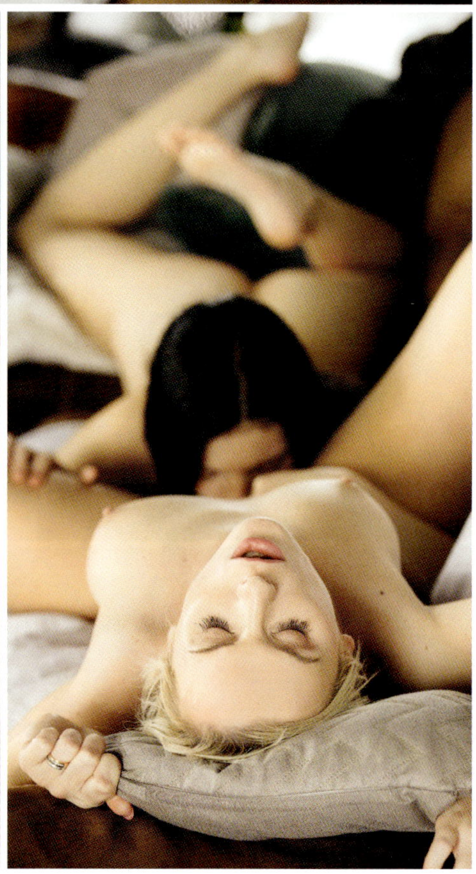

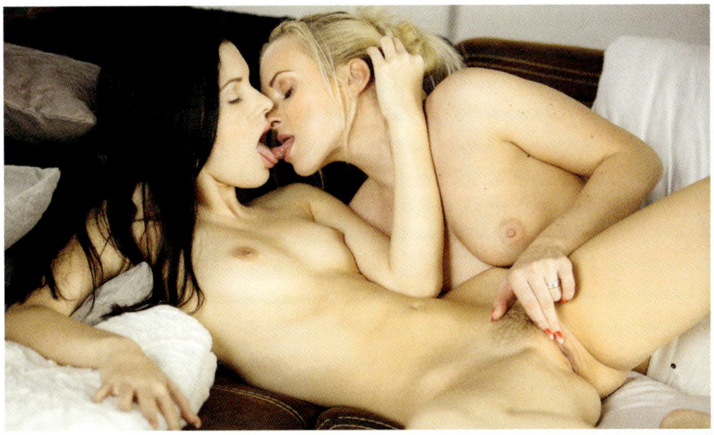

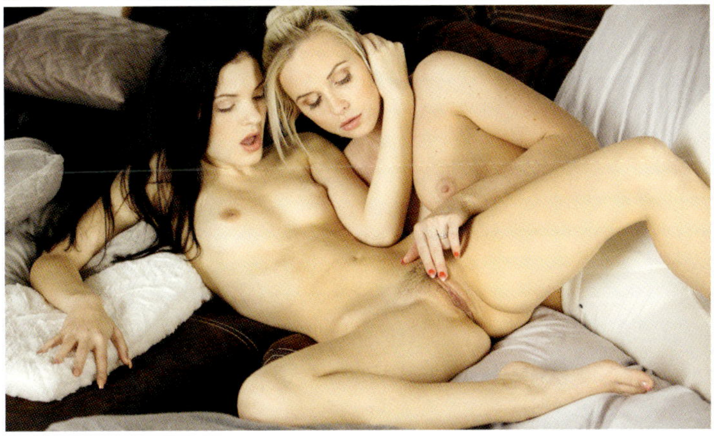

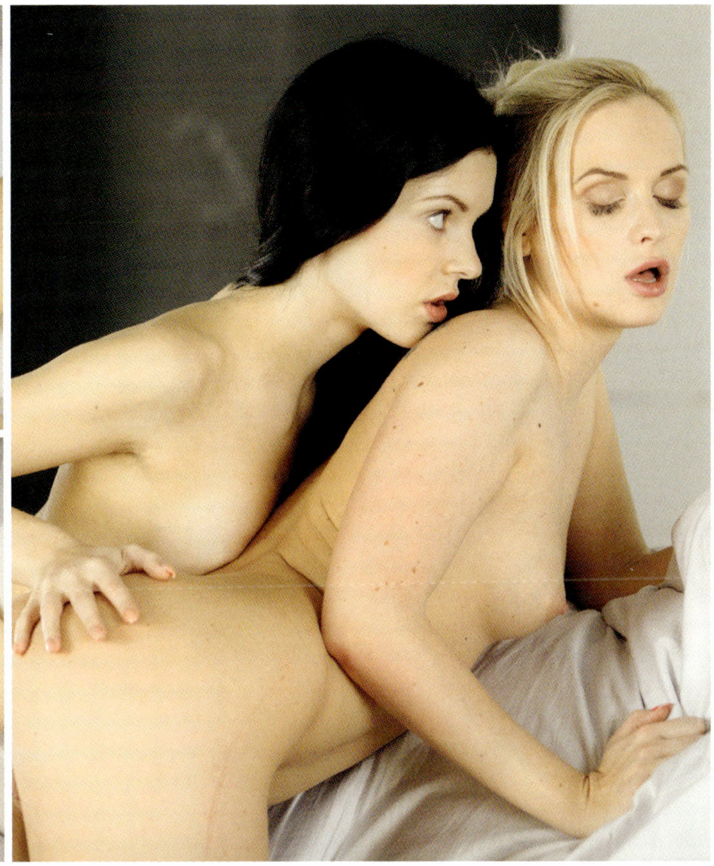

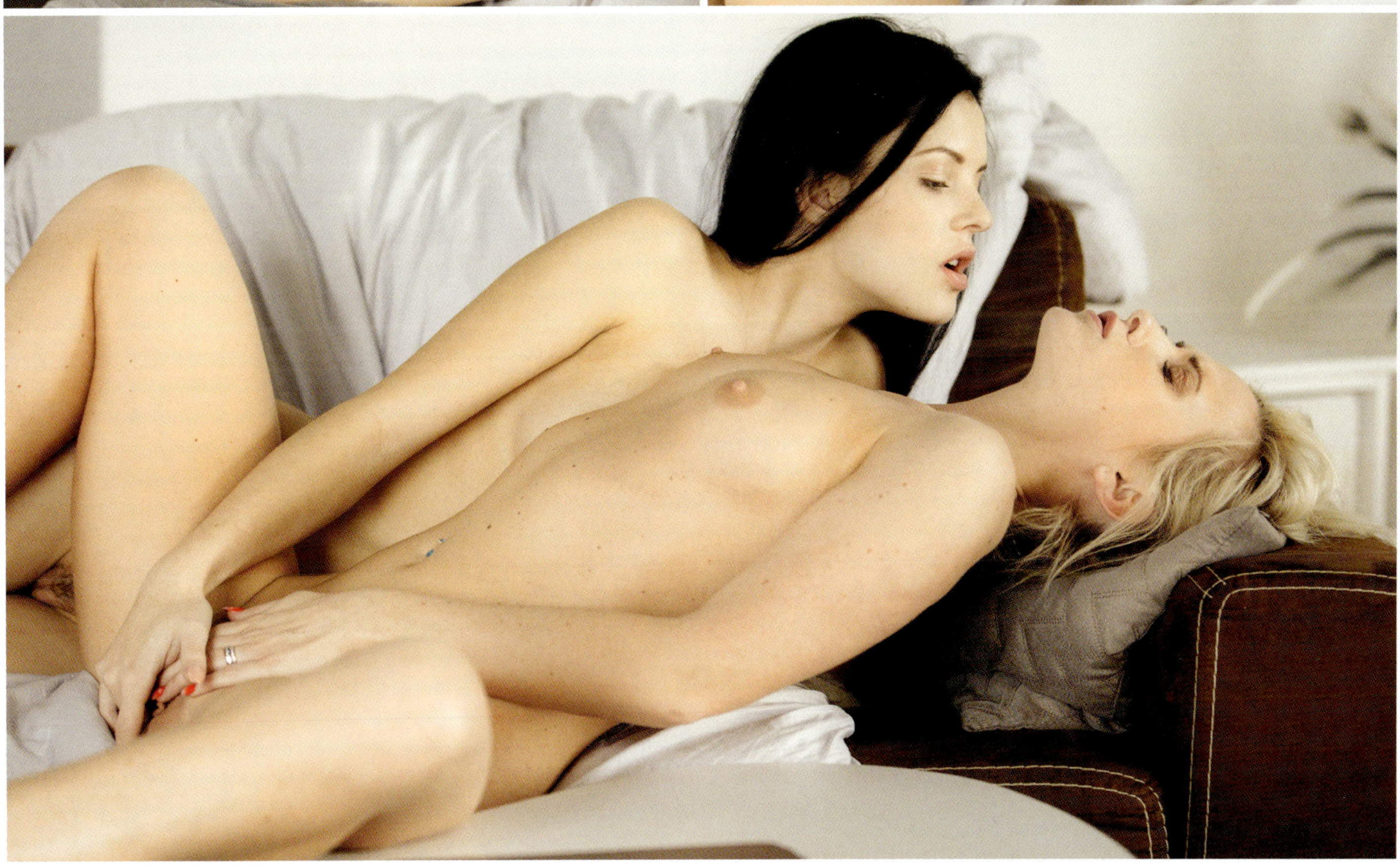

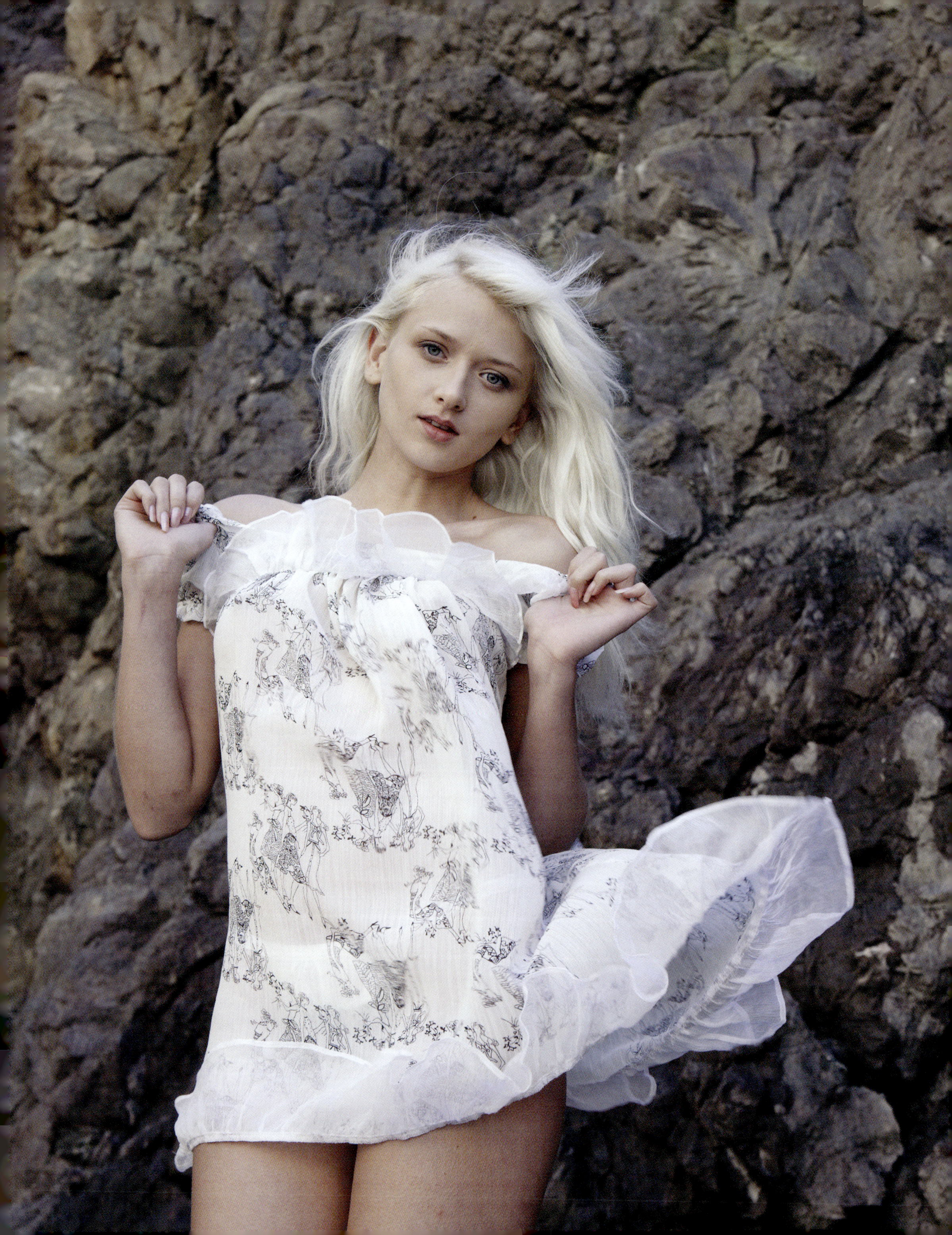

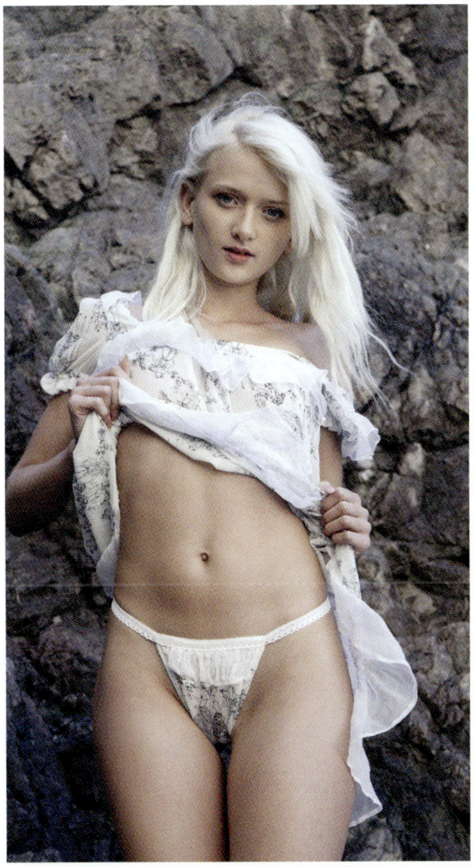

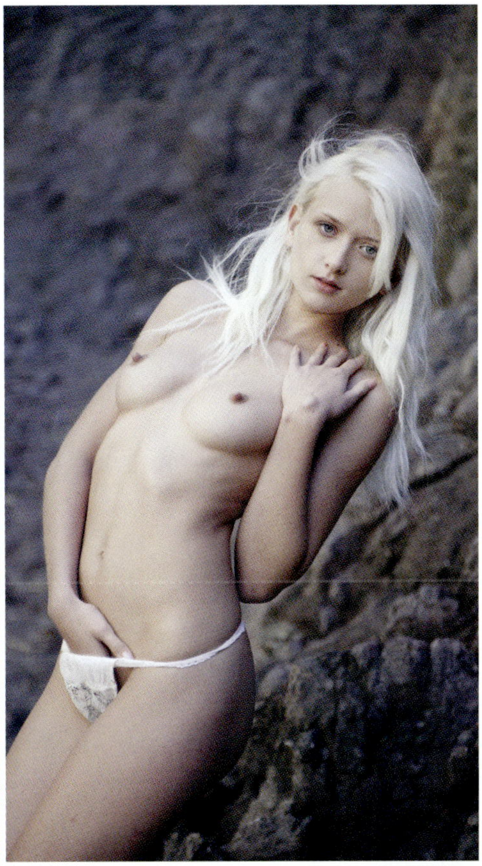

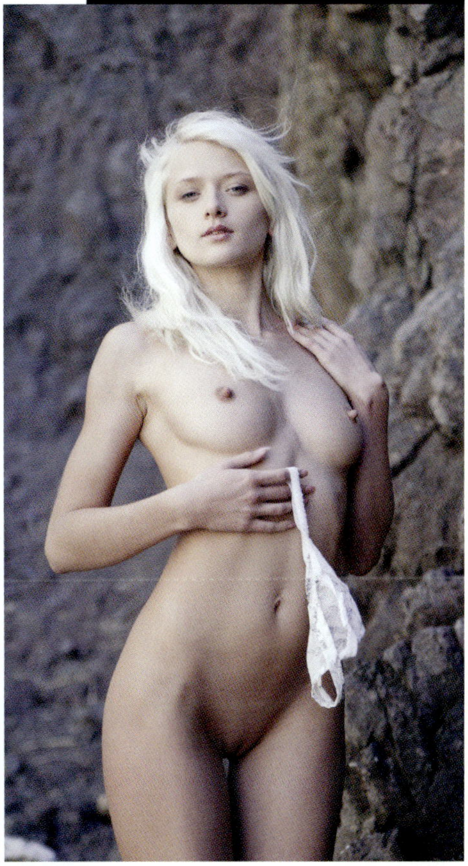

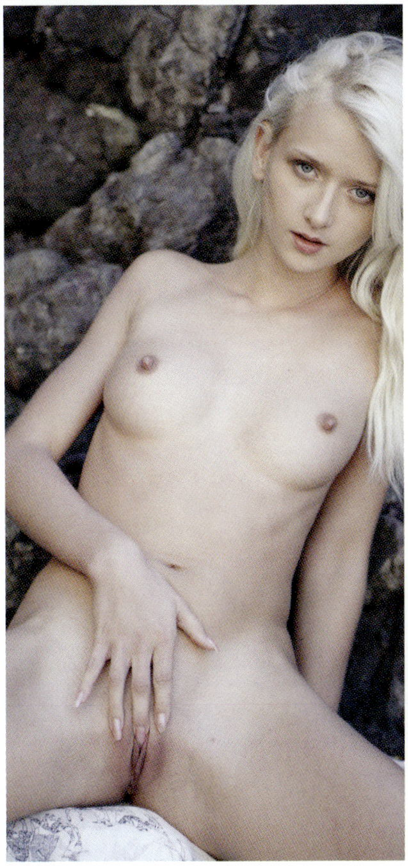

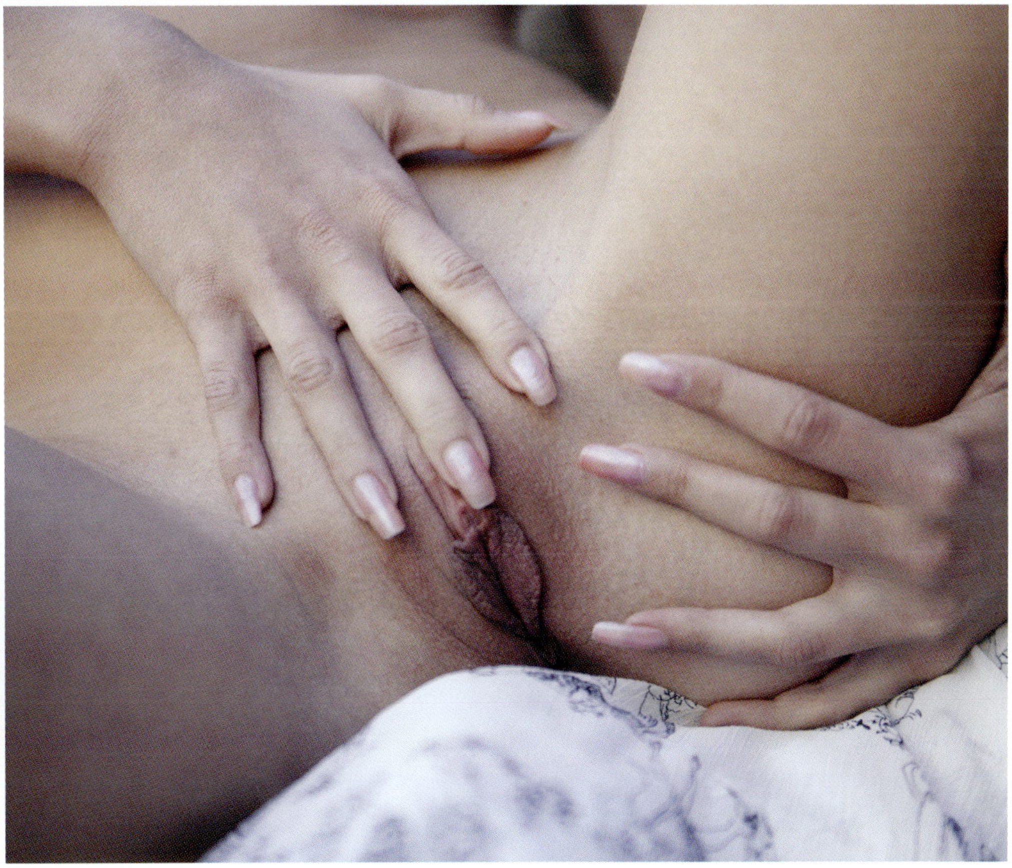

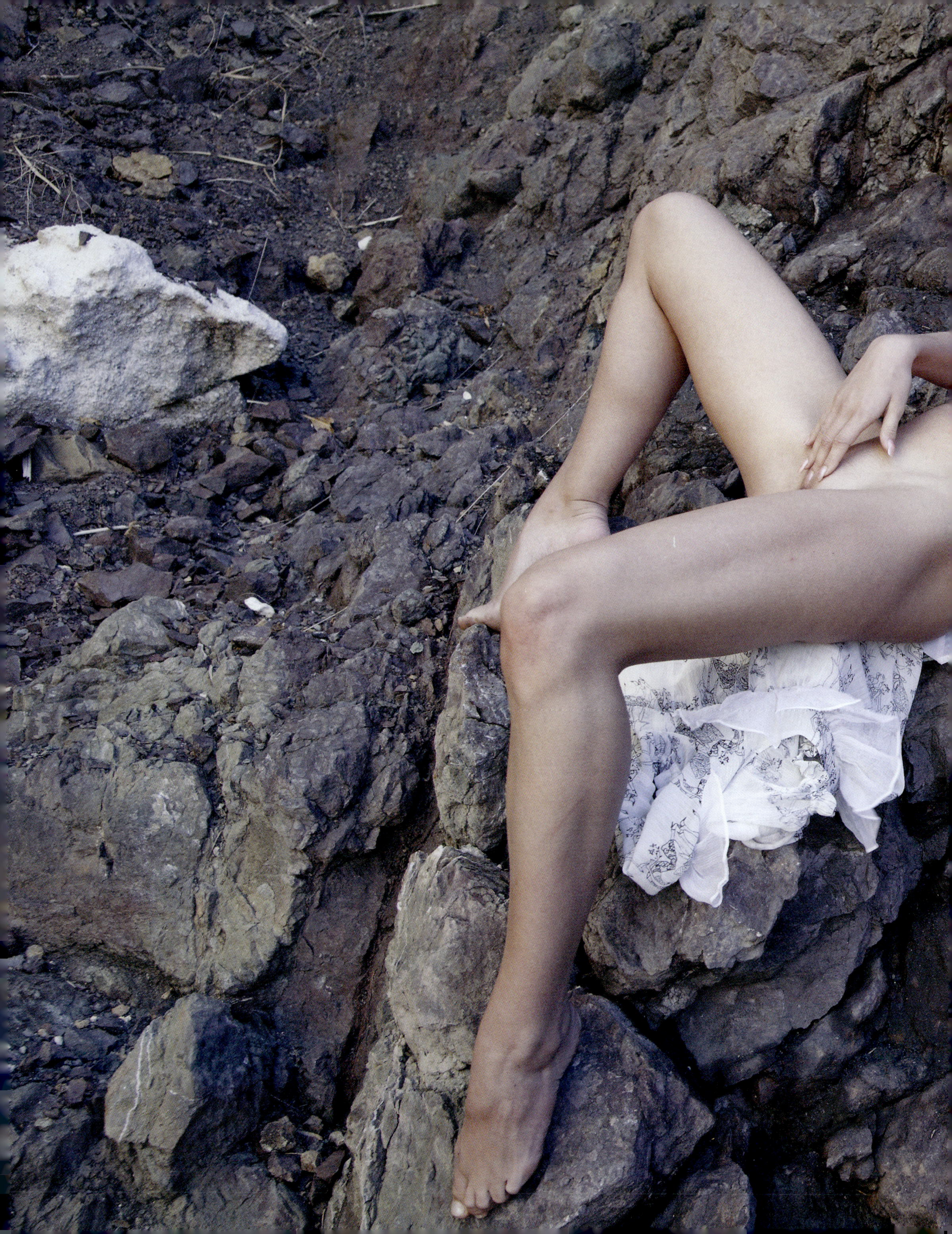

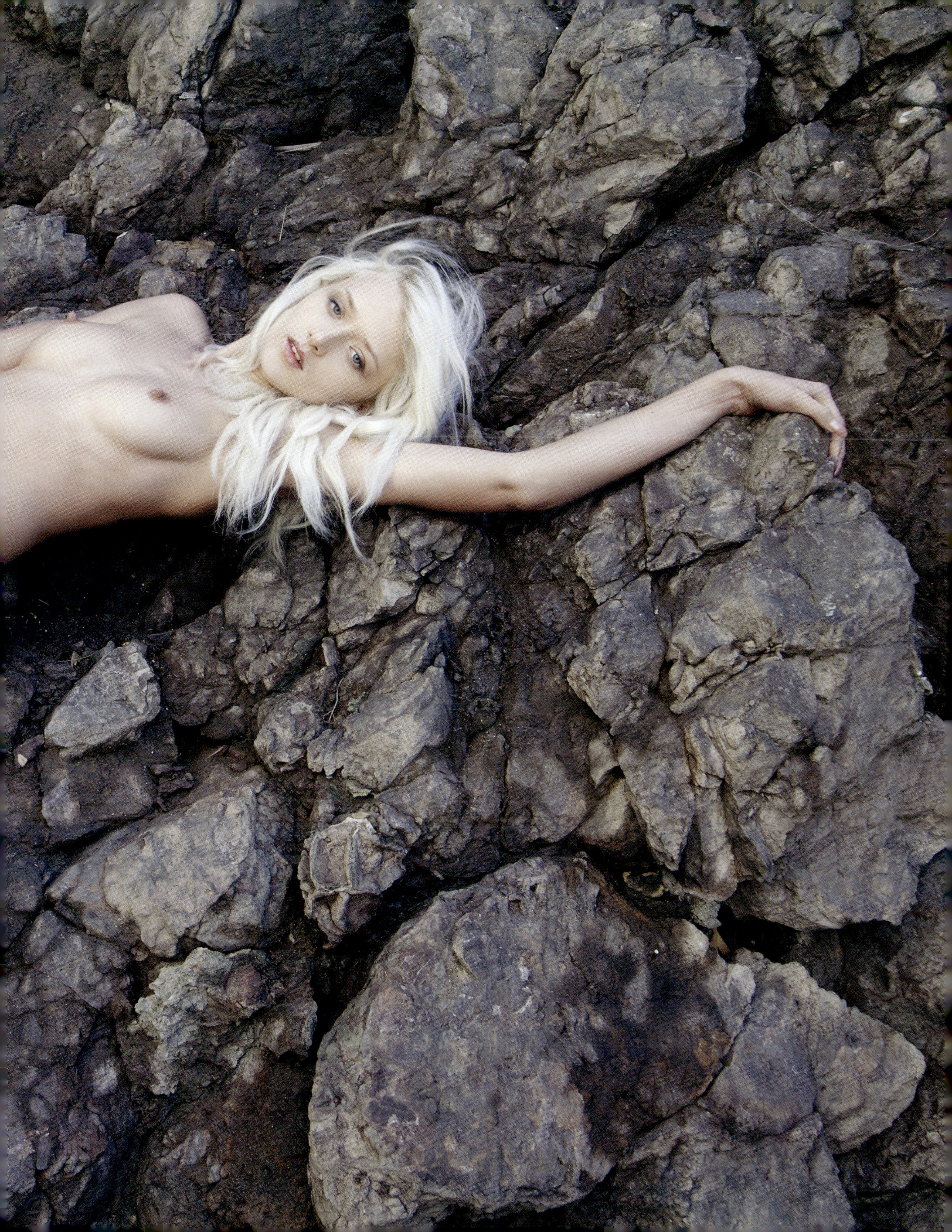

Nedda A

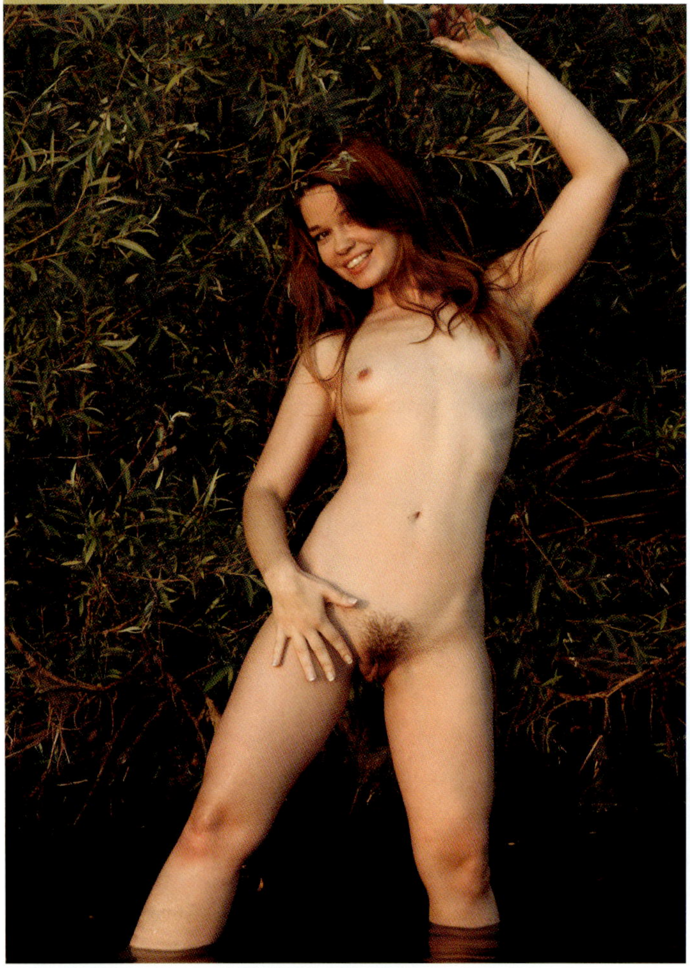

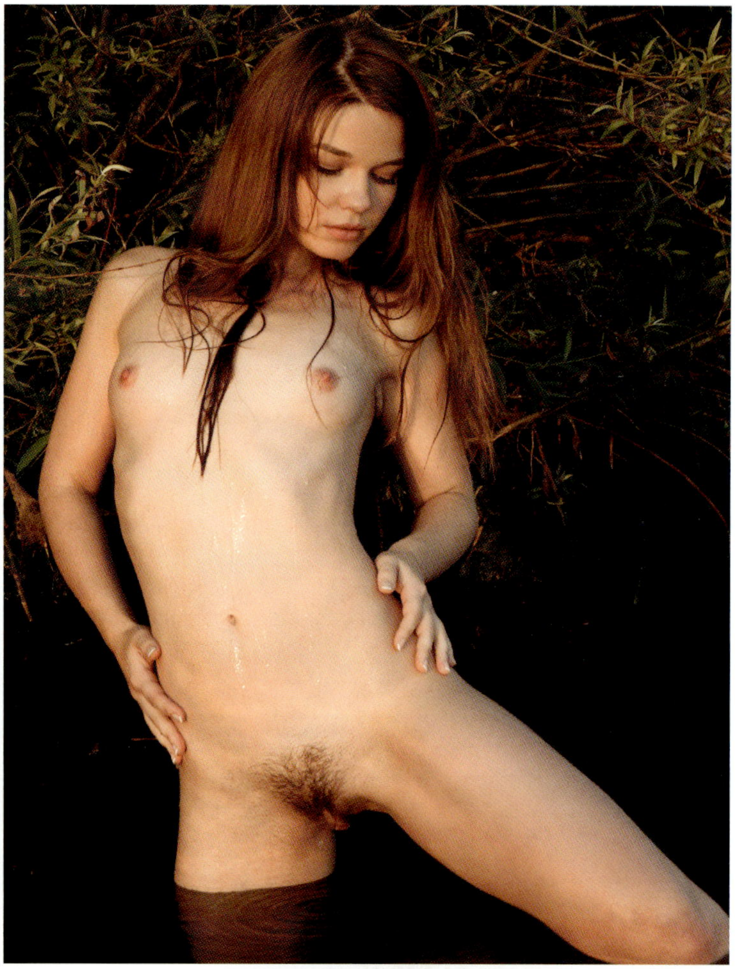

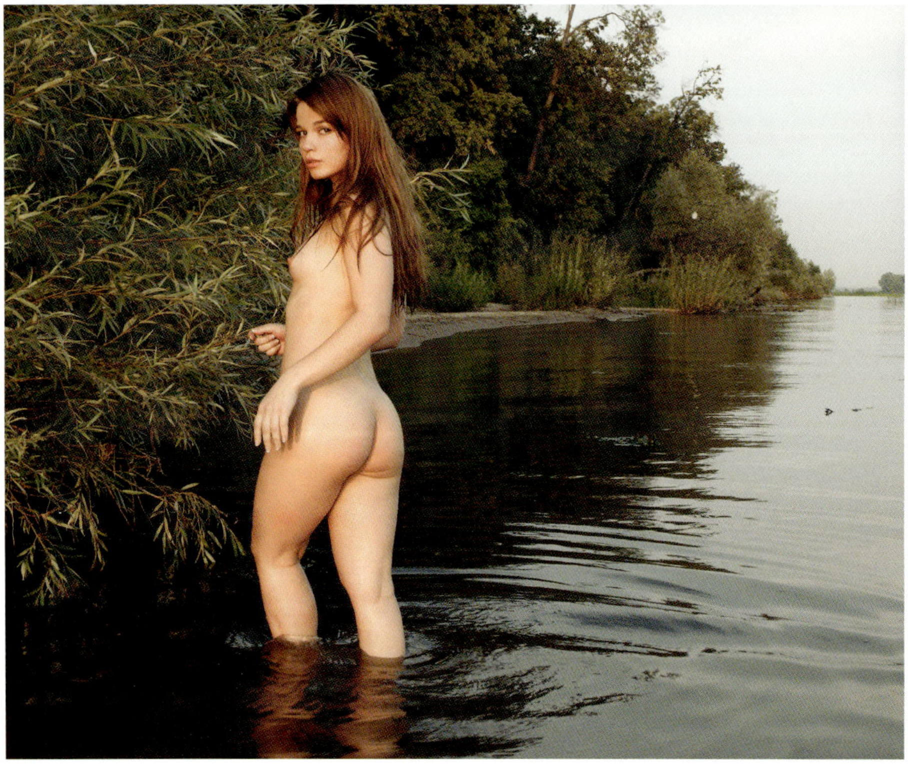

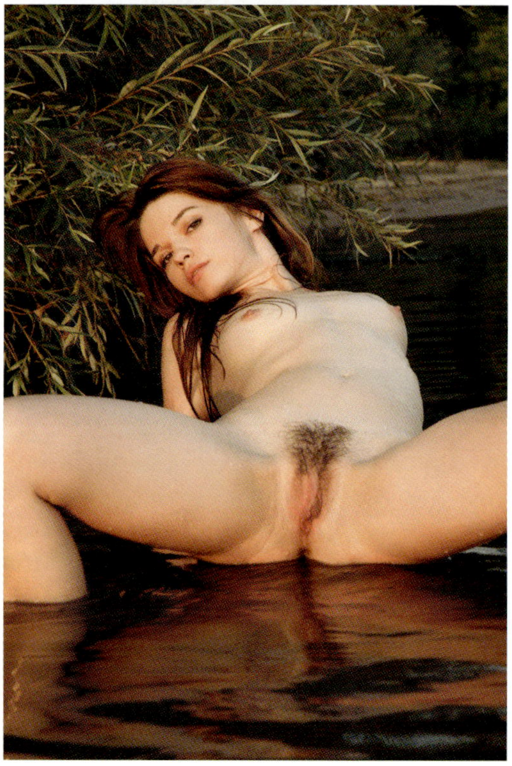

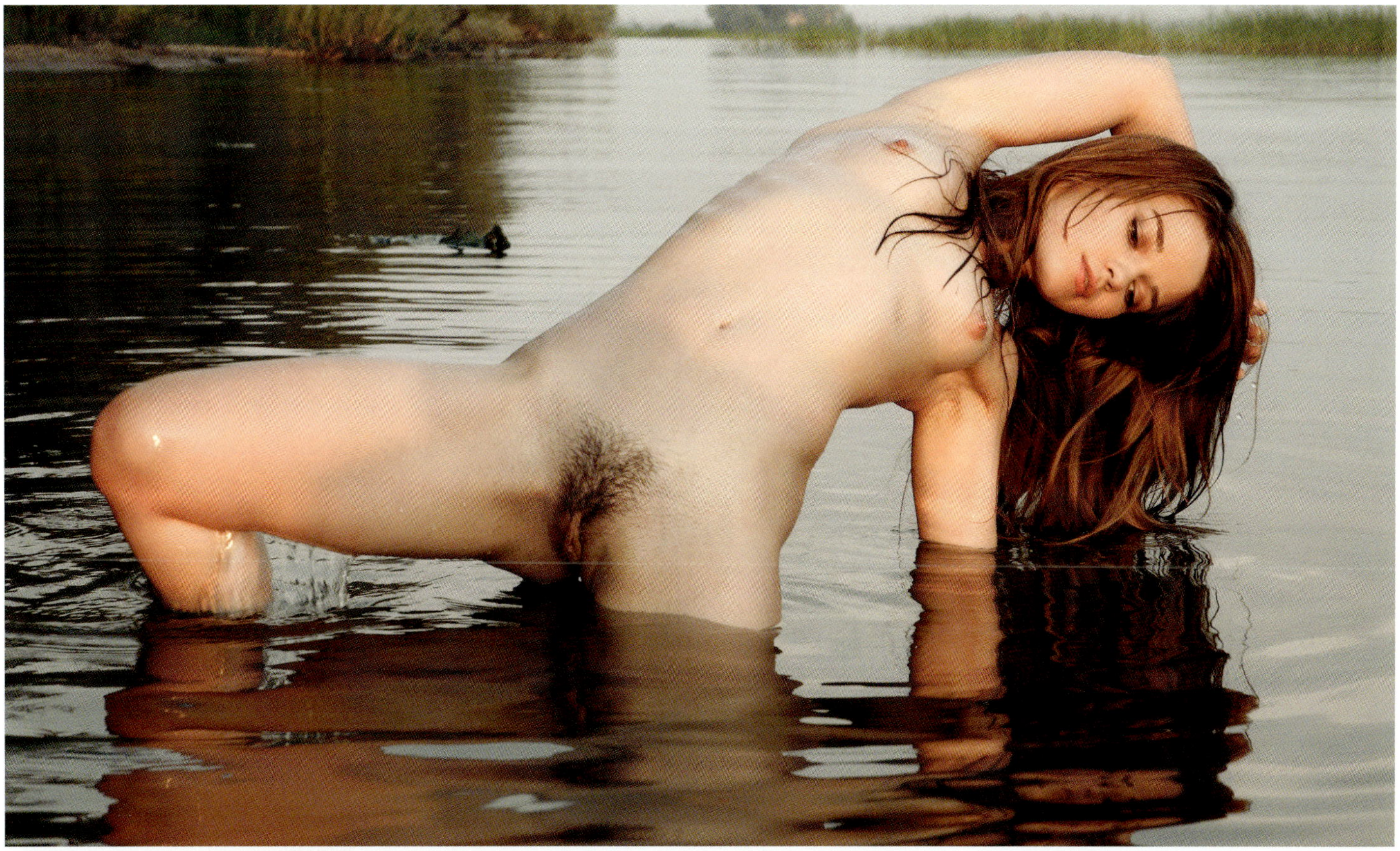

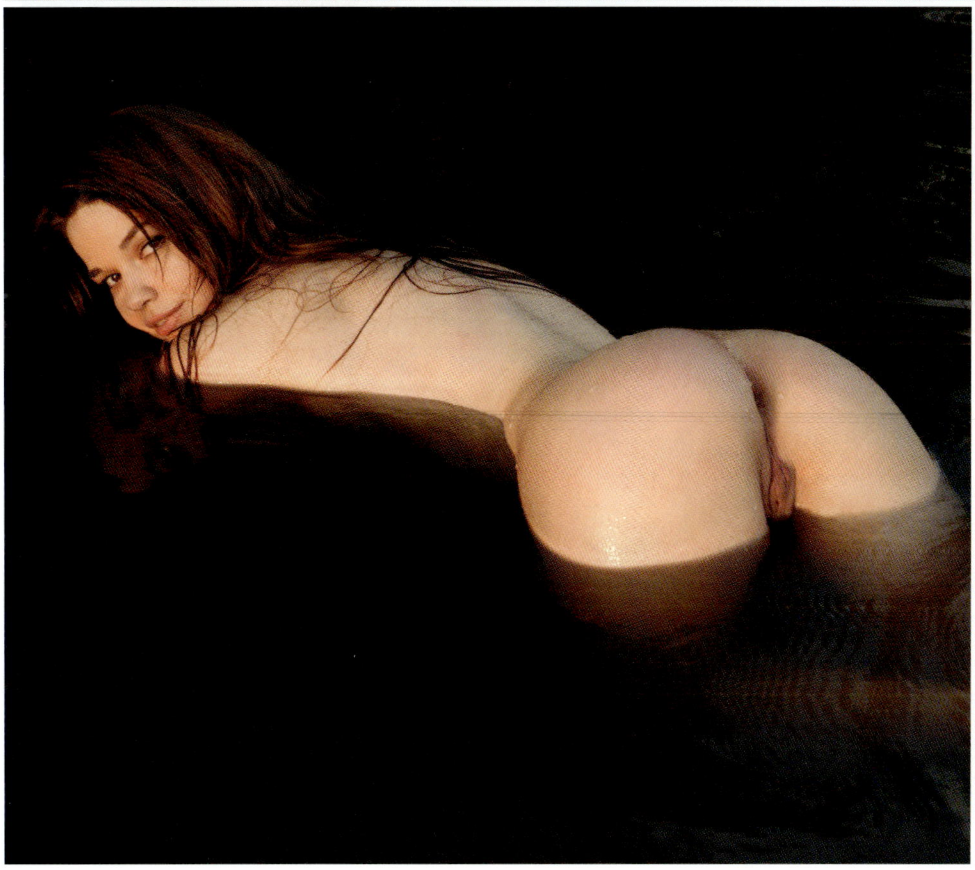

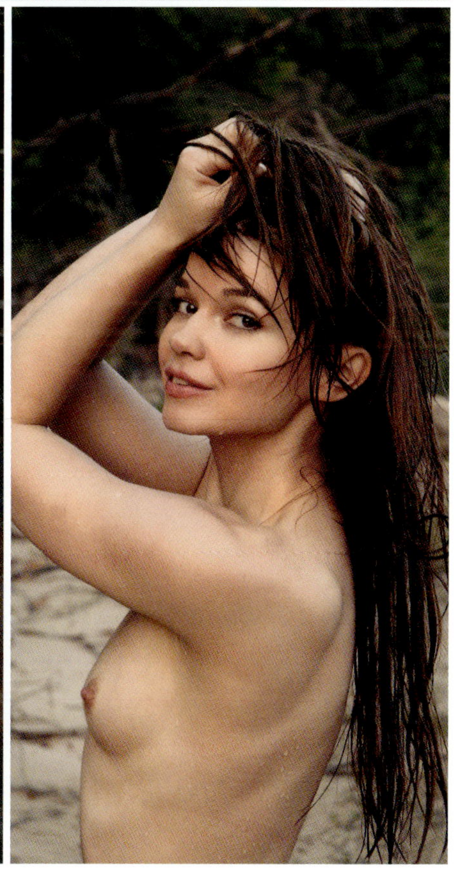

Aislin
Veronica Leal

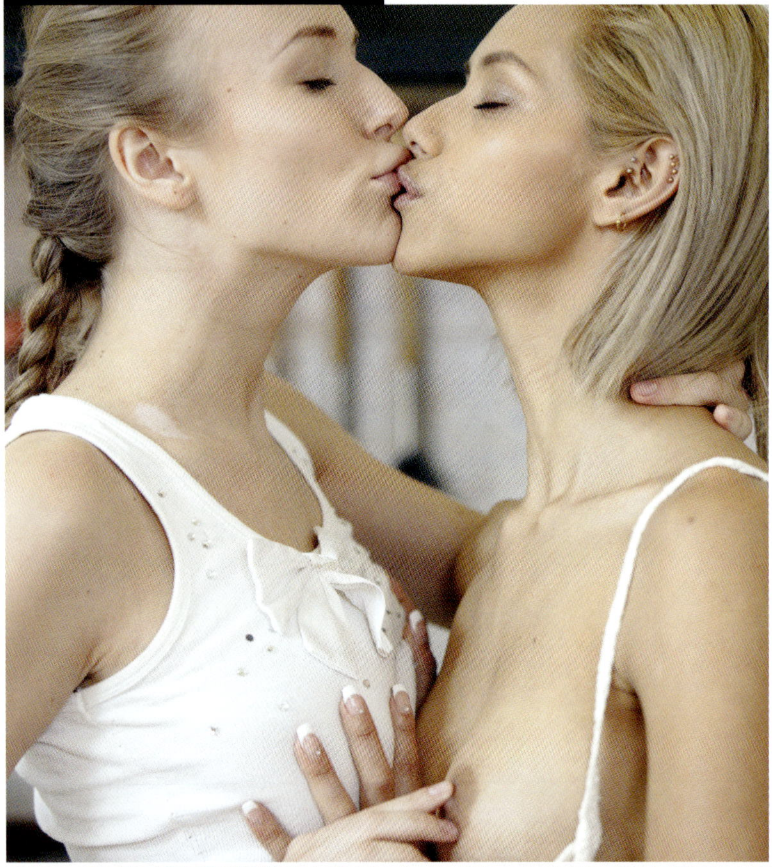

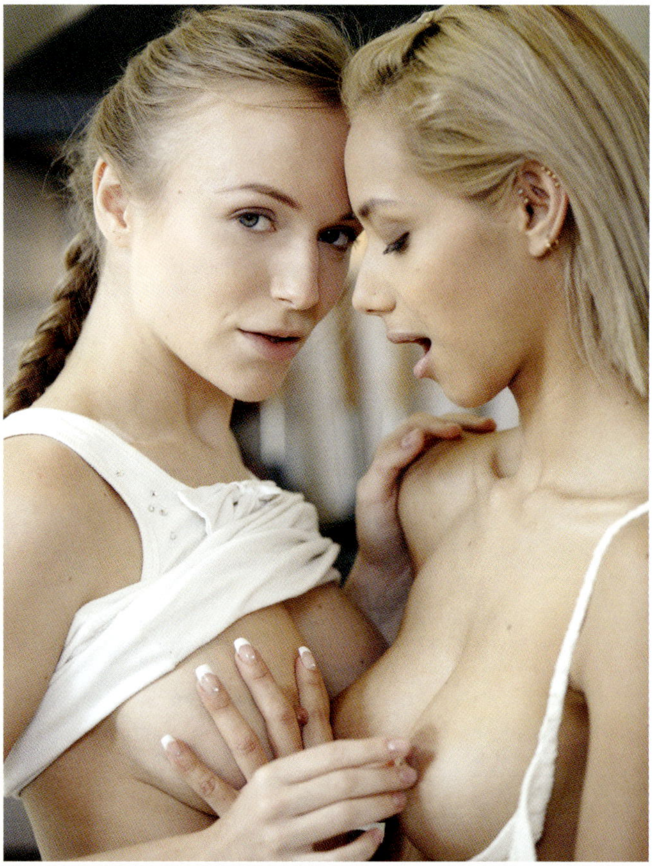

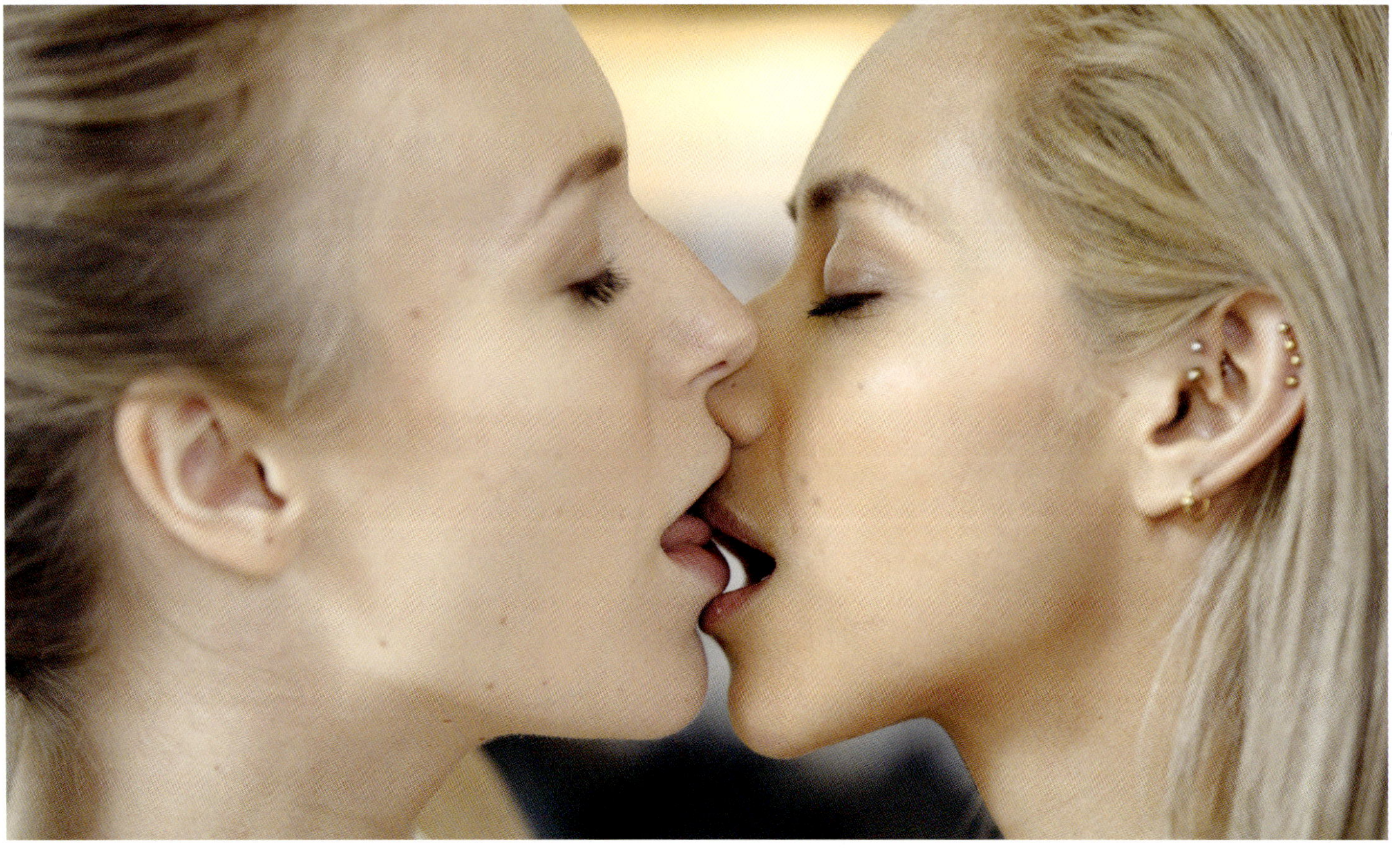

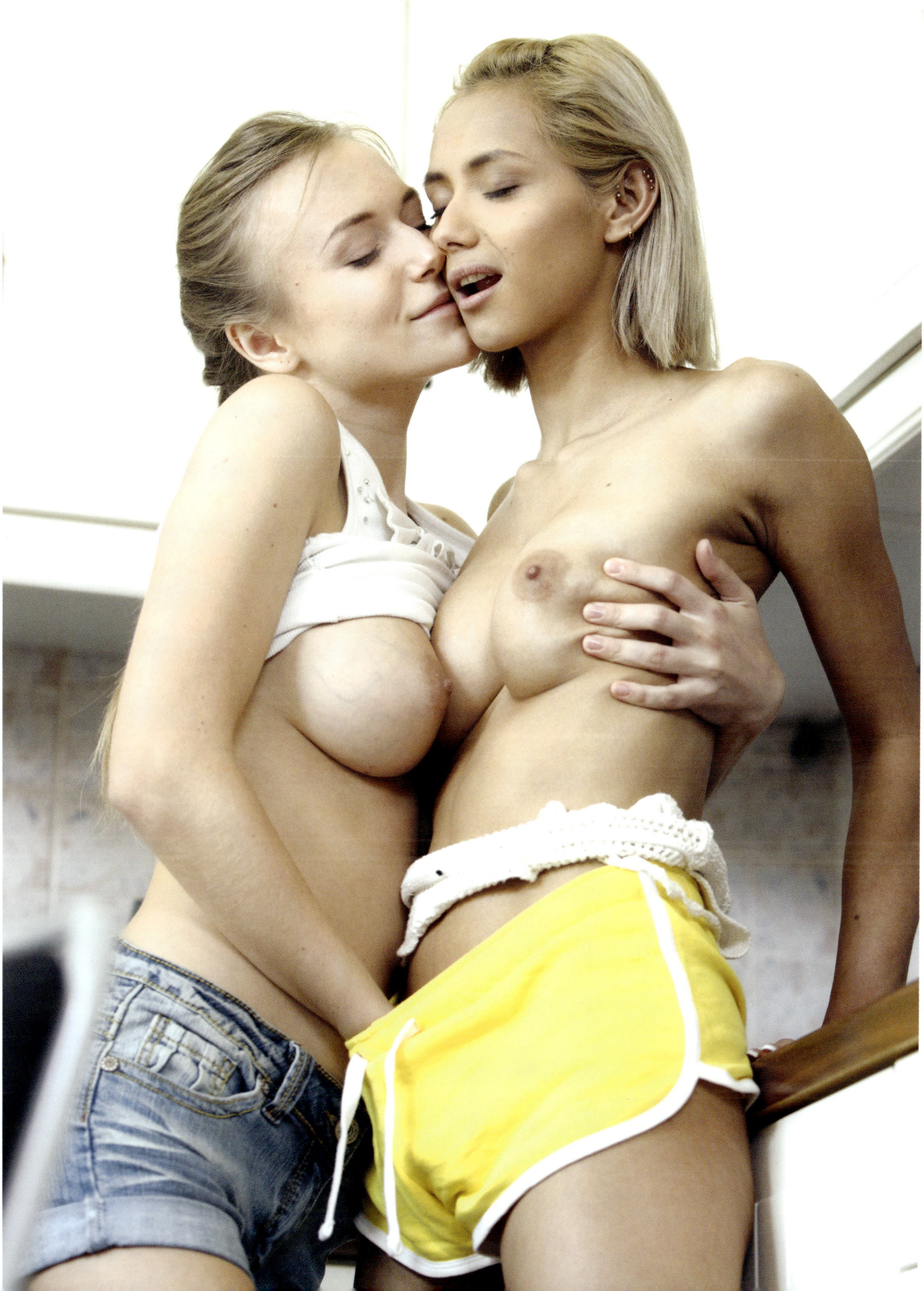

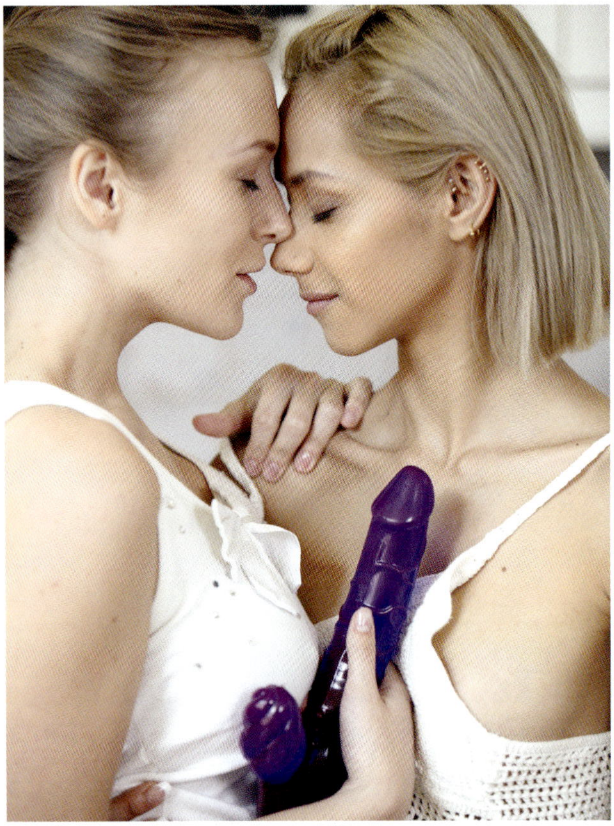

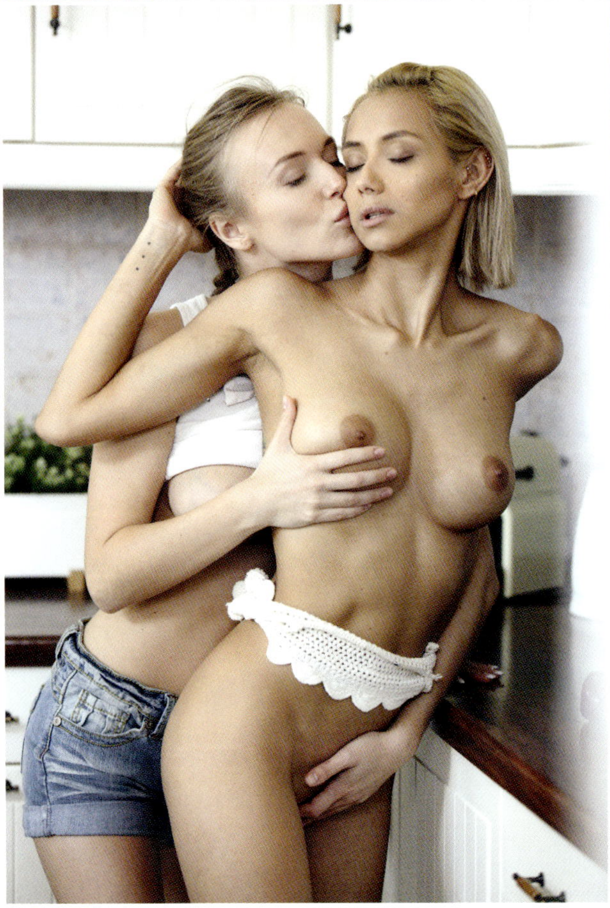

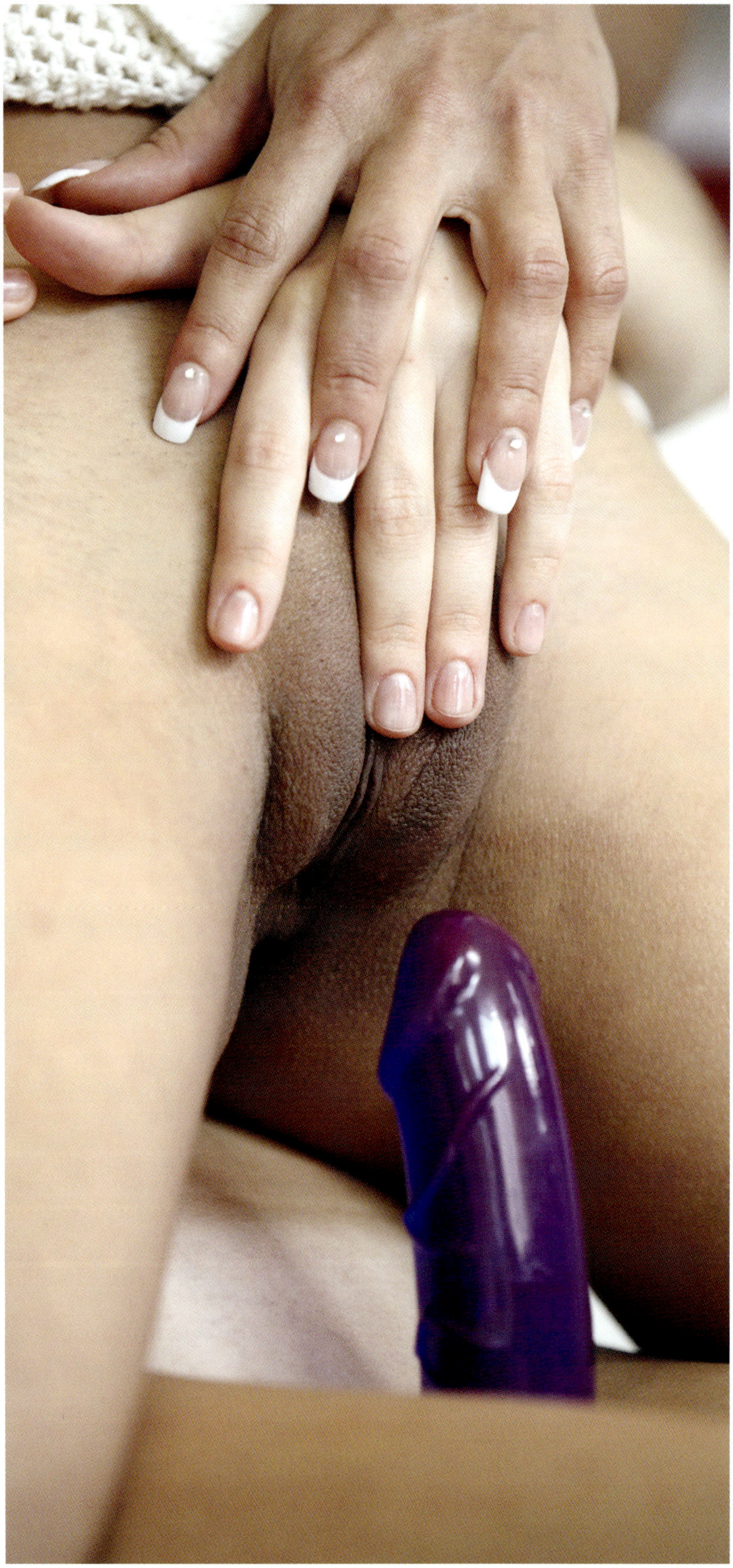

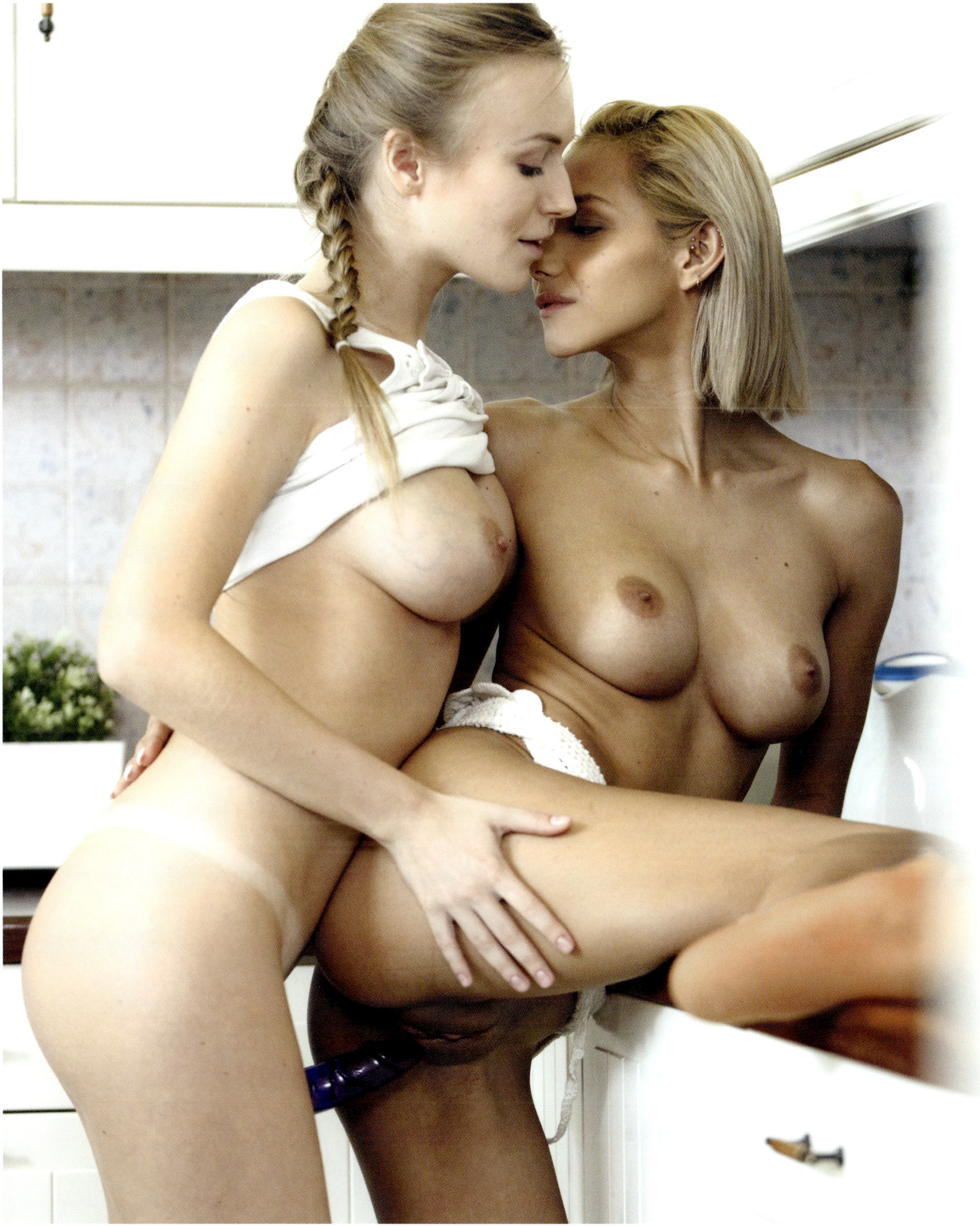

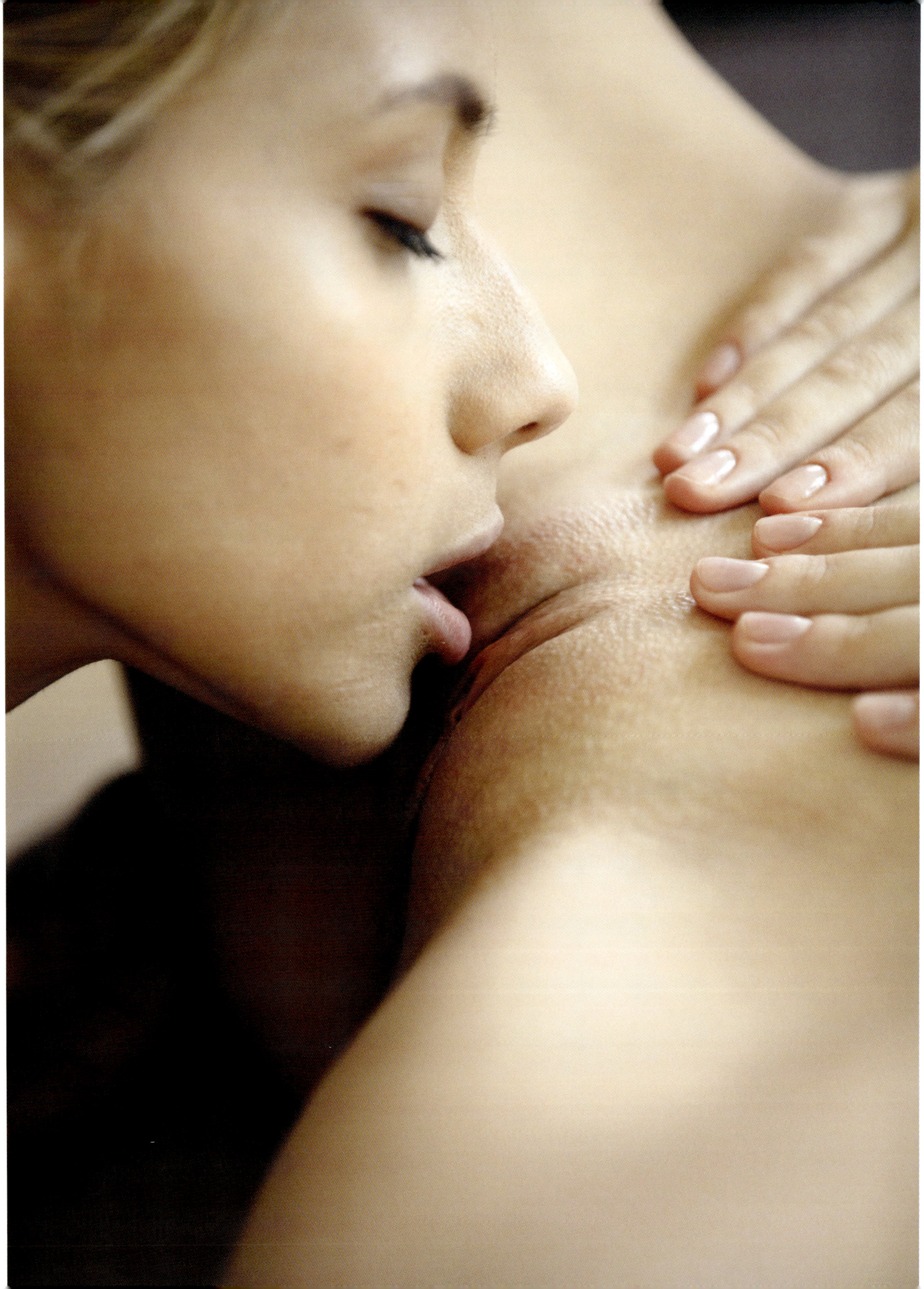

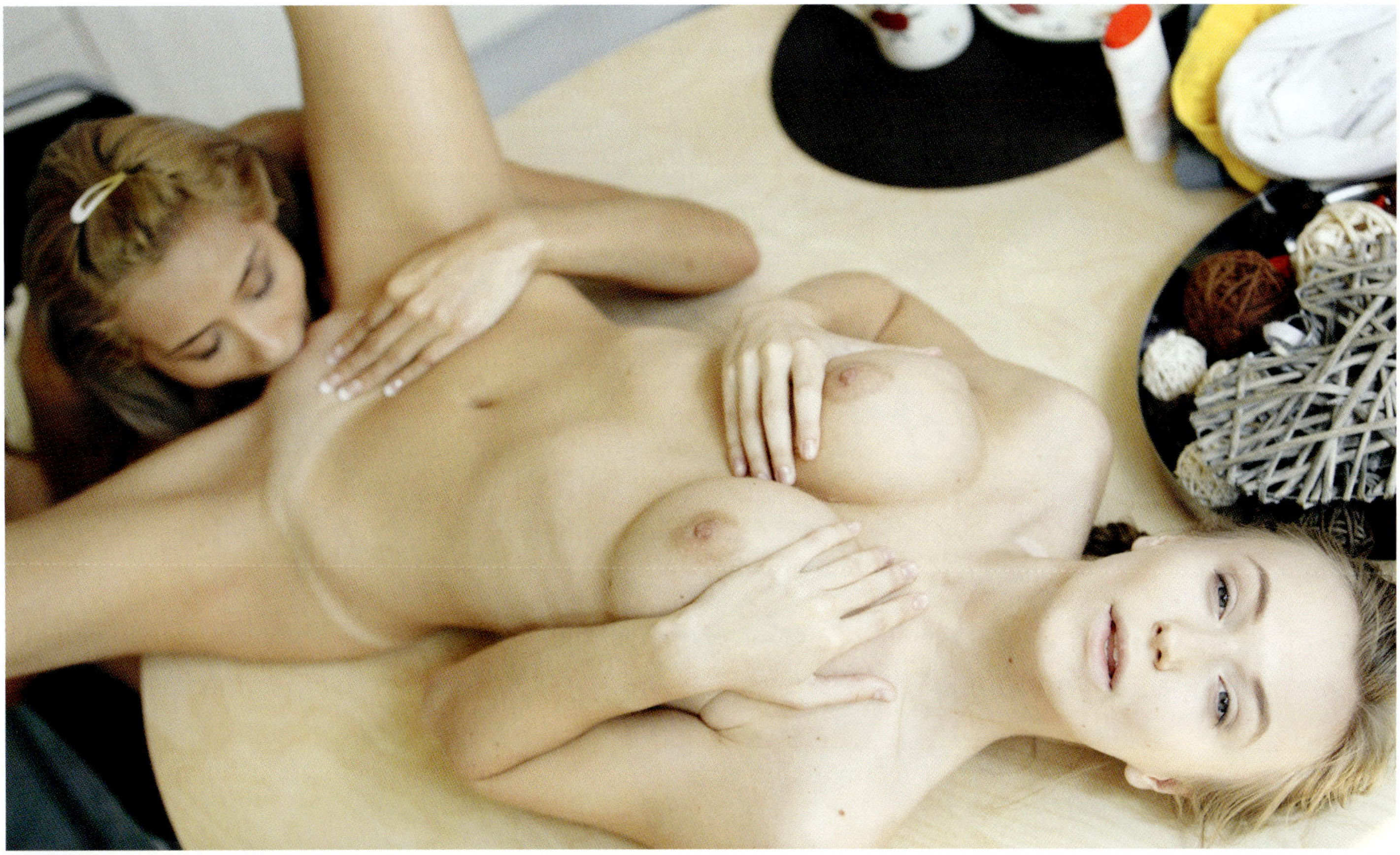

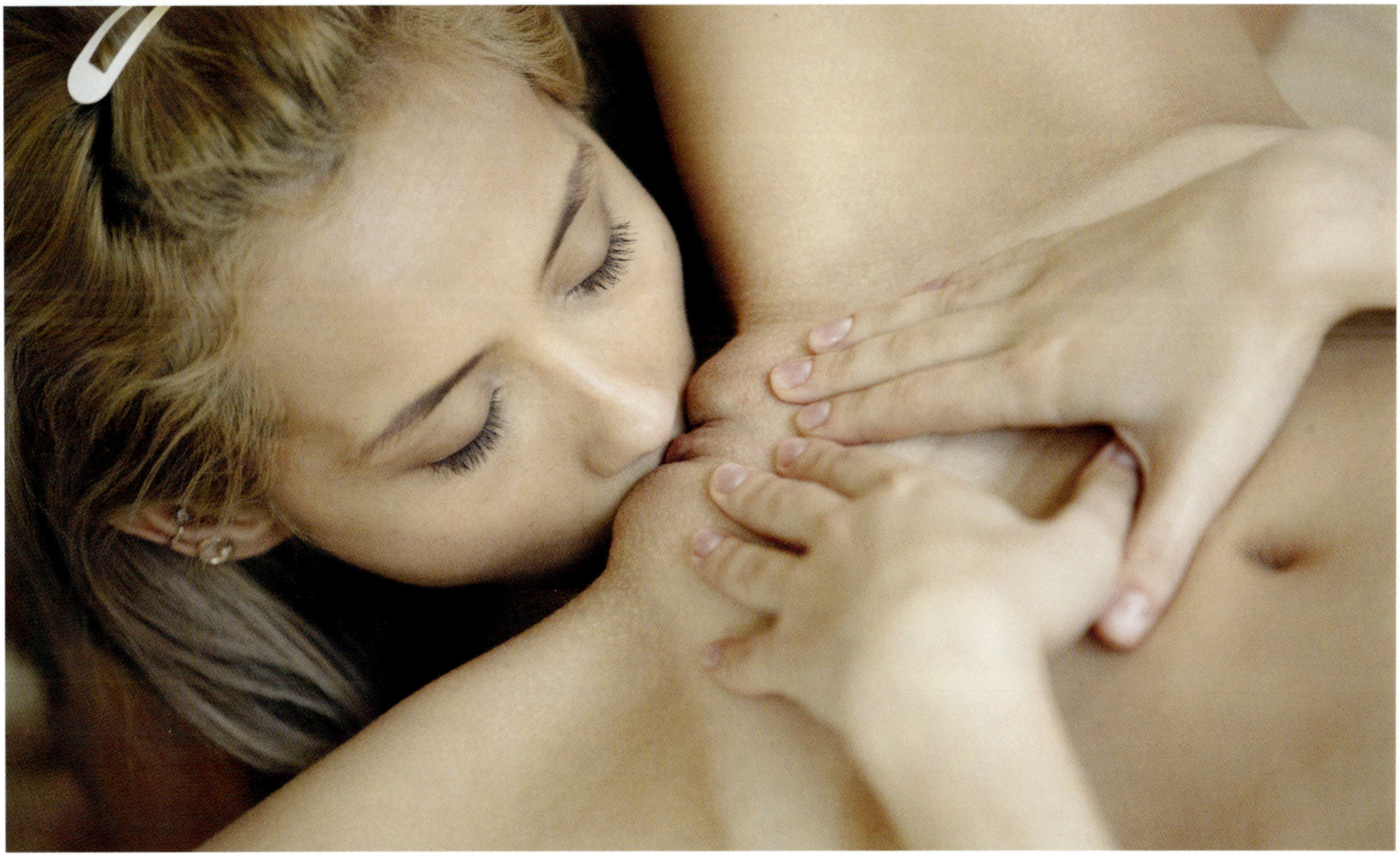

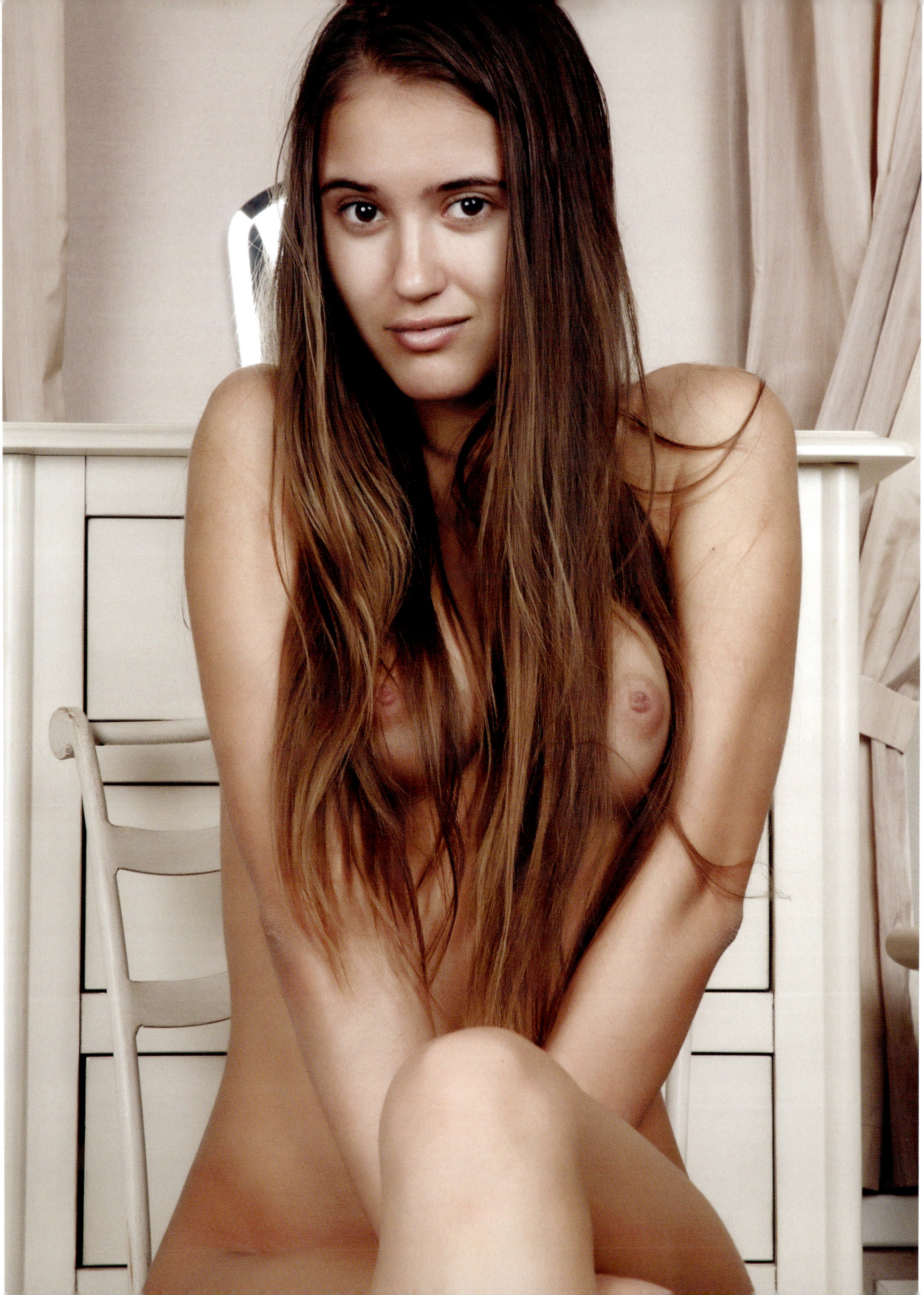

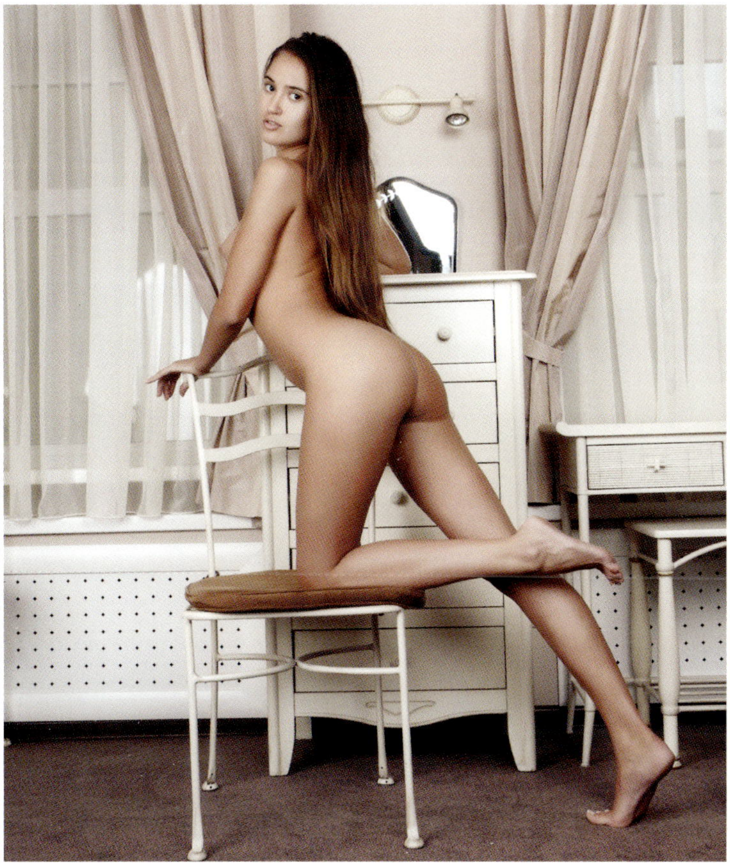

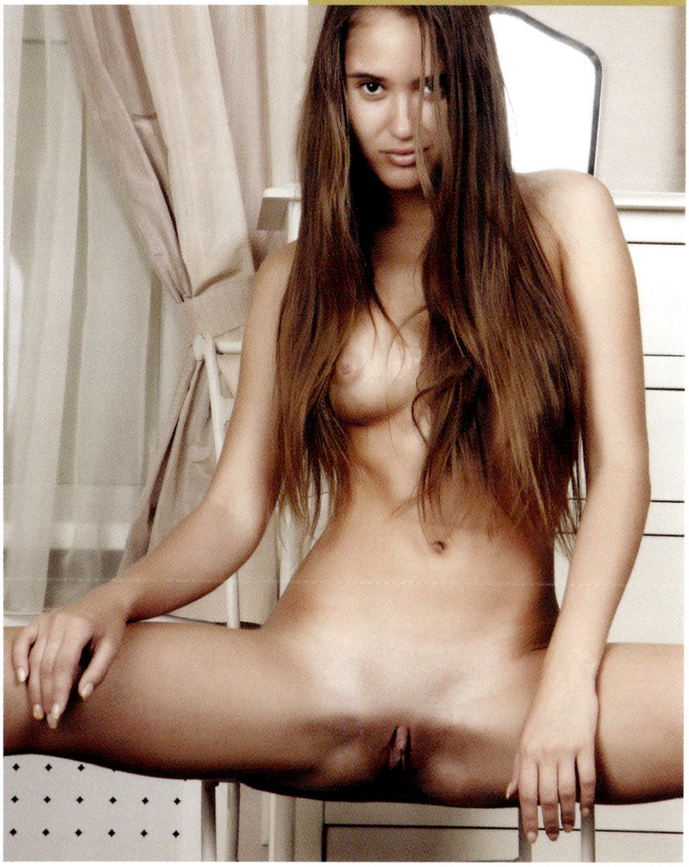

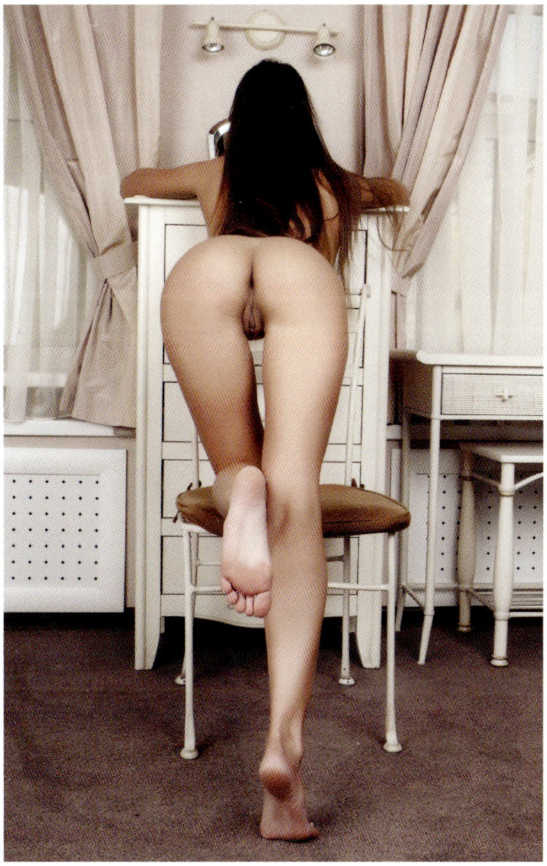

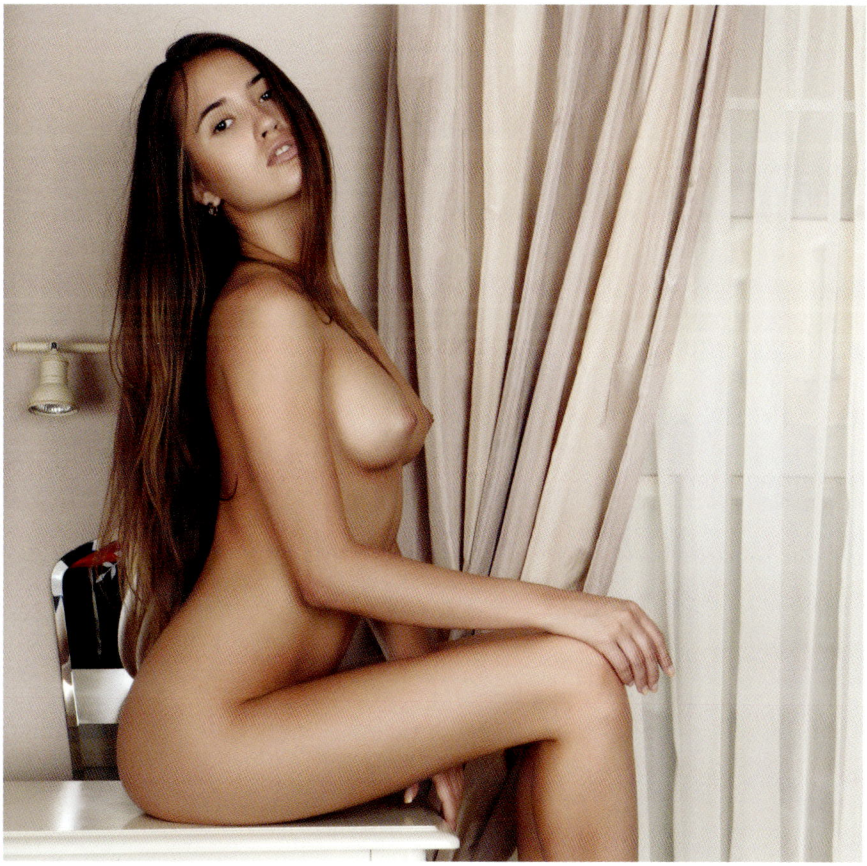

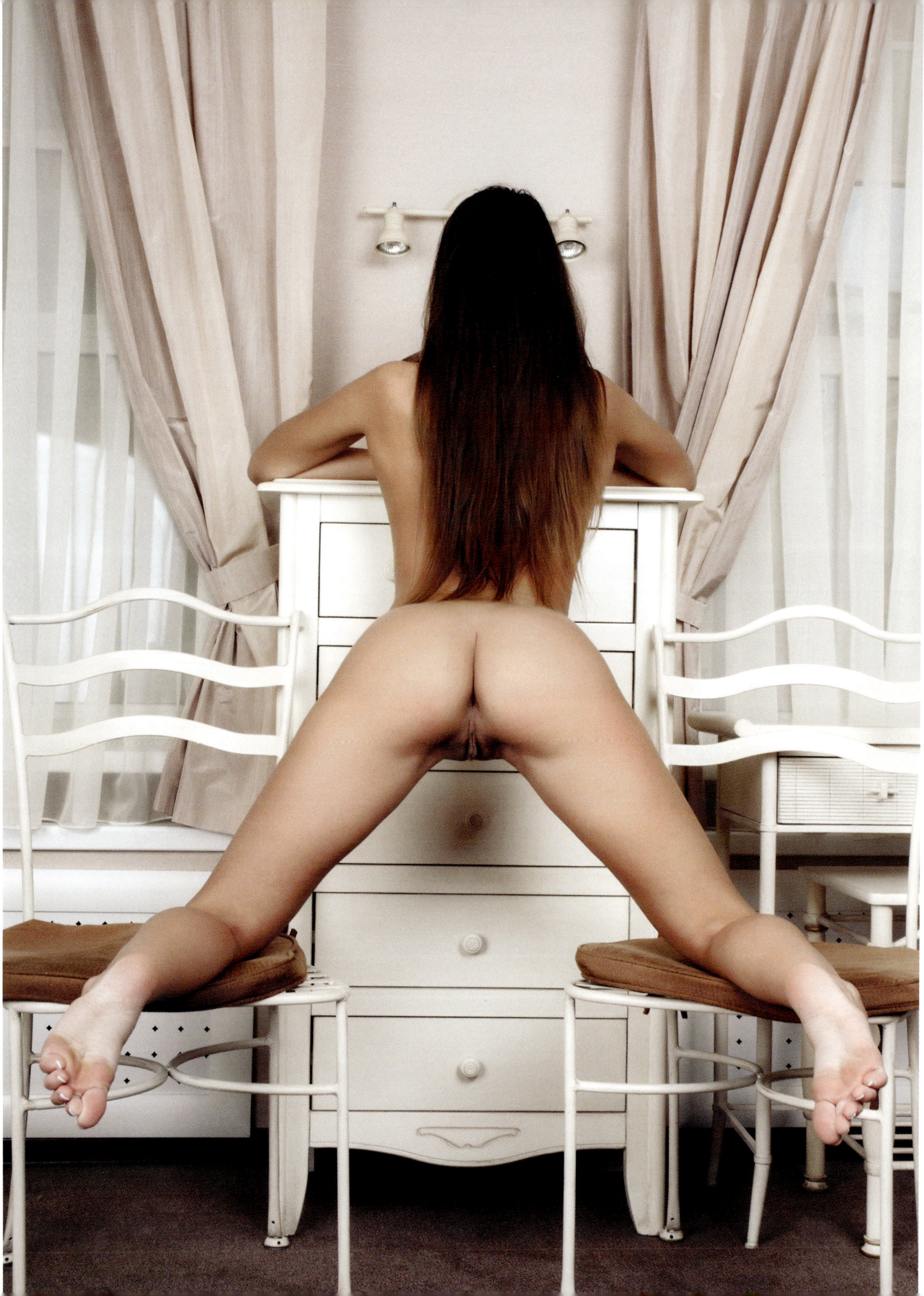

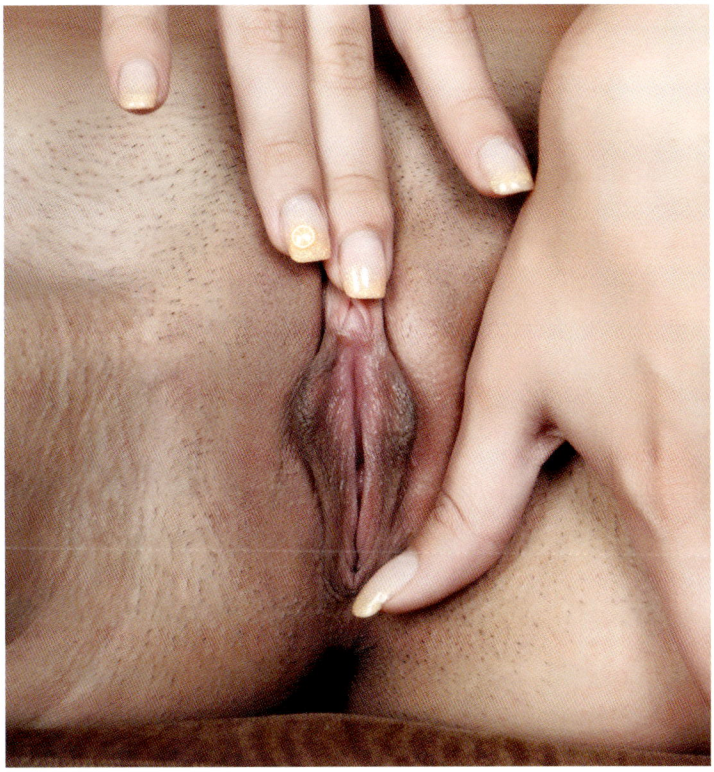

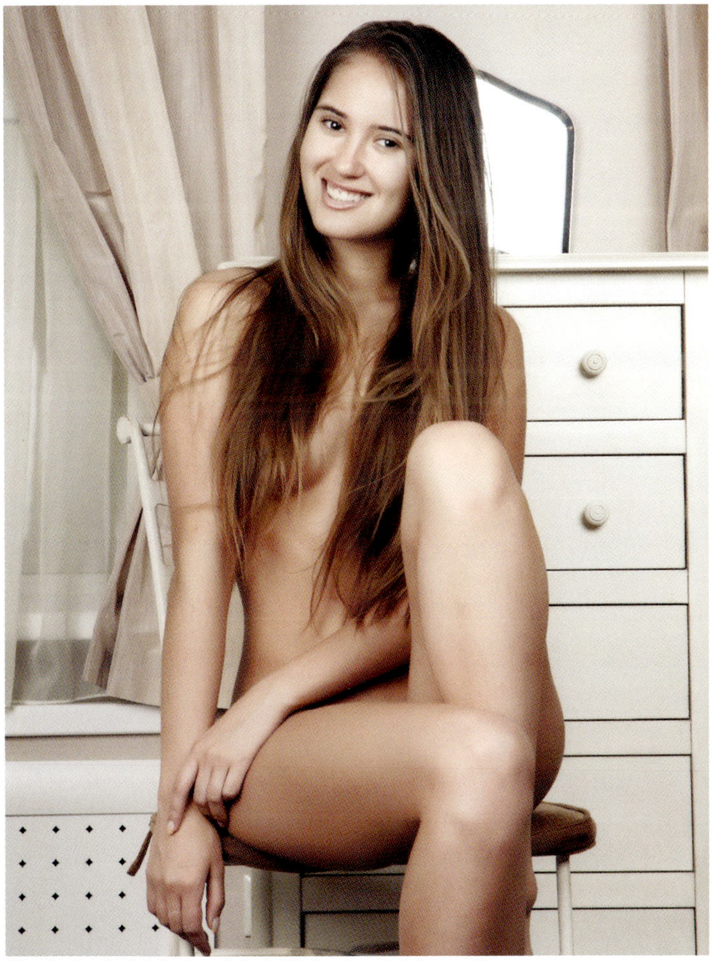

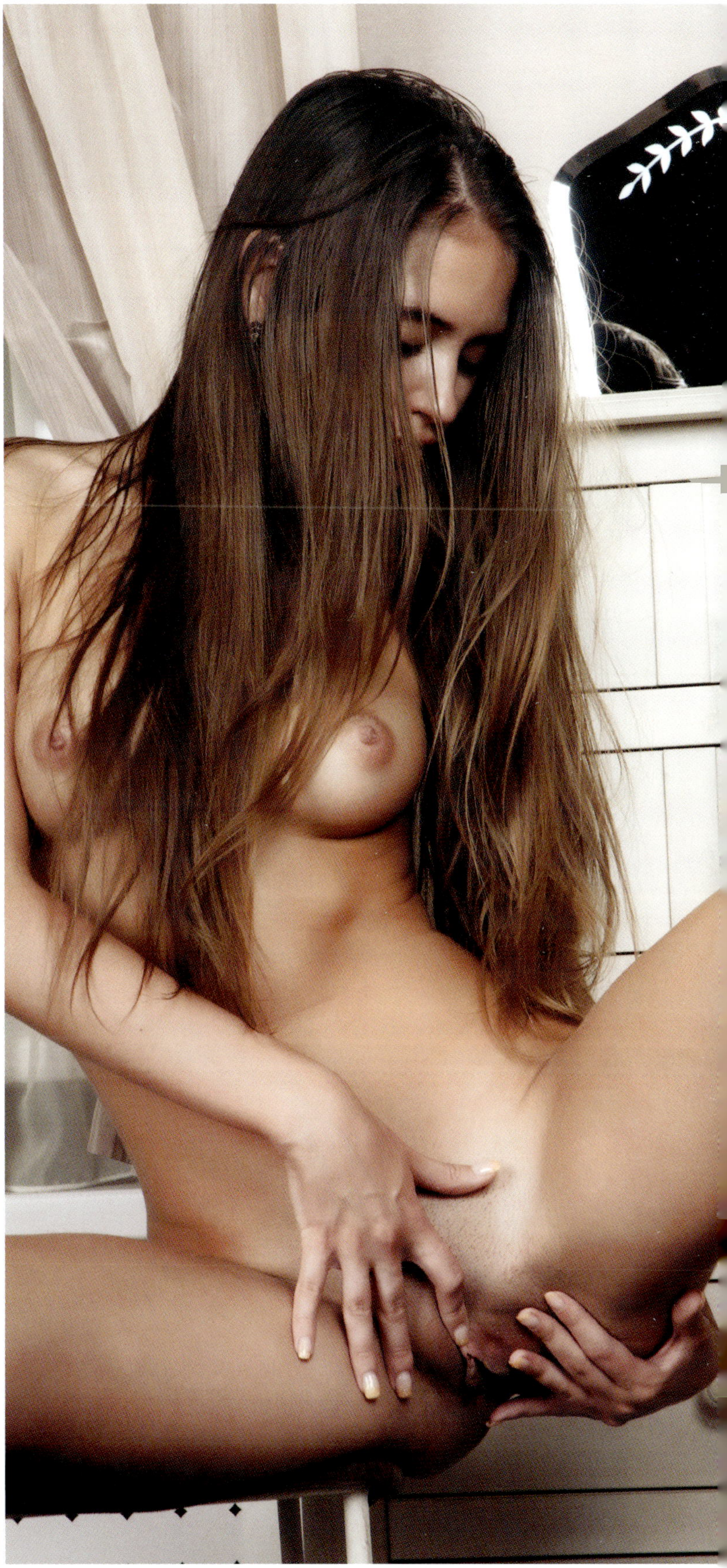

Foxy Alissa
Nikki Hill

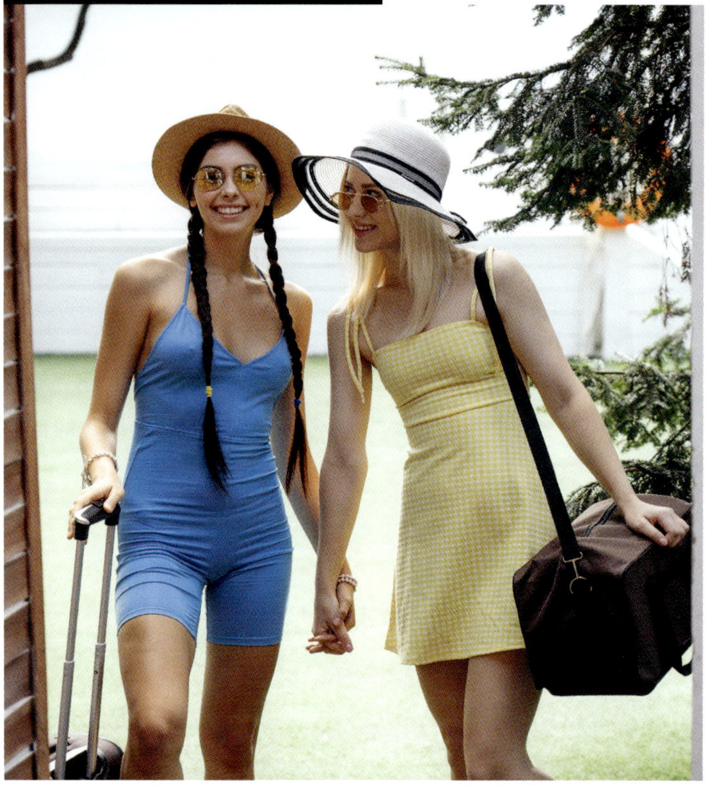

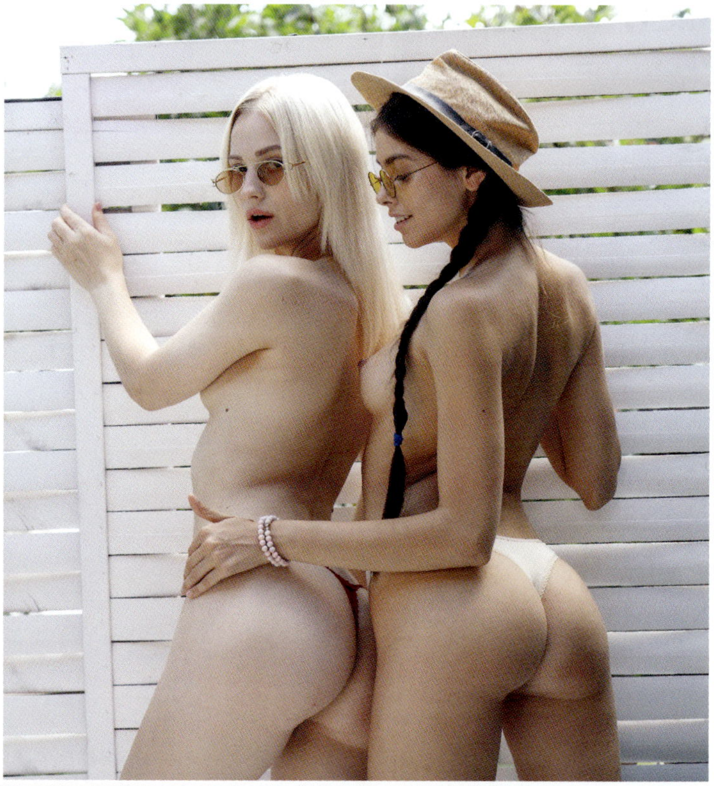

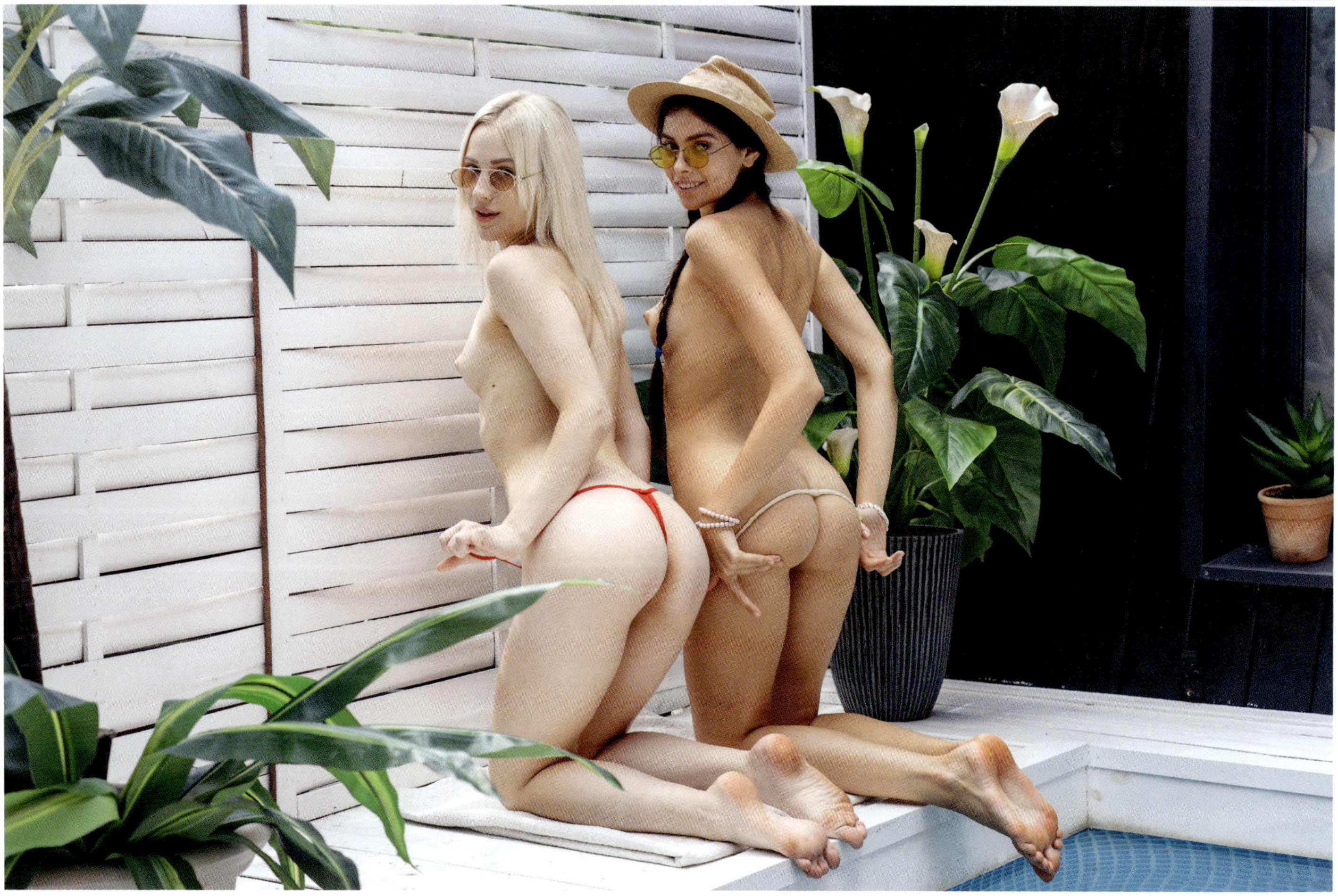

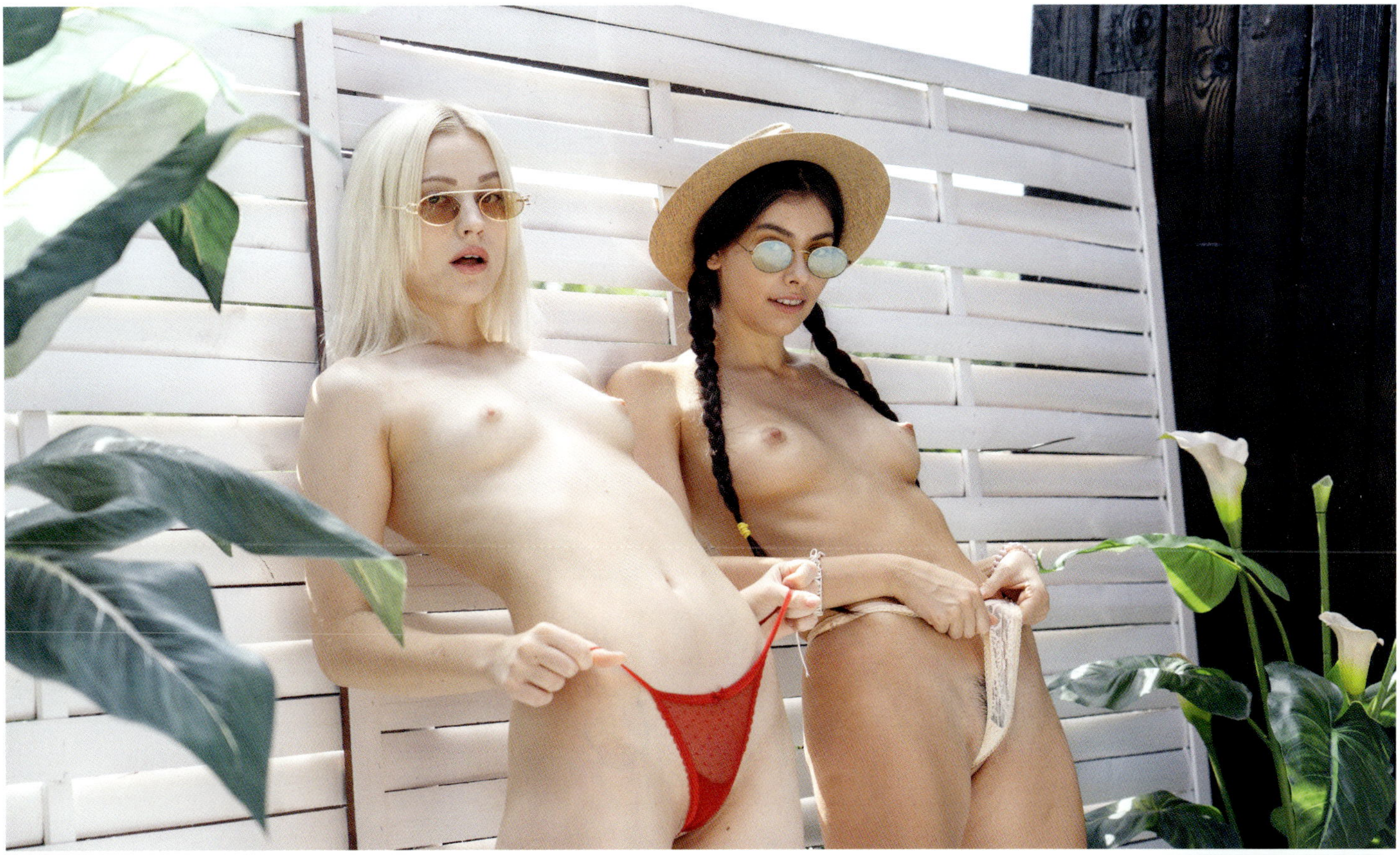

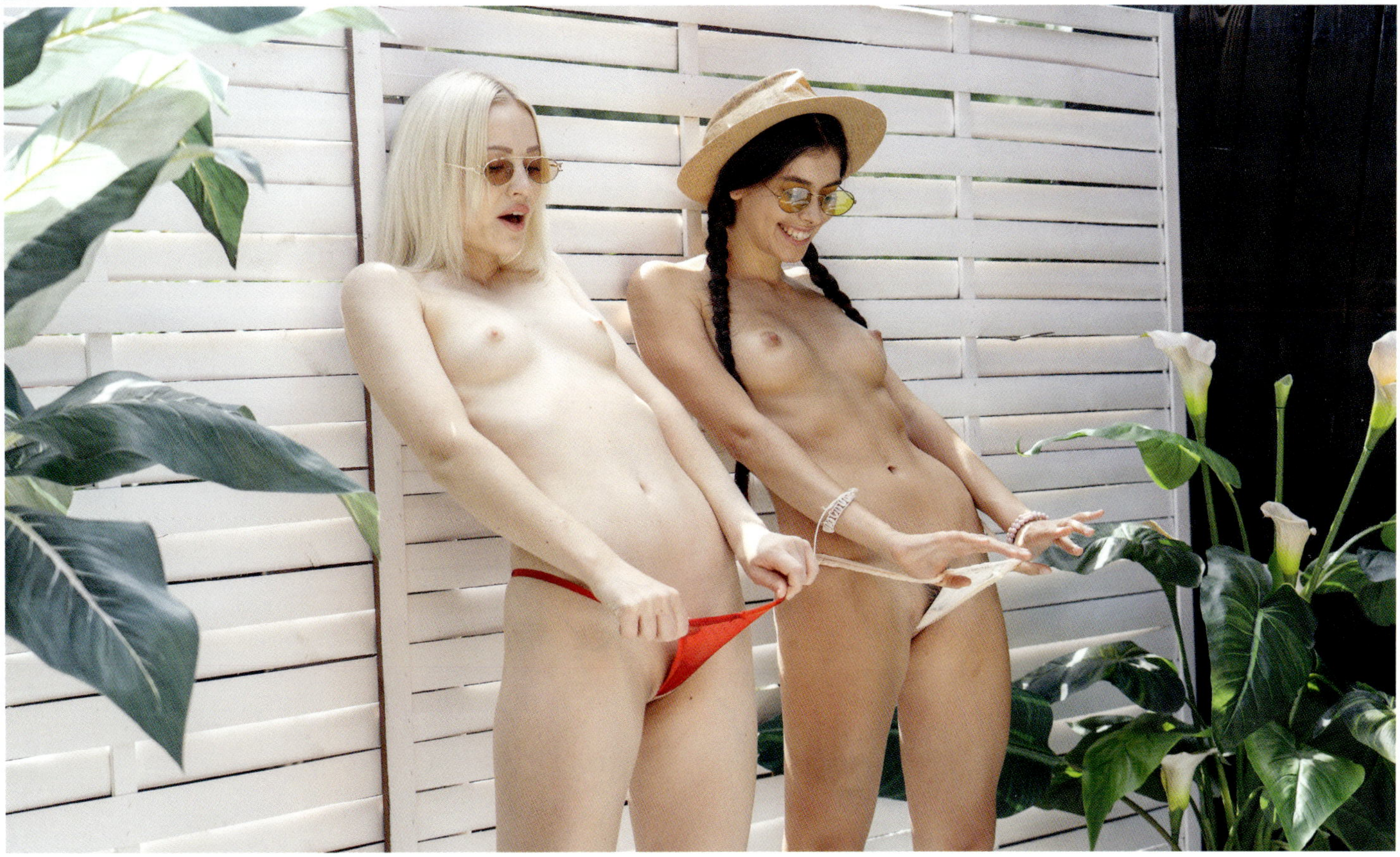

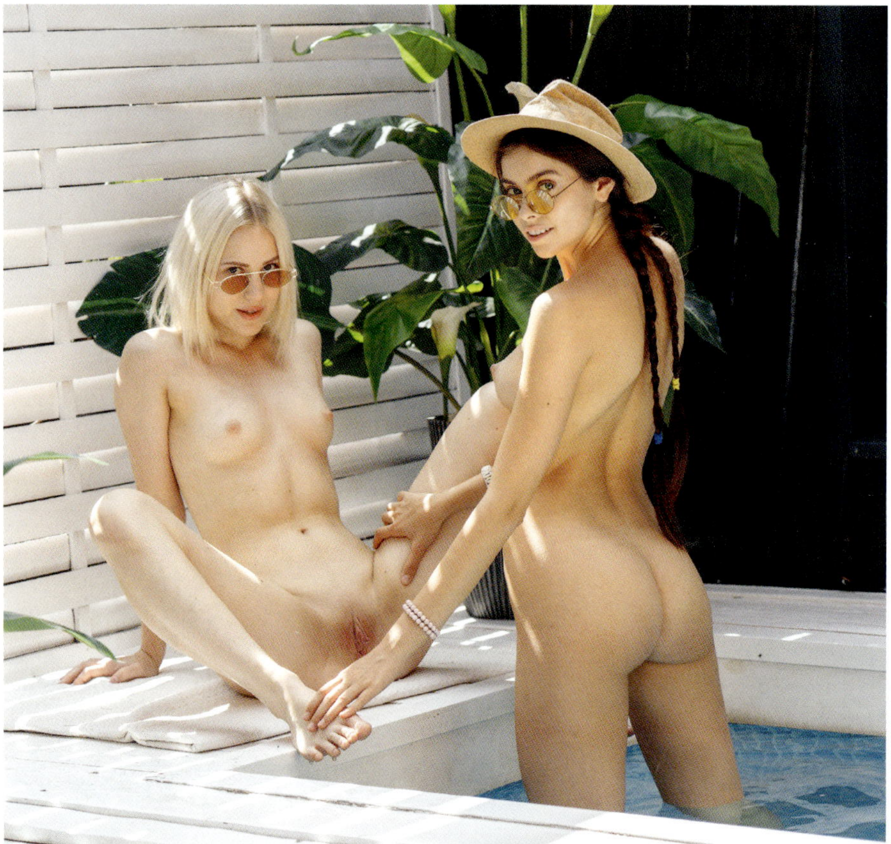
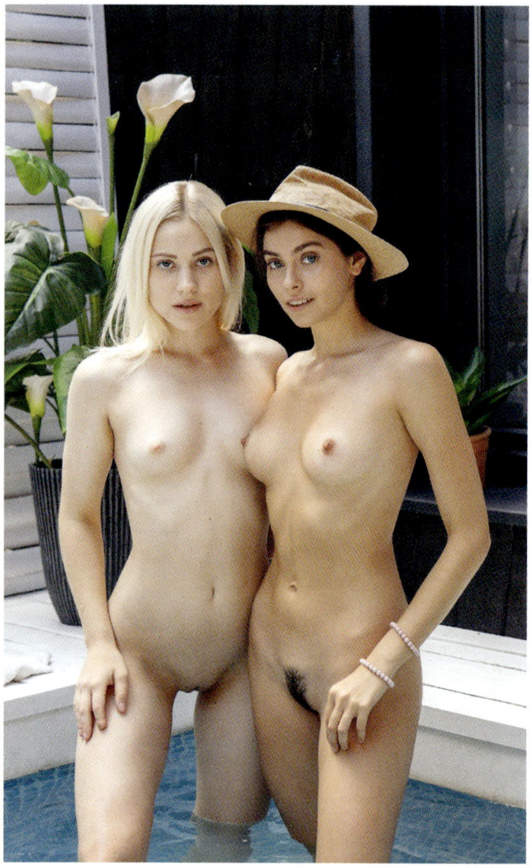
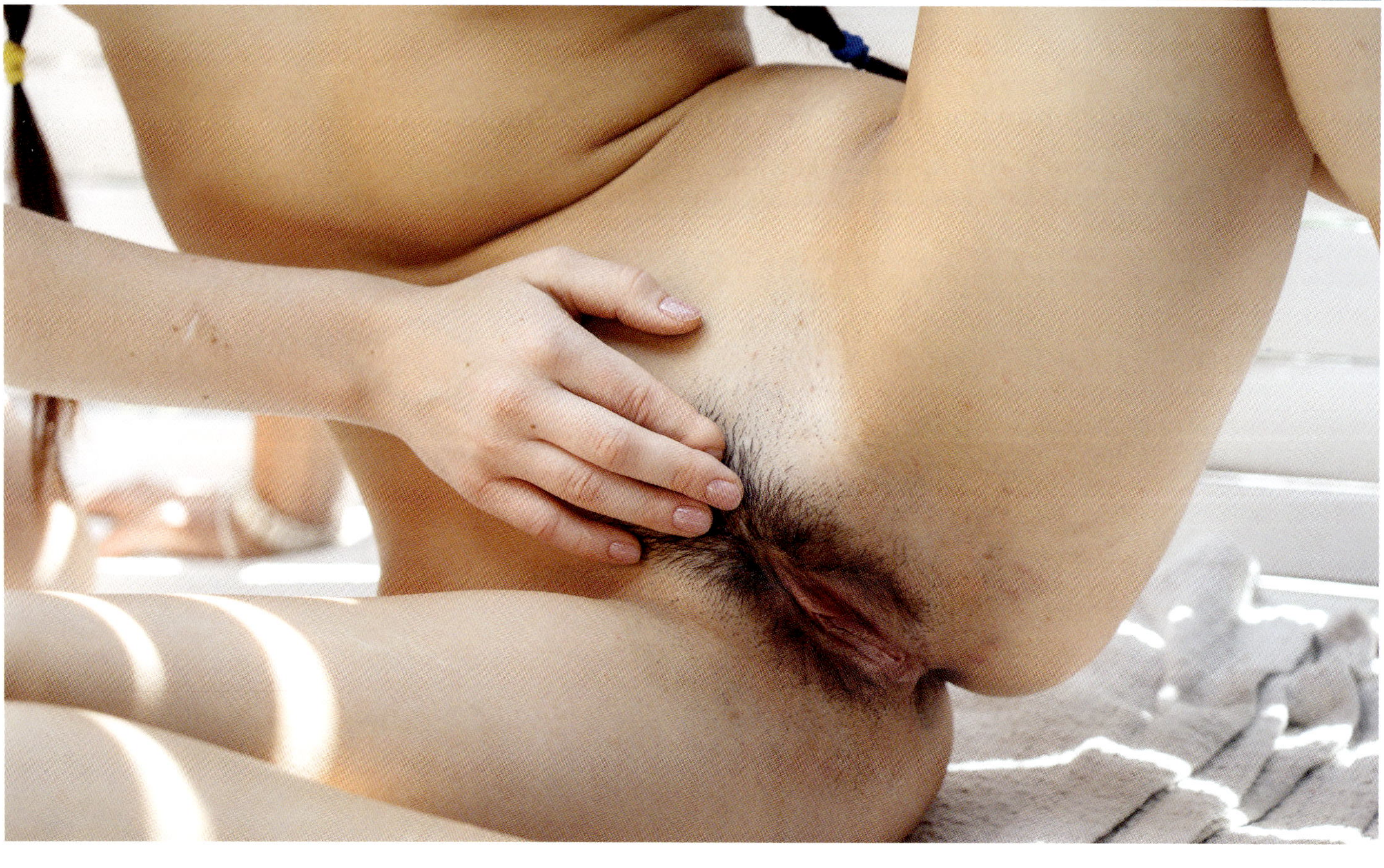

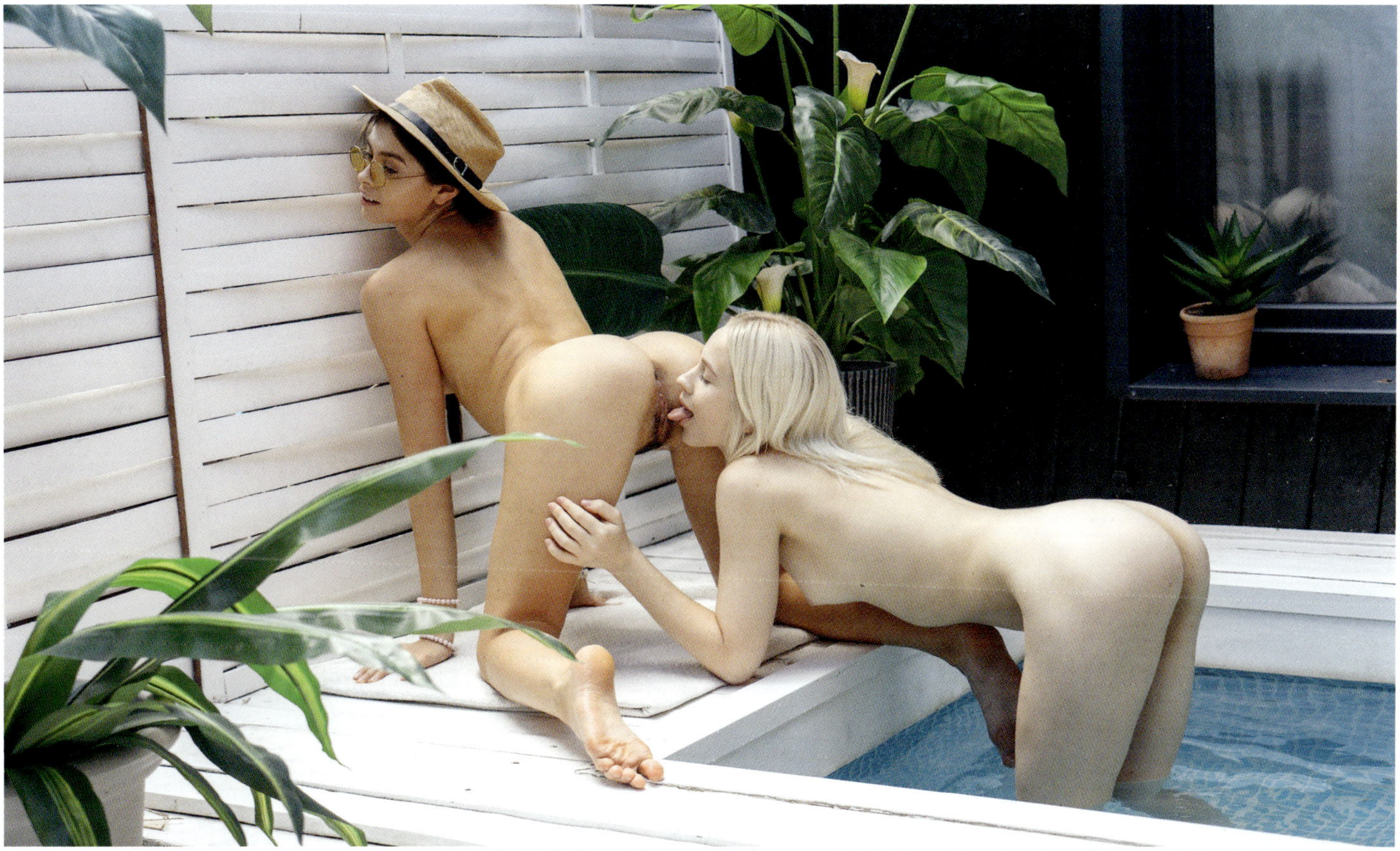

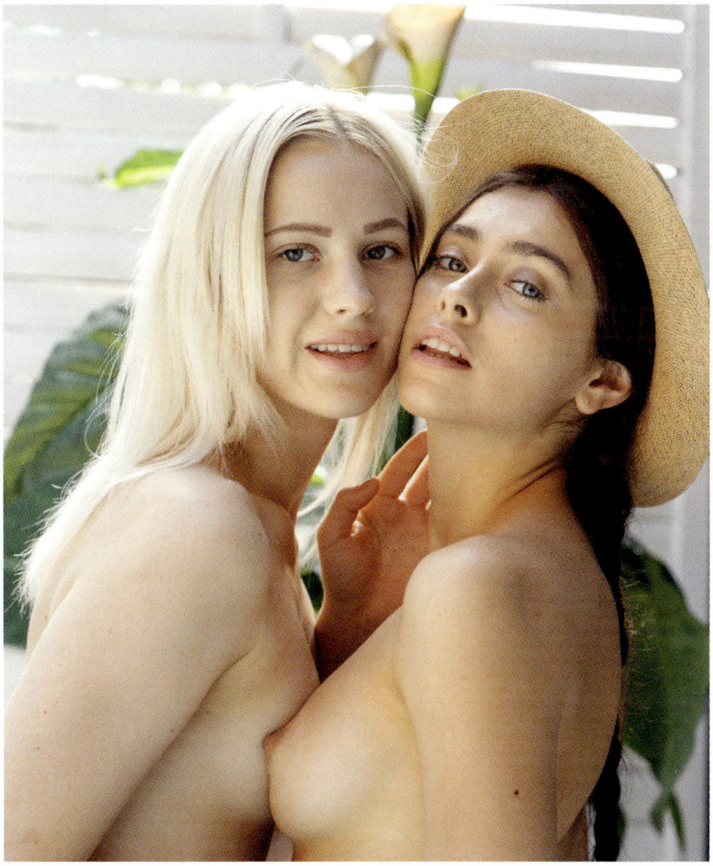

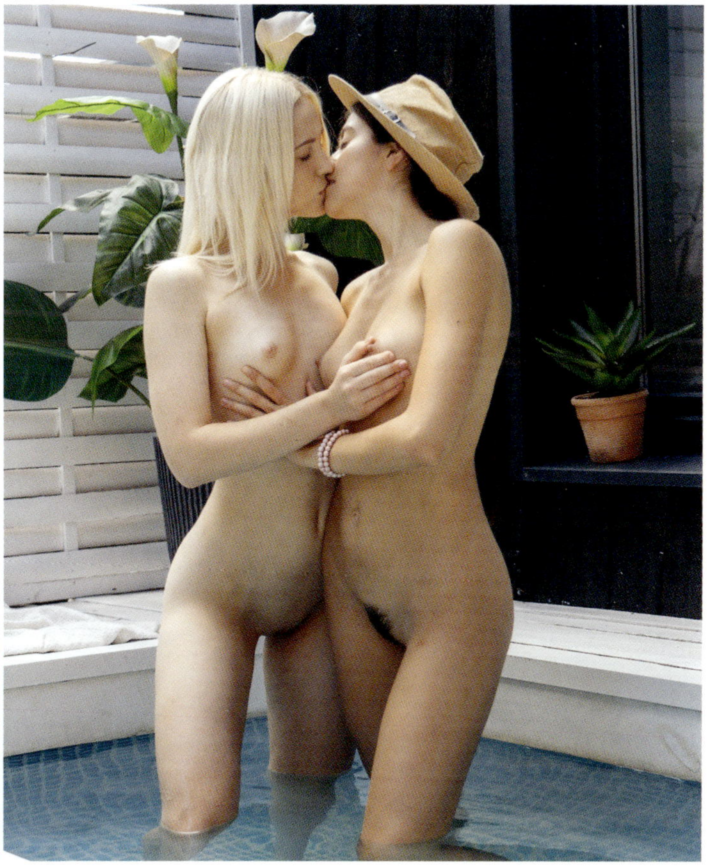

Kylie D

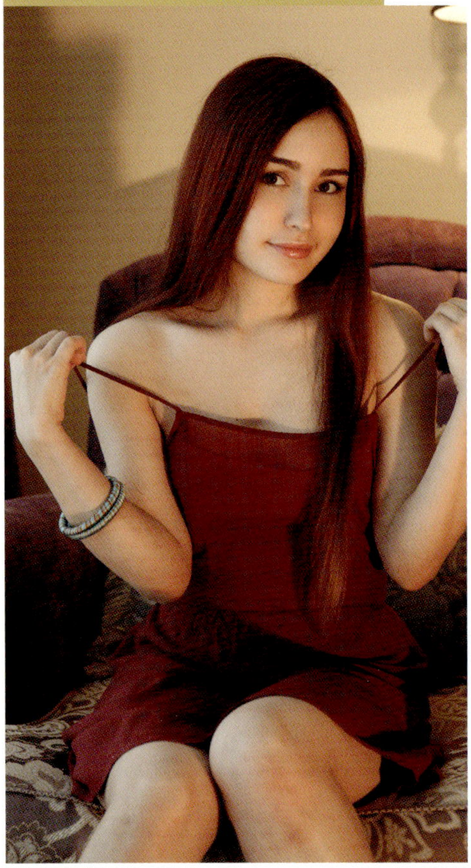

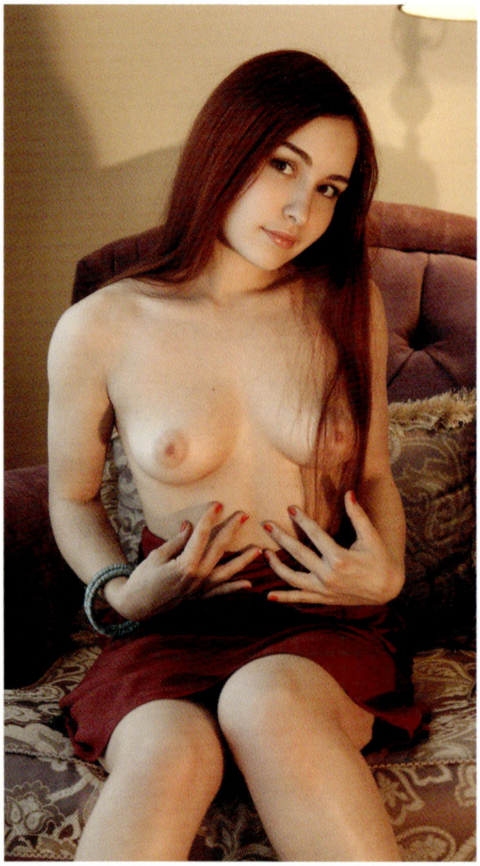

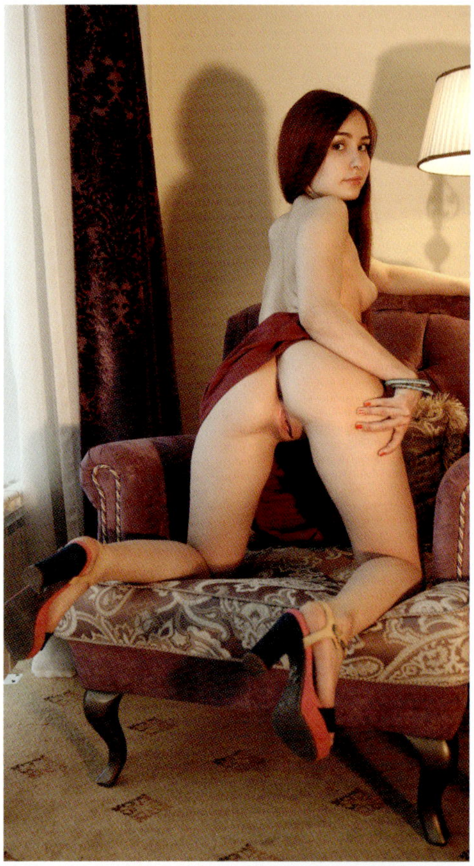

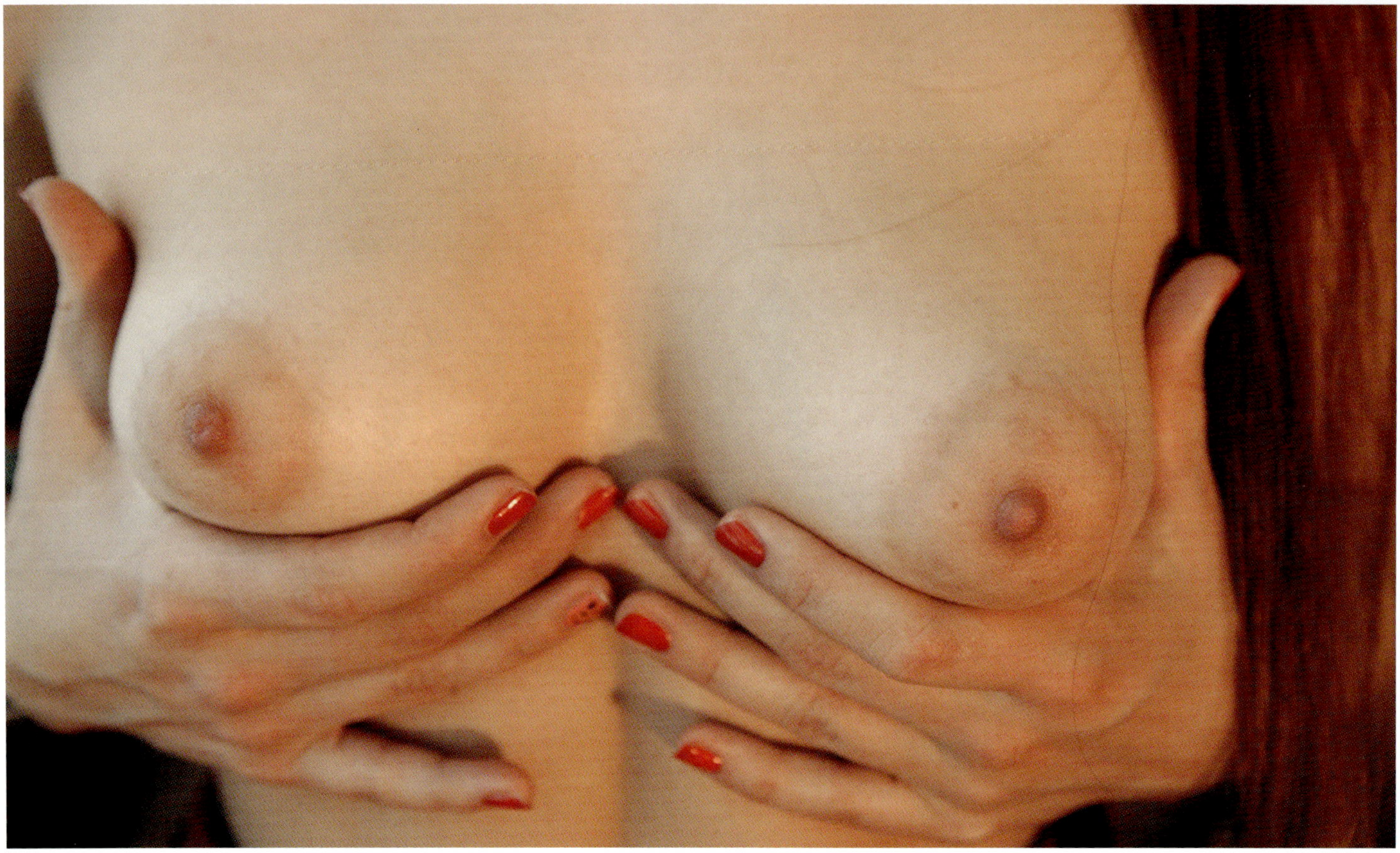

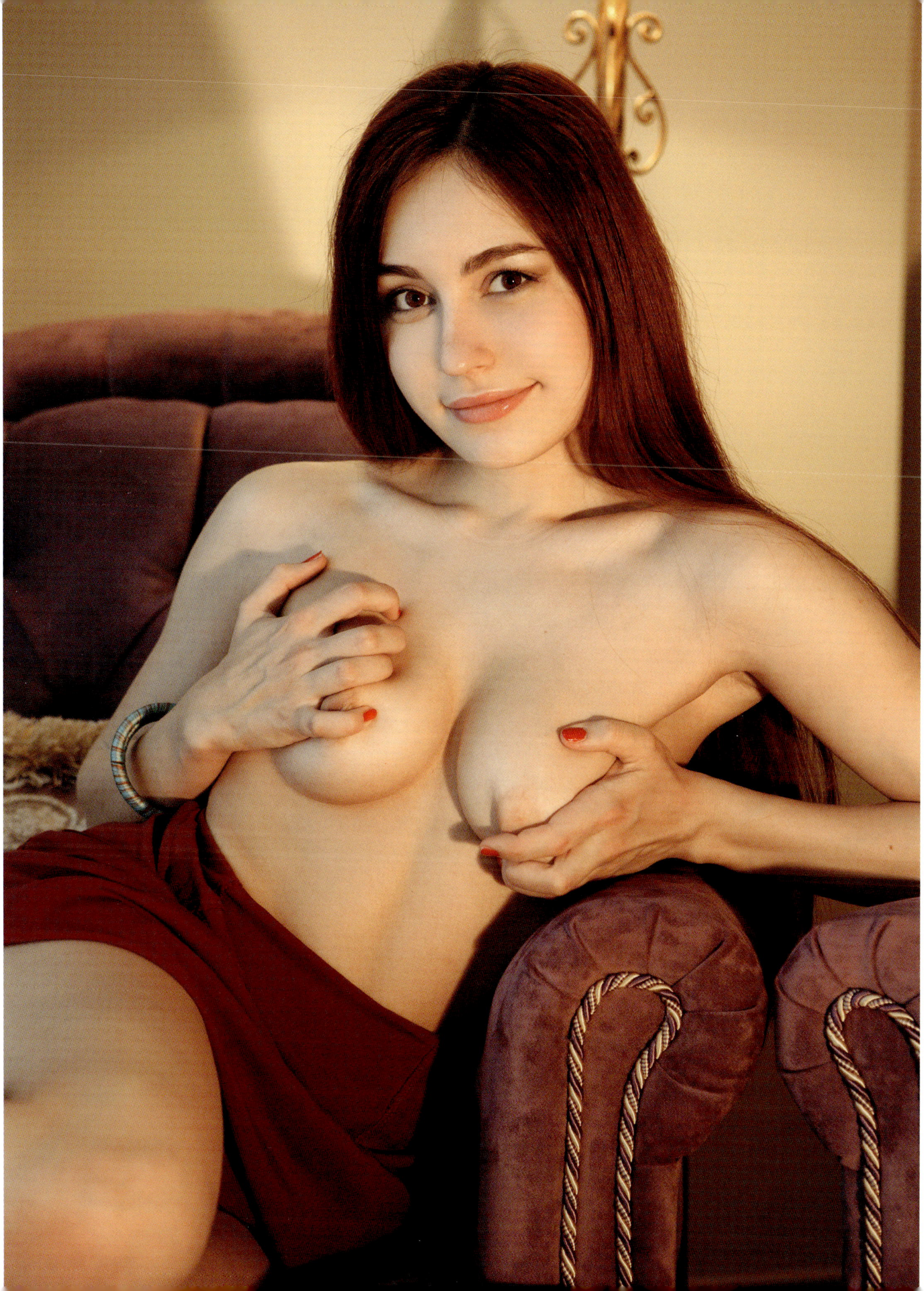

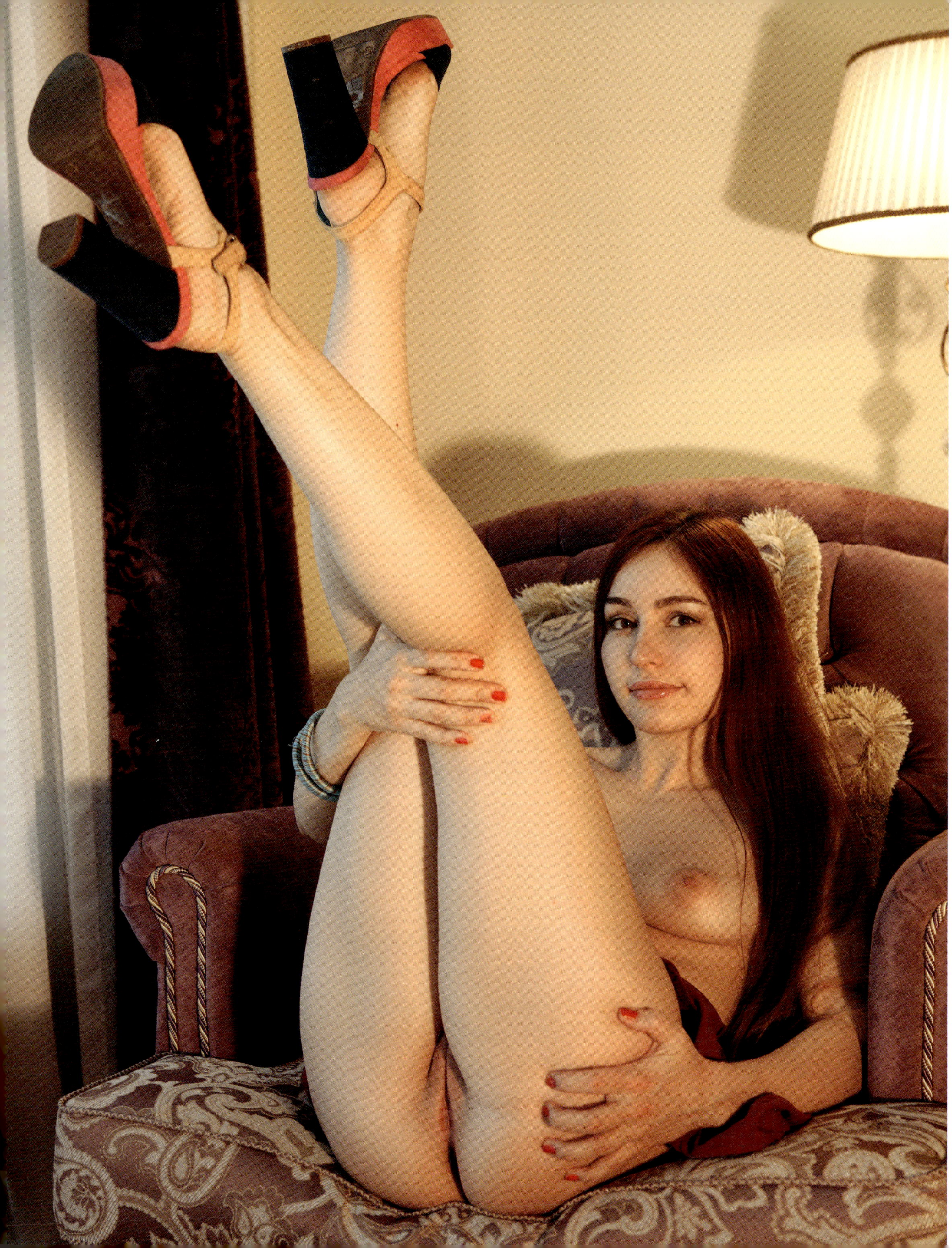

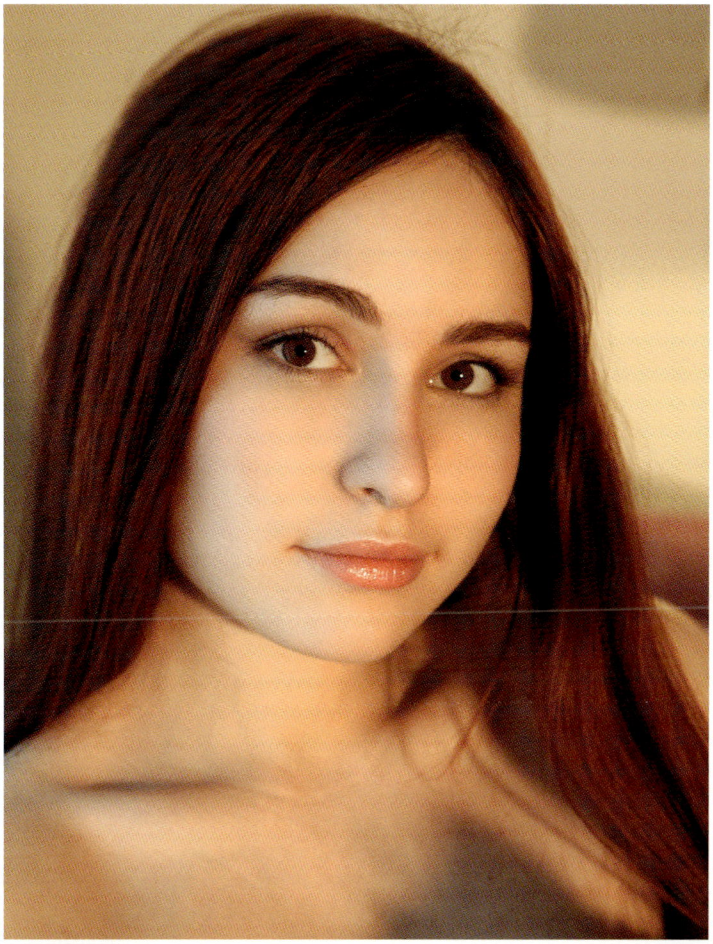

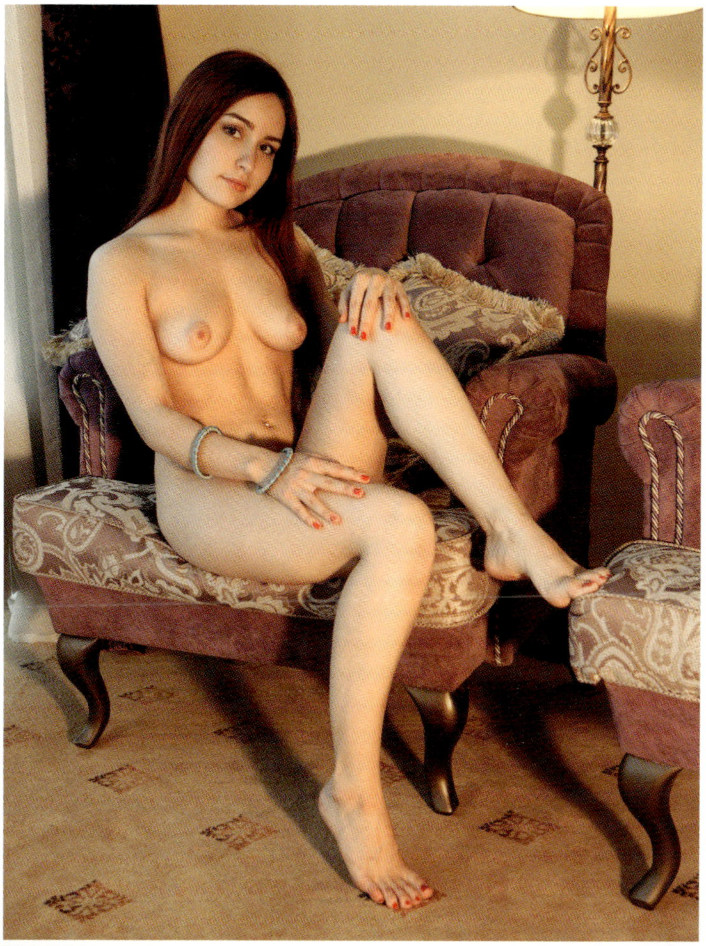

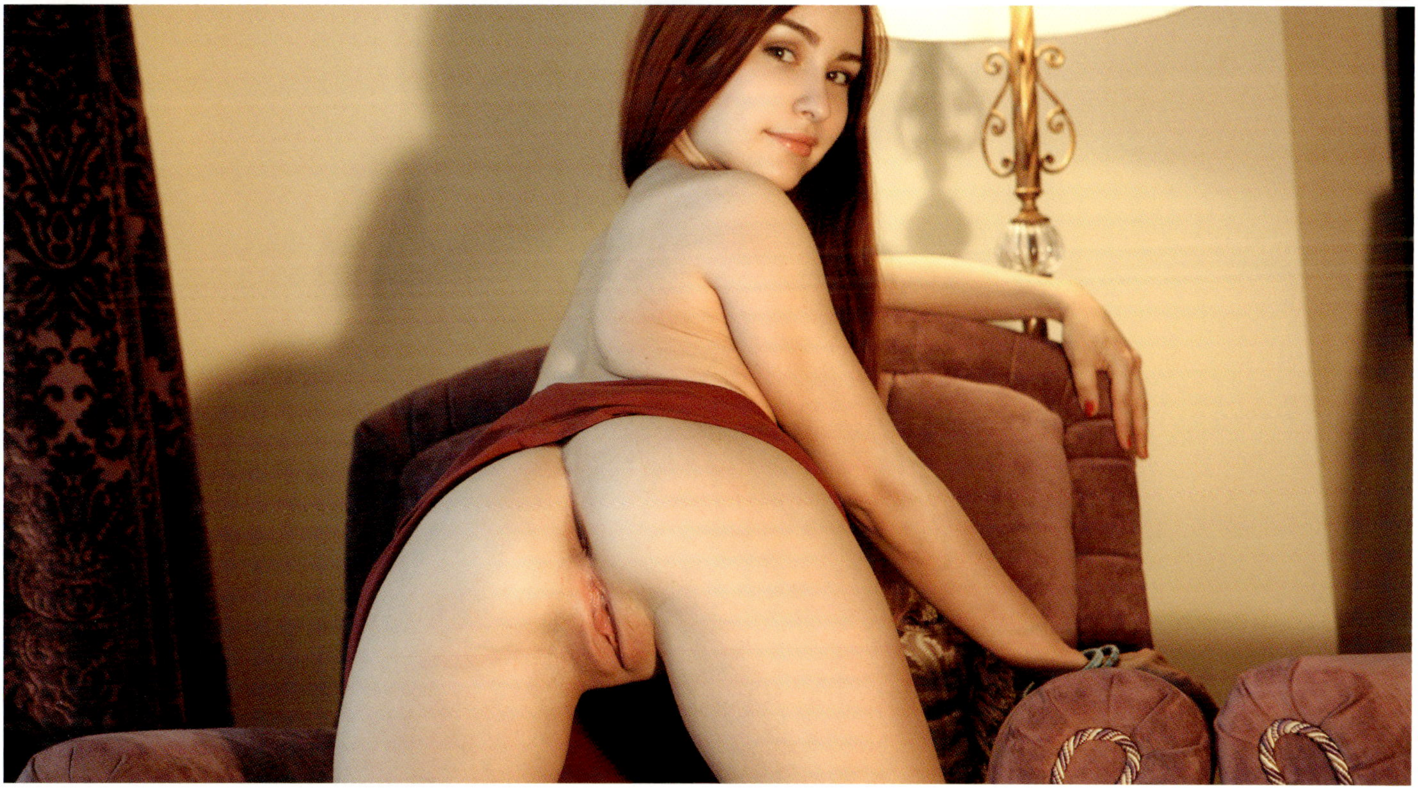

Anoli Angel
Nïka N

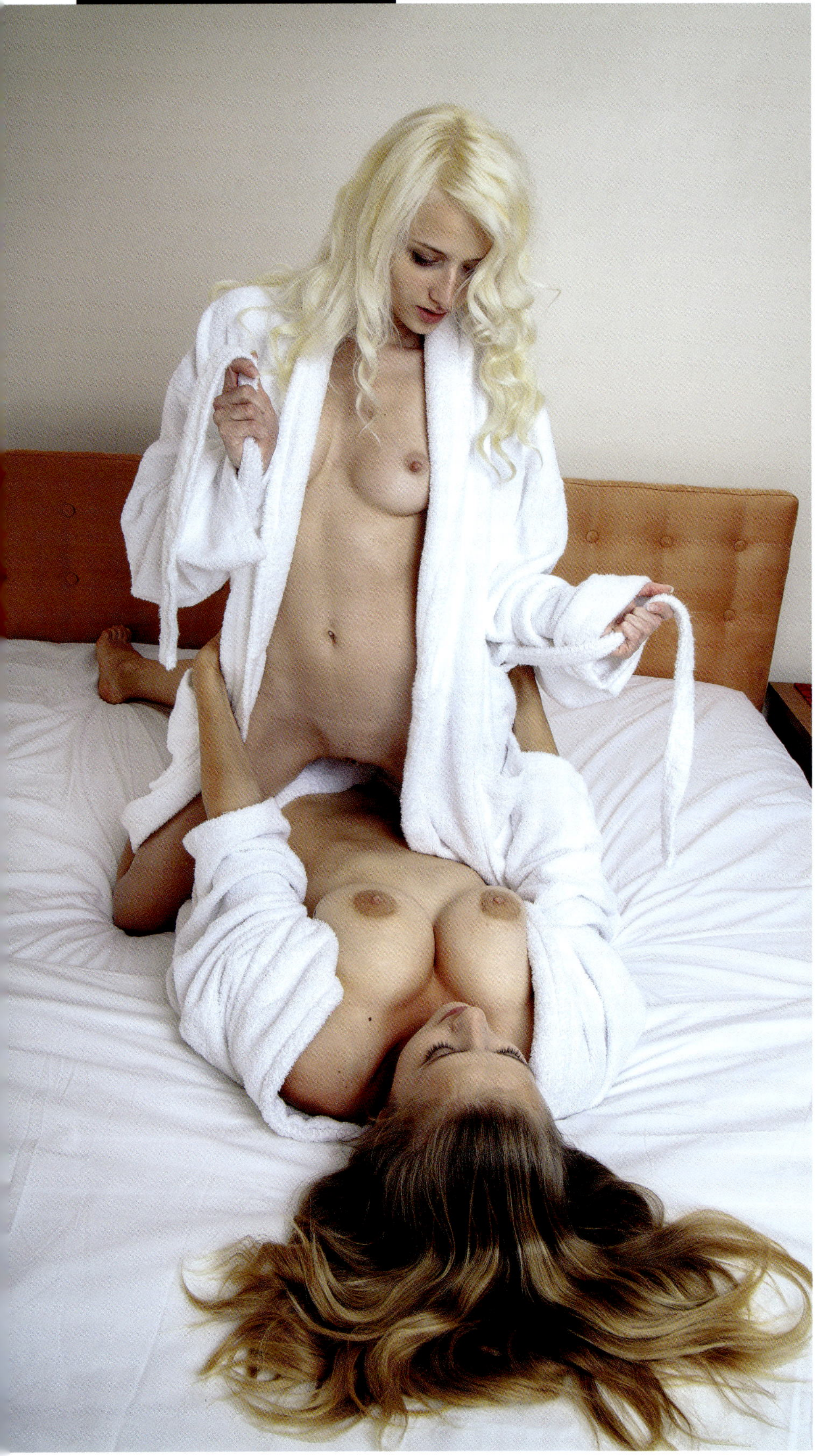

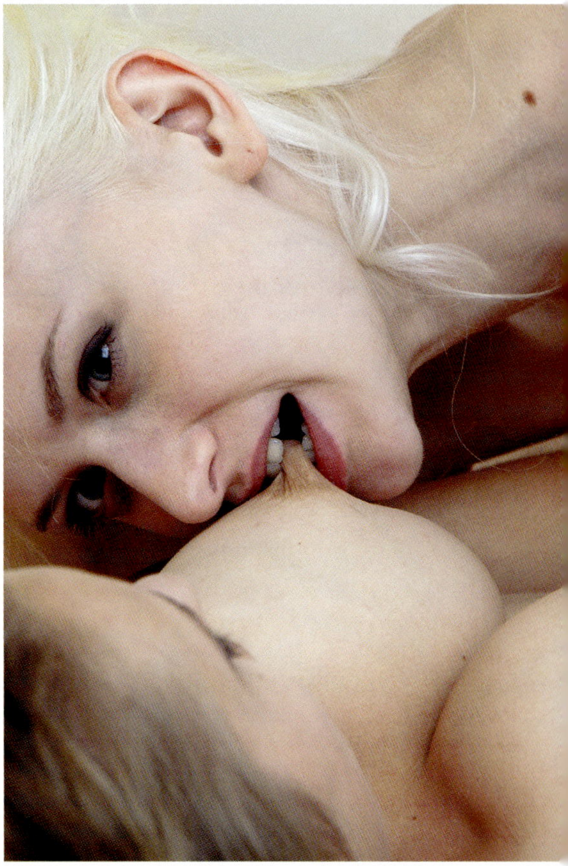

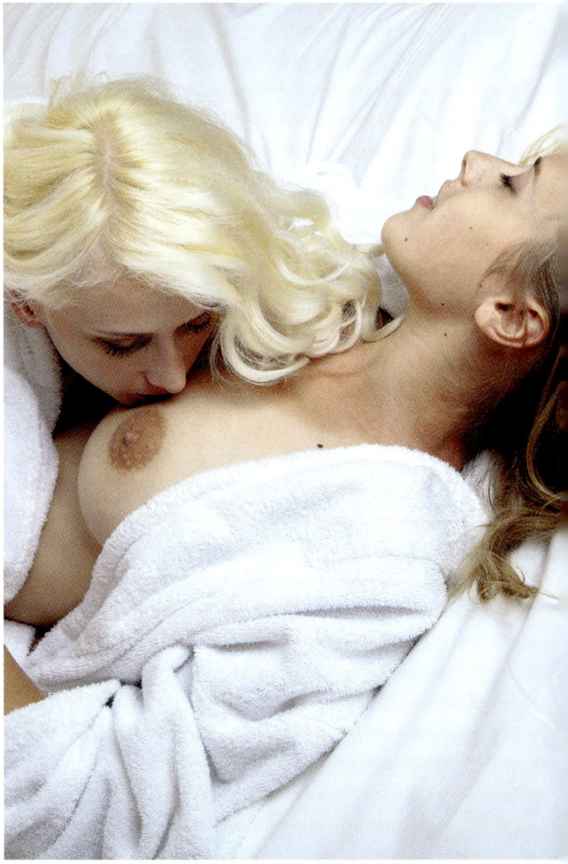

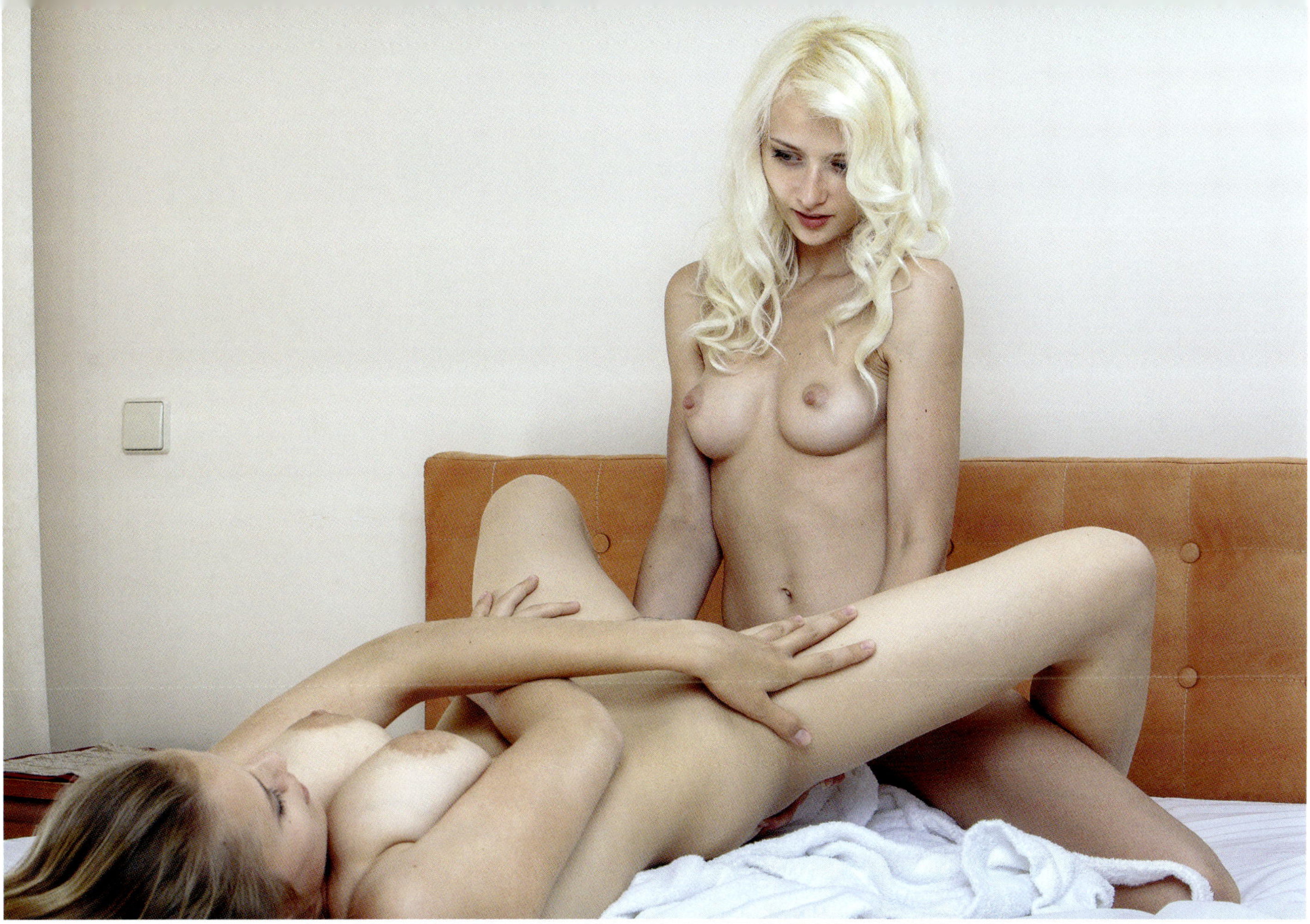

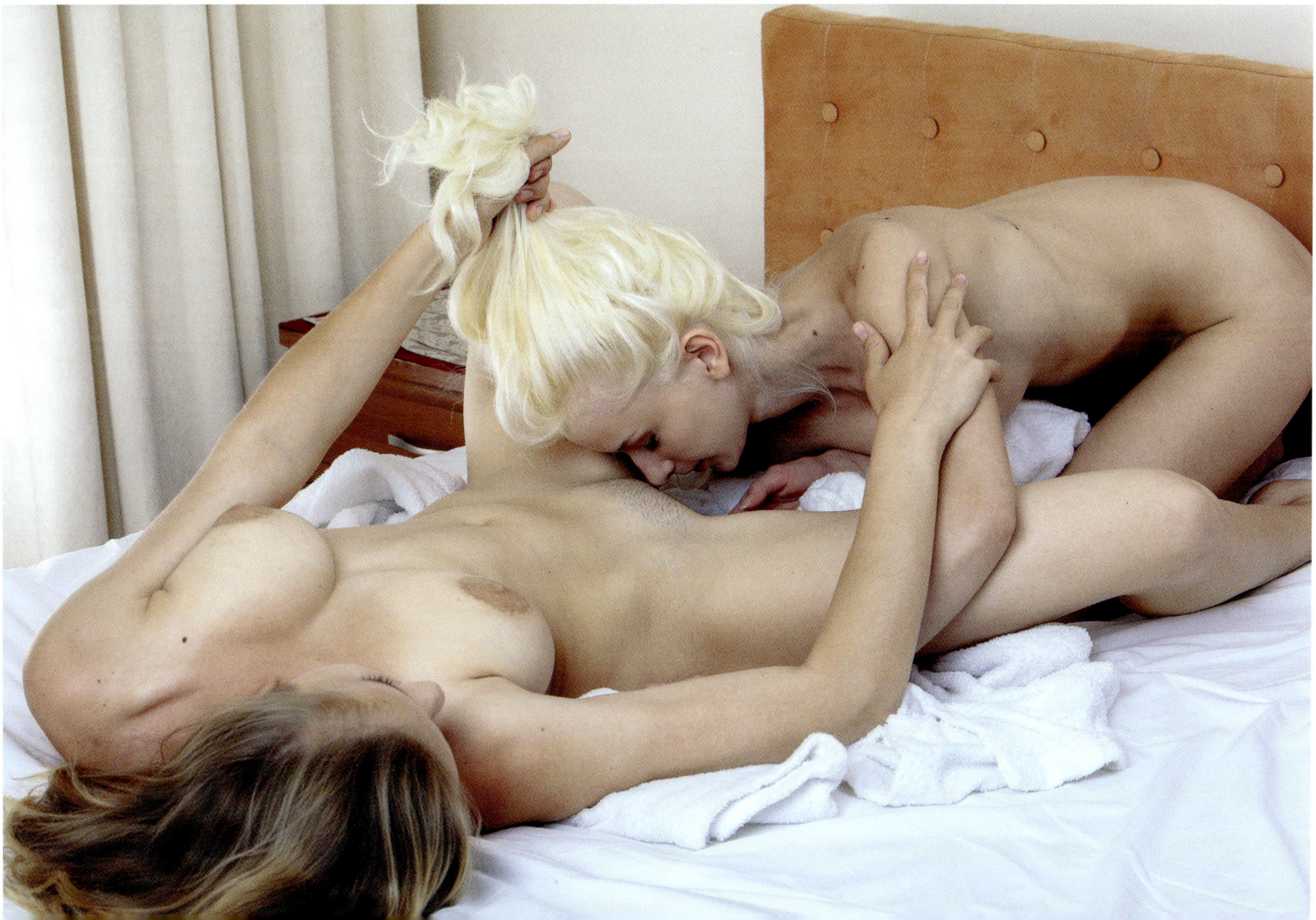

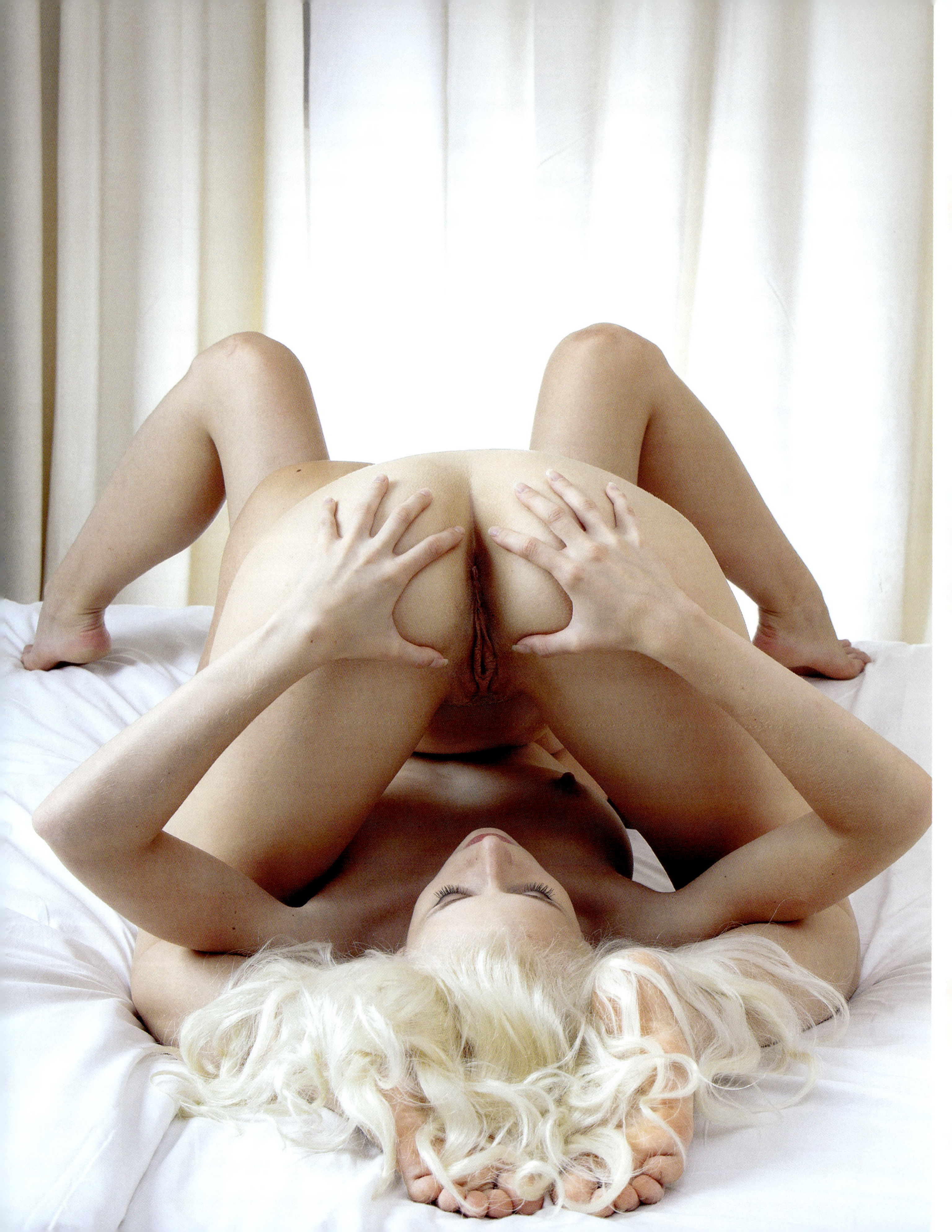

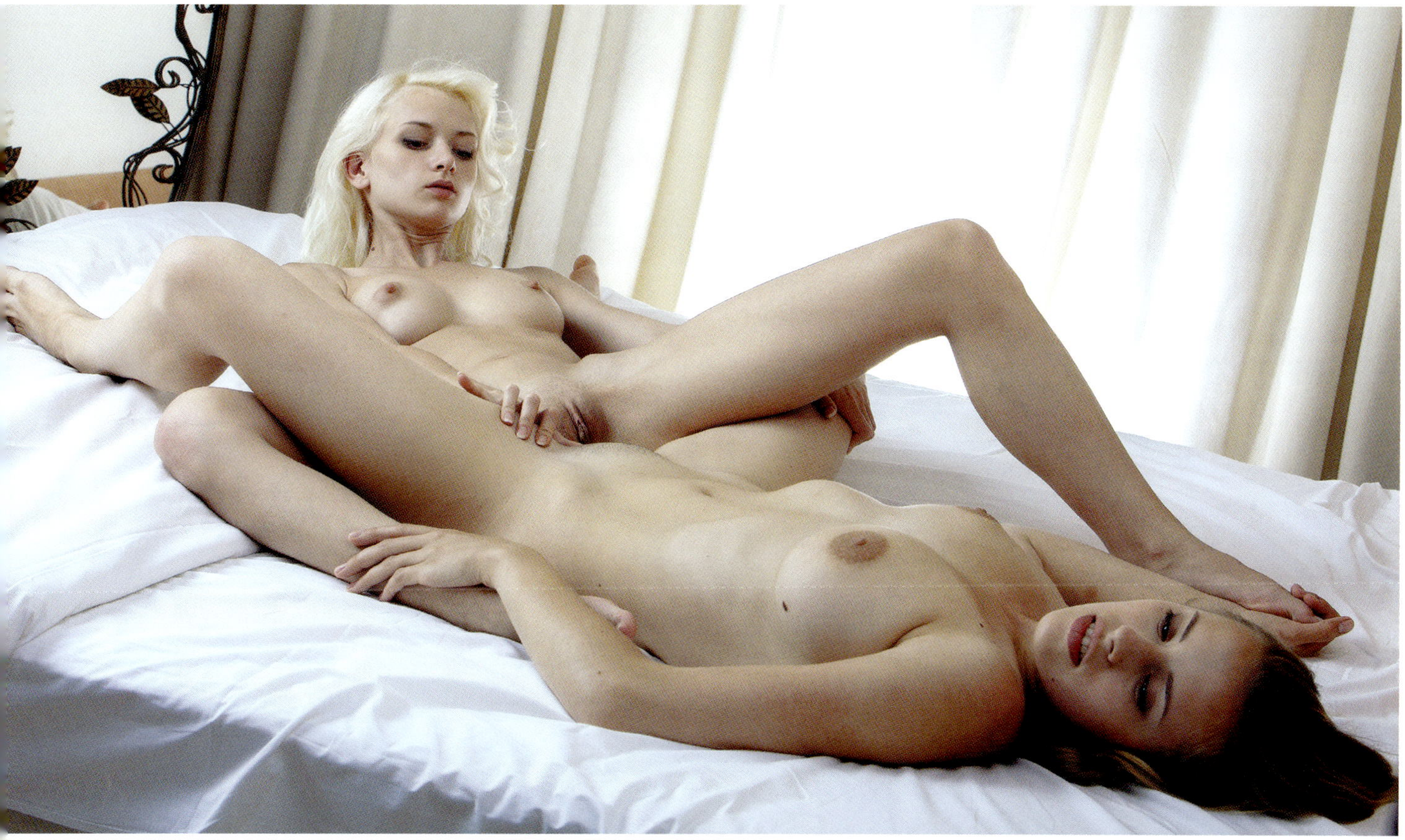

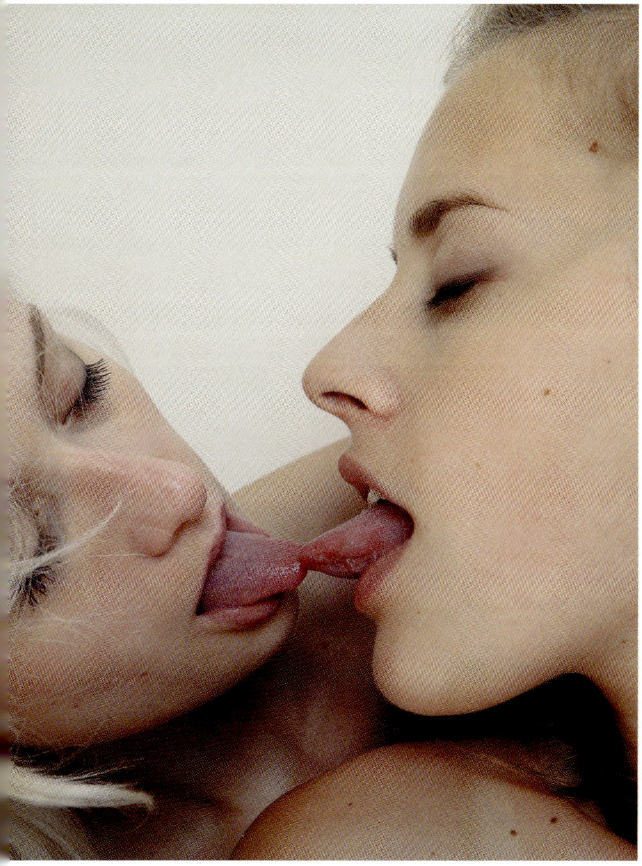

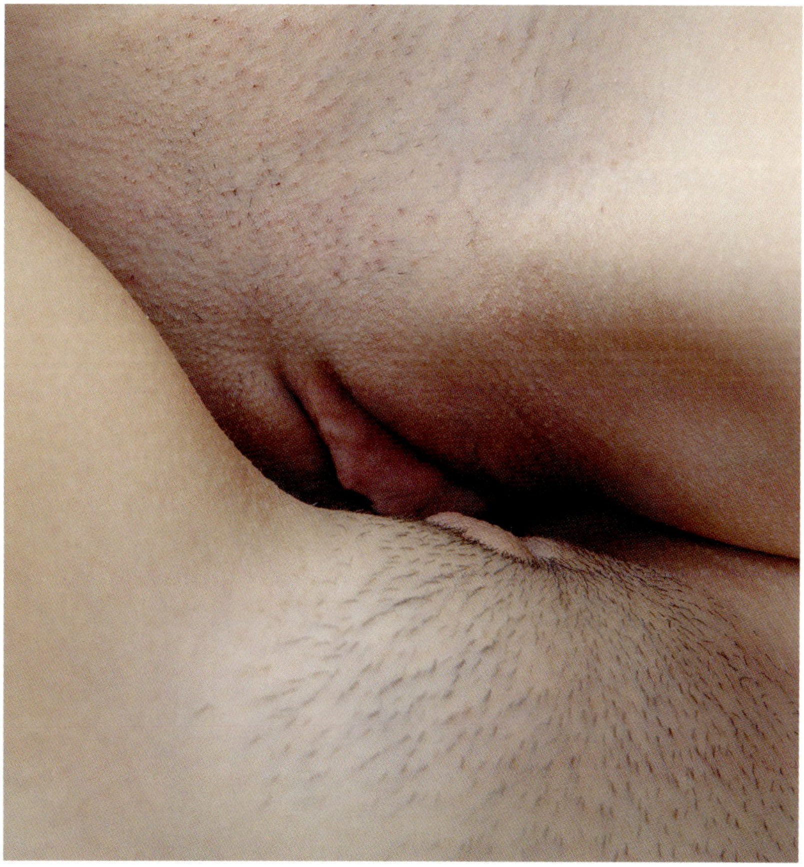

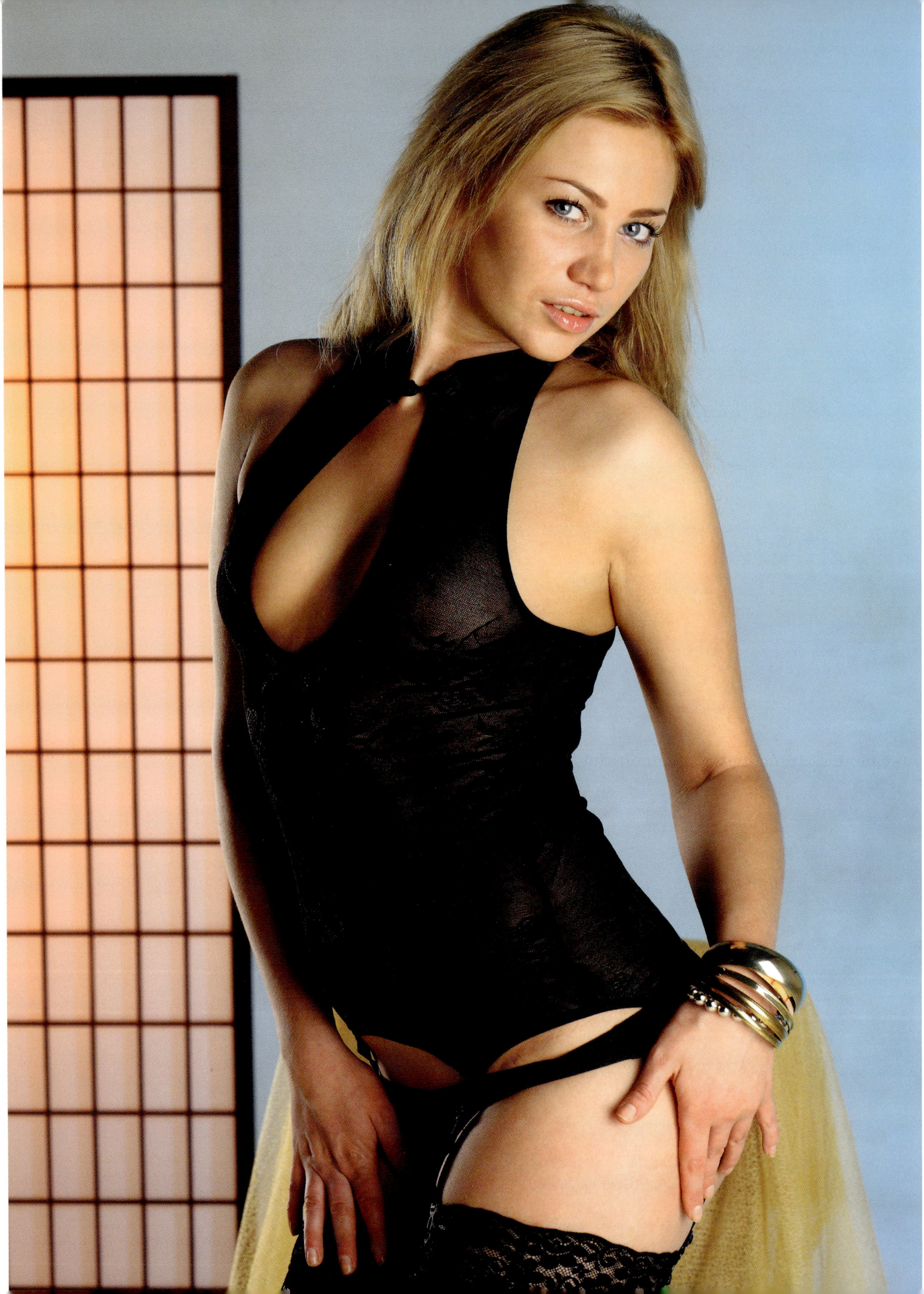

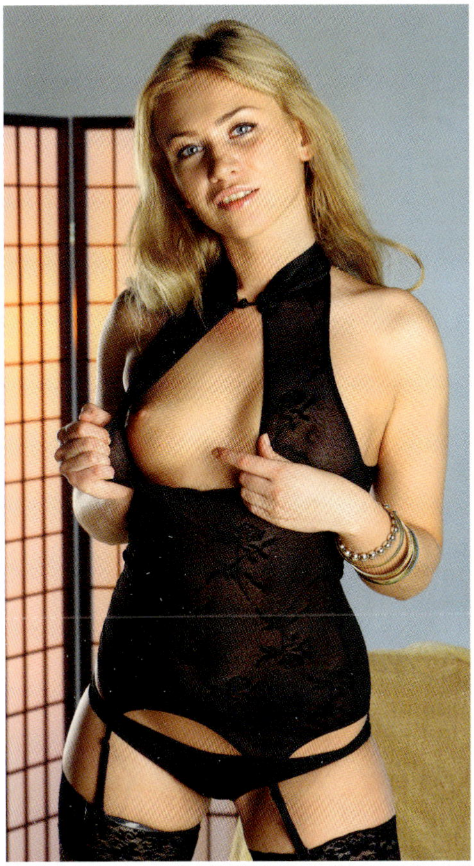
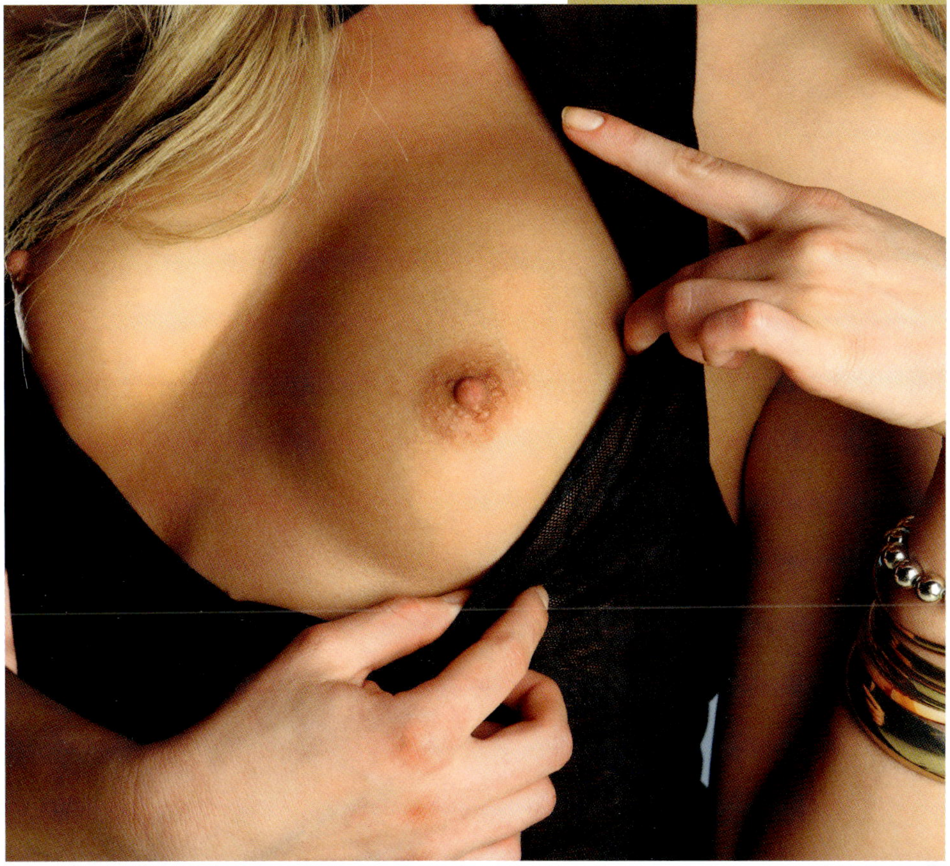
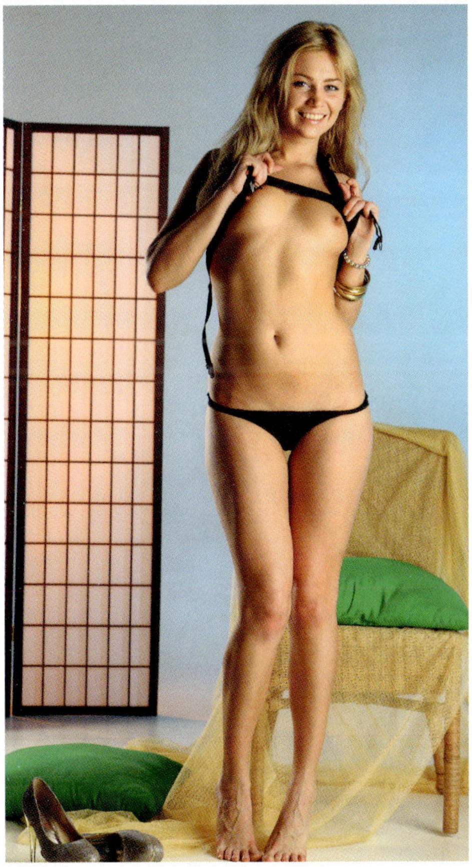
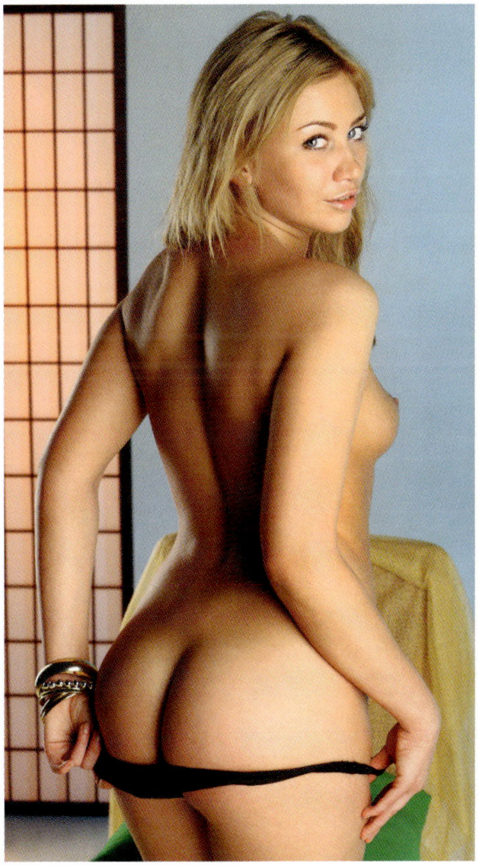
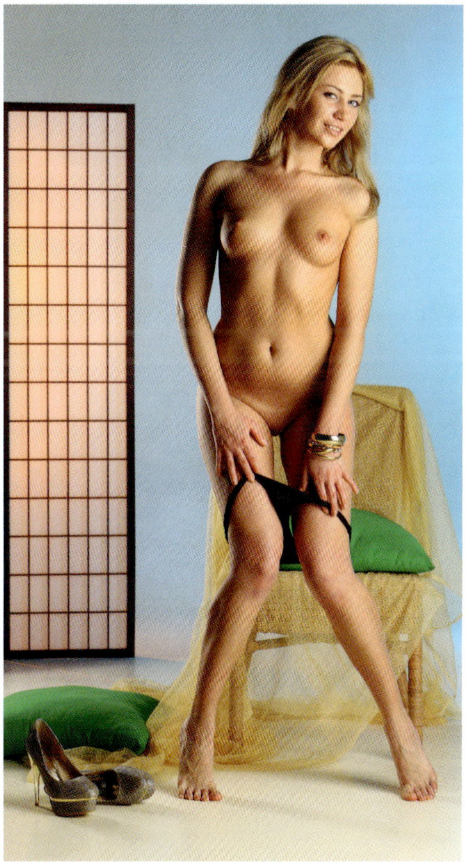

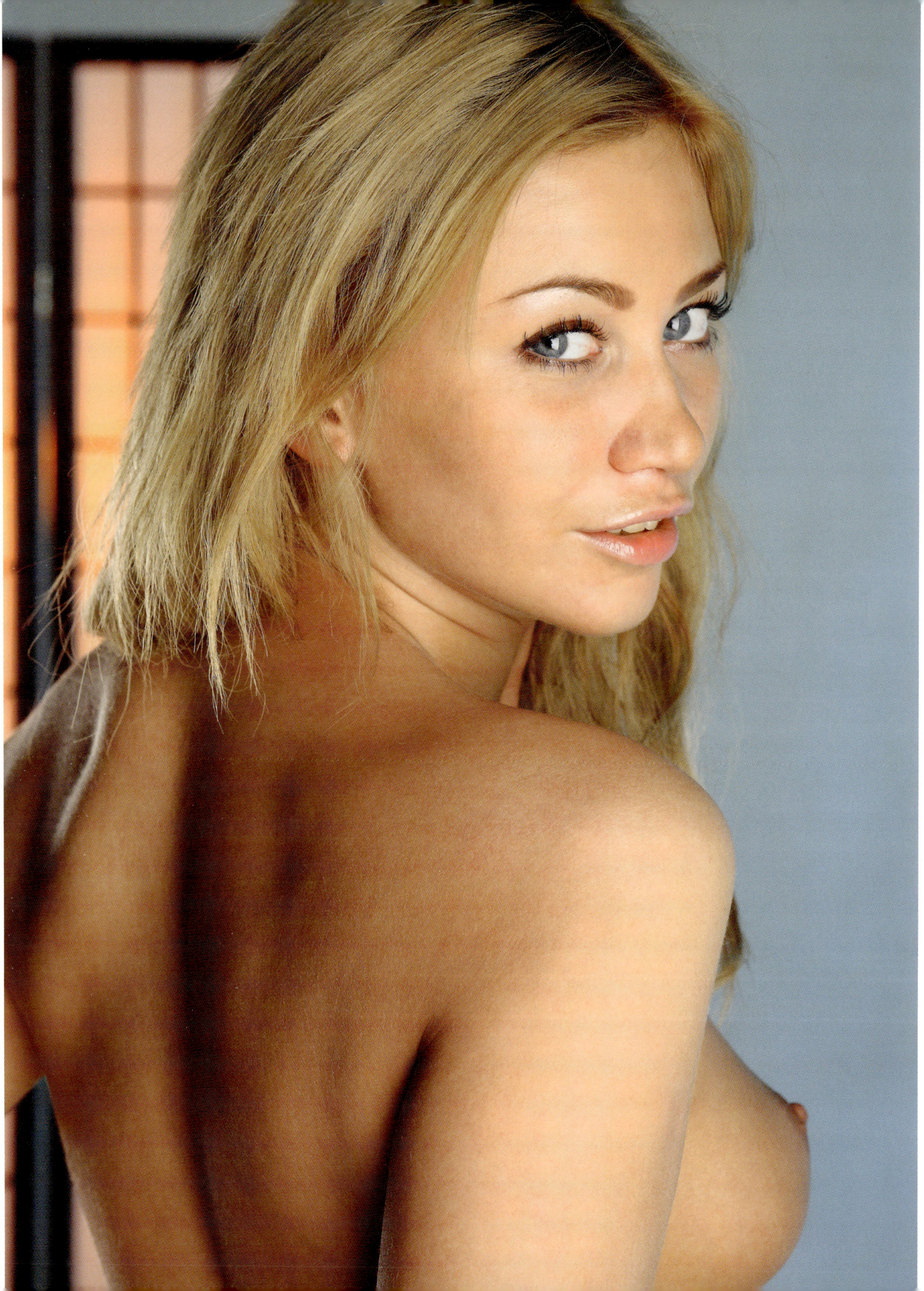

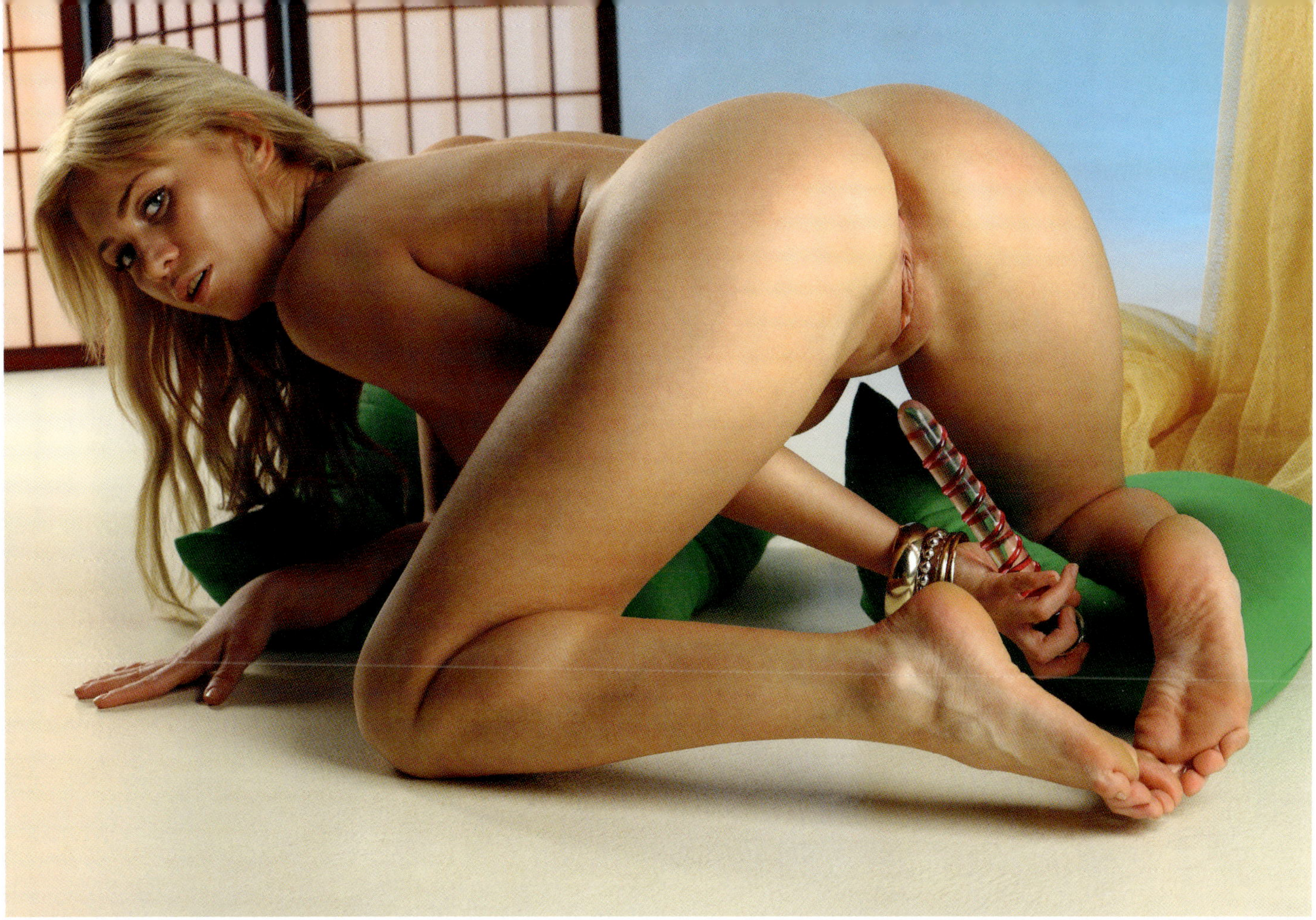

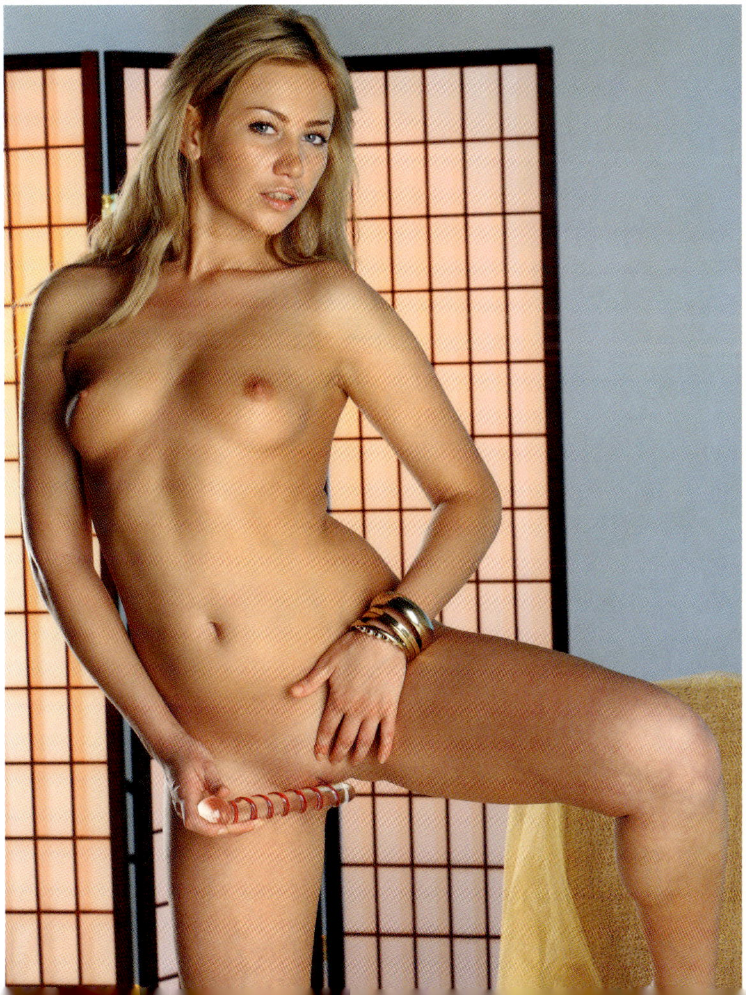

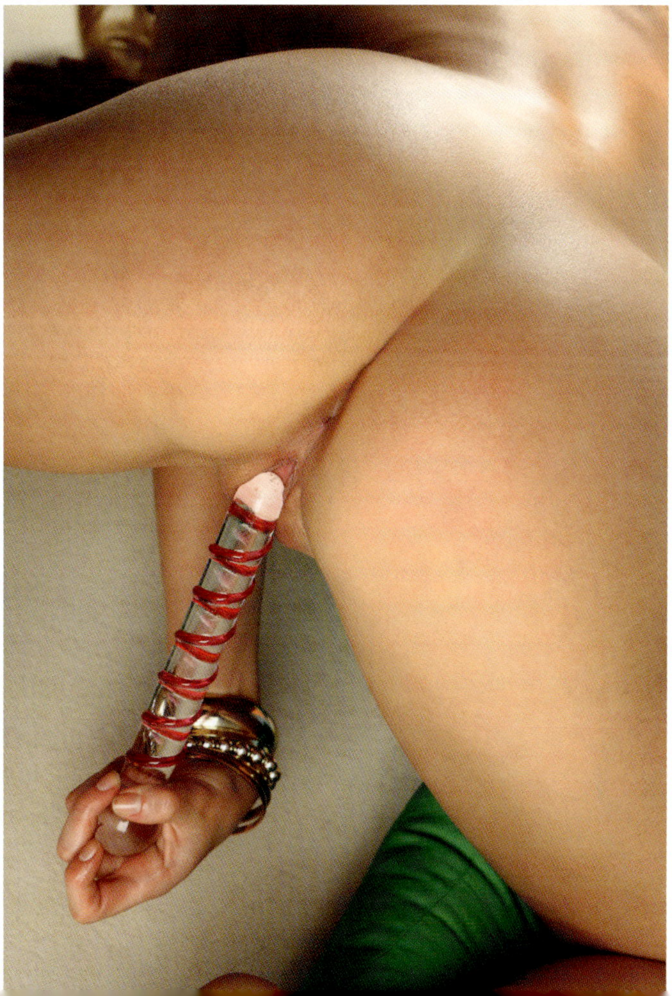

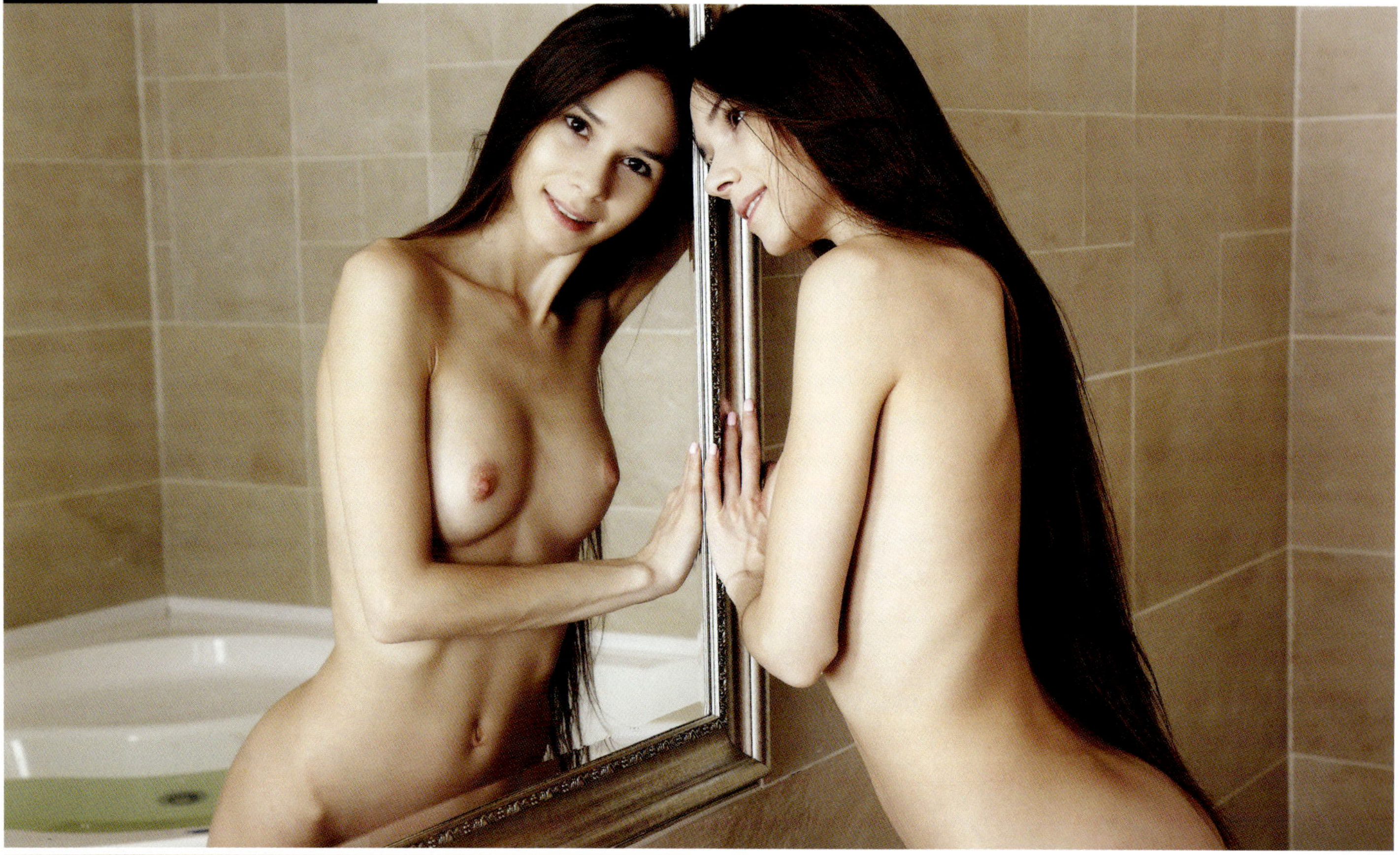

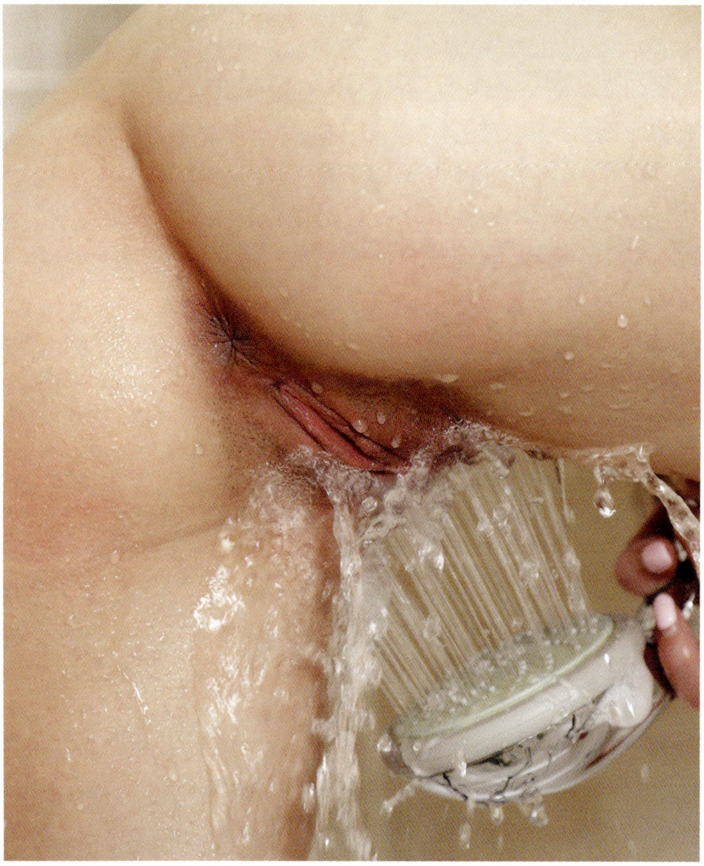

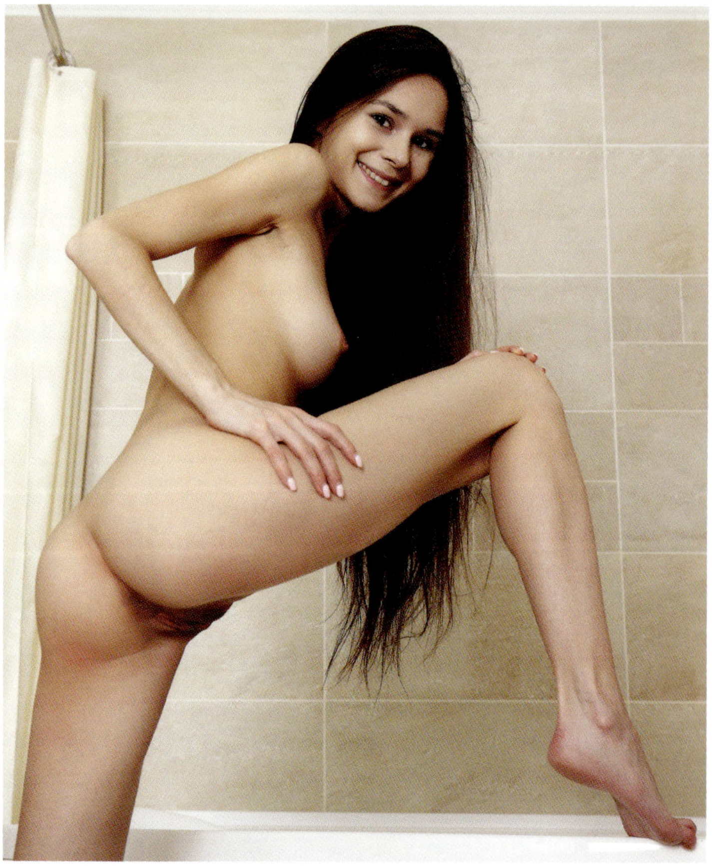

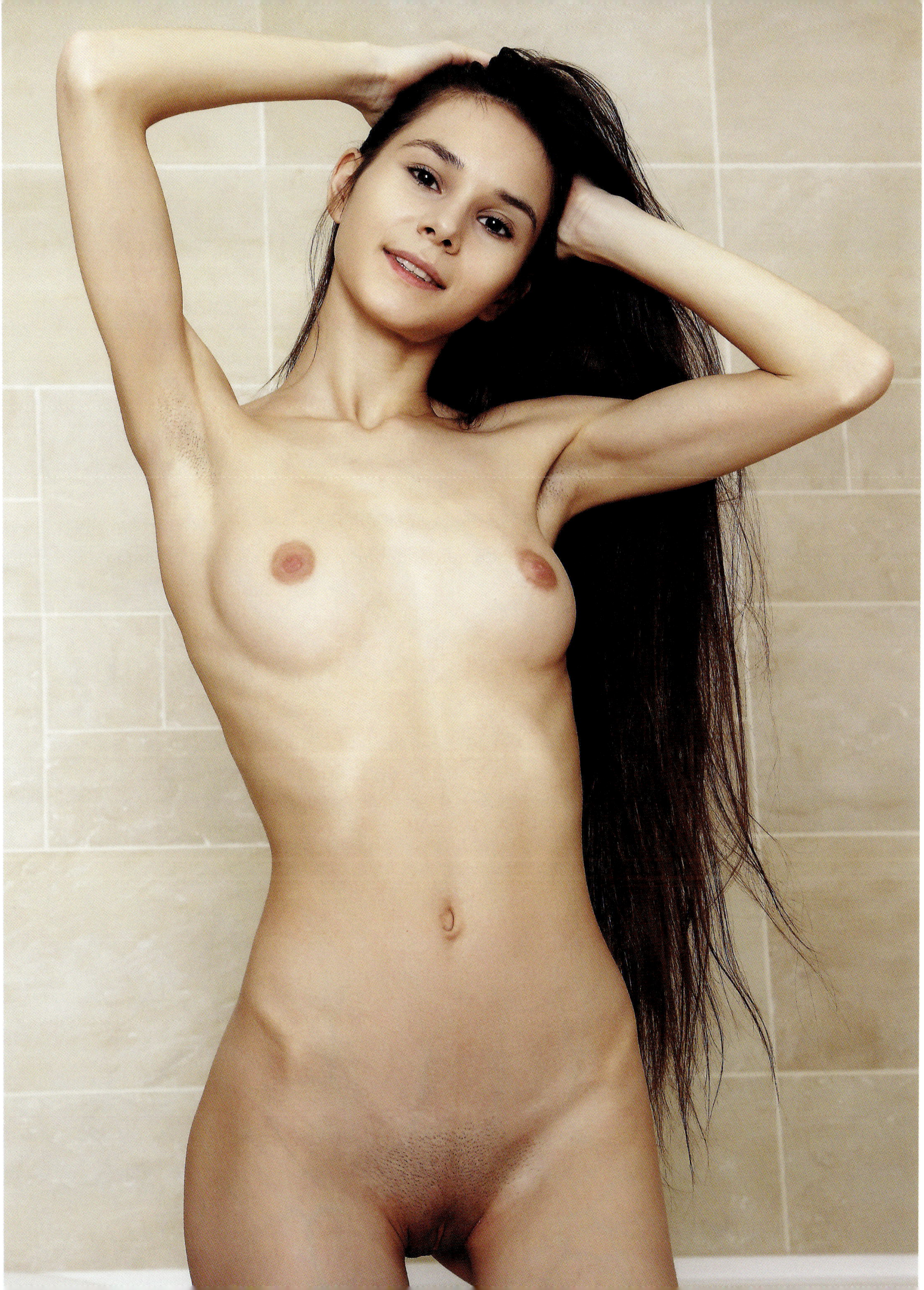

Gina Gerson
Lucy Heart

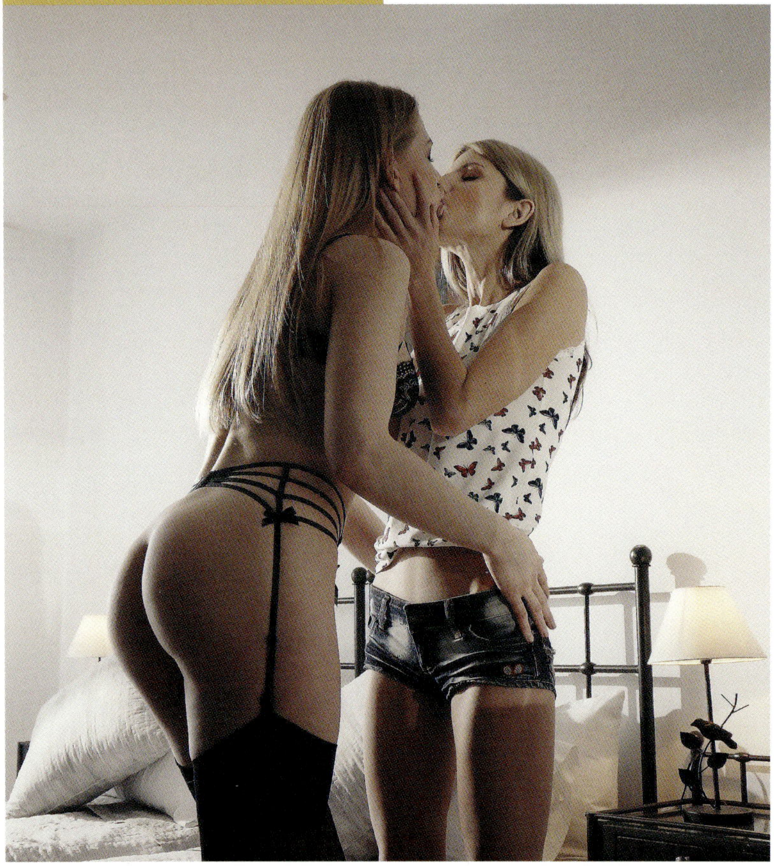

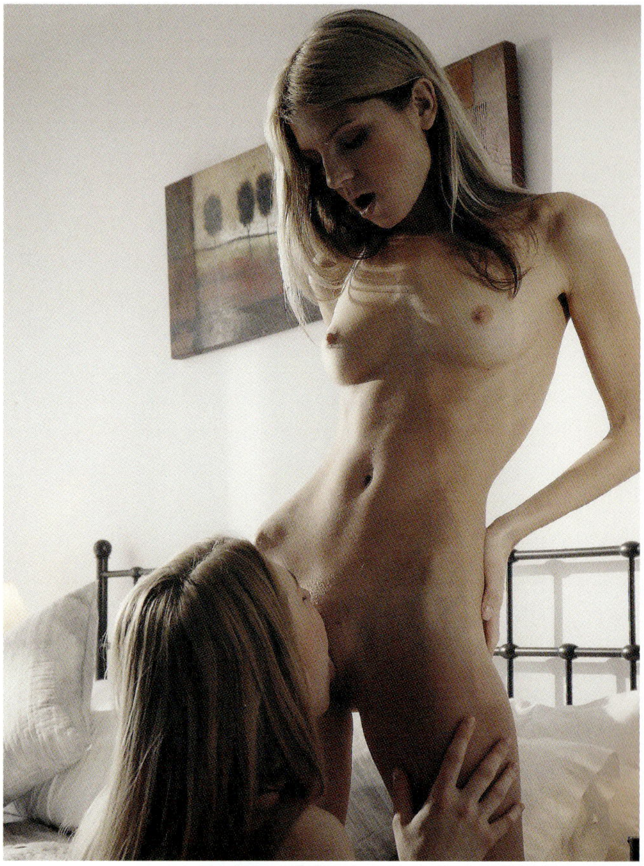

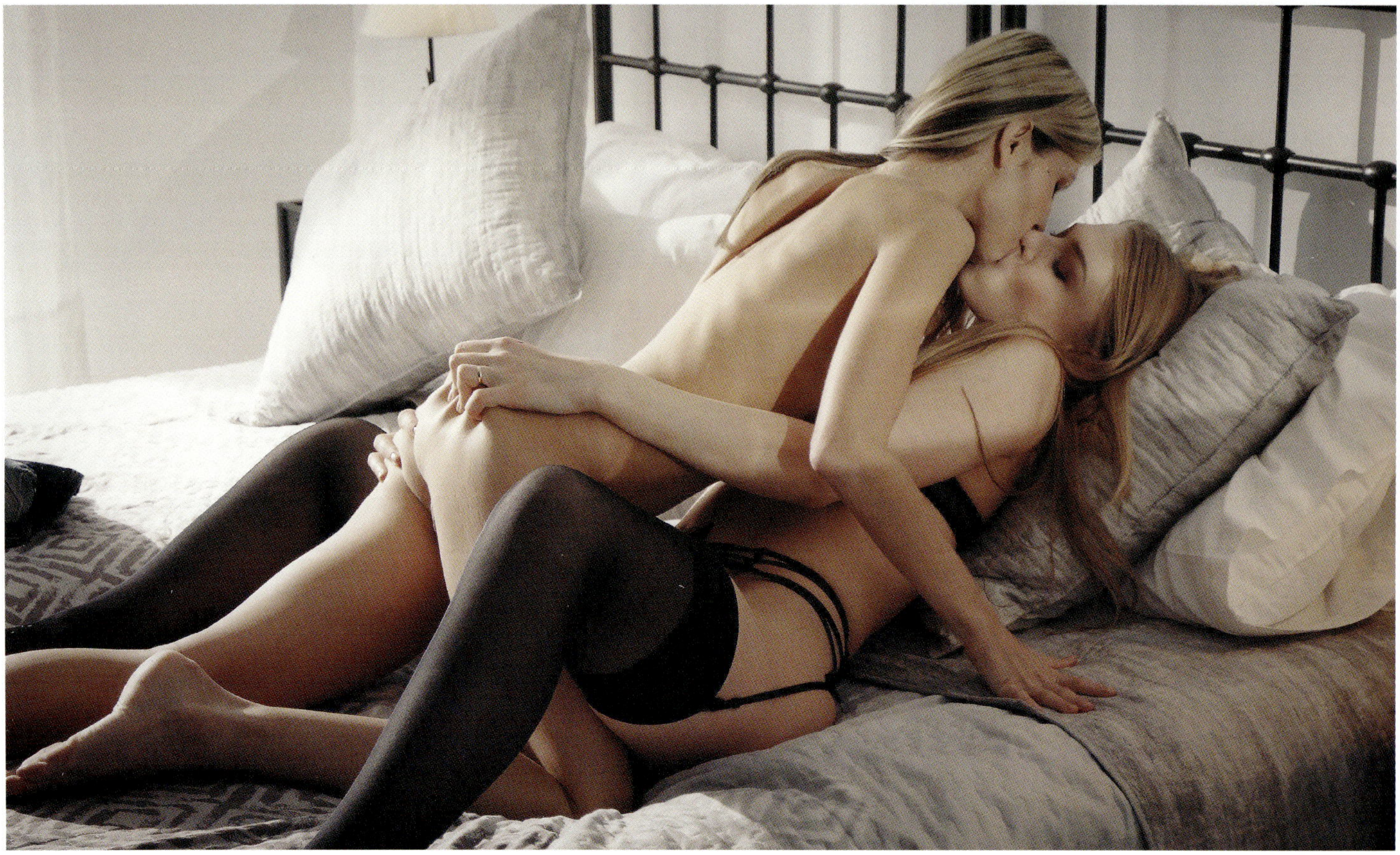

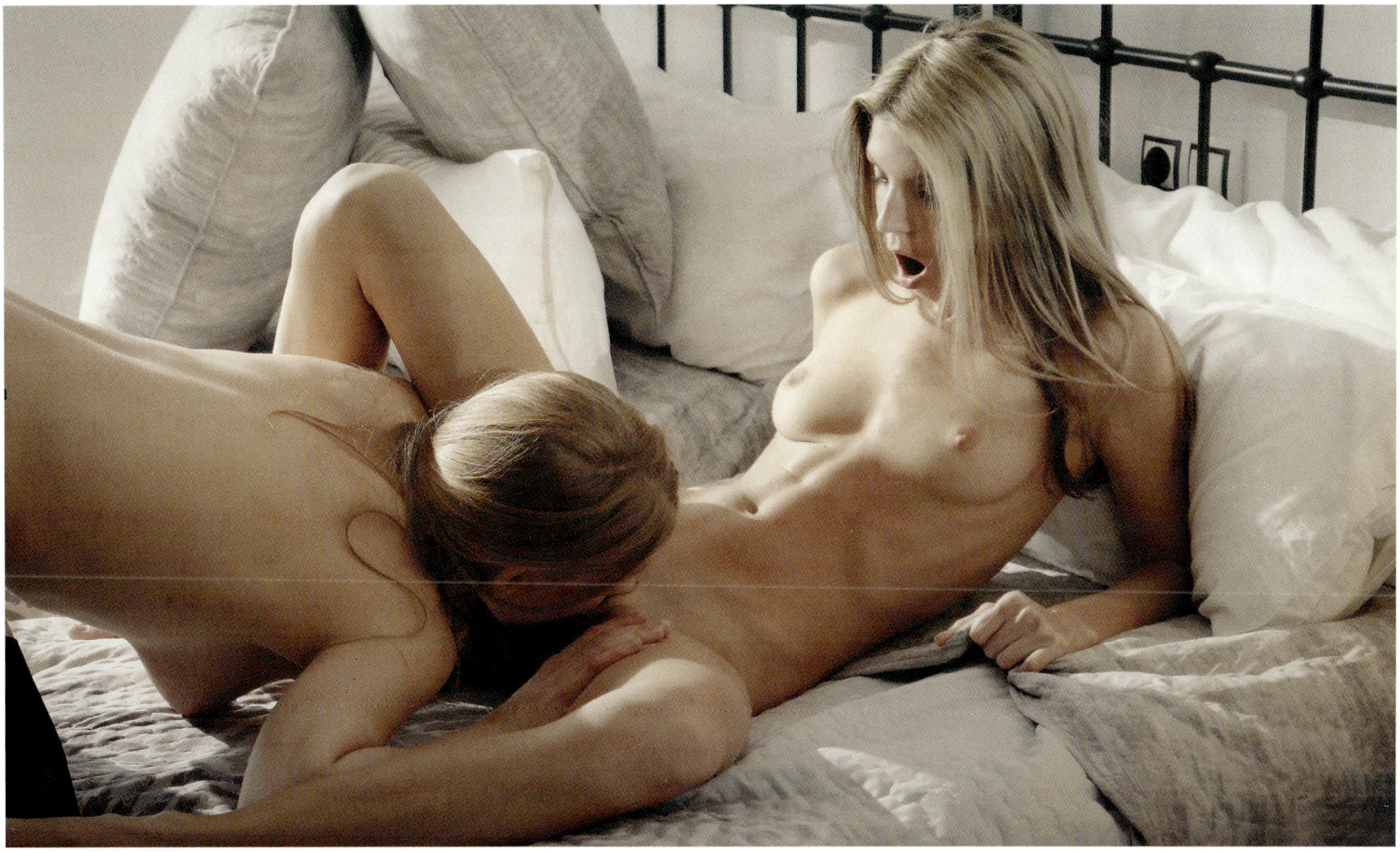

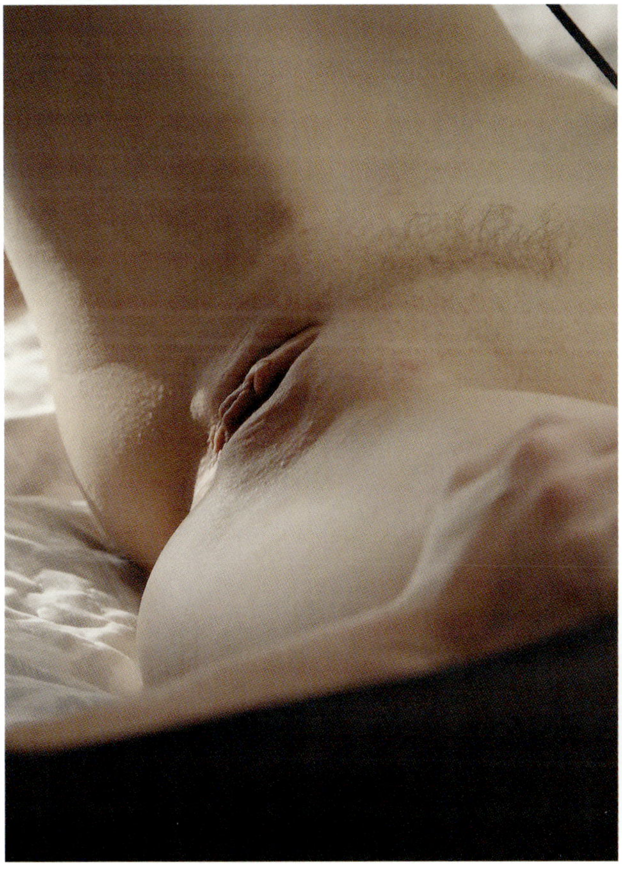

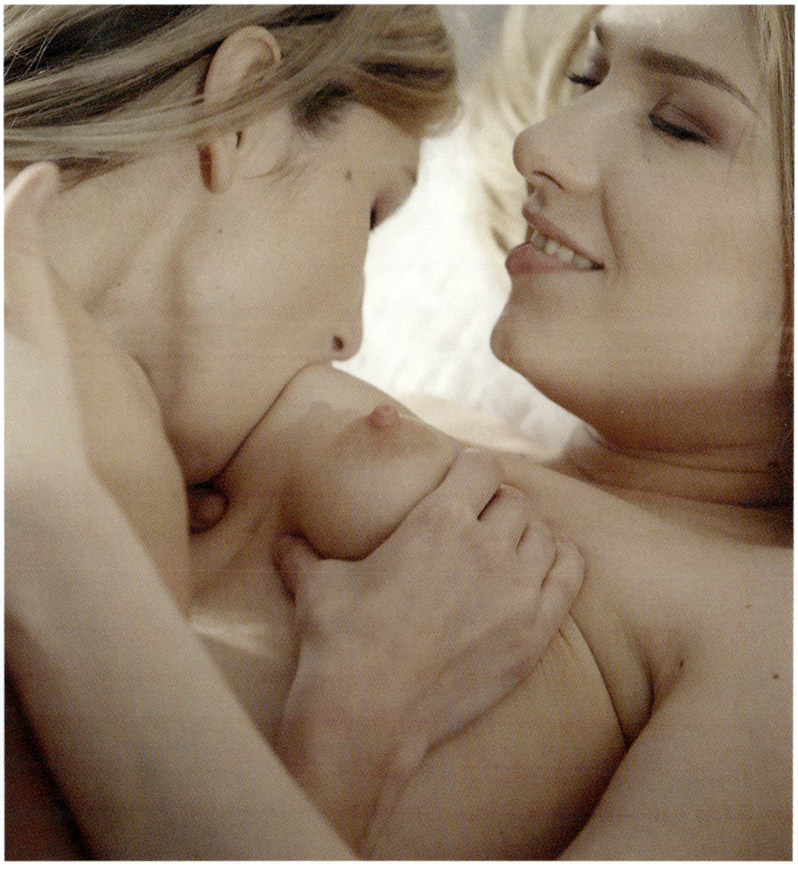

Milena D
Nika N

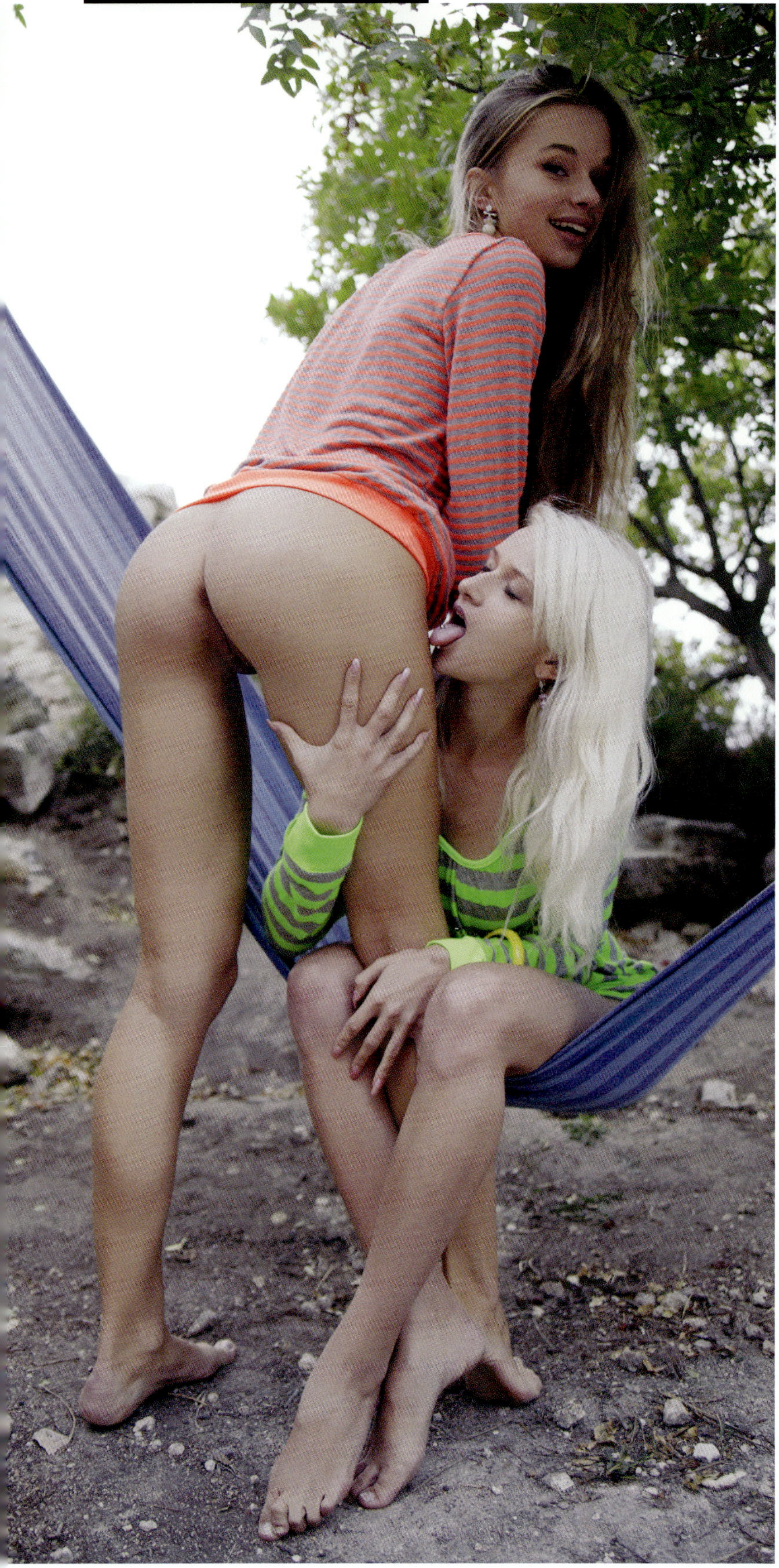

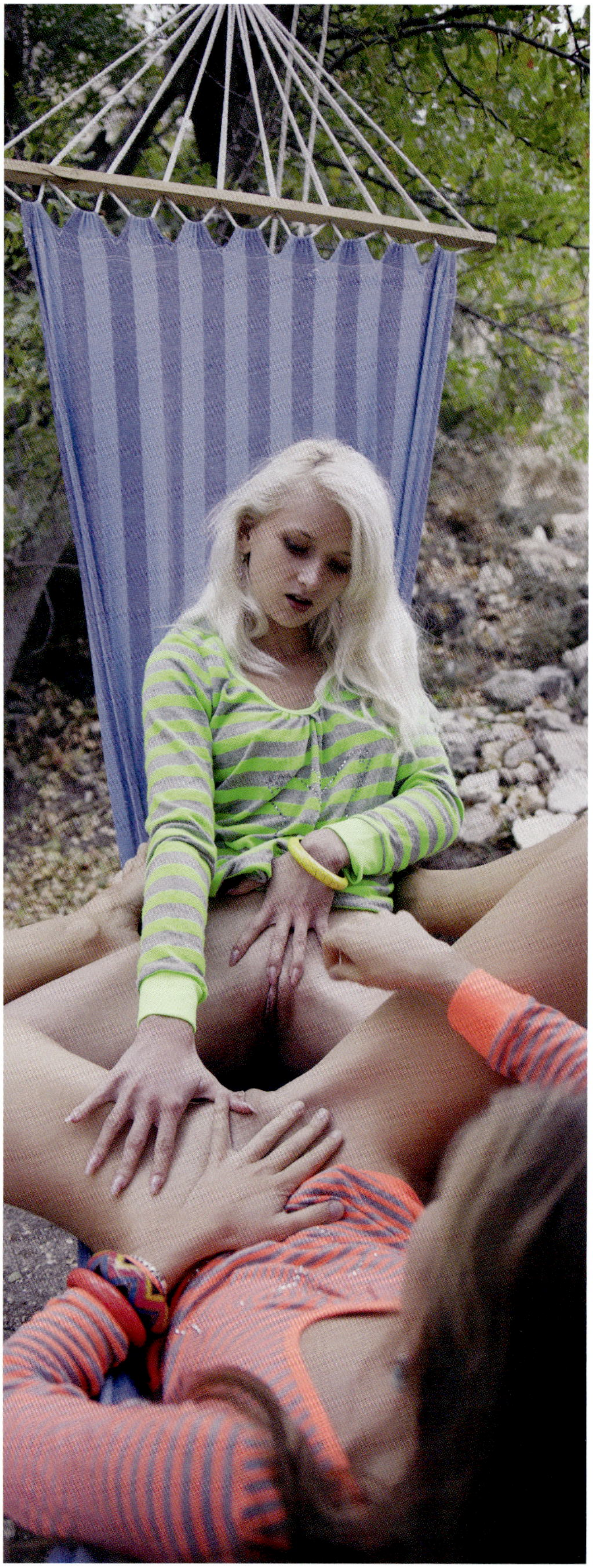

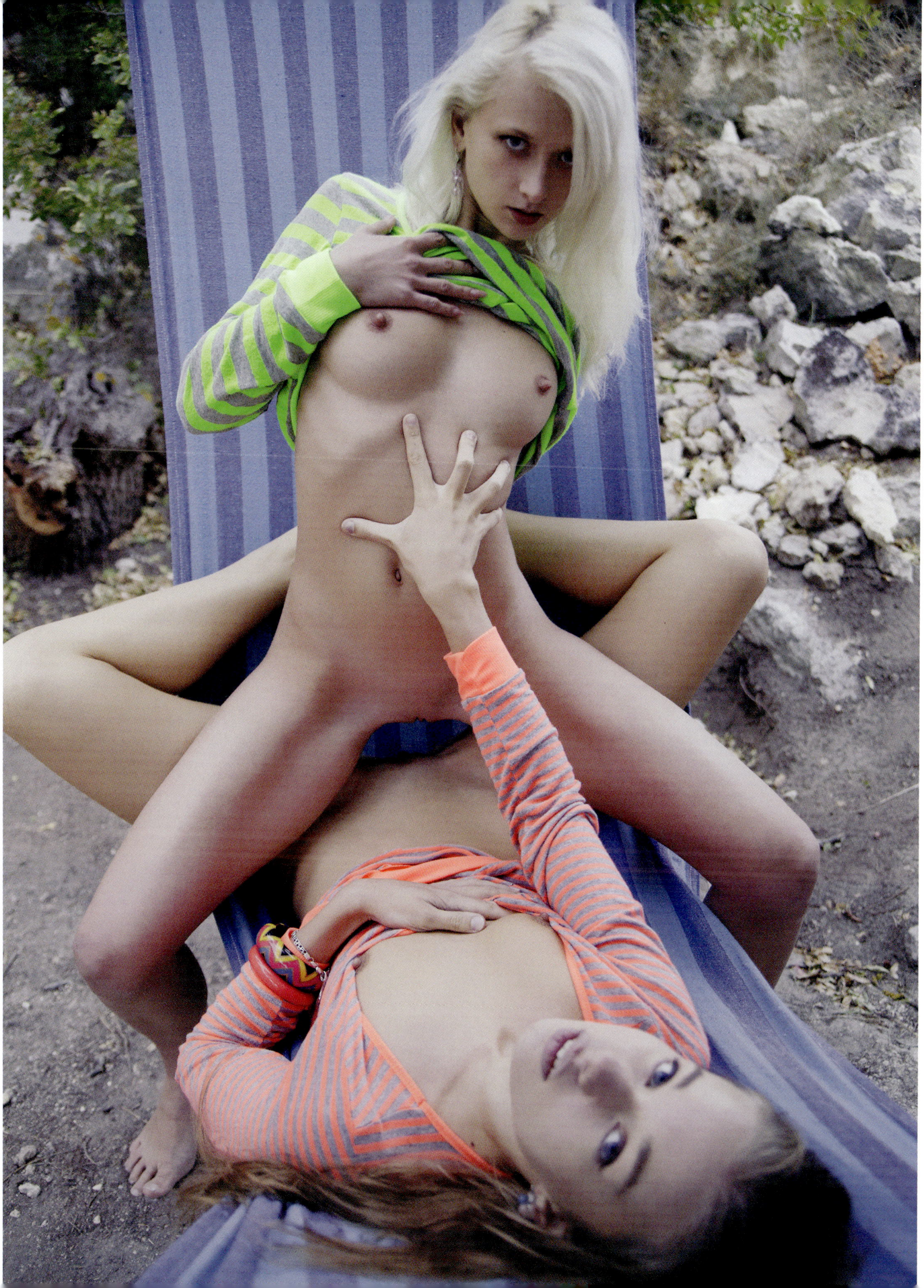

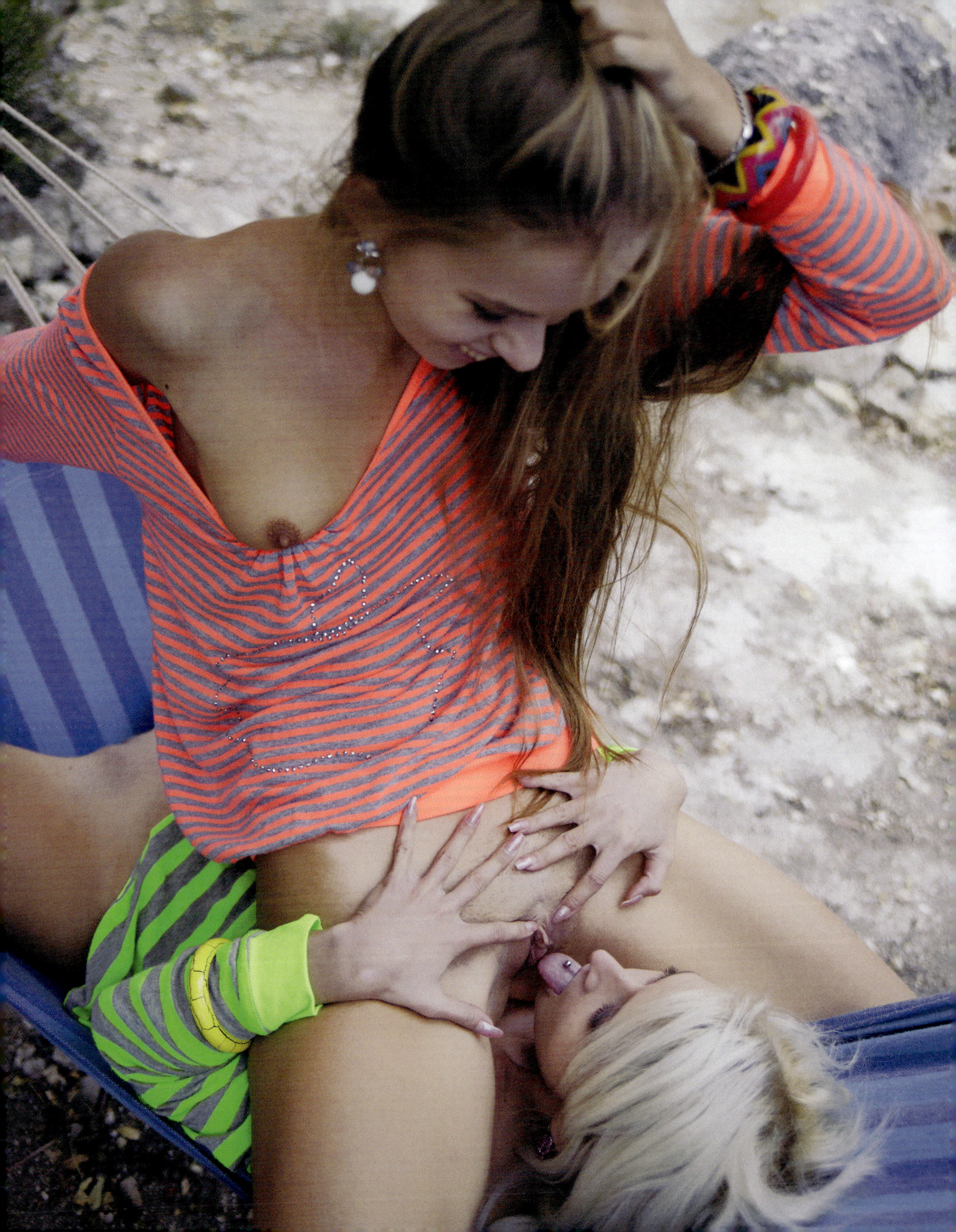

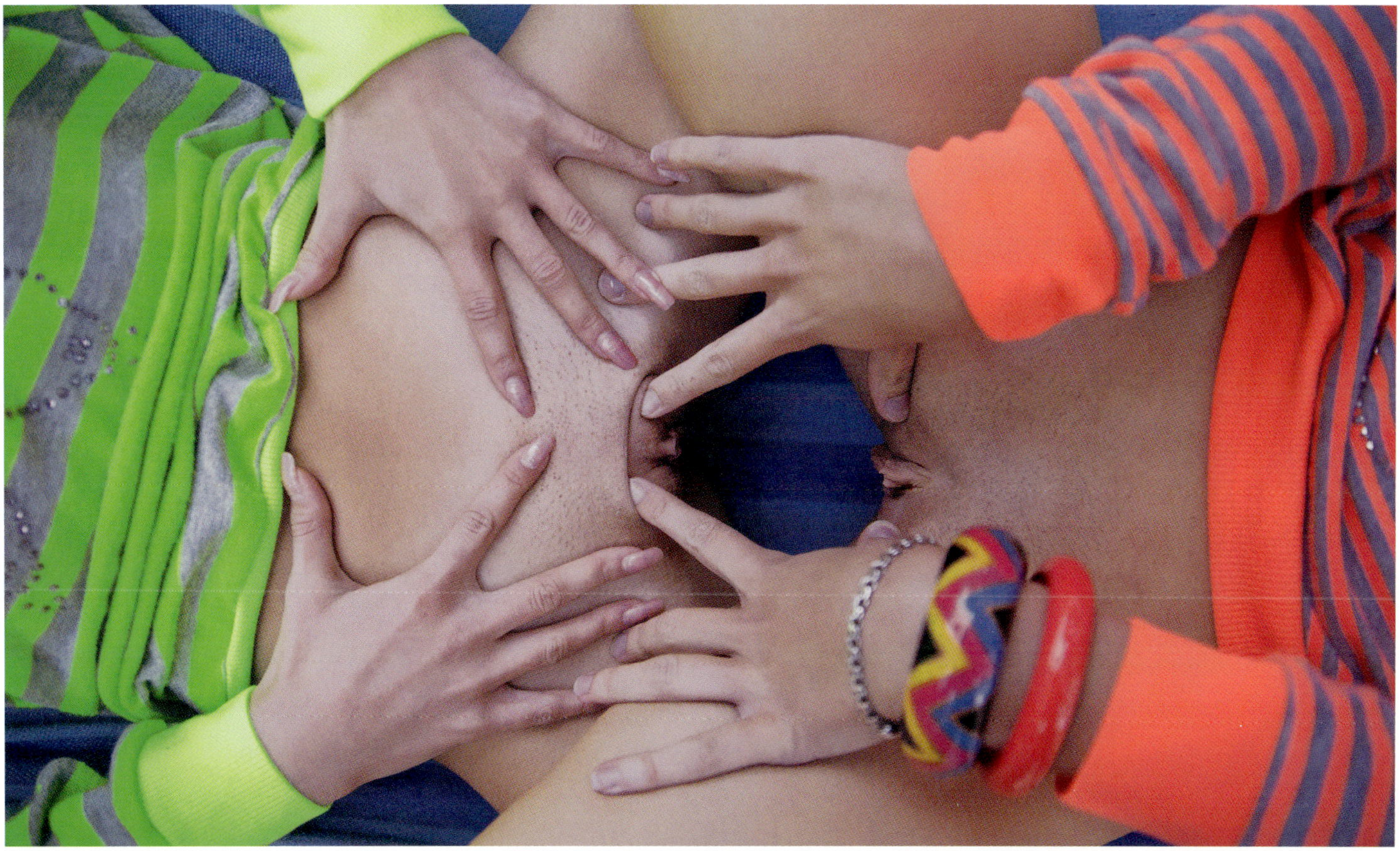

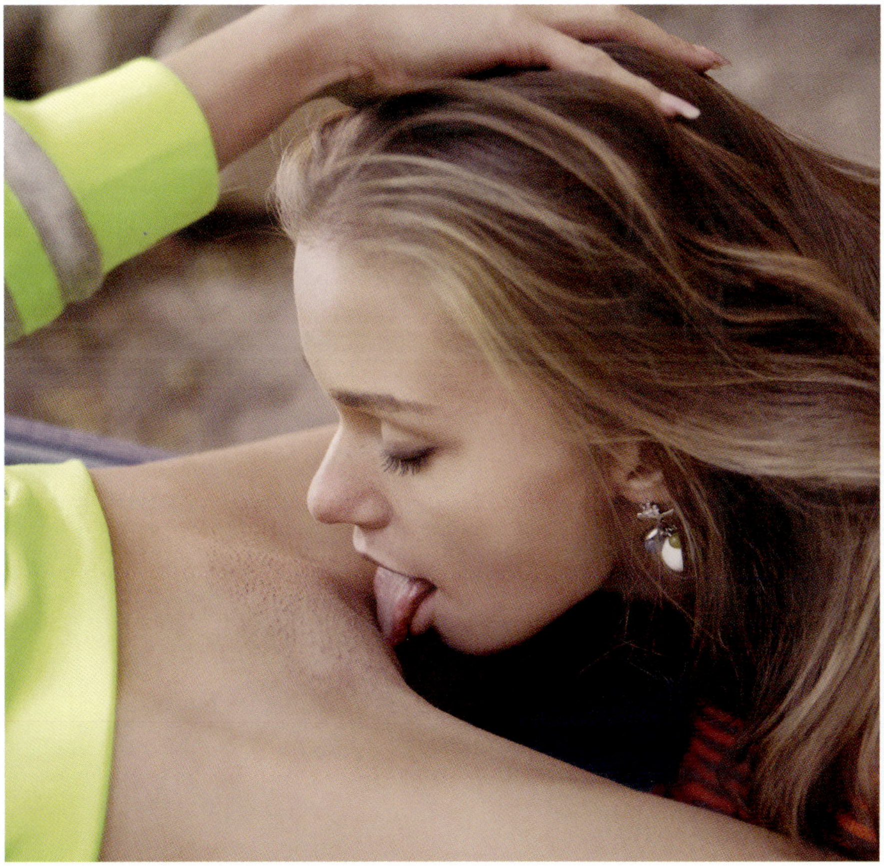

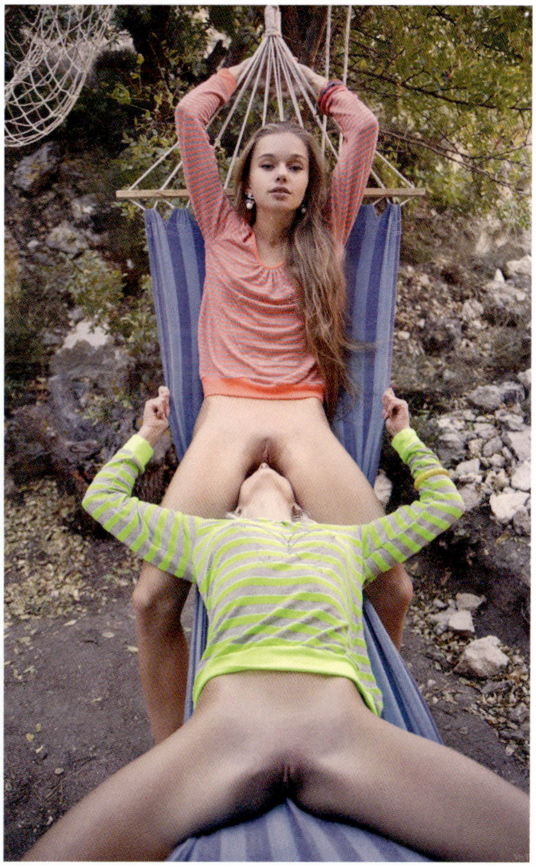

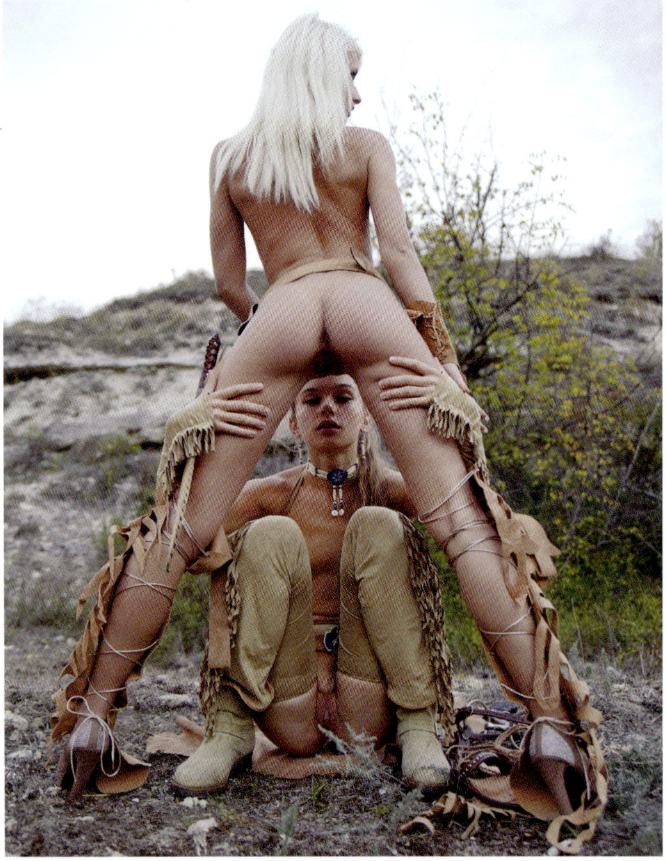
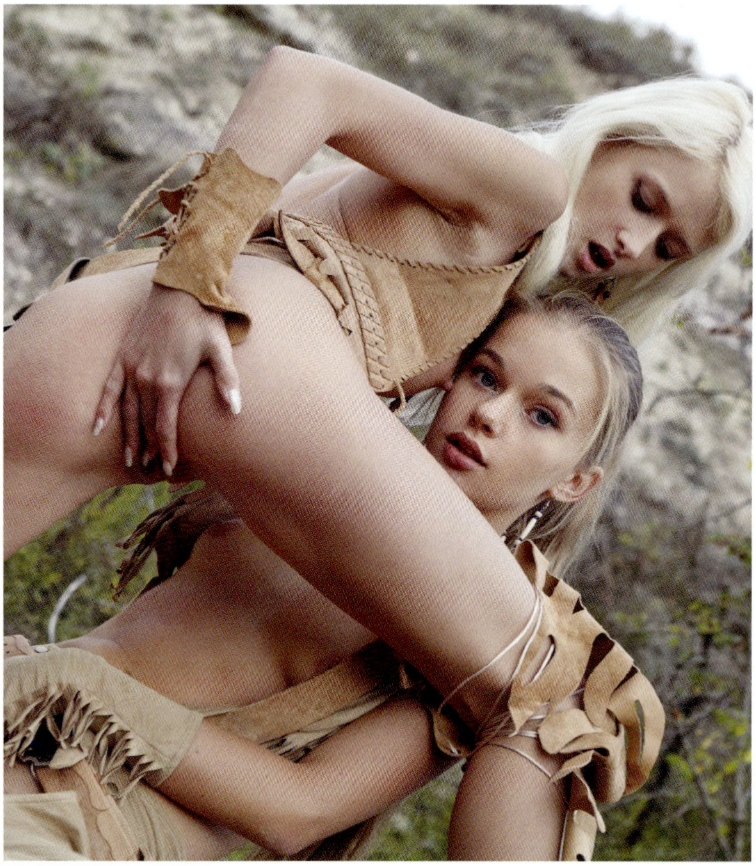
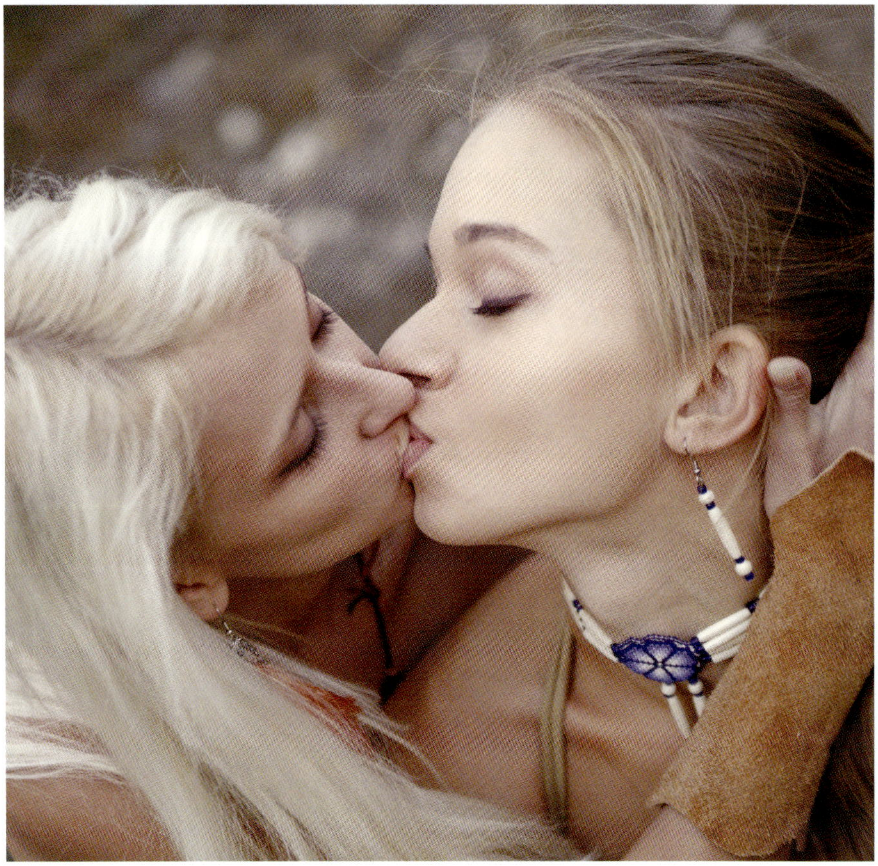
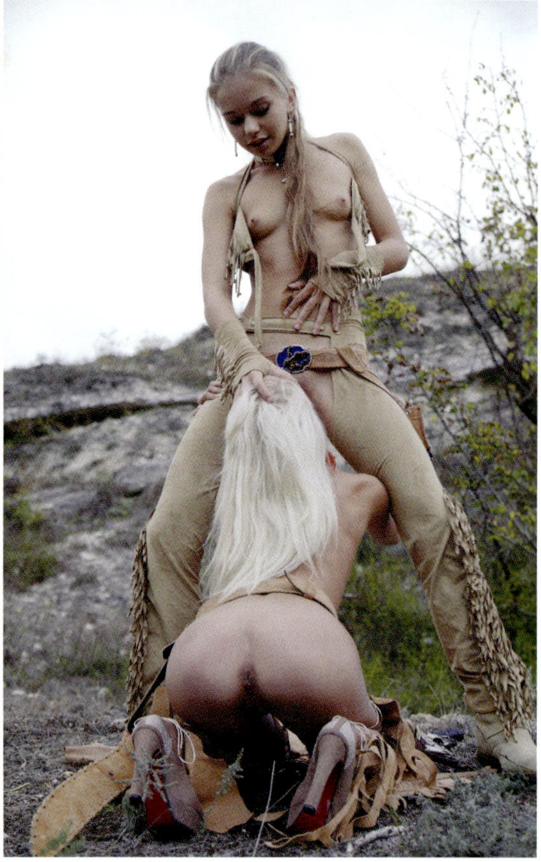

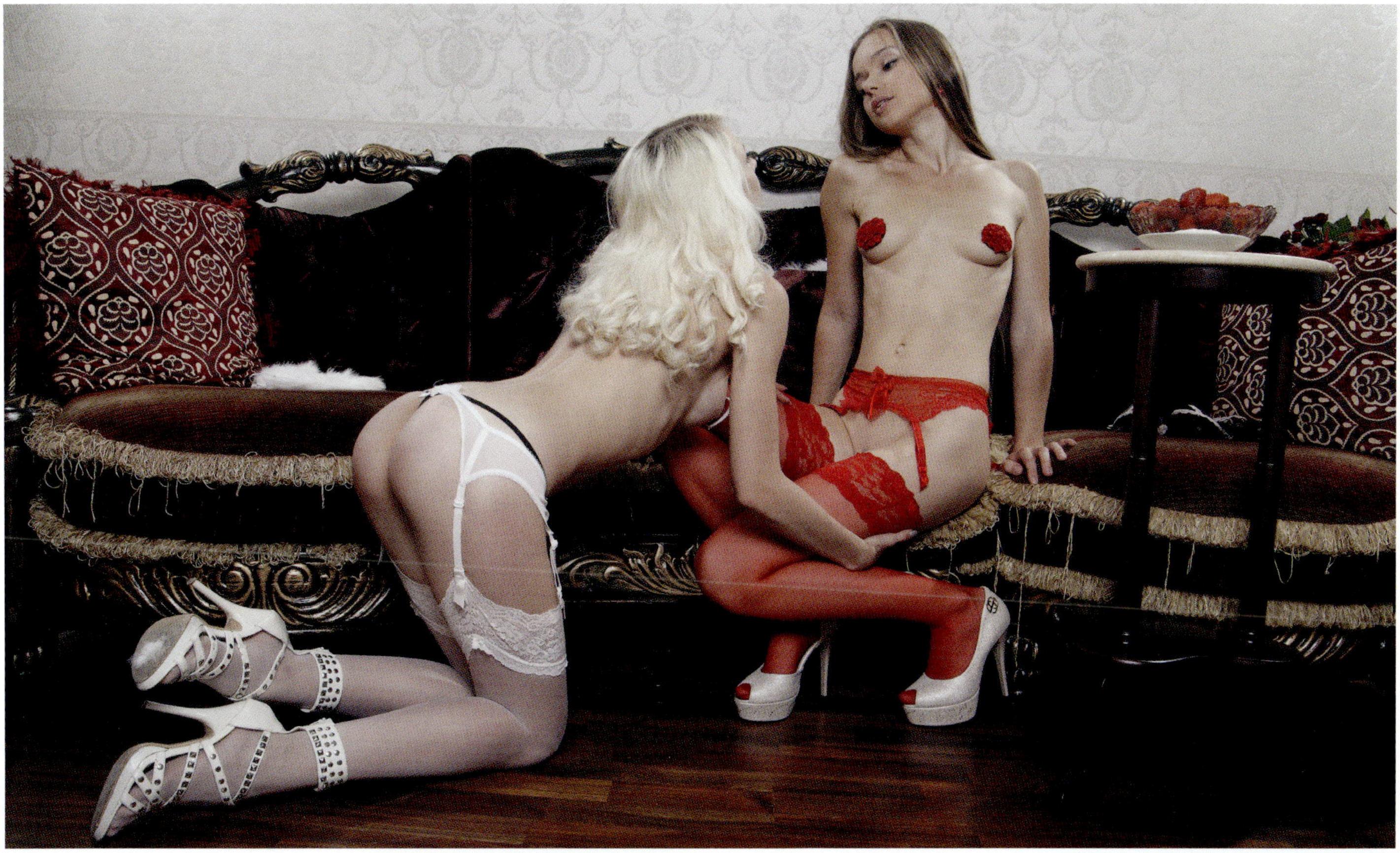

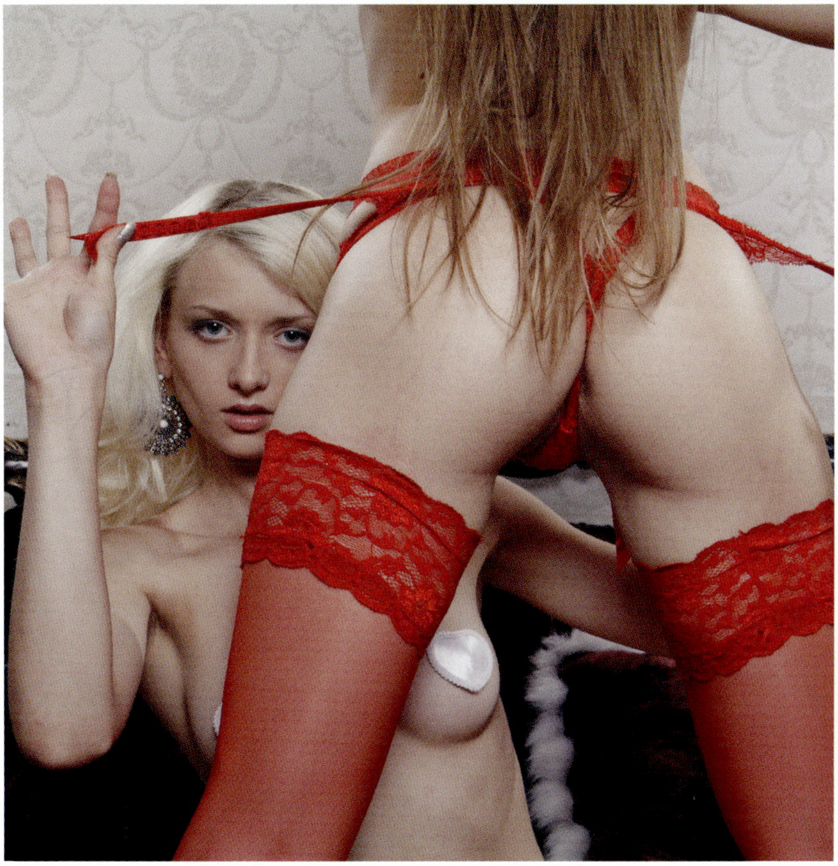

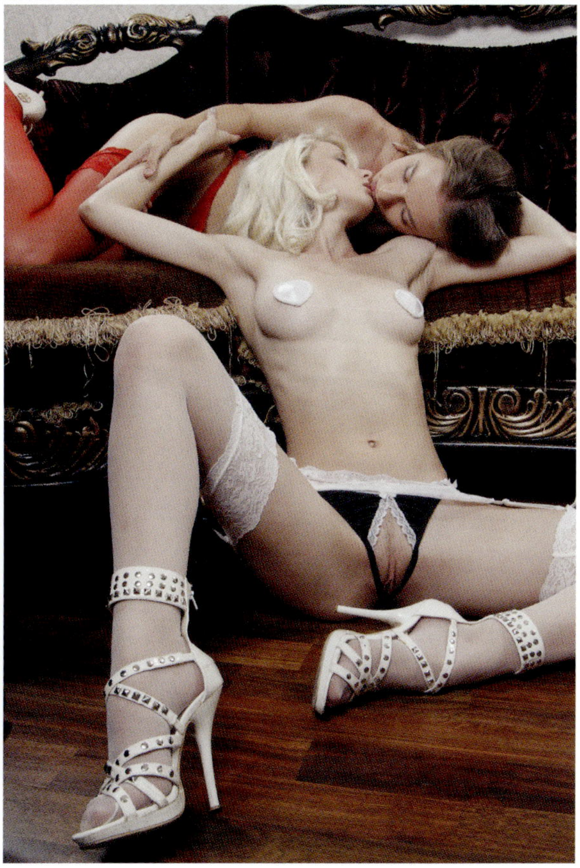

Eve Sweet Foxy Alissa Kelly Collins

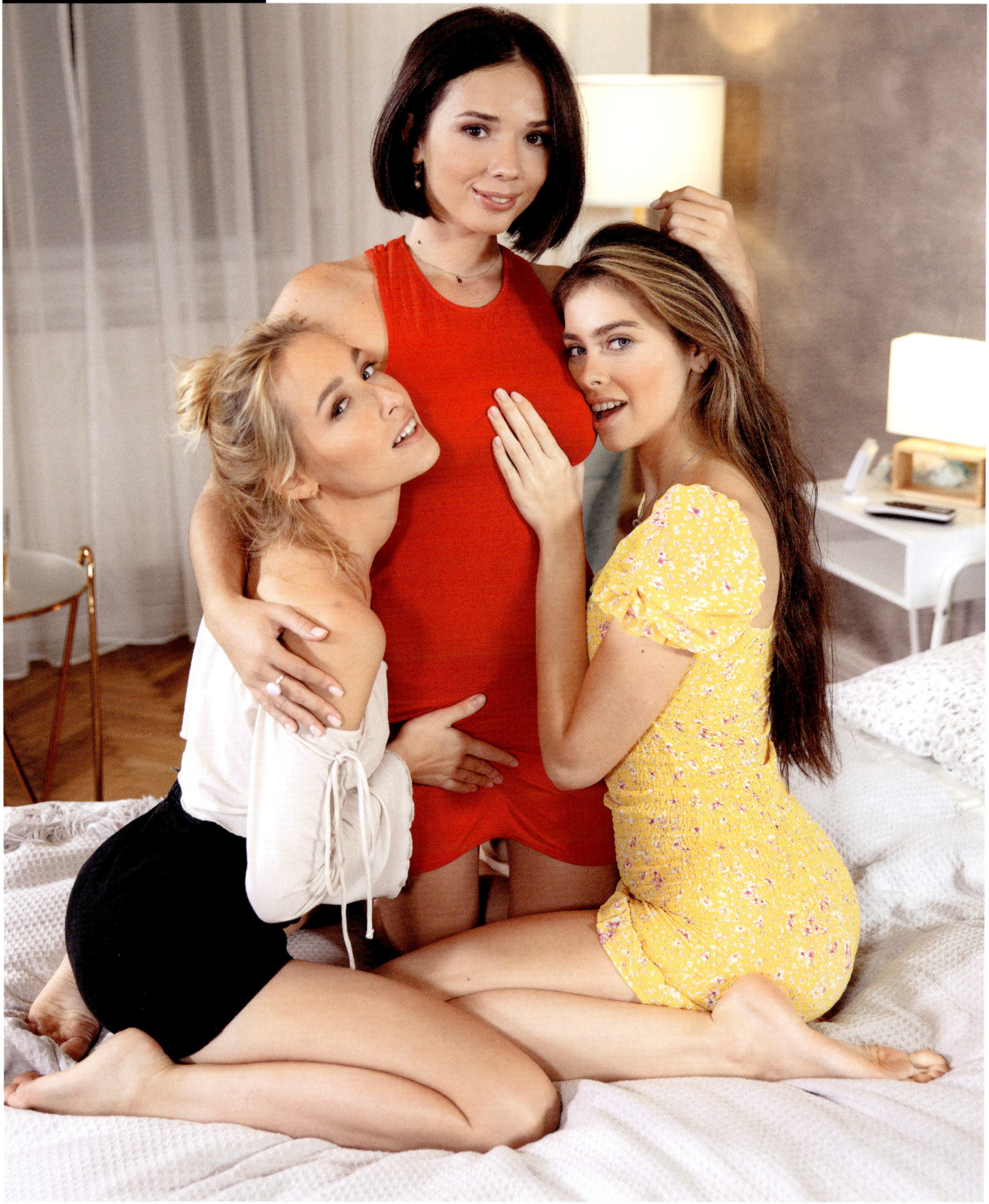

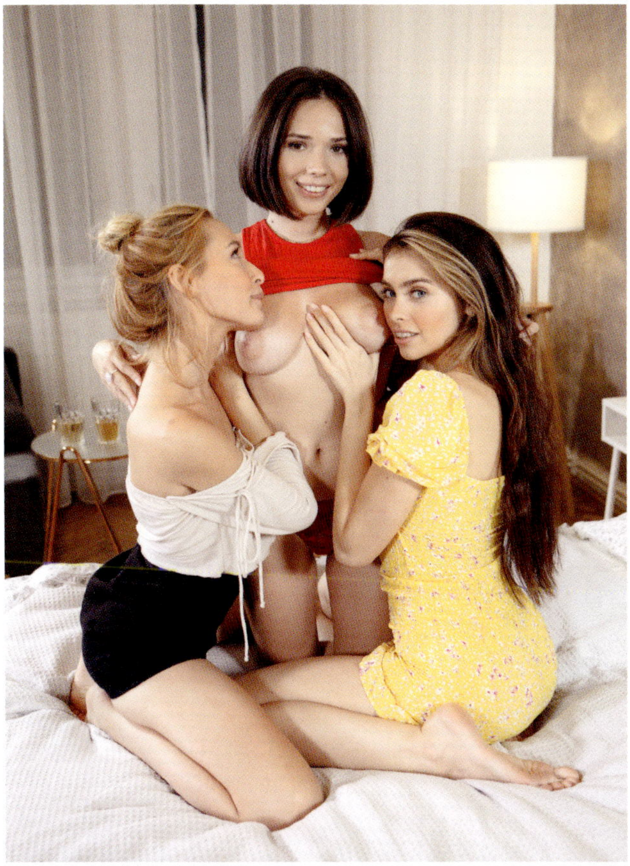
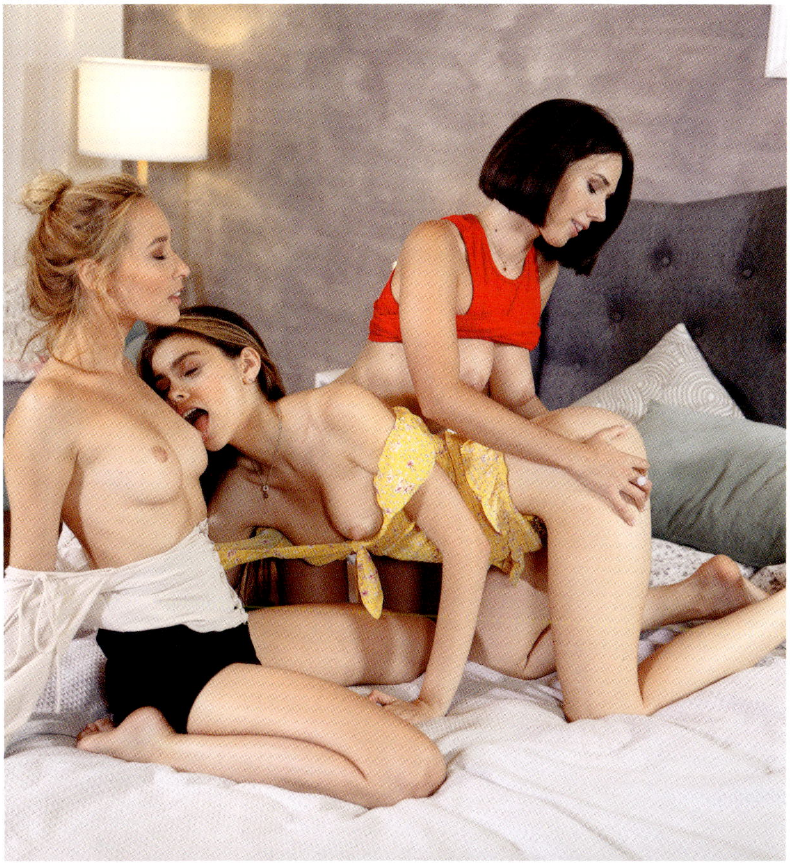
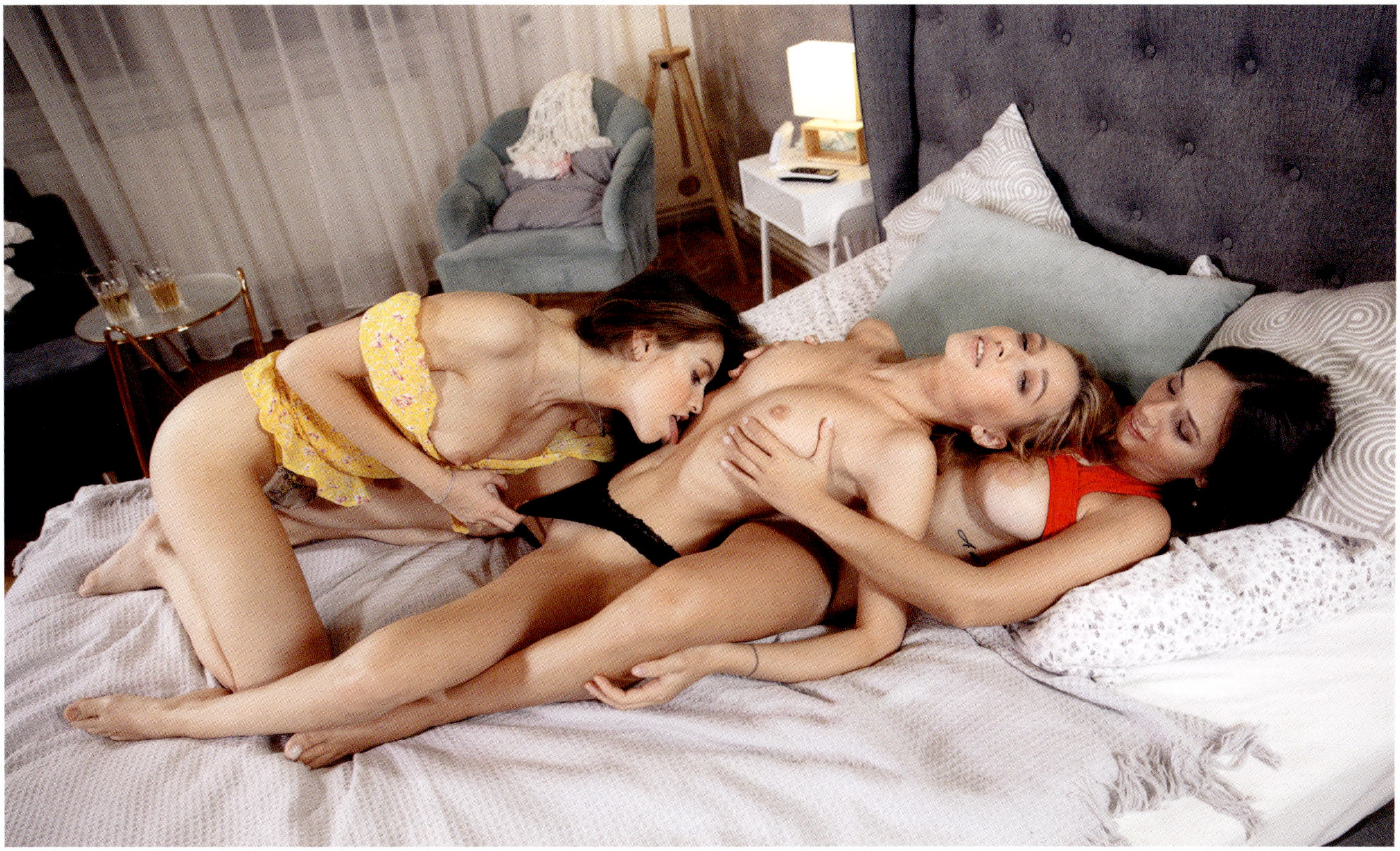

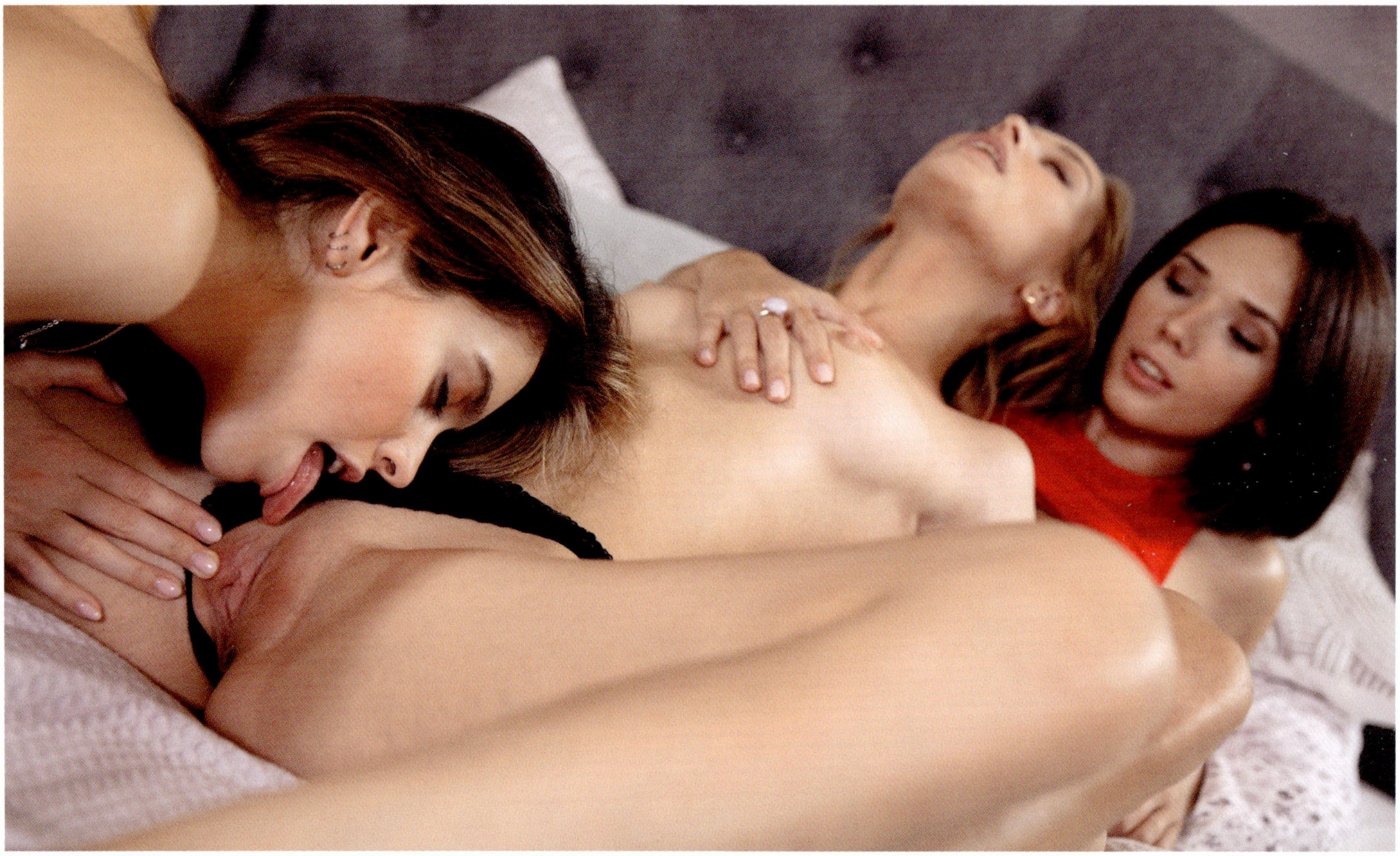

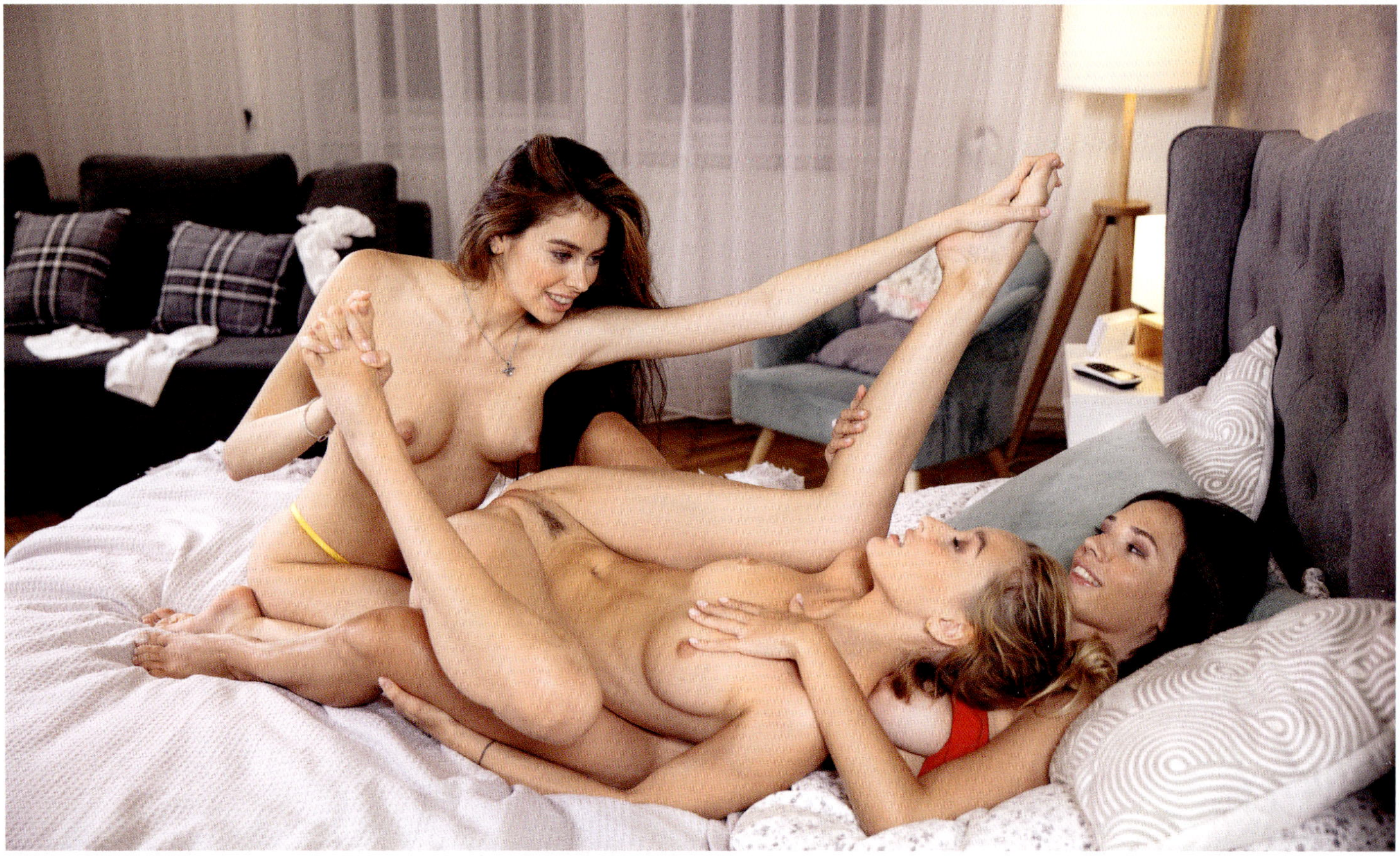

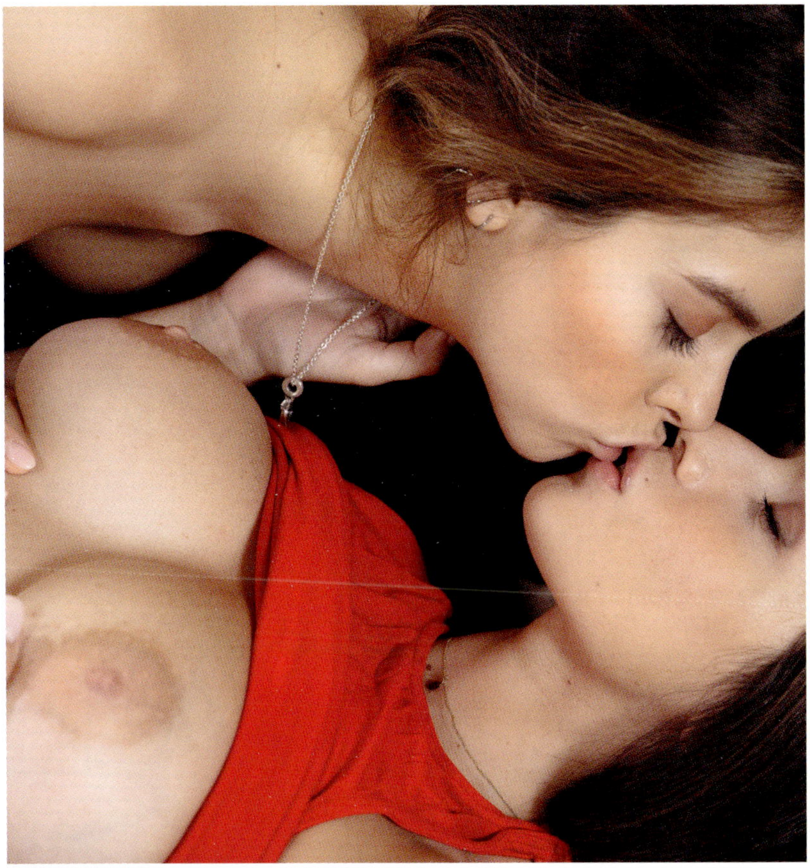
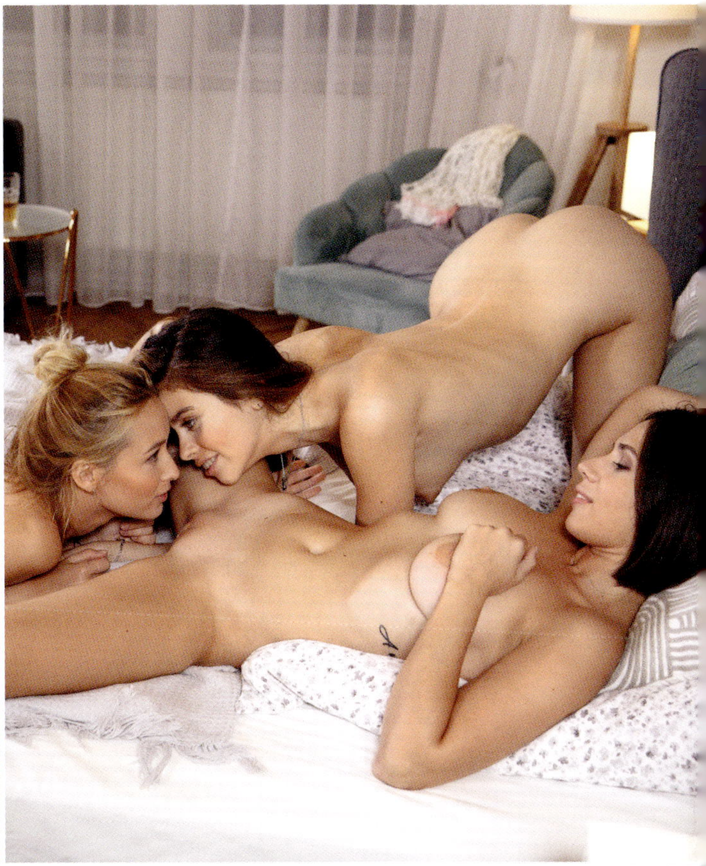
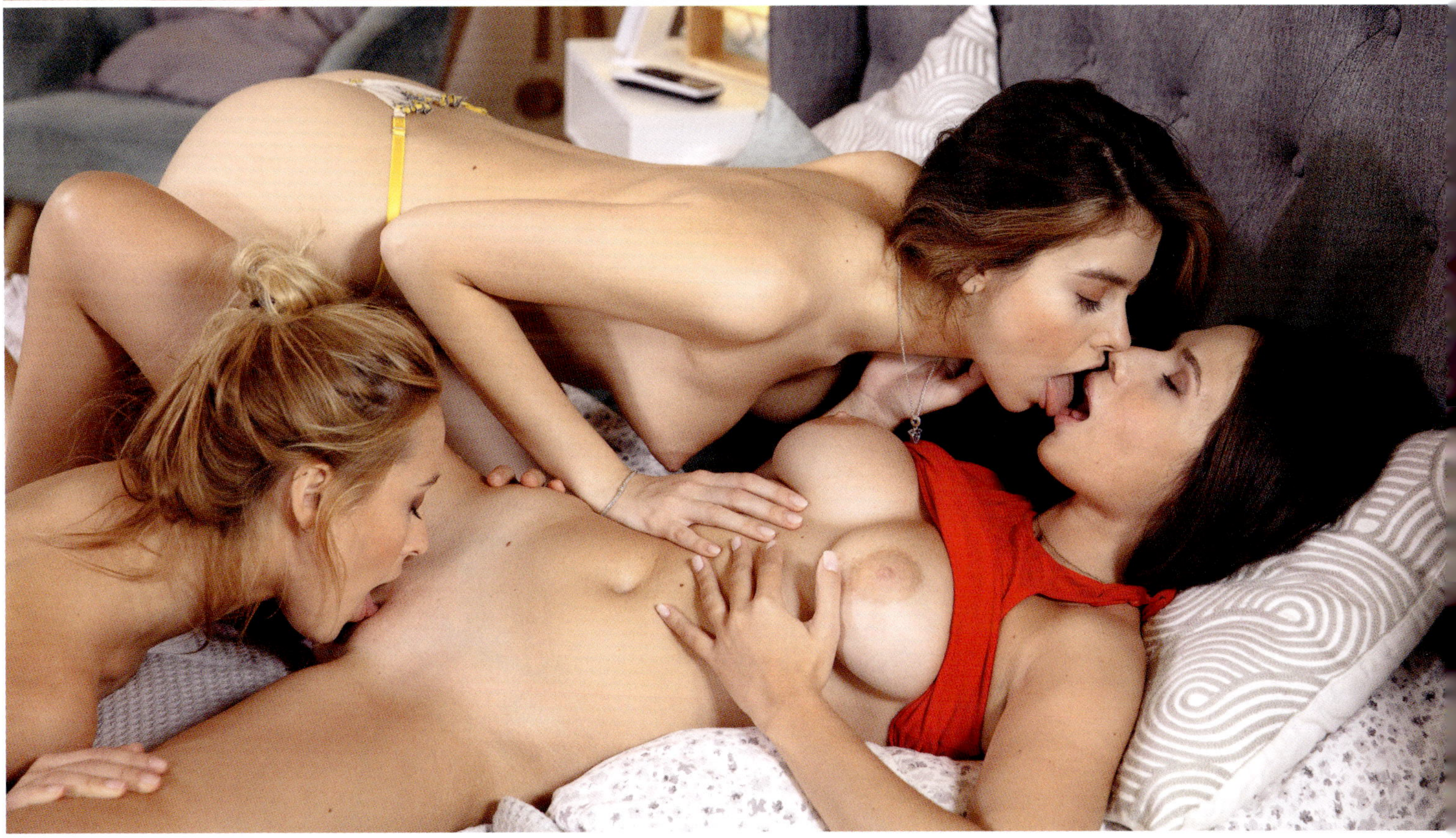

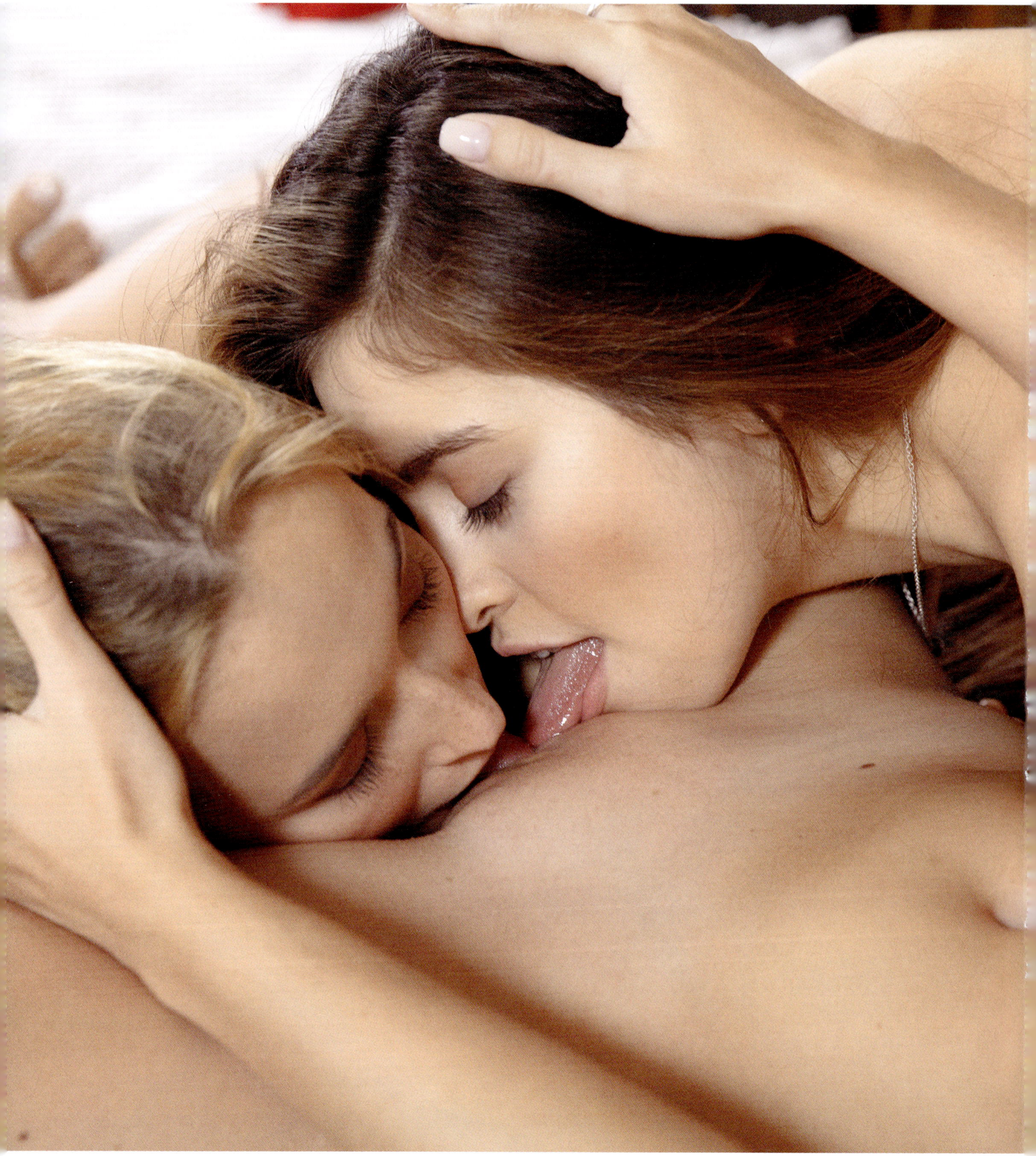

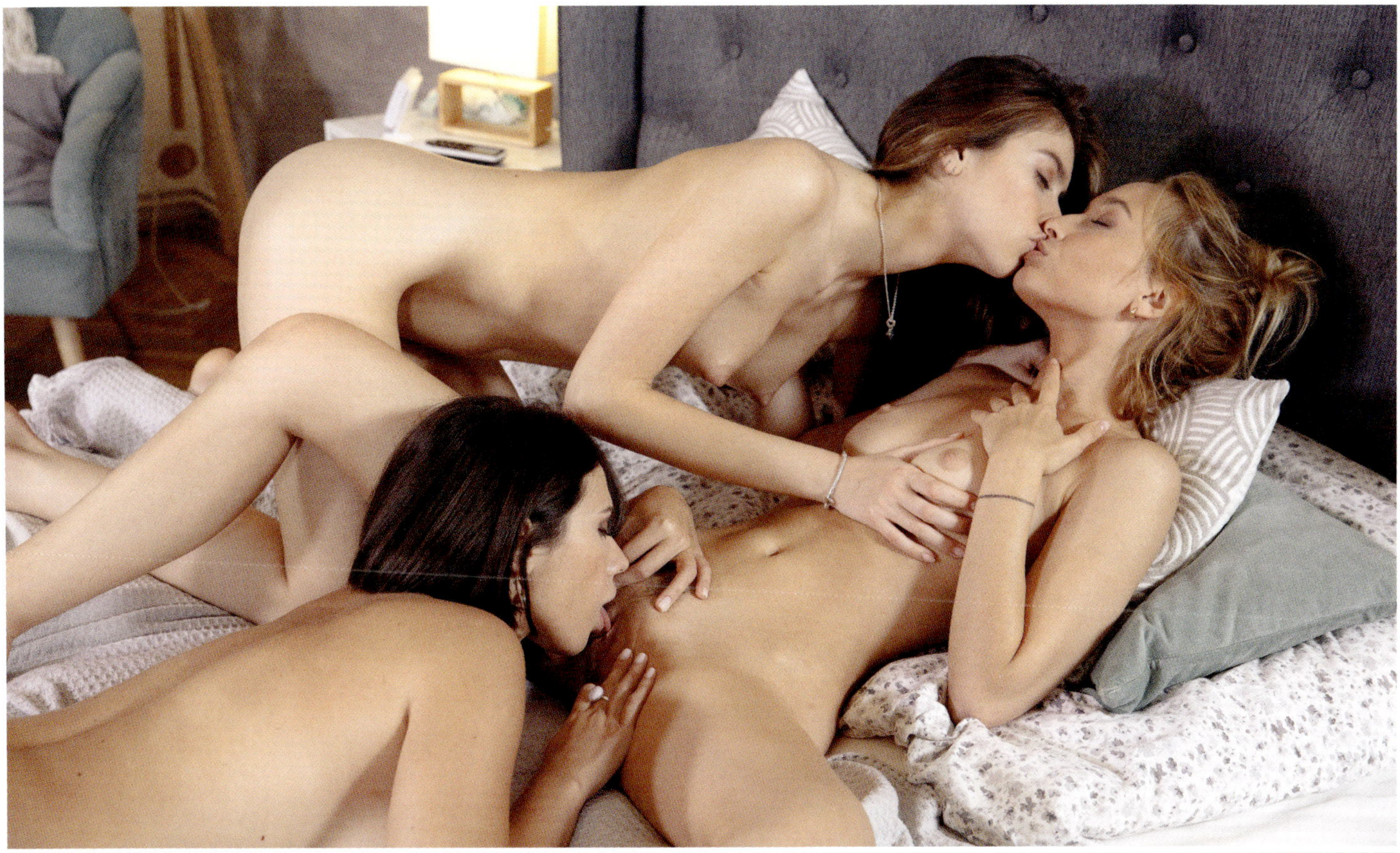

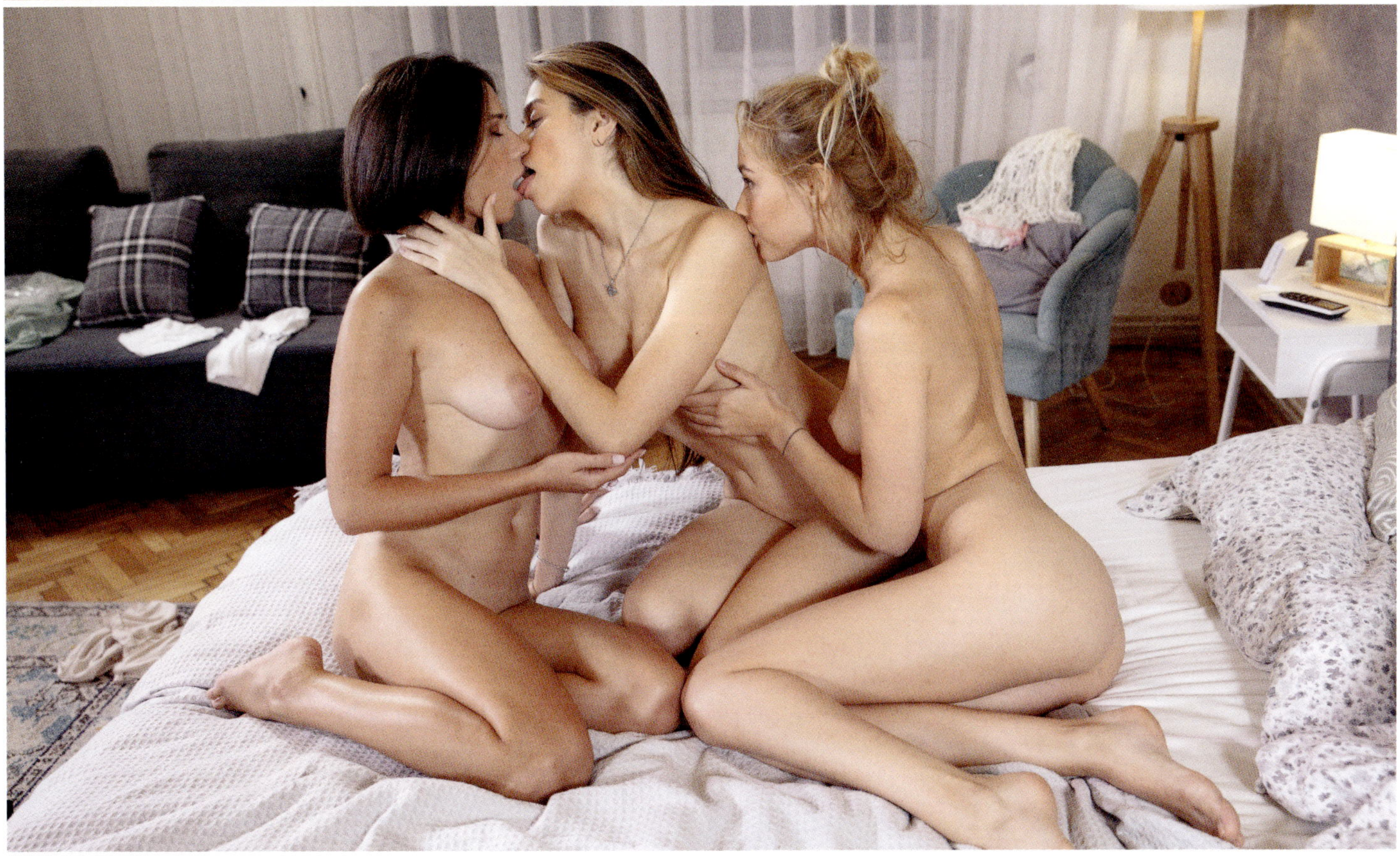

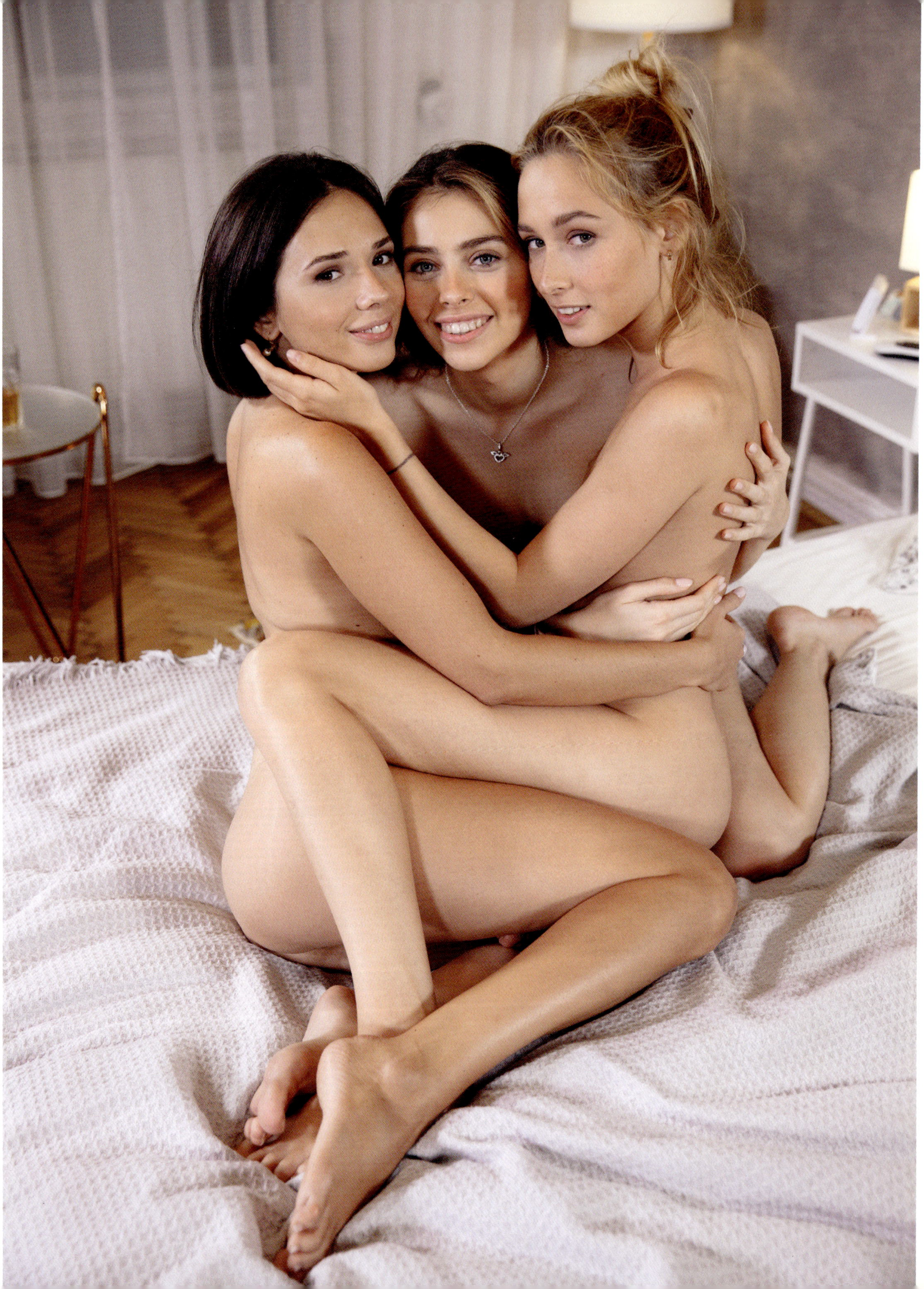

COLLECT THEM ALL: OUR BEAUTIFUL METART PHOTO BOOKS

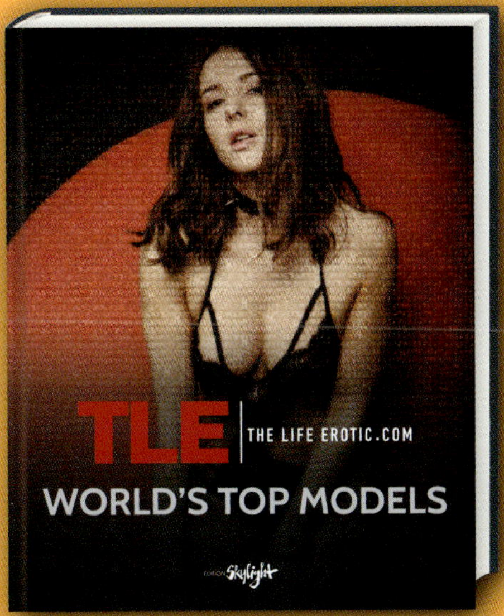

192 pp. with over 400 pictures.
ISBN 978-3-03766-697-5

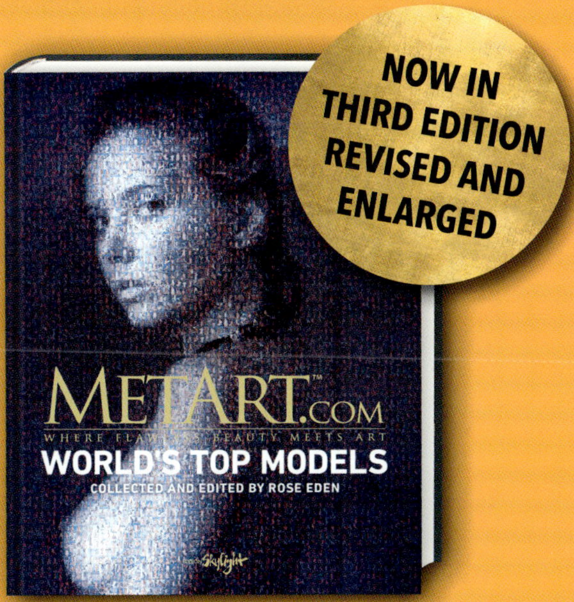

328 pp. with over 600 pictures.
ISBN 978-3-03766-708-8

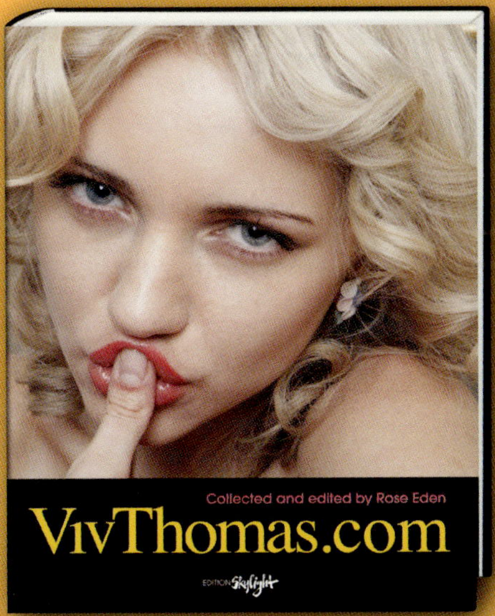

192 pp., with over 350 pictures.
ISBN 978-3-03766-719-4

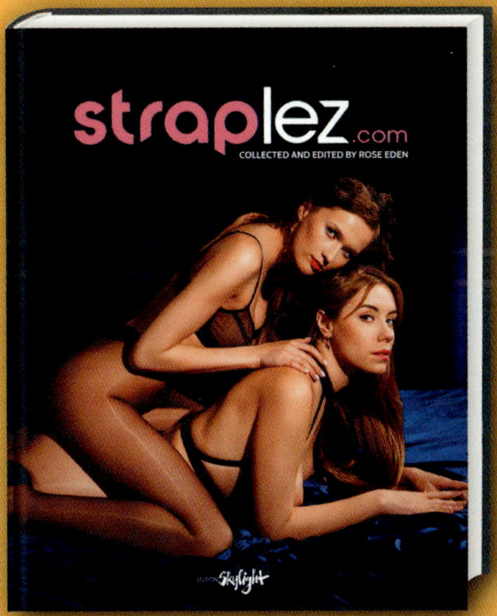

160 pp., with over 350 pictures.
ISBN 978-3-03766-702-6

WWW.EDITION-SKYLIGHT.COM

COLLECT THEM ALL: OUR MOST BEAUTIFUL

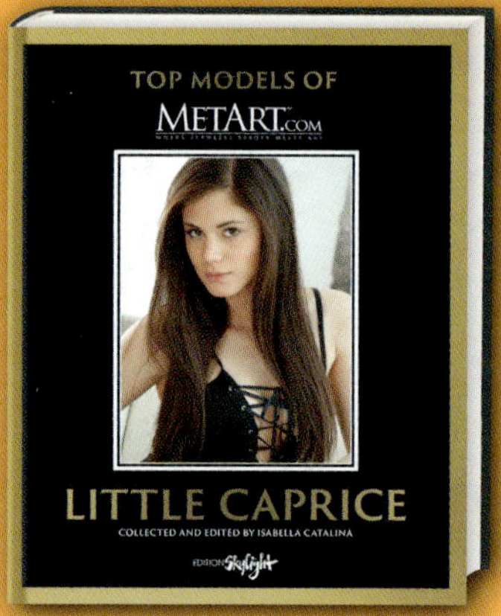

ISBN 978-3-03766-659-3

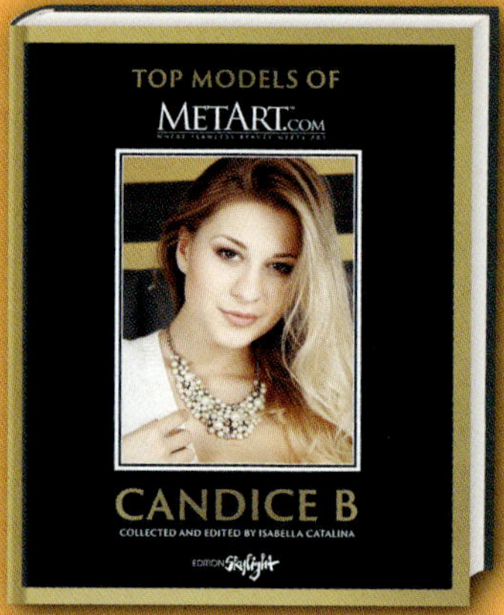

ISBN 978-3-03766-660-9

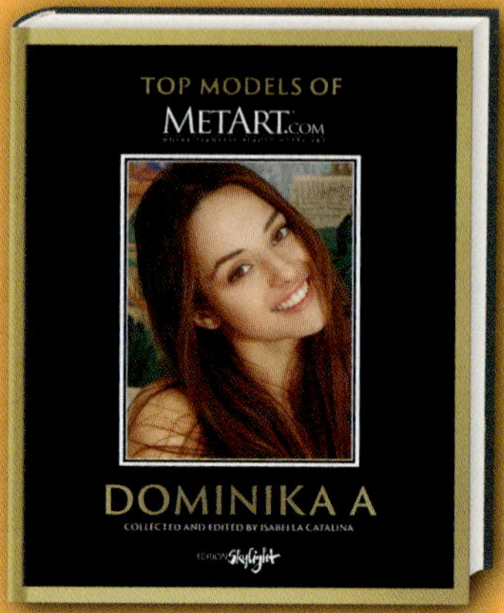

ISBN 978-3-03766-679-1

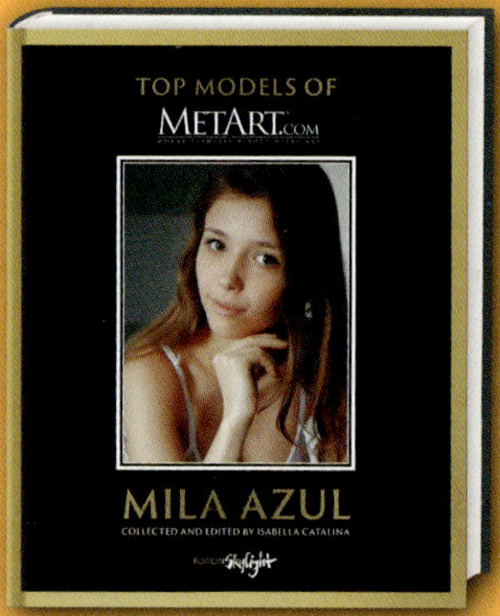

ISBN 978-3-03766-680-7

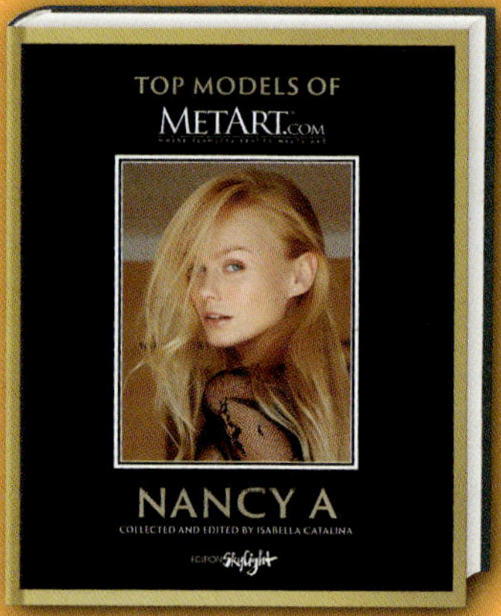

ISBN 978-3-03766-687-6

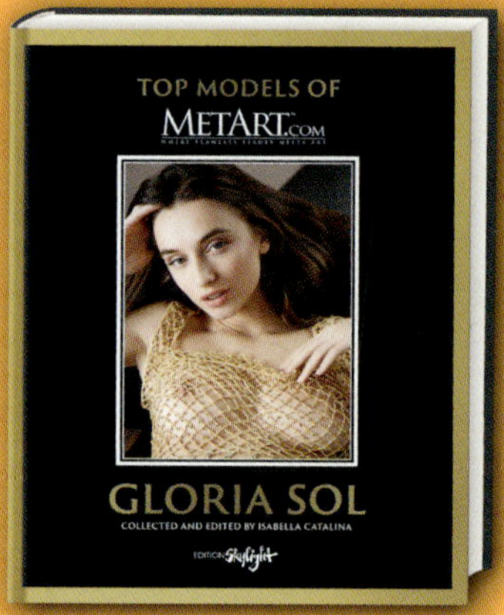

ISBN 978-3-03766-688-3

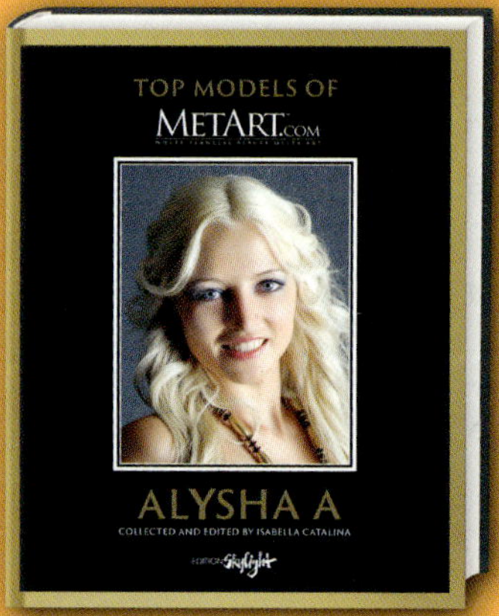

ISBN 978-3-03766-692-0

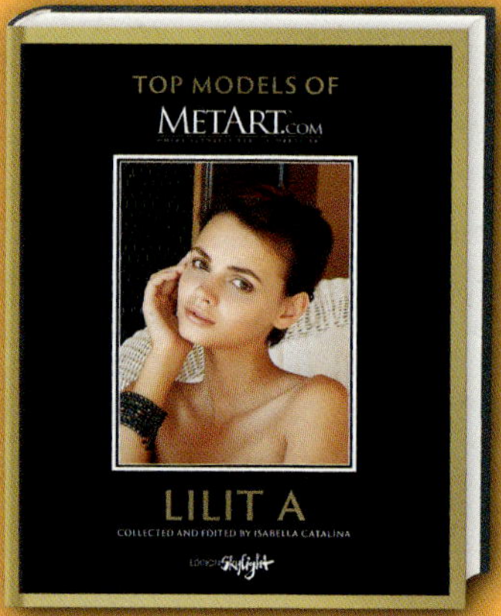

ISBN 978-3-03766-693-7

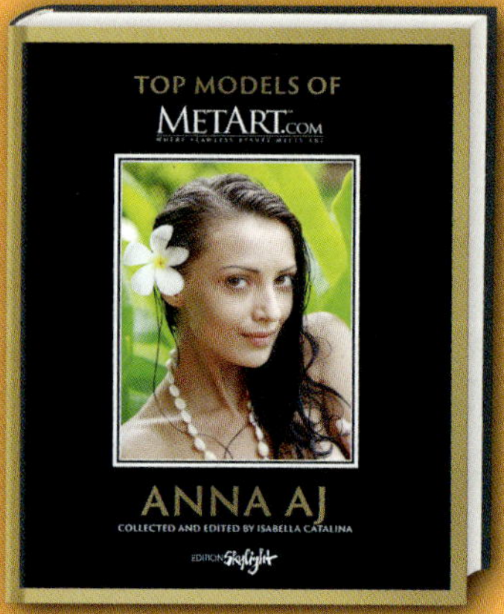

ISBN 978-3-03766-695-1

WWW.EDITION-SKYLIGHT.COM